⇜ CATO ⇝
SUPREME COURT
REVIEW

2014 — 2015

☙ CATO ❧
SUPREME COURT
REVIEW

2014 — 2015

CENTER FOR CONSTITUTIONAL STUDIES

INSTITUTE
Washington, D.C.

THE CATO SUPREME COURT REVIEW (ISBN 978-1-939709-86-8) is published annually at the close of each Supreme Court term by the Cato Institute, 1000 Massachusetts Ave., N.W., Washington, D.C. 20001-5403.

CORRESPONDENCE. Correspondence regarding subscriptions, changes of address, procurement of back issues, advertising and marketing matters, and so forth, should be addressed to:

Publications Department
The Cato Institute
1000 Massachusetts Ave., N.W.
Washington, D.C. 20001

All other correspondence, including requests to quote or reproduce material, should be addressed to the editor.

CITATIONS: Citation to this volume of the Review should conform to the following style: 2014-2015 Cato Sup. Ct. Rev. (2015).

DISCLAIMER. The views expressed by the authors of the articles are their own and are not attributable to the editor, the editorial board, or the Cato Institute.

INTERNET ADDRESS. Articles from past editions are available to the general public, free of charge, at www.cato.org/pubs/scr.

ISBN 978-1-939709-86-8 (Paperback)
ISBN 978-1-939709-87-5 (Digital)

Printed in the United States of America.

Cato Institute
1000 Massachusetts Ave., N.W.
Washington, D.C. 20001
www.cato.org

Contents

FOREWORD

Roberts' Rules: Deference Trumps Law

*Roger Pilon**

The Cato Institute's Center for Constitutional Studies is pleased to publish this 14th volume of the *Cato Supreme Court Review*, an annual critique of the Court's most important decisions from the term just ended, plus a look at the term ahead—all from a classical Madisonian perspective, grounded in the nation's first principles, liberty through limited government. We release this volume each year at Cato's annual Constitution Day conference. And each year in this space I discuss briefly a theme that seemed to emerge from the Court's term or from the larger setting in which the term unfolded.

As many have said, this was an unusual "liberal" term for the Roberts Court, at least as defined by outcomes consistent with modern liberal views in the larger political community. And it was, as also widely noted, partly because of the docket this term, but also because the Court's four liberals voted as a block 90 percent of the time, which meant that to carry the day in a given case only one of the five more conservative justices needed to join them. As in the past, that role was filled most often by the Court's two moderate conservatives, Chief Justice John Roberts and Justice Anthony Kennedy. Both joined the liberals in the first of the term's two most high-profile cases, *King v. Burwell*, upholding the Affordable Care Act; and Kennedy wrote for the liberal side in *Obergefell v. Hodges*, which made same-sex marriage the law of the land.

Two decisions do not make a term, of course. But a look at the reasoning of both justices in those emblematic cases, including that of Roberts in his blistering *Obergefell* dissent, may shed at least some light on both Roberts' noted "minimalism" and why, despite their

---

* Vice president for legal affairs at the Cato Institute, founder and director of Cato's Center for Constitutional Studies, B. Kenneth Simon Chair in Constitutional Studies, and founding publisher of the *Cato Supreme Court Review*.

numbers, the Court's conservatives seem often to come up short. Conservatives lost both cases, liberals won both, while for classical liberals like the editors of this *Review* it was a split.

We take it as given that legal reasoning, far from a free-standing matter, is a function of the role of a judge—to apply the law to the facts before the court, which first means reading the law correctly. That begins with the plain text of the law. And it ends there, unless it is necessary to move, as relevant and in rough order, from text to original understanding, structure, function, history (including precedent), and policy, all with an eye toward securing and preserving the rule of law. That brings us, not surprisingly, to the decision that effectively reversed that order of things, the first of those two emblematic cases.

King v. Burwell

Let us stipulate that it would be surprising if a statutory scheme as complicated, as rushed to completion and passage, and as ill-thought-out as the 900-page Affordable Care Act (ACA) were to admit of anything but multiple interpretations. All the more reason when a passage is clear and unambiguous on its face for a judge to latch on to it as an anchor in a potential political firestorm. That is not, however, what Chief Justice Roberts did in *King v. Burwell*. Writing for a majority of six, and drawing heavily on his reading of the policy behind the ACA, he rejected what he allowed was "the most natural reading" of the text at issue, finding instead that it was ambiguous when read in the context of "the statute as a whole." Writing for the dissent, Justice Antonin Scalia put it best, alluding to *NFIB v. Sebelius*, the Court's 2012 go-round with the ACA: "Under all the usual rules of interpretation, the Government should lose this case. But normal rules of interpretation seem always to yield to the overriding principle of the present Court: The Affordable Care Act must be saved."

That was clear from the start: Step by step, Roberts bent over backwards to save not only the ACA but Congress itself from itself. The question before the Court was really quite simple: Does a provision of the ACA that authorizes tax credits for qualified individuals who purchase health insurance through "an Exchange established by the State" *also* authorize subsidies for qualified individuals who purchase insurance through an exchange established by the federal government? Interpreting the provision on its terms, the IRS had initially said no, but the Obama administration prevailed upon it to rule otherwise, thus making tax subsidies available in the 34 states that had declined to establish exchanges. And Roberts, thinking the question too important to be left to an agency to decide, found that when the ACA says "Exchange established by the State" it means, as Scalia put it, "Exchange established by the State or the Federal Government." "That is of course quite absurd," Scalia added, "and the Court's 21 pages of explanation make it no less so."

Roberts' argument had two steps: first, to show that the provision at issue, appearances aside, is ambiguous; second, to show that one of its permissible meanings—the one that makes tax credits available not just through state but through federal exchanges as well—is compatible with "the statute as a whole."

He began, therefore, by saying that the meaning—or ambiguity—of certain words may become apparent only "when placed in context. So when deciding whether the language is plain we must read the words 'in their context and with a view to their place in the overall statutory scheme.'" In other words, perhaps Congress didn't mean what its words plainly say. Notice that this would seem to get things backward from the start. We ordinarily look to context to clarify ambiguous text, not to discover ambiguity in clear text, much less, as Scalia said, as an excuse to *rewrite* clear text—adding that the more unnatural the proposed rewrite, "the more compelling the contextual evidence must be to show that it is correct."

As contextual evidence purporting to show that "state" includes "federal," consider just the first two of several points Roberts raised. Looking beyond the provision that establishes state exchanges—the provision at issue—he pointed to the later section of the Act that authorizes federal exchanges. That provision provides that if a state does not establish an exchange, the secretary of health and human services shall establish and operate "such exchange" within the state. By using the phrase "such exchange," Roberts wrote, that section "instructs the Secretary to establish and operate the same Exchange that the State was directed to establish" under the earlier section. "In other words," he concluded, "State Exchanges and Federal Exchanges are equivalent—they must meet the same requirements, perform the same functions, and serve the same purposes."

Notice the work that Roberts is asking the general phrase "such exchange" to do: It is to import into federal exchanges all the features of exchanges established by states, including tax credits, and to do so in the face of a provision that expressly authorizes tax credits only for exchanges "established by the State," an authorization that is missing from the section of the Act that authorizes federal exchanges. That is a substantial leap, first, because, as Roberts grants, the two exchanges are established by different sovereigns, but second, and more to the point, an exchange established by the federal government is *not* an exchange "established by the State," the *sine qua non* of tax credit eligibility. (Moreover, both here and elsewhere, Roberts failed to seriously address the idea that Congress may have had a good reason for omitting tax credits for federal exchanges, a point I will discuss more fully below.)

But Roberts' second point purporting to show that federal exchanges are "established by the State" for tax credit purposes shows only a further difficulty of drawing that inference, as he himself recognized: "After all," he wrote, "the Act defines 'State' to mean 'each of the 50 States and the District of Columbia'—a definition that does not include the Federal Government." So here too we must read "established by the State" in context, "with a view to [its] place in the overall statutory scheme." And the section of the Act authorizing state exchanges provides that all exchanges "shall make available qualified health plans to qualified individuals." But another section, he continued, defines "qualified individual" in part as

> an individual who "resides in the State that established the Exchange." And that's a problem: If we give the phrase "the State that established the Exchange" its most natural meaning, there would be *no* "qualified individuals" on Federal Exchanges. But the Act clearly contemplates that there will be qualified individuals on *every* Exchange. As we just mentioned, the Act requires all Exchanges to "make available qualified health plans to qualified individuals"—something an Exchange could not do if there were no such individuals.

True. But how does that observation serve to show that federal exchanges are "established by the State" for tax credit purposes? That inference is a *non sequitur*. Here, Scalia responded with a homely example of directions given to a class of people, although they apply only to some in the class. And he went on to show that the balance of Roberts' contextual arguments not only did not show that the text at issue was ambiguous, but that Congress had good reasons for distinguishing state and federal exchanges. As he concluded, "reading the Act as a whole leaves no doubt about the matter: 'Exchange established by the State' means what it looks like it means."

Nonetheless, having concluded that the phrase "an Exchange established by the State" is ambiguous when read in context, Roberts turned next to the second step in his argument, to show that only one of the phrase's permissible meanings—the one that makes tax credits available in federal as well as state exchanges—"produces a substantive effect that is compatible with the rest of the law." By contrast, the plain reading would destabilize the individual insurance market in any state with a federal exchange, he argued, creating the very "death spirals" that Congress sought to avoid. Explaining how that would happen, he concluded that Congress meant for those credits to apply in both exchanges.

Not surprisingly, this venture into policy and into the question of what Congress intended generated a challenge from the dissent about whether Roberts had correctly discerned Congress's intent. And here things got interesting. Scalia began by observing that if Roberts' dire predictions were accurate, they "would show only that the statutory scheme contains a flaw; they would not show that the statute means the opposite of what it says." And he added that "no law pursues just one purpose at all cost," noting, in particular, that the ACA "displays a congressional preference for state participation in the establishment of Exchanges."

By way of background, under the federalism principles the Court recognized in 1992 in *New York v. United States*, Congress could not simply "dragoon" states into creating exchanges. But for political reasons, apparently, neither did Congress want to replace our traditional state-centered health insurance arrangements with a federal system. So like the incentives Congress offered states to participate in Medicaid, here too, to encourage states to establish exchanges, Congress offered incentives in the form of tax credits for their citizens. Indeed, MIT Professor Jonathan Gruber, one of the principal advisors to the congressional and administrative staff that drafted the ACA, addressed the point directly in a January 2012 speech, when it looked like states might not be responding to those incentives:

> I think what's important to remember politically about this, is if you're a state and you don't set up an exchange, *that means your citizens don't get their tax credits*. But your citizens still pay the taxes that support this bill. So you're essentially saying to your citizens, you're going to pay all the taxes to help all the other states in the country. I hope that's a blatant enough political reality that states will get their act together and realize there are billions of dollars at stake here in setting up these exchanges, and that they'll do it (emphasis added).

Well 34 states did not do it. Whatever their reasons—Scalia listed various burdens states would take on if they established exchanges—there certainly would be less reason if tax credits were available under *either* scenario. "So even if making credits available on all Exchanges advances the goal of improving healthcare markets," Scalia noted, "it frustrates the goal of encouraging state involvement in the implementation of the Act."

Focusing on only the first of those goals, Roberts responded feebly that the section of the Act that establishes federal exchanges refutes the incentives argument by providing that

> if a State elects not to establish an Exchange, the Secretary "shall . . . establish and operate such Exchange within the State." The whole point of that provision is to create a federal fallback in case a State chooses not to establish its own Exchange. Contrary to petitioners' argument, Congress did not believe it was offering States a deal they would not refuse—it expressly addressed what would happen if a State *did* refuse the deal.

Actually, the Act's provision for federal exchanges does not refute the incentives argument. To be sure, *a* point of what Congress did was to create a federal fallback. But it was not "the *whole* point" of what it did. By not providing for tax credits for federal exchanges, as it had done for state exchanges, Congress *also* sought to incentivize states to create their own exchanges.

It is noteworthy at least that an argument that relies so heavily on judicial discernment of congressional intent should give such short shrift to so central a feature of Congress's scheme. The mere fact that two-thirds of the states had declined to establish exchanges should alone have alerted the Court to the very real possibility, given the dire consequences that the Court said would follow were the law read as written, that there was a flaw in the scheme and that it would fall to the Congress and not to the Court to fix it. Not that Roberts was unsolicitous of the point: Noting that the Court's role is "more confined" than Congress's, he wrote that the Court "must respect the role of the Legislature, and take care not to undo what it has done." But if holding Congress to its own words would undo its scheme, it is not the Court that would be undoing what Congress had done. Congress would have undone itself. It is not the role of the Court to serve as handmaiden to the legislature by rewriting what the legislature has written.

Here again, Scalia said it best: "The Court's insistence on making a choice that should be made by Congress both aggrandizes judicial power and encourages congressional lassitude." In a case of statutory interpretation where the text is clear, as here, deference is due to what Congress wrote, not to what it should have written. It is no small irony that Chief Justice Roberts, known for his judicial modesty and minimalism, deferred to his understanding of what Congress meant rather than to what it wrote.

Obergefell v. Hodges

Misdirected deference was a problem in *Obergefell v. Hodges* as well, but mainly for the dissenters—Chief Justice Roberts, who wrote the main dissent, and Justices Scalia, Clarence Thomas, and Samuel Alito, each of whom wrote a dissent. Whereas deference in this case should again have gone to the text—here, the text of the Fourteenth Amendment—theirs went to "tradition" and hence to the state respondents that had refused to recognize same-sex marriages. And in Roberts' dissent we see the same pattern we saw in his opinion for the Court in *King*, an obsession with the role of the Court that superseded a focus on the law. To develop those points more fully, let us first look briefly at Justice Kennedy's opinion for himself and the Court's four liberals, which had its own share of misdirection, then at the dissents, especially that of Roberts.

If the Court's opinion in *King* was as much policy as law, its opinion in *Obergefell* was even more so, yet it need not have been since there was a simple and straightforward answer to the question before the Court: If a state licenses, recognizes, and affords benefits for opposite-sex marriages, must it do so for same-sex marriages as well? It must. Pursuant to the Fourteenth Amendment's Equal Protection

Clause, unless a state has a compelling reason for discriminating against same-sex marriages, it must treat them as it treats opposite-sex marriages. In other words, such "policy" as is reflected in that conclusion is entailed by the law that is the Equal Protection Clause. And it is that law to which the Court should have deferred in overriding the decisions of the state respondents to discriminate against same-sex marriages.

Unfortunately, Kennedy rested his otherwise correct conclusion to that effect mainly on the Fourteenth Amendment's Due Process Clause. Only at the end of his opinion did he turn to the Equal Protection Clause, incompletely and as something of an afterthought. Waxing at once rhapsodic and banal—Scalia barely contained himself—Kennedy found that a fundamental "liberty" and hence a fundamental "right" of same-sex couples to marry was supported by "four principles and traditions": respect for individual autonomy and choice, the unique association entailed by marriage, the well-being of children reared by couples, and social order and stability.

But as Thomas pointed out in dissent—drawing on the theory of the Constitution and the Lockean state-of-nature, natural-rights theory that underpins it—no state prevented same-sex couples from marrying. They were perfectly free to go to any willing clergyman who would marry them and the state would not have interfered with their liberty or their right to do so. What they wanted, he saw, was a state *license*, the state's positive *recognition* of the marriage, and the *legal benefits* that go with the state's recognition. But those are not "liberties" protected under the Due Process Clause, said Thomas. They are *privileges* the state affords pursuant to its general police power. And he was right.

Thus, the right to marry someone of the same sex is a natural right that anyone would enjoy in the state of nature. But once we leave that state and enter into civil society, if an actual state grants the privileges of marriage—as all states do—those privileges cannot be denied to any person who meets the criteria for being granted them (about which more below). Their denial is then properly litigated against the state under the Equal Protection Clause, not the Due Process Clause. Unfortunately, Thomas never developed those points, nor did Kennedy get to the heart of the matter in his brief and gauzy discussion of equal protection, which he used only to "shore up" his due process analysis, Thomas said. But neither did the other dissents.

Instead, each focused almost exclusively on the Court's mistaken due process analysis.

However misdirected, the conservatives' arguments are worth examining, if only to see why that crucial fifth vote is so often lost. In general, the dissents all noted the Constitution's silence concerning marriage, the resulting limited role of the Court in addressing the question before it, and the role of the people in their states in deciding whether same-sex marriage should be recognized. But they directed their fire mainly at the majority's resort to "substantive due process" whereby the Court finds unenumerated rights under the Constitution's Due Process Clauses.

The Fourteenth Amendment's Due Process Clause prohibits states from depriving "any person of life, liberty, or property, without due process of law." Narrowly read, with an emphasis on democratic decision-making in the states, that clause would allow majorities to deprive minorities of life, liberty, and property as long as "due process of law" is afforded. That is how many conservatives read it. Indeed, Thomas railed against "the dangerous fiction of treating the Due Process Clause as a font of substantive rights." And Scalia wrote that "the Constitution places *some* constraints on self-rule—constraints adopted *by the People themselves* when they ratified the Constitution and its Amendments" (first emphasis added). Scalia went on to cite a few of those constraints—"enumerated" rights—but he concluded that aside from those, the "powers 'reserved to the States respectively, or to the people' can be exercised as the States or the People desire," quoting thus from the Tenth Amendment.

Conspicuous by its absence in any of the four dissents was any mention of the Ninth Amendment: "The enumeration in the Constitution of certain rights shall not be construed to deny or disparage others *retained by the people*." Clearly, we cannot "retain" what we do not first have to be retained; nor can we enumerate in a constitution the infinite number of rights we retained when we established and empowered government in the first place. That is one of the reasons the Ninth Amendment was written and ratified—to make it clear that we have both enumerated *and* unenumerated rights. And just as clearly, it was to protect those rights—both enumerated *and* unenumerated—that the Due Process Clauses were written.

It is at this point—this "most sensitive category of constitutional adjudication" as he put it—that we pick up Roberts' argument, for it is here, he wrote, that the petitioners' claim rests. Noting first that the Court "has interpreted the Due Process Clause to include a 'substantive' component that protects certain liberty interests against state deprivation 'no matter what process is provided,'" Roberts pointed next to the "obvious concerns" this raises about the judicial role, then to the Court's 1997 decision in *Washington v. Glucksberg*, which purported to give judges guidance in finding unenumerated rights. There the Court held that to be "fundamental," implied rights must be "objectively, deeply rooted in this Nation's history and tradition," and "implicit in the concept of ordered liberty, such that neither liberty nor justice would exist if they were sacrificed."

Obviously, Roberts will go on to argue that an unenumerated right to same-sex marriage will not satisfy those criteria because it is not "deeply rooted in this Nation's history and tradition." But the broader problem with the *Glucksberg* criteria should be equally obvious: If any right at issue before the Court is already deeply rooted, it is likely already protected; and if it is not deeply rooted, then it is likely not to get protected. Barely noticing that problem, Roberts focused instead on what plainly for him was the far more serious problem—an unrestrained judiciary. Indeed, almost to the point of obsession, he went on to cite the 1905 case of *Lochner v. New York* no fewer than 16 times as emblematic of the dangers of substantive due process under a willful judiciary. Yet his arguments, apparently uninformed by recent scholarship on the case, fell far short.

The *Lochner* Court overturned a New York statute that limited the hours bakers could work, citing the freedom of contract and adding that the statute could not be justified as a health and safety measure. Enacted on behalf of large unionized bakeries facing competition from small, often immigrant-owned rivals, the statute was a textbook example of special-interest legislation, but Roberts dressed it up in the garb of democratic legitimacy. And he charged the majority with "unprincipled" judicial policymaking, adopting "naked policy preferences," and "empowering judges to elevate their own policy judgments to the status of constitutionally protected 'liberty,'" as if that were what the majority was doing. Trotting out the familiar Holmesian tropes in dissent—that the case was "decided upon an economic theory which a large part of the country does not entertain" and that "the Fourteenth Amendment does not enact Mr. Herbert Spencer's Social Statics," as if those were constitutionally cognizable concerns—Roberts even quoted Holmes' contention to the effect that "the Constitution 'is not intended to embody a particular economic theory'" (actually, Holmes wrote "*a* constitution"). *The* Constitution, *our* Constitution, protects property, contract, and liberty, of course, which should settle the question of its neutrality as between capitalism and socialism.

The point of this obsession with *Lochner* becomes clear once Roberts draws what he sees as the parallels with *Obergefell*. "Ultimately," he wrote,

> only one precedent offers any support for the [Obergefell] majority's methodology: *Lochner* v. *New York*. The majority opens its opinion by announcing petitioners' right to "define and express their identity." The majority later explains that "the right to personal choice regarding marriage is inherent in the concept of individual autonomy." This freewheeling notion of individual autonomy echoes nothing so much as "the general right of an individual to be *free in his person* and in his power to contract in relation to his own labor" (here quoting *Lochner*, emphasis added by Roberts).

And Roberts continued in this vein: "The truth is that today's decision rests on nothing more than the majority's own conviction that same-sex couples should be allowed to marry because they want to." Is that a problem—allowing same-sex couples to marry "because they want to"? For the chief justice, apparently, it is. For he added: "Whatever force that belief may have as a matter of moral philosophy, it has no more basis in the Constitution than did the naked policy preferences adopted in *Lochner*." In other words, Roberts reads the guarantees of the Fourteenth Amendment narrowly—which means that *he reads the powers of the states broadly*. And what justifies that broad reading here? In the nearest Roberts came to answering that question, he spoke of "the States' 'legitimate state interest' in 'preserving the traditional institution of marriage'" as "the union of a man and a woman." But apart from mere tradition, what privileges that conclusory definition? Each of the dissents set forth a few of the by-now familiar policy rationales for rejecting same-sex marriage; but like the health and safety rationales in *Lochner*, those rationales have grown increasingly unconvincing and unable to withstand scrutiny, especially in the face of pleas like those of the petitioners to be free to marry whomever they choose.

In the end, then, Roberts' argument turns on the definition of marriage, plus the question of who decides, as he signaled it would early on. But by settling on the states' definition, as he did, he begged the very question before the Court. It is a circular argument—unless, of course, states are unrestrained in exercising that power. But that was the whole point of the Fourteenth Amendment, to *restrain* the police power of the states, and to do so in a principled way, repairing to life, liberty, property, due process, and the equal protection of the laws. If, without sufficient justification, as just noted, states discriminate by virtue merely of their definition of marriage, thereby denying benefits to some that are available to others, the denial of those benefits amounts to harming those so denied.

Kennedy had it backwards, then, a point Thomas saw but never developed: The Due Process Clause harm is a function of the Equal Protection Clause denial of recognition and benefits. And the equal-protection problem becomes even clearer once we look critically at the traditional definition of marriage and recognize that marriage, at bottom, is a contract pertaining to certain personal commitments. As with all contracts, therefore, it should fall to the parties to set the terms, not to the state—especially not in a discriminatory manner. To be sure, there may be limited scope for licensure regarding consent and evidence of marriage, which *can* be justified in a non-discriminatory way; and enforcement is always an issue, as with any contract. But none of that distinguishes same-sex from opposite-sex marriage contracts.

Justice Kennedy may have rested his conclusion upholding same-sex marriage on the wrong constitutional foundation, but it was not without salutary effect. For his venture down the path of substantive due process induced his conservative critics to follow him, which brought to the surface both the substantive and the methodological infirmities that have so often afflicted their Fourteenth Amendment jurisprudence. Substantively, conservatives too often fail to credit the fact that the law at issue prohibits actions that harm no one, whether it restricts the sale and use of contraceptives (*Griswold v. Connecticut*), interracial marriage (*Loving v. Virginia*), same-sex sodomy (*Lawrence v. Texas*), or much else. Here is Roberts, for example:

> Near the end of its opinion, the majority offers perhaps the clearest insight into its decision. Expanding marriage to in-

clude same-sex couples, the majority insists, would "pose no
risk of harm to themselves or third parties." This argument
again echoes *Lochner*, which relied on its assessment that "we
think that a law like the one before us involves neither the
safety, the morals nor the welfare of the public, and that the
interest of the public is not in the slightest degree affected by
such an act."

Kennedy was right: same-sex marriage harms no one. But so was
Justice Rufus Peckham right in *Lochner*: freedom of contract harms
no one.

And conservative methodological infirmities (and more) were
captured in this instructive, albeit opaque, Roberts passage, which
directly follows the passage above:

Then and now, this assertion of the "harm principle" sounds
more in philosophy than law. The elevation of the fullest individual self-realization over the constraints that society has
expressed in law may or may not be attractive moral philosophy. But a Justice's commission does not confer any special
moral, philosophical, or social insight sufficient to justify
imposing those perceptions on fellow citizens under the pretense of "due process." There is indeed a process due the people on issues of this sort—the democratic process. Respecting
that understanding requires the Court to be guided by law,
not any particular school of social thought.

Note first that, in fact, the "harm principle" does sound very much
in law, starting with the law of torts. Beyond that, however, whether
the "perceptions" Roberts mentions refers to the harm principle or to
a justice's "moral, philosophical, or social insights," it is clear at least
that he has severed "life, liberty, and property" from "due process,"
leaving that phrase to denote simply "the democratic process." That
enables "*the* people"—which means, at best, the majority, but more
often some special interest—to run roughshod over the lives, liberties, and property of *actual* people, and all in the name of a Court
"guided by law"—as if the Fourteenth Amendment did not incorporate "a particular school of social thought," namely, the one that elevates life, liberty, property, equal protection, and due process above
majoritarian rule.

But the methodological problem is deeper still. It concerns ultimately the very conception of the Constitution and how to treat

claims brought under the Fourteenth Amendment. In brief, both liberals and conservatives have gone about their substantive-due-process jurisprudence backwards. Both have asked the Court either to recognize the unenumerated rights at issue or to not do so, which has driven the Court to try to discern rights pursuant to the *Glucksberg* formula. But the proper question, as is implicit in the Ninth Amendment, is not whether there is a right but whether the state has a justification for the restriction it has imposed or the discrimination it has practiced. Once the plaintiff has filed his prima facie complaint, that is, the burden should be on *the state* to justify its police power action. That power, after all, is not unlimited. In fact, it is authorized mainly to protect our rights and to provide those "public goods" that might otherwise not be provided by private markets owing to high transaction costs, free-rider problems, and the like, as economists have argued. The further it strays from those basic purposes, especially if it ventures into morals legislation, the more difficult it is to justify it in a plural society dedicated to liberty and tolerance, as this case illustrates. Indeed, from *Lochner* to *Griswold, Loving, Lawrence,* and more, what rights are those police power laws protecting?

Thus, what we have in these *Obergefell* dissents is the latest iteration of the error we find in the late Judge Robert Bork's discussion of his "Madisonian dilemma." America was founded on two opposing principles, he wrote, which must continually be reconciled:

> The first principle is self-government, which means that in *wide* areas of life majorities are entitled to rule, if they wish, simply because they are majorities. The second principle is that there are nonetheless *some* things majorities must not do to minorities, *some* areas of life in which the individual must be free of majority rule" (emphasis added).

Unfortunately, that gets Madison exactly backward. America's first *political* principle may indeed have been self-government, but its first *moral* principle—and the reason we instituted government at all— was individual liberty, which the Declaration of Independence makes plain for all to see and the Fourteenth Amendment incorporated at last in the Constitution as against the states. That means that in "wide areas" individuals are entitled to be free simply because they are born so entitled, while in "some" areas majorities are entitled to rule not because they are inherently so entitled but because we have authorized them to, as a practical compromise.

That gets the order right: individual liberty first, self-government second, as a means toward securing that liberty. And that, precisely, is what too many conservatives get backwards, as is evident in the dissents here. At an intuitive level, Justice Kennedy seems to appreciate that order of things—not always, but often, even if his reasoning and rhetoric sometimes cloud the matter, as here. And that is at least part of the reason the Court's conservatives come up short on occasion. In at least some Fourteenth Amendment cases, the Court's liberals, plus Kennedy, seem to have a better grasp of the principles of the matter than the conservatives.

But another reason is the lingering overhang of the "judicial restraint" school of which Bork was perhaps the most prominent member. We see that here, in both decisions. In *King*, Chief Justice Roberts seemed driven to keep the Court out of the political process that had produced the Affordable Care Act, and so he ignored the plain text before him—resulting, ironically, in the very "judicial activism" that school condemned. And in *Obergefell* he seemed driven again to keep the Court out of the political process that had produced such discriminatory state actions, thus ignoring the plain text of the Fourteenth Amendment's Equal Protection Clause, which prohibited those actions. Judicial "modesty" and "minimalism" aside, better it would have been to focus on the law than on judicial behavior, especially if the latter distracts one from an accurate reading of the law.

Introduction

*Ilya Shapiro**

This is the 14th volume of the *Cato Supreme Court Review*, the nation's first in-depth critique of the Supreme Court term just ended, plus a look at the term ahead. We release this journal every year in conjunction with our annual Constitution Day symposium, less than three months after the previous term ends and two weeks before the next one begins. We are proud of the speed with which we publish this tome—authors of articles about the final cases have no more than a month to provide us full drafts—and of its accessibility, at least insofar as the Court's opinions allow. I'm particularly proud that this isn't a typical law review, whose submissions' esoteric prolixity is matched only by their footnotes' abstruseness. Instead, this is a book of essays on law intended for everyone from lawyers and judges to educated laymen and interested citizens.

And we are happy to confess our biases: We approach our subject matter from a classical Madisonian perspective, with a focus on individual liberty that is protected and secured by a government of delegated, enumerated, separated, and thus limited powers. We also try to maintain a strict separation of law and politics; just because something is good policy doesn't mean it's constitutional, and vice versa. Moreover, just because being faithful to the text of a statute might produce unfortunate results doesn't mean that judges should take it upon themselves to rewrite the law and bail out the politicians. Accordingly, just as judges must sometimes overrule the will of the people—as when legislatures act without constitutional authority or trample individual liberties—resolving policy and political problems caused by poorly conceived or inartfully drafted legislation must be left to the political process.

---

* Senior fellow in constitutional studies, Cato Institute, and editor-in-chief, *Cato Supreme Court Review*.

Statistics and Trends

Following a term that saw a record level of unanimity, the 2014–2015 term regressed to the mean. Thirty of the 74 cases decided on the merits (41 percent) ended up 9-0.[1] The previous term it was 66 percent, but that term was the real outlier, given that the preceding five terms registered 36, 44, 46, 45, and 49 percent, respectively. Five more cases were decided by 8–1 margins, which brings us to nearly half the docket. And recall that the superficial harmony of the term that ended in June 2014 papered over real doctrinal differences, producing many narrow rulings that were often accompanied by strident concurrences—dissents in all but name. Many of those scorching writings were produced by Justice Antonin Scalia, who this year, if anything, only turned up the heat.

The term produced 19 5–4 decisions (26 percent, the second-highest of the last six years), including in such contentious areas as campaign finance (*Williams-Yulee v. Florida Bar*), same-sex marriage (*Obergefell v. Hodges*), environmental regulation (*Michigan v. EPA*), and the death penalty (*Glossip v. Gross*). And that doesn't even include the big ~~Obamacare~~ RobertsCare case, *King v. Burwell*, which came out 6–3—as did another 10 cases (15 percent of the total). That means that 41 percent of the rulings were either 5-4 or 6-3, demolishing last term's 22 percent—and higher than any term in recent memory (30 percent is the average of the preceding five terms). In other words, the Court is still of one mind on many issues—typically lower-profile cases—but continues to be split on constitutional rights and civil liberties, as well as certain types of criminal procedure cases that produce heterodox but consistent divisions.

The increase in split judgments naturally resulted in significantly more dissenting opinions, 68, whereas the previous term there were 32 and the average going back to 2000-2001 is 55.9. Not surprisingly, the total number of all opinions (majority, concurring, and dissenting) was also high—186, up from 146 last term and the highest since 2009–2010—and the average of 2.51 opinions per case was up slightly

---

[1] These figures include eight summary reversals (without oral argument), seven of which were unanimous. All statistics taken from Kedar Bhatia, Final Stat Pack for October Term 2014, SCOTUSblog (June 30, 2015; updated July 5, 2015), http:// www.scotusblog.com/2015/06/final-stat-pack-for-october-term-2014. For more detailed data from previous terms, see SCOTUSblog, Statpack Archive, http://www. scotusblog.com/reference/stat-pack (last visited Aug. 18, 2015).

from the average of the preceding decade. Justice Clarence Thomas wrote the most opinions (37, including 19 dissents), followed by Justices Samuel Alito (30) and Scalia (28), after which there's a big drop to the next number (16 each by Justices Stephen Breyer and Sonia Sotomayor). Justice Thomas also produced the most opinion pages (432), more than tripling those of Justice Ruth Bader Ginsburg (143).

Some of this "divisive" dynamic—which, again, followed a "unified" term, so take all of this with a grain of salt—can be attributed to the Court's controlling its docket such that four justices can decide to take a case guaranteed to prove controversial. But of course no justice generates his or her own cases, so if fewer non-ideological circuit splits or bald errors in complicated legal areas emerge from the lower courts—this term saw many fewer patent cases than the previous term, for example—there may be less opportunity for technical agreement. Such are the vicissitudes of the litigation calendar. Nevertheless, any way you slice it, the Court was definitely more discordant than it has been in the recent past—so Chief Justice John Roberts didn't manage to orchestrate the minimalistic unity he craves.

The Court reversed or vacated 53 lower-court opinions (72 percent), which is essentially the same as last term and in line with recent years. Of the lower courts with significant numbers of cases under review, the U.S. Court of Appeals for the Eighth Circuit attained a 1–7 record (88 percent reversal), narrowly "beating" the Fifth Circuit (2-6, 75 percent). Traditional "big loser" Ninth Circuit did suffer the most reversals, but also the most affirmances, for a respectable record in this context of 6–10.

None of the stats thus far are that remarkable, falling generally within the modern norm, without much if any significance for the Court's ebbs and flows. What is remarkable, however, is *which* justices were in the majority. After six straight years being most often on the winning side, Justice Anthony Kennedy dropped to third (65 of 74 cases, or 88 percent). In that time, Chief Justice Roberts tied Kennedy for that honor twice and was second three times—and yet this term he dropped to sixth (80 percent). So who took their places? Amazingly, it was Justices Breyer (92 percent) and Sotomayor (89 percent). Still, Justice Kennedy maintained his typical lead in those 5–4 cases, being in the majority in 14 of them—eight times with the "liberals," five times with the "conservatives," and once in a heterodox coalition. But even here Justice Breyer tied him and Justice Sotomayor was only one case behind (with Justice Ginsburg one more back).

Justice Thomas had enjoyed a long run of success in 5–4 cases—he was second to Kennedy in October Terms 2010–2013—but this year he was ahead only of Justice Scalia (by one case) and didn't author any of the majority opinions. Not surprisingly, Thomas was also the justice most likely to dissent (39 percent of all cases and 66 percent of divided cases)—most memorably in *Obergefell*. He takes over from Justice Sotomayor, who went from worst to (almost) first. Thomas also maintained his status as the leading "lone dissenter"—since 2006–2007 he's averaged 1.8 solo dissents per term, nearly double his closest colleague—writing three dissents in 8–1 cases. Justices Alito and Sotomayor each wrote one solo dissent. Chief Justice Roberts and Justice Elena Kagan have still *never* written one of those during their entire tenures (ten and five terms, respectively).

Justice Scalia, despite being on the winning side of six 5–4 rulings, made the most of his opportunities and authored three such decisions. He was particularly active on the last three days that the Court handed down opinions, producing important majority opinions in *Johnson v. United States* and *Michigan v. EPA*, memorable dissents in *King v. Burwell*, *Obergefell v. Hodges*, and *Arizona State Legislature v. Arizona Independent Redistricting Commission*, and a notable concurrence in *Glossip v. Gross* (which he read from the bench, the fourth justice to do so in that case).

More big news comes out of an examination of judicial-agreement rates. The top six pairs of justices most likely to agree, at least in part, were all from the "liberal bloc." Heck, the three tied for first all involved Justice Breyer—with Justices Ginsburg, Sotomayor, and Kagan, by definition, each pair at 94.4 percent—the most unlikely "Mr. Congeniality" in recent memory. The top conservative pairing consisted of Chief Justice Roberts and Justice Scalia, coming in seventh at 83.8 percent, which is a steep drop from the sixth slot. Justices Thomas and Sotomayor voted together less than anyone else (in only 37 of 74 cases, or 50 percent). Indeed, the next three-lowest pairings also involve Justice Thomas, with Justices Breyer (51.4 percent), Kagan (54.1), and Ginsburg (55.4). Justices Scalia and Sotomayor were on opposite ends of all of the 5–4 cases, as were Justices Alito and Kagan.

My final statistics are more whimsical, relating to the number of questions asked at oral argument—and how funny they were. Not surprisingly, Justice Scalia maintained his perch as the Supreme Court's most frequent interlocutor, with an average of 22 questions per argument. That was up from his 19.6 average from two terms ago, made Scalia the top questioner in 43 percent of cases, and put him in the top three 63 percent of the time. Justice Ginsburg again asked the first question most often (in 29 percent of cases), followed by Justice Sotomayor (21 percent). Justice Thomas continued his non-questioning ways. With respect to laughter—or "[laughter]," as it's noted on oral-argument transcripts—Scalia maintained his commanding lead, followed by a "not-so-close" Justice Breyer.[2] And Justice Kagan finally lived up to her potential, matching Chief Justice Roberts for third spot on the laugh track.

Statistics aside, this term, which was supposed to give a bit of a breather to Court-watchers, was obviously overshadowed by two cases. I won't belabor them here because this volume features not just two articles on RobertsCare and one on same-sex marriage, but also a trenchant foreword by Roger Pilon that synthesizes the two rulings by way of explaining what both liberals and conservatives get wrong about judging. Looking back on the term, in sum, we do see a few trends: fewer unanimous rulings; more results that experts classify as "liberal" than "conservative"—though that's largely due to the vagaries of the docket—and the lockstep voting of the Democratic appointees, contrasted against the inscrutability of Chief Justice Roberts and Justice Kennedy.

Despite the highs and lows of the term, however, when the dust cleared, there was one aspect of continuity that's particularly gratifying to me: Cato continued its winning streak in cases in which we filed amicus briefs. While not as dominating as in the previous two terms—when we went 15–3 and 10–1, respectively—we still managed to pull off an 8–7 record. I'm also proud to note that we were the

---

[2] This part of the analysis comes from Boston University law professor Jay Wexler, who tracks such things. See Kimberly Robinson, A Sikh, a Jew, a Muslim and a Catholic: Funniest Moments from the Supreme Court's 2014 Term, U.S. Law Week Blog, Bloomberg BNA (July 27, 2015), http://www.bna.com/sikh-jew-muslim-b17179933918. For Wexler's work in this area going back a decade, see Jay Wexler, SCOTUS Humor, http://jaywex.com/wordpress/scotus-humor (last visited Aug. 18, 2015).

only organization in the country to support those challenging both state marriage laws and the IRS's reworking of the Affordable Care Act. So it was a pretty good year for liberty, though obviously not without its disappointments—even beyond *King v. Burwell*.

Moreover, we fared way better than the U.S. government, which compiled an 8-13 record. Curiously, for the first time ever, both Cato and the feds found ourselves on the winning side of one case (see below)—but that was against a state government, so some Leviathan had to lose there. UCLA law professor Adam Winkler, writing at *Slate*, attributed the government's poor performance to its "conservative" positions on criminal justice.[3] I don't buy the ideological characterization: Justices Scalia and Thomas often vote against the prosecution, so does that mean they're "liberal," in contrast to "law-and-order conservative" Justices Breyer and Kagan? But the larger point is correct: many of the government losses, including two unanimous ones, were in criminal cases. (Overcriminalization, anyone?)

But regardless—and regardless of its RobertsCare victories—this administration is easily the worst performer of any before the Court in modern times[4] (and probably ever, though it's more relevant to compare Obama to Bush, Clinton, Bush, and Reagan than, say, Benjamin Harrison). Whether you look overall—where Obama is below 50 percent, against a historical norm of 70 percent—or just at unanimous cases—where he has a record average of nearly four unanimous losses per term—it's not a pretty picture. There are three basic reasons for this: expansive executive action (including overzealous prosecution), envelope-breaking legal theories, and the fact that, regardless of his reasoning, Justice Kennedy tends to act like a libertarian in close cases. If the administration wants to improve its standing before the Court, I humbly suggest that it follow Cato's lead, advocating positions (and engaging in actions) that are grounded in law and that reinforce the Constitution's role in securing and protecting liberty.

---

[3]Adam Winkler, Is the Supreme Court More Liberal Than Obama?, Slate (June 30, 2015), http://www.slate.com/articles/news_and_politics/jurisprudence/2015/06/supreme_court_liberal_on_criminal_justice_issues_clarence_thomas_sided_with.html.

[4] See Oliver Roeder, Despite This Week's Victories, Obama Has Struggled at the Supreme Court, FiveThirtyEight (June 26, 2015), http://fivethirtyeight.com/datalab/despite-this-weeks-victories-obama-has-struggled-at-the-supreme-court.

Finally, before I whet your appetite for the articles to come, a few words on the consequences of the marriage case for which this term will become known. Just because the ruling was expected doesn't make it any less momentous. In sometimes-soaring rhetoric, Justice Kennedy explained that the Fourteenth Amendment's guarantee of both liberty and equality means that there's no valid reason to deny this particular institution—the benefit of these particular laws—to gay and lesbian couples. Okay, fair enough: there's a constitutional right for gay and lesbian couples to get marriage licenses—at least as long as everyone else gets them.

But where do we go from here? What about people who disagree, in good faith, with no ill intent toward gay people? Will ministers, to the extent they play a dual role in signing state licenses, have to officiate at big gay weddings? Will bakers and photographers have to work them? What about employment-discrimination protections based on sexual orientation—around half the states lack them, but are they now required? And what about tax-exempt status for religious schools, an issue that came up during oral argument?

It's unclear, to be honest—much depends on whether Kennedy remains on the Court to answer these questions in his own hand-waving way—but all of these examples, including marriage-licensing itself, show the folly inherent in government insinuation into the sea of liberty upon which we're supposed to sail our ship of life.

If the government didn't get involved in regulating private relationships between consenting adults—whether sexual, economic, political, athletic, educational, or anything else—we wouldn't be in that second-best world of adjudicating competing rights claims. If we maintained that broad public non-governmental sphere, as distinct from both the private home and state action, then we could let a thousand flowers bloom and each person would be free to choose a little platoon with which to associate. But that live-and-let-live world is rapidly contracting, so we're forced to fight for carve-outs of liberty amidst a sea of mandates, regulations, and other authoritarian "nudges."[5]

In any event, good for the Court. And while I echo Justice Kennedy's hope that both sides now respect each other's liberties and

[5] See Ilya Shapiro, Hobby Lobby and the Future of Freedom, 23 Nat'l Affairs 132 (Spring 2015), available at http://object.cato.org/sites/cato.org/files/articles/hobby_lobby_for_natl_affairs_28published28.pdf.

the rule of law, I stand ready to defend anybody's right to offend or otherwise live his or her life in ways I might not approve.

Articles

Turning to the *Review*, the volume begins as always with the previous year's B. Kenneth Simon Lecture in Constitutional Thought, which in 2014 was delivered by Judge Diane Sykes of the U.S. Court of Appeals for the Seventh Circuit. Judge Sykes's lecture focused on "Minimalism and Its Limits," describing the pitfalls judges face when they try too hard not to affect the real world. While jurists ought not to think of themselves as legislators and rewrite the laws they're tasked with interpreting, they shouldn't hesitate to make legal rulings and let the political chips fall where they may. Too much deference to the political branches amounts to an abdication of the judicial role, after all. "At a time of deep political polarization," Judge Sykes says, "the modesty and consensus values claimed by judicial minimalism seem especially attractive." "But strong avoidance and deference doctrines are not the answer. . . . The Court's legitimacy arises from [the Constitution] and is best preserved by adhering to decision methods that neither expand, nor contract, but *legitimize* the power of judicial review."

It's altogether fitting then, and ironic, that as we move next to the 2014–2015 term, we start with two articles on a case exhibiting both judicial overreach and over-deference, *King v. Burwell*. The progenitors of the lawsuits against the IRS tax-credit rule at issue, Jonathan Adler of Case Western and my Cato colleague Michael Cannon, present a comprehensive overview of *King* and related lawsuits. Those who followed the litigation know that it turned on the ACA provision that authorizes tax credits (subsidies) for buying health insurance on exchanges "established by the State." A six-justice majority found that this seemingly clear text nevertheless allowed credits for purchases made on the *federal* exchange. Cannon elsewhere found this interpretive legerdemain to be akin to "six Humpty Dumptys playing Calvinball."[6] The consequences of this judicial rewriting are dire for the health care system and the rule of law, of course, but also for federalism. "The Court's decision to disregard Congress's express

---

[6] Michael F. Cannon, Six Humpty Dumptys Playing Calvinball, SCOTUSblog (June 26, 2015), http://www.scotusblog.com/2015/06/symposium-six-humpty-dumptys-playing-calvinball.

plan has deprived states of a power Congress granted them, and that many states were eager to use," Adler and Cannon write. "And it creates uncertainty about whether citizens can trust that federal statutes mean what they say."

Vanderbilt's Jim Blumstein has a similar take on *King*, though if anything he's even less charitable to John Roberts. "Effectively reading pivotal statutory text out of a statute seems well beyond the umpire or referee function much proclaimed by the chief justice during his confirmation process." Invoking the biblical story regarding Joseph's interpretation of Pharaoh's dreams, Blumstein posits that "the Court in *King* looked to the dreams of the drafters of the ACA . . . and took measures to accommodate, empower, and implement those dreams." Who needs to do the hard work of textual exegesis when judges simply know what Congress wanted to do? Blumstein is much more alarmed by *King* than he was by *NFIB v. Sebelius*—the individual-mandate case he wrote about in these pages three years ago—labelling the ruling "institutionally corrosive."

We got the principal author of Cato's brief in *Obergefell v. Hodges*, Yale law professor Bill Eskridge, to write about the same-sex marriage cases. In a preview of his forthcoming book on the subject, Eskridge colorfully describes how members of the LGBT community have moved "from outlaws to 'inlaws.'" While not uncritical of Justice Kennedy's majority opinion—it's disappointing that he didn't engage the clear original-meaning evidence regarding the Equal Protection Clause[7]—Eskridge recognizes it as a "landmark decision." The result was wholly expected given the rapid shifts in popular opinion on the subject, as well as the Court's ruling on the Defense of Marriage Act two years ago in *United States v. Windsor*—which Kennedy also authored, as he did the case that struck down sodomy laws in 2003, *Lawrence v. Texas*. Still, the Supreme Court, Eskridge write, "is not the primary engine for the process by which Americans work through the implications of gay rights, but that process will,

---

[7] Cf. Roger Pilon, Fair Decision in Same-Sex Marriage, but Based Mostly on Faulty Logic, Nat'l L.J., July 20, 2015, available at http://www.cato.org/publications/commentary/fair-decision-same-sex-marriage-based-mostly-faulty-logic; Ben Domenech, Symposium Contribution, Gay Marriage Is Here—Now What?, The Federalist (June 27, 2015) ("It would have been much better if Justice Kennedy had just quoted from the entirety of [Cato's] Obergefell v. Hodges amicus brief, and written at the end: 'This!'"), http://thefederalist.com/2015/06/27/gay-marriage-is-here-now-what.

assuredly, bring new equality–liberty clashes to the Court in the next decade."

My colleague Walter Olson makes his debut in the *Review* with an article on a case in which Cato was on the losing side of an 8–1 decision, *EEOC v. Abercrombie & Fitch*. This was the one where the clothing retailer declined to hire a teenager who was wearing a headscarf—for religious reasons, as it turns out—which violated the chain's (since-relaxed) "Look Policy." Justice Scalia called this case "easy" when he announced the ruling, but there are plenty of complexities here that Olson does well to tease out. For example, are employers simply supposed to indulge whatever religious stereotypes they have in dealing with job applicants who seem to present some manifestation of religiosity? If someone shows up with a cross around her neck, does that indicate something about how they dress—whether modestly or like Madonna—and if an applicant wears a yarmulke, does that mean you can't schedule him for Saturday shifts? Amazingly, the case brought together the Becket Fund for Religious Liberty, Americans United for Separation of Church and State, the ACLU, and the Christian Legal Society—all on the same side and against both Cato and a rare joint brief by the Chamber of Commerce and the National Federation of Independent Business (the leading advocate for small businesses). Don't expect another religious-accommodation case like it.

Next, Roger Clegg of the Center for Equal Opportunity returns to our journal for a look at what may have been the term's most surprising ruling—and one that was overlooked because it came down the same day as *King v. Burwell*. The case had a mouthful of a name—*Texas Department of Housing and Community Affairs vs. The Inclusive Communities Project*—and asked whether the Fair Housing Act allows claims for "disparate impact" liability. That is, the FHA, like all civil-rights statutes, prohibits the use of race in decisions relating to housing (including development plans, mortgage-financing, and many other areas)—but does there have to be intentional discrimination, or can race-neutral policies that have a statistically disparate impact on particular racial groups also land you in hot water? Although all appellate courts to have decided the question have permitted disparate-impact claims, the federal government so feared the Supreme Court's response that it facilitated settlements in two other such cases that the high court took up in the last four years.

And for good reason: after oral argument, it seemed that there were clearly four votes against disparate impact—with Justice Scalia, of all people, as the swing vote (and it seemed that his view might be that the law did contemplate disparate impact, but that this made the law unconstitutional). But it was not to be. Justice Kennedy wrote a majority opinion that left the door open to disparate-impact claims but gave plenty of language to both plaintiffs' and defendants' lawyers.

Then we have Tim Sandefur, principal attorney at Pacific Legal Foundation and Cato adjunct scholar, for a fascinating take on the most interesting antitrust case in recent memory. *North Carolina Board of Dental Examiners v. FTC* was so unusual that it was the first one ever where Cato filed a brief supporting the federal government! Here, the state governing board of dentists was trying to prevent non-dentists from performing a procedure that's so safe that people can do it on themselves: teeth-whitening. The Court ultimately ruled that such a board can get the antitrust immunity given to "state action" only if the state is indeed actively supervising the regulatory activities—not merely giving its imprimatur to a self-interested cartel. Come to think of it, this is really the flip-side of all those economic-liberty cases brought by PLF, the Institute for Justice, and a host of other libertarian public-interest law firms. Sandefur writes: "Legal barriers to entry such as licensing laws raise the cost of living and deprive entrepreneurs of economic opportunity and their constitutionally protected right to pursue the lawful vocation of their choice."

Following that remarkable case comes one with a truly bizarre factual scenario (which I'll try to describe without making any bad puns). In *Yates v. United States,* a Gulf Coast fisherman was caught by a fish-and-wildlife inspector with undersized grouper—and was eventually prosecuted for violating the anti-shredding provision of the Sarbanes-Oxley Act of 2002 (which was enacted in response to the turn-of-the-century financial-accounting scandals). It seems that when John Yates (presumably) cast overboard the evidence of his fishing infractions, he provided an opportunity for an overzealous prosecutor to use a provision meant for anyone who "knowingly alters, destroys, mutilates, conceals, covers up, falsifies, or makes a false entry in any record, document, *or tangible object* with the intent to impede" any federal investigation. Here to help us untangle this net—darn it, I was so close to a pun-free summary—is John Malcolm, who directs the Edwin Meese Center for Legal and Judicial Studies at the Heritage Foundation. Malcolm, an experienced prosecutor now heavily involved in the movement against overcriminalization, notes that "while it should not be unduly onerous for the federal government to prosecute those who engage in what is arguably criminal conduct, it shouldn't be like shooting fish in a barrel either."

Staying with the criminal law but moving to its constitutional aspects, Louisville law professor Luke Milligan tackles *Los Angeles v. Patel*, the "no-tell motel" case. At issue here was an ordinance in the City of Angels that required places of public accommodation to maintain certain guest records, and to make those records available at any time to police (without a warrant). A group of hotel operators sued the city, arguing that this provision violated the Fourth Amendment's protection against unreasonable search and seizure. It was an unusual lawsuit in that most Fourth Amendment cases involve allegations that law enforcement officers made an unconstitutional search in a particular situation—typically finding drugs or guns that a criminal defendant wants to exclude from evidence as being "fruit of the poisonous tree." Milligan argues that the key to *Patel* isn't a mere determination of whether a given search is "unreasonable"—or even whether most would be under the L.A. ordinance—but instead goes to understanding the right "to be secure" from such searches. So "the original meaning of the Fourth Amendment appears to have played a silent but important role."

BakerHostetler's Andrew Grossman, a prolific adjunct scholar for Cato's Center for Constitutional Studies—we got him in a trade with Heritage for a bag of pocket Constitutions and three interns to be named later—covers *Michigan v. EPA*, the term's big environmental case. And he makes this exceedingly complicated administrative-law case look simple. The Court ruled that an EPA regulation ostensibly aimed at mercury but really targeting greenhouse gases was illegal because the agency didn't follow the proper procedures in promulgating it. In a nutshell, Grossman writes, "*Michigan* establishes as a baseline principle of administrative law that agencies must give some consideration to costs when regulating under statutes that do not preclude them from doing so." In other words, this wasn't even about the propriety of using a bogus pretext (mercury emissions, which are already exceedingly low) to pursue policy that's been legislatively stymied (carbon-dioxide emissions related to ~~global~~

~~warming~~ ~~climate change~~ bad weather). The EPA didn't even bother trying to justify imposing billions of regulatory costs to reap (speculative) millions in benefits; not good enough, said the justices.

From the War on Coal we turn to the War on Raisins. Former federal judge Michael McConnell, now director of Stanford's Constitutional Law Center, provides an eminently readable essay about a case that he actually argued at the Supreme Court—twice. In a story that sounds like it was ripped from an Ayn Rand novel, the Raisin Administrative Committee, which of course dates back to the New Deal, requires all raisin producers to withhold some of their crop from the market each year, and instead to deliver it to the government. The government, in its infinite wisdom, does whatever it wants with those raisins, from putting them in school lunches, to letting them rot, to selling them to large packers (think Sun-Maid) and using the proceeds for export subsidies. All in the name of "stabilizing" prices, you see, and all for the benefit of those farmers. But the issue here wasn't "really, this is still a thing?" Instead, it was whether taking these raisins—47 and 30 percent of the crop, respectively, in the years relevant to the litigation—constituted a "taking" of private property without just compensation under the Fifth Amendment. "Seems like an easy question," McConnell says, stating the obvious. "Yet the case took three published opinions in the [Ninth Circuit] . . . and two trips to the U.S. Supreme Court. It even earned a mock investigative report on Comedy Central." If you've lost Jon Stewart, you've lost America.

Speaking of dry and shriveled doctrines, Adam White—new to the *Review* but a frequent contributor to *National Affairs*, *City Journal*, *The Weekly Standard*, and more—considers how much deference courts must give agencies with respect to interpretive rules (and what makes for an "interpretive" rule as opposed to some other kind). It's a pretty thorny question, and one that, if you follow the logical thread, goes to the heart of the administrative state. After all, White points out, "agencies wield immense powers delegated to them by Congress. . . . [which delegations] violate the Constitution only in the most extreme cases—namely, when Congress's grant of power to the agency is so open-ended as to contain no 'intelligible principle' guiding and limiting the agency's discretion." Thus most of our "law" is made not in the gleaming-marble halls and mahogany-paneled committee rooms of Congress but in the bowels of Washington's less-attractive federal buildings. In the context of *Perez v. Mortgage*

Bankers Association—which asked whether mortgage-loan officers are entitled to overtime pay (a question whose answer only matters to said officers and their employers)—White sensibly concludes that "Congress must take seriously the extent to which the [Administrative Procedure Act] fails to impose meaningful constraints upon agency discretion . . . and the extent to which [the resulting] rules receive deference from the courts."

If that's not deferential enough for you, our final article on the term just past features Emory law professor Sasha Volokh's chugging through the "private nondelegation" doctrine. The issue arises in *Department of Transportation v. Association of American Railroads* in the context of certain "metrics and standards"—regulations addressing the performance and scheduling of passenger rail services— which Congress has allowed Amtrak to set. Surely there's something wrong with allowing an entity to set the regulations by which it (and its competitors) operate. The Supreme Court doesn't really dispute that; but still, Amtrak (and the government) win this one because, at least for these purposes, Amtrak *is* the government. Amtrak may not be part of the government for other purposes, however—it's apparently Schrödinger's rail company. Moreover, as Justices Thomas and Alito point out in separate concurrences, Amtrak's being part of the government raises other constitutional issues. As Volokh puts it, the ruling "is the narrowest, most fact-based, most Amtrak-specific decision one could imagine," leaving many questions unanswered.

The volume concludes with a look ahead to October Term 2015 by John Elwood and Conor McEvily, who are appellate lawyers at the Washington office of Vinson & Elkins. As of this writing—before the term starts—the Court has 35 cases on its docket, down from last year's 39 (which was further down from previous years), such that we can expect about 70 opinions at term's end. Here are some of the issues: whether public employees can be forced to subsidize unions whose activities they don't support (*Friedrichs v. California Teachers Association*); whether and how racial preferences can be used in college admissions (*Fisher v. University of Texas at Austin*); whether state legislative districts should be drawn to equalize people or eligible voters (*Evenwel v. Abbott*); whether a class action can proceed on a statistical theory of damages and where certain class members weren't injured (*Tyson Foods v. Bouaphakeo*); and whether a criminal defendant has a right to use untainted assets to pay for her legal defense (*Luis v. United States*). These cases don't quite reach the high profile of recent terms, but they should be enough to shift the "liberals ascendant" narrative that came out this past June. As Elwood and McEvily conclude, "we would hesitate to say that this is another candidate to be the Term of the Century, [but] we can all agree that OT2015 is a strong contender to be the outstanding term of the third fifth of the 20-teens."

* * *

This is the eighth volume of the *Cato Supreme Court Review* that I've edited. The process gets a bit more comfortable each year but the workload certainly doesn't—which is why we've promoted Trevor Burrus to managing editor. This way I can still take credit for producing the wonderful book you hold in your hands, but can more effectively slough off the blame for any errors. Trevor has been a big help over the years with both the *Review* and our amicus brief program, so I'm delighted to be working more closely with him.

I'm also most thankful to our authors, without whom there would literally be nothing to edit or read. We ask leading legal scholars and practitioners to produce thoughtful, insightful, readable commentary of serious length on short deadlines, so I'm grateful that so many agree to my unreasonable demands every year.

My gratitude further goes to my colleagues Bob Levy, Tim Lynch, and Walter Olson, who provide valuable counsel and editing in legal areas less familiar to me. I used to joke that Jonathan Blanks "makes the trains run on time" in our department—no relation to the Amtrak case noted above—and he proved so good at his job that he's now a research associate with our Project on Criminal Justice. Taking his spot in the lineup is sensational rookie Anthony Gruzdis (who's also a star for Cato's softball team, so the metaphor is doubly apt). Anthony previously worked as a corporate paralegal, so he has special skills in dealing with hot-headed lawyers and arcane court rules alike. He also ably stepped into Jon's shoes in keeping track of legal associates Gabriel Latner and Randal John Meyer and legal interns Thomas Berry, Robert Fountain, and Devin Watkins—who in turn performed many thankless tasks without (much) complaint. Neither the *Review* nor our Constitution Day symposium would be possible without them.

Finally, thanks to Roger Pilon, the founder of Cato's Center for Constitutional Studies, who has advanced liberty and constitutionalism for longer than I've been alive. I'm confident that Roger is pleased with how his journal has turned out, and how its production runs like clockwork—though not without his editorial hand and oversight as he otherwise enjoys the summer. My career has benefited greatly from the high standard of excellence and integrity that he sets. Roger also demonstrates, especially if you catch him after-hours, what it is to be a happy warrior.

I reiterate our hope that this collection of essays will secure and advance the Madisonian first principles of our Constitution, giving renewed voice to the Framers' fervent wish that we have a government of laws and not of men. In so doing, we hope also to do justice to a rich legal tradition in which judges, politicians, and ordinary citizens alike understand that the Constitution reflects and protects the natural rights of life, liberty, and property, and serves as a bulwark against the abuse of government power. In these heady times when the People are demanding government accountability and an end to unconstitutional actions of various kinds—and anger is afoot, real anger at where the political class has taken us—it's more important than ever to remember our proud roots in the Enlightenment tradition.

We hope you enjoy this 14th volume of the *Cato Supreme Court Review*.

Minimalism and Its Limits

*by Diane S. Sykes**

Next month [October 2014] the curtain rises on the 10th term of the Roberts Court. From the beginning, Chief Justice Roberts has been explicit about wanting to foster greater consensus on the Court. It's often suggested that the Court's legitimacy would be enhanced by fewer 5–4 rulings along the usual conservative/liberal fault line. In his confirmation-hearing testimony, and more fully in his first major public address, the Chief Justice articulated his view that although differences among the justices should not be "artificially suppressed," a greater degree of consensus in the Court's decisions would bring "clear [jurisprudential] benefits."[1] He explained that unanimous or near-unanimous decisions "promote clarity and guidance for the lawyers and for the lower courts trying to figure out what the Supreme Court meant."[2] More fundamentally, he said, "The rule of law is strengthened when there is greater coherence and agreement about what the law is."[3] And he famously set for himself this guiding principle: "If it's not necessary to decide more to dispose of a case, in my view it is necessary not to decide more. The broader the agreement among the justices, the more likely it is that the decision is on the narrowest possible ground."[4]

Much of the early commentary about the Court's 2013–2014 term focused on the significant increase in the number of unanimous judgments. For the first time since the 1940s, almost two-thirds of

---

* Circuit Judge, U.S. Court of Appeals for the Seventh Circuit. This is the 13th annual B. Kenneth Simon Lecture in Constitutional Thought, delivered at the Cato Institute on September 17, 2014.

[1] Chief Justice John G. Roberts, Jr., Address at the 2006 Georgetown Law Center Commencement Ceremony (May 21, 2006), http://www.law.georgetown.edu/webcast/eventDetail.cfm?eventID=144.

[2] *Id.*

[3] *Id.*

[4] *Id.*

the Court's merits opinions were unanimous on the bottom line, if not necessarily in their reasoning. This is generally thought to be a striking and welcome development. In some key respects it is, although it's important to note that a significant part of the Court's docket each term consists of technical statutory or procedural issues that do not engage the philosophical differences among the justices. Still, the uptick in bottom-line agreement is remarkable, especially in cases raising difficult constitutional questions. In this category the Court achieved this greater degree of consensus (if that's what it is) mostly by following the Chief's maxim about narrow decisions, applying one technique or another of judicial minimalism. This dynamic will undoubtedly fuel the ongoing debate about whether the Roberts Court is committed to minimalism and, if so, whether that's a good thing.

I should probably begin by defining the term. Modern judicial minimalism as a distinctive theory of decision-making is usually credited to Professor Cass Sunstein of Harvard Law School, who coined the term and is the leading academic proponent of this approach to judging.[5] Sunstein proposes that judges should generally "avoid broad rules and abstract theories, and attempt to focus their attention only on what is necessary to resolve particular disputes."[6] He advocates the practice of "saying no more than necessary to justify an outcome, and leaving as much as possible undecided."[7] Minimalist judging of the Sunstein variant proceeds along two dimensions. First, judicial opinions should be narrow rather than wide, deciding the case at hand while avoiding pronouncing rules for resolving future cases.[8] Second, judicial opinions should be shallow rather than deep, avoiding large theoretical controversies and issues of basic principle. Judicial opinions should rely instead on incompletely theorized agreements that enable judges with diverse philosophical commitments to join in bottom-line judgments, leaving the more fundamental questions of principle undecided.[9]

[5] See Cass R. Sunstein, One Case at a Time: Judicial Minimalism on the Supreme Court (1999).

[6] *Id.* at 9.

[7] *Id.* at 3–4.

[8] *Id.* at 10–14.

[9] Cass R. Sunstein, Radicals in Robes: Why Extreme Right-Wing Courts Are Wrong for America 28 (2005).

Modern minimalism is justified primarily on pragmatic grounds. Minimalist decision methods (so the argument goes) account for the limitations on judicial competence—in particular, the limits on the judge's ability to accurately assess the consequences of a decision one way or the other. Narrow, shallow decisions reduce the risk and cost of error. Minimalist decisions are also said to be more pluralistic, demonstrating respect for diverse perspectives by leaving fundamental matters of principle unaddressed. Minimalism recommends itself for other reasons, too. It claims to promote stability and predictability, to maintain flexibility for future courts, and to empower democratic deliberation by giving political decision-makers room to maneuver and respond to constitutional questions left open by the Supreme Court.[10]

On the surface the theory sounds like it's limited to process values, but it's not. Substantively, minimalism starts from a presumption of deference to the political branches. It self-consciously avoids invalidating acts of the legislative and executive branches either by upholding them on the merits or by using various techniques for avoiding constitutional questions. The point of defaulting to deference is to "recognize[] the limited role of the federal judiciary and [to] make[] a large space for democratic self-government."[11] Minimalism also advocates a strong version of *stare decisis*; consistent adherence to precedent promotes stability and predictability, thereby preserving the Court's institutional interests.[12] On a more philosophical level, modern minimalism promotes itself as a hedge against judicial supremacy. It calls on judges to go slowly and in small steps.

The emphasis on incrementalism and gradualism evokes the philosophy of Edmund Burke, who viewed governance as a practical endeavor guided by experience grounded in skepticism of grand political theories.[13] Burke counseled deference to long-settled practices and traditions tested by experience and the collective wisdom of society accumulated over generations. He held the common law in high regard.[14]

---

[10] Sunstein, One Case at a Time, *supra* note 5, at 51–54.

[11] Sunstein, Radicals in Robes, *supra* note 9, at *xv*.

[12] *Id.* at 28.

[13] See Cass R. Sunstein, Burkean Minimalism, 105 Mich. L. Rev. 353, 369–70 (2006).

[14] *Id.*

Of course, the Founding generation didn't need a theory of judicial minimalism. The common-law tradition, as it was understood and practiced at the time, was itself essentially minimalist, and important minimalist features are embedded in our constitutional design. The common law as applied in the courts of the new American states was based on English customary law, and in the Blackstonian tradition it was found, not made.[15]

The philosophical terrain was also different than it is now. The Framers inherited a strong natural-rights tradition, but they also understood that because natural-rights principles are quite general—today we would say "underdetermined"—the judges of the new federal judiciary, like their counterparts in the states, would be called upon to exercise a substantial element of judgment in individual cases. As a constraint on that authority, Article III limits the judicial power to cases or controversies that are explicitly *judicial* in nature. The Framers rejected a more active political role for judicial review by deciding against a Council of Revision.[16] Beyond the constraining effect of the case-or-controversy limitation, the Framing generation generally understood that federal judges would follow long-established norms of judicial practice. They would be bound down by rules and precedents, to paraphrase *The Federalist No. 78*.[17] This was thought to be a sufficient check against arbitrary decisions based on will rather than judgment.

That was the "old" form of judicial minimalism; it was swept away by the legal realism of the 20th century. The "new" judicial minimalism is a response to the realist idea that, inescapably, appellate judges engage in discretionary lawmaking when they decide cases, including and especially cases of constitutional interpretation. If judges *make* constitutional law, then we need some theory or method to guide them in that enterprise.

Now, no one in this audience needs to be reminded of the normative constitutional theories that have been in contention since the New Deal, but I'll remind you anyway because it helps to place the new minimalism in proper historical perspective. The

---

[15] William Blackstone, 1 Commentaries, *71.

[16] See Jonathan T. Molot, Principled Minimalism: Restriking the Balance Between Judicial Minimalism and Neutral Principles, 90 Va. L. Rev. 1753, 1762 (2004).

[17] The Federalist No. 78, at 439 (Alexander Hamilton) (Clinton Rossiter ed., 1961).

"living constitution" school of thought held sway in the decades that spanned the Warren Court and the early years of the Burger Court. This evolutionary approach authorized judges to interpret the core principles of the Bill of Rights and the Fourteenth Amendment in a way that reflects contemporary values and allowed them to adapt the Constitution's broad language to address modern conditions and problems. In practice this theory produced the "rights revolution" of the 1950s and '60s, which was aggressively interventionist in implementing social, political, and legal reform by judicial decree. The results were in some cases a virtue and in others, well, not so much.[18] But in all cases the theory empowered the judiciary to deploy the Constitution as a malleable instrument of social and legal change at the expense of the democratic process.

The conservative counterrevolution began in earnest in the 1980s and initially focused on restoring the practice of "restraint," understood as judicial deference to the policy choices and value judgments of the political branches. In the early years, the primary concern was to stand athwart the jurisprudence of the Warren Court yelling "Stop!" (Apologies to William F. Buckley Jr.) But the emphasis on restraint did not address how the Constitution *ought* to be interpreted and applied. That would come later, as originalism was recovered, developed, and refined.

The animating principles of originalism arise from the legal justification for judicial review—the duty to decide cases according to law, including the law of the Constitution. Briefly stated, the basic theory is this: Because our Constitution is written, unlike the British Constitution, and because it is supreme law adopted by the people as the original sovereign that brought the American government into being, constitutional interpretation ought to be grounded in the public meaning of the text as understood at the time of ratification.

On this view, constitutional adjudication begins with an inquiry into the meaning and scope of the provision in question based on the Constitution's original meaning. Anchoring constitutional adjudication in the document's text, structure, and history is thought to best legitimize the power of judicial review. We all know *Marbury v.*

---

[18] For one view of the era, see J. Harvie Wilkinson III, Cosmic Constitutional Theory 13–32 (2012).

Madison:[19] The judiciary's authority to set aside a validly enacted law in the name of the Constitution arises by inference from the judge's duty to apply the law in individual cases. Originalism holds that the interpretive inquiry into the law of the Constitution ought to be grounded in, and tethered to, the principles fixed in its text and structure.

Originalism first established a foothold in the legal academy and eventually arrived at the Supreme Court. Professor Sunstein's minimalism is a response to the rise of originalism and is meant to counter it. Minimalist theory occupies some common ground with what has come to be known as judicial pragmatism, which is a flexible approach to judging that focuses on the consequences of judicial decisions. The aim of pragmatism is to achieve good overall outcomes, although its practitioners differ in their accounts of what is a good outcome. Minimalism and pragmatism are overlapping theories of consequentialist judging. Both mix law with practical politics.

This brings me to my final point about modern judicial minimalism: the theory is flexible about when judges should proceed minimally. It explicitly acknowledges that not every case calls for a minimalist ruling. As Sunstein puts it, "[T]he pragmatic foundations [of minimalism] suggest that constitutional law should not be insistently or dogmatically minimalist."[20] In other words, "there are times and places in which minimalism is rightly abandoned."[21] There's a nonexclusive, multifactor test for determining when it's best to issue a minimalist decision and when it's best to go maximalist—but you probably guessed that already.

It should be clear from this description that although minimalism is an approach to judging, it's *not* a theory of constitutional interpretation. Unlike originalism, it's not a method for determining the meaning, scope, and application of the Constitution. Instead, it's a theory of deference. Judges should defer to the political branches of government and to the decisions of prior courts—except when they shouldn't.[22] It's also a theory of avoidance. Judges should not make

[19] 5 U.S. (1 Cranch) 137 (1803).

[20] Cass R. Sunstein, Of Snakes and Butterflies: A Reply, 106 Colum. L. Rev. 2234, 2234 (2006).

[21] *Id.*

[22] See Tara Smith, Reckless Caution: The Perils of Judicial Minimalism, 5 N.Y.U. J.L. & Liberty 347, 374 (2010).

broad pronouncements on foundational matters of constitutional principle—except when they should. Got that?

As you've probably gathered, minimalism can and has been criticized for offering "no genuine guidance to judges."[23] As the philosopher Tara Smith observes, "[T]he instruction to the judiciary to 'minimize your impact' is hollow."[24] Critics have also attacked minimalism for "privileg[ing] the doctrinal status quo."[25] Sai Prakash, a law professor at the University of Virginia, notes that whereas originalism privileges the original public meaning of the Constitution, "minimalism—because it is precedent focused—tends to privilege the views of the Warren and Burger Courts."[26] Other critics have argued that by promoting shallow decision-making—especially in cases involving broad constitutional principles like free speech and equality—the theory permits judges to smuggle in their own unstated and unexamined ethical assumptions and preferences.[27] And as I have already noted, the pragmatic flexibility in minimalist theory provides no rule or standard for deciding when it should apply and when it should not.[28]

For my part, I tend to side with the critics. A unifying theory of minimalism is both unworkable and unwise. The Article III constraints on judicial power already enforce a degree of minimalism, and all judges respect and reason from precedent. We have well-established doctrines to ensure that judges do not unnecessarily decide constitutional questions, and the norm of analogical reasoning has a natural constraining effect. In other words, minimalism is inherent in standard judicial method. We do not need a heavy theoretical thumb on the scales. What's important is how the traditional sources of law and legal interpretation—text, structure, history, canons of interpretation, precedent, and other well-established tools of the judicial craft—are prioritized, weighted, and applied.

---

[23] *Id.* at 363.

[24] *Id.*

[25] Saikrishna Prakash, Radicals in Tweed Jackets: Why Extreme Left-Wing Law Professors Are Wrong For America, 106 Colum. L. Rev. 2207, 2212 (2006) (reviewing Cass R. Sunstein, Radicals in Robes).

[26] *Id.* at 2213–14.

[27] See, e.g., Steven D. Smith, The Disenchantment of Secular Discourse 26–37 (2010).

[28] See Tara Smith, *supra* note 22, at 373–74; Prakash, *supra* note 25, at 2215–17.

So with the theory now in place and my own position confessed, let's return to the question of the extent to which our current Supreme Court relies on minimalist methods. I've selected four representative examples from the more important constitutional cases of the 2013–2014 term—three unanimous, one not.

McCullen v. Coakley was the abortion-clinic protest buffer-zone case.[29] A Massachusetts law established a 35-foot buffer zone around the entrance to abortion clinics and made it a crime for anyone other than employees, patients, and their escorts to enter. The Court unanimously held that the law violated the First Amendment. But the justices were sharply divided on the rationale. Chief Justice Roberts wrote for himself and Justices Ruth Bader Ginsburg, Stephen Breyer, Sonia Sotomayor, and Elena Kagan. He first addressed whether the buffer-zone law was a content-based restriction on speech. This inquiry determined the standard of review. Content-based laws are presumptively unconstitutional and get strict judicial scrutiny; content-*neutral* laws are subject to a more relaxed standard of review. The Chief held that the Massachusetts law was content neutral but failed intermediate scrutiny because it burdened more speech than necessary.

Justice Antonin Scalia concurred in the judgment only, excoriating the Court for gratuitously deciding the content-neutrality question. If the statute was unconstitutional under the less demanding standard of review, then there was no need to address content neutrality, the predicate for strict scrutiny. In other words, resolving the question was logically unnecessary once the Court concluded that the Massachusetts law flunked the more lenient standard of review; the Court could have taken a minimalist approach and reserved the question for another day. To no one's surprise, Justice Scalia also thought the Court was wrong about content neutrality; he explained his view that the Massachusetts law flagrantly targeted antiabortion speech. Justices Anthony Kennedy and Clarence Thomas joined his concurrence. Justice Samuel Alito separately concurred, although he essentially agreed with Justice Scalia that the buffer-zone law discriminated on the basis of viewpoint.

Justice Scalia was quite right that a more limited approach—assuming but not deciding the content-neutrality question—would

[29] 134 S. Ct. 2518 (2014).

have gotten the job done in *McCullen*. The Massachusetts law would fail, but the Court would not pronounce judgment on the constitutionality of abortion-clinic buffer zones more generally. That kind of decision would have been minimalist in the sense of deciding no more than necessary. Instead, by deciding the question as he did, the Chief achieved a unanimous judgment, and he did so by writing an opinion that might be characterized as minimalist in a more *substantive* sense. By ruling that the Massachusetts law was content neutral, the Court signaled that buffer-zone laws are permissible *if* properly tailored. That holding leaves room for political decision-makers to maneuver in this speech-sensitive area. If the decision on content neutrality had gone the other way, *all* abortion-clinic buffer-zone laws would be presumptively unconstitutional, and the Court's controversial decision in *Hill v. Colorado*[30] —which upheld a buffer-zone law—would have to be overruled or strictly limited to its facts. Indeed, the *McCullen* certiorari grant had included that very question, as Justice Scalia noted in his concurrence. The Chief's content-neutrality holding allowed the Court to avoid overruling a precedent.

In notable contrast, in *McCutcheon v. Federal Election Commission*,[31] another important free-speech case decided earlier in the term, the Court specifically *declined* to address a key question about the standard of review *precisely because* doing so would have meant revisiting a long-standing precedent. *McCutcheon* raised a challenge to the federal limits on the aggregate amount a person may contribute to candidates and political committees in a single election cycle. In *Buckley v. Valeo*,[32] the seminal 1976 campaign-finance decision, the Court drew a distinction, for First Amendment purposes, between campaign *contributions* and campaign *expenditures*: Limits on contributions to candidates are evaluated under intermediate scrutiny and may be justified based on the government's interest in preventing corruption or its appearance; but limits on expenditures get strict scrutiny and usually flunk. The contribution/expenditure distinction—and the different standards of review—were specifically challenged in *McCutcheon*. The Court sidestepped the question, finding it unnecessary to "parse the differences between the two standards"

---

[30] 530 U.S. 703 (2000).

[31] 134 S. Ct. 1434 (2014).

[32] 424 U.S. 1 (1976).

because the aggregate limits were unconstitutional even under the more lenient test.[33]

When *McCullen* was later decided, Justice Scalia saw something amiss in the Court's earlier decision to avoid the predicate standard-of-review question in *McCutcheon*—yet decide it now in *McCullen*. He bluntly confronted the Court in his *McCullen* concurrence: "What has changed since [*McCutcheon*]?" "Quite simple," he said, "This is an abortion case, and *McCutcheon* was not."[34] The Chief responded that "[a]pplying any standard of review other than intermediate scrutiny in *McCutcheon* . . . would have required overruling a precedent."[35] Yes, but the same was true in *McCullen*; *Hill v. Colorado* was on the line if strict scrutiny applied, though perhaps it could have been limited or distinguished, neither of which were viable options if the Court had taken the plunge and revisited the contribution/expenditure distinction in *McCutcheon*. Overruling this aspect of *Buckley* was fraught with consequences for our politics; deciding the content-neutrality question in *McCullen* was not.

Thanks to Marcia Coyle of *The National Law Journal*, we have a window on the Chief's thinking in *McCullen*. In a revealing interview with Justice Ginsburg in August 2014, the veteran Supreme Court reporter asked the Justice why she had joined the Chief's opinion in *McCullen*. Justice Ginsburg replied that the Chief "made a very important case that . . . regulation[s] [on abortion-clinic] protests are content-neutral. That was the most important thing to me about the [C]hief's decision."[36] She continued: "My initial view was this is permissible legislation but if you looked at the record, it was so sparse. . . . It wasn't necessary to have that 35-foot zone."[37] She also observed that Massachusetts had already "gone back and changed [its buffer-zone law]."[38] How interesting! The Chief joined with his more liberal colleagues to leave open the possibility of regulation in this area. The Court's content-neutrality holding may be debatable, but there is clear deference to political policymakers here.

---

[33] McCutcheon, 134 S. Ct. at 1446.

[34] McCullen, 134 S. Ct. at 2542 (Scalia, J., concurring) (footnote omitted).

[35] *Id.* at 2530 (majority opinion).

[36] Marcia Coyle, Ginsburg on Rulings, Race, Nat'l L.J., Aug. 22, 2014.

[37] *Id.*

[38] *Id.*

Harris v. Quinn[39] is another example of the Court's complex relationship with the minimalist impulse to avoid confrontations with precedent. The question in *Harris* was whether Illinois violated the First Amendment by requiring in-home caregivers to pay public-employee union dues even if they did not support the union's activities. In *Abood v. Detroit Board of Education*,[40] the Court had rejected a claim by public-school teachers that requiring them to pay union dues violated their right to free speech and association. The in-home caregivers in *Harris*, however, were not public-sector employees in the usual sense. They were employed primarily by their private customers; the State's role was limited to compensating them with Medicaid funds. The issue in *Harris* was whether *Abood* controlled, and if so, whether it should be overruled.

The Court broke 5–4 along the usual conservative/liberal fault line. Writing for the majority, Justice Alito held that the First Amendment prohibited the collection of union dues from the in-home caregivers. The decision was carefully limited to quasi-public employees; the Court left *Abood* intact.

The interesting thing about Justice Alito's opinion is its extended discussion of *Abood*'s "questionable foundations,"[41] with particular emphasis on the conceptual and practical distinctions between private- and public-sector collective bargaining and the special problem in public-sector cases of "distinguishing . . . between union expenditures that are made for collective-bargaining purposes and those that are made to achieve political ends."[42] For the dissenters, this was all just "gratuitous dicta."[43] (Now we see the shoe on the other foot!) Justice Kagan, writing for herself and Justices Ginsburg, Breyer, and Sotomayor, pointedly criticized her colleagues for failing to suppress the urge to "tak[e] potshots at *Abood*."[44] Her complaint is understandable but misplaced. The first question in *Harris* was whether the rule of *Abood* was controlling; that necessarily required the Court to decide whether to extend the holding of the case

[39] 134 S. Ct. 2618 (2014).
[40] 431 U.S. 209 (1977).
[41] 134 S. Ct. at 2638.
[42] *Id.* at 2632.
[43] *Id.* at 2645 (Kagan, J., dissenting).
[44] *Id.*

to quasi-public employees. The majority concluded that it should not, and that conclusion required an explanation. True, a minimalist justice might have said less, but under-reasoned decisions can seem arbitrary and evasive. In the minimalist taxonomy, perhaps *Harris* is best classified as an opinion of *narrow deepness*. The opinion is *narrow* because it is limited to its facts. But it is also *deep* because the constitutional principle is carefully explained.

I'll spend just a few moments on *Noel Canning*, the Recess Appointments Clause case.[45] As in *McCullen* the Court was unanimous in the judgment but split 5–4 on the rationale. All nine justices agreed that President Obama lacked the authority to make three recess appointments to the NLRB when the Senate was in *pro forma* session in January 2012. Justice Breyer, writing for a majority that included Justice Kennedy and the left side of the bench, held that the *"pro forma* sessions count as sessions, not as periods of recess."[46] But on the remaining questions in the case—the meaning of the term "recess" and whether the vacancy must actually "happen" during a recess—Justice Breyer deferred to presidential practice, which since the Civil War era had shown increased reliance on the recess-appointment power. Based on this historical experience, Justice Breyer held that the term "recess" included *intra*-session recesses and that the vacancy need not "happen" during a recess.

The minimalist data point in Justice Breyer's opinion is this: He thought it best not "to upset the compromises and working arrangements that the elected branches of Government have themselves reached."[47] Judicially updating the Clause to reflect the more expansive, modern-day understanding required the Court to set some artificial barriers on the President's use of this power. Justice Breyer declared that a recess of three days is too short to permit an appointment without Senate consent; a recess of more than ten days is generally long enough; and a recess between three and ten days may or may not qualify, depending upon exigencies.

Justice Scalia's concurrence is both rigorously originalist and emphatic that the Court's duty in structure-of-government cases is to enforce the original boundaries of the separation of powers, not to

[45] NLRB v. Noel Canning, 134 S. Ct. 2550 (2014).
[46] *Id.* at 2574.
[47] *Id.* at 2560.

endorse practices that seem more prudent in light of modern experience.[48] He was joined by the Chief and Justices Thomas and Alito.

The last case I'll mention is the term's most important federalism challenge: *Bond v. United States.*[49] The facts were unusual; the case illustrates how an aggressive charging decision by a local U.S. Attorney can resurface a profound but long dormant constitutional question. In 2006 Carol Anne Bond learned that her best friend was pregnant and that her own husband was the child's father. She responded to this betrayal by repeatedly trying to injure her now ex-friend by assaulting her with toxic chemicals. On many occasions over a period of seven months, Bond applied the chemicals to items that her rival would touch—a mailbox, a car door, a doorknob at her house. The victim was not seriously injured, but postal inspectors put the house under surveillance and caught Bond stealing mail from the victim's mailbox and putting chemicals in the muffler of her car.

Bond was charged with mail theft, but prosecutors also threw in charges of possessing and using a chemical weapon in violation of the Chemical Weapons Convention Implementation Act,[50] adopted in 1998 to implement the international Convention on Chemical Weapons.[51] The Act defines "chemical weapon" very broadly and included Bond's conduct. She argued that the crime was purely local, and that the chemical-weapons statute exceeded the enumerated powers of Congress and invaded powers reserved to the states by the Tenth Amendment. The first time her case was before the Court, back in 2011, the justices addressed only the question of standing: May an individual assert a Tenth Amendment challenge? The Court unanimously said "yes," the Constitution's federal structure "protects the liberty of all persons within a State by ensuring that laws enacted in excess of delegated governmental power cannot direct or control their actions."[52]

When the case returned to the Court on the merits, the government specifically disclaimed any reliance on the Commerce Power and defended the statute based solely on the Necessary and Proper

[48] *Id.* at 2617 (Scalia, J., concurring).

[49] 134 S. Ct. 2077 (2014).

[50] 18 U.S.C. § 229(a)(1).

[51] 134 S. Ct. at 2083–85.

[52] Bond v. United States, 131 S. Ct. 2355, 2364 (2011).

Clause as applied to the authority of the national government to make treaties. This argument rested largely on a single statement in the 1920 decision in *Missouri v. Holland.*[53] While the first appeal in *Bond* raised a narrow question of standing, this time the stakes were very different. The case pressed hard on the boundaries of the Necessary and Proper Clause and its interplay with the Treaty Power. It also tested the Court's willingness to enforce the Tenth Amendment. To complicate matters, the case called into question a long-standing but largely unexamined precedent. A perfect storm.

The Court unanimously reversed Bond's conviction, but again the justices were divided on the rationale. Writing for himself and five of his colleagues, the Chief Justice avoided the high-stakes constitutional question and the uncomfortable need to reconsider *Holland* by construing the statute so that it did not reach Bond's conduct. The Chief began his statutory analysis by noting that "Congress legislates against the backdrop of certain unexpressed presumptions," including "those grounded in the relationship between the Federal Government and the States."[54] In light of this "federalism presumption," the Chief found the statute ambiguous based on its "improbably broad reach."[55] So he trimmed the statute to cover only the possession and use of chemicals "of the sort that an ordinary person would associate with instruments of chemical warfare."[56]

Once again, Justice Scalia cried foul. In yet another concurrence that reads like a dissent, he accused the Court of shirking its duty to decide the case by turning a "federalism-inspired interpretive presumption" on its head.[57] Background principles of federalism may be useful in choosing between two plausible readings of an ambiguous statute, but here the Court was using the statute's "disruptive effect on the 'federal-state balance'" as a reason to find an "utterly clear" statute ambiguous.[58] This interpretive move, he said, distorted the law and held the potential for future mischief. The vagueness of the Court's "ordinary person" test for criminal liability raised a whole

---

[53] 252 U.S. 416, 432 (1920).

[54] Bond, 134 S. Ct. at 2088 (citation omitted).

[55] *Id.* at 2090.

[56] *Id.*

[57] *Id.* at 2095 (Scalia, J., concurring).

[58] *Id.* at 2095–96.

new set of constitutional concerns. The Court had delivered "a supposedly 'narrow' opinion which, in order to be 'narrow,' set[] forth interpretive principles never before imagined that will bedevil our jurisprudence (and proliferate litigation) for years to come."[59] Justice Scalia was joined by Justices Thomas and Alito in concluding that the statute exceeded Congress's power under the Necessary and Proper Clause as applied to the Treaty Power.

Stepping back, these cases reflect what I think is indeed a noteworthy feature of the Roberts Court at age 10: its preference for using minimalist techniques to avoid or soften or at least postpone confrontation with the political branches in structurally or politically sensitive cases. Although the constitutional-avoidance doctrine was not specifically mentioned in *Bond*, the Chief's analysis exemplifies the modern version of the doctrine. The original or "classic" avoidance canon dates to the Marshall Court.[60] As described by Justice Joseph Story, the basic rule is this: if a statute "admits of two interpretations, one of which brings it within, and the other presses it beyond the constitutional authority of [C]ongress, it will become [the Court's] duty to adopt the former construction . . . unless [the other] conclusion is forced upon the Court by language altogether unambiguous."[61]

The avoidance canon underwent a subtle but important change in the twentieth century. The modern version directs judges to construe statutes to avoid constitutional *doubt*. This much broader idea of constitutional avoidance took hold in the New Deal era and was cemented in a famous concurring opinion by Justice Louis Brandeis in the 1936 case of *Ashwander v. Tennessee Valley Authority*.[62] Critics charge that the modern version of the doctrine distorts rather than preserves the separation of powers. As my colleague Frank Easterbrook has memorably put it, modern avoidance doctrine "acts as a

---

[59] *Id.* at 2102.

[60] William K. Kelley, Avoiding Constitutional Questions As A Three-Branch Problem, 86 Cornell L. Rev. 831, 842–46 (2001).

[61] United States v. Coombs, 37 U.S. (12 Pet.) 72, 75–76 (1838) (Story, J.).

[62] 297 U.S. 288, 345 (Brandeis, J., concurring) ("It must be evident to any one that the power to declare a legislative enactment void is one which the judge, conscious of the fallibility of the human judgment, will shrink from exercising in any case where he can conscientiously and with due regard to duty and official oath decline the responsibility." (quoting 1 Cooley, Constitutional Limitations (8th ed.) 332)).

roving commission to rewrite statutes to taste."[63] On this view "the constitutional-doubt canon is simultaneously unfaithful to the statutory text *and* an affront to . . . the political branches."[64] In other words, judicial amendment of statutes in the name of constitutional avoidance both distorts the law and displaces the prerogatives and responsibilities of the political branches. But, as Judge Easterbrook has noted, the justices are addicted to it.[65] There are many recent examples, perhaps the most controversial of which is *NFIB v. Sebelius*,[66] the challenge to the individual-insurance mandate in the Affordable Care Act.

Sometimes these avoidance techniques simply delay the confrontation. In *Shelby County v. Holder*,[67] decided in June 2013, the Court struck down the coverage formula in Section 4 of the Voting Rights Act, the trigger for the preclearance requirement in Section 5 of the Act. Four years earlier in *Northwest Austin Municipal Utility District v. Holder*,[68] the Court had transparently signaled its discomfort with the coverage formula, which was based on a decades-old baseline that did not reflect changes in voting and discriminatory election practices when Congress reauthorized the Act in 2006. In a decision by Chief Justice Roberts, the Court sidestepped the tough constitutional question about the validity of this part of the Act by issuing a narrow decision holding that the petitioner in the case—a Texas utility district—could bail out of the preclearance requirement. To reach this conclusion, however, the Court had to stretch the statutory definition of "political subdivision" well beyond its text. *Northwest Austin* was nearly unanimous; only Justice Thomas would have reached the constitutional question.

Northwest Austin might be understood as an example of minimalism as a signaling device or a form of temporary abstention to allow the political branches to correct an identified constitutional defect. Although the Court avoided the constitutional question, it took pains

[63] Frank H. Easterbrook, Do Liberals and Conservatives Differ in Judicial Activism?, 73 U. Colo. L. Rev. 1401, 1405 (2001).

[64] *Id.* at 1406 (emphasis added).

[65] *Id.*

[66] 132 S. Ct. 2566 (2012).

[67] 133 S. Ct. 2612 (2013).

[68] 557 U.S. 193 (2009).

to explain that the preclearance requirement and its application to a limited set of states cut against basic principles of federalism and equal sovereignty, clearly signaling what it wanted Congress to do. When Congress did not address the formula and the issue returned to the Court in *Shelby County*, the Court was direct about its methodology. With the Chief Justice again writing, this time for a five-justice majority, the Court candidly explained its use of the avoidance doctrine in *Northwest Austin*:

> [I]n 2009, we took care to avoid ruling on the constitutionality of the Voting Rights Act when asked to do so . . . . But in issuing that decision, we expressed our broader concerns about the constitutionality of the Act. Congress could have updated the coverage formula at that time, but did not do so. Its failure to act leaves us today with no choice but to declare § 4(b) unconstitutional.[69]

The "no choice" language is interesting. A nearly unanimous Court used a minimalist decision as a soft-power tool to give the political branches an opportunity to correct an identified constitutional problem. But a narrow majority proceeded to judgment on the ultimate constitutional question when the political fix was not forthcoming. Minimalism simply put off the constitutional day of reckoning. In other contexts, however, the Court is slow to circle back to important structural questions left open.

In some areas of constitutional law, the Roberts Court has been decidedly nonminimalist. *Citizens United*,[70] the game-changing campaign-finance decision, is a prominent example—although it too was preceded by a minimalist compromise. In a plurality decision in the 2007 case of *Federal Election Commission v. Wisconsin Right to Life*,[71] the Chief Justice had crafted a narrow, as-applied remedy to avoid striking down the federal ban on political speech sponsored by corporations. When that remedy was shown to be seriously inadequate, the Court revisited the matter in *Citizens United*, invalidating the ban as an unconstitutional restriction on core political speech.

---

[69] 133 S. Ct. at 2631.

[70] Citizens United v. FEC, 558 U.S. 310 (2010).

[71] 551 U.S. 449 (2007).

Riley v. California,[72] handed down in June [2014], is another good example of anti-minimalism at work; we now have a clear rule that the police must obtain a warrant to search a cell phone seized incident to an arrest.[73] *Hosanna-Tabor*,[74] which recognized a ministerial exception to workplace discrimination laws under the Religion Clauses, is another example of anti-minimalism. These decisions are notable for giving us clear, foundational statements about what the law is, which in the end is the Court's duty.

At a time of deep political polarization, the modesty and consensus values claimed by judicial minimalism seem especially attractive. Restraint is indeed a judicial virtue. Judicial mistakes on constitutional questions are extraordinarily difficult to fix. Arrogating too much power to the judiciary distorts our politics and undermines our ability to democratically shape and alter our basic legal, social, and economic institutions. But strong avoidance and deference doctrines are not the answer. They may serve prudential or political concerns, but they are not necessary to enforce the separation of powers and indeed may undermine that critical feature in our constitutional design. The Court's legitimacy arises from the source of its authority—which is, of course, the Constitution—and is best preserved by adhering to decision methods that neither expand, nor contract, but *legitimize* the power of judicial review. The Court's primary duty, in short, is not to minimize its role or avoid friction with the political branches, but to try as best it can to get the Constitution right.

---

[72] 134 S. Ct. 2473 (2014).

[73] *Id.* at 2495.

[74] Hosanna-Tabor Evangelical Lutheran Church & Sch. v. EEOC, 132 S. Ct. 694 (2012).

King v. Burwell and the Triumph of Selective Contextualism

*Jonathan H. Adler and Michael F. Cannon**

I am altering the deal. Pray I don't alter it any further.[1]

Introduction

King v. Burwell presented the question of whether the Patient Protection and Affordable Care Act of 2010 (ACA) authorizes the Internal Revenue Service to issue tax credits for the purchase of health
insurance through exchanges established by the federal government. The *King* plaintiffs alleged an IRS rule purporting to authorize tax credits in federal exchanges was unlawful because the text
of the ACA expressly authorizes tax credits only in exchanges "established by the State." Led by Chief Justice John Roberts, the Supreme Court conceded the plain meaning of the operative text, and
that Congress defined "State" to exclude the federal government.
The Court nevertheless disagreed with the plaintiffs, explaining
that "the context and structure of the Act compel us to depart from
what would otherwise be the most natural reading of the pertinent
statutory phrase."[2] Voting 6–3, the Court effectively rewrote the

* Adler is the Johan Verheij Memorial Professor of Law and director of the Center
for Business Law & Regulation at the Case Western Reserve University School of Law.
Cannon is director of health policy studies at the Cato Institute. The authors were
intimately involved in *King v. Burwell* and related litigation. They were the first to
publicly question the lawfulness of the disputed IRS rule, developed many of the legal
arguments raised in the resulting legal challenges, and filed multiple amicus curiae
briefs in *King* and related cases. The authors thank Andrew Peterson for his research
assistance.

[1] Star Wars: Episode V - The Empire Strikes Back (Lucasfilm 1980).

[2] King v. Burwell, 135 S. Ct. 2480, 2495 (2015).

statutory text in order to ensure the ACA would "improve health insurance markets, not . . . destroy them."[3]

King was the Supreme Court's third ACA case in four years. In 2012, the Court upheld the constitutionality of the act in *National Federation of Independent Business v. Sebelius*, but only after rejecting a Commerce Clause justification for the individual mandate (construing it instead to be a use of the taxing power) and eliminating the requirement that states must implement the ACA's Medicaid expansion in order to keep receiving federal Medicaid grants.[4] Then, in 2014, in *Hobby Lobby Stores v. Burwell*, the Court concluded the Obama administration had failed to accommodate religious objections to the so-called "contraception mandate" as required under the federal Religious Freedom Restoration Act.[5]

NFIB saved the ACA, but left the statute scarred. *Hobby Lobby* rebuked the Department of Health and Human Services' implementation of the new law. By comparison, 2015's *King v. Burwell* was a resounding victory for the Obama administration. This third trip to One First Street was the charm.

While portions of the Court's *King* opinion may constrain agency interpretive authority in future cases, the opinion green-lighted the administration's efforts to implement the ACA without regard for the limitations contained in the ACA's text.[6] Even if the Court did not accept the specific arguments offered by the solicitor general, it gave

[3] *Id.* at 2496.

[4] 132 S. Ct. 2566 (2012). On *NFIB* see David B. Rivkin, Jr., Lee A. Casey, and Andrew M. Grossman, NFIB v. Sebelius and the Triumph of Fig-Leaf Federalism, 2011–2012 Cato Sup. Ct. Rev. 31 (2012); James F. Blumstein, Enforcing Limits on the Affordable Care Act's Mandated Medicaid Expansion: The Coercion Principle and the Clear Notice Rule, 2011–2012 Cato Sup. Ct. Rev. 67 (2012).

[5] 134 S. Ct. 2751 (2014). See Richard A. Epstein, The Defeat of the Contraceptive Mandate in Hobby Lobby: Right Results, Wrong Reasons, 2013–2014 Cato Sup. Ct. Rev. 35 (2014). See also Wheaton Coll. v. Burwell, 134 S. Ct. 2806 (2014) (mem.). This order generated opinions, but was not a decision on the merits after oral argument.

[6] This result is particularly troubling given the administration's pattern of modifying the meaning of the ACA in the course of implementing it. See Brief of Amici Curiae Cato Institute and Prof. Josh Blackman in Support of Petitioners, King v. Burwell, 135 S. Ct. 2480 (2015) (No. 14-114); see also Jonathan H. Adler, The Ad Hoc Implementation and Enforcement of Health Care Reform, in Liberty's Nemesis (D. Reuter & J. Yoo, eds., forthcoming); Grace-Marie Turner, 51 Changes to ObamaCare . . . So Far, Galen Institute (June 9, 2015), http://www.galen.org/newsletters/changes-to-obamacare-so-far.

the Obama administration nearly everything it wanted. The Court expanded the ACA beyond what its congressional supporters ever had the votes to enact. It just had to disregard portions of the ACA's text and selectively consider statutory structure and context to do it.

This article proceeds as follows. Part I demonstrates, via the ACA's unique legislative history, how having states operate the law's exchanges was an indispensable purpose of the act. The ACA literally would not have become law if the federal government were given primary responsibility for operating exchanges. Part II explains how the statutory language at issue in *King* is clear, unambiguous, and serves that congressional purpose—even if some ACA supporters did not know about or approve of that language. Part III discusses how and why the IRS departed from the plain meaning of that language, and the academic and legal challenges that followed. Part IV gives an overview of the Supreme Court's *King* decision. Part V shows how the majority misused statutory context to find the ACA is ambiguous. Part VI shows the Court's claim that it is "implausible" that Congress intended that language is demonstrably false. Part VII discusses the significance of the Court's decision not to apply the *Chevron* deference-to-agencies doctrine in *King*. Part VIII connects Chief Justice Roberts's approach to *King* to his "saving constructions" in *NFIB v. Sebelius*, which together have produced a law that is now materially different from Congress's plan. Part IX offers concluding thoughts.

I. State-Run Exchanges: An Essential Part of Congress's Plan

After 100 years marked by more failures than successes, advocates of universal health insurance coverage were heartened when a wave election in 2008 gave Democrats control of the presidency and both chambers of Congress. Crucially, one Republican senator's subsequent party switch also gave Democrats a 60-seat, filibuster-proof majority in the U.S. Senate that lasted from July 2009 until January 2010.[7] The House passed its health care bill in November 2009.[8] The Senate followed suit, passing the ACA—the merged product of

[7] This history is recounted in Jonathan H. Adler & Michael F. Cannon, Taxation Without Representation: The Illegal IRS Rule to Expand Tax Credits under the PPACA, 23 Health Matrix 119, 124–26 (2013); see also Brief of Amici Curiae Jonathan H. Adler & Michael F. Cannon, King v. Burwell, 135 S. Ct. 2480 (2015) (No. 14-114).

[8] Affordable Health Care for America Act, H.R. 3962, 111th Cong. (2009).

health care bills passed by the Senate Health, Education, Labor, and Pensions (HELP) Committee and the Senate Finance Committee—on December 24, 2009. The ACA passed the Senate by a vote of 60–39, overcoming a GOP filibuster without a vote to spare.

The ACA's authors never intended it to become the final bill.[9] Their goal was simply to marshal 60 votes behind something they could later merge with the House bill. A special-election upset put an end to such hopes. In January 2010, Massachusetts voters elected Republican Scott Brown to fill the Senate seat vacated by the death of Sen. Edward M. Kennedy (D-MA). Brown's victory put an end to the Senate Democrats' filibuster-proof majority. At that moment, the ACA became the only health care bill that could become law, because neither a House-Senate compromise nor any other bill could overcome a GOP filibuster.

Whatever the ACA's shortcomings, if Democrats wanted comprehensive health care legislation, it would have to be the ACA, because voters had blocked them from enacting anything more expansive. Despite serious reservations,[10] House Democrats approved the ACA as-is, making only minor changes through the budget reconciliation process, and sent it to the president's desk. One of those reservations would prove significant.

The ACA employed the basic framework House and Senate Democrats had agreed upon before the legislative process began: Medicaid coverage for everyone below a given poverty threshold and heavily regulated private health insurance for everyone else. The latter regulations banned discrimination on the basis of pre-existing conditions, and then, to combat the resulting instability, both required individuals to obtain coverage (an individual mandate) and subsidized premiums for low- and moderate-income households. Economists liken this scheme to a three-legged stool because it has the quality that without each of those three elements in place, the scheme collapses.

---

[9] Timothy S. Jost, Yes, the Federal Exchange Can Offer Premium Tax Credits, Health Reform Watch Blog (Sept. 11, 2011), http://www.healthreformwatch.com/2011/09/11/yes-the-federal-exchange-can-offer-premium-tax-credits ("No one intended the current ACA to become the final law. It was the Senate bill, enacted after the House bill, which was to go through conference before the final [bill] was enacted.").

[10] See Harold Pollack, 47 (Now 51) Health Policy Experts (Including Me) Say "Sign the Senate Bill," The New Republic (Jan. 22, 2010).

The ACA differed from the House bill in at least one significant respect: it gave states primary responsibility for administering its health-insurance "Exchanges," allowing the federal government to operate exchanges only where states failed to do so themselves.[11] The House bill created a single, nationwide exchange administered by the federal government.

Whatever substantive reasons individual Senate Democrats may have had for preferring state-run exchanges—for example, local control, deflecting criticisms that the ACA was a federal takeover of health care[12]—what matters for our present purposes is that state-run exchanges were an absolute political necessity. Key Democratic senators threatened not to support a final bill unless states operated the exchanges.[13] All other ACA supporters had no choice but to relent. Defeating a GOP filibuster required 60 votes, and Senate

[11] See U.S. Rep. Doggett: Settling for Second-Rate Health Care Doesn't Serve Texans, My Harlingen News (Jan. 11, 2010), http://www.myharlingennews.com/?p=6426 (letter from 11 House Democrats to President Obama and House Speaker Nancy Pelosi expressing concern about the ACA and "states with indifferent state leadership that are unwilling or unable to administer and properly regulate a health insurance market-place"); see also Terry Gross, Next Up: Turning Two Health Care Bills into One, Fresh Air (WBUR News) (Jan. 12, 2010), http://www.wbur.org/npr/122483567 ("GROSS: So getting to the exchanges, in the House bill, it's a national insurance exchange. In the Senate bill, it's state-oriented . . . Mr. COHN: Absolutely, and this is a very important difference that frankly has gotten little attention."). See also Julie Rovner, House, Senate View Health Exchanges Differently, NPR (Jan. 12, 2010), http://www.npr.org/templates/story/story.php?storyId=122476051.

[12] Senate Democratic Policy Comm., Fact Check: Responding to Opponents of Health Insurance Reform (Sept. 21, 2009), http://dpc.senate.gov/reform/reform-factcheck-092109.pdf ("There is no government takeover or control of health care in *any* senate health insurance reform legislation. . . . *All* the health insurance exchanges, which will create choice and competition for Americans' business in health care, are run by states" (emphasis added)).

[13] On the Record (Fox News broadcast, Apr. 13, 2010), http://www.foxnews.com/story/2010/04/14/sen-ben-nelson-his-side-cornhusker-kickback.html ("I had requirements. The requirements were no government run plan, no federal exchange, national exchange, and adequate language to deal with abortion. Those were requirements."). See also Patrick O'Connor & Carrie Brown, Nancy Pelosi's Uphill Health Bill Battle, Politico, Jan. 9, 2010 ("Two key moderates—Sen. Ben Nelson (D-Neb.) and Sen. Joe Lieberman (I-Conn.)—have favored the state-based exchanges over national exchanges."); Reed Abelson, Proposals Clash on States' Roles in Health Plans, N.Y. Times, Jan. 13, 2010 ("Senator Ben Nelson, Democrat of Nebraska, is a former governor, state insurance commissioner and insurance executive who strongly favors the state approach. His support is considered critical to the passage of any health care bill.").

Democrats had no votes to spare. Following Scott Brown's election, no other bill could have cleared Congress. The ACA *would not have passed* without a system of state-run exchanges. This was not only a distinct part of Congress's plan, but indeed a *sine qua non* of the ACA.

This congressional purpose was neither hidden nor its existence in dispute. Democrats in both chambers emphasized the ACA's exchanges would be state-run. They scarcely mentioned the possibility of federal exchanges.[14] Shortly after enactment, HHS Secretary Kathleen Sebelius testified, "I think it will very much be a State-based program."[15] President Obama predicted, "by 2014, each state will set up what we're calling a health insurance exchange."[16] They did not foresee that 34 states would refuse.

II. Clear Language that Serves a Congressional Purpose

The ACA's text reflects Congress's preference for state-run exchanges. Section 1311 directs, "Each State shall . . . establish an . . . Exchange."[17] Like the Finance and HELP bills, the ACA authorized unlimited start-up funds for state-run exchanges.[18] To provide an incentive for states to establish exchanges, it conditioned renewal of those grants on states making progress toward establishing an exchange and implementing other parts of the act.[19] Like the Finance and HELP bills, it provided no start-up funding for federal exchanges.[20]

---

[14] See Adler & Cannon, *supra* note 7, at 148–50 (reviewing discussion of exchanges in the Congressional Record).

[15] Departments of Labor, Health & Human Services, Education, & Related Agencies Appropriations for 2011: Hearing Before a Subcomm. on Appropriations, House of Representatives, 111th Cong. 171 (Apr. 21, 2010) (statement of Kathleen Sebelius, Sec'y, Dep't of Health & Hum. Servs.).

[16] Remarks on Health Insurance Reform in Portland, Maine, 2010 Daily Comp. Pres. Doc. 220 (Apr. 1, 2010).

[17] 42 U.S.C. § 18031(b)(1).

[18] *Id.* § 18031(a).

[19] *Id.*

[20] In the Health Care and Education Reconciliation Act of 2010, Congress did appropriate $1 billon "for Federal administrative expenses to carry out [the ACA]." Health Care and Education Reconciliation Act, Pub. L. No. 111-152, § 1005, 124 Stat. 1029 (2010); but see J. Lester Feder, HHS May Have to Get 'Creative' on Exchange, Politico (Aug. 16, 2011), http://www.politico.com/news/stories/081161513.html ("The general pot of money that the ACA makes available for implementation is surprisingly

The statutory language at issue in *King* likewise serves Congress's purpose of encouraging states to establish exchanges. Section 1401 of the ACA created a new Internal Revenue Code Section 36B, which authorizes refundable "premium-assistance tax credits" for "applicable taxpayers" who meet certain criteria. One criterion is that recipients enroll in coverage "through an Exchange established by the State under section 1311 of the Patient Protection and Affordable Care Act."[21]

Notably, Section 36B's tax-credit eligibility rules bear no mention of exchanges established by the federal government. Indeed, "established by the State under Section 1311" twice distinguishes state-established exchanges from federal exchanges, authority for which appears in Section 1321.[22] The eligibility rules contain no language broadly authorizing credits through "an[y]" exchange, as the ACA does with small-business tax credits.[23] Instead, Section 36B's tax-credit eligibility rules are tightly, even artfully worded. Every reference to exchanges is to "an Exchange established by the State under section 1311." That requirement appears twice explicitly and seven more times by cross-reference.[24] Section 36B plainly authorizes tax credits solely through state-established exchanges,[25] a condition that serves Congress's purpose of encouraging state-run exchanges by creating an incentive for states to establish them.

---

small, given that it is ushering in a series of new regulations covering a sector that accounts for a major chunk of the American economy. It only appropriates $1 billion for all federal administrative costs. 'Everyone expects that billion dollars not to be adequate,' said Edwin Park of the Center on Budget and Policy Priorities[.]"). In other words, (1) the ACA became law with zero funding for federal exchanges, (2) Congress only later added a general implementation fund that *could* be used for federal exchanges, but (3) that fund was insufficient to fund responsibilities HHS was expected to undertake, much less federal exchanges.

[21] PPACA § 1401(c)(2)(A)(i); 26 U.S.C. § 36B(c)(2)(A)(i).

[22] PPACA § 1321(c); 42 U.S.C. § 18041(c).

[23] PPACA § 1421(b)(1); 26 U.S.C. § 45R(a)(1).

[24] See 26 U.S.C. § 36B(b)(2)(A), (c)(2)(A)(i) (direct language); 26 U.S.C. § 36B(b)(3)(B), (b)(3)(B)(i), (b)(3)(C), (b)(3)(D), (b)(3)(E), (c)(2)(A)(ii), (e)(A) (cross-references).

[25] Congressional Research Service, Legal Analysis of Availability of Premium Tax Credits in State and Federally Created Exchanges Pursuant to the Affordable Care Act, Congressional Distribution Memorandum (Jul. 23, 2012) ("[A] strictly textual analysis of the plain meaning of the provision would likely lead to the conclusion that the IRS's authority to issue the premium tax credits is limited only to situations in which the taxpayer is enrolled in a state-established exchange.").

The broader context of the ACA supports the plain meaning of Section 36B. As noted above, Section 1311 creates a parallel financial incentive for states to establish exchanges.[26] The act explicitly defines the District of Columbia as a "State," bringing a D.C.-established exchange within the meaning of "an Exchange established by the State."[27] It explicitly treats any U.S. territory that establishes a compliant exchange as a "State."[28] The House and HELP bills contained language explicitly creating full equivalence between exchanges established by states and those established by HHS.[29] Yet Congress rejected those bills in favor of the ACA, which includes no language defining federal exchanges as having been "established by the State," or otherwise making federal exchanges equivalent to state-established exchanges for purposes of Section 36B.

Remarkably, there is no discussion of the status of tax credits in federal exchanges in the *Congressional Record*, contemporaneous media reports, or known communications among the ACA's drafters and supporters. The only exception of which we are aware supports the plain meaning of Section 36B. In January 2010, all 11 House Democrats from Texas complained that, as in other federal programs that condition benefits on state cooperation, residents of states that fail to establish exchanges would not receive "any benefit" from the ACA, and "will be left no better off than before Congress acted."[30]

There are several reasons for the lack of publicly available contemporaneous discussion of this issue.[31] Due to the ACA's peculiar his-

---

[26] 42 U.S.C. § 18031(a).

[27] 42 U.S.C. § 18024(d).

[28] 42 U.S.C. § 18043(a)(1).

[29] See Adler & Cannon, *supra* note 7, at 158–59.

[30] See *supra* note 11.

[31] Contemporaneous emails, notes, memoranda, and other documents generated by the ACA's drafters, legislative counsel, and House negotiators in 2009 and 2010 presumably would include at least some discussion of this issue. Unfortunately, congressional Democrats have not made those records available, and the individuals responsible for drafting 36B have not discussed the issue publicly. See Robert Pear, Four Words That Imperil Health Care Law Were All a Mistake, Writers Now Say, N.Y. Times, May 25, 2015, available at http://www.nytimes.com/2015/05/26/us/politics/contested-words-in-affordable-care-act-may-have-been-left-by-mistake.html ("The words were written by professional drafters—skilled nonpartisan lawyers—from the office of the Senate legislative counsel, then James W. Fransen . . . The language of the Finance Committee bill was written largely by Mr. Fransen and a tax expert, Mark J. Mathiesen

tory, there was never a conference report. "Congress wrote key parts of the Act behind closed doors," the *King* majority wrote, "rather than through the traditional legislative process."[32] The public debate was dominated by hot-button issues like a "public option" and abortion funding.[33] A general consensus that all states would establish exchanges made this restriction uninteresting. The fact that nobody expected the ACA to become the final law made it unimportant.

Nevertheless, the limited legislative history that exists suggests this feature was deliberate. The "established by the State" requirement originated in the first draft of the Senate Finance Committee's bill, appearing once explicitly and five more times by cross-reference. It survived multiple revisions throughout the drafting process, including revisions to the adjacent cross-reference.[34] There is no evidence whatsoever that Senate Democrats even considered altering the meaning of that requirement. Instead, under the supervision of Senate leaders and White House officials, drafters inserted *additional* mentions of this requirement—a second explicit mention and two more cross-references to it—shortly before the ACA went to the Senate floor.[35]

... Mr. Fransen did not respond to a message seeking comment, and other attempts to reach him were not successful." Note that this passage contradicts the article's title; Section 36B's writers did not comment.).

[32] King, 135 S. Ct. at 2492 (internal quotation marks omitted).

[33] See Gross, *supra* note 11 (noting that exchanges were "not a hot-button issue like abortion or the public option.").

[34] Compare, e.g., S. 1796, 111th Cong. (2009), § 1205, proposing 26 U.S.C. § 36B(b)(2)(A)(i) ("and which were enrolled in through an exchange established by the State *under subpart B of title XXII of the Social Security Act*" (emphasis added)), with PPACA § 1401, creating 26 U.S.C. § 36B(b)(2)(A) ("and which were enrolled in through an Exchange established by the State *under [section] 1311 of the Patient Protection and Affordable Care Act*" (emphasis added)).

[35] Compare America's Healthy Future Act of 2009, S. 1796, 111th Cong. (2009), § 1205, proposing 26 U.S.C. § 36B(c)(2)(A)(i) (limiting credits to those "covered by a qualified health benefits plan *described in subsection (b)(2)(A)(i),*" a cross-reference to plans "enrolled in through an exchange established by the State" (emphasis added)), with PPACA § 1401, 26 U.S.C. § 36B(c)(2)(A)(i) ("covered by a qualified health plan described in subsection (b)(2)(A) *that was enrolled in through an Exchange established by the State under section 1311*" (emphasis added)). See, e.g., David M. Herszenhorn & Robert Pear, White House Team Joins Talks on Health Care Bill, N.Y. Times (Oct. 15, 2009), http://www.nytimes.com/2009/10/15/health/policy/15health.html; Perry Bacon Jr., Small Group Now Leads Closed Negotiations on Health-Care Bill, Wash. Post (Oct.

Other legislation proposed by the ACA's authors contained similar provisions. The HELP bill—as the government and its amici conceded—created the same three-legged stool yet conditioned exchange subsidies on states implementing that bill's employer mandate.[36] Those who drafted and supported this bill were willing to cut off exchange subsidies in intransigent states.

As this history indicates, ACA supporters actively considered conditioning tax credits on state cooperation, and were willing to tolerate the instability that would result from imposing community-rating price controls without offering premium subsidies, in order to serve their purpose of getting states to implement the new federal program.

III. The Road to *King*

Government officials and independent analysts were aware of Section 36B's limitations on tax-credit eligibility when constitutional challenges to the act were still before lower courts. In late 2010, employee-benefits attorney Thomas Christina made a presentation at the American Enterprise Institute highlighting the fact that the ACA authorizes tax credits for those who enroll "through an Exchange established by the State under section 1311," but not for those who enroll through federal exchanges.[37] One of us heard Christina's presentation in early 2011 while researching federal-state relations under the ACA versus other approaches to "cooperative federalism." The resulting paper, discussing the limitation on tax credits in Section

---

18, 2009), http://www.washingtonpost.com/wp-dyn/content/article/2009/10/17/AR2009101701810.html.

[36] Brief for the Respondents, King v. Burwell, 135 S. Ct. 2480 (2015) (No. 14-114) ("[T]he Senate HELP Committee bill made tax credits conditional on state action in certain respects."); Brief of Amici Curiae Members of Congress & State Legislatures, Halbig v. Sebelius, 758 F.3d 390 (D.C. Cir. 2014) (No. 14-5018), ("[I]f a state chose not to adopt specified insurance reform provisions and make state and local government employers subject to specified provisions of the statute, 'the residents of such State shall not be eligible for credits.'"); Timothy Jost, Health Insurance Exchanges in Health Care Reform Legal and Policy Issues, Washington & Lee Public Legal Studies Research Paper Series (Oct. 23, 2009) (describing the HELP bill: "A state's residents will only become eligible for federal premium subsidies...if the state provides health insurance for its state and local government employees.").

[37] Thomas Christina, What to Look for Beyond the Individual Mandate (And How to Look for It), Am. Enter. Inst. (Dec. 6, 2010).

1401 among other aspects of the ACA, was presented at a health law conference that spring.[38] None of the numerous health law experts and government officials in attendance, including the Kansas Insurance Commissioner,[39] raised any objection to the plain-meaning interpretation of Section 36B.

According to a later congressional investigation, a Treasury official overseeing ACA implementation became aware of this feature of the act in March 2011 via media coverage of Christina's presentation.[40] This discovery concerned IRS officials. Soon thereafter, the IRS dropped the statutory requirement that tax-credit recipients must enroll "through an Exchange established by the State" from their draft regulations.[41]

The IRS's decision to focus more closely on this question was no doubt motivated by growing resistance to ACA implementation in dozens of states.[42] A wave election in 2010 swept into office many state governors and legislators opposed to implementing the law.[43] If states could block tax credits by refusing to establish exchanges, they could expose the full cost of exchange coverage to enrollees, which could affect the act's popularity and viability. Despite the potential

[38] See Jonathan H. Adler, Cooperation, Commandeering or Crowding Out? Federal Intervention and State Choices in Health Care Policy, 20 Kans. J. L. & Pub. Pol'y 199 (2011).

[39] See Sandy Praeger, A View from the Insurance Commissioner on Health Care Reform, 20 Kan. J.L. & Pub. Pol'y 186 (2011).

[40] See Staff of H. Comm. on Oversight and Gov't Reform, 113th Cong., Administration Conducted Inadequate Review of Key Issues Prior to Expanding Health Law's Taxes and Subsidies (Comm. Print 2014), http://oversight.house.gov/wp-content/uploads/2014/02/IRS-Rule-OGR-WM-Staff-Report-Final1.pdf [hereinafter Oversight Report]; Thomas D. Edmondson, Opponents of New Federal Health Care Law Wage Constitutional War in Courts, Daily Tax Report, Bloomberg BNA (Jan. 4, 2011), http://object.cato.org/sites/cato.org/files/articles/bna-dtr-article.pdf.

[41] See Oversight Report, *supra* note 40, at 17.

[42] See David K. Jones, Katharine W. V. Bradley and Jonathan Oberlander, Pascal's Wager: Health Insurance Exchanges, Obamacare, and the Republican Dilemma, 39 J. Health Pol., Pol'y & L. 97 , 130 (2014) ("The pervasive resistance to Obamacare was so strong that many states decided to cede control of the exchanges to the federal government.").

[43] See *id.*; see also Brendan Nyhan, The Effects of Health Care Reform in 2010 and Beyond, Brendan-Nyhan.com (Mar. 8, 2012), http://www.brendan-nyhan.com/blog/2012/03/the-effects-of-health-care-reform-in-2010-and-beyond.html ("Democratic incumbents who voted yes [on the PPACA] performed significantly worse than those who did not.").

for unlimited start-up funds and other entreaties by HHS, 34 states ultimately refused to establish exchanges.

After consultations with HHS, on August 17, 2011, the IRS proposed a regulation providing "a taxpayer is eligible for the credit . . . through an Exchange established under section 1311 *or 1321* of the Affordable Care Act"—that is, without regard for whether the exchange was established by a state or the federal government.[44] Though IRS officials had discussed whether this approach was permissible under Section 36B, the *Federal Register* notice included no mention of the contrary statutory language, much less any basis for the IRS's departure from it.[45] Nevertheless, many noticed and raised objections to the proposed rule.[46]

The IRS did not heed these concerns. On May 23, 2012, it promulgated a final regulation purporting to authorize tax credits in exchanges established by HHS under Section 1321.[47] The rule circumvented the statutory text by (1) declaring eligible taxpayers could obtain a tax credit if a qualifying insurance plan was purchased on "an Exchange"[48] and then (2) adopting a definition of "Exchange" that HHS had promulgated (in coordination with the IRS) that

---

[44] U.S. Dep't of the Treasury, IRS, Health Insurance Premium Tax Credit, Fed. Reg. 76 (Aug. 17, 2011) (proposed rule), at 50934 (emphasis added).

[45] See Oversight Report, *supra* note 40; Lisa Rein, Six Words Might Decide the Fate of Obamacare at the Supreme Court, Wash. Post, Mar. 1, 2014, http://www.washingtonpost.com/politics/why-six-words-might-hold-the-fate-of-obamacare-before-the-supreme-court/2015/03/01/437c2836-bd39-11e4-b274-e5209a3bc9a9_story.html.

[46] See, e.g., David Hogberg, Oops! No Obamacare Tax Credit Via Federal Exchanges?, Inv. Bus. Daily, Sept. 7, 2011, http://news.investors.com/090711-584085-oops-no-obamacare-tax-credit-via-federal-exchanges-.htm; Jonathan H. Adler & Michael F. Cannon, Another ObamaCare Glitch, Wall Street J., Nov. 16, 2011, available at http://online.wsj.com/article/SB10001424052970203687504577006322431330662.html; see also Rep. David Phil Roe, U.S. House of Reps., Letter to Douglas Shulman, Comm'r, IRS (Nov. 4, 2011), http://roe.house.gov/UploadedFiles/Letter_to_IRS_Commissioner_regarding_tax_credits_under_PPACA_-_11.03.11.pdf, Sen. Orrin G. Hatch, U.S. Senate, Letter to Timothy Geithner, Treasury Sec'y, and Douglas Shulman, Comm'r, IRS (Dec. 1, 2011), http://www.cato.org/sites/cato.org/files/documents/12.1.11_premium_credit_letter_to_geithner_and_shulman.pdf.

[47] 77 Fed. Reg. 30378 (2012).

[48] 26 CFR § 1.36B–2 (2013).

purported to create full equivalence between state-established and federal exchanges.[49]

The IRS acknowledged opposition to its interpretation, yet offered no more than a single conclusory paragraph in response, lacking any reference to relevant statutory text or other legal authority for its action:

> The statutory language of section 36B and other provisions of the Affordable Care Act support the interpretation that credits are available to taxpayers who obtain coverage through a State Exchange, regional Exchange, subsidiary Exchange, and the Federally-facilitated Exchange. Moreover, the relevant legislative history does not demonstrate that Congress intended to limit the premium tax credit to State Exchanges. Accordingly, the final regulations maintain the rule in the proposed regulations because it is consistent with the language, purpose, and structure of section 36B and the Affordable Care Act as a whole.[50]

The IRS purported to rely on the "relevant legislative history," yet cited no legislative history to support the rule, perhaps because no such legislative history exists. This bears emphasis: to this day, neither the government, nor the Supreme Court, nor anyone else has identified even a single contemporaneous statement of any kind asserting that the ACA authorizes, or that its supporters intended for it to authorize, tax credits in federal exchanges.

The IRS rule created two types of legally cognizable injuries. First, the ACA's employer mandate penalizes large employers if one or more employees are eligible for or receive a tax credit under Section 36B.[51] By offering tax credits in non-establishing states, the IRS rule injures employers in those states by exposing them to penalties. Second, the individual mandate penalizes taxpayers who do not obtain coverage, but only if coverage is "affordable."[52] By offering tax credits in non-establishing states, the IRS rule makes coverage "afford-

---

[49] 45 CFR § 155.20 (2013) (defining "Exchange" as "an Exchange serving the individual market . . . regardless of whether the Exchange is established and operated by a State . . . or by HHS.").

[50] U.S. Dep't of the Treasury, IRS, Health Insurance Premium Tax Credit, 77 Fed. Reg. 30, 377 (May 23, 2012) (final rule).

[51] 26 U.S.C. § 4980H.

[52] 26 U.S.C. § 5001A(e)(1).

able" for millions of taxpayers, and thus exposes them to penalties from which they would otherwise be exempt.

Injured parties soon began challenging the IRS rule in federal court. In September 2012, the state of Oklahoma became the first plaintiff, claiming injury as an employer (*Oklahoma v. Burwell*). In May 2013, a group of employers and individuals from multiple states filed a second challenge (*Halbig v. Burwell*). In September 2013, four Virginia residents challenged the rule (*King v. Burwell*). In October 2013, the state of Indiana and dozens of Indiana school districts filed a fourth challenge (*Indiana v. IRS*).

At district court, the government prevailed in *Halbig* and *King*, while the challengers prevailed in *Oklahoma*.[53] On July 22, 2014, panels of the D.C. Circuit (*Halbig*) and the Fourth Circuit (*King*) issued conflicting rulings for and against the challengers, respectively, within hours of each other. In *Halbig*, the full D.C. Circuit granted the government's request for *en banc* review. The *King* plaintiffs appealed their loss to the Supreme Court, which granted certiorari in November 2014.

IV. The Court's *King* Ruling

The Supreme Court sided with the federal government, though not on the grounds urged by the solicitor general or most commentators. The chief justice's opinion for the Court was joined by Justice Anthony Kennedy and the Court's four "liberal" justices—Ruth Bader Ginsburg, Stephen Breyer, Sonia Sotomayor, and Elena Kagan—none of whom concurred separately. The Court's arch-textualist, Justice Antonin Scalia, authored a sharp, and at times caustic and sarcastic, dissent, joined by Justices Clarence Thomas and Samuel Alito.

Chief Justice Roberts explained that while Section 36B may appear clear, it was actually "ambiguous" when viewed in a broader context.[54] In the ordinary case, a finding of ambiguity would trigger deference to the implementing agency under the *Chevron* doctrine.[55]

---

[53] Halbig v. Sebelius, 27 F. Supp. 3d 1 (D.D.C. 2014); King v. Sebelius, 997 F. Supp. 2d 415 (E.D. Va. 2014); Oklahoma v. Burwell, No. 6:11-cv-00030 (E.D. Okla. Sept. 30, 2014).

[54] King, 135 S. Ct. at 2490–91.

[55] See Chevron USA v. Nat. Res. Def. Council, 467 U.S. 837 (1984).

King was not an ordinary case, however.[56] Rather than defer to the IRS's interpretation, the Court resolved the ambiguity itself. Turning again to the broader statutory context, and the potential effects of enforcing Section 36B as written, the Court concluded that the ACA should be read to authorize tax credits in federal exchanges. Though the text of Section 36B authorizes tax credits for insurance purchased on exchanges "established by the State under section 1311," this language will henceforth be read to authorize tax credits for insurance purchased on exchanges established by states under Section 1311 *or* by the federal government under Section 1321.

Roberts's primary rationale was that a "fair construction" of the statute requires more than giving meaning to discrete phrases— and cannot be constrained by the semantic meaning of ordinary terms, or even statutorily defined terms, such as "State." The chief justice wrote that it is the Court's job to avoid, "if at all possible," an interpretation that would undermine the ACA's goal of improving health insurance markets—such as an interpretation that, when combined with the intervening decisions of dozens of states not to establish exchanges, could create a "death spiral" of increasing costs and declining coverage.[57] Therefore the statutory language was to be stretched so as to conform to "what we see as Congress's plan."[58] If that required ignoring some portions of the text, or subverting another purpose of the statute, so be it. The chief justice decided where the Court should go and was determined not to let the text get in the way.[59] But to make it work, the Court's majority would have to find

[56] King, 135 S. Ct. at 2488–89 ("In extraordinary cases, however, there may be reason to hesitate before concluding that Congress has intended such an implicit delegation." (quoting FDA v. Brown & Williamson Tobacco Corp., 529 U.S. 120, 159 (2000))).

[57] King, 135 S. Ct. at 2496.

[58] *Id.*

[59] As commentators have noted, the chief justice has been similarly aggressive and creative in his interpretation of other statutes. See, e.g., Nw. Austin Mun. Utility Dist. No. One v. Holder ("NAMUDNO"), 557 U.S. 193 (2009), Richard L. Hasen, Constitutional Avoidance and Anti-Avoidance by the Roberts Court, 2009 Sup Ct. Rev. 181, 182 (2009) ("[I]n *NAMUDNO*, the Court applied the [constitutional avoidance] canon to adopt an implausible reading of a statute that appeared contrary to textual analysis, congressional intent, and administrative action."); Bond v. United States, 134 S. Ct. 2077 (2014); Nicholas Quinn Rosenkranz, Bond v. United States: Concurring in the Judgment, 2013–2014 Cato Sup. Ct. Rev. 285, 287 (2014) ("[Roberts' opinion is] an object lesson in dodgy statutory interpretation.").

a way to dispense with "the most natural reading" of the relevant statutory provisions.[60]

Before looking at what the majority did, it is worth noting which arguments the Court did *not* adopt. It did not accept the primary arguments offered by the solicitor general. It did not accept that "established by the State" was a "statutory term of art,"[61] nor did it claim the text clearly compelled its result, as the government also urged. Indeed, not a single justice adopted those arguments. To the contrary, the Court claimed the relevant text was ambiguous. While some critics maintained the plaintiffs' arguments were frivolous or absurd, not a single justice expressed this view in an opinion.[62] According to Chief Justice Roberts's opinion for the Court, the plaintiffs' "arguments about the plain meaning of Section 36B are strong."[63]

Though the Court claimed to be following "Congress's plan," it did not rely much on traditional sources of legislative history to determine Congress's unstated purpose, and was quite selective in the sources of legislative history it did cite. Nor did the Court take the suggestion offered by some commentators that it should rely upon the scoring of the ACA by the Congressional Budget Office[64] or *ex*

[60] King, 135 S. Ct. at 2495.

[61] See Brief for the Respondents at 20–25, King v. Burwell, 135 S. Ct. 2480 (2015) (No. 14-114).

[62] Many commentators were quite dismissive of arguments against the IRS rule. One prominent critic called them "screwy," "nutty," and "stupid" (Erika Eichelberger, Conservatives Insist Obamacare Is on Its Deathbed, Mother Jones (Jan. 24, 2013), http://www.motherjones.com/print/214256). Others charged that the litigation was "frivolous" (Harold Pollack, If the Latest Obamacare Lawsuit Succeeds, Obamacare Is in Big Trouble, Wash. Post, Feb. 3, 2014, http://www.washingtonpost.com/blogs/wonkblog/wp/2014/02/03/if-the-latest-obamacare-lawsuit-succeeds-obamacare-is-in-big-trouble/); that it was "a conspicuously weak case that should never have reached the Supreme Court"; that it was "obvious" the ACA authorizes those provisions in federal exchanges; or that King was nothing but a "trolling exercise" (Harold Pollack, The Greatest Trolling Exercise in the History of Health Policy Is Over, Politico (blog) (June 25, 2015), http://www.politico.com/magazine/story/2015/06/health-care-supreme-court-king-burwell-119446.html). Not all commentators took this position, however. See Sarah Kliff, The Accidental Case Against Obamacare, Vox.com (May 26, 2015) ("'When I read prominent people saying this case was frivolous, I winced a bit,' says Nicholas Bagley, an assistant law professor at the University of Michigan who has written extensively on the King challenge. 'This is a serious lawsuit.'").

[63] King, 135 S. Ct. at 2495.

[64] See, e.g., Abbe Gluck, The "CBO Canon" and the Debate over Tax Credits on Federally Operated Health Insurance Exchanges, Balkinization (July 10, 2012), http://

post comments offered by legislators and staff to explain the inconvenient wording of the relevant provisions.[65] Though the Court admitted the ACA was the result of "inartful drafting,"[66] it did not claim the relevant language was a scrivener's error.

Some thought the Court might rely upon federalism principles to side with the government, out of a concern that conditioning tax credits on state cooperation would be unduly coercive.[67] Several amici raised federalism concerns of various stripes,[68] and Justice Kennedy seemed amenable to such an approach at oral argument.[69]

---

balkin.blogspot.com/2012/07/cbo-canon-and-debate-over-tax-credits.html; Dylan Scott, BOOM: The Historic Proof Obamacare Foes Are Dead Wrong on Subsidies, Talking Points Memo (Aug. 1, 2014), http://talkingpointsmemo.com/dc/obamacare-halbig-cbo-scores. For an explanation of why the CBO score did not actually establish the correctness of the government's position see David Ziff, TPM's Halbig/PPACA "BOOM" Goes Boom, Ziff Blog (Aug. 1, 2014), https://ziffblog.wordpress.com/2014/08/01/tpms-halbigppaca-boom-goes-boom.

[65] See, e.g., Robert Pear, Four Words, *supra* note 31 ("The answer, from interviews with more than two dozen Democrats and Republicans involved in writing the law, is that the words were a product of shifting politics and a sloppy merging of different versions. Some described the words as 'inadvertent,' 'inartful' or 'a drafting error.' But none supported the contention of the plaintiffs, who are from Virginia."); but see text accompanying note 31, *supra*. Doug Kendall, Carvin's Cornhusker Quandry in King, Huffington Post (Jan. 30, 2015), http://www.huffingtonpost.com/doug-kendall/carvins-cornhusker-quanda_b_6581690.html (quoting Senator Nelson as saying, "I *always* believed that tax credits should be available in all 50 states regardless of who built the exchange, and the final law also reflects that belief as well." (emphasis in original)); but see Michael F. Cannon, King v. Burwell: In 2013, Nelson Admitted He Didn't Know If ACA Offered Subsidies in Fed. Exchanges, Forbes.com (Feb. 10, 2015), http://www.forbes.com/sites/michaelcannon/2015/02/10/king-v-burwell-in-2013-nelson-admitted-he-didnt-know-if-aca-offered-subsidies-in-fed-exchanges/ ("In other words, if we want to know what Nelson *actually* intended to become law, asking Ben Nelson is not an option. Our only option is to read the bill.").

[66] King, 135 S. Ct. at 2492.

[67] See, e.g., David G. Savage, Obamacare Defense Is Tailored for Key Supreme Court Justices, L.A. Times, Feb. 26, 2015, available at http://www.latimes.com/business/healthcare/la-na-court-health-argument-20150226-story.html.

[68] See Brief of the Commonwealth of Virginia, et al., as Amici Curiae in Support of Affirmance, King v. Burwell, 135 S. Ct. 2480 (2015) (No. 14-114); Brief for Professor Thomas W. Merrill, et al., as Amici Curiae Supporting Respondents, King v. Burwell, 135 S. Ct. 2480 (2015) (No. 14-114); Brief of Amici Curiae Jewish Alliance for Law & Social Action (JALSA), et al., in Support of Respondents, King v. Burwell, 135 S. Ct. 2480 (2015) (No 14-114).

[69] Transcript of Oral argument at 16, King v. Burwell, 135 S. Ct. 2480 (2015) (No. 14-114) ("JUSTICE KENNEDY: Let me say that from the standpoint of the dynam-

Yet there was no mention of federalism in the Court's opinion. If such concerns did influence the justices, they did not see the need to mention them.

Perhaps tellingly, the Court openly adopted a non-textualist approach to interpreting the ACA. As Professor Abbe Gluck observed, "*King* is one of the only major text-oriented statutory interpretation decisions in recent memory in which the majority opinion barely includes a single canon of interpretation."[70] Moreover, the chief justice's opinion expressly rejects some interpretive canons that textualists hold dear. As Gluck noted, "This is not Antonin Scalia's textualism"[71] —a point Justice Scalia's dissent made clear. Instead, the Court adopted a "fair construction" of the statute over the plain meaning of relevant provisions and congressionally provided definitions.[72]

The problem with the Court's "fair construction" is that it considered only those parts of the statute that, once isolated, could be used to cast doubt on the intentionality of Section 36B, while it dismissed, disregarded, or distorted other provisions that completely dispel those doubts. If this is a "fair construction," it is one that elevates judicial construction over legislative action.[73]

V. Desperately Seeking Ambiguity

Chief Justice Roberts went to extraordinary lengths to find the act ambiguous. He conceded "the most natural reading of the pertinent statutory phrase"[74] is that tax credits are available "only" through

---

ics of Federalism, it does seem to me that there is something very powerful to the point that if your argument is accepted, the States are being told either create your own Exchange, or we'll send your insurance market into a death spiral.").

[70] Abbe Gluck, Congress Has a "Plan" and the Court Can Understand It—The Court rises to the challenge of statutory complexity in King v. Burwell, SCOTUSBlog (June 26, 2015), http://www.scotusblog.com/2015/06/symposium-congress-has-a-plan-and-the-court-can-understand-it-the-court-rises-to-the-challenge-of-statutory-complexity-in-king-v-burwell.

[71] *Id.*

[72] King, 135 S. Ct. at 2492.

[73] See Antonin Scalia & Bryan Garner, Reading Law: The Interpretation of Legal Texts 57 (2012) (noting that for a court to find legislative purpose "in the absence of a clear indication in the text is to provide the judge's answer rather than the text's answer to the question").

[74] King, 135 S. Ct. at 2495.

"an Exchange established by the State under [Section 1311]."[75] He implicitly conceded the ACA is otherwise silent on the question presented: the Court failed to identify even a single piece of statutory text or scrap of legislative history in which any member of Congress claimed the ACA *would* offer tax credits in federal exchanges. That should have resolved the matter.[76] Nevertheless, Roberts still managed to find the operative text ambiguous "when read in context."[77]

There was no disagreement among the justices that statutory structure, design, and context are useful in *resolving* latent ambiguities in statutory provisions.[78] As Justice Scalia counseled in dissent, "Statutory design and purpose matter only to the extent they help clarify an otherwise ambiguous provision."[79] Yet the majority not only used statutory context to *resolve* ambiguity, but to *create* the ambiguity in the first place. Worse, the majority considered text selectively and adopted inconsistent presumptions about the applicability of statutory provisions bearing on the question. Though Roberts conceded that "established by the State" is clear on its face and the *only* statutory text that speaks directly to the question presented, by the time he was done, he rendered that provision not only ambiguous but meaningless. It was as if the majority was determined to shoehorn inconvenient statutory text into a preconceived narrative of how the statute should operate. After all, as Roberts explained, the statute *must* be read this way "if at all possible."

The Court's judgment ultimately rested on a conclusion that the relevant text was "ambiguous"—or could at least be read as such in context. But what was ambiguous? Not the word "State," given that Congress took pains to define this term to exclude federal

---

[75] *Id*. at 2489.

[76] See Brown & Williamson, 529 U.S. at 133 (noting that contextual interpretation must yield to an "insuperable textual barrier"); Conn. Nat'l Bank v. Germain, 503 U.S. 249, 253–54 (1992) ("[I]n interpreting a statute a court should always turn first to one, cardinal canon before all others . . . courts must presume that a legislature says in a statute what it means and means in a statute what it says there. When the words of a statute are unambiguous, then, this first canon is also the last." (citations omitted)).

[77] *Id*. at 2490.

[78] See *id*. at 2492 (noting the "fundamental canon of statutory construction that the words of a statute must be read in their context and with a view to their place in the overall statutory scheme" (quoting FDA v. Brown & Williamson Tobacco Corp., 529 U. S. 120, 133 (2000))); *id*. at 2502 (Scalia, J., dissenting).

[79] See King, 135 S. Ct. at 2502. (Scalia, J., dissenting).

exchanges.[80] Perhaps "establish" is ambiguous, but not in a way that muddies whether it is the state or HHS that is doing the establishing.

Consider in more detail the analysis underlying the majority's conclusion that the statute is "properly viewed as ambiguous" on the question of whether it authorizes tax credits in federal exchanges.[81] As the Court accepted, "the most natural reading of the pertinent statutory phrase"[82] is that the ACA authorizes tax credits "only" through "an Exchange established by the State under [Section 1311]."[83] Under this language, for tax credits to issue, "three things must be true: First, the individual must enroll in an insurance plan through 'an Exchange.' Second, that Exchange must be 'established by the State.' And third, that Exchange must be established 'under [Section 1311]."[84]

The first requirement, that tax credits are only available for the purchase of insurance through "an Exchange," is uncontroversial, as is the proposition that both state and federal exchanges satisfy this initial requirement, even though limiting tax credits to exchange-based insurance purchases limits their availability and potentially undermines the legislative purpose of subsidizing insurance.[85] Section 1321 requires the HHS secretary to "establish" an exchange in any state that fails to do so (or otherwise fails to comply with relevant ACA requirements) and indicates that this exchange should be the practical equivalent of the exchange for which it substitutes. Federal and state exchanges may be "established by different sovereigns,"[86] the Court wrote, but both enable consumers to engage in comparison shopping and facilitate government regulation of health insurance offerings.[87]

---

[80] See 42 U.S.C. § 18024(d).

[81] King, 135 S. Ct. at 2491.

[82] Id. at 2495.

[83] Id. at 2489.

[84] Id.

[85] Actually, the government has ignored this tax-credit eligibility requirement as well. Ricardo Alonso-Zaldivar, Health Law Fix for State-Run Websites, Assoc. Press, Feb. 28, 2014 ("HHS said state residents who were unable to sign up because of technical problems may still get federal tax credits if they bought private insurance outside of the new online insurance exchanges.").

[86] King, 135 S. Ct. at 2489.

[87] See Max Baucus, Reforming America's Health Care System: A Call to Action, S. Fin. Comm., Nov. 12, 2008, at 17 ("The Exchange would be an independent entity, the *primary purpose* of which would be to organize affordable health insurance options,

Next the Court turned to the phrase "established by the State." This language would seem to be clear and unambiguous. Any member of Congress who had bothered to read the relevant provisions would have understood what it meant.[88] As Chief Justice Roberts conceded, "it might seem that a Federal Exchange cannot fulfill this requirement."[89] Lest there be any doubt, as the majority conceded, the ACA defines "State" in a manner "that does not include the Federal Government."[90]

Despite the plain meaning of "established by the State," despite the statutory definition of "State," despite the consistent (and conventional) usage of the word "establish" throughout the statute, and despite the majority's acknowledgement that the plaintiffs offered "the most natural reading of the pertinent statutory phrase," the majority asserted that "when read in context, 'with a view to [its] place in the overall statutory scheme,' the meaning of that phrase 'established by the State' is not so clear."[91] Other provisions of the statute, the majority wrote, "suggest that the Act may not always use the phrase 'established by the State' in its most natural sense."[92]

The Court cites just one statutory provision, found in Section 1312, to substantiate its claim that other provisions of the ACA "suggest" that "established by the State" "may not" mean what it says. Yet not only does that provision not contradict or other undermine

---

create understandable, comparable information about those options, and develop a standard application for enrollment in a chosen plan" (emphasis added)); Praeger, *supra* note 39, at 190 ("The main purpose of the exchanges will be to facilitate the comparison and purchase of coverage by individuals and small businesses."); see also Michael F. Cannon, ObamaCare's Exchanges Perform More than a Dozen Functions Besides Issuing Subsidies (Updated), Cato@Liberty, (June 27, 2014), http://www.cato.org/blog/obamacares-exchanges-perform-more-dozen-other-functions-besides-issuing-subsidies.

[88] Note, however, that not all may have read the statute. For example, Senator Max Baucus, one of the ACA's chief architects, remarked that it would be a "waste [of his] time to read every page of the bill," since it's "statutory language," and that's what "experts" are for. Jordan Fabian, Key Senate Democrat Suggests that He Didn't Read Entire Healthcare Reform Bill, The Hill (Aug. 25, 2010), http://thehill.com/blogs/blog-briefing-room/news/115749-sen-baucus-suggests-he-did-not-read-entire-health-bill.

[89] King, 135 S. Ct. at 2489–90.

[90] *Id.* at 2490.

[91] *Id.* (quoting FDA v. Brown & Williamson Tobacco Corp, 529 U.S. 120, 133 (2000)).

[92] *Id.*

a straightforward interpretation of "established by the State," it does not even utilize that phrase.

Section 1312 defines "qualified individuals," in relevant part, as those who "reside[] in the State that established the Exchange."[93] The majority thinks this casts doubt on the plain meaning of "established by the State." Why? If the Court were to interpret such language as drawing distinctions between state-established and federal exchanges, the majority reasoned, then "there would be *no* 'qualified individuals' on Federal Exchanges."[94] Federal exchanges would therefore not be able to meet several requirements the act imposes with respect to qualified individuals. For example, explains Chief Justice Roberts, "the Act requires all Exchanges to 'make available qualified health plans to qualified individuals'—something an Exchange could not do if there were no such individuals."[95]

The majority's argument fails on three levels. First, as Justice Scalia notes in dissent, it would be perfectly reasonable for Congress to create a category of enrollees that is unique to state-established exchanges:

> Imagine that a university sends around a bulletin reminding every professor to take the "interests of graduate students" into account when setting office hours, but that some professors teach only undergraduates. Would anybody reason that the bulletin implicitly presupposes that every professor has "graduate students," so that "graduate students" must really mean "graduate or undergraduate students"? Surely not. Just as one naturally reads instructions about graduate students to be inapplicable to the extent a particular professor has no such students, so too would one naturally read instructions about qualified individuals to be inapplicable to the extent a particular Exchange has no such individuals.[96]

The majority responds that Congress would have had no reason to detail requirements related to "qualified individuals" if there were to be no qualified individuals in federal exchanges. Yet such reasons abound, both in the ACA and its legislative history. Sections

[93] 42 U.S.C. § 18032(f)(1)(A).

[94] King, 135 S. Ct. at 2490.

[95] *Id.*

[96] King, 135 S. Ct. at 2501 (Scalia, J., dissenting).

1311, 1321, and other provisions make clear that many Senate Democrats feared that states might not implement the ACA as well or as faithfully as the secretary would. The ACA therefore provides wide discretion to the secretary, while states get detailed instructions.[97] There is thus nothing about the "qualified individuals" definition that casts doubt on the meaning of "established by the State." Any anomalies the majority identifies flow not from the text, but from the majority's atextual assumptions about Congress's plan.

Second, context further shows that the "qualified individuals" definition casts no doubt on what Congress meant by "established by the State," and instead supports the plain meaning of that phrase. There is a *reason* why Section 1312 defines "qualified individuals" in terms of "the State that established the Exchange." In Sections 1311, 1312, and 1313, Congress is speaking to states. Those sections direct states to establish exchanges and detail related requirements. Section 1312 defines "qualified individuals" in terms of "the State that established the Exchange" because the whole point of these sections is that Congress is presuming that states *will* establish exchanges.

Context also shows the "qualified individuals" definition still has applicability to federal exchanges, despite the fact that they are not established by states. In the very next section, Section 1321, Congress drops the presumption that each state will establish an exchange, and explains what the secretary "shall" do if states fail to establish exchanges. Section 1321 directs the secretary to "issue regulations setting standards for meeting the requirements under this title," which encompasses regulations for both state-established and federal exchanges, and to implement "such . . . requirements" if a state fails to do so. That is, if Sections 1311, 1312, or 1313 impose requirements on state-established exchanges that would be inappropriate in the case of a federal exchange, Section 1321 authorizes the secretary to issue and enforce a parallel requirement. In this case, it authorizes the HHS secretary to develop a "qualified individuals" definition appropriate to federal exchanges—that is, that qualified individuals must reside in the state "within" which "the Secretary . . . establish[es]" an Exchange.[98] The only ambiguity that exists is whether the ACA *requires* the secretary to develop a "qualified individuals" definition

97 See PPACA § 1321; 42 U.S.C. § 18041.
98 See *id.* at (a), (c).

for federal exchanges or (per Justice Scalia) merely *authorizes* her to do so. In neither case does Section 1321's "qualified individuals" definition cast doubt on the meaning of "established by the State."

Thus it is not true that giving the phrase "established by the State" its plain meaning would mean there would be no qualified individuals in federal exchanges. Context shows that Congress covered that contingency. Unfortunately, the Court only looked to part of the context—the part that supported its preconceived understanding of "Congress's plan."

Third, even if one were to conclude that the provisions relating to "qualified individuals" created an anomaly, this does not "suggest," let alone demonstrate, that other language used in other parts of the statute is ambiguous. The majority's reliance on the "qualified individual" provision on this point is even more curious given the majority's refusal to consider the operation of the phrase "established by the State" in other parts of the ACA. "Because the other provisions cited by the dissent are not at issue here," the majority meekly explains in a footnote, "we do not address them."[99] The majority did not even address the reference to exchanges "established by the State" *in Section 1311*, despite that section's obvious relevance to the question at hand.[100] So much for considering the statute as a whole.

When the majority turns to consider whether an exchange established by the federal government as required under Section 1321 could qualify as an exchange established "under Section 1311," it takes further liberties with the statutory text. Here, the majority claims that the statutory definition of an "Exchange" forces the conclusion that Section 1321 "authorizes the Secretary to establish an Exchange under Section [1311], not (or not only) under Section [1321]."[101] The relevant text does nothing of the kind.

The linchpin of the majority's argument here is the statutory definition of "Exchange" provided for in ACA Section 1563: "The term 'Exchange' means an American Health Benefit Exchange established under section 1311 of the Patient Protection and Affordable Care

---

[99] King, 135 S. Ct. at 2493 n.3.

[100] 42 U.S.C. § 18031(f)(3) ("AUTHORITY TO CONTRACT.— (A) IN GENERAL.—A State may elect to authorize an Exchange *established by the State* under this section to enter into an agreement with an eligible entity to carry out 1 or more responsibilities of the Exchange." (emphasis added)). See *infra* note 112 and accompanying text.

[101] King, 135 S. Ct. at 2490–91.

Act."[102] According to the majority, "every time the Act uses the word 'Exchange,' the definitional provision *requires* that we substitute the phrase 'Exchange established under section [1311].'"[103] The statute flatly contradicts this claim.

Section 1563 adds that definition of "Exchange" to the Public Health Service Act to conform that statute to the ACA. Section 1551 then conforms the ACA to the PHSA by circuitously importing that and other PHSA definitions back into the ACA. Contrary to the majority opinion, however, Section 1551 expressly provides that PHSA definitions are *not* to be applied "every time" the relevant terms are mentioned in the ACA. Section 1551 provides that PHSA definitions "shall apply" to the ACA "unless specifically provided for otherwise."[104] With respect to federal exchanges, the ACA specifically provides that they are established under Section 1321.[105] Thus the PHSA definition that exchanges are "established under Section 1311" does not apply. The majority's claim that the ACA "requires" the Court to insert this definition of "Exchange" into Section 1321 is simply false. The majority erases the distinction between Section 1311 exchanges and Section 1321 exchanges only by ignoring Congress's express instructions. After it cavalierly interprets a universal definition of "State" to be conditional, the majority then interprets a conditional definition of "Exchange" to be universal—all in the name of "what we see as Congress's plan."

Having sufficiently tampered with two statutory definitions, the majority then proceeds to claim that federal exchanges established under Section 1321 are also established under Section 1311. "All of the requirements that an Exchange must meet are in Section [1311]," the majority asserts.[106] Therefore, a federal exchange must be "established under Section 1311" or else "literally none of the Act's requirements would apply to them."[107] Again, the statute flatly contradicts the majority's claims.

[102] 42 U.S.C. § 300gg-91(d)(21).

[103] King, 135 S. Ct. at 2491 (emphasis added).

[104] PPACA § 1551.

[105] 42 U.S.C. § 18041(c)(1). See also 45 CFR § 155.20 (2013) ("*Federally-facilitated Exchange* means an Exchange established and operated within a State by the Secretary under section 1321(c)(1) of the Affordable Care Act.").

[106] King, 135 S. Ct. at 2491.

[107] *Id.*

It is not true that "all of the requirements" for exchanges are contained in Section 1311. Sections 1312 and 1313 also impose requirements on exchanges.[108] The reconciliation amendments imposed reporting requirements on exchanges codified in Section 36B of the Internal Revenue Code—the provisions created by Section 1401—and those requirements *distinguished* between Section 1311 and Section 1321 exchanges.[109] Section 1321 imposes requirements on exchanges when it obligates the HHS secretary to "issue regulations setting standards" for exchanges to meet "the requirements under this *title*" (that is, not just Section 1311), and further authorizes the secretary to impose "such *other* requirements as the Secretary determines appropriate" (that is, beyond what the ACA itself requires).[110]

Indeed, far from conflating state-run and federal exchanges, Section 1321 draws a bright line between the two. It authorizes the secretary to write rules for both Section 1311 exchanges and Section 1321 exchanges, which remain distinct. This authority includes the ability to write separate rules for federal exchanges in cases where the rules for state-established exchanges would make no sense.

The majority's selective contextualism creates anomalies that exist nowhere under a plain-meaning interpretation of Section 36B and the act's broader context. For example, the ACA prohibits the use of federal funds for the operating expenses of Section 1311 exchanges.[111] Under a plain-meaning interpretation, where Section 1311 and 1321 exchanges are distinct, this poses no problems. Section 1321 authorizes the secretary to draft a parallel rule appropriate to federally administered exchanges (for example, that they may use federal funds, but must be self-sufficient). If the majority were correct that federal exchanges *are* Section 1311 exchanges, however, it would create the anomaly that federal exchanges must somehow operate with no federal funds. Likewise, Section 1311 grants states the power to choose whether "an Exchange established by the State" may contract out certain exchange functions. If the majority were correct that federal exchanges are "established by the State under Section 1311," it would create an anomaly where states that did not

---

[108] See, e.g., 42 U.S.C. § 18032(d)(4), § 18033(a)(1).

[109] 26 U.S.C. § 36B(f)(3).

[110] 42 U.S.C. § 18041(a), (c) (emphasis added).

[111] 42 U.S.C. § 18031(d)(5).

establish exchanges could dictate whether a federal agency may contract with outside entities.[112] The majority's selective contextualism creates such anomalies by ignoring these and other provisions that reveal Congress's actual plan to be quite different from what the majority imagines.

True to form, the majority does devote attention to a part of Section 1321 that, once isolated, it uses to cast doubt on the clear line Section 36B draws between state-established and federal exchanges. To support its conclusion that the phrase "Exchange established by the State under Section [1311]" could refer to *"all* Exchanges—both State and Federal—at least for purposes of the tax credits," it points to Section 1321's instructions to the HHS secretary.[113] This provision provides that should a state fail to create the "required Exchange," the secretary shall "establish and operate such Exchange within the State."[114]

According to the majority, "by using the words 'such Exchange,' the Act indicates that State and Federal Exchanges should be the same."[115] The majority is correct in that this language indicates the exchange established by the secretary should perform the same general functions as those established by states under Section 1311. Section 1321 anticipates this by expressly authorizing the secretary to adopt regulations providing that HHS exchanges will operate like state exchanges. Yet this is not enough to fulfill the requirements of Section 36B, as the relevant language speaks both to the type of exchange in which tax credits are to be available, as well as the sovereign that has established it.[116] So even if "such Exchange" could be read to make a Section 1321 exchange legally equivalent to a Section 1311 exchange, it is still not an exchange "established by the State."

This understanding is confirmed by consideration of other relevant provisions of the statute. Section 1323 provides that when a U.S. territory creates "such an Exchange," the territory "shall be treated

---

[112] 42 U.S.C. § 18031(f)(3). See *supra* note 100.

[113] King, 135 S. Ct. at 2491.

[114] 42 U.S.C. § 18041 (c).

[115] King, 135 S. Ct. at 2491.

[116] See *id.* at 2489–90 ("State and Federal Exchanges are established by different sovereigns"); see also Halbig v. Burwell, 758 F.3d 390, 400 (D.C. Cir. 2014) ("[S]ubsidies also turn on a third attribute of Exchanges: who established them.").

as a State."[117] The fact that Congress considered it necessary to insert that explicit equivalence language shows that Congress did not consider the word "such" to have the meaning the majority claims. Similarly, when Congress sought to create full equivalence between actions undertaken by the federal and state governments it did so explicitly. Section 1322, for instance, conditions recognition of an organization as a "qualified nonprofit health insurance issuer," in part, on the state adopting insurance market reforms or "the Secretary ha[ving] implemented [the reforms] for the State."[118] Congress knew full well how to authorize the federal government to stand in the state's shoes. It did not do so here. The phrase "such Exchange" may indicate that federal exchanges have the same intrinsic characteristics as a state-established exchange, but tax-credit eligibility hinges on the extrinsic characteristic of *which* sovereign established the exchange.

The majority seeks further support for its conclusion that the relevant language is ambiguous by pointing to "several provisions that assume tax credits will be available on both State and Federal Exchanges."[119] Yet the first two provisions the majority cites in support of this proposition are taken from Section 1311—the very section that instructs states to create exchanges in the first place. That Section 1311 includes provisions that assume tax credits will be available in Section 1311 exchanges is hardly surprising given that Section 1401 provides tax credits in exchanges "established by the State under Section 1311." These provisions lend no support for the majority's position. At best, they beg the question.

The majority also points to Section 36B's requirements that both state and federal exchanges report information on health insurance purchases, including information about any tax credits provided."[120] In the majority's view it "would make little sense" to require reporting on tax credits were such credits not available in federal exchanges.[121] Yet even under the majority's interpretation, these reporting requirements apply to instances where tax credits are not available.

[117] 42 U.S.C. § 18043(a)(1).
[118] 42 U.S.C. § 18042(c)(6).
[119] King, 135 S. Ct. at 2491.
[120] 26 U.S.C. § 36B(f)(3).
[121] King, 135 S. Ct. at 2492.

This requirement obligates all exchanges to report information on all enrollees, yet not all those who purchase insurance on exchanges are eligible for tax credits due to income or other characteristics. Further, as the D.C. Circuit noted in *Halbig*, "even if credits are unavailable on federal Exchanges, reporting by those Exchanges still serves the purpose of enforcing the individual mandate—a point the IRS, in fact, acknowledged."[122]

Having walked through "Exchange established by the State under Section [1311]," the majority now concludes that this phrase "is properly viewed as ambiguous."[123] Yet the majority's tortured path came at the expense of plain language and Congress's express commands. That's not all. In his dissent, Justice Scalia summarized some of the other steps the majority took in its quest to find ambiguity:

> To mention just the highlights, the Court's interpretation clashes with a statutory definition, renders words inoperative in at least seven separate provisions of the Act, overlooks the contrast between provisions that say "Exchange" and those that say "Exchange established by the State," gives the same phrase one meaning for purposes of tax credits but an entirely different meaning for other purposes, and (let us not forget) contradicts the ordinary meaning of the words Congress used. On the other side of the ledger, the Court has come up with nothing more than a general provision that turns out to be controlled by a specific one, a handful of clauses that are consistent with either understanding of establishment by the State, and a resemblance between the tax-credit provision and the rest of the Tax Code. If that is all it takes to make something ambiguous, everything is ambiguous.[124]

Indeed.

VI. A Most Plausible Implausibility

Having concluded that the relevant statutory text is "ambiguous," the majority turns "to the broader structure of the Act to determine the meaning of Section 36B."[125] Rather than consider the text of

---

122 758 F. 3d. at 403.

123 King, 135 S. Ct. at 2491.

124 *Id.* at 2502–03 (Scalia, J., dissenting).

125 *Id.* at 2492.

the ACA, however, the majority focused instead on the "statutory scheme"—the aforementioned three-legged stool—and concluded that tax credits simply must be available in federal exchanges. Otherwise, the act would threaten to "destabilize" the individual insurance market in any state that failed to establish its own exchange. The idea that Congress would allow such a result, the majority reasoned, was "implausible."[126] Section 36B's tax credits "are necessary for Federal Exchanges to function like their State Exchange counterparts, and to avoid the type of calamitous result that Congress plainly meant to avoid."[127]

The majority hangs its resolution of this purported ambiguity upon its assumption that Congress would not have enacted a provision that threatened to undermine its goal of expanding health insurance coverage. More specifically, the majority concluded that Congress would not have imposed costly restrictions on health insurance providers, such as community-rated premiums, without also imposing mandates and providing subsidies to stabilize markets. However reasonable this assumption may seem in the abstract, the ACA's legislative history flatly contradicts it. The ACA's leading advocates considered, supported, and in some cases enacted provisions that would undermine the very coverage expansions the majority claims Congress would never undermine. While the majority assumes ACA supporters would not support community rating without also providing for subsidies and a mandate to combat the resulting instability, they did exactly that, over and over again, including where the Court claimed Congress wouldn't.

Both the ACA and the House bill created a long-term-care entitlement program called the Community Living Assistance Services and Supports (CLASS) Act. Each bill imposed community-rated premiums *and* an explicit prohibition on subsidies that might reduce the resulting instability.[128] ACA supporters enacted these provisions

---

[126] *Id.* at 2493–94.

[127] *Id.* at 2496.

[128] 42 U.S.C. § 300ll-7(b) ("No taxpayer funds shall be used for payment of benefits under a CLASS Independent Benefit Plan. For purposes of this subsection, the term 'taxpayer funds' means any Federal funds from a source other than premium."). Richard S. Foster, Ctr. for Medicare & Medicaid Servs., Estimated Financial Effects of the "America's Affordable Health Choices Act of 2009" (H.R. 3962), as Passed by the House on November 7, 2009 (2009), at 10.

despite repeated warnings that "voluntary, unsubsidized, and non-underwritten insurance programs such as CLASS face a significant risk of failure as a result of adverse selection by participants."[129] The CLASS Act promptly collapsed, and Congress repealed it.[130] According to Chief Justice Roberts, the CLASS Act doesn't count because it is "a comparatively minor program" and not part of "the general health insurance program—the very heart of the Act."[131] Again, so much for reading the statute as a whole.

That objection cannot be raised against Congress's imposition of the ACA's prohibitions on pre-existing-condition exclusions and discrimination based on health status with respect to children. In the market for child-only health insurance policies, the ACA imposed these measures beginning September 23, 2010—more than *three years* before it provided subsidies or imposed a purchase mandate.[132] Those markets either constricted or completely collapsed in two-thirds of the states.[133] These facts belie the majority's claims that Congress deemed all three legs of the stool "should take effect on the same day—January 1, 2014,"[134] and that ACA supporters subordinated *everything* to their desire "to avoid adverse selection in the *health* insurance markets."[135]

Moreover, in developing the ACA, Congress indisputably considered provisions that would condition tax credits and other subsidies for the purchase of insurance on state cooperation, and advanced legislation that could force exchanges to operate without the benefit of premium subsidies. The HELP bill, for example, withheld premium subsidies in any state that refused to implement that bill's employer

---

[129] *Id.*at 11. See also Am. Academy of Actuaries, Critical Issues in Health Reform: Community Living Assistance Service and Supports Act (CLASS) (2009).

[130] American Taxpayer Relief Act of 2012, Pub. L. No. 112-240, § 642, 126 Stat. 2313, 2358 (2013) (repealing the CLASS Act).

[131] King, 135 S. Ct. at 2494 n.4.

[132] Pub. L. 111–148, § 1255 ("the provisions of [42 U.S.C. 300gg–3] (as amended by section 1201), as they apply to enrollees who are under 19 years of age, shall become effective for plan years beginning on or after the date that is 6 months after the date of enactment of this Act").

[133] S. Comm. on Health, Educ., Labor & Pensions, 112th Cong., Ranking Member Rep. Enzi: Health Care Reform Law's Impact on Child-Only Health Insurance Policies 5 (Aug. 2, 2011).

[134] King, 135 S. Ct. at 2487.

[135] *Id.* at 2494 n.4 (emphasis in original).

mandate. The result, in non-cooperating states, would have been exchanges selling health insurance subject to even more destabilizing community-rating price controls than the ACA imposes, but without any subsidies to rescue those markets. All 12 HELP Committee Democrats, a group that included several of the ACA's authors, voted in favor of that bill and that provision. One cannot reasonably argue the plain meaning of Section 36B is *implausible* when even the government and its amici concede that the ACA's authors supported another bill that also could have destroyed health insurance markets in uncooperative states.[136] And yet, to determine what ACA supporters were thinking, the Court relied on testimony delivered by a nonmember of Congress *to* the HELP Committee, and *ignored* legislation produced *by* the HELP Committee—that is, by a dozen of the ACA's authors and supporters—that dispositively shows ACA supporters accepted conditioning exchange subsidies on state cooperation.[137]

Similarly, the Finance bill conditioned small-business tax credits on states implementing that bill's community-rating price controls.[138] Senate Democrats dropped these provisions from the Finance and HELP bills at the same time they reinforced the Finance provisions conditioning tax credits on states establishing exchanges.

Congress was willing to risk even more destruction with the ACA's Medicaid expansion. As the ACA was originally drafted, state refusal to expand Medicaid would result in the loss of health insurance subsidies for the most vulnerable segments of society. Even after the Court severed the Medicaid expansion from traditional Medicaid in *NFIB*, it remains the case that a state's refusal to accept the expansion exposes the poorest of the working poor to higher health insurance

---

[136] See *supra* note 36.

[137] King, 135 S. Ct. at 2486. See also Confirmation Hearing on the Nomination of John G. Roberts, Jr. to Be Chief Justice of the United States, Hearing Before the Committee on the Judiciary, U.S. Senate, 109th Cong., First Session, S. HRG. 109–158, (Sept.12–15, 2005) (explaining the use of legislative history to resolve textual ambiguities "requires a certain sensitivity . . . . All legislative history is not created equal.").

[138] See S. 1796, 111th Cong. (2009), § 1221(a), proposing 26 U.S.C. § 45R(c)(2) ("STATE FAILURE TO ADOPT INSURANCE RATING REFORMS. — No credit shall be determined under this section . . . for any month of coverage before the first month the State establishing the exchange has in effect the insurance rating reforms . . . ."); S. Rep. No. 111-89, at 48 (2009), http://www.gpo.gov/fdsys/pkg/CRPT- 111srpt89/pdf/CRPT-111srpt89.pdf ("If a State has not yet adopted the reformed rating rules, qualifying small business employers in the State are not eligible to receive the credit.").

costs in the individual market, while depriving them of tax credits to subsidize insurance purchases. This is because Section 36B requires individuals to earn at least 100 percent of the federal poverty line to be eligible for subsidies.[139] It also remains the case that a state's refusal to participate in traditional Medicaid would eliminate subsidies for the poorest of the poor. One cannot reasonably argue it is *implausible* that Congress would give states the power to "destroy" coverage for 8.5 million *moderate*-income individuals when it is undisputed that Congress gave and continues to give states the power to destroy coverage for 50 million *low*-income individuals.

Chief Justice Roberts's conclusion that it is "implausible" that Congress could have intended Section 36B to work as written is simply false. ACA supporters offered too many similar proposals to claim Congress could not have meant what it said in Section 36B.[140]

Beyond the health care context, Congress often enacts laws that rely upon state cooperation, and that risk severe adverse consequences should states fail to comply. It often enacts statutes with conflicting goals; the ACA contains conflicting goals in its very title. It often enacts legislation that undermines its stated goals or upsets the expectations of individual legislators.[141] Environmental law is replete with such examples, including pollution-control laws that increase pollution[142] and species-conservation laws that undermine species conservation.[143] It is indisputable that portions of the ACA undermine other stated goals and produce results that some

[139] See King, 135 S. Ct. at 2495 (quoting definition of "applicable taxpayer" eligible for tax credits).

[140] See Brief of Amici Curiae Jonathan H. Adler and Michael F. Cannon at 22–28, King v. Burwell, 135 S. Ct. 2480 (2015) (No. 14-114).

[141] See generally, Steven M. Gillon, That's Not What We Meant to Do: Reform and Its Unintended Consequences in the Twentieth Century (2000).

[142] One of the best-known examples is documented in Bruce Ackerman & William Hassler, Clean Coal, Dirty Air: Or How the Clean Air Act Became a Multibillion-Dollar Bail-Out for High-Sulfur Coal Producers (1981); see also Jonathan H. Adler, Clean Fuels, Dirty Air, in Environmental Politics: Public Costs, Private Rewards (1992).

[143] See, e.g., Jonathan H. Adler, Money or Nothing: The Adverse Environmental Consequences of Uncompensated Land Use Controls, 49 B.C. L. Rev. (2008); Jonathan H. Adler, Introduction to Rebuilding the Ark: New Perspectives on Endangered Species Act Reform (Jonathan H. Adler, ed., 2011).

supporters failed to anticipate, such as when the law threw millions out of their existing insurance plans.[144]

What is unique about the ACA was not that Congress passed a law with conflicting goals, or that the law threatened to withhold valuable benefits and impose a more punitive regulatory structure on non-cooperating states, but that so many states refused to cooperate. Moreover, as the large number of state amici supporting the *King* petitioners illustrates, many states preferred that deal to the one the majority offers them.[145]

Ironically, the Court's reliance upon its predetermined sense of "Congress's plan" may doom one of Congress's goals. As the *New York Times* noted just after the decision was released, *King* may have "killed state-based exchanges."[146] This is because, absent the threat of losing tax credits, the ACA offers states minimal inducement for the difficult and thankless task of creating and operating exchanges.[147] The idea that Congress conditioned tax credits on state cooperation, under the assumption that most (if not all) states would fall quickly into line, is more plausible than the idea Congress enacted a law encouraging federal exchanges in every state. Indeed, some senators

[144] See Angie Drobnic Holan, Lie of the Year: 'If You Like Your Health Care Plan, You Can Keep It,' PolitiFact (Dec. 12, 2013, 4:44 PM). This example, in particular, shows that many who supported the ACA in Congress either did not understand the law for which they voted, or were willing to deliberately misrepresent it in order to ensure its passage. Either way, the frequency with which members of Congress and the president were willing to say "if you like your health insurance plan, you can keep it" should illustrate the danger of relying upon "Congress's plan" when it is not embodied in the text of the statute at issue.

[145] See, e.g., Brief of Amici Curiae Indiana and 39 Indiana Public School Corporations, King. v. Burwell, 135 S. Ct. 2480 (2015) (No. 14-114); Brief of Amici Curiae Oklahoma, et al., King v. Burwell, 135 S. Ct. 2480 (2015) (No. 14-114).

[146] See Margot Sanger-Katz, Obamacare Ruling May Have Just Killed State-Based Exchanges, The Upshot, N.Y. Times, June 25, 2015, available at http://www.nytimes.com/2015/06/26/upshot/obamacare-ruling-may-have-just-killed-state-based-exchanges.html?abt=0002&abg=0.

[147] Ricardo Alonso-Zaldivar, High Costs Plague Some State-Run Health Insurance Markets, Associated Press (Jul. 27, 2015) ("Now that the Supreme Court has ruled the Obama administration can keep subsidizing premiums in all 50 states through HealthCare.gov, no longer is there a downside for states turning to Washington . . . The pendulum probably will swing toward a greater federal role in the next couple of years, said Jim Wadleigh, director of Connecticut's Access Health.").

who voted for the ACA made clear that was an option they would not support. And yet that is the law *King* gives us.[148]

VII. *Chevron's* Domain vs. *King's* Dominion

As noted above, the Court's *King* opinion rests on its conclusion that the relevant statutory language, when read in context, is ambiguous. Under normal circumstances, this would mean the government wins under step two of the *Chevron* doctrine, which provides that when a statute is ambiguous, courts should defer to the interpretation of the implementing agency. Not here. Instead, the chief justice explained, resolving the ambiguity was the job of the Court because the underlying question—whether tax credits are available for the purchase of health insurance in federally established exchanges— was sufficiently "extraordinary," and of such "deep economic and political significance," that it should not be left to an administrative agency, particularly one (like the IRS) lacking "expertise in crafting health insurance policy of this sort."[149] This meant that it was up to the Court to resolve the ambiguity it had discovered in the ACA, in this case by molding the relevant language to conform to the Court's understanding of Congress's plan.

There was precedent for the Court's refusal to apply *Chevron* deference. The Supreme Court similarly refused to defer to the Food and Drug Administration on whether tobacco could be regulated under the Food, Drug, and Cosmetic Act[150] and the Environmental Protection Agency on whether greenhouse gases constituted "pollutants" under the Clean Air Act.[151] The chief justice had also urged a narrow conception of *Chevron's* domain in *City of Arlington v. Federal Communications Commission*, though in dissent.[152]

---

[148] See Marc Levy, Penn. Withdraws Its Healthcare Marketplace Plan After Supreme Court Ruling, Insurance Journal (June 26, 2015), http://www.insurancejournal.com/news/east/2015/06/26/373202.htm; Randall Chase, Delaware Opts Against Setting Up State Health Insurance Exchange, Insurance Journal (Aug. 10, 2015), http://www.insurancejournal.com/news/east/2015/08/10/378007.htm ("The court's ruling upholding the subsidies in all states—not just those operating their own exchanges —was a major factor").

[149] King, 135 S. Ct. at 2489 (citation omitted).

[150] FDA v. Brown & Williamson Tobacco Corp., 529 U.S. 120, 159–60 (2000).

[151] Massachusetts v. EPA, 549 U.S. 497, 528–32 (2007).

[152] City of Arlington v. FCC, 133 S. Ct. 1863, 1880 (2013) (Roberts, C.J., dissenting).

The rationale for refusing to apply *Chevron* deference in such cases is that such deference is only appropriate where Congress would have wanted the implementing agency to exercise such authority. That is, agencies get *Chevron* deference when a statute is ambiguous *and* it is reasonable to believe Congress meant to delegate interpretive authority to the agency. Based on his *City of Arlington* dissent, it seems that the chief justice is committed to this principle. Whether a consistent majority of the Court concurs is an open question.[153]

The chief justice was unwilling to presume Congress had delegated the IRS authority to construe provisions of the Internal Revenue Code, because Congress had failed to expressly delegate such authority. Yet he had little difficulty presuming that Congress had authorized the payment of billions of dollars in refundable tax credits, not to mention the resulting penalties, without expressly providing so. Such authorization was to be found, if at all, in Congress's unstated "plan." What makes this inconsistency all the more striking is the Court's failure to engage with the precedents expressly counseling against assuming that Congress authorizes expenditures or tax benefits obliquely.[154]

Electing not to apply *Chevron* in *King* also allowed the majority to sidestep the fact that the IRS had never provided much of an explanation for its rule. As noted above, the IRS offered no more than a cursory and conclusory justification for its interpretation of Section 36B, failing to provide any substantive response to critical public comments on the proposed rule. Compared with the sort of legal analysis that typically accompanies important rulemakings of this type, the IRS's concise statement was utterly lacking. Under the

---

153 The same may be true of Justice Kennedy, who authored *Gonzales v. Oregon*, 546 U.S. 243 (2006) (holding that the Attorney General's interpretation of "legitimate medical purpose" under the Controlled Substance Act did not merit *Chevron* deference). Justices Ginsburg, Kagan, and Sotomayor joined Justice Scalia's broad application of *Chevron* deference in *City of Arlington v. FCC* and Justice Breyer concurred in the result. Of those joining the *King* majority, only Justice Kennedy joined Chief Justice Roberts's dissent.

154 See, e.g., United States v. Wells Fargo Bank, 485 U.S. 351, 354 (1988) (citing "the settled principle that exemptions from taxation are not to be implied; they must be unambiguously proved"); see also Yazoo & Miss. Valley R.R. Co. v. Thomas, 132 U.S. 174, 183 (1889) (holding that tax credits and the like "must be expressed in clear and unambiguous terms").

traditional standards of judicial review of agency action, it is hard to see how what the IRS did could constitute reasoned decisionmaking.

In other words, the IRS expanded its power by doing the opposite of what the ACA says, provided no justification until forced to do so by Congress and the courts, for years thereafter offered a constantly shifting series of post-hoc rationalizations, and still got away with it. The solicitor general's claim that "established by the State" was an undefined statutory term of art, for example, made its first appearance in the government's merits brief before the Supreme Court, years after the IRS rule was finalized. By assuming the role of final interpreter for itself, the Court was able to uphold the substance of the IRS rule without passing judgment on the IRS's manifestly unreasonable rulemaking.[155]

While this approach to *Chevron* did not come at the expense of the administration's preferred outcome in *King*, it may hamper other administrative initiatives in the future. As commentators have already noted, this aspect of the *King* decision gives opponents of agency action a new arrow for their legal quivers.[156] When confronted with particularly ambitious agency interpretations, challengers can argue the question at issue should not be left to the agency—and the higher the stakes, the more compelling this argument will be. One example of where *King* could affect other agencies is the Environmental

---

[155] This also enabled the Court to avoid confronting the "fundamental rule of administrative law" that courts "must judge the propriety" of agency actions "solely by the grounds invoked by the agency." See SEC v. Chenery Corp., 332 U.S. 194 (1947). As the *Chenery* Court explained, courts have no warrant for substituting their arguments for those offered by the agency:

> If those grounds are inadequate or improper, the court is powerless to affirm the administrative action by substituting what it considers to be a more adequate or proper basis. To do so would propel the court into the domain which Congress has set aside exclusively for the administrative agency.

Id. at 196.

[156] See Chris Walker, What King v. Burwell Means for Administrative Law, Notice & Comment, Yale J. Reg. (June 25, 2015), http://www.yalejreg.com/blog/what-king-v-burwell-means-for-administrative-law-by-chris-walker; The Obamacare Sidestep: Professor Freedman on King v. Burwell, Environmental Law Program (June 2015), http://environment.law.harvard.edu/2015/06/the-chevron-sidestep/; Cass R. Sunstein, The Catch in the Obamacare Opinion, Bloomberg View (June 25, 2015), http://www.bloombergview.com/articles/2015-06-25/the-catch-in-the-obamacare-opinion.

Protection Agency's Clean Power Plan.[157] So while many in the Obama administration cheered the outcome in *King*, the Court's rationale may have given officials in some agencies something to worry about. Then again, it remains to be seen whether there really are five consistent votes on the Court for this approach.

VIII. Altering the Deal

King was not the first time that the chief justice would stretch the ACA's text in service of his notion of how the statute should read. Roberts's opinion in *NFIB* adopted multiple saving constructions of the statutory text so as to overcome potential constitutional infirmities. The result, as in *King*, was a statute quite different from the one Congress actually enacted.

One of the most controversial aspects of the ACA is the so-called "individual mandate"—a requirement that individuals obtain qualifying health insurance or pay a penalty. Roberts's controlling opinion in *NFIB* found the individual mandate as written—a command imposed under Congress's power to regulate interstate commerce—to be unconstitutional.[158] Roberts nevertheless declined to invalidate the provision because he concluded that the assessment for noncompliance could be characterized as a "tax" and therefore justified as a use of Congress's taxing power.[159] That Congress termed the assessment a penalty instead of a tax—and that the ACA's supporters repeatedly disclaimed that the penalty was a "tax" because it would not have passed otherwise—was not enough to let the plain text of the law guide Roberts's understanding.

Nor did it matter that this interpretation could constrain the individual mandate's operation in the future: Roberts concluded that the assessment could be considered a tax rather than a penalty because the amount was significantly less than the cost of buying coverage, and therefore was not large enough to coerce individuals into purchasing health insurance.[160] But that means that the mandate will be

---

[157] See Jonathan H. Adler, Could *King v. Burwell* Spell Bad News for the EPA?, The Volokh Conspiracy, Wash. Post (July 3, 2015), https://www.washingtonpost.com/news/volokh-conspiracy/wp/2015/07/03/could-king-v-burwell-spell-bad-news-for-the-epa/.

[158] NFIB, 132 S. Ct. 2566, 2600–01 (2012).

[159] *Id.*

[160] *Id.* at 2595–96.

less effective in fulfilling its stated purpose of preventing adverse selection.[161] If the assessment is significantly less than the cost of purchasing qualifying health insurance, many uninsured individuals will lack a sufficient incentive to purchase insurance before they are sick. The logical response to this problem would be to increase the assessment, but Roberts's *NFIB* opinion limits Congress's ability to do so because—at some unknown amount—a higher assessment ceases to be a constitutional tax and becomes an unconstitutional penalty.[162] This may have made sense to the chief justice at the time, but it is hard to square with either the statutory text or the statutory purpose he described in *King*.[163]

Roberts also took liberties with the ACA's text in upholding the Medicaid expansion. Like six of his colleagues, the chief justice concluded that it was unconstitutional for Congress to condition a state's receipt of all Medicaid funding on acceptance of the ACA's Medicaid expansion.[164] Leveraging longstanding state participation in the Medicaid program, and reliance upon significant federal support, was impermissibly coercive.

Rather than invalidate the Medicaid expansion in its entirety, however—let alone the ACA as a whole—the chief justice opted to rewrite the relevant ACA provisions to separate the old Medicaid program from the new. Although Congress had constructed the Medicaid expansion as an extension of the existing program by simply including the expansion among the conditions imposed on receipt of all Medicaid funds, the chief justice concluded that these were in fact two separate programs that states could consider separately. The relevant statutory language was effectively replicated, with one version continuing to set conditions on receipt of old Medicaid funds and another version incorporating the conditions of the Medicaid expansion. Here again, the chief justice's opinion adopted an interpretation of the ACA at odds with the relevant statutory language in the

---

[161] King, 135 S. Ct. at 2486 ("Congress adopted a coverage requirement to 'minimize this adverse selection and broaden the health insurance risk pool to include healthy individuals, which will lower health insurance premiums.'" (citing 42 U. S. C. § 18091(2) (I))).

[162] See Randy E. Barnett, No Small Feat: Who Won the Health Care Case (and Why Did so Many Law Professors Miss the Boat)?, 65 Fla. L. Rev. 1331, 1339 (2013).

[163] Cf. King, 135 S. Ct. at 2485–87.

[164] NFIB, 132 S. Ct. at 2601–07.

name of a never-expressed congressional plan. Again, Roberts adopted an interpretation that undermined the purpose of the relevant provisions; since *NFIB*, dozens of states have declined to implement the ACA's Medicaid expansion—which the ACA's supporters clearly sought to ensure in all 50 states.[165] By decoupling the Medicaid expansion from the continued receipt of traditional Medicaid funding, the chief justice made it much easier for states to refuse to participate in the expansion.[166]

In *NFIB* the chief justice took liberties with the statutory text, even at the expense of statutory purpose, to prevent the ACA's constitutional infirmities from dooming the statute. In *King*, he took liberties with the text to prevent the ACA's political and operational infirmities from frustrating "Congress's plan." In so doing, the chief justice revealed that his willingness to stretch statutory text is not confined to cases of constitutional avoidance, and that providing a statute that "works" is as much a job for the courts as it is for Congress.

There is no indication in the statute or its legislative history that it was part of Congress's plan to enact an inflexible tax rather than a flexible penalty; or to offer states a choice of either implementing the Medicaid expansion or preserving the status quo ante; or to make tax credits available in federal exchanges. The only "plan" that makes sense of Roberts's saving constructions is a desire to prevent the ACA's constitutional, political, and operational infirmities from threatening its survival.

---

[165] PPACA proponents emphasized that the Medicaid expansion was not a new program, but a change to the existing Medicaid program, which every state had implemented. See Brief of Senate Majority Leader Harry Reid, House Democratic Leader Nancy Pelosi, and Congressional Leaders and Leaders of Committees of Relevant Jurisdiction as Amici Curiae in Support of Respondents (Medicaid) at 6, NFIB v. Sebelius, 132 S. Ct. 2566, (2012) (No. 11-400). This is the only way to understand the purpose of the minimum income requirement for tax credit eligibility. See 26 U.S.C. § 36B.

[166] See Noam N. Levey, Court's Decision Could Widen Medicaid Gap, L.A. Times, June 29, 2012, available at http://articles.latimes.com/2012/jun/29/nation/la-na-court-impact-20120629; Stacey Butterfield, Changes to Medicaid Divide States, Doctors, ACP Internist (2013), http://www.acpinternist.org/archives/2013/10/medicaid.htm (quoting Sara Wilensky as saying "the toughest thing about Medicaid expansion, post-Supreme Court decision, is that what was supposed to be uniform across the country is now being decided on a state-by-state basis."). As of July 20, 2105, 19 states had refused to expand Medicaid under the PPACA.

IX. Conclusion

Whether the members of Congress who supported the ACA were aware of it or not, "the most natural reading of the pertinent statutory phrase" shows they voted to present states with a choice. States could either create health insurance exchanges, in which case eligible citizens would receive tax credits, and many individuals and employers who failed to purchase coverage would face penalties, or states could choose not to create exchanges, in which case residents would receive no subsidies, but face fewer penalties. Like the choice Congress presented states via the Medicaid expansion, this choice was stark. No doubt few in Congress anticipated states would act like "separate and independent sovereigns" and "defend their prerogatives by adopting the simple expedient of not yielding to federal blandishments."[167] What makes the ACA unique is not that it offered states this sort of choice, but that a majority of states chose not to cooperate.

Chief Justice Roberts framed the Court's *King* ruling as a service to "democracy." "[I]n every case," he wrote, the Court "must respect the role of the Legislature, and take care not to undo what it has done."[168] Yet that is precisely what the majority did. By elevating an unexpressed congressional plan over the plan Congress expressly laid out in statute, the majority altered the deal Congress offered states. Indeed, the Court went to great lengths to do so.

Reaching its conception of Congress's plan required the majority to change the meaning of "established by the State" from its natural or plain meaning; to change the meaning of that phrase in some parts of the statute but not others; to treat a universal definition as conditional, and a conditional definition as universal; to conclude that Congress would allow adverse selection in long-term-care insurance, but not health insurance; to ignore that Congress indeed tolerated significant adverse selection in health insurance; to isolate select statutory text for the purpose of casting doubt on the operative text; to ignore all other text and context that eliminate such doubts; to rely on legislative history that supported its understanding of Congress's plan, but ignore legislative history that supports the plain

---

[167] NFIB, 132 S. Ct. 2566, 2603 (2012) (internal quotation marks omitted).
[168] King, 135 S. Ct. at 2496.

meaning; and to make broad assumptions about the way Congress legislates that are contrary to what we actually observe.

If it is "possible" to interpret "established by the State" to mean "established by the State or federal government," are there any provisions of the ACA that cannot be rewritten to fulfill "what we see as Congress's plan"? The ACA explicitly denies tax credits to those who purchase coverage outside of an exchange, to many dependents who do not have access to "affordable" employer coverage,[169] and even to those with incomes below 100 percent of the poverty line, many of whom aren't eligible for Medicaid. If "Congress's plan" is simply to "improve health insurance markets," should those limitations on tax-credit eligibility stand in the way? Should the IRS disregard all ACA provisions that limit eligibility for tax credits? Will the Court ratify those revisions of the statute?

These questions are not academic. The IRS has already expanded eligibility for tax credits to certain undocumented immigrants, individuals below 100 percent of the poverty line, and others in direct contravention of the clear limits imposed by Section 36B.[170] Is pretending that 99 percent is greater than 100 percent also part of Congress's plan? Those tax credits will trigger penalties against employers. Must those employers also pay taxes from which the ACA clearly exempts them?

The only answer the majority provides—the only limitation it envisions on the judicial power to override plain text in the service of "what we see as Congress's plan"—is what is "at all possible." That stands in stark contrast to the rule laid out by five of the six justices in the *King* majority just one year earlier:

> [T]his Court does not revise legislation...just because the text as written creates an apparent anomaly as to some subject it does not address. Truth be told, such anomalies often arise from statutes...Rejecting a similar argument that a statutory anomaly...made "not a whit of sense," we explained in one recent case that "Congress wrote the statute it wrote"—

---

[169] Tricia Brooks, The Family Glitch, Health Affairs, Nov. 10, 2014, available at http://www.healthaffairs.org/healthpolicybriefs/brief.php?brief_id=129 ("Some low-to-moderate-income families may be locked out of receiving financial assistance to purchase health coverage through the Marketplaces.").

[170] See, e.g., Andy S. Grewal, Lurking Challenges to the ACA Tax Credit Regulations, Bloomberg BNA Tax Insights, 98 DTR J-1 (May 2015).

> meaning, a statute going so far and no further. . . . This Court
> has no roving license, in even ordinary cases of statutory
> interpretation, to disregard clear language simply on the view
> that...Congress "must have intended" something broader.[171]

It is also not much of a limitation. If judges may deprive select words of all meaning, construe select phrases to mean their opposite, ignore Congress's express instructions, and treat text, context, legislative history, and a statute's competing purposes as buffets from which they may select only the items that serve "what we see as Congress's plan," then judges will find very little is impossible. It remains to be seen whether this approach to statutory interpretation will be applied across the board, or is limited to the law "[w]e should start calling . . . SCOTUSCare."[172]

The Court's decision to disregard Congress's express plan has deprived states of a power Congress granted them, and that many states were eager to use. It has altered the balance of power between the federal government and the states. It has reduced democratic accountability for the ACA, and perhaps other acts of Congress. It has subjected tens of millions of employers and individuals to penalties from which the ACA plainly exempts them.[173] And it creates uncertainty about whether citizens can trust that federal statutes mean what they say.[174]

---

[171] Michigan v. Bay Mills Indian Community, 134 S. Ct. 2024, 2033–34 (2014) (internal citations omitted).

[172] King, 135 S. Ct. at 2507 (Scalia, J., dissenting); see also *id.* at 2497 ("[N]ormal rules of interpretation seem always to yield to the overriding principle of the present Court: The Affordable Care Act must be saved."). Cf. Ilya Shapiro, Scalia's Obamacare Argument Is Stronger Than Roberts', CNN.com, June 26, 2015, http://www.cnn.com/2015/06/26/opinions/shapiro-supreme-court-obamacare ("Scalia renamed the law at issue 'SCOTUSCare,' but really it deserves the moniker RobertsCare.").

[173] See Michael F. Cannon, Benefits Of 'King v. Burwell': More Jobs, Higher Incomes & 70 Million Freed From Illegal Taxes, Forbes.com (June 24, 2015); Michael F. Cannon, King v. Burwell Expanded Obamacare Even More Than You Know, National Review Online (July 29, 2015).

[174] See Star Wars *supra* note 1 ("This deal is getting worse all the time."); see also Robot Chicken: Star Wars Episode II (Adult Swim broadcast, Nov. 16, 2008), https://youtu.be/WpE_xMRiCLE (illustrating the perils of *post hoc* deal alterations).

Mistaken Paradigms and Interpreting Dreams: Some Reflections on *King v. Burwell*

*James F. Blumstein**

Introduction

In *King v. Burwell*, the Supreme Court addressed the question of whether federal subsidies for the purchase of medical insurance were available to income-qualified individuals who purchased on federally run exchanges.[1] It ruled that such subsidies, provided for by a regulation promulgated by the Internal Revenue Service, were available.

In reaching this conclusion, the Court upheld the IRS regulation but disregarded the operative language of the Affordable Care Act.

The ACA's text authorizes federal subsidies for medical insurance purchased on an exchange "established by the State" but is silent about authorizing such subsidies for medical insurance purchased on an exchange established by the federal government. The Court, somewhat remarkably, regarded the pivotal statutory language in the ACA as "surplusage," and described the straight-forward language as "not . . . a particularly useful guide to a fair construction of the statute."[2] This acknowledged disregard of quite plain statutory language raises serious questions about the appropriate method used by the Court in interpreting the ACA (or any other statute).

Effectively reading pivotal statutory text out of a statute seems well beyond the umpire or referee function much proclaimed by the chief justice during his confirmation process. The approach to

---

* University Professor of Constitutional Law and Health Law and Policy, Vanderbilt University.

[1] 135 S. Ct. 2480 (2015).

[2] *Id.* at 2483.

statutory interpretation embraced in *King* invites nonlegislative actors such as courts and agencies to identify and embrace a broad statutory narrative and then shoehorn the legislative text into that story line. The *King* approach anthropomorphizes statutes, assuming that there is a clear and coherent statutory vision, with all components serving a set, designed function. That is not how legislation emerges from the legislative process, and pursuing that "coherent statutory vision" allows for what happened in *King*—the Court used this anthropomorphization to allow perceived broad statutory objectives and structures to trump clear statutory language. The Court turned away from what the ACA did to what the ACA's drafters should have done or meant to do (as the Court divined it).

The *King* approach turns statutory interpretation into a secular version of the Genesis story of Joseph, who gained power and influence by interpreting the dreams of the Egyptian pharaoh.

Genesis 41 tells the story of the Egyptian pharaoh dreaming of seven attractive cows being eaten by seven ugly cows, and seven plump ears of grain being swallowed by seven blighted ears of grain. When asked to interpret the pharaoh's dreams, Joseph concluded that the cows were not cows but years, and the same for the ears of grain. Invoking divine guidance, Joseph saw the pharaoh's dreams as signaling seven years of plenty followed by seven years of famine, and he recommended a sensible policy—a food savings plan during the good times to ensure food availability during the years of famine.

In *King*, the Court found that the ACA's language, which authorized subsidies for purchases of medical insurance on an exchange "established by the State," also called for the availability of subsidies on exchanges established not by the state but by the federal government. That was the case even though the ACA (Section 1304(d)) actually defined the term "State" so as not to include the federal government.[3] As with the Biblical story of Joseph, the Court in *King* looked to the dreams of the drafters of the ACA (and those of advocates for universal medical care coverage over many decades) and took measures to accommodate, empower, and implement those dreams. In the process, the Court treated the legislative work product actually produced by Congress as unhelpful surplusage. To use a more

---

[3] 42 U.S.C. § 18024(d) (codifying Section 1304(d) of the ACA).

modern metaphor, *King* turns statutory interpretation into a Ror-schach test.

The *King* approach has significant separation-of-powers implica-tions, transferring enormous powers to nonlegislative entities such as agencies and courts. The consequence of the decision in *King* also has significant federalism implications—diminishing state auton-omy and states' roles in two ways.

First, the outcome of *King* diminishes states' roles and withdraws states' authority. By determining whether or not to set up an ex-change, states would have served as gatekeepers to federal subsidies under the ACA, a role that states now play with respect to expanding ACA-based coverage under state Medicaid programs.

Second, *King* eliminates the role that states play under the ACA in striking the appropriate balance between (1) providing access to federal subsidies for their residents who have incomes that qualify for federal subsidies, and (2) providing a safe harbor (and competi-tive advantage) for their employers who face taxes/penalties if their employees secure federal subsidies. Under the ACA's employer man-date for employers with 50 or more full-time employees, employ-ers are penalized (substantially) if the employer does not provide ACA-compliant health benefits and if one of its employees receives a subsidy on an exchange. So no exchange means no subsidy and, therefore, no employer-mandate tax or penalty. [4]

[4] Petitioners' interpretation of the ACA subsidy provisions empowers (and does not coerce) states (1) by establishing states as gatekeepers to the federal exchange-based subsidies, and (2) by allowing states to provide a tax safe harbor to large employers whose medical insurance policies do not comply with the comprehensiveness and affordability requirements of the ACA and who are thereby subject to a substantial fine/tax. That fine/tax is triggered when one employee receives a subsidy on an ex-change. This form of state empowerment is the antithesis of federal coercion through use of conditions on federal spending programs, such as the functionally forced ex-pansion of Medicaid under the ACA held invalid in *Nat'l Fed. of Indep. Bus. v. Se-belius,* 132 S. Ct. 2566 (2012) ("NFIB"). Unlike expanded Medicaid, which made use of after-the-fact leveraging and took place at the level of contract modification, the exchange-based subsidy was an admittedly new program and therefore occurred at the contract-formation stage, where courts traditionally allow the parties more flex-ibility. At contract modification, principles of fairness attach in the performance of an ongoing contractual relationship; that is not the case at contract formation. In *NFIB,* the Court viewed the ACA Medicaid expansion not as a foreseeable, organic part of pre-existing Medicaid but an unanticipated add-on—a new program that, to survive constitutional scrutiny, had to be treated as a contract formation situation, not a con-tract modification. Had the ACA's expanded Medicaid provisions been mandated on

The approach embraced by the Court in *King* allows courts and agencies to have their way with statutory text when that text does not yield results in accord with the drafters' pharaoh-like dreams, as interpreted by a court or an agency based on gossamer and much-contested claims of statutory context, purpose, or structure.

But how can we be confident that the dreams, as interpreted by a court or an agency, reflect the preferences of the drafters rather than those of latter-day advocates or the interpreters themselves? And, in a democratic nation governed by the rule of law, can we really accept legislation by dreams or governance by dreams and their interpretation? Doesn't that empower modern, secular Josephs in ways that are troubling to democracy and the rule of law? After all, the rule of law, going back centuries, relies in large measure on statutory text as the guardian of democratic accountability and empowerment and as the embodiment of the statutory lawmaking function.

The Constitution assigns that lawmaking role primarily to Congress, although the Constitution also contemplates a role for the president, with his concurrence or non-concurrence (veto) serving as a part of the lawmaking process. And the Supreme Court has been the vigorous guardian of the constitutional formalities of that

---

states as a form of contract modification, that would have been unconstitutionally coercive as a violation of the principle that states cannot be forced to participate in federal programs (the "anti-commandeering" principle). The ACA's Medicaid enhancements and inducements were held valid, but only when seen as a contract-formation situation, in which states had real choices to opt-in or not, without the threat of loss of pre-existing Medicaid funding. Under the plaintiffs' interpretation in *King*, the states were in a contract-formation situation regarding exchange-based subsidies; they could set up an exchange and thereby allow subsidies to flow on those exchanges, or not; no threat to a pre-existing program existed, and no fiscal harm to the state as compared to the *status quo ante* existed. Moreover, under *New York v. United States*, 504 U.S. 144 (1992), a claim of coercion must focus on state budgetary expenses and obligations, not the loss of benefits to a state's residents as would have been the case if the plaintiffs' interpretation of the subsidy provisions of the ACA had been accepted by the *King* Court. See James Blumstein on the *King* Oral Argument, Volokh Conspiracy, Wash. Post, Mar. 3, 2015, http://www.washingtonpost.com/news/volokh-conspiracy/wp/2015/03/05/james-blumstein-on-the-king-oral-argument; James F. Blumstein, Enforcing Limits on the Affordable Care Act's Mandated Medicaid Expansion: The Coercion Principle and the Clear Notice Rule, 2011–2012 Cato Sup. Ct. Rev. 67 (2012); James F. Blumstein, *NFIB v. Sebelius* and Enforceable Limits on Federal Leveraging: The Contract Paradigm, the Clear Notice Rule, and the Coercion Principle, 6 J. of Health & Life Sciences L. 123 (Feb. 2013).

lawmaking process—formalities that solemnize and ensure the integrity of that process.

For example, the Court has rejected innovations like the legislative veto because that short-circuits the authority of one house (the Constitution contemplates bicameralism) and undermines the authority of the president when Congress acts without the president's involvement (the absence of "presentment").[5] The Court has also rejected a line-item-veto innovation because that transferred lawmaking power from Congress to the president.[6] But the Joseph interpretation-of-dreams approach to statutory interpretation, as reflected in *King*, looks in a very different direction. It admittedly treats operative statutory terms as "surplusage," problems to be overcome, when those terms do not fit the broader statutory dream as interpreted by a nonlegislative body. As in the story of Joseph, where "cows" and "grain" were treated as "years," the term "state"—albeit an ACA-defined term that does not include the federal government—is treated as including the federal government for purposes of making available tax subsidies to income-qualified purchasers of medical insurance on federally run exchanges.

In short, *King* does not paint a pretty portrait of where the art of statutory interpretation now is. No matter what one thinks of the outcome in terms of health policy, the Court's approach in *King*—purportedly saving the law from itself by disregarding its own textual provisions—is, well, stunning, even Orwellian. The ugly cow of the story of Joseph in the Bible (Genesis 41) has swallowed the plump one—in this case, the one actually enacted by Congress.

I. The ACA's Structure and Text

A. Types of Exchanges Under the ACA and Their Significance

Under the ACA, there are two kinds of exchanges, marketplaces in which sellers of medical insurance offer medical insurance policies and consumers can shop for such policies. Under Section 1311, states "shall" establish an exchange. The parties and the Court recognized that that mandatory language is unenforceable because, under the anti-commandeering principle, the federal government cannot force

---

[5] See INS v. Chadha, 462 U.S. 919 (1983).

[6] See Clinton v. New York, 524 U.S. 417 (1998).

states to participate in federal programs.[7] Yet the mandatory language, unenforceable though it may be, remains in the statutory text and expresses a strong preference for states to establish and operate an exchange.

The role of states in running exchanges was an important feature of the ACA as drafted in the Senate. While states, the Senate drafters came to realize, could not be compelled to establish exchanges, states could be given a right of first refusal, so that no federal exchange could be set up in a state unless a state chose not to establish an exchange or otherwise failed to do so. And states could be incentivized to set up exchanges, consistent with the anti-commandeering principle. The ACA drafted in the House contemplated a federally run exchange, a significant difference between the versions drafted in the Senate and the House; and it was the Senate version that ultimately became the law in this regard.

In what I have previously referred to as likely an "oops" provision, Section 1321 of the ACA recognizes the unenforceability of the mandatory provisions of Section 1311; states cannot be ordered to establish an exchange (although, as noted, they can be incentivized to do so).[8] Section 1321 sets up a fallback provision—namely a mandatory duty on the part of the federal government to establish "such" an exchange if a state elects not to set up an exchange under Section 1311. Absent the fallback provision of Section 1321, the ACA would have failed because states could not be compelled to set up exchanges, and no federal alternative would have been present. The federal government's obligation (or opportunity) to establish an exchange arises only when a state chooses not to or otherwise fails to establish an exchange under Section 1311.

King draws an erroneous inference about the ACA's exchange-fallback provision (Section 1321). The readily apparent role of the fallback provision, which requires the federal government to establish

---

[7] See NFIB, 132 S. Ct. 2566 (2012) (Anti-commandeering principle has a functional dimension so that Congress cannot force states to expand Medicaid on pain of losing pre-existing Medicaid funds); Printz v. United States, 521 U.S. 898 (1997) (Congress cannot force local officials to conduct background checks); New York v. United States, 505 U.S. 144 (1992) (Congress cannot force states to "take title" of radioactive waste).

[8] *Id.*; South Dakota v. Dole, 483 U.S. 203 (1987) (Congress may attach reasonable conditions to funds disbursed to the states without running afoul of the Tenth Amendment.).

an exchange where states choose not to or fail to do so, is to avoid the anti-commandeering problem if Section 1311 stood alone—impermissibly mandating states to establish an exchange.

Plaintiffs contended that the ACA, in order to overcome the anti-commandeering problem, incentivized states to establish an exchange by limiting subsidies to income-qualified persons who purchased medical insurance through exchanges established by a state. Evidence of this preference for state-run exchanges is that the ACA (Section 1311) retains the mandatory language despite its acknowledged unenforceability and gives states the first shot at establishing an exchange (precluding the federal government from establishing an exchange if the states act). But the drafters of the ACA miscalculated: States did not find the incentives sufficient, and nearly two-thirds decided not to establish such an exchange. The result under the ACA, plaintiffs argued, was that subsidies were unavailable in the two-thirds of states that did not establish an exchange.

In response to plaintiffs' contention that drafters of the ACA believed that the incentives for states to establish exchanges constituted "a deal that [states] would not refuse," the Court in *King* stated that the fallback provision (Section 1321) "refutes [that] argument." Why so? Well, according to the Court, the "whole point" of the fallback provision was "to create a federal fallback in case a State chooses not to establish its own Exchange." So, therefore, this demonstrates that "Congress did not believe it was offering States a deal they would not refuse" because the fallback provision "expressly addressed what would happen if a State *did* refuse the deal".[9]

This reasoning gets it backwards.

The fallback provision was a constitutional necessity under the anti-commandeering principle. Under that principle, states have a constitutionally protected right not to set up an exchange, even though Section 1311 of the ACA seemingly mandates states to establish such exchanges. The ACA was constitutionally obligated to achieve its goal of state-established exchanges by use of incentives, not mandates or functional coercion.

Incentives encourage behavior, but do not mandate it; such is the nature of an incentive and the constitutional anti-commandeering principle. Treading too close to the mandate line through use

---

[9] King, 135 S. Ct. at 2494 (emphasis in original).

of incentives risks running afoul of the anti-commandeering bar, which has a functional, not merely a formal, dimension.

That is, regulatory commandeering has a functional counterpart that applies to the use of conditions on federal spending. That functional counterpart was recognized in the portion of *NFIB v. Sebelius* that dealt with ACA-prescribed states' expansion of Medicaid. The ACA threatened states with the loss of all pre-existing Medicaid funding if they did not expand Medicaid to cover the ACA-prescribed category of eligible persons (covering persons with incomes up to 138 percent of the federal poverty level). *NFIB* held invalid that linkage between states' pre-existing Medicaid program funding and their ACA-imposed obligation to cover all persons with incomes below 138 percent of the federal poverty level.[10]

The presence of the fallback provision in Section 1321 was a response to a constitutional necessity; and that constitutional necessity, the anti-commandeering principle, was what obligated the ACA's drafters to embrace an incentives strategy. In addition, that incentives strategy had to leave real choices for states because the incentives could not be excessively coercive in practice. So, of course, the ACA recognized—it constitutionally had to recognize—that states might not accept the incentives. The ACA provided for a fallback provision in order to ensure the constitutional and practical viability of the ACA's exchange-based structure.

The Court erred by drawing an inference that the existence of a fallback provision regarding exchanges meant that the ACA did not embrace an incentives structure in order to encourage states to establish their own exchanges. To be constitutional, such an incentives structure had to allow for real choice, which means that some (or, as it turned out, many) states will not be drawn to action by the incentives offered. The fallback exchange provision only acknowledges the constitutional game plan; it is entirely consistent with plaintiffs' assertion that the carrot offered to states for establishing exchanges was access for a state's residents to federal tax subsidies (and the correlative stick was the absence of eligibility of a non-electing state's residents to those federal subsidies).

The Court's opposite inference—that the existence of the federal exchange fallback refutes plaintiffs' contention that the incentives

[10] NFIB, 132 S. Ct. at 2607–08.

were designed to incentivize states to establish exchanges and were expected to do the job—does not and cannot withstand analytical scrutiny; it disregards the constitutional game plan and the dilemma posed by that game plan, as reflected by the anti-commandeering principle. The Court, here, is caught with its analytical toga down.

B. *The Subsidy Provisions*

An entirely different ACA provision—Section 1401—deals with subsidies for income-qualified persons who purchase medical insurance. Income-qualified persons are those who have incomes in the range of 100–400 percent of the federal poverty level.

Under the ACA, subsidies are not available for all purchases of medical insurance by income-qualified individuals.

For example, subsidies under the ACA are not available for such purchases if income-qualified individuals purchase medical insurance outside an exchange. Persons can buy medical insurance outside an exchange, but no subsidies attach. So, the structure of the ACA precludes the contention that all those who are income-qualified receive universal subsidies through the ACA for their purchases of medical insurance.

Similarly, no subsidies on exchanges are available for persons who do not qualify for a state's Medicaid program but whose income is below 100 percent of the federal poverty level. Such persons are not income-qualified for subsidies on an exchange. Those persons were assumed by the ACA's drafters to be covered by states' expansions of their pre-existing Medicaid programs, which, until the decision in *NFIB* made such state decisions optional, were considered an automatic outcome; no state could risk its entire pre-existing Medicaid program funding by declining to expand pre-existing Medicaid, and such was the risk under the ACA before the Supreme Court invalidated that condition in *NFIB*.

Under the Supreme Court's 2012 decision in *NFIB*, states are not obliged to extend their pre-existing Medicaid programs to include all persons whose income is below 100 percent of the federal poverty level and who are thereby ineligible for the ACA's federal subsidies on a state-established exchange.[11] Nearly half the states have chosen not to extend (or not yet to extend) their Medicaid programs, even

---

[11] *Id*. at 2608.

though the matching terms under the ACA are very attractive. That leaves a significant number of persons in poverty who reside in non-expanding states and are uncovered by Medicaid, yet who are ineligible for federal subsidies on the exchanges.

In short, the ACA does not provide for universal subsidies—either for income-qualified persons who purchase medical insurance outside an exchange or for non-income-qualified persons (those with incomes below 100 percent of the federal poverty level) who are not covered by Medicaid but whose income is too low to qualify for subsidies on a federal exchange. On the other hand, the ACA does provide that income-qualified persons who purchase medical insurance on an exchange "established by the State under Section 1311" are eligible for federal subsidies. These subsidies are available on a sliding scale for persons whose income falls in the range of 100–400 percent of the federal poverty level.

By its terms, the ACA makes no comparable provision for subsidies to accrue to income-qualified persons who purchase medical insurance on the fallback federally run exchanges. Concluding that the lack of such a provision in the ACA was a gap in the ACA, the IRS determined to fill that gap. By regulation, it decided that federal subsidies should apply to income-qualified persons who purchase medical insurance through federal fallback exchanges. The IRS concluded that such an extension of subsidies was consistent with the ACA (even if not directly authorized by it).

As described earlier, the IRS regulation is a double-edged sword. It expands benefits to income-qualified employees in states that choose not to set up exchanges (and therefore have federally run exchanges). At the same time, the rule triggers potentially substantial taxes/penalties for some employers whose health plans do not comply with the comprehensiveness and affordability mandates of the ACA and that have at least one employee who receives a subsidy on an exchange.

This all seems very straightforward. No subsidies are available outside the exchanges. And subsidies on the exchanges are only available to those who are income-qualified and not covered by Medicaid. Two types of exchanges are provided for; Section 1401 of the ACA provides for subsidies only on exchanges "established by the State under Section 1311." No comparable provision authorizes subsidies on federally run exchanges established under Section 1321.

And no provision exists in the ACA, with respect to federal subsidies, for a gap-identification or gap-filling role for the IRS.[12]

The federal government is charged with establishing an exchange—"such" exchange—where the states elect not to set one up. But these are exchanges, at best, established not by a state but *in lieu of* an exchange established by a state. The ACA defines the term "state" so that it does not include the federal government.[13]

Had the ACA enacted subsidies on both types of exchanges—those established by a state and by the federal government—it would not have taken much to achieve that objective. The term "state," for example, could have been defined to include the federal government, but the ACA defines a "state" so as to exclude the federal government. Or the operative subsidy provision could have been generic— subsidies are available when medical insurance is purchased on an exchange, in contrast to the lack of such subsidies when medical insurance is purchased outside an exchange. Or, even simpler, the language could have authorized subsidies for state-established or federally established exchanges.

Under the circumstances, the operative subsidy provisions of the ACA (if not ignored) cannot reasonably be understood as enacting or authorizing subsidies on federally run exchanges. What the ACA did (as distinct from what its drafters arguably should have done or

[12] In the face of this straightforward language and exchange structure, one might question whether the IRS had gap-filling authority. See, e.g., United States v. Home Concrete & Supply, LLC, 132 S. Ct. 1839, 1843 (2012) (plurality opinion of Breyer, J.) (Where statutory language on a "particular issue" is clear cut, a court will infer that "Congress did *not* delegate gap-filling authority to an agency" regarding the precise question in issue.) (emphasis in original). The Court's unwillingness to rely on the *Chevron* doctrine, which traditionally grants deference to agency decisionmaking (see discussion of *Chevron, infra*), might be explained, at least in part, by reservations about whether the ACA had delegated gap-filling authority to the IRS on the tax subsidy issue. The Court in *King* said as much: "[H]ad Congress wished to assign that question [whether tax credits are available on federally run exchanges] to an agency, it surely would have done so expressly." King, 135 S. Ct. at 2489.

[13] The term "state" is defined in Section 1304(d) of the ACA so that it does not include the federal government. 42 U.S.C. § 18024(d) (defining the term "state" to include each of the 50 states and the District of Columbia). The ACA's definition of a "state" is applicable to Title I of the ACA, which includes Sections 1311, 1321, and 1401. Those sections mandate the establishment of exchanges and govern the subsidy provisions. Where, with respect to territories, the definition of "state" was to be expanded, the ACA deemed the territories to be treated as a state if they sought funding to establish an exchange. 42 U.S.C. § 18043(a)(1).

perhaps meant to do) is altogether clear; and the Court did not really dispute that, labeling this analysis the most "natural" interpretation of the ACA's terms.

II. The ACA's Text Should Govern

A 1980 case, arising in the context of an equal protection challenge, points the way to the conclusion that what Congress *did*, not what it might have intended to do or arguably should have done, is what should be given effect by a court.

In *United States Railroad Retirement Board v. Fritz*, the Supreme Court dealt with a statute that fundamentally restructured the railroad retirement system—somewhat as the ACA fundamentally restructured the American health care system.[14] Under pre-existing law, railroad industry retirees who had worked for both railroad and non-railroad employers could qualify for both Social Security benefits and railroad retirement benefits. These "windfall" benefits threatened the financial viability of the railroad retirement system.

Congress cut back on these retirement benefits, preserving them for some categories of workers but not for others. The line drawn in the statute—between those whose dual benefits were preserved and those whose benefits were curtailed—was subject to constitutional challenge under equal protection.

In his dissent, Justice William Brennan asserted that the "purposes" of the statute were "clear."[15] Committee reports stated the goal of retaining all "vested" retiree rights based on considerations of fairness and the legitimate expectations of retirees.[16] Justice Brennan criticized the resolution reached by Congress—curtailing such benefits for some pre-existing beneficiaries—because that resolution did not preserve pre-existing rights for all beneficiaries. Congress's resolution as reflected in the statute was at odds with the "principal purpose" of the law—"to preserve the vested earned benefits of retirees who had already qualified for them."[17]

The Court's response to that line of analysis—that the "purpose" of the statute, to preserve preexisting benefits for all beneficiaries,

---

[14] 449 U.S. 166 (1980).

[15] *Id.* at 185 (Brennan, J., dissenting).

[16] *Id.* at 185–86 (Brennan, J., dissenting).

[17] *Id.* at 186 (Brennan, J., dissenting).

trumped the terms of the statute itself—was clear-cut: The "plain language of [the statute] marks the beginning and end of our inquiry."[18] The terms of the enacted law control; and resort to ostensible but unenacted provisions cannot be used analytically to overcome a law's terms.

The approach in the *Fritz* case has its counterpart in interpreting statutes such as the ACA. "There is . . . no more persuasive evidence of the purpose of a statute than the words by which the legislature undertook to give expression to its wishes."[19] The terms of the statute must govern,[20] unless they are unclear or "ambiguous." The Court in *King* conceded as much. So how did the Court overcome the clear meaning of the ACA's operative provisions regarding the scope of the subsidy? This is where Chief Justice Roberts shed the robes of Holmes and donned those of Houdini.

A. Statutory Anomalies

The Court looked to other provisions of the ACA and concluded that there could be interpretive concerns (statutory anomalies) if the ACA's provisions regarding subsidies were applied in other contexts. Most significantly, the Court looked to a provision regarding the definition of a "qualified individual"—a person to whom all exchanges must make health plans available.[21] The ACA defines a "qualified individual" as a person who "resides in the State that established the Exchange." The Court found this to be a "problem," because such a definition would mean that no qualified individuals existed for federally run exchanges since, in those states, there would be no exchange established by the state.[22]

---

[18] *Id.* at 176.

[19] Griffin v. Oceanic Contractors, 458 U.S. 564, 571 (1982).

[20] Devotion to specific statutory terms, even if odd, has a long tradition. *United States v. Locke*, 471 U.S. 84 (1985) is a good example. Congress in that case specified a filing deadline of December 30, even though it was customary for a deadline to track the end of a month, and December has thirty-one days. Despite the risk of confusion, which triggered the litigation, the agency adopted and the Supreme Court affirmed the December 30 deadline, not extending it to December 31. The congressional will, as reflected in the terms of the statute, was respected. Neither the agency nor the Court took it upon itself to undo or redo the straightforward textual command.

[21] King, 135 S. Ct. at 2490.

[22] *Id.*

Well, does that make the subsidy provision ambiguous? Hardly. It has nothing to do with the subsidy provision. And one must wonder about the Court's attempt to anthropomorphize the statute by inferring that Congress would not "intend" to establish a regime without any qualified individuals to whom federally run exchanges must offer their services. The anthropomorphization of the ACA—trying to determine and then implement a single, unifying theme for the entire ACA—seems wrongheaded and hopelessly naïve, as reflected in the Court's *Fritz* decision. Resort to purpose can illuminate text, not serve to eviscerate it. Statutory interpretation deserves better.

The interpretive issue is what to do with the "qualified individual" provision, should the issue arise. That provision does not and cannot shed light on why the operative subsidy provision warrants interpretive interment. At most, the "qualified individual" provision would support an inference that the drafters assumed that state-run exchanges would be the norm, probably because of the unenforceable mandatory "shall" language in Section 1311 or, plausibly, because of the incentives built into the ACA's subsidy provisions.[23]

In any event, the provisions regarding qualified individuals cannot reasonably or sensibly transform clear-cut and straightforward language regarding subsidies into ambiguous language.

B. Consequences

The Court in *King* also looked to consequences or outcomes of plaintiffs' position if it prevailed. The Court was influenced by the argument that a significant reduction in subsidies (because so many states had chosen not to establish an exchange) would interfere with the working of the insurance markets in states with federally run exchanges. The insurance market reforms—no consideration of pre-existing medical conditions by insurance companies when accepting customers in the individual market ("guaranteed issue")—were

---

[23] The workaround embraced by the D.C. Circuit in *Halbig v. Burwell*, was its observation that exchanges must offer services to a "qualified individual," but that others could make use of the exchanges as well. Halbig v. Burwell, 758 F.3d 390 (D.C. Cir. 2014). The D.C. Circuit's approach comports with the ACA's terminology, and its adoption has the virtue of focusing on the specific interpretive concern—rather than forcing the total disregard and evisceration of a clear statutory term in a different portion of the ACA (and thereby allowing federal subsidies not expressly or even impliedly provided for by Congress when enacting the ACA).

nationwide in scope, and the Court concluded that those nationwide reforms would not work in non-electing states without the availability of tax subsidies on federally run exchanges. An insurance death spiral in individual markets in non-electing states would result, because the pool of the insured would become sicker, would be more expensive to insure, would drive up premium prices, and would result in the departicipation or non-participation of healthier individuals who could sign up (once enrollment opened up) if they became ill. The risk to individuals of non-insurance would diminish, the price of insurance would increase, and, without subsidies, many more persons would not be required to sign up under the individual mandate because they were not obliged to spend more than 8 percent of their income on medical insurance premiums. From this, the Court reasoned as follows: "So it stands to reason that Congress meant for those provisions [tax subsidies] to apply in every State as well."[24]

This is back to the world of Joseph and the pharaoh, of course. There is no claim that Congress did, in fact, act on what it ostensibly meant to do or how it meant for things to work. Only through anthropomorphization—after-the-fact inferring that there is a single guiding (invisible?) principle that must govern all interpretation, particularized and controlling language to the contrary notwithstanding—could this type of "it stands to reason" analysis trump operative language in the ACA or any statute and assign that otherwise-controlling language to the ignominious status of "surplusage."

The "it stands to reason" analysis—the focus on consequences to conclude "that Congress meant for" the tax subsidies "to apply in every State"—relies on broad considerations of abstract "purpose" or "intent." That style of analysis gives effect to these types of amorphous purposes or objectives at the expense of trashing, not illuminating, actually enacted terms.

The plaintiffs claimed that Congress used incentives for states to set up exchanges—by allowing states to serve as gatekeepers to tax subsidies for their residents. One potential outcome of such a constitutionally mandated strategy was the possibility that states would choose a pathway that preferred business climate objectives and safe harbor protection for its businesses against the employer-mandate

---

[24] King, 135 S. Ct. at 2493–94.

tax. That would conduce toward discouraging the formation of state-established exchanges and no tax subsidies for a state's residents when they purchased medical insurance. If there were adverse effects on the individual insurance market or on individual beneficiaries, those were foreseeable consequences (some would say risks) of the terms of the ACA as enacted and the federalism-based structural design that empowered states to make such choices. If that state-based preference were deemed unacceptable by the legislatively accountable branch, the Congress, then Congress or the states themselves through their political process are charged with making that determination and deciding whether and how to remedy that unacceptable outcome.

Plaintiffs' claim was plausible—and according to Jonathan Adler and Michael Cannon correct.[25] But it should not have to be correct, only plausible when it has the statutory text behind it. The *King* Court's finding otherwise is an admitted rewriting of the terms of the ACA—albeit in furtherance of a perceived overarching purpose. But pursuit of and identification of such an overarching purpose by a court or an agency results in the undoing and redoing of the terms of the ACA itself and reflects an unrealistic and false attempt to anthropomorphize the ACA. It purports to identify a single, coherent purpose or policy that can, through nonlegislative intervention, trump the work actually done by Congress as enacted into law with adherence to the formalities of lawmaking.

This type of analysis transfers enormous power away from the legislative branch at the federal level and from the political processes at the state level. And it turns the Court into something of a "Dream Team," overturning the work of Congress based on fuzzy, subjective, and indeterminate efforts at constructing a statutory worldview that does not exist and derives from the judicial imagination. Such judicial power does not or at least should not exist. And it calls into question just what is going on in the judicial process.

---

[25] Jonathan H. Adler & Michael F. Cannon, Taxation Without Representation: The Illegal IRS Rule to Expand Tax Credits under the PPACA, 23 Health Matrix 119 (2013).

III. The Roadmap to Ambiguity: Undoing and Redoing the ACA's Text

A. The "Context" Issue

The *de rigueur* mantra—akin to a *deus ex machina* in the *King* Court's rendering—is the concept of "context." This is the Court's "Shazam." Say it loud and say it often—look at context, not at a set of words in isolation. That seems reasonable, when helping to understand what words mean; but what about when the words are clear on their own terms? The use of context not to clarify but to disregard (and even effectively excise as in *King*) legislative terminology is destructive of *legislative* supremacy in lawmaking.

Given the chief justice's affinity to a baseball metaphor when describing a court's role—just calling balls and strikes—it might be useful to invoke a legendary (and perhaps apocryphal) Yogi Berra story.

Yogi was a great catcher with the New York Yankees, who trained in St. Petersburg, Florida. As legend has it, a young woman was standing outside the Yankees' training facility, dressed in shorts and a tank top, when Yogi emerged from the dressing room. Seeing Yogi dressed in a T-shirt and shorts, the young woman commented: "You look cool, Yogi." Looking back at the similarly clad young woman, Yogi responded: "You don't look so hot yourself."

Now, this is a case for context. Was Yogi slurring the young woman, using a connotative expression suggesting that she did not look attractive? Or was Yogi responding in a more denotative manner, recognizing that both he and the young woman were dressed to account for the hot Florida weather and that, accordingly, she would not be hot despite the weather conditions? Context, in this situation, illuminates the words spoken. Was Yogi using the term "hot" in a literal manner, regarding the hot Florida weather? Or was he using the term in the more idiomatic sense, which would gratuitously cast aspersions on the young woman's appearance?

Consideration of context in the Yogi story provides real insight to the meaning of a set of words; it does not disregard Yogi's words but gives them accurate meaning. It would be entirely appropriate to ask whether, for example, Yogi had previously known or encountered the young woman, so that he would not welcome her comments or might construe them to be related to his own appearance (after all being "cool" can have a colloquial meaning that refers to appearance, not temperature-related comfort). Was Yogi being provoked to make an acerbic, not a conversational, retort? Or was Yogi just making a perhaps infelicitous comment about the temperature-adaptive or weather-adaptive character of the young woman's choice of clothing? Context in the Yogi situation clarifies and illuminates Yogi's meaning, but it does not eviscerate his words or assign them to the trash bin of "surplusage."

The use of "context" in *King* was altogether different—not an attempt to understand the underlying meaning of specific and controlling terms in a statute, using "context" to inform the meaning of the words as used. It was an attempt to divine an overarching statutory "context" and then place (or disregard, as the matter warrants) those critical and controlling words into that overarching statutory "context" so as to ignore the words themselves, not inform their meaning. That exercise was performed in the name of the higher cause of fulfilling a purportedly overarching statutory objective as divined by the Court—as effectively presented in court filings and extra-judicial postings by the statute's agenda-driven maximalist advocates, and as inferred from other provisions of the statute.

King's resort to "context" provides an executive agency or a court with what amounts to a "Get Out of Jail Free" card—an opportunity to undo and redo the particularized and restrictive terms of a statute, thereby vesting enormous discretion and power with nonlegislative actors. As reflected in the *King* case, this use of Houdini-like methods improperly allows for nonlegislative disregard for clear, legislatively adopted terminology in a statute—much like Justice Brennan's rejected claim in *Fritz* that the retiree-benefits fix, as embodied in statutory law, was at odds with the overall purpose or objective of the law.

B. Purpose, Structure, and Consequences of the ACA

Once the *King* Court concluded that the "context" of the ACA made the otherwise-clear language of the subsidy provision "not so clear," that opened the door; it allowed the Court to delve into broader, amorphous considerations of purpose, structure, and consequences. But there again, the narrative the Court embraced was, at best, an uncertain one.

The Court contended that Congress would intend subsidies to be available on federal and state exchanges so as to avoid an insurance market death spiral. But, of course, Congress did not so provide when it would have been very easy to so provide. That type of reasoning is *ex post* and far from legislative or even legislatively authorized gap-filling—especially so when alternative narratives that conform to the language regarding the availability of subsidies are available.

Such an alternative narrative includes the comprehensive work of Jonathan Adler and Michael Cannon (and more than one amicus brief) demonstrating that the subsidy strategy was designed to incentivize states to set up exchanges when drafters realized that states could not be commanded to set up those exchanges.[26] Under that line of argument, the legislative preference, as formulated in the Senate version that became the ACA, was for state-established exchanges. When the drafters realized that such state-established exchanges could not be mandated (despite the mandatory language of Section 1311), they purposefully and knowingly embraced an incentives approach, as permitted under the anti-commandeering cases. Those incentives, it turned out, were insufficient to induce most states to establish an exchange,[27] but that provides no warrant for

[26] *Id.* See also Jonathan H. Adler & Michael F. Cannon, *King v. Burwell* and the Triumph of Selective Contextualism, 2014–2015 Cato Sup. Ct. Rev. 35 (2015).

[27] A question was raised by supporters of the government's position in *King* about whether states had clear notice that their failure to establish an exchange would mean no subsidy for their residents on the federally run exchange. In *NFIB*, the Court had ruled that imposition of the ACA's expanded Medicaid mandate did not provide states with adequate notice at the relevant time—when they signed up for Medicaid—so the additional conditions could not be imposed on states as a condition for retaining preexisting Medicaid funding. See Blumstein, 2011–2012 Cato Sup. Ct. Rev., *supra* note 4, at 93–99; Blumstein, 6 J. of Health & Life Sciences L., *supra* note 4, at 130–35. This Clear Notice requirement for conditions on federal spending programs derives from *Pennhurst State Sch. & Hosp. v. Halderman*, 451 U.S. 1 (1981). The notice issue in *King* is very different. The claim is that states lacked adequate notice of the consequences when they declined to establish an exchange. But the exchange and subsidy aspects of the ACA were new programs—contract formation. There was no after-the-fact imposition of conditions on a pre-existing program. If states decided to set up an exchange under the ACA, that would be a new program with the statute setting forth the relevant and straightforward terms and conditions. To the extent that the states were lulled by the challenged IRS rule, the strongest argument on this point, states still have the option to set up an exchange and secure for their residents the ability to qualify for subsidies.

the IRS or the Supreme Court to fill a perceived gap that is not a gap contemplated by the terms of the ACA itself.

Another plausible narrative, or consequence, is that the structure of the ACA empowers states, allowing them to serve as gatekeepers. This is a federalism narrative.

The plaintiffs' theory would establish states as gatekeepers to subsidies in their states—much as they are gatekeepers with regard to expanded Medicaid under the Court's 2012 *NFIB* decision. Further, states would be empowered to provide a tax safe harbor to large employers in their states. The large-employer mandate obliges employers with 50 or more employees to provide qualifying medical insurance to their full-time employees (30 hours) or face a substantial tax/penalty. The tax/penalty is $2000 per employee per year (after an exemption for the first 30 employees). The key is that the tax is triggered when one employee receives an ACA subsidy.

If a state controls access to subsidies (for example, by not setting up an exchange), it can bar subsidies by not establishing an exchange; states can thereby provide a safe harbor to their employers from the bite of the employer mandate/tax. The political process in such states would be charged with determining what to prioritize—strong business climate with its economic benefits and with some non-qualifying medical benefits for workers versus expanded subsidies for residents with incomes in the 100–400 percent of the federal poverty level. Under *King*, such state empowerment as provided for under the terms of the ACA does not exist, a real federalism cost.[28]

In addition, there are important separation-of-powers costs that stem from *King*. The ACA empowers the IRS to make various implementing regulations, but there is no indication that the IRS is authorized to determine whether the terms of the ACA regarding subsidies leave a statutory gap and if so how to fill that gap.

Legislative gap-filling in this context is a job for Congress, not the courts or the IRS. The IRS regulation challenged in *King* reflects executive-branch overreaching, and it is disappointing that the Supreme Court did not see that the IRS regulation in the *King* case was part of a broader mosaic of executive-branch overreaching that the

---

[28] This narrative also belies the claim, made by some supporters of the government's position in *King*, that the linkage between the availability of a subsidy and the obligation of a state to set up an exchange was coercive. For discussion of this point, see note 4, *supra*.

courts can and should rein in. This is especially true regarding tax subsidies, where enormous expenses are at stake and are being implemented based, at best, on an ambiguous legislative platform.

IV. *Chevron* and Related Issues

Pre-existing case law, stemming back over 100 years, seemingly had established a legislative clear-statement rule for authorizing tax credits. That is, tax credits "must be expressed in clear and unambiguous terms."[29]

That earlier doctrine is in tension with the more recent approach in the *Chevron* case, which mandates deference to agency rulemaking where an underlying statute is ambiguous.[30] *King* provided the Court with an opportunity to address and resolve that tension. In an earlier decision, the Supreme Court had held that an agency, faced with an ambiguous underlying statute, retained its deference under *Chevron* in rulemaking, even in matters related to taxation.[31] That is the so-called *Chevron* Step 2 analysis; but the Court had not addressed the question of the vitality of the earlier "clear statement" mandate in the context of determining whether agency rulemaking granting tax credits is warranted—that is, *Chevron* Step 1.

The *King* Court did not directly address that earlier clear-statement doctrine or its relationship to the *Chevron*-style analysis, a missed opportunity.

As noted, a case could be made that the *Chevron* rule, which calls for judicial deference to agency rulemaking when an underlying statute is ambiguous, was in tension with the earlier tax-subsidy, clear-statement doctrine. But the Court in *King* expressly declined to invoke the *Chevron* framework, so one would think that the earlier tax-subsidy, clear-statement doctrine would still be the right precedent to use. Resolution of the tension on this issue—did *Chevron* erode the pre-existing tax-subsidy, clear-statement doctrine?—would have been an important clarification. But, again, the Court missed its mark, ignoring the issue entirely in its opinion. The Court left the inference that the older case law regarding tax subsidies is no longer operative since the IRS's tax subsidy under the ACA was

---

[29] Yazoo & Miss. Valley R.R. Co. v. Thomas, 132 U.S. 174, 183 (1889).

[30] Chevron U.S.A., Inc. v. NRDC, 467 U.S. 837 (1984).

[31] Mayo Found. v. United States, 562 U.S. 44 (2011).

upheld based on a law considered by the Court to be ambiguous, not clear, as required by the pre-existing doctrine. But the *King* Court left this to inference by not dealing with the status of the tax-subsidy, clear-statement rule in the modern context.

Another issue of importance arises from the Court's refusing to apply the *Chevron* framework to this case.

Under *Chevron*, an agency receives deference for its regulations when a statute authorizes agency action but is ambiguous about how an agency should resolve a set of policy options deemed reasonable under the operative legislation. In *King*, the Court found the ACA to be ambiguous; so presumably under *Chevron* an agency can resolve policy options and receive judicial deference. That does not mean that an agency can, based purely on political preferences, undo previous agency action.[32] But an agency can make changes where it chooses and defends alternative policy prescriptions authorized by underlying legislation.[33]

In this case, a putative Republican president could redo the Obama administration's IRS regulation. For example, the IRS in the future could embrace the federalism goals outlined earlier, empowering states to choose between business climate considerations and tax subsidies for its residents. That would reflect an enhanced gatekeeping role for states, allowing states to provide a safe harbor from employer-mandate taxation for noncompliance with the ACA. A future IRS could analogize such a state decisionmaking role as comparable to states' roles in providing a safe harbor from federal antitrust legislation under the antitrust "state action" doctrine.[34] Under *Parker*, states can insulate private parties from federal antitrust enforcement when states adopt a policy that prefers regulation to competition and actively supervises private conduct to ensure that state policies are being adhered to.[35]

At the *King* oral argument, the question of a possible redo of the IRS regulation by a future administration was raised by the chief

---

[32] See, e.g., Motor Vehicle Manufacturers Assn. v. State Farm Mutual Auto. Ins. Co., 463 U.S. 29 (1983).

[33] See, e.g., FCC v. Fox Television Stations, Inc., 556 U.S. 502 (2009).

[34] See Parker v. Brown, 317 U.S. 341 (1943).

[35] See FTC v. Ticor Title Ins. Co., 504 U.S. 621 (1992). That "active supervision" component played a central role in the Court's refinement of *Parker* immunity this term. See North Carolina St. Bd. of Dental Examiners v. FTC, 135 S. Ct. 1101 (2015).

justice. Some have interpreted the Court's avoidance of reliance on the *Chevron* framework as a signal that future administrations will not be afforded an opportunity to redo the existing IRS regulations by limiting tax subsidies to state-established exchanges. The contention is that the *King* Court left no room for agency flexibility in embracing alternative interpretations of the ACA subsidy provisions going forward.

This is an intriguing issue—and that commentary is not clearly unfounded—but I think that this set of conclusions overreads the *King* opinion. An ostensible reason, seemingly apparent from oral argument, that the Court likely chose not to embrace the type of deference mandated by *Chevron* is that the IRS regulation was providing for enormous increases in federal tax subsidies—something that past precedent allowed only when legislation clearly authorized those subsidies.[36] As I noted earlier, the Court did not expressly link its analysis to this earlier doctrine, but it did express its concern about granting such deference to an agency when the ACA was, at best, ambiguous.

King does not necessarily apply symmetrically with respect to the increase or decrease of the availability of federal tax credits.[37] The reason for skepticism in situations such as *King* about non-explicit deference to the IRS—given the history—is that tax credits are being increased without clear statutory authorization by Congress. Where tax credits are being reduced, the concerns about clear legislative authorization are diminished, and greater deference in that circumstance would seem not inappropriate. But the issue is surely fair to raise, and only time will tell if a Republican administration is elected in 2016 and if it seeks to revisit these issues administratively.

---

[36] See Yazoo & Miss. Valley R.R. Co., 132 U.S. at 183.

[37] See Nat'l Cable & Telecoms. Ass'n v. Brand X Internet Servs., 545 U.S. 967, 982 (2005) ("A court's prior judicial construction of a statute trumps an agency construction otherwise entitled to *Chevron* deference only if the prior court decision holds that its construction follows the unambigious terms of the statute and thus leaves no room for agency discretion"). *King* held that the ACA was ambiguous and not unambigious on the subsidy question, so *Brand X* would suggest a role for agency rulemaking of the type discussed.

V. Judicial Role Considerations

A. A Paradigm Mistake

Finally, one comes to the question of judicial role. The chief justice received much criticism in some quarters for his rescuing of the ACA in the *NFIB* case by deeming the individual mandate a constitutionally valid "tax," rather than a constitutionally questionable "penalty" (the term adopted in the text of the ACA itself).[38] I saw the penalty/tax issue as one of political accountability: if Congress and the Obama administration wanted the legal benefits of labeling the individual mandate as a tax, they should not be allowed to play political dodge-ball games by labeling the individual mandate in the ACA itself a penalty and not a tax.

But I also have recognized and respected the chief justice's broader view from 30,000 feet that the Court would put itself into a difficult position institutionally to strike down the entire ACA on constitutional grounds when that legislation was the signature product of an administration that also had a super-majority in both the Senate and the House at the time of enactment. That meant going the extra mile to find a reasonable pathway toward upholding the ACA, consistent with the requirement that the pathway is reasonable under principles undergirding the rule of law.[39]

In 2012, for the Court to invalidate the entire ACA would have been a judicial trumping of both other branches. It would have been seen as and treated as a political confrontation during the 2012 presidential election, and it would have placed the Court's institutional role in the political crosshairs of a fierce political and partisan campaign. The Court would have stood against the political branches, and one can arguably understand the impetus of the chief justice for restraint in those circumstances.

The posture in *King* was altogether different; by not recognizing that difference, the Court made a significant paradigm mistake.

The issue in *King* was legislative interpretation, not constitutional interpretation; statutory interpretation is undoubtedly within the Court's job description, and the Court's legitimacy is beyond

---

[38] See, e.g., Ilya Shapiro, Like Eastwood Talking to a Chair: The Good, the Bad, and the Ugly of the Obamacare Ruling, 17 Tex. Rev. L. & Pol. 1 (Fall 2012).

[39] See James F. Blumstein, Understanding the Faulty Predictions Regarding the Challenges to Health Reform, 2014 U. Ill. L. Rev. 1251 (2014).

criticism in that sphere. In such a role, the Court was not in confrontation with the other branches. It was not being asked to trump the politically accountable branches. It was asked to referee a dispute that pitted the IRS, an executive branch agency, against Congress. If plaintiffs had prevailed, Congress would have been empowered to determine whether a problem with the ACA existed and if so how to resolve it. That is, in *King* the Court was not aligned against both the Congress and the president; it was being asked by plaintiffs to give effect to what Congress did, not what it may have intended to do, and in the process to empower Congress as the institution to determine whether a fix was needed (and if so what that fix might be).

But the Congress of 2015 is under new management compared with the Congress that enacted the ACA in 2010. If anything, that should have increased the Court's unwillingness to use its Houdini approach to safeguard the purported broad purposes of the enacting Congress by allowing for perceived drafting gaps to be filled nonlegislatively by judicial inference or IRS action. That is, from an institutional perspective, there was a strong case for the Supreme Court to hold the enacting Congress to the text of what it had enacted. The institutional or judicial-restraint concerns that may have led the chief justice in *NFIB* to find a way to save the ACA from constitutional invalidation were not present in *King*.

Adopting the plaintiffs' "natural" interpretation of the ACA's subsidy provisions in *King* would have created an opportunity for dialogue, an approach that should have appeal to a Frankfurterian such as the chief justice. A ruling for plaintiffs would undoubtedly have had some destabilizing short-run practical consequences, but many of those concerns could have been resolved remedially through a transition phase.[40] A ruling for plaintiffs would also have increased the likelihood that the party in control of Congress (Republicans) and the president (a Democrat) would have to have a political conversation about future changes to the ACA. And, to the extent that congressional Republicans had no participation in the enactment of the ACA and enjoyed a certain political validation from their legislative takeover—shared to some degree with the president through his reelection—a ruling for plaintiffs might have forced some discussion

---

[40] See the discussion of the procedural posture of the case, dealing with a motion to dismiss, in Part V.B, *infra*.

about health reform legislation that would have had the fingerprints on it of both parties.

Where the terms of the ACA were clear cut, the Court had a duty under the rule of law to enforce its terms; but in the face of admitted statutory ambiguity, at most, the Court had no obligation to enforce the purported broad general purposes, policy preferences, or objectives of the ACA when they were not embedded as enactments in the actual terms of the ACA itself—and when giving effect to such broad goals necessarily resulted in condemning the operative provisions of the enacted text to the never-never status of "surplusage." Such statutory surgical repair is a role for Congress—especially a Congress under new management.

The Court concluded that its interpretation "respect[ed] the role of the Legislature" and that the Court should "not undo what [Congress] has done." The Court said it must respect and secure "a fair understanding of the legislative plan." But that led to the wrong outcome when such a "fair understanding" necessitated actually undoing and redoing what Congress actually did—in the process labeling the operative statutory language surplusage and therefore inoperative. *King* did not respect Congress; it disempowered Congress as an institution, implicitly buying into the government's position that Congress could not be counted on to "fix" the problems that would arise if plaintiffs' position were accepted.

But it is precisely Congress that must determine whether what it actually did needs fixing and if so in what manner; use by the Court of its own interpretation of the ACA's "legislative plan" so as to trump the terms of the ACA itself reflects a significant paradigm mistake about the Court's role regarding interpretation of the ACA. *King* reflected no deference to what Congress did in the ACA or what role Congress would or should play if the ACA's statutory terms were given effect.

B. Procedural Posture: Considering a Motion to Dismiss

The Supreme Court, after all is said and done, is a court. Courts operate with rules. The chief justice noted at oral argument that the case was before the Supreme Court on a motion to dismiss.[41]

---

[41] See Jim Blumstein on Why the Procedural Posture of King v. Burwell Might Matter, Volokh Conspiracy, Wash. Post (June 24, 2015), http://www.washingtonpost.com/

In a proceeding under a motion to dismiss, the focus is on the pleadings, not extrinsic evidence or considerations. Yet the Court's opinion is replete with analysis that turned on extrinsic facts, such as predictions about a death spiral in the individual medical insurance marketplace. The Court, critically, relied on the "calamitous result" on insurance markets in states that have not established exchanges, concluding that Congress "plainly meant to avoid" that outcome. Accordingly, the Court, despite the terms of the ACA itself, concluded that tax credits are "allow[ed]" for "insurance purchased on any Exchange created under the [ACA]" in order to avoid the calamitous results Congress wanted to avoid. These observations have little if any role in a motion-to-dismiss proceeding.

Without consideration of extrinsic factors, such as the effect of plaintiffs' interpretation of the ACA's subsidy provisions on the functioning of the individual market for medical insurance in states with federally run exchanges, the Court would have had no basis for ruling against plaintiffs' position. The Court seemed to recognize this when it stated that "[r]eliance on context and structure in statutory interpretation" calls for "great wariness lest what professes to be mere rendering becomes creation and attempted interpretation of legislation becomes legislation itself."[42] In *King*, however, the Court decided that "such reliance is appropriate" because of the consequences of giving effect to the terms of the ACA itself. And without such reliance, by the Court's own acknowledgment, the interpretive outcome in *King* would have to have been different.

Reliance on such "it stands to reason" type of inferences was, therefore, pivotal to the Court's casting aside the ACA's clear and operative language—that subsidies were available to income-qualified persons who purchased medical insurance on exchanges established by a state and that the ACA made no comparable provision regarding subsidies to income-qualified persons who purchased medical insurance on federally run exchanges.

But such reliance in the context of ruling on a motion to dismiss is inappropriate or at least highly questionable since such reliance goes well beyond the pleadings. If it were to act like a court, the Supreme

---

news/volokh-conspiracy/wp/2015/06/24/jim-blumstein-on-why-the-procedural-posture-of-king-v-burwell-might-matter.

[42] King, 135 S. Ct. at 2495–96 (citations omitted).

Court, by the terms of its own analysis, would have reversed the lower courts' grant of the government's motion to dismiss. That would not have meant granting of judgment to the plaintiffs, given the Court's thoughts regarding context and structure. It would, however, have meant remanding for consideration, in a procedurally proper forum and manner, of the types of extrinsic factors that the Court deemed so crucial to reaching an understanding of the ACA's subsidy provisions. A remand could also have included fact-finding or consideration of context in a summary judgment proceeding. The subsidies would have remained in place during the pendency of those proceedings, since the result of the Court's action would only be a denial of a motion to dismiss, not a judgment for plaintiffs.[43]

The Court's treatment of and reliance on extrinsic matters in the procedural posture of the matter—ruling on a motion to dismiss—further calls into question just what was going on and why in the Court's deliberations.[44] The Court's reasoning in the context of ruling on a motion to dismiss went well beyond accepted and customary boundaries for a motion-to-dismiss proceeding.

The Court's stretching not only the interpretive but also the procedural boundaries raises the question, again, of just what is going on—an issue raised in dissent by Justice Antonin Scalia. It seems that, as described earlier, this is the Court's paradigm mistake—its determination that the institutional roles of the Court in the

---

[43] Moreover, had the Court given effect to the operative language in the ACA, by limiting subsidies to state-established exchanges, the procedural posture of the case would also have resulted in reversal of the motion to dismiss granted by the lower courts. It would not and could not have resulted in a judgment for plaintiffs. So, additional proceedings in the lower courts would have been needed to translate the reversal of the motion to dismiss into an enforceable judgment—plenty of time for the political process to play out or for an orderly transition to take place without upsetting existing insurance contracts or undoing those settled expectations.

[44] The Court's decision to hear the case suggested a strong interest in addressing the broad issues raised; if, upon further analysis, the Court took a different view than the one presented by plaintiffs, then it still had to live within the parameters of the procedural posture—review of the lower courts' granting of a motion to dismiss. In that posture, the Court could not properly affirm the granting of a motion to dismiss if it confined itself to examining the pleadings. In order to reach the analytical outcome it did, the Court had to and did consider extrinsic circumstances and projected (and contested) consequences regarding the putative impact of a ruling for plaintiffs on the insurance markets; in a motion-to-dismiss proceeding, consideration of such extrinsic factors beyond the pleadings is at the very least procedurally questionable.

constitutional case of *NFIB* and in the statutory case of *King* are the same or analogous. Yet avoiding use of its constitutional authority to trump both political branches by overturning the ACA did raise non-trivial concerns regarding the Court's role. In *King*, on the other hand, the Court was being asked to interpret the terms of a statute, not confronting both other branches. The communication of the interpretive question—giving effect to clear text of a statute—would have been easy and straightforward. There was no confrontation with both the politically accountable branches, only empowering the Congress and the states consistent with the terms and text of the ACA.

But again the government and its backers won the case at 30,000 feet, characterizing it as a political attack on the ACA. The Court unnecessarily and unwarrantedly shied away from giving effect to the terms of the ACA and thereby empowering Congress for no real institutional reason. All the Court had to do was enforce the terms of the ACA—respecting Congress's work product and its role in modifying that work product if Congress deemed that to be warranted—and disavow any involvement in the political process. As in the *Fritz* case, the Court would have focused on what Congress did and would have stayed within the procedural parameters of how courts function.

VI. How Far Does Executive Discretion Extend?

After *King*, one is left to wonder what extensions to federal subsidies could be implemented by executive action under the ACA. If broad purposes trump, and even relegate, directly on-point statutory language to mere "surplusage," can the IRS do even more?

Under the ACA, subsidies on exchanges are now available to purchasers on both federally established and state-established exchanges. But those eligible for such subsidies must be income-qualified—that is, persons having incomes in the range of 100–400 percent of the federal poverty level. The 100–400 percent of the federal poverty level range was adopted in the ACA under the assumption that persons with lower incomes (under 100 percent of the federal poverty level) would be covered under states' ACA-expanded Medicaid programs. But in *NFIB* the Supreme Court ruled that the ACA went too far in assuring (effectively coercing) coverage of an expanded population under states' Medicaid programs.

The result of *NFIB* is that states may opt into expanded Medicaid with attractive financial incentives, but they have a genuine choice; they no longer must put at risk their pre-existing Medicaid programs if they choose not to expand Medicaid. And nearly half of the states have, to this point, declined to expand their Medicaid programs to cover the ACA's preferred population.

The result is that, in non-expanding states, persons with incomes under 100 percent of the federal poverty level may not be covered by Medicaid and yet are too poor to qualify for tax subsidies on an exchange. This seems like an utterly irrational outcome in terms of eligibility for federal subsidies.

The income-qualification guidelines are clearly specified in the ACA—100–400 percent of the poverty line. But *NFIB* also makes it abundantly clear that Congress in the ACA had a clear preference that persons in poverty have medical coverage and federal financial support for that coverage; indeed, so clear was that objective that Congress overreached by effectively (and unconstitutionally) mandating that states expand their Medicaid programs to cover all those who would otherwise not be eligible for subsidies on an exchange.

Given this "context" and these "purposes," is the IRS free to issue regulations that extend subsidies on exchanges to those who are not eligible for their state's Medicaid program but who now do not qualify for subsidies on exchanges because their incomes are too low? Or, even more far-reaching, does the ACA by itself authorize federal subsidies for such persons on the exchanges, despite the textual constraints of the ACA itself, given the access-oriented overarching objectives of the ACA?

This type of expansion has not been under consideration, at least openly, but wouldn't the type of reasoning in *King* lend itself to this type of executive-branch-driven expansion of subsidy availability? Or even a court-based claim by a person in the no-man's-land between Medicaid ineligibility (too much income) and ineligibility for exchange-based subsidy (too little income)? If operative and controlling statutory terms or provisions are consigned to the Orwellian world of "surplusage," overborne by resort to such amorphous and malleable concepts as overall "purpose" or "structure" or "context," why is such an IRS regulation expanding subsidies—which are indisputably in accord with Congress' overall access-oriented objectives—or even litigation on this theory unsupportable?

One can imagine a limitation on litigation or a distinction on administrative action, but just asking the question and having to do more than say "the provisions of the ACA do not provide for such subsidies" indicates just how broad and undisciplined the Court's decision in *King* really is. Maybe we should stay tuned on this.

VII. Conclusion

In sum, the Court's opinion in *King* was highly disappointing and institutionally corrosive; its unpersuasive, interpretation-of-dream-like reasoning and analysis lend support to the inference that the issue was decided at 30,000 feet—at the level of broad institutional role and policy considerations that resulted from a paradigm mistake about the Court's role. The Court missed an opportunity to empower Congress (and indirectly the states) by ruling for plaintiffs. In the process, the unsatisfying and unpersuasive use of Shazam tactics in reaching its outcome undermines its own institutional credibility— precisely the opposite of its stated goal of staying out of the political realm by deferring to what Congress purported to do in enacting the ACA. This is particularly the case when the Court, in (Lewis) Carrollinian fashion, concludes that the key operative language— about availability of federal subsidies on exchanges established by a state—is not to be illuminated through non-textual techniques but to be ignored.

The Marriage Equality Cases and Constitutional Theory

*William N. Eskridge Jr.**

On June 26, 2015, the Supreme Court in *Obergefell v. Hodges* ruled that the Fourteenth Amendment bars states from refusing to issue marriage licenses to same-sex couples or declining to recognize their valid out-of-state marriages.[1] Justice Anthony Kennedy's opinion for the Court started: "The Constitution promises liberty to all within its reach, a liberty that includes certain specific rights that allow persons, within a lawful realm, to define and express their identity."[2] The Court had long recognized the right to marry as a fundamental right protected against deprivation by the Due Process Clause. The bulk of the Court's opinion focused on the values of that constitutional liberty, holding that the values of marriage for individual spouses, for children, and for society apply with equal force to lesbian and gay couples (long excluded from the institution) as to straight couples.[3]

"The right of same-sex couples to marry that is part of the liberty promised by the Fourteenth Amendment," Justice Kennedy continued, "is derived, too, from that Amendment's guarantee of the equal protection of the laws."[4] The Equal Protection Clause has special bite when states discriminate against a minority with regard to a fundamental liberty, and so equality works together with liberty to require heightened judicial scrutiny of the states' reasons for any kind of marriage exclusion.[5] The Court found no weighty, much less com-

---

* John A. Garver Professor of Jurisprudence at Yale Law School.

[1] Obergefell v. Hodges, 135 S. Ct. 2584 (2015).

[2] *Id.* at 2593. Justice Kennedy's majority opinion was joined by Justices Ruth Bader Ginsburg, Stephen Breyer, Sonia Sotomayor, and Elena Kagan.

[3] *Id.* at 2597–602.

[4] *Id.* at 2602.

[5] E.g., Zablocki v. Redhail, 434 U.S. 374, 383 (1978); Loving v. Virginia, 388 U.S. 1, 11 (1967).

pelling, public-regarding justifications for policies adopted in Michigan, Ohio, Kentucky, and Tennessee for denying marriage licenses to same-sex couples.[6]

The primary dissenting opinion, by Chief Justice John Roberts, sadly and somberly regretted that the majority was announcing a "dramatic social change" that "has no basis in the Constitution or this Court's precedent[s]."[7] "[A]cross all . . . civilizations," the chief justice insisted, marriage has "referred to only one relationship: the union of a man and a woman."[8] Because the Court was redefining marriage in a way that no culture had ever done (according to him), the Court's previous right-to-marry cases were not on point. With no precedent really supporting this significant shift in family law policy, the dissenting justices charged the majority with legislating rather than judging and with violating the democratic premises of our system of government.[9]

I am one of the millions of Americans who cheered when the Supreme Court handed down its opinion in *Obergefell*. This opinion means a great deal to lesbian, gay, bisexual, and transgender Americans. *Obergefell* is a landmark decision. As much as it is celebrated today, it will be not just celebrated but will be a cornerstone of constitutional law in the decades to come. Because of its importance, and the analytical effort that went into the decision from all angles—including by people and groups supporting what they consider "traditional" marriage—it might be useful to consider the opinions and the debate within the Court in light of theories of constitutional decisionmaking.

I shall consider three theories, starting with the Constitution's original public meaning. *Obergefell* is a missed opportunity for that theory. Although its holding is quite insightfully defensible under original-meaning originalism, the Court ignored that approach to constitutional law. Even worse, the dissenting justices who relied on

[6] Obergefell, 135 S. Ct. at 2606–07.

[7] *Id.* at 2612 (Roberts, C.J., joined by Scalia & Thomas, J.J., dissenting).

[8] *Id.* That statement is flat wrong, as historians and anthropologists have documented same-sex marriages in dozens of cultures in human history, including many in North America. See William N. Eskridge Jr., The Case for Same-Sex Marriage 27–44 (1996).

[9] Obergefell, 135 S. Ct. at 2616–18, 2624–26; accord, *id.* at 2626–31(Scalia, J., joined by Thomas, J., dissenting); *id.* at 2640–43 (Alito, J., joined by Scalia & Thomas, JJ., dissenting).

originalist argumentation cherry-picked the historical record and ignored the rich background of the term "equal protection" that would have lent support to the majority's holding.

In contrast, *Obergefell* did follow the path of common-law constitutionalism, as both the majority and dissenting justices purported to neutrally apply precedent to resolve this highly charged case. Ad hoc case-by-case decisionmaking continues to be the theory that best approximates the approach actually followed by the Supreme Court, even in the big cases. This common-law decisionmaking, however, is not an easily defensible approach when the Court is making "big moves," as it did in *Obergefell*. In the hard cases, precedent will not constrain the exercise of judicial judgment. The lesson suggested by *Obergefell* is that when the Court makes a big move, its methodology will be one of creatively misreading precedent, rather than mechanically applying it. But if a common-law court is creatively applying precedent, is that not cause for concern, especially in the big cases? What guides the justices, apart from their own preferences?

Deliberative theories of constitutional decisionmaking ask the Court to consider political process reactions before it applies the Constitution, especially when it is making a big move. Like common-law constitutionalism, this theory captures the Court's methodology in *Obergefell*, and deliberative theories suggest sources of constraint. Deliberative theories ask the Court to consider legislative debates, public opinion, academic commentary, state constitutionalism, presidential election campaigns, and citizen referenda and initiatives. One lesson of *Obergefell* is that deliberative theories of judicial review need to consider not just the democratic legitimacy of the Court's judgment and its coherence with precedent and our constitutional traditions, but also the ongoing evolution of our *pluralist* republic. The lesbian and gay rights social movement won a place at the table in *Obergefell* and other recent triumphs, but Justice Kennedy sought to assure traditionalists that they had not lost their place at the table—though they do have to share it now. What I call a pluralism-respecting approach to constitutional cases urges the Court to apply the Fourteenth Amendment to invite new social groups into the political process, on terms of equality, but without marginalizing older groups that have been resistant.

I. Original Public Meaning: A Missed Opportunity

Original-meaning theories ask what meaning constitutional text and structure would have had to a neutral reader of the English language at the time of the framing; this approach rejects a narrow focus on "original intent," namely, the subjective expectations the Framers of a constitutional provision had for its application to specific issues.[10] Thus, an original-meaning approach is not interested in how constitutional Framers would have addressed the precise issue that has become salient today—but addresses instead the general meaning constitutional text and structure would have had to neutral readers of the era.[11]

Theorists and supporters of original meaning defend that jurisprudence as superior because it is (they claim) the only method of constitutional interpretation that neutrally applies the Constitution and actually constrains judges.[12] As far as I can determine, there is no empirical evidence to support that claim, and skeptical scholars have relentlessly attacked it, both empirically across large populations of cases[13] and in connection with specific cases, such as the recent gun-control cases.[14]

---

[10] Steven G. Calabresi, A Critical Introduction to the Originalism Debate, 31 Harv. J.L. & Pub. Pol'y 875 (2008) (providing an account of the turn to original meaning in 1985); Vasan Kesavan & Michael Stokes Paulsen, The Interpretive Force of the Constitution's Secret Drafting History, 91 Geo. L.J. 1113, 1134–48 (2003) (providing a broader account of the shift from "original intent" to "original meaning" jurisprudence in the 1980s).

[11] See, e.g., Robert Bork, The Tempting of America: The Political Seduction of the Law 75–77, 143–45, 154–55 (1990); Antonin Scalia, A Matter of Interpretation (1997); Clarence Thomas, The Higher Law Background of the Privileges or Immunities Clause of the Fourteenth Amendment, 12 Harv. J.L. & Pub. Pol'y 63 (1989).

[12] Bork, Tempting of America 143–45 (1990); Antonin Scalia & Bryan A. Garner, Reading Law (2012); Randy Barnett, An Originalism for Nonoriginalists, 45 Loy. L. Rev. 611 (1999); Antonin Scalia, Originalism: The Lesser Evil, 57 U. Cin. L. Rev. 849 (1989).

[13] E.g., Frank Cross, The Theory and Practice of Statutory Interpretation 177–79 (2009) (empirical examination of original meaning in statutory interpretation, finding that it is no more constraining than other methods); Peter J. Smith, Sources of Federalism: An Empirical Analysis of the Court's Quest for Original Meaning, 52 UCLA L. Rev. 217 (2004) (finding that justices relying on original meaning in federalism cases are selective in the sources they are willing to credit).

[14] For critical analysis of the Supreme Court's enforcement of the original meaning of the Second Amendment, see Richard A. Posner, In Defense of Looseness: The Supreme Court and Gun Control, The New Republic (Aug. 27, 2008) (denouncing the Court's

Additionally, critics maintain that original meaning has a narrow appeal, namely only to those Americans who are (like Justice Antonin Scalia and the late Judge Robert Bork) politically conservative and personally hierarchical, traditionalist, or libertarian.[15] The limited constituency of originalism risks further shrinkage if that theory were to stand against landmark precedents like *Brown v. Board of Education*—and so it is no coincidence that original-meaning theorists have been busy justifying previous landmark decisions, such as *Brown*, as consistent with their methodology.[16]

The marriage equality cases offered supporters a golden opportunity to demonstrate that original meaning is more than looking out over the crowd and picking out your friends. For the reasons that follow, I believe marriage equality is required by original meaning; if the conservative justices had taken these arguments seriously and *voted against their presumed political biases*, that would have been powerful evidence that original meaning has more bite than any other theory of constitutional decisionmaking. Even if those justices had found themselves unpersuaded by original meaning arguments, they could have pulled off an original-meaning coup if they could have demonstrated, decisively, why those arguments are wrong and could have persuaded some commentators to change their minds.

Obergefell was a complete disappointment along these lines. The five justices in the majority ignored original meaning, as did two of the four dissenting justices. And the two justices who relied on original meaning ignored the best arguments presented to them and widely discussed in public commentary on marriage equality.[17]

---

opinion as exactly the opposite of what original meaning would have dictated) available at www.newrepublic.com/article/books/defense-looseness; J. Harvie Wilkinson III, Of Guns, Abortion, and the Unraveling Rule of Law, 95 Va. L. Rev. 253 (2009) (raising concerns that the Court was not evaluating the original-meaning evidence in a neutral manner). But see Alan Gura, Heller and the Triumph of Originalist Judicial Engagement: A Response to Judge Harvie Wilkinson, 56 UCLA L. Rev. 1129 (2009).

[15] Jamal Greene, Nathaniel Persily & Stephen Ansolabehere, Profiling Originalism, 111 Colum. L. Rev. 356, 373–75 (2011).

[16] E.g., Bork, Tempting of America, 75–77, 143–45 (defending *Brown*); Steven G. Calabresi & Julia T. Rickert, Originalism and Sex Discrimination, 90 Tex. L. Rev. 1 (2011) (defending the Court's sex discrimination jurisprudence).

[17] See, e.g., Brief of Amicus Curiae Cato Institute, William N. Eskridge Jr., and Steven Calabresi in Support of Petitioners, Obergefell v. Hodges 135 S. Ct. 2584 (2014) (No. 14-556). Obviously, this is a brief that reflects my own views. See also Doug Kendall

As the dissenters charged, much of Justice Kennedy's opinion reads like a policy document endorsing a generally libertarian philosophy, state respect for the dignity of all citizens, and a very high opinion of marriage as the foundation of family *and* society *and* government, "without which there would be neither civilization nor progress."[18] Although Kennedy connected the wonderfulness of marriage with his understanding of libertarian philosophy, he did not connect either to the original meaning of the Fourteenth Amendment's requirement that "no State shall deny any person life, liberty, or property without due process of law." Indeed, Justice Thomas's dissenting opinion demonstrated that due process "liberty" has traditionally been freedom *from* government interference in our private lives.[19] Even *Loving v. Virginia* involved traditional liberty, he argued, because Virginia criminally prosecuted the different-race couple who had been validly married in the District of Columbia. Marriage is a highly regulatory institution. Its function is more disciplinary than liberating. Each spouse gives up a lot of liberties (including sexual freedoms) when he or she gets married.

In my view, Justice Kennedy was presenting a serious understanding of liberty. One role of government is to provide a productive structure within which each of us makes choices, always seeking to create a distinctively flourishing life. The "liberty" in the marriage cases is a freedom to marry the partner who will make you happy and enable your joint flourishing, and this is a liberty the government ought to respect, on an equal basis. Lesbian and gay Americans would not flourish in different-sex marriages, and so their freedom is effectively circumscribed if they do not have access to dignifying, reinforcing, benefit-conferring civil marriage. As Justice Thomas thoughtfully observed, however, there was no effort by the Court to link this positive conception of liberty to original meaning.

If it is notable that Justice Kennedy essentially ignored this line of reasoning, it is also notable that Justice Thomas ignored important

---

& Ilya Shapiro, The Constitutional Case for Marriage Equality, Huffington Post (Feb. 28, 2013), http://www.huffingtonpost.com/doug-kendall/the-constitutional-case-f_b_2781874.html; Steven G. Calabresi & Hannah M. Begley, Originalism and Same-Sex Marriage (2015), available at http://papers.ssrn.com/sol3/papers.cfm?abstract_id=2509443.

[18] Obergefell, 135 S. Ct. at 2601 (quoting Maynard v. Hill, 125 U.S. 190, 211 (1888)).

[19] *Id.* at 2631–37 (Thomas, J., dissenting).

original-meaning arguments supporting the majority's holding. Steven Calabresi and Andrea Mathews have powerfully argued that original *meaning* solves the problem for originalism long posed by the application of original intent to *Loving v. Virginia*, the different-race marriage case.[20] Few originalists have argued that *Loving* is consistent with their theory because the Framers of the Fourteenth Amendment repeatedly assured congressional and ratifying supporters that anti-miscegenation laws were consistent with equal protection as they understood it.[21] Once the focus of inquiry is no longer the subjective expectations of the framers and becomes the objective meaning of the text created by the constitutional amendment process, however, Calabresi and Mathews maintain that *Loving* becomes not only defensible but clearly correct. The original meaning of the Fourteenth Amendment was to protect the right of all Americans to enter into voluntary contracts, including marital contracts backed up by the full authority of the state.[22] Indeed, the privileges and immunities (or liberties) protected by the text of the Fourteenth Amendment in 1868 would surely have included the right to marry, as most state constitutions then (and now) included specific protection for marriage rights.[23]

Even informed by the Calabresi and Mathews analysis, Justice Kennedy would have to respond to the dissenters' argument, that a "fundamental right to marry" in American culture has traditionally (and perhaps embedded in the Constitution and its Reconstruction Amendments) been grounded in the policy of channeling procreative sexuality into domesticating marriage.[24] The majority opinion treated marriage as an institution fulfilling individual needs for personal fulfillment and expression—which is the more recent model for civil marriage but is not the only model. Why should demo-

[20] Steven G. Calabresi & Andrea Mathews, Originalism and *Loving v. Virginia*, 2012 BYU L. Rev. 1393 (2012).

[21] *Id.* at 1394–95 (collecting and analyzing examples of originalist skepticism or silence on *Loving*); see *id.* at 1399–413 (broader examination of original intent jurisprudence and the desegregation cases).

[22] See *id.* at 1413–33 (defense of *Loving*, based upon a detailed examination of the original meaning of the Privileges or Immunities Clause of the Fourteenth Amendment).

[23] *Id.* at 1437–63.

[24] See Obergefell, 135 S. Ct. at 2641–42 (Alito, J., joined by Scalia & Thomas, J.J., dissenting).

cratically accountable state legislatures (and not life-tenured federal judges) not be making the choice between these two models?

In short, Justice Kennedy's opinion not only substantially ignored original meaning, but was vulnerable to original-meaning objections. The more deeply the majority grounded its analysis in substantive due process liberty, the more discordant the analysis was with a historical case for its asserted right. Joined only by Justice Scalia, Justice Thomas made a serious original meaning case for the proposition that "liberty" is constitutionally protected only as a matter of "due *process*" (and not as a substantive matter) and that the protected "liberty" does not include positive rights such as the thousands associated with civil marriage.[25] Is it possible that original-meaning theory proved its neutrality through the analysis of Justice Thomas? Surprisingly, though, the dissenters made their originalist case by ignoring the best original-meaning arguments.

For example, the Calabresi-Mathews defense of *Loving* is grounded in the original meaning of the Equal Protection Clause, which Justice Thomas ignored entirely. The majority relied, in part, on the Equal Protection Clause, which was the main provision invoked by the petitioners; rejecting all claims for a constitutional right to marriage equality, the dissenters were obliged to demonstrate why the equal protection claim, like the due process claim, was not supported by original meaning analysis. The liberty focus of the Court's debate obscures the best original-meaning argument for marriage equality, one that was offered to the Court in great detail.

Unlike the Fourteenth Amendment's Due Process Clause, which was copied from the Fifth Amendment equivalent, and the Privileges or Immunities Clause, which is similar to language in Article IV, the Equal Protection Clause was new language added to the Constitution by the Fourteenth Amendment. What public meaning did that language have in 1868? This was a term of art with an established legal meaning. As early as the Jacksonian era, "equal protection" was an expression of the old principle that government must legislate for the common good and must avoid "class legislation" that favored one class of citizens with special benefits or denigrated one class with special disabilities.[26] Conscience Whigs, anti-slavery

---

[25] *Id.* at 2631–37 (Thomas, J., joined by Scalia, J., dissenting).

[26] Andrew Jackson, Veto Report (July 10, 1832), in 2 A Compilation of the Messages and Papers of the Presidents: 1789–1897, at 590 (James D. Richardson ed., 1896) (early

Democrats, and Republicans in the 1840s and 1850s popularized the term "equal protection" and deepened its meaning to include social "castes" as well as economic "classes."[27]

When the Fourteenth Amendment was drafted and debated, Americans understood that a guarantee of "equal protection of the laws," by its terms, "abolishes all class legislation in the States," thereby "securing an equality of rights to all citizens of the United States, and of all persons within their jurisdiction."[28] State legislatures ratifying the Fourteenth Amendment discussed the Equal Protection Clause in precisely these terms.[29]

What are the hallmarks of class or caste legislation? Contemporary authors explained what judges and advocates meant by class legislation—and theirs was a broad reading of equality. "Under a system of caste, personal liberty and the right of property are controlled by laws restraining the activity of a class of persons, more or less strictly defined, to a particular course of life, and allowing only a limited enjoyment of property and relative rights."[30] Thus, "a statute would not be constitutional which should proscribe a class or party for opinion's sake, or which should [identify] particular individuals from a class or locality, and subject them to peculiar rules, or impose upon them special obligations or burdens, from which others in the same locality or class are exempt. . . . Special privileges are obnoxious, and discriminations against persons or classes are still more so."[31]

------

deployment of the term "equal protection" to target "class legislation"). See generally William N. Eskridge Jr., Original Meaning and Marriage Equality, 52 Hous. L. Rev. 1067 (2015).

[27] E.g., Ohio Const. of 1851, art. I, § 2 (specific constitutional provision for "equal protection"); Charles Sumner, Equality before the Law: Unconstitutionality of Separate Colored Schools in Massachusetts (1870). Argument of Charles Sumner, Esq., before the Supreme Court of Massachusetts in the Case of Sarah C. Roberts v. City of Boston [1849], at 7, 9–10, 13 (1870). See generally Melissa L. Saunders, Equal Protection, Class Legislation, and Colorblindness, 96 Mich. L. Rev. 245, 253–54 & n.34 (1997) (reporting other state constitutional provisions).

[28] Cong. Globe, 39th Cong., 1st Sess. 2766 (1866) (first quotation in text); *id.* at 2502 (second quotation).

[29] William E. Nelson, The Fourteenth Amendment: From Political Principle to Judicial Doctrine 67, 73, 79 (1988); Steven G. Calabresi & Julia T. Rickert, Originalism and Sex Discrimination, 90 Tex. L. Rev. 1, 35–42 (2011).

[30] John C. Hurd, Topics of Jurisprudence Connected with Conditions of Freedom and Bondage 44 (1856); accord Wally's Heirs, 10 Tenn. (2 Yer.) at 555–57.

[31] Thomas M. Cooley, A Treatise on the Constitutional Limitations Which Rest upon the Legislative Power of the States of the American Union 390–91, 393 (1868).

Is exclusion from the definition of marriage class or caste legislation within the original meaning of the Fourteenth Amendment? It may be fairly debatable whether a state affording all normal rights to lesbian and gay persons but retaining its ancient definition of marriage as one man, one woman has violated the original meaning of equal protection. But none of the states in *Obergefell* offered the Court such a regime.

Michigan, one of the states defending its recent and broadly written marriage exclusion, had long treated lesbian and gay citizens as presumptive criminals whose consensual intimacy subjected them to potential life sentences in prison.[32] Michigan also created a regime for civilly committing people convicted of sex offences who "appear to be psychopathic, or a sex degenerate" or a "sex pervert."[33] Such "perverts" could be committed for an indeterminate time in a state mental hospital and, possibly, sterilized.[34] In 1948, Michigan's Liquor Control Commission informed bars that they would lose their liquor licenses if they served "homosexuals."[35] Because anti-gay discrimination was grounded upon the view that lesbians and gay men were sterile, predatory, and anti-family, it went without saying that Michigan openly discriminated against lesbian and gay families. Thus, state judges often denied lesbian and gay parents custody of—and sometimes barred visitation with—their own biological children.[36]

In the 20th century, Michigan created a caste regime demonizing gay people and imposing special disabilities upon them. To be sure, gay people pushed back at the end of the century—but instead of repealing its anti-gay caste regime, Michigan *expanded* it. Thus, the legislature amended Michigan's marriage code to exclude lesbian and gay marriages, to promote the "welfare of society and its children,"[37] even though thousands of Michigan children would have benefitted from the marriage of their gay parents. In 2004, acting for the benefit of "future generations of children," the voters amended the state constitution to ensure that "the union of one man and one woman

[32] Mich. Penal Code §§ 750.158, 750.338–338a (current codification of the state consensual sodomy [anal sex] and gross indecency [oral sex] laws).

[33] 1935 Mich. Pub. Acts 87–88, 141.

[34] 1929 Mich. Pub. Acts 281 (authorizing the sterilization of incarcerated "moral degenerates and sexual perverts").

[35] Mich. Liquor Comm'n, Admin. Rule 436-3 (1948).

[36] Hall v. Hall, 95 Mich. App. 614, 615 (1980) (per curiam).

[37] 1996 Mich. Pub. Act 324 (codified at Mich. Comp. Laws § 551.1).

in marriage shall be the only agreement recognized as a marriage or similar union for any purpose."[38] The Michigan Supreme Court applied this sweeping bar to deprive lesbian and gay municipal employees of health insurance and other contract-based benefits.[39] After some cities and the state civil service commission created a new category of "other qualified persons" who could be awarded employment benefits without seeming to recognize a "similar union" for gays, the legislature overrode those humane efforts and reinstated the contract-based discrimination.[40]

April DeBoer and Jayne Rowse, a female couple rearing an ever-increasing number of adopted children, challenged Michigan's pervasive exclusion of them from the normal guarantees of state family law. (Theirs was one of the four clusters of state marriage-exclusion challenges that the Supreme Court consolidated under the *Obergefell* caption.) If you take seriously the original public meaning of the Equal Protection Clause in 1868, it is hard to avoid the conclusion that the intricate array of anti-gay discriminations do not violate that constitutional provision—a conclusion that becomes all the more compelling in light of the Calabresi-Mathews demonstration that the Fourteenth Amendment has even sharper teeth when the state is denying a despised class the right to civil marriage.

Yet neither Justice Thomas nor any of the other dissenting justices even considered this original-meaning argument. If they had considered it, is there any chance they would have changed their votes? Apparently, not a chance, because applying original meaning seems like looking out over the crowd and picking out your friends. Just as original-intent theory struck out in *Brown v. Board of Education,* so original meaning theory has struck out in *Obergefell v. Hodges.* Does this suggest that original meaning is dead as a theory of constitutional decisionmaking? Of course not. What it does mean is that this theory missed a golden opportunity to reveal its power to constrain judges and to inform decisionmaking for a hotly contested issue.

---

[38] Mich. Const. art. I, § 25.

[39] See National Pride at Work, Inc. v. Governor of Michigan, 748 N.W.2d 524 (2008).

[40] Public Employee Domestic Partner Benefit Restriction Act, 2011 Mich. Pub. Act 297 (a discrimination found to be unconstitutional caste legislation in Bassett v. Snyder, 59 F. Supp. 3d 837, 839 (E.D. Mich. 2014)).

II. Common Law Constitutionalism: Creative Misreadings

Because it is a legal document that is very old, relatively short, and infrequently amended, the U.S. Constitution's text and structure may not determinatively answer most of the novel interpretive issues of the day. Original meaning is a serious methodology for giving content to constitutional text and structure, but it does not seem to constrain or even guide the justices in landmark cases such as *Brown* and *Obergefell*.

In that event, the Supreme Court might follow the example of Ulysses, who strapped himself to the mast of his ship, to avoid following the tempting Siren song to ruin. Knowing that any justice is tempted to read constitutional text to reflect her or his political preferences, the Court might adopt a "Thayerite" strategy of invalidating state and federal laws only when the political process has made a "clear mistake," violating the plain meaning of the Constitution.[41] This is, obviously, a strategy the Supreme Court has rejected and is certainly not the strategy taken by the Court in *Obergefell*, which is an ambitious reading of the Fourteenth Amendment's open-textured language. (This is also not a strategy the *Obergefell* dissenters have taken in other constitutional cases, such as *Shelby County v. Holder*, which was as ambitious a reading of the Constitution by Chief Justice Roberts as that by Justice Kennedy in *Obergefell*.[42])

Ignoring original meaning and rejecting a strong Thayerite presumption, Justice Kennedy's opinion in *Obergefell* appealed to a different, and highly popular, strategy of constitutional theory—what David Strauss has called "common law constitutionalism."[43] Under this theory, text and original meaning are not serious constraints on a Court applying broad constitutional provisions such as the Due Process, Equal Protection, and Free Speech Clauses. What does con-

---

[41] James Bradley Thayer, The Origin and Scope of the American Doctrine of Constitutional Law, 7 Harv. L. Rev. 129, 144 (1893); see Adrian Vermeule, Judging Under Uncertainty: An Institutional Theory of Legal Interpretation (2006) (proposing a similarly stingy approach to judicial review).

[42] Compare Shelby County, Ala. v. Holder, 133 S. Ct. 2612, 2618–31 (2013), with *id.* at 2632–52 (Ginsburg, J., dissenting) (strong objection to the Court's dynamic interpretation of the constitutional text and precedent).

[43] David A. Strauss, Common Law Constitutional Interpretation, 63 U. Chi. L. Rev. 877 (1996); see also David A. Strauss, The Irrelevance of Constitutional Amendments, 114 Harv. L. Rev. 1457 (2001).

strain the justices is the common law tradition, which requires them to follow precedent, take its reasoning as well as results seriously, and advance the law case by case through analogy of new problems to older decisions.

The heart of Justice Kennedy's opinion is precisely this appeal to precedent. Repeatedly, the Supreme Court has recognized the right to marry as constitutionally fundamental and has insisted on the rights of interracial couples, deadbeat dads, and even convicted prisoners to marry the spouses of their choice.[44] From more than a century of constitutional case law, Justice Kennedy deduced four principles undergirding the right to marry—respect for individual autonomy and choice, the unique association entailed by marriage, the well-being of children reared by couples, and social order and stability.[45] Justice Kennedy maintained that these underlying constitutional values apply just as much to lesbian and gay couples as to straight couples. As presented, this is an eloquent statement of why gay people ought to be given the same marriage rights as other citizens, a proposition also supported by the Court's precedents striking down state "homosexual sodomy" laws[46] and part of the Defense of Marriage Act.[47]

As Chief Justice Roberts objected in dissent, Justice Kennedy's deployment of precedent involved a significant recharacterization of the Court's prior decisions, all but one of which assumed that protected marriage involved potential procreation.[48] The Chief Justice's bigger point is that the Court was deploying precedent instrumentally, to "redefine" marriage in the face of millennia of traditional practices and thereby to effect a "dramatic social change." Most of

---

[44] See *Obergefell,* 135. Ct. at 2598–2601 (citing and discussing Loving v. Virginia, 388 U.S. 1 (1967) (interracial couples); Zablocki v. Redhail, 434 U.S. 374 (1978) (deadbeat dads); Turner v. Safley, 482 U.S. 78 (1987) (prisoners)).

[45] Obergefell, 135 S. Ct. at 2599–2601.

[46] Lawrence v. Texas, 539 U.S. 558 (2003).

[47] United States v. Windsor, 133 S. Ct. 2675 (2013).

[48] Thus, *Loving* involved interracial couples, who were denied marriage rights because Virginia feared "mongrelization" through procreation that was not racially pure. *Turner v. Safley* involved some inmates who were serving life sentences and would not have been able to procreate, even theoretically, and so the Court's protection extended beyond the usual assumptions. (Additionally, Missouri *allowed* procreating inmates to marry, and the Court's judgment only protected inmates that the state conceded were not procreating. Turner, 482 U.S. at 97–99.)

the theorists of common law constitutionalism (such as the Columbia School theorists Henry Monaghan and Thomas Merrill) defend this approach to constitutional interpretation as incrementalist, cautious, and respectful of the nation's traditions.[49] Even fans of Justice Kennedy's opinion should admit that it took a big step, well beyond the holdings of the Court's earlier precedents.

Although unremarked by the dissenters, Justice Kennedy also garbled some of the precedents he was synthesizing. The newer precedents emphasized individual autonomy and marriage as a special situs for human flourishing for the spouses, as Justice Kennedy emphasized.[50] And the Court has, in the older cases, given great weight to marriage as the best context for children and indeed as the "keystone of our social order."[51] What Justice Kennedy jumbled together is that most of the precedents celebrating marital childrearing[52] and all the precedents emphasizing social order[53] were premised on the assumption of traditional marriage, as a situs not of individual spousal fulfillment, but as a situs of spousal self-sacrifice for the good of the procreated family.

Indeed, this understanding of marriage, as intimately linked with the possibility of procreation by the spouses, was probably the basis for the Court's summary disposition of the first marriage equality case, *Baker v. Nelson*.[54] In 1971–72, Jack Baker and Mike McConnell had made almost exactly the same argument accepted in *Obergefell*, namely the protection of their fundamental right to marry under both the Due Process and Equal Protection Clauses of the Fourteenth Amendment.[55] The county attorney had responded that their

[49] Henry Monaghan, *Stare Decisis* and Constitutional Adjudication, 88 Colum. L. Rev. 723 (1988); Thomas W. Merrill, Originalism, *Stare Decisis*, and the Promotion of Judicial Restraint, 22 Const. Comment. 271 (2005); Ernest Young, Rediscovering Conservatism: Burkean Political Theory and Constitutional Interpretation, 72 N.C. L. Rev. 619 (1994).

[50] Obergefell, 135 S. Ct. at 2599–600.

[51] *Id.* at 2600–01.

[52] E.g., Pierce v. Society of Sisters, 268 U.S. 510 (1925); Meyer v. Nebraska, 262 U.S. 399 (1926).

[53] E.g., Maynard v. Hill, 125 U.S. 190, 211 (1888). Justice Kennedy also invoked de Toqueville, who also assumed traditional marriage.

[54] Baker v. Nelson, 191 N.W.2d 185, 186 (Minn. 1971), appeal dismissed, 409 U.S. 810 (1972).

[55] Jurisdictional Statement at 12, Baker v. Nelson, 409 U.S. 810 (1972) (No. 71-1027).

claim would redefine marriage, which was a major policy change well beyond the competence and legitimacy for judges to effect.[56] The Supreme Court had, unanimously, dismissed Baker and McConnell's appeal for lack of a "substantial federal question."[57] Although summary dispositions do not carry the full weight of *stare decisis* that decisions after full briefing and argument do, they still count as precedents and imposed upon the *Obergefell* Court a higher burden of justification.

Again, more focus on the Court's equal-protection precedents would have addressed these analytical gaps in the Court's common law reasoning. The Court's 19th- and early 20th-century marriage jurisprudence had been delivered against the traditional background norm that "the good husband is the good citizen."[58] In the course of the 20th century, that gendered background norm gave way to a more modern understanding that not only can a "good wife" be a "good citizen" and unselfish caregiver, but so can a "good wife" married to another woman, as Michigan plaintiffs DeBoer and Rowse had been since 2007 (without state recognition). Indeed, Justice Kennedy explicitly invoked the Court's constitutional sex discrimination jurisprudence in his discussion of the dynamics of equal protection. As his opinion observed, American family law was deeply gendered until the last generation, and the Court itself cleared away much of the nation's gendered family law.[59] Kennedy could have carried this discussion further, to argue that women's constitutional equality has rendered the procreation imperative in the constitutional right to marry inadmissible.

The central point of the chief justice's dissent is that Justice Kennedy was reading the Court's precedents very dynamically—and of course Kennedy's response was that the chief justice was mischaracterizing precedent himself. Their debate reminds us that precedent in a heavily contested area of the law is not the constraining mechanism that common law constitutionalism makes it out to be.

---

[56] Memorandum from Hennepin County Attorney George C. Scott to Hennepin County District Court Clerk Gerald R. Nelson, May 22, 1970, in University of Minnesota, Tretter Collection, McConnell Files, Box 21.

[57] Baker v. Nelson, 409 U.S. 810 (1972), about which more below.

[58] Walter Berns, Marriage Anyone?, First Things, April 1996, available at http://www.firstthings.com/article/1996/04/002-marriage-anyone (viewed Aug. 1, 2015).

[59] Obergefell, 135 S. Ct. at 2603–04.

As David Cole has put it, the justices, especially in the great cases, not only pick and choose precedents they like and recharacterize prior decisions, but engage in a process of *creative misreading* of the precedents they do discuss.[60] For Justice Kennedy, *Loving v. Virginia*, a case pitting hysterical fears of interracial procreation against the central (anti-racism) agenda of the Fourteenth Amendment, became a case about individualized marriage. For Justice Thomas, *Loving's* great equal-protection core was overshadowed by a libertarian feature that played virtually no role in the Court's reasoning in that case. This process of misreading or recharacterizing precedent recurs in the debate among the justices in *Obergefell*.

Justice Kennedy's opinion in *Obergefell* is a far cry from the Burkean approach to common-law constitutionalism advocated by the Columbia School and virtually all judges who would dare say anything in support of such a theory. Instead, it is an example of common law *modernization*.[61] Justice Kennedy's opinion modernized the Fourteenth Amendment to account for two momentous changes in the United States, changes driven by the needs and preferences of Americans in the modern era.

One is the shift in the American family, and family law, away from a notion of marriage as creating a lifetime unity to what sociologist Andrew Cherlin calls "individualized marriage."[62] That family law has accommodated and even encouraged individualized marriage (through no-fault divorce, marital rape laws, promotion of birth control and family planning, promotion of adoption, and allowance of assisted reproduction) may be poor policy, but it is the marriage regime available to straight couples—but not to lesbian and gay couples until recently. When the *Obergefell* dissenters complained that the majority was redefining marriage, they were missing Cherlin's point, that Americans had redefined marriage through their choices. Following those choices, Michigan had redefined marriage, away from the communitarian, children-based vision of traditional mar-

[60] David Cole, Agon at the Agora: Creative Misreadings in the First Amendment Tradition, 95 Yale L.J. 857 (1986).

[61] David A. Strauss, The Modernizing Mission of Judicial Review, 76 U. Chi. L. Rev. 859 (2009); cf. Jack Balkin, Living Originalism (2011) (repackaging a modernizing common law constitutionalism as "originalism," in a tour de force of creative misreading).

[62] Andrew J. Cherlin, The Marriage Go-Round 88 (2009); Andrew J. Cherlin, Deinstitutionalization of American Marriage, 66 J. Marriage & Fam. 848, 851 (2004).

riage and toward a liberal, choice-based regime where almost anybody can marry and just as easily get divorced—everyone, that is, except for lesbian and gay couples.

The other shift has been the advance of lesbians, gay men, bisexuals, and transgender persons from outlaws to "inlaws" in one generation. In the 1970s, when the Supreme Court dismissed the appeal in *Baker v. Nelson*, gay people were presumptive criminals in most states (including liberal Minnesota), and their outlaw status, repeatedly reaffirmed by the Supreme Court, legitimated the many state discriminations against them.[63] Indeed, the status of gay people as outlaws or, in the more tolerant states, social outcasts rested upon a core stereotype of them as antithetical to family. Denying child visitation to a gay (biological) parent in 1985, an Ohio court explained that "given its concern for perpetuating the values associated with conventional marriage and the family as the basic unit of society, the state has a substantial interest in viewing homosexuality as errant sexual behavior which threatens the social fabric, and in endeavoring to protect minors from being influenced by those who advocate homosexual lifestyles."[64]

In the last generation, stereotypes such as these have eroded, as hundreds of thousands of LGBT persons have come out of the closet and entered public life—increasingly as committed partners and as parents. For decades, social scientists have documented that LGBT persons are capable parents and that children flourish under their care.[65] As the *Obergefell* majority observed, hundreds of thousands of children are presently being raised in lesbian and gay households; discrimination against their parents' committed relationship is, even according to many traditional marriage supporters, harmful to those children as well.[66] Does that new but documented concern not raise

[63] On the pervasive anti-gay state discriminations, see William N. Eskridge Jr., Gaylaw: Challenging the Apartheid of the Closet (1999).

[64] Roberts v. Roberts, 489 N.E.2d 1067, 1070 (Ohio Ct. App. 1985); accord, S. v. S., 608 S.W.2d 64 (Ky. Ct. App. 1980); Hall, 95 Mich. App. at 615. See generally Angela Simon, The Relationship Between Stereotypes and Attitudes Toward Lesbians and Gays, in Stigma and Sexual Orientation 62–63 (Gregory Herek, ed., 1998).

[65] See, e.g., Brief of the American Psychological Association et al. as Amici Curiae, Hollingsworth v. Perry, 133 S. Ct. 2652 (2013) (No. 12-144).

[66] Obergefell, 135 S. Ct. at 2600–01; see DeBoer v. Snyder, 973 F. Supp. 2d 757, 771 (E.D. Mich. 2013) (findings of fact on this point).

equal-protection problems? That is, is the state not discriminating against the children raised within lesbian and gay families by denying them the security and other advantages claimed for marriage from its traditionalist defenders?

So LGBT persons have moved from outlaws to inlaws, a process completed by the *Obergefell* Court through a modernized and dynamic reading of the Fourteenth Amendment and the Court's precedents. Although the dissenting justices did not deny the foregoing changes in American society, they questioned the legitimacy of the unelected Court's modernizing family law through constitutional activism. In a representative democracy, the proper engine for family law modernization is the state legislatures, many of which had already updated their law in precisely the manner the Court was imposing on all the states. Are the five majority justices wiser than their four dissenting colleagues, the large majority of state legislators and governors, and the people who for hundreds of years supported traditional marriage (or even its modern individualized version for straight couples)? "Just who do we think we are?" wondered Chief Justice Roberts.[67]

Again, more attention to the Equal Protection Clause might have answered these concerns more satisfactorily than the liberty-supported-by-equality approach taken by the majority. The Equal Protection Clause, read literally, seems strongly inconsistent with the massively discriminatory regime Michigan offered DeBoer and Rowse, for example. Even as narrowed by original meaning, the clause bars "class" or "caste" legislation, which also characterized the Michigan regime. The most irresponsible straight couple could get married in Michigan, and then divorced overnight, while the committed lesbian couple unselfishly devoted to their (now) five children were not afforded the dignity of the same marriage license that the state hands out like lollipops at the dentist's office to straight couples. This is such an upside-down understanding of "traditional" marriage as to challenge the rationality of the discrimination.

---

[67] Obergefell, 135 S. Ct. at 2612 (Roberts, C.J., dissenting); see also DeBoer, 772 F.3d at 406–07 (Sutton, J., for the majority in the lower court) (conceding the "costs to the plaintiffs of allowing the States to work through this profound policy debate," but urging, from a "Burkean sense of caution," that courts should allow "state democratic forces" to solve the problems caused by the state's own longstanding anti-gay caste regime when "evolving community mores show they should be fixed").

But is this analysis not anti-democratic? Yes. Constitutionalism is anti-democratic in the short term. The proudest moments of the Equal Protection Clause, in particular, have been when the Court wielded it to protect despised minorities—and its most shameful moments have come when the Court ratified discriminatory treatment of Japanese-American citizens, for the most notorious example,[68] and felony criminalization of "homosexual sodomy," to take a more recent example.[69] "The idea of the Constitution 'was to withdraw certain subjects from the vicissitudes of political controversy, to place them beyond the reach of majorities and officials and to establish them as legal principles to be applied by the courts.'"[70]

If that is the case, was *Baker v. Nelson* wrongly decided in 1972? Mike McConnell and Jack Baker made almost exactly the same argument that Justice Kennedy accepted in *Obergefell*. Although *Obergefell* explicitly overruled *Baker*, it did not say, as Justice Kennedy said in *Lawrence*, that the discredited precedent was wrong the day it was decided. Indeed, it is doubtful that any justice on the current Court would have voted differently in 1972—or perhaps even in 2013, when no justice reached the merits in *Hollingsworth v. Perry*, the Fourteenth Amendment challenge to California's constitutional exclusion of same-sex couples from marriage in Proposition 8.[71] Justice Kennedy's modernizing version of common-law constitutionalism suggests that it was premature in 1972 for the justices to settle the issue of marriage equality, because the changes in the American family, in state family law, and in the status of LGBT persons had not undergone the sea change that had become clear by 2015.

[68] Korematsu v. United States, 323 U.S. 214 (1944) (interpreting the equal protection component of the Fifth Amendment's Due Process Clause to allow imprisonment of Japanese-American citizens without any demonstrated basis).

[69] Obergefell, 135 S. Ct. at 2606, discussing Bowers v. Hardwick, 478 U.S. 186 (1986) (rejecting a due process challenge to a Georgia statute making consensual sodomy a felony, with a mandatory minimum term of one year in jail and a maximum of 20 years), overruled by Lawrence v. Texas, 539 U.S. 558, 578 (enforcing a due process liberty right to engage in consensual sodomy in private places).

[70] Obergefell, 135 S. Ct. at 2605–06, quoting W.V. Bd. of Educ. v. Barnette, 319 U.S. 624, 638 (1943).

[71] Hollingsworth v. Perry, 133 S. Ct. 2652 (2013) (holding that the defenders of Prop 8 did not have constitutional standing, thereby rendering the appellate federal courts without jurisdiction to hear the constitutional challenges to Prop 8; dissenting justices argued that the defenders had standing, but did not reach the merits).

But of course all those changes were clear by 2013 and perhaps even by 2003, when the Court decided *Lawrence v. Texas* and the Massachusetts Supreme Court decided *Goodridge v. Department of Public Health.*[72] Justice Kennedy was very probably unwilling to write an *Obergefell*-type landmark in 2003, when his *Lawrence* opinion scrupulously avoided mention of marriage rights (in contrast to Justice Scalia's cassandric dissenting opinion, which predicted the Court's trajectory on the marriage issue). Something more is going on with the Court's modernized version of common law constitutionalism than new circumstances. Consider a third way of understanding constitutional decisionmaking.

III. Pluralism-Respecting Judicial Review: Equality over Time

Speaking for the five justices in the majority, Justice Kennedy's opinion responded to the dissenters' claim that the nation was unsettled on the need for marriage equality. This was certainly true in 1972, when the Court dismissed the appeal in *Baker v. Nelson,* and may have been true in 2013, when the Justices declined to evaluate Proposition 8. But Justice Kennedy rejected the view that the Constitution demanded more deliberation on this issue in 2015:

> Yet there has been far more deliberation than this argument acknowledges. There have been referenda, legislative debates, and grassroots campaigns, as well as countless studies, papers, books, and other popular and scholarly writings. There has been extensive litigation in state and federal courts. Judicial opinions addressing the issue have been informed by the contentions of parties and counsel, which, in turn, reflect the more general, societal discussion of same-sex marriage and its meaning that has occurred over the past decades. As more than 100 *amici* make clear in their filings, many of the central institutions in American life—state and local governments, the military, large and small businesses, labor unions, religious organizations, law enforcement, civic groups, professional organizations, and universities—have devoted substantial attention to the question. This has led to an enhanced understanding of the issue—an understanding

---

[72] Goodridge v. Dep't. of Pub. Health, 798 N.E.2d 941 (Mass. 2003) (requiring marriage equality under the state constitution).

> reflected in the arguments now presented for resolution as a matter of constitutional law.[73]

This discussion baffled the dissenters and will likely draw fire from commentators, but in my view it was quite thoughtful. And it reflects a deliberation-based theory for judicial review.

The parent of this theory is Professor Alexander Bickel, whose endorsement of the "passive virtues" suggested that judicial review is more complicated than simple enforcement of original meaning or application of constitutional text in a common law manner.[74] In contrast to John Hart Ely's representation-reinforcing theory of judicial review, which urged courts to protect politically marginalized social groups,[75] Bickel's theory cautioned that the Supreme Court is "the least dangerous" branch, because it has no lawmaking, taxing, or enforcement authority.[76] Hence, its ability to enforce constitutional values is hemmed in by the justices' ability to persuade the country of the correctness (or at least plausibility) of its pronouncements. Even when the logic of original meaning and of precedent seem to support a particular constitutional ruling, the Court ought to hesitate before making broad pronouncements until the country is at rest on the matter.

The passive virtues are techniques of substantive avoidance and postponement until a constitutional issue is ripe for national settlement. Thus, the Court in 2013 avoided decision in the Proposition 8 Case (*Hollingsworth*) by dismissing the appeal for lack of appellate standing (a classic passive-virtue device). Likewise, *Baker v. Nelson* may have been an example of the passive virtues in action; although dismissal of the appeal was a substantive judgment, it carried less precedential effect. Accordingly, *Obergefell* could overrule *Baker v. Nelson* without faulting the Court's strategy in that case, because the Court recognized that the country was not ready for gay marriage in 1972; even LGBT people were apprehensive, as most were still hovering in

---

[73] Obergefell, 135 S. Ct. at 2605 (citations omitted); see Appendices to the Court's opinion, listing state and federal judicial opinions as well as statutes recognizing marriage equality.

[74] Alexander M. Bickel, The Least Dangerous Branch: The Supreme Court at the Bar of Politics (1962).

[75] John Hart Ely, Democracy and Distrust: A Theory of Judicial Review (1980).

[76] Bickel is appropriating and updating Federalist 78, where Hamilton explained why the judiciary was "the least dangerous branch" for these reasons.

the closet. Nor was the country ready in 2003, when most states were responding to the possibility of gay marriage by amending their constitutions (by overwhelming margins) to prevent such a development—and any other kind of relationship recognition for good measure, as Michigan did in 2004. But *Lawrence v. Texas* encouraged LGBT persons to come out of the closet and engage in public debate, seeking equality in family recognition as well as other arenas.[77]

Both the majority and dissenting justices were impressed with the rapidity by which LGBT groups have been able to persuade most Americans that marriage equality is an idea whose time has come. Since 2011, more Americans have supported marriage equality than have opposed it, and the margin of approval will probably increase in the next five years. The dissenting Justices raised a few related concerns, however, about the Court's willingness to settle the debate in favor of nationwide marriage equality. Why not let the democratic process take its course, and let marriage equality come through the democratic process? And will nationwide marriage equality not marginalize a new religious minority, namely, those Americans still supporting traditional marriage?

In my view, a pluralism-facilitating approach to judicial review provides Justice Kennedy with answers to both of these questions—answers that help explain features of his opinion that are otherwise elliptical.[78]

The United States is a (1) constitutional (2) democracy embedded within a (3) pluralist political system. Overlooked by scholars both before and after Professor Bickel, the pluralist features of America's constitutional democracy help explain and justify *Obergefell*. A pluralist political system is one whose goal is the accommodation of the interests of as many salient groups as possible, without disturbing the ability of the state and the community to press forward with collective projects.[79] In a pluralist democracy, social, economic, and

[77] Obergefell, 135 S. Ct. at 2604.

[78] The discussion that follows is adapted from William N. Eskridge Jr., Pluralism and Distrust: How Courts Can Support Democracy by Lowering the Stakes of Politics, 114 Yale L.J. 1279 (2005), as well as William N. Eskridge Jr., A Pluralist Theory of Equal Protection, 11 U. Pa. J. Const. L. 1239 (2009).

[79] See Robert A. Dahl, Pluralist Democracy in the United States: Conflict and Consent (1967); Nicholas R. Miller, Pluralism and Social Choice, 77 Am. Pol. Sci. Rev. 734 (1983).

ideological groups compete for the approval and support of representatives and the electorate. The polity, in turn, encourages groups to participate in the marketplace of politics.

The 20th century saw an evolving landscape of American pluralism, generating wave after wave of new identity-based social movements. Those movements sought to change public opinion about norms involving race, sex/gender, sexual orientation, and disability, and worked through the political process to change the law. Those movements reflected a multicultural pluralism, in which an increasing array of groups or subgroups would work from within their own communities to assert the equal citizenship of its members within the larger culture.[80] Because many cohesive minority groups are also the objects of governmental as well as private discrimination and abuse, they formed law-reforming social movements to challenge social norms demonizing them and policies disadvantaging them. Social movements, in turn, inspired countermovements. The states-rights response to the civil-rights movement is one example, the pro-life movement in response to *Roe v. Wade* is another. The LGBT-rights movement has inspired a traditional-family-values (TFV) countermovement that successfully opposed marriage equality for many decades.[81]

Although the Framers of the Constitution did not anticipate our modern multifaceted pluralism, they appreciated the fragility of democracy when the "stakes" of pluralist politics get too high. Stakes get high when the system becomes embroiled in bitter disputes that drive salient, productive groups away from engagement in pluralist politics.[82] Such politics not only needs all established social groups to participate, but also needs new social groups seeking to secure political goals. Unfortunately, groups will disengage when they believe that participation in the system is pointless due to their permanent defeat on issues important to them, or due to their perception that the process

[80] See Will Kymlicka, Multicultural Citizenship (1996); Stephen Macedo, Diversity and Distrust: Civic Education in a Multicultural Democracy (2000).

[81] For a history of the LGBT-rights movement and its corresponding TFV countermovement, see William N. Eskridge Jr., Dishonorable Passions: Sodomy Law in America, 1861–2003 (2008).

[82] On the dangers of high-stakes issues in a pluralist system, see Adam Przeworski, Democracy and the Market: Political and Economic Reforms in Eastern Europe and Latin America 36–37 (1991).

is stacked against them, or when the political process imposes fundamental burdens upon them or threatens their group identity or cohesion. At the founding of our nation, religion was the classic example of high-stakes pluralist politics; the religion clauses of the First Amendment sought to lower the stakes of religion-based politics by preventing one religion from securing state endorsement *and* by assuring state tolerance of religious minorities.[83] Today, issues such as abortion and same-sex marriage are the paradigm for high-stakes politics.

When a minority group is seeking tolerance from a suspicious majority, judicial review enforcing basic liberties, including free speech and association, can protect minorities and give them an opportunity to make their case for inclusion. *Lawrence v. Texas* played that role for sexual minorities in 2003. Based upon a libertarian reading of the Due Process Clause, the Court held that the state cannot criminalize private, consensual "homosexual sodomy." Justice Kennedy's opinion there highlighted an equal protection bonus: nor can the state discriminate against gay people as presumptive outlaws. *Lawrence* energized the LGBT-rights movement generally, and the marriage-equality movement in particular. Between *Lawrence* (2003) and *Obergefell* (2015), recognition of marriage equality for LGBT persons went from zero states to at least 36, as illustrated by the maps below.

■ Same-sex Marriage Recognized   ☐ No Recognition for Lesbian or Gay
■ Civil unions, Domestic P'ships, etc. Relationships, Unions or Marriages.

Marriage Equality, June 26, 2003 (*Lawrence*)

[83] Stephen Holmes, Passions and Constraint: On the Theory of Liberal Democracy 202–08, 222–27 (1995).

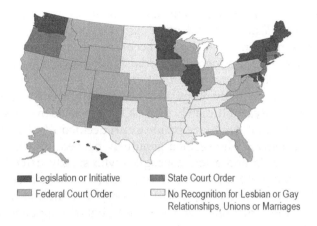

Legislation or Initiative   State Court Order
Federal Court Order   No Recognition for Lesbian or Gay
Relationships, Unions or Marriages

Marriage Equality, June 25, 2015 (Day before *Obergefell*)

As the second map illustrates, 11 of the 36 states achieved marriage equality by legislation, and another six achieved marriage equality by state-court decree that could have been overridden by a state constitutional amendment (but there was enough political mobilization to head off such a move). The *Obergefell* dissenters protested that marriage equality was sweeping the country only because unelected federal judges were imposing it (the second-lightest gray states). Why not let the process play out politically, rather than judicially?

Justice Kennedy's analysis, quoted above, suggests that there has been a national conversation, with the fact-based argumentation pushing strongly in the direction of marriage equality. The supporters of traditional marriage in this national conversation had run out of arguments for excluding lesbian and gay couples from civil marriage. They still had good arguments for advocating stable marriages as a good situs for rearing children, but they did not have good arguments for thinking that gender complementarity is necessary for this institution and for childrearing. Although their arguments were, essentially, exhausted, supporters of traditional marriage likely would have held most of the nonrecognition states for a decade or more, because the political process in places like Texas, Alabama, Mississippi, Louisiana, Arkansas, and even the midwestern and plains states were just too strongly stacked against sexual minorities.

A Bickelian justice might still have hesitated, but the Bickelians in the *Obergefell* majority did not. Possibly decisive for them were deliberative moments that did not occur, as well as those that did. In May 2012, Vice President Biden and President Obama came out in favor of marriage equality on national television—to general acclaim and with virtually no pushback from Governor Romney and Representative Ryan, ultimately their GOP opponents in the November 2012 election. When the Supreme Court decided *Windsor* in 2013, the only American who seemed genuinely peeved with the Court was Justice Scalia and a few colleagues who stoutly defended the constitutionality of the Defense of Marriage Act. The nonreaction to Edie Windsor's triumph suggested not only that Americans really had turned the corner on marriage equality, but that opponents were losing intensity as well as numbers.

So the five majority justices felt it was the right time to insist on marriage equality in *Obergefell*. As in *Windsor*, it seemed like the only American completely riled up by the decision was Justice Scalia, who wrote an intemperate dissenting opinion, denouncing the majority for a "judicial Putsch" and ridiculing Justice Kennedy's words, logic, and even his level of linguistic generality.[84] To express outrage and disrespect for majority opinions he especially dislikes, Justice Scalia sometimes concludes his dissents with "I dissent," rather than "I respectfully dissent."[85] In *Obergefell*, he simply ended his opinion; tellingly, its last word was "impotence."

A pluralism-respecting theory of judicial review should attend not just to new social groups, but also to older ones. Justice Alito and other dissenters expressed concern that marriage equality "will be used to vilify Americans who are unwilling to assent to the new orthodoxy."[86] By imposing marriage equality on all the states, moreover, the Court is closing off havens for diversity of belief about marriage and other matters of spiritual concern.[87]

The *Obergefell* majority sought to allay these concerns. Nothing in recognition of equality in civil marriages, Justice Kennedy advised,

[84] Obergefell, 135 S. Ct. at 2629–31, especially n. 22 (Scalia, J., dissenting).

[85] See, e.g., King v. Burwell, 135 S. Ct. 2480, 2507 (2015) (Scalia, J., dissenting in the Affordable Care Act Case, handed down the day before *Obergefell*).

[86] Obergefell, 135 S. Ct. at 2642 (Alito, J., joined by Scalia & Thomas, J.J., dissenting); accord *id.* at 2638–39 (Thomas, J., joined by Scalia, J., dissenting).

[87] *Id.* at 2643 (Alito, J., dissenting).

prevents religious organizations and persons from continuing to recognize only one-man, one-woman marriages consistent with their faith traditions. Indeed, the First Amendment affirmatively protects the freedom of religious organizations and persons "to teach the principles that are so fulfilling and so central to their lives and faiths" and to advocate and live "the family structure they have so long revered."[88]

As before, the dissenting justices have a deeper point that the Court did not address. Once the media, most Americans, the state and federal governments, and now the U.S. Constitution line up decisively in favor of marriage equality for LGBT persons, there will be enormous pressure on traditionalist organizations to change their tone and on many religious individuals to hold their tongues on this issue in public discourse. As LGBT people learned in the 1950s, normalization is a more powerful force than state regulation—and normalization silences. Just as LGBT persons are still streaming out of their closets, now persons of faith and other skeptics of marriage equality are likely to slip into their own closets.

I believe that Justice Kennedy, in particular, is mindful of these concerns. Indeed, they may have motivated him to focus on the fundamental right to marry, rather than classification-based equal protection scrutiny, because the liberty-based analysis allowed the Court to avoid any mention of "animus"—and to avoid taking a position on whether sexual orientation is a suspect classification. With the latter question unanswered, the Court retains the option of protecting religious liberty interests in future cases.

This suggests yet another deep point about *Obergefell* and why the Equal Protection Clause is, in the end, the central constitutional assurance at stake in this and subsequent cases. Contrary to the rhetoric one often sees in Supreme Court opinions, *equality* is a process more than a declared status. As a formal matter, LGBT Americans

---

[88] *Id.* at 2607 (opinion of the Court). First Amendment protections include not just those of the Free Exercise Clause—see Hosanna-Tabor Evangelical Lutheran Church & Sch. v. EEOC, 132 S. Ct. 694 (2012) (protecting churches against application of anti-discrimination laws to "ministerial" personnel)—but also (potentially) the Free Speech Clause and the general freedom of association that the amendment has long been understood to guarantee. Of course, Justice Kennedy only spoke of teaching and advocating religious views, omitting any guidance that would be relevant to the hot debate regarding wedding vendors and others who don't want to participate in same-sex ceremonies.

now have all the legal rights and responsibilities that everyone else has in most states. As an informal matter, social equality is still a project in the works—and now citizens who still believe in "traditional marriage" fear that they will suffer social and economic discrimination. The Supreme Court is not the primary engine for the process by which Americans work through the implications of gay rights, but that process will, assuredly, bring new equality–liberty clashes to the Court in the next decade.

A Hijab and a Hunch: *Abercrombie* and the Limits of Religious Accommodation

Walter Olson*

"This is really easy," ad-libbed Justice Antonin Scalia from the bench just before announcing the Court's decision in *EEOC v. Abercrombie & Fitch Stores*, the hijab case.[1] And indeed, amid the term's storms and squalls, *Abercrombie* came off as something of a respite of sunny harmony. It united justices across the usual lines and Scalia's opinion for all but one of his colleagues was hailed by liberal Court-watchers. Even the lone naysayer, Justice Clarence Thomas, expressed relatively cordial disagreement, suggesting the plaintiff might have won her case on a different theory.[2]

The Equal Employment Opportunity Commission, a federal agency oft battered by Roberts Court jurisprudence, found solace as well. It had represented a sympathetic young plaintiff, Samantha Elauf, the largely undisputed facts of whose case were both easy to grasp (she wanted to wear her religious head covering while working at a clothing store) and literally colorful (the hue of a scarf figured as one bit of evidence). The direct stakes were unusually low for a Supreme Court case—Elauf had won a trial verdict of just $20,000, which the appellate court had snatched away—but that just underscored that everyone was in the case for the principle of the thing.

Public discussion of the case, too, managed to be lively but mostly not strident. This was remarkable because *Abercrombie* assembled elements that in other contexts might have made for a combustible mix: stereotyping, Islam, and the exposure of women's bodies to the male gaze, just for a start. The year before, the collision of religious accommodation in the workplace with women's interests and gender

---

*Senior fellow, Cato Institute Center for Constitutional Studies; associate editor, *Cato Supreme Court Review*.

[1] 135 S. Ct. 2028 (2015).

[2] *Id.* at 2037–38 (Thomas, J., concurring in part and dissenting in part).

roles had generated nationwide fits of hyperbole in the case of *Burwell v. Hobby Lobby*, with a Supreme Court majority said to be on the verge of imposing on a once-free nation a Handmaid's Tale-like dystopia of gender inequality and subordination. In fact, even as it calmly discussed the *Abercrombie* case, America's pundit class was gripped by a fury of contention over attempts in Arizona and Indiana to adopt local versions of the Religious Freedom Restoration Act, based on the 1993 federal enactment at issue in *Hobby Lobby*. Perhaps one difference—but surely not the only one—was that in the A&F case conservative religious belief and the interests of employers were ranged against each other rather than being on the same side.

The breadth of amicus support on Elauf's side was impressive: the Becket Fund for Religious Liberty, Americans United for Separation of Church and State, the Orthodox Church in America, the gay-advocacy Lambda Legal Defense and Education Fund, the American Jewish Committee, and so on. The ACLU, National Association of Evangelicals, American Islamic Congress, and Christian Legal Society not only backed the plaintiff, but did so all on the same brief.

The resulting decision seemed to be a crowd-pleaser as well, perhaps because it quietly kicked some of the more difficult issues down the road. It was hailed by groups on every side of law-and-religion debates, by feminists and anti-feminists, by supporters and scathing critics of Islamic practices. And when so many contestants can see their own hopes reflected in a Court pronouncement, one thing seems sure: someone is going to wind up disappointed.

Would a Headscarf Fit the Look?

If you were committed to the virtue of bodily modesty, Abercrombie & Fitch (A&F) might sound like the very last place you'd want to work. Described by the *New Yorker* as "one of the most successful—and most hated—brands in retail history,"[3] A&F had built its business plan around what had been called the "sexualized marketing"[4] of "young, beautiful, and barely clothed" models whose "sculpted

[3] Christopher Glazek, The Story Behind 'Fitch the Homeless', New Yorker, June 19, 2013.

[4] David Yi, Abercrombie & Fitch Kicks Out Shirtless Models, Ending an Era of Abs, Mashable, Apr. 24, 2015, available at http://mashable.com/2015/04/24/abercrombie-fitch-end-of-an-era/.

torsos" and suggestive postures hinted at an anything-goes party scene.[5] Appalled parents wrote letters of protest to its Columbus, Ohio headquarters, which (at least for a time) only seemed to help its sales.

It's not quite so paradoxical, though, that 17-year-old Samantha Elauf might find herself filling out an application form there. Along with its main college-age brand, the company also ran a middle- and high-schooler chain called Abercrombie Kids. The tamer apparel items on offer at Kids, unlike the crop tops and tight shorts for which its older sibling was known, would probably not get you sent to the principal's office. (The retailer, which has more than 400 locations in the United States as well as operations overseas, also operates under the Hollister brand.) There was a Kids store at Woodland Hills Mall in Tulsa, Oklahoma, and Samantha's friend Farisa Sepahvand, who worked there, urged Samantha to apply.

A&F was famously obsessed with presentation, its outlets often resembling theatrical sets as much as conventional stores. Sales-floor staffers were called "models" and had to have a consistent look that promoted the type of garments the company sold, though they didn't have to be actual A&F goods. Certain types of shoes were required, female employees were forbidden to wear necklaces and bracelets, and so forth. It was called the Look Policy.

Would Samantha Elauf's headscarf, which she wore in line with her Islamic faith, be acceptable? She approached an acquaintance who was a manager at the store—he wasn't going to be a decision maker on her own application—who remembered having worked with a sales staffer who wore a yarmulke, which had been fine even though the Look Policy banned "caps." He thought a headscarf would be okay too, even though the company didn't sell scarves, but advised her to wear a color other than black. A&F didn't like black clothes and found them inconsistent with the Look.

At the interview, Elauf did wear a black headscarf; applicants were not required to wear clothing compliant with the Look Policy at this meeting, although the company did use it to evaluate their overall fashion sense. It was something of a scripted affair, and neither the

[5] Robert Klara, The Rise and Fall of the World's Most Hated Clothing Brand, AdWeek, Nov. 2, 2014, available at http://www.adweek.com/news/advertising-branding/rise-and-fall-worlds-most-hated-clothing-brand-161153.

topic of the headscarf nor religion, it was later agreed, had come up. In any event, Elauf must have made a good impression, because the hiring manager recommended she be offered a job. But the manager was unsure how to proceed on the headscarf question. Piecing together bits of information—the teenager had never been seen around the mall bareheaded, for example—the manager "assumed" that she was probably Muslim and "figured" that was why she wore the scarf.[6] These words would prove significant later.

When she (the local hiring manager) consulted a district manager to ask how the company's policy would apply, he vetoed the hiring. As far as he was concerned, a headscarf violated the Look Policy, period. Later, there was a conflict of testimony: the hiring manager said the topic of religion came up and the district manager had dismissed it as no reason to make an exception. But the district manager denied that and remembered no discussion of religion. (That was one of the few conflicts in what was otherwise largely an agreed factual record in the case.) Although testimony indicated that he was aware that many Muslim women cover their heads as a religious practice, he saw the situation at hand as a simple breach of company policy.

Had he called corporate headquarters on that, it is not impossible that they might have given him the go-ahead for the scarf. As early as 2006, A&F had approved a headscarf exception to its policy. In the next few years, it began granting many more exceptions; of course, this was the period in which the Elauf case was going public, and lawyers would have been getting involved. By 2010, A&F's general counsel specifically said the company made every reasonable effort to grant head-covering as a religious accommodation. But by then it was in court with Elauf, who had never gotten a call back after the district manager's decision. Her friend at the store passed along word that it had been because of the headscarf, and the EEOC filed suit on her behalf in 2009.

Up Through the Courts

Title VII of the Civil Rights Act of 1964, as amended, makes it an unlawful employment practice "to fail or refuse to hire" any individual "because of such individual's . . . religion,"[7] and provides that

---

[6] EEOC v. Abercrombie & Fitch Stores, Inc., 731 F.3d 1106, 1113, 1128 (10th Cir. 2013).

[7] 42 U.S.C. § 2000e-2(a).

the "term 'religion' includes all aspects of religious observance and practice, as well as belief, unless an employer demonstrates that he is unable to reasonably accommodate to an employee's or prospective employee's religious observance or practice without undue hardship on the conduct of the employer's business."[8] The District Court for the Northern District of Oklahoma, applying this law to the facts as submitted by the parties, granted the EEOC summary judgment as to liability. It also determined that the accommodation sought would not pose an undue hardship to the company. In a religious-accommodation dispute under Title VII of the Civil Rights Act an employer can establish undue hardship by proving that cost or disruption exceeds a *de minimis* level, but the court found A&F had failed to meet even that not-very-demanding hardship standard. Following a trial, a jury awarded Elauf $20,000.

A panel of the U.S. Court of Appeals for the Tenth Circuit, in an opinion by Judge Jerome Holmes, joined by Judge Paul Kelly, Jr., overturned the EEOC's grant of summary judgment and instead granted summary judgment to Abercrombie. In partial dissent, the third judge on the panel, Senior Judge David Ebel, agreed with the overturning of the summary judgment to the EEOC but would have remanded for trial, finding that the disputable issues were too great to justify a counter-award to Abercrombie.[9]

Along the way, Abercrombie had struck out on various points. Aside from its arguments on undue hardship, it had gotten nowhere trying to challenge whether Elauf really held (to quote a formula announced in earlier cases) "a bona fide religious belief that conflicts with an employment requirement."[10] It got her to admit, for example, that she went to mosque only occasionally, and didn't pray daily. She regarded female relatives who didn't cover their heads as still being good Muslims. Although she did follow some observances such as refraining from drink and gambling and observing the Ramadan fast, it was hard to classify her as a purist or strict Muslim.

[8] 42 U.S.C. § 2000e(j).

[9] 731 F.3d at 1143 (10th Cir. 2013) (Ebel, J., concurring in part and dissenting in part).

[10] See, e.g., Knight v. Connecticut Dep't of Pub. Health, 275 F.3d 156, 167 (2d Cir. 2001); Bruff v. North Mississippi Health Services, Inc., 244 F.3d 495, 500 (5th Cir. 2001); EEOC v. USPS, 94 F.3d 314, 317 (7th Cir. 1996); Chalmers v. Talon Co. of Richmond, 101 F.3d 1012 (4th Cir. 1996), cert. denied 522 U.S. 813 (1997).

Not only did this line of argument probably cost the company sympathy, but it was almost a sure loser legally as well. The courts have been generous toward religious accommodation complainants on what qualifies as a bona fide religious belief. Title VII itself by its terms protects "all aspects of religious observance and practice," and the courts have interpreted that in what has been called an individualist spirit, not requiring participation in or obedience to a well- established church (or any church at all), or what any book or authority may deem correct theological views or behavior. So long as the religious belief that generates a workplace conflict is sincere, they will ordinarily not inquire as to whether it hangs together logically or plausibly with other religious views or practices. And there was no hint that Elauf was in any way insincere, or had any deceptive or self-serving reason to wear the covering.

In principle, showing that a complainant does not consistently follow a religious tenet might help a defendant with the "conflict" part of the formula. That's because a bona fide belief that is sincerely held, but which the believer seldom gets around to acting on, may not truly come into conflict with a job requirement. (A Christian believer who sleeps in and misses church nearly every Sunday, even if feeling sincerely guilty about that failing, is not necessarily entitled to get out of a Sunday assignment at work.) But that was a useless argument here: Elauf had worn a headscarf in public consistently since age 13. For her the conflict was indisputably genuine.

But Had There Been Notice?

Abercrombie's winning argument at the Tenth Circuit, and the one that reached the high court, was on the issue of notice: the courts had recognized reasonable accommodation as a process departing from the ordinary course of an employment relationship, and the law put control over when to initiate it in the hands of the employee alone. In the 2000 case of *Thomas v. National Association of Letter Carriers*, the Tenth Circuit had declared that to have a case for failing to accommodate a religious belief an employee must "show that . . . he or she informed his or her employer of this belief."[11] Other circuits' opinions had used similar language,[12] and so had the EEOC's own 2008 compliance manual:

[11] Thomas v. Nat'l Assoc. of Letter Carriers, 225 F.3d 1149, 1155 (10th Cir. 2000).

[12] See, e.g., Dixon v. Hallmark Cos., 627 F.3d 849, 855 (11th Cir. 2010).

An applicant or employee who seeks religious accommodation must make the employer aware both of the need for
accommodation and that it is being requested due to a conflict between religion and work. The employee is obligated to
explain the religious nature of the belief or practice at issue,
and cannot assume that the employer will already know or
understand it.[13]

According to yet another EEOC document, "obligation to accommodate begins when an individual notifies the employer of the need for
an accommodation."[14] That seemed clear enough.

The EEOC's comeback to this was basically: stop being so literal-
minded. The "critical fact is the existence of the notice itself, not how
the employer came to have such notice," its brief argued.[15] Suppose
Elauf had sent a relative to the store to explain her need for an accommodation. Would the company not be on notice simply because
the message had come from someone other than her? Notice could
be given implicitly, by the circumstances of the situation. Cases from
the U.S. Courts of Appeals for the Eighth, Ninth, and Eleventh Circuits could be read as holding that the notice requirement was met
once the employer had enough information to figure out a conflict,
whether or not the employee had stated it in so many words.[16]

Besides, the Supreme Court itself had warned in its foundational
pronouncement on the subject, *McDonnell Douglas*, that the elements
of a plaintiff's initial discrimination case might need to be modified
to fit particular factual situations.[17] In a 1983 case, the Court had confirmed that the application of the well-known *McDonnell Douglas* formula was "never intended to be rigid, mechanical, or ritualistic."[18]

The functional point being served here (continued the EEOC and
its amici) was that ordinarily in an accommodation situation the

---

[13] EEOC Compliance Manual, No. 915.003 § 12-IV (July 2008), available at www.
eeoc.gov/policy/docs/religion.html.

[14] 45 Fed. Reg. 72610 (Oct. 31, 1980).

[15] Abercrombie, 731 F.3d at 1122 (10th Cir. 2013) (quoting the EEOC's brief).

[16] Brown v. Polk Cnty., 61 F.3d 650, 654 (8th Cir. 1995) (en banc); Heller v. Ebb Auto
Co., 8 F.3d 1433, 1439 (9th Cir. 1993); Dixon v. Hallmark Cos., 627 F.3d 849 (11th Cir.
2010).

[17] McDonnell Douglas Corp. v. Green, 411 U.S. 792 (1973).

[18] USPS Bd. of Governors v. Aikens, 460 U.S. 711, 715 (1983) (quoting Furnco Constr.
Co. v. Waters, 438 U.S. 567, 577 (1978)).

worker knows something that the employer does not know, and the analysis might be different if an employer had somehow been ambushed by a worker withholding the need for an accommodation on purpose, say to build a legal case. But that's not what had happened here: A&F *did* have a reasonable grasp of the likelihood that Elauf would need an accommodation, and she had not tried to keep it hidden; she had even inquired of a manager, even if he couldn't speak for the company. She simply had no reason to expect that the scarf would leave her without so much as a callback.

Judges Holmes and Kelly were unconvinced. To begin with, the weight of legal authority supported actual notice to the employer, not implied notice by roundabout means. But Elauf would lose even under a standard below that of actual notice, they said, because the company's awareness did not amount to knowing for a fact that she needed an accommodation; at most, it rose to a level of informed guesswork.[19]

As it happened, the EEOC itself could be cited as authority on this point too. The commission had called as an expert witness an authority on Islam, Georgetown professor John Esposito, who testified that many women adopt the hijab for non-religious reasons; it can make it easier to fit in with a circle of friends, be a way of signaling membership in family or nationality, and so forth. The EEOC's own guidance, the judges noted, had pointed out that some persons follow practices for religious reasons that others follow for purely secular reasons, and that the same person may switch from one motive to another at different times in life. A cross worn daily around the neck might betoken a devout Christian faith or might be a remembrance of a beloved grandmother who had worn it.

In other words, knowing that Elauf was of Muslim background and regularly wore a headscarf didn't add up to "knowing" that it would clash with her job duties. For all the company could predict, she might have been wearing it diffidently to please elders in her family, and be glad of the excuse of a new job to tell them she would now sometimes be going bareheaded. After the Tenth Circuit refused to grant en banc rehearing, the Court granted certiorari on the question of the role of notice and knowledge.

---

[19] Abercrombie, 731 F.3d at 1142.

Employers' Burden of Knowledge

At oral argument, these were the first questions out of the gate. Can someone have knowledge without notice, or notice without reasonable grounds for knowledge? If you come up with an informed guess that X is true, have you been put "on notice of" X? What if you instead have a wild, reckless hunch about something that turns out to be true?

Ian Gershengorn, the principal deputy solicitor general, represented the EEOC before the Supreme Court and began his oral argument by criticizing the Tenth Circuit for requiring an allegation that an employer "know, rather than just correctly understand" the need for an accommodation. "I don't understand," Justice Scalia broke in. "What is the difference between knowing and correctly understanding?" Gershengorn tried to clarify: "Our position is that when you figure, when you assume, when you—when it signifies to you that a religious accommodation is needed, that is sufficient notice for an employer to be on notice." Justice Kennedy wondered why the commission seemed to be taking care to stay away from the word "know." If the standard were "less than certainty, how much less than certainty is it?" asked Justice Elena Kagan. "Two out of three. Is that sufficient? . . . Under 50 percent? . . . Or even a 40 percent chance [that] this practice is religious"? But Justice Sonia Sotomayor, foreshadowing the Court's eventual direction, said the percentages weren't what mattered: "Isn't the issue the reason that they acted?" If they turned someone down because they didn't want to get into some hassle over accommodation, wasn't that the problem right there, even if the accommodation need wouldn't have been very likely to pan out? [20]

But if the advice was "have as much of a hunch as you like about someone's religious scruples, just don't act on it," that was advice not easily taken. In a case like this, acting on the hunch would often be indistinguishable from not acting on it; a manager who failed to draw any scarf–religion connection in his mind, but simply stuck with the facially neutral job rule, might have made the same decision as one with a bad motive. Neither the EEOC nor anyone else was claiming that employers had to drop any and all rules that might sometimes conflict with someone's religious observance. So

---

[20] Transcript of Oral Argument at 3–9, Abercrombie & Fitch, 135 S. Ct. 2028 (2015).

it seemed that what was being asked of employers was some sort of positive action-taking.

That led to the question on almost everyone's mind: if managers were worried about something, why didn't they just ask? "You could raise the policy," the EEOC lawyer offered at oral argument.[21] Then the applicant would have a chance to answer the question or respond to the overture, putting the employer closer to a resolution of some kind. Title VII's demand for religious accommodation of workers had itself often been described as a process of mutual (if awkward and, on one side, forced) dialogue: the two sides would go back and forth exploring the possibilities until finding (if they could) some arrangement agreeable to both. For the employer to initiate such a conversation, if the worker hadn't, would seem to fit that spirit.

Of course, there were a few problems with that. "Questions about an applicant's religious affiliation or beliefs," according to the EEOC's own guidance, "are generally viewed as non job-related and problematic under federal law."[22] In line with that guidance, Abercrombie itself at the time of the Tulsa incident had told its managers not to inquire about religion.

What about getting at the issue less directly: "Would wearing our standard employee attire pose a problem for you?" Well, questions in a job interview intended to flush out protected-group status are held suspect, no less than direct questions. As A&F's brief pointed out, under EEOC guidelines "employers generally may not ask applicants whether they are available during normal business hours. . . . If an employer asks anyway and then declines to hire someone who said she needed an accommodation, "[t]he Commission will infer that the need for an accommodation discriminatorily influenced a decision to reject [the] applicant" and will put the "burden . . . on the employer to demonstrate that factors other than the need for an accommodation were the reason for rejecting the qualified applicant."[23] Lawyers representing the employee in a private claim for damages likewise

---

[21] *Id.* at 20.

[22] EEOC, Pre-Employment Inquiries and Religious Affiliation or Beliefs, available at http://www.eeoc.gov/laws/practices/inquiries_religious.cfm.

[23] Brief of Respondent at 55, Abercrombie & Fitch, 135 S. Ct. 2028 (2015) (referring to 29 C.F.R. § 1605.3(b)(2) and (b)(3)).

can introduce such questions as evidence that religion was on the employer's mind.

The EEOC is not so unrealistic as to think employers can be kept entirely from asking about, say, schedule availability before taking on new staff. What it prescribes instead is a painfully artificial structuring of the process: the employer is supposed to advise applicants to answer scheduling questions *as if* they could be sure of getting reasonable accommodation for religious conflicts, and then, after a job offer is made, reveal the truth in a further round of disclosure, with the employer left in the position of withdrawing the job offer if it doesn't like the news (thus painting the biggest possible sue-me target on its chest).[24] Bizarre and strained as this process may sound, it actually parallels the longstanding trend in employment law on other topics where information that is obviously job-related may still furnish grounds for discrimination. In the context of the Americans with Disabilities Act, for example, disability-related inquiries are barred outright, rather than merely discouraged as suspect, and the employer is supposed to ask about the ability to handle job prerequisites with roundabout language along the lines of "*Given reasonable accommodation,* would you be able to lift fifty pounds / climb a ladder / lead a building evacuation in an emergency?" If such formulas are vaguely workable at companies with legal staffs and large human resources departments, yet not in informal hiring at smaller employers, well, those are just the rules of the game.

Probing for more information from certain applicants who look as if they might need one, or pre-emptively offering an accommodation, runs into a further problem: which applicants should be singled out for such special handling? How much of a hunch does it take, and what happens if the hunch is itself based on imperfect, perhaps stereotypical information?

The set of practices the EEOC was now urging, A&F protested in its brief, "necessarily devolves into a totality-of-the-stereotypes standard."[25] Yet according to the commission's own "Best Practices" compilation, employers should "avoid assumptions or stereotypes

[24] On requiring employers to don sue-me vests, compare the recent movement for "ban the box" laws prohibiting pre-offer inquiries about criminal records (employer must make job offer before opening envelope that reveals rap sheet, and then withdraw offer if it dislikes the envelope's contents).

[25] Brief of Respondent, *supra* note 23, at 53.

149

about what constitutes a religious belief or practice or what type of accommodation is appropriate." Moreover, managers "should be trained not to engage in stereotyping based on religious dress and grooming practices."[26] Just as it knew its interviewers were not supposed to ask questions that might flush out religious practices and beliefs, so Abercrombie had also instructed its managers not to make assumptions about employees or their wishes based on presumed religion. It had been a diligent honor student in following the guidance from the federal teacher, only to be flunked after all. Once again, employers were being placed in a sued-if-you-do, sued-if-you-don't position.

There remained possible but one final, headlong leap into the chasm of utter absurdity: why not ask *all* the applicants *all* the questions? Specifically, if employers couldn't probe about religious objections, and couldn't ask different questions from one applicant to the next, why couldn't they compile ahead of time a list of all the ways a job listing might conflict with anyone's religious practices—scheduling, garb, contact with taboo substances, non-availability of prayer breaks, and so forth—and pre-announce to each applicant the whole list to start a discussion? Some did take that idea seriously, which is why the Court at oral argument that morning found itself staring into that very chasm. As Chief Justice John Roberts mused, it would take a "code of conduct that presumably would go on for several pages," or perhaps recited over 20 minutes to make sure the applicant had heard and understood. And yet inevitably even then it would fall short of achieving its goal fully. There is not some set, countable number of sincerely held religious beliefs held within the human heart, but an infinite potential for them. Some believers sincerely ascribe a pious or taboo significance to a particular number or letter of the alphabet, or a certain form found in a shape or picture, or a certain direction from which to walk into or out of a building, or the presence or absence of a certain animal. As the EEOC's compliance manual noted, Title VII protects a religious belief or practice that may happen to arise "in the person's own scheme of things" and "even if few—or no—other people adhere to it." Even if seven lawyers on seven laptops spent seven years working up the resulting

---

[26] EEOC, Best Practices for Eradicating Religious Discrimination in the Workplace, available at http://www.eeoc.gov/policy/docs/best_practices_religion.html.

checklist, they could never hope to anticipate every accommodation request in a truly exhaustive way.

Public Employers' Anxieties

While dozens of religious and social-change organizations joined amicus briefs on the EEOC's side, the only ones to file on Abercrombie's—aside from the Cato Institute, which publishes this journal—were major employer organizations. Some represented the private sector, including the National Federation of Independent Business, U.S. Chamber of Commerce, and Equal Employment Advisory Council. But public-sector employer groups, which are sometimes hesitant to step into disputes about discrimination law, were perhaps even more notable in their outspokenness; they included the National Council of State Legislatures, the National League of Cities, the National Association of Counties, the National School Boards Association, and quite a few more.

Why would they find significant questions of public-sector management lurking in this dispute about teen clothing sales? In part it's because on issues of religion in the workplace, public-sector employers are distinctively whipsawed by multiple sources of liability. On display of religious symbols at a workplace, for example, they may have to contend with possible liability under the First Amendment (if, say, they restrict employees' speech improperly) and the Establishment Clause (if, say, they give the impression of endorsing that same speech). Title VII liability for not accommodating employees' religious practices—an exposure they share with private employers—then gets layered on top of that.

For the EEOC, as for Abercrombie, some of its legal tactics worked better than others. The commission's briefs held discussion of its own former employer guidance to a minimum, even as it quietly revamped its guidance to reflect its new litigating positions.[27] As was its custom, it also asked the Court to give deference as an expert

---

[27] EEOC, Religious Garb and Grooming in the Workplace: Rights and Responsibilities, available at http://www.eeoc.gov/eeoc/publications/qa_religious_garb_grooming.cfm ("Religious Garb Guidance"). On the EEOC's change of guidance on notice, see Brief for National Council of State Legislatures et al. as Amici Curiae Supporting Respondent at 22, EEOC v. Abercrombie & Fitch, 135 S. Ct. 2028 (2015), available at https://www.nsba.org/sites/default/files/reports/EEOC%20v.%20AF%20-%20Amicus%20Brief%20January%202015.pdf.

agency to its latest (as distinct from its recent) interpretation of the law.[28] It refrained from proposing the drawing of any clear line on what should count as sufficient implicit notice, for all the attention being paid to that troublesome question. And—shrewdest of all, perhaps—it changed its underlying theory of the case from the one that had lost below. Instead of presenting the case as an accommodation case *simpliciter*, a theory it had advanced as recently as its certiorari briefing, it urged that it be considered as a matter of "intentional discrimination" falling under the heading of "disparate treatment."[29]

The Supreme Court's Ruling

A. The Majority: Motive Matters, Not Knowledge

Whether as an elaborate collective prank or simply because it enjoys thinking issues through, the Court often gives its liveliest attention in oral argument to points that do not wind up forming the basis of its decision. And so it was again this time. Justice Scalia, writing for the Court, found that notice, knowledge, and certainty were not, after all, the crux of this case: motive was. To prove intentional discrimination under Title VII, Scalia wrote, "an applicant need only show that his need for an accommodation was a motivating factor in the employer's decision." Title VII makes it unlawful for an employer to refuse to hire "because of" a religious practice, and unlike some other branches of discrimination law, it has settled on a relatively relaxed standard for "because of"; namely, that the employee's religious practice be a "motivating factor." "It is significant that § 2000e–2(a)(1) [the central ban on discrimination, or disparate treatment, in

---

[28] *Abercrombie* was the second case of the term in which the Court, while giving the EEOC a victory, had disregarded its claims to be owed expert agency deference; in both cases the commission had recently altered its position. See Walter Olson, Young v. UPS: Bias Plaintiffs Win at the Supreme Court, Cato at Liberty (Mar. 25, 2015) (discussing *Young v. UPS*, 135 S. Ct. 1338 (2015)), available at http://www.cato.org/blog/young-v-ups-job-bias-plaintiffs-win-scotus. On the commission's less-than-stellar track record in recent cases, see Walter Olson, The EEOC Loses (and Loses. and Loses.) in Federal Court Again, Cato at Liberty (Sept. 30, 2014), available at http://www.cato.org/blog/more-courts-smack-down-eeoc.

[29] Brief of Petitioner at 19, Abercrombie & Fitch, 135 S. Ct. (2015).

Title VII] does not impose a knowledge requirement. As Abercrombie acknowledges, some antidiscrimination statutes do." [30]

So the law in this case bans acting on bad motive, without directly inquiring into knowledge. Scalia offers an example: an employer who "thinks" but does not "know for certain" that a certain applicant will need Sabbath accommodation and acts with that as "a motivating factor" will be liable, at least in cases where the applicant actually does need it. In passing, he dismisses Abercrombie's argument that it had treated religious practice no worse than non-religious practice: "Title VII does not demand mere neutrality with regard to religious practices—that they be treated no worse than other practices. Rather, it gives them favored treatment."[31] This was the same decision promptly hailed in the newspapers by Americans United for Separation of Church and State.[32]

B. Justice Thomas: Accommodation Not a Freestanding Claim

Used to going his own way on employment discrimination issues—he was the longest serving chairman of the EEOC—Justice Clarence Thomas wrote a separate concurrence/dissent that was mostly a dissent. He quoted the Court's own words in a 1979 case, which themselves invoked a quote from decades earlier (hence the nested quotes): "'Discriminatory purpose'—i.e., the purpose necessary for a claim of intentional discrimination—demands 'more than . . . awareness of consequences. It implies that the decisionmaker . . . selected or reaffirmed a particular course of action at least in part 'because of,' not merely 'in spite of,' its adverse effects upon an identifiable group.'"[33] A&F had plainly adopted its Look Policy for non-religious and facially neutral reasons. To be sure, sometimes an employer applying a neutral rule has nonetheless engaged in intentional discrimination, if, for example, it turns down a religious exemption though routinely granting secular ones. But A&F's decision

---

[30] 135 S. Ct. at 2032.

[31] *Id.* at 2034.

[32] Robert Barnes, Supreme Court Allows Suit by Muslim Woman Who Says Headscarf Cost Her a Job, Wash. Post, June 1, 2015 (quoting Gregory Lipper of Americans United), available at http://www.washingtonpost.com/national/supreme-court-allows-suit-by-muslim-woman-who-says-head-scarf-cost-her-a-job/2015/06/01/977293f0-088c-11e5-9e39-0db921c47b93_story.html.

[33] Personnel Administrator of Mass. v. Feeney, 442 U.S. 256, 279 (1979).

maker appeared to have applied the policy mechanically, with no special animus or worse treatment, and in the absence of an outright request for accommodation. To Thomas, this was a "classic case of an alleged disparate impact." It would still be open to challenge on that basis, and might result in liability unless A&F could prove that the policy was grounded in "business necessity."[34]

All nine justices united on one point of importance to practicing lawyers: these religious accommodation cases had all up to now been put in the wrong box. Thomas: "many lower courts, including the Tenth Circuit below, wrongly assumed that Title VII creates a freestanding failure-to-accommodate claim distinct from either disparate treatment or disparate impact."[35] While Thomas would have put accommodation into the disparate-impact rather than the disparate-treatment box, there was not a single vote on the court for keeping to the three-box arrangement that had heretofore been standard teaching. Not only had lower courts routinely accepted a three-box scheme, but the EEOC had done so too, both in its compliance manual—"A religious accommodation claim is distinct from a disparate treatment claim, in which the question is whether employees are treated equally," it had recited[36]—and even in its argument petitioning for certiorari in this very case. But if everyone had behaved up to now as if there were three boxes, so much the worse for everyone. From now on, there would be only two.

C. The Aftermath: "Really Easy"

In a separate concurrence, Justice Samuel Alito wrote to warn the Court that it did not dispose of the knowledge-and-notice problem quite so easily. An inquiry into motive is still going to raise questions of knowledge, since it would be absurd to impose liability on an employer with no "inkling" that a religious conflict tended to disqualify a potential worker. The majority opinion dismissed this point as dicta, though Scalia conceded in a footnote that it is at least "arguable" that an employer shouldn't be legally expected to offer

---

[34] 135 S. Ct. at 2037–38. (Thomas, J., concurring in part and dissenting in part).

[35] *Id.* at 2041.

[36] *Id.* (quoting the EEOC Compliance Manual, *supra* note 13).

an accommodation unless it at least "suspects" a given worker will need one.[37]

It is perhaps a tribute to Justice Scalia's high tolerance for complication that a case like this could strike him as "really easy." The lower courts had divided among three viewpoints in their consideration, and the Supreme Court then divided between two viewpoints neither of which agreed with any of those below. The EEOC changed the theory on which it argued the case partway through, and then suffered the mild indignity of seeing all five camps of judicial sentiment reject years' worth of its own (the EEOC's) regulatory guidance on multiple points. If that counts as "really easy," what would a hard case look like?

At any rate, the justices sent the case back for further consideration, which didn't last long; the parties settled almost immediately for a modest sum. Shortly before, in the spring of 2015, the parent Abercrombie company had announced that it planned to tone down its sexualized promotions and fashion photography, and would also move away from its former "controversial long-standing policy of hiring based on body type or physical attractiveness."[38]

Employment Law: The Age of Accommodation

For all that the *Abercrombie* case ended in some semblance of accord, the remarkable array of constituencies it brought together on the plaintiff's side is not likely to reunite in future cases. Accommodation mandates have been one of the huge growth areas of employment law over the past generation, a trend that shows every sign of continuing. Yet religious accommodation in some ways runs along its own track, and it is worth looking more closely at how the two came to diverge.

It can truly be said that we live in an age of accommodation in employment law, and the most powerful force in ushering in that age was the 1990 enactment of the Americans with Disabilities Act (ADA).[39] Like earlier civil rights laws, it set forth a protected group, in this case the disabled, against whom discrimination is prohib-

---

[37] *Id.* at 2035. (Alito, J., concurring in the judgment).

[38] Yi, Mashable, *supra* note 4.

[39] See Walter Olson, The Excuse Factory: How Employment Law Is Paralyzing the American Economy Chs. 6 & 7 (1997).

ited. Unlike most earlier laws, it also instituted far-reaching new requirements for "reasonable accommodation" of covered persons in employment and other areas. And while Title VII had earlier incorporated a mandate of accommodation of employees' religious practice, ADA went so much farther that its difference of degree amounted to something of a difference in kind.

This marked an important shift in thinking. Discrimination law, even as slightly modified by the religious accommodation mandate, had long been driven by concepts of equal treatment, in which differing talents could make their way once prejudice and animus were removed. Now, increasingly, the goal was to correct inequalities of endowment: the employer would be asked to invest freely to provide the deaf with captioning, the paraplegic with a new built environment suited for wheelchairs, the slow with extra time to complete tasks, and so forth. For some years the tendency in the courts was to confine the right to accommodation to "traditional" disabled groups such as the blind and deaf, but advocates were deeply discontented at these limits, and persuaded Congress by an overwhelming majority that the law should cover a much wider range of impairments. At this point, lawyers often advise employers that it is not worth a losing ADA fight on whether an employee qualifies as disabled, and the goal should be to keep some control over the cost of accommodation.

Other laws have followed a similar path, with the ban on pregnancy discrimination now including a right to accommodation, which can often involve light duty, reassignment of duties, and extra time spent away from work. The milestone Family and Medical Leave Act,[40] while not quite couched in terms of discrimination per se, sought to extend the idea of scheduling accommodation, already familiar from the religious and disability areas, to workers more broadly. Moves were soon afoot to establish a more general entitlement to paid leave, with no reasons given.

As accommodation advanced as an objective, the tone and language used to describe it also began to change. With organized disability advocates in the lead, it was argued that accommodation was not just an exercise in generosity that a wealthy society might be asked to extend, but a matter of rights being denied: the failure to build more ramps was akin to laws enforcing racial separation.

[40] 29 U.S.C. § 2601 et seq.

Accommodation rights needed to be absolute, immediate, and as little constrained by cost as possible.

Unless you were an employer, this was immensely popular stuff—new benefits for all these nice people, maybe even for everyone, and the boss is paying! It also guaranteed a healthy docket for enforcers of the new laws and private lawyers, because the supply of possible accommodations is without end, even as employers resist demands that they see as expensive or disruptive. In 2014 the EEOC received 9,765 filings alleging lack of reasonable ADA accommodation, compared with 1,541 complaints of disability discrimination for hiring and 14,736 for discharge. Religion was a far less active area, with 582 filings for failure to extend accommodation, compared with 1,748 for discharge and 313 for hiring. Even so, religious discrimination has been a growth area at the EEOC, with filings more than doubling from 1997 to 2014, and its share of the overall commission docket nearly doubling from 2.1 to 4.0 percent, with a particularly sharp increase in the years 2004–2008.[41]

If most human resources managers experience disability accommodation as far more of a headache than religious accommodation, one reason lies in the way courts have interpreted the two statutes in starkly different fashions. One key term that appears in both areas of law—"undue hardship" to an employer—gets defined in almost comically opposite ways. In disability accommodation, courts routinely refuse to find undue hardship even when employers have been battered by the cost, disruption, and inconvenience of trying to accommodate a worker. In religious accommodation, by contrast, they follow a *de minimis* standard; even a little bit of employer cost, disruption, or inconvenience is undue.

The history of the Title VII religious accommodation requirement sheds light on this divergence. While the Civil Rights Act of 1964 said nothing on the topic of accommodation for employees' religious practices, the newly established EEOC three years later issued regulations proclaiming such a right as an implication of the law. But a

---

[41] EEOC, Enforcement and Litigation Statistics, available at http://www.eeoc.gov/eeoc/statistics/enforcement. For a recent survey of developments in religious accommodation, see J. Gregory Grisham & Robbin W. Hutton, Religious Accommodation in the Workplace: Current Trends Under Title VII, 15 Engage 60 (July 2014), available at http://www.fedsoc.org/publications/detail/religious-accommodation-in-the-workplace-current-trends-under-title-vii.

closely divided Supreme Court declined to go along, in the case of *Dewey v. Reynolds Metals* affirming a Sixth Circuit ruling that the terms of a union contract did not have to be set aside to accommodate a worker's Sabbath observance.[42] In 1972 Congress proceeded to introduce a new statutory right to accommodation, in an amendment offered by Democratic Sen. Jennings Randolph of West Virginia, himself a member of the Saturday-Sabbath-keeping Seventh Day Baptists. Curiously—and introducing an element of confusion whose echo can still be heard more than 40 years later in the *Abercrombie* case—Randolph inserted the relevant language not as a new section of prescriptions or prohibitions, as might seem natural, but as a change to the definition of religion itself, which he altered as follows:

> The term 'religion' includes all aspects of religious observance and practice, as well as belief, unless an employer demonstrates that he is unable to reasonably accommodate an employee's or prospective employee's religious observance or practice without undue hardship on the conduct of the employer's business.[43]

As one commentator observed, it was almost as if Congress was saying that if a religious observance or practice couldn't feasibly be accommodated in the workplace, it didn't really count as religion.[44]

The Randolph Amendment in its terse language left plenty of leeway for interpretation, and in two major cases that followed, the Court gave accommodation rights a narrow reading. In *TWA v. Hardison*, announcing the rule that still prevails today, it decided that undue hardship was reached when an employer's cost exceeded *de minimis* levels.[45] In *Ansonia Board of Education v. Philbrook*, it further found that so long as an employer had offered some reasonable accommodation that would permit the employee to work without

---

[42] Dewey v. Reynolds Metals Co., 402 U.S. 689 (1971).

[43] See, e.g., Sara S. Silbiger, Heaven Can Wait: Judicial Interpretation of Title VII's Religious Accommodation Requirement Since Trans World Airlines v. Hardison, 53 Fordham L. Rev. 839 (1985).

[44] See Andrew Little, Title VII and Religious Accommodation: An Evidentiary Approach To the Undue Hardship Standard Under Trans World Airlines v. Hardison, 21 Southern L. J. 225 (2011).

[45] Trans World Airlines, Inc. v. Hardison, 432 U.S. 63 (1977).

violating his beliefs, it did not have to engage in further exploration or agree to some other accommodation that might work better for the employee.[46]

No one doubted the ideological polarities in these cases: the support for a broader mandate of religious accommodation was coming from the Court's left wing. The dissenters in *Hardison* were Justices William Brennan and Thurgood Marshall, while in *Philbrook* they were Marshall and John Paul Stevens, Brennan having cast his vote with the conservatives.

Law school commentators criticized these rulings as too lenient toward employers, suggesting that a threshold of, say, "significant" difficulty or expense would be preferable to the *Hardison* standard, and that some obligation to follow through on an affirmative and interactive search for better accommodation would be preferable to *Philbrook's* "if some reasonable fix has been offered, call it a day" standard.[47] The EEOC, trying to make the best of it for plaintiffs, promoted a liberal position on many of the issues courts had not settled: for example, it sought to minimize customer and co-worker morale and upset as factors that might enter into undue hardship.

In 1994 Rep. Jerry Nadler (D-N.Y.) introduced the first version of the Workplace Religious Freedom Act (WRFA), a measure soon taken up and long championed in the Senate by Sen. John Kerry (D-Mass.) with support from liberal stalwarts like Sen. Ted Kennedy (D-Mass.) and later Sen. Hillary Rodham Clinton (D-N.Y.). The exact provisions of WRFA changed over the years, but the idea was to toughen accommodation burdens on employers, often in ways reminiscent of the ADA.[48] The version considered in 2004, for example, would have (1) obliged employers to make a wider range of accommodations having a "temporary or tangential impact on the [employee's] ability to perform" so-called "essential" job functions; (2) replaced the *de minimis*

---

[46] Ansonia Bd. of Educ. v. Philbrook, 479 U.S. 60 (1986).

[47] See, e.g., Dallan Flake, Bearing Burdens: Religious Accommodations That Adversely Affect Coworker Morale, 76 Ohio State L. J., 169 (2015), available at http://moritzlaw. osu.edu/students/groups/oslj/files/2015/07/10-Flake.pdf. See also, EEOC Religious Garb Guidance, *supra* note 27 ("Customer preference is not a defense to a claim of discrimination.").

[48] See also, Gregory M. Baxter, Note, Employers Beware: The Workplace Religious Freedom Act of 2000, 2 Rutgers J. L. & Religion 6 (2000) (analyzing the 2000 version), available at http://lawandreligion.com/sites/lawandreligion.com/files/Baxter.pdf.

cost standard with one of "significant difficulty and expense" taking into account the employer's size and number of facilities, so that larger employers would be expected to bend further; and (3) required that an accommodation "remove" the underlying conflict, a phrase with imprecise meaning but which was expected to stiffen the limp *Philbrook* standard. But WFRA was and is stoutly resisted by employer groups, and none of the bills have picked up enough support to pass.

The Parallel Track: *Employment Division* and RFRA

Meanwhile the groundwork was being laid for a controversy much better known in our own day, that over the Religious Freedom Restoration Act (RFRA). The Court's resistance to religious accommodation demands in the statutory Title VII environment of *Hardison* and *Philbrook* were advance tremors of a far bigger jolt to come, this time in First Amendment law itself. That earthquake came with *Employment Division v. Smith* in 1990, and it confirmed that the accommodationist zeal for which the Warren Court had been known was no more.[49] For 30 years, during the so-called *Sherbert/Yoder* era, the Court had construed the Free Exercise Clause to encompass broad rights of accommodation for religious belief and practice when they came into conflict with otherwise applicable law.[50] Writing for the majority in *Smith*, Justice Scalia rang down the curtain on this experiment; henceforth the Court would decline a broad constitutional role in heading off conflicts between religious conviction and legal duties, though it recognized Congress as having broad discretion to step into the gap to do so through legislation. The line-up of dissenters was familiar: Blackmun, Brennan, and Marshall.

Congress promptly took up the challenge: it passed RFRA by a unanimous House and near-unanimous Senate vote. The law, which was signed and took effect in 1993, pushed further than *Sherbert/Yoder* in one important respect: it required the government to use the least restrictive means when accommodating belief, a distant echo of the literature criticizing the *Philbrook* court for contenting itself with a bare minimum of accommodation. A minority of states proceeded

[49] Employment Div., Dept. of Human Resources of Oregon v. Smith, 494 U.S. 872 (1990). Another important precursor case was Estate of Thornton v. Caldor, 472 U.S. 703 (1985) (Connecticut law mandating that private employers grant Sabbath leave to employees violates Establishment Clause).

[50] Sherbert v. Verner, 374 U.S. 398 (1963); Wisconsin v. Yoder, 406 U.S. 205 (1972).

to enact individual "mini-RFRAs." At the federal level, at least, statutory RFRA now filled the crater where constitutional *Sherbert/Yoder* had late stood.[51]

Over the next 20 years, RFRA and its state equivalents were to change from a progressive enthusiasm (albeit one also widely supported by conservatives and centrists) to something drawing ardent support on the Right amid increasingly heated criticism from the Left. And yet this whole curious trajectory could have been observed earlier in the parallel, smaller-gauge politics of WRFA. The first signs must have seemed promising for supporters: prominent Republicans identified with their party's social-conservative wing, including future presidential candidates Sen. Rick Santorum (R-Pa.) and Rep. Bobby Jindal (R-La.), began speaking up enthusiastically for WRFA. At the same time, the coalition on the left for the bill began to show signs of fracturing. Matters came to a head in 2004 when the previously supportive American Civil Liberties Union declared that in its view the legislation needed to be rethought and rewritten. In a letter, the ACLU released an analysis of the 113 reported federal cases between 1977 (the *Hardison* year) and 2002 in which employees had lost Title VII religion cases on issues of either reasonable accommodation or undue hardship.[52] Of these, it said, 83 "involved the scheduling of religious holidays or the wearing of religious clothing or a beard." Those were not so controversial. However, of the other 30, it found many alarming. The plaintiffs included:

- employees who wished to chide co-workers or agency clients about lifestyles they saw as sinful, or proselytize retail customers, mental patients and prison inmates at their workplace;[53]

---

[51] See Marci A. Hamilton, The Establishment Clause During the 2004 Term: Big Cases, Little Movement, 2004–2005 Cato Sup. Ct. Rev. 159 (post-Smith developments); Richard W. Garnett & Joshua D. Dunlap, Taking Accommodation Seriously: Religious Freedom and the *O Centro* Case, 2005–2006 Cato Sup. Ct. Rev. 257, 264 ("[T]he doctrinal landscape—if not the results for litigants in actual cases—changed markedly" after *Smith*).

[52] Laura Murphy & Christopher Anders, ACLU Letter on the Harmful Effect of S. 893, The Workplace Religious Freedom Act, on Critical Personal and Civil Rights, ACLU, June 2, 2004, available at https://www.aclu.org/letter/aclu-letter-harmful-effect-s-893-workplace-religious-freedom-act-critical-personal-and-civil.

[53] Spratt v. County of Kent, 621 F. Supp. 594 (W.D. Mich. 1985), aff'd, 810 F.2d 203 (6th Cir. 1986) (prison inmates); Baz v. Walters, 782 F.2d 701 (7th Cir. 1986) (psychiatric patients); Chalmers v. Tulon Co. of Richmond, 101 F.3d 1012 (4th Cir. 1996) (co-

- two truck drivers and an emergency worker who asked to avoid overnight shifts spent in the company of women;[54]
- employees seeking to display symbols that they held to be of religious significance, but which co-workers found upsetting[55];
- police officers who asked to be excused from protecting abortion clinics;[56]
- a counselor who gave advice on relationship issues as part of an employee assistance counseling program, but believed it wrong to counsel gay employees on relationships.[57]

To make religious accommodation law more stringent across the board would be to tip some of these cases from losers to winners. While the ACLU said it would continue to support a scaled-down version of the bill to cover garb, grooming, and holidays issues, it opposed the broad forms of the bill it had previously supported. Social-conservative backers of WRFA, not surprisingly, took a different view. They saw some or many of the cases that bothered the ACLU as deserving sympathy or outright support.[58] In their view, adherents of conservative religious views were emerging as (in effect) a religious minority whose interests were stepped on by the dominant culture. The pharmacy employee who wished to ask co-workers to

workers); Knight v. Conn. Dep't of Public Health, 275 F.3d 156 (2nd Cir. 2001) (visiting nurse's clients); Anderson v. U.S.F. Logistics (IMC), Inc., 274 F.3d 470 (7th Cir. 2001) (clients).

[54] Virts v. Consolidated Freightways Corp. of Delaware, 285 F.3d 508 (6th Cir. 2002); Weber v. Roadway Express, Inc., 199 F.3d 270 (5th Cir. 2000); Miller v. Drennon, 1991 WL 325291 (D.S.C. 1991), aff'd, 966 F.2d 1443 (4th Cir. 1992) (emergency medical technician).

[55] Wilson v. U.S. West Commc'ns, 58 F.3d 1337 (8th Cir. 1995) (anti-abortion button); Kaushal v. Hyatt Regency Woodfield, 1999 WL 436585 (N.D. Ill. 1999) (swastika); Swartzentruber v. Gunite Corp., 99 F. Supp.2d 976 (N.D. Ind. 2000) (burning cross).

[56] Rodriguez v. City of Chicago, 156 F.3d 771 (7th Cir. 1998); Parrott v. District of Columbia, 1991 WL 126020 (D.D.C. 1991).

[57] Bruff v. N. Miss. Health Servs., Inc. 244 F.3d 495 (5th Cir. 2001), cert. denied 534 U.S. 952 (2001).

[58] While not all the case dismissals on the ACLU list were controversial in their outcome, many set out fact patterns that were to recur repeatedly in the years since then. See, for example, Peterson v. Hewlett-Packard Co., 358 F.3d 599, 602 (9th Cir. 2004) (employee's religious objections to employer's pro-gay messages). For more discussion of a number of cases on the ACLU list, see EEOC Informal Guidance Letter, Dec. 21, 2004, available at http://www.eeoc.gov/eeoc/foia/letters/2004/titlevii_religious_expression.html.

handle requests for contraception, or the office worker who wished to sit out pro-alternative-lifestyle sensitivity training, were not asking for anything more radical than those before them who refused to serve in the wartime military, recite the Pledge of Allegiance, or comply with official school-leaving ages. Now that it was their turn to ask for protection, why weren't they getting more help from those who had long spoken up for the practice of minority religions?

Those who follow Title VII issues had had at least 10 years' advance warning when, in 2014, the once-sleepy RFRA issue burst into furious headlines with *Hobby Lobby*, Arizona, and Indiana. And the same was true a few months later when some conservative governors announced that they would seek to recognize accommodation rights for county and other local clerks not to sign certificates for same-sex marriages.[59]

Conclusion: A Consensus Unlikely to Last

For almost as long as there has been an ideological spectrum, religious accommodations have tended to cut across it both ways. The Right tends to prize the role religion plays in society, yet also prizes the rule of law with its dispassionate application of neutral rules to all. And as regards Title VII in private employment, at least, each advance for obligatory accommodation represents a retreat for the principles of freedom of association and employment at will that undergird the liberty of the marketplace. Even in the government workplace, conservatives might have mixed feelings about widening the scope for litigation or giving public employees new ways of digging in against managers, as new rights sometimes do.

Progressives, for their part, have often spoken up for religious minorities scorned and misunderstood by American elites and majorities. Yet an equally durable strain of progressive thought finds democratic value in the equal application of law, and fears that public programs and standards will disintegrate if individual opt-out rights are provided too freely under the heading of conscience exemptions. Religion-based exceptions, unless accompanied by equal

[59] For a legal critique of the clerk exemptions, see Kara Loewentheil & Katherine Franke, Public Rights/Private Conscience Project Memorandum, Proposed Conscience or Religion-Based Exemption for Public Officials Authorized to Solemnize Marriages, (June 30, 2015), available at http://web.law.columbia.edu/sites/default/files/microsites/gender-sexuality/marriage_exemptions_memo_june_30.pdf.

rights of accommodation for strongly held secular scruples of conscience, also grant official elevation to religion over the secular—"gives them favored treatment," as Scalia noted in passing.[60]

EEOC v. Abercrombie & Fitch was the rare case in which an expansion of workplace religious accommodation managed to slip through without tripping these alarms. It seems unlikely that the next big case will be as uncontroversial.

[60] Abercrombie, 135 S. Ct. at 2034.

Silver Linings Playbook: "Disparate Impact" and the Fair Housing Act

Roger Clegg*

I. Introduction

In *Texas Department of Housing and Community Affairs v. Inclusive Communities Project ("Inclusive Communities")*,[1] the Supreme Court at last resolved the issue of whether "disparate impact" causes of action may be brought under the Fair Housing Act (FHA), which was first passed in 1968 and then substantially amended and expanded in 1988. In brief, disparate-impact cases result in liability if a defendant's actions—typically involving a selection criterion of some sort—have a disproportionate adverse effect on a racial or other group, even if the criterion was selected without discriminatory motive and is nondiscriminatory by its terms and in its application. By contrast, disparate-treatment cases, which are indisputably covered by the Act, are triggered when a defendant's actions are taken because the plaintiff is a member of such a racial or other group.

The issue was before the Court in 1988 and 2003.[2] Later, in the two terms preceding this year's decision, the Court granted review of petitions presenting this same question, but both cases settled at the eleventh hour.[3] It should be noted that the issue of whether a disparate-impact cause of action may be brought under a civil rights statute is

---

*Roger Clegg (Rice U., B.A., 1977; Yale Law School, J.D., 1981) is president and general counsel of the Center for Equal Opportunity. The center joined an amicus brief supporting petitioners in the case discussed in this article that was filed by the Pacific Legal Foundation and joined by the Cato Institute and several other organizations as well.

[1] 135 S. Ct. 2507 (2015).

[2] Huntington v. Huntington Branch, NAACP, 488 U.S. 15 (1988); City of Cuyahoga Falls v. Buckeye County Hope Fund, 538 U.S. 188 (2003).

[3] As noted in the first footnote of Justice Samuel Alito's dissent in *Inclusive Communities*, those cases were Gallagher v. Magner, 132 S. Ct. 548 (2011); and Township

---

a recurrent one for the Court; the question has been decided for Title VII of the 1964 Civil Rights Act (yes); Section 2 of the Voting Rights Act (no); and the Age Discrimination in Employment Act (yes).[4]

Justice Anthony Kennedy wrote the 5–4 majority opinion in *Inclusive Communities*, in which he was joined by Justices Ruth Bader Ginsburg, Stephen Breyer, Sonia Sotomayor, and Elena Kagan. Justice Samuel Alito's dissent was joined by the remaining justices; Justice Clarence Thomas also wrote a separate dissenting opinion, which focused on and criticized the origins of the disparate-impact approach in *Griggs v. Duke Power Co.*[5]

The Court's decision is disappointing. It fails to follow the clear language of the statute and will not only result in unfair liability for many defendants, but will encourage race-based decisionmaking in the housing area—exactly what the Fair Housing Act was meant to prohibit. The only silver linings are that Justice Kennedy's opinion itself recognizes these problems, and some of the language toward the end might be useful in stemming the worst abuses.

To elaborate: The question presented in this case was, "Are disparate-impact claims cognizable under the Fair Housing Act?" Under a disparate-impact claim, discriminatory motive is irrelevant: It need not be alleged or proved, and it doesn't even matter if the defendant proves that there was no actual disparate treatment. If a policy or procedure results in a disproportion of some sort—on the basis not only of race, color, or national origin but also (under the FHA) of religion, sex, or familial status (that is, having children)—then that's enough, even if the policy is nondiscriminatory by its terms, in its intent, and in its application. The defendant can prevail only by showing—to the satisfaction of a judge or jury who may know or care nothing of the defendant's needs—some degree of "necessity" for

---

of Mount Holly v. Mt. Holly Gardens, 133 S. Ct. 2824 (2013). See further discussion in Part II.B, *infra*.

[4] The Title VII and ADEA decisions are discussed below and in all three opinions in the case at hand. Mobile v. Bolden, 446 U.S. 55 (1980), determined as a practical matter that Section 2 of the Voting Rights Act prohibited only disparate treatment; that statute has since been amended, although the extent to which it now allows disparate-impact lawsuits is unresolved. See Roger Clegg & Hans A. von Spakovsky, "Disparate Impact" and Section 2 of the Voting Rights Act (Mar. 17, 2014), available at http://www.heritage.org/research/reports/2014/03/disparate-impact-and-section-2-of-the-voting-rights-act.

[5] 401 U.S. 424 (1971).

the policy. This numbers-driven, we-don't-much-care-about-your-reasons approach inevitably results in pushing potential defendants away from perfectly legitimate and race-neutral policies and toward race-based decisionmaking: again, just the opposite of what civil rights laws are supposed to do.

This article will begin by summarizing the various opinions in the case, and will then explain some of the problems with the disparate-impact approach, both generally and with respect to housing discrimination in particular. It will then discuss what might be done to address these problems in the future, through litigation and through legislation.

II. Summary of the Opinions

A. Majority Opinion

Majority opinions typically begin by laying out the facts of the case, noting the applicable statutes or other laws, and tracing the litigation's procedural history, and Justice Kennedy's opinion here is no exception. But then, and ominously for those hoping that he would ground his opinion in statutory text rather than junk social science, he adds a second section to the overture. In that section, he paints with a broader brush about the intractability and evil of housing segregation, citing the notoriously liberal Kerner Commission Report (formally, the "Report of the National Advisory Commission on Civil Disorders"). He concludes that, after the assassination of Dr. Martin Luther King Jr. in April 1968, and the ensuing "social unrest in the inner cities," "Congress responded by adopting the Kerner Commission's recommendation and passing the Fair Housing Act."[6]

---

[6] Inclusive Communities, 135 S. Ct. at 2516. Justice Kennedy also references the Kerner Commission in his conclusion, citing its "grim prophecy that '[o]ur Nation is moving toward two societies, one black, one white—separate and unequal.' The Court acknowledges the Fair Housing Act's continued role in moving the Nation toward a more integrated society." *Id.* at 2525–26. On the other hand, "At a 1998 lecture commemorating the 30th anniversary of the report, Stephan Thernstrom, a history professor at Harvard University, stated, 'Because the commission took for granted that the riots were the fault of white racism, it would have been awkward to have had to confront the question of why liberal Detroit blew up while Birmingham and other Southern cities—where conditions for blacks were infinitely worse—did not. Likewise, if the problem was white racism, why didn't the riots occur in the 1930s, when prevailing white racial attitudes were far more barbaric than they were in the 1960s?'" An Unfilled Prescription for Racial Equality, Bay State Banner (Feb. 28, 2008), available at http://www.baystate-banner.com/issues/2008/02/28/news/blackhistory02280890.htm.

Part II of Justice Kennedy's opinion resolves the question presented in the case, namely "whether, under a proper interpretation of the FHA, housing decisions with a disparate impact are prohibited."[7] But "[b]efore turning to the FHA," Kennedy thinks it first "necessary to consider two other antidiscrimination statutes that preceded it."[8] The two statutes are Title VII of the 1964 Civil Rights Act[9] and the Age Discrimination in Employment Act.[10] He proceeds to discuss them, the Court's decisions about them, and what those decisions mean for the current dispute. Turning, finally, to the language in the Fair Housing Act itself, Kennedy argues that Title VII and the ADEA and the Court's decisions about them somehow reveal a disparate-impact cause of action cloaked in the FHA's text.

Justice Kennedy then purports to adduce other evidence in favor of this interpretation of the FHA. He argues that, when the 1988 amendments were added, Congress was aware of the fact that "all nine Courts of Appeals to have addressed the question had concluded that the Fair Housing Act encompassed disparate-impact claims."[11] He notes that the 1988 amendments also "included three exemptions from liability that assume the existence of disparate-impact claims."[12] Finally, Kennedy asserts, "Recognition of disparate-impact claims is consistent with the FHA's central purpose,"[13] which he apparently thinks is about "zoning laws and other housing restrictions that function unfairly to exclude minorities from certain

---

[7] Inclusive Communities, 135 S. Ct. at 2516.

[8] Id.

[9] 42 U.S.C. §§ 2000e et seq. (2012).

[10] 29 U.S.C. §§ 621 et seq. (2012).

[11] Inclusive Communities, 135 S. Ct. at 2519.

[12] Id. at 2520. This claim had been discussed at the case's oral argument before the Court. See Transcript of Oral Argument at 9–10, Inclusive Communities, 135 S. Ct. 2507 (2015) (No. 13-1371), available at http://www.supremecourt.gov/oral_arguments/argument_transcripts/13-1371_g4ek.pdf. It is a dubious one, as the author explained in two posts on National Review Online. An Observation after the Disparate-Impact Oral Argument (Jan. 21, 2015), http://www.nationalreview.com/bench-memos/396883/observation-after-disparate-impact-oral-argument-today-roger-clegg; Three Short Trialogues on Disparate Impact and the Fair Housing Act (Feb. 2, 2015), http://www.nationalreview.com/bench-memos/397592/three-short-trialogues-disparate-impact-and-fair-housing-act-roger-clegg.

[13] Inclusive Communities, 135 S. Ct. at 2521.

neighborhoods without any sufficient justification. Suits targeting such practices reside at the heartland of disparate-impact liability."[14]

So far, so bad, but these are all arguments that one would expect to find in an opinion upholding the disparate-impact approach under the FHA. At this point, however, Justice Kennedy shifts gears, and provides some welcome relief that was not so predictable in a decision in plaintiff's favor. As I summarize this part of his opinion, I will go into a fair amount of detail and quote more heavily, since— as I discuss later—what Justice Kennedy says here will be of use to future litigants who want to limit the damage done by disparate-impact lawsuits.

In this latter part of the opinion, Justice Kennedy begins by noting "the serious constitutional questions that might arise under the FHA" if "liability were imposed solely on the basis of a statistical disparity." After all, it could take a race-conscious measure to prevent, or a race-conscious remedy to mitigate, a disparate racial impact; yet public actors are constitutionally mandated not to deny to any person the equal protection of the laws. In part to address that dilemma, Justice Kennedy would lessen the burden on defendants to rebut disparate-impact claims.

Defendants need not "reorder their priorities"; the problem is said to be with "arbitrarily" creating a disparate impact.[15] On remand, wrote Justice Kennedy, the lawsuit "may be seen simply as an attempt to second-guess which of two reasonable approaches a housing authority should follow"; again, it should be stressed that "reasonable" is a low bar, compared to the "necessity" standard that a plaintiff's lawyer would prefer.[16] Defendants must be given "leeway to state and explain the valid interest"—that word "valid" again— "served by their policies."[17]

In the disparate-impact area, the definition of the defendant's rebuttal burden is important—rather like determining the level of "scrutiny" that courts will apply in reviewing the constitutionality of a statute. Defendants favor "rational basis" scrutiny, a low bar demanding only a "valid" or "legitimate" justification for legislation.

[14] *Id.* at 2521–22.

[15] *Id.*

[16] *Id.*

[17] *Id.*

Plaintiffs prefer "strict" scrutiny, which requires that the legislation be "essential" or at least "necessary."

Justice Kennedy says that the "business necessity" standard used in employment cases is "analogous" to what he has in mind, but he then seems to mix standards when he refers to a policy that is "necessary to achieve a valid interest." Worse, he says that this is something that the defendant must "prove."[18] To complete the muddle, Justice Kennedy ends the analogizing by concluding, "To be sure, the Title VII framework may not transfer exactly to the fair-housing context, but the comparison suffices for present purposes."[19] Present purposes?

Leaving the employment analogy behind, the opinion next alludes to a problem that Chief Justice Roberts identified at oral argument, namely that it seems unfair to subject defendants to disparate-impact lawsuits when they have to choose between two alternatives and either one could credibly be claimed to create a disparate impact.[20]

But then, in perhaps the most opinion's most interesting twist, Justice Kennedy asserts that plaintiffs must "point to a defendant's policy or policies causing that [alleged] disparity." "A robust causality requirement ensures that '[r]acial imbalance . . . does not, without more, establish a prima facie case of disparate impact' and thus protects defendants from being held liable for racial disparities they did not create."[21] Without this limit, he says, the pressure for racial quotas would raise "serious constitutional questions."[22] But it is one thing—albeit a welcome thing—to require a specific policy to be identified as causing the disparate impact; yet suggesting that a racial imbalance is not enough to make out a prima facie case arguably goes further than that, and saying that a defendant cannot be held liable for disparities he didn't create could, if taken to its logical conclusion, dramatically change litigation in this area. For example, Duke Power Co. did not create the racial disparities in high-school

[18] As discussed at note 76, *infra*, the Court, citing Fed. R. Evid. 301, rejected such burden-shifting under Title VII; Congress then reversed that.

[19] *Id.* at 2523.

[20] See *id.*; Transcript of Oral Argument, *supra* note 12, at 39–45. Note that Justice Kennedy himself seemed to agree with Chief Justice Roberts on this point. *Id.* at 44.

[21] Inclusive Communities, 135 S. Ct. at 2523 (citing Wards Cove Packing Co. v. Atonio, 490 U.S. 642, 653 (1989)).

[22] *Id.*

graduation rates or test-score performances at issue in *Griggs,* but it was found liable nonetheless.

Then Justice Kennedy once more suggests that the plaintiff's case may be doomed on remand, referring again to the "serious constitutional concerns" that pushing defendants to adopt racial quotas would raise.[23] More broadly, "Courts should avoid interpreting disparate-impact liability to be so expansive as to inject racial considerations into every housing decision."[24]

Justice Kennedy adds: "The limitations on disparate-impact liability discussed here are also necessary to protect potential defendants against abusive disparate-impact claims."[25] It would be a bad thing if the threat of such lawsuits discouraged low-income housing or other "legitimate objectives"—again, a low bar compared to "necessity."[26] The opinion reiterates that "valid" priorities set by defendants, public or private, are legal. The FHA should target those policies devoted "solely" to creating "artificial, arbitrary, and unnecessary barriers" that could "set our nation back in its quest to reduce the salience of race in our social and economic system."[27] "[R]emedial orders must be consistent with the Constitution," should be aimed at discrimination that is "arbitrar[y]" and "invidious[]," and should be as "race-neutral" as possible.[28] Conversely, "[r]emedial orders that impose racial targets or quotas might raise more difficult constitutional questions."[29]

It's noteworthy, by the way, that Justice Kennedy refers to Justice Alito's "well-stated principal dissenting opinion in this case."[30] Compared to the heated exchanges one typically observes between justices in high-stakes civil rights cases, this salute is remarkable, and suggests that Kennedy found the dissent's arguments to be well-taken.

---

[23] *Id.*
[24] *Id.* at 2524.
[25] *Id.*
[26] *Id.*
[27] *Id.* (quoting Griggs, 401 U.S. at 431) (internal quotation marks omitted).
[28] *Id.*
[29] *Id.*
[30] *Id.*

Finally, Justice Kennedy indulges himself by citing the point he made in an earlier case—*Parents Involved in Community Schools v. Seattle School Dist. No. 1*—that it's all right to use "race-neutral" methods to "foster diversity and combat racial isolation."[31] Just how a policy that aims at a particular racial result can be said to be "race-neutral" is a matter that Justice Kennedy leaves unaddressed; presumably the answer lies in whether the result is, in Justice Kennedy's eyes, a desirable one. Thus, a racist but neutrally worded "grandfather clause" in voting law would still have to go,[32] but politically correct siting of low-income housing is fine.

B. Dissenting Opinions

Much of Justice Alito's dissent—which is about one-and-a-half times longer than the majority opinion—will be cited later in my own, broader critique of the disparate-impact approach, so I give only a brief summary of it here. He begins with an attention-grabbing sentence: "No one wants to live in a rat's nest."[33] That's a reference to an earlier case, presenting the same issue being decided here, involving a claim by slumlords that the City of St. Paul's stepped up enforcement of health and safety ordinances would have a "disparate impact" on racial minorities because of the resulting rent increases for them. As Justice Alito says in ending his overture, "Something has gone badly awry when a city can't even make slumlords kill rats without fear of a lawsuit."[34]

Having gotten the reader's attention, Justice Alito in Part I discusses why the FHA's prohibitions against discrimination are, as a textual matter, aimed only at disparate treatment. Part II continues, "The circumstances in which the FHA was enacted only confirm what the text says."[35] Part III focuses on the 1988 amendments to the FHA and how they, in particular, contain nothing that supports a disparate-impact approach to its enforcement, and Part IV distinguishes *Griggs* and subsequent Court decisions from this case. The

---

[31] *Id.* at 2525 (citing Parents Involved, 551 U.S. 701, 789 (2007) (Kennedy, J., concurring in part and concurring in the judgment).

[32] See, e.g., Guinn v. United States, 238 U.S. 347 (1915).

[33] Inclusive Communities, 135 S. Ct. at 2532 (Alito, J., dissenting).

[34] *Id.*

[35] *Id.* at 2537.

practical problems with extending the disparate-impact approach from employment to the housing area are discussed in Part V, and Part VI concludes the dissent by rejecting the majority's "pretext," "federalism," and "purpose" arguments.

Justice Thomas joins Justice Alito's dissent "in full" but writes separately "to point out that the foundation on which the Court builds its latest disparate-impact regime—*Griggs v. Duke Power Co.*—is made of sand."[36] In Part I of his dissent, Justice Thomas analyzes the text of Title VII of the 1964 Civil Rights Act, and, finding no support for the disparate-impact approach there, then explains how the real author of the approach was not Congress but the federal bureaucrats at the Equal Employment Opportunity Commission (which Justice Thomas chaired for a time, from 1982 to 1990—well after that particular bit of mischief had been completed and become entrenched). In Part II, he discusses why, statutory text aside, it makes no sense to equate racial imbalances with racial discrimination, since they can have all kinds of other causes and, indeed, "do not always disfavor minorities."[37] Without a plausible remedial justification, there is no justification at all, since "'racial balancing' by state actors is 'patently unconstitutional.'"[38] And, in Part III, Justice Thomas laments that the Court has spread its error in *Griggs* for Title VII first to the Age Discrimination in Employment Act and, now, to the Fair Housing Act, where it will have unintended and unfortunate consequences.

III. Problems with the Disparate-Impact Approach

A. In General[39]

As noted, under a disparate-impact claim of discrimination, discriminatory motive is irrelevant: It need not be alleged or proved, and it doesn't even matter if the defendant proves that there was no discriminatory motive. If a policy or procedure results in a

[36] *Id.* at 2526 (Thomas, J., dissenting).

[37] *Id.* at 2530.

[38] *Id.* (citation omitted).

[39] The author has critiqued the disparate-impact approach at length in a monograph, Disparate Impact in the Private Sector: A Theory Going Haywire (Dec. 2001), available at https://www.aei.org/wp-content/uploads/2011/10/Briefly-Disparate-Impact.pdf. That monograph drew from his earlier article, The Bad Law of "Disparate Impact," 138 Public Interest 79 (Winter 2000), available at http://www.nationalaffairs.com/doclib/20080709_20001386thebadlawofdisparateimpactrogerclegg.pdf.

disproportion of some sort, then that's enough, even if the policy is nondiscriminatory by its terms, in its intent, and in its application. The defendant can prevail only by showing—to the satisfaction of a judge or jury who may know or care nothing of the defendant's needs—some degree of "necessity" for the policy.

Now, suppose that you are a potential defendant and that you have some nondiscriminatory selection criterion that has helped you run your business well, but the criterion has a disparate impact on some group. You know you are vulnerable to a lawsuit, which you may or may not win, depending on the judge or jury you draw, and you know that lawsuits are expensive, win or lose. If you don't want to get sued—and who does?—the potential of a disparate-impact lawsuit is going to push you to do one of several things, none of which is good. You might keep the criterion but apply it in a way that gets your numbers right—in other words, you will adopt surreptitious quotas. Or you might get rid of the criterion altogether, and just accept the fact that your business will not be run quite as well as it could be. Or you might decide to replace the old criterion with a new one, which you will choose and/or apply in a race-conscious way. You might, that is, now choose a criterion because of the racial outcomes that will result, or choose some criterion that can be applied in a biased way so that the resulting racial double standard will ensure that the numbers come out right. No matter what, you are no longer using the criterion you freely chose because you thought it to be the best, but are instead weighing race—directly or indirectly—in what you do.

In other words, we're supposed to stop judging people by the content of their character, and start judging them by the color of their skin. In addition to this moral dilemma, there is this overwhelming practical one: There is probably *no* selection or sorting criterion that doesn't have a disparate impact on some group or subgroup.

And here's the most fundamental point of all: If a business, agency, or school has standards for hiring, promoting, admissions, or offering a mortgage that aren't being met by individuals in some racial or ethnic groups, there are three things that can be done. First, the standards can be relaxed for those groups. That's what racial preferences do. Second, the government or aggrieved private party can attack the standards themselves. That's what the disparate-impact approach to enforcement does. Third, one can examine the underlying reason *why* a disproportionate number of individuals in some groups aren't meeting the standards—such as failing public schools or being born out of wedlock—and do something about *that*. But this option holds little interest on the political left.

Speaking of which, the Obama administration has made no secret of its love for disparate-impact civil rights enforcement, and has been aggressive in applying it to every imaginable situation. In employment, for example, the government complains if fire or police departments administer physical or written tests that have politically incorrect results,[40] or if companies use criminal background checks;[41] in voting, it objects if voter ID is required;[42] in education, it is hostile to school discipline policies if they have a disproportionate racial or ethnic result;[43] it has even insisted on drawing distinctions between acceptable and unacceptable pollution, depending on the skin color and national origin of those affected by the pollution.[44] The disparate-impact approach is also employed to require the use of a foreign language—on driver's license exams, for example—on the theory that using only English might have a disproportionate effect on the basis of national origin.[45] And it has been used to pressure banks with regard to their lending requirements,[46] even though

[40] See, e.g., Roger Clegg, The Obama Administration Sues the Jacksonville Fire Department, National Review Online (Apr. 23, 2012), http://www.nationalreview.com/corner/296812/obama-administration-sues-jacksonville-fire-department-roger-clegg.

[41] See, e.g., Roger Clegg, EEOC Opposes Criminal Background Checks, National Review Online (June 13, 2013), http://www.nationalreview.com/corner/351011/eeoc-opposes-criminal-background-checks-roger-clegg.

[42] See, e.g., John Fund & Hans von Spakovsky, Democrats Losing Long War against Voter ID, Washington Examiner (Oct. 6, 2014), http://www.washingtonexaminer.com/democrats-losing-long-war-against-voter-id/article/2554195.

[43] See, e.g., Roger Clegg, How the Obama DOJ's School-Discipline 'Guidance' Will Hurt Well-Behaved Poor Kids, National Review Online (Jan. 8, 2014), http://www.nationalreview.com/corner/367901/how-obama-dojs-school-discipline-guidance-will-hurt-well-behaved-poor-kids-roger-clegg.

[44] See, e.g., Roger Clegg, Make Sure Your Pollution Is Racially Fair, National Review Online (May 13, 2015), http://www.nationalreview.com/corner/418327/make-sure-your-pollution-racially-fair-roger-clegg.

[45] See, e.g., Alexander v. Sandoval, 532 U.S. 275 (2001).

[46] See, e.g., Ari Karen, How Disparate Impact Ruling Affects Lenders' Daily Operations, National Mortgage News (July 6, 2015), http://www.nationalmortgagenews.

many believe this to have been a contributing cause of the mortgage meltdown and the following recession.

B. *Under the Fair Housing Act in Particular*[47]

While the points that will be made in this section obviously did not carry the day with the Supreme Court, they are useful as part of an analysis of Justice Kennedy's opinion—and, more important, because many of the points made here can still be made in future cases involving the use of disparate impact in other areas.

1. Text

Disparate-impact claims may now be brought under the Fair Housing Act, which applies not only to race, color, or national origin, but also to religion, sex, or familial status (that is, having children). This approach is flatly inconsistent with the Act's text. The text uses not only the phrase "because of" race but also "on account of" and "based on."[48] All of these phrases are naturally read to require a showing of motive or intent—that is, disparate treatment. The phrase "on account of" also appears in a section of the Act that bans coercion and intimidation of those exercising fair-housing rights, and intent is clearly implied there. The "because of" and "on account of" language also is used to delineate certain fair-housing violations as crimes, and criminal prosecutions cannot be based on a disparate-impact theory.[49] A construction of the Fair Housing Act that interprets a phrase one way in one section and another way elsewhere is implausible.

The disparate-impact approach renders superfluous many of those provisions in the statute regarding the disabled. For instance, the failure to make or allow "reasonable modifications" and "reasonable

---

com/news/regulation/how-disparate-impact-ruling-affects-lenders-daily-operations-1055261-1.html.

[47] The National Association of Mutual Insurance Companies submitted excellent testimony at congressional hearings on this issue in November 2013. A General Overview of Disparate Impact Theory: Hearing before the Subcomm. on Oversight & Investigations, House Comm. on Fin. Servs., 113th Cong. 110–33 (2013), available at http://www.gpo.gov/fdsys/pkg/CHRG-113hhrg86686/pdf/CHRG-113hhrg86686.pdf.

[48] See 42 U.S.C. §§ 3604, 3631 (2012).

[49] Justice Alito's dissent makes these points. Inclusive Communities, 135 S. Ct. at 2533–37 (Alito, J., dissenting).

accommodations" could have been attacked under a disparate-impact theory without those provisions.

The federal government's brief stressed three provisos—which, it was argued, were aimed at specific kinds of possible disparate-impact causes of action—to suggest that any other disparate-impact cause of action must be permissible. The three provisos specified that occupancy limits for dwellings were permissible, that conduct against people because they had convictions for the illegal manufacture and distribution of illegal drugs is not prohibited by the statute, and that real-estate appraisals may take into consideration factors other than race, color, national origin, etc. But in the first two instances the nonprotected characteristics are close enough to protected characteristics that Congress likely wanted to spell out what was and wasn't protected a bit more. That is, drug crimes—which were especially unpopular when this proviso was enacted, another explanation for why politicians might have found it attractive to go on record against them—get close to the line of disability, since addiction is often viewed as a disability; likewise, occupancy limits get close to the line prohibiting discrimination on the basis of familial status. As for the exemption for real-estate appraisals, perhaps the appraiser lobby was really effective—that sort of thing happens sometimes, which is why good lobbyists are well-paid. In all events, according to the Supreme Court's interpretation of the statute, now anyone can be liable under a disparate-impact cause of action except for real-estate appraisers—and what, exactly, is the logic in that? [50]

2. History

If there is no textual support for a disparate-impact cause of action in the original act or its 1988 amendments, and since, as Justice Alito noted, the act's history points in the other direction as well, the remaining argument to support disparate impact in fair housing law is that many lower courts had recognized a disparate-impact cause of action under the original 1968 version of the Act. Congress thus implicitly endorsed the approach when it reenacted the statute in 1988 with full knowledge of those decisions.[51]

[50] The three provisos are discussed at greater length in the sources cited at note 12, *supra*. Justice Alito's dissent also discusses them. *Id.* at 2541.

[51] See, e.g., *id.* at 2537, 2540–41.

But, as Justice Alito also pointed out, Congress likewise knew that the Supreme Court had not resolved this question.[52] During the summer of 1988, while the amendments were still before Congress, the Justice Department was arguing to the Supreme Court that it ought to grant certiorari in a Second Circuit case and rule against a disparate-impact approach. In other words, Congress could hardly be said to have been endorsing settled case law by passing the 1988 legislation, because no settled case law existed.

3. Deference

During the course of this litigation, the Department of Housing and Urban Development (HUD) did conveniently mint new regulations that endorse the disparate-impact approach, and the government argued that the Court should defer to the agency's interpretation of the statute. But, as Justice Alito's dissent discusses, there are very good reasons why these regulations are entitled to little deference. It is interesting, by the way, that the majority opinion does not give such deference as a reason for its decision.

First and foremost, the meaning of the statute is clear: only actual discrimination—"disparate treatment"—is banned. Further, the Fair Housing Act has been on the books since 1968, and during that time the executive branch has sometimes endorsed the disparate-impact approach and sometimes not. For example, President Reagan explicitly rejected the approach in signing the 1988 amendments to the Act,[53] and his Justice Department argued against it in a brief to the Supreme Court; the Bushes didn't think much of it, either. The Obama administration, on the other hand, was attempting to game the system here; it orchestrated a rather shady deal with the City of St. Paul to get it to withdraw an earlier term's petition for writ of certiorari that had been granted (the case had been fully briefed and was about to be argued), and meanwhile worked on promulgating new regulations. "We were afraid we might lose disparate impact in the Supreme Court because there wasn't a regulation," said Sara Pratt, a HUD official.[54]

---

[52] *Id.* at 2538–39.

[53] This is noted in Justice Alito's dissent. *Id.* at 2540–41.

[54] The shady circumstances were noted in both dissents. See *id.* at 2529 n.4, 2543 n.8; see also Mary Kissel, HUD's Shady St. Paul Dealings, Wall St. J. (Oct. 31, 2012), avail-

In any event, the principle of deference is trumped in this case by the "constitutional-doubt canon," as Justice Scalia calls this long-honored principle in his book *Reading Law: The Interpretation of Legal Texts*.[55] The Supreme Court has repeatedly acknowledged—and that includes all nine justices in this case—that a statute mandating the disparate-impact approach also can encourage race-conscious decisionmaking; this of course raises serious constitutional issues. (Note that the racial classifications that the approach would require in the FHA are more constitutionally problematic than, say, the age classifications that the Court has accepted under the Age Discrimination in Employment Act.) The approach raises further constitutional problems here by altering the state-federal balance in far-reaching ways.[56] For example, it renders race-neutral state rules—such as rules for preserving order in public-housing projects—suspect. The approach will also result in federal micromanagement of insurance practices, which is at odds with the McCarran-Ferguson Act—a point emphasized in a recent federal district court decision striking down the HUD regulations.[57]

4. Coherence

One would also expect that, if a statute contemplates use of the disparate-impact approach, it would answer some fundamental questions like how to measure the kind and degree of disparate impact that is required and what sort of rebuttal is needed.[58] But there's none of that. What's more, the resulting problems are myriad and severe.

---

able at http://www.wsj.com/articles/SB10001424052970203707604578090581653496960; NAMIC testimony, *supra* note 47, at 122, 124.

[55] "A statute should be interpreted in a way that avoids placing its constitutionality in doubt." Antonin Scalia & Bryan Garner, Reading Law: The Interpretation of Legal Texts 247–51 (2012).

[56] See Roger Clegg & Ralph W. Kasarda, Take the *Mt. Holly* Case, National Review Online (June 7, 2013), http://www.nationalreview.com/bench-memos/350506/take-mt-holly-case-roger-clegg-ralph-w-kasarda.

[57] American Insurance Ass'n v. HUD, No. 13-00966 (RJL), 2014 WL 5802283 (D.D.C. Nov. 7, 2014).

[58] One of the amicus briefs filed in the case focused on the frequent misuse of statistics in disparate-impact cases. See Brief Amicus Curiae of James P. Scanlan, Inclusive Communities, 135 S. Ct. 2507 (2015) (No. 13-1371).

For example, what should decisionmakers do if a practice has a disparate impact in one location but not in another? It is astonishing to interpret a national civil rights statute in a way that makes conduct in one city illegal while allowing exactly the same conduct in another city, just because of the different racial makeup of the two cities. Or suppose the impact ebbs and flows over time? And what should landlords do if a policy (for instance, excluding violent felons as tenants) has an unfavorable disparate impact on *potential* tenants of a particular race, but is welcomed by the *incumbent* tenants who are predominately of that same race?

And what if a practice is favorable for some racial minority groups (say, Asian Americans) but not for others (say, Latinos)—and, what's more, the opposite is at the same time true for some minority *sub*groups (e.g., the practice is unfavorable for Hmong but favorable for Asian Americans more broadly)? Is there any way that a potential defendant could know that a policy will have a disparate impact on the basis of, say, religion (e.g., it turns out to favor most Jews over most Muslims)—and, here again, what if that policy's disparate impact gets more complicated the more one delves into it (Shiites do well with it compared to Hasidim)? And remember, also, that "majority" groups—whites and men and Christians, for example—must be able to bring these lawsuits, too, or you've added an even greater equal-protection problem.

Thus, for example, in the mortgage lending context: (a) a foreclosure policy may have no disparate impact on a particular group in pre-recession 2006, but a severe one in 2009; (b) an income requirement may have no disparate impact on Latinos in Nashville but a severe one in Denver; and (c) the use of, say, credit scoring may have a disparate impact on Latinos but not Asians, even if there's no disparate impact on Cubans but a severe one on the Hmong. Geographic disparities are especially problematic: Companies with identical policies in different locations could have very different liability risks, or the same company might be liable in one city but not in the other, but only if city-by-city data control rather than aggregate statistics.

There's an even more fundamental problem, noted by Chief Justice John Roberts at oral argument[59] and in both the majority opinion[60]

---

[59] See note 20, *supra*.

[60] Inclusive Communities, 135 S. Ct. at 2523.

and Justice Alito's dissent[61]: It is often hard to say whether the impact a practice has on a group is adverse or not. In fact, all three cases that the Court has taken recently illustrate this. In *Magner v. Gallagher*, was it bad for African Americans that landlords who disproportionately rented to blacks were being cited for violating safety and health code requirements? In *Mount Holly v. Mount Holly Gardens Citizens in Action*, was the urban renewal there bad for African Americans?

And in the present case, is it bad for African Americans that low-income housing is being disproportionately located in black areas? Poor black people might prefer to have housing opportunities near where they already live rather than far away, and they could complain about the disparate impact of deliberately changing the system so that they had fewer such opportunities. Yes, social engineers might prefer that blacks relocate to white areas, but that goal of greater integration might also be met in some cities or counties by encouraging non-blacks (not just whites, but also Latinos and Asians) to live in black areas.[62]

These problems make it difficult to decide not only whether there is a disparate impact in the first place, but also how to weigh properly the defendant's rebuttal, which in the public housing context—versus, say, employment—will often involve balancing myriad and hard-to-quantify interests. That is, it is relatively straightforward to ask an employer how a selection criterion will help hire more productive employees. But the reason for a particular zoning decision, for example, might involve all kinds of considerations: health, safety, aesthetics, traffic, money, nonracial politics, you name it.[63]

Two final points. First, it's frequently asserted that we must allow "disparate impact" causes of action because actual discrimination—disparate treatment—is difficult to prove. Indeed, this is

[61] *Id.* at 2548–49 (Alito, J., dissenting).

[62] Soon after the oral argument before the Court, the chairman of another Texas organization—who appears to be just as committed to helping racial minorities and is also one of the case's plaintiffs—published an op-ed complaining that what's needed is more low-income housing in minority areas, not less. Richard Knight, Supreme Court Case Could Deprive Areas of Needed Low-Income Housing Credits, Dallas Morning News (Feb. 9, 2015), available at http://www.dallasnews.com/opinion/latest-columns/20150209-richard-knight-supreme-court-case-could-deprive-areas-of-needed-low-income-housing-credits.ece.

[63] Justice Alito makes a similar point in his dissent. 135 S. Ct. at 2549–50 (Alito, J., dissenting).

the principal justification for the disparate-impact approach.[64] But this is simply not true: The overwhelming majority of housing cases brought and won by the federal government are disparate-treatment cases, as anyone who reads the Department of Justice's press releases every day (as we do at the Center for Equal Opportunity) can attest. Within a month of the Court's decision, the Obama administration posted press releases about successful disparate-treatment housing cases—one involving "testers" (a particularly easy and available way to prove housing discrimination) and the other involving a defendant who had actually placed ads indicating illegal preferences.[65] And Justice Alito's dissent notes, correctly, "Disparate impact can be *evidence* of disparate treatment."[66]

Relatedly, many on the other side argue that you need the disparate-impact approach in order to go after segregated housing patterns. These arguments, indeed, may have carried the day with Justice Kennedy.[67] But of course that's not true if the segregation stems from actual discrimination, proof of which can be reinforced by adducing the same sort of statistical evidence that is used in a disparate-impact case. But if there's no actual discrimination, then using the disparate-impact approach raises all the usual problems noted above. For example, how much racial balancing is to be required? What if the reasons for the racial imbalance reflect voluntary decisions or economic realities? What sort of remedies will be required (like deliberate assignments on the basis of race), and what if those remedies end up hurting people (including minorities) on

---

[64] It's odd for the government to argue for redefining an offense to make it easier to prove. It's as if the government were to say that, because it is hard for us to prove arson, we are going to make it a crime if you allow a building you own to burn down—even if you can prove that the building burned down by accident—since that way all we have to prove is that you owned the building and it did burn down, and that's easy.

[65] See Press Release, Dep't of Justice, Justice Department Obtains $251,500 Settlement in Housing Discrimination Lawsuit Against Effingham, Illinois, Landlord (July 15, 2015), http://www.justice.gov/opa/pr/justice-department-obtains-251500-settlement-housing-discrimination-lawsuit-against-effingham; Press Release, Dep't of Justice, Justice Department Sues Nevada Housing Provider for Discriminating Against Families with Children (July 10, 2015), http://www.justice.gov/opa/pr/justice-department-sues-nevada-housing-provider-discriminating-against-families-children.

[66] Inclusive Communities, 135 S. Ct. at 2550 (Alito, J., dissenting) (emphasis in original).

[67] Justice Alito addresses these arguments at the end of his dissent. *Id.* at 2550–51.

the basis of race? And so on. Finally, if racial imbalances in housing patterns are a result of voluntary choices by individuals, then it's unclear why the government needs to fix that situation.

IV. Going Forward

A. Litigation

While the Supreme Court's ruling here is misguided, potential litigants should not lose sight of this counterintuitive fact: The law is actually better now than it was before Justice Kennedy wrote the opinion.

This is true partly because the bar was so low. All the courts of appeals to entertain this issue had adopted this approach, too, and the Obama administration and its allies in the civil rights establishment were already interpreting the law this way. So things could not have gotten a lot worse, no matter what the Court had done.

It is also true, however, that the law is now better because Justice Kennedy's opinion recognizes that the disparate-impact approach can lead to very bad results. As the summary of the second part of the opinion above sets out, the Court has now set some limits on the law that will be useful. For example, Kennedy warns the lower courts against "second-guess[ing]" the nondiscriminatory reasons for challenged policies, requires a "robust causality requirement" rather than relying simply on racial disproportions, recognizes that "racial quotas" and "racial considerations" and "abusive . . . claims" can result from threatened and actual lawsuits, and cautions that any "remedial orders must be consistent with the Constitution."[68] He all but says that he expects the plaintiffs to lose in this case. He even calls Justice Alito's dissent, which of course makes similar points, "well-stated."[69]

Given that the Court was unanimous, then, in recognizing the constitutional problems and bad policy results that can arise from the disparate-impact approach, litigators should continue to press courts to reject or at least limit the approach. For example, the door is still open for courts to reject disparate impact under the Equal

[68] See *id*. at 2522–24.
[69] *Id*. at 2524.

Credit Opportunity Act,[70] to limit it under Section 2 of the Voting Rights Act,[71] and to strike down disparate-impact regulations that have been promulgated under Title VI of the 1964 Civil Rights Act.[72] Those regulations have been used, for example, to challenge school discipline, policing policies, and English-language requirements where they have a disproportionate effect on this-or-that racial or ethnic group.

Note that the approach that Justice Kennedy took in writing the majority opinion here is reminiscent of two employment discrimination cases decided in back-to-back terms in the late 1980s: *Watson v. Fort Worth Bank & Trust*[73] (in which Justice Kennedy did not participate) and *Wards Cove Packing Co. v. Atonio*[74] (in which he did). In *Watson*, the Court also decided to apply the disparate-impact approach to a new area—subjective employment practices—but a plurality then felt obliged to set out some limits on how that approach ought to be implemented, in order to avoid its abuse. A year later, in *Wards Cove*—in which Justice Kennedy joined Justice White's opinion for the Court—a majority of the justices then endorsed those limitations.

The limitations in Justice Kennedy's opinion now are similar to those laid out in *Watson* and, especially, *Wards Cove*; they are also what one would expect, given the nature of disparate-impact lawsuits and the potential abuse of them.[75] To begin with, simply point-

---

[70] See, e.g., Buckley Sander LLP, Disparate Impact Under FHA and ECOA: A Theory Without a Statutory Basis (July 13, 2012), available at http://www.buckleysandler.com/uploads/36/doc/disparateimpactwhitepaper.pdf; Buckley Sander LLP, Disparate Impact under the Equal Credit Opportunity Act after Inclusive Communities (June 29, 2015), available at http://www.lexology.com/library/detail.aspx?g=d472a830-c597-4da2-8ce8-801154360359.

[71] See, e.g., Roger Clegg & Hans A. von Spakovsky, "Disparate Impact" and Section 2 of the Voting Rights Act (Mar. 17, 2014), available at http://www.heritage.org/research/reports/2014/03/disparate-impact-and-section-2-of-the-voting-rights-act.

[72] The legal problems with Title VI regulations using a disparate-impact standard are set out in Letter from Roger Clegg & Edward Blum to Merrily Friedlander (Feb. 14, 2002), available at http://www.ceousa.org/attachments/article/836/bilingual.comment.pdf.

[73] 487 U.S. 977 (1988).

[74] 490 U.S. 642 (1989).

[75] In employment cases, the courts have also discussed a surrebuttal stage, where the plaintiffs can prevail if they can show that, while the defendant's use of the challenged criterion is justified, there is some other criterion that will serve the defendant's interests just as well and with less of a disparate impact. See, e.g., Wards Cove, 490

ing to raw statistical disparities ought not to be enough if the law is to be consistent with addressing actual discrimination and discouraging racial quotas. There must be "causation"—that is, a link must be shown between a particular challenged practice and the racially disproportionate results. Second, the defendant must have an opportunity to show that, even if challenged practice does lead to a disparity, its valid justifications mean that the practice should be allowed to stand. Defendants will want to argue, of course, that the justifications need not be a matter of dire necessity, but simply pursuant to a legitimate, nondiscriminatory interest. A third important element is whether the defendant's burden here is one of *production* or actual *proof*. The general rule in civil litigation is the former, as indicated in Federal Rule of Evidence 301, and defendants should press for that rule.[76] Justice Kennedy's opinion, while disappointing, has at least left the door open to defendants to try to make good case law on all three points.[77]

U.S. at 660–61; see also 42 U.S.C. § 2000e-2(k)(1)(A)(ii) (2012). This is dubious in the employment context (for one thing, it will always be the case that a criterion can be tweaked in some minor way that will improve the employer's numbers). In the housing context, a surrebuttal process would be even worse, given the difficulty in quantifying the defendant's interest. See Part III.B.4 at 181–82, *supra*.

[76] These three elements were also addressed by Congress in the legislation that was introduced and, in less extreme form, passed in the wake of *Wards Cove*. See Roger Clegg, A Brief Legislative History of the Civil Rights Act of 1991, 54 La. L. Rev. 1459 (1994). That legislation adopted a causation requirement, shifted the burden of proof to the defendant at the rebuttal stage, and largely punted on defining the rebuttal. The Court noted in *Wards Cove*, 490 U.S. at 660, that "proof" doesn't always mean "persuasion," which may come in handy given Justice Kennedy's unfortunate use of the word "prove" (see Part II.A at 170, *supra*).

[77] Others have also noted these silver linings in Justice Kennedy's opinion. See, e.g., Michael Foreman, Texas Department of Housing v. Inclusive Communities Project: Two Steps Forward, One Step Back?, CaseText (July 9, 2015), https://casetext.com/posts/texas-department-of-housing-v-inclusive-communities-project-two-steps-forward-one-step-back; ABA Banking Journal, ABA Staff Analysis Explores Disparate Impact Ruling (July 7, 2015), http://bankingjournal.aba.com/2015/07/aba-staff-analysis-explores-disparate-impact-ruling; Buckley Sander LLP, Disparate Impact under the Equal Credit Opportunity Act after Inclusive Communities (June 29, 2015), available at http://www.lexology.com/library/detail.aspx?g=d472a830-c597-4da2-8ce8-801154360359; Melanie Brodie et al., The Supreme Court Recognizes but Limits Disparate Impact in its Fair Housing Act Decision, JD Supra (June 29, 2015), http://www.jdsupra.com/legalnews/the-supreme-court-recognizes-but-limits-45493/ (for a nearly identical version of this analysis that appeared earlier, see also Paul Hancock & Andrew C. Glass, Symposium: The Supreme Court Recognizes but Limits Disparate

B. Legislation

While much can be accomplished through litigation in stemming the abuses of the disparate-impact approach to civil rights enforcement, ultimately there is no substitution for action by Congress, which ought now to amend the Fair Housing Act. And, while at it, Congress should clarify that, in other contexts as well, the disparate-impact approach is invalid.

Most civil rights laws have no "disparate impact" provisions—rather, they prohibit actual disparate treatment—but they have been expanded to include disparate impact through agency interpretation and unwarranted court rulings. The FHA is, of course, a case in point. Thus, Congress should make clear that laws prohibiting discrimination do not extend to mere disparate impact.[78] The Center for Equal Opportunity (CEO) has drafted legislation, the "Civil Rights Clarification Act of 2015," to do just that in a way that includes the FHA and a number of other statutes.[79]

Note that our proposed legislation doesn't include Title VII of the Civil Rights Act of 1964 or the Voting Rights Act of 1965, because they explicitly mention the disparate-impact approach or, at least, go beyond mentioning "disparate treatment." Ideally, Congress should amend those two laws to eliminate those provisions. (Section 2 of the Voting Rights Act uses a "results" test, which is not as bad, though

---

Impact in Its Fair Housing Act Decision, SCOTUSblog (June 26, 2015), http://www.scotusblog.com/2015/06/paul-hancock-fha); Trey Garrison, Hurdles Remain for Disparate Impact Claims in Housing Despite SCOTUS Ruling, Housing Wire (June 26, 2015), http://www.housingwire.com/articles/34319-hurdles-remain-for-disparate-impact-claims-in-housing-despite-scotus-ruling; Robert N. Driscoll, A Win for Disparate Impact, but Not a Total Loss for Lenders, 19 No. 5 Consumer Fin. Services L. Rep. 2 (July 12, 2015), available at http://www.mcglinchey.com/A-Win-For-Disparate-Impact-But-Not-A-Total-Loss-For-Lenders-07-12-2015; Robert Helfand, Not-So-Sudden Impact: Insurers Face A New Breed Of Claim Under the Fair Housing Act (Part 2 of 3), JD Supra Business Advisor (Aug. 4, 2015), available at http://www.jdsupra.com/legalnews/not-so-sudden-impact-insurers-face-a-58688. There has already been an encouraging federal district court decision: City of Los Angeles v. Wells Fargo & Co., No. 2:13-cv-09007-ODW(RZx) (C.D. Cal. July 17, 2015).

[78] Even before the Court's decision, Rep. Scott Garrett of New Jersey had introduced H.R. 2577, an appropriations rider that passed the House and forbid any funds being used to enforce HUD's disparate-impact regulation. It might also be possible to persuade (another) administration not to bring disparate-impact lawsuits, even if that administration has authority to do so.

[79] See Appendix A, *infra*.

it raises many of the same problems.) At the very least, Congress could amend these statutes to provide defendants with an affirmative defense against disparate-impact claims: Where a defendant can demonstrate its nondiscriminatory intent for conduct that resulted in a disparate impact, it should not be liable for discrimination based on a disparate-impact claim. Justice Scalia has hinted at such an approach, noting that while disparate impact might be "an evidentiary tool used to . . . 'smoke out' . . . disparate treatment," existing laws that authorize disparate-impact claims "sweep too broadly . . . since they fail to provide an affirmative defense for good-faith [conduct]."[80] Indeed, "[i]t is one thing to free plaintiffs from proving an employer's illicit intent, but quite another to preclude the employer from proving that its motives were pure and its actions reasonable."[81] CEO has drafted legislation to this effect as well, calling it the "Good Faith Civil Rights Act of 2015."[82]

V. Conclusion

The disparate-impact approach to civil rights enforcement is untenable as a matter of law and policy. It second-guesses nondiscriminatory selection criteria and encourages race-based decisionmaking.

Those are disturbing abuses of federal power at the expense of liberty and limited federal government. As a general matter, the presumption should be that the decisions of private, state, and local actors are no business of the federal government; an exception can be made in extraordinary circumstances of, for example, racial discrimination, but the disparate-impact approach is used precisely when racial discrimination has *not* been shown. And the problem is compounded here since it will be the federal government that is encouraging racial discrimination.

While Justice Kennedy's opinion for the Court in *Texas Department of Housing and Community Affairs v. Inclusive Communities Project* unfortunately now allows this approach under the Fair Housing Act, it recognizes the problems with it, leaving the door open to future litigation that limits this approach under that statute, as well as to litigation that challenges or limits the approach under other statutes.

[80] Ricci v. DeStefano, 557 U.S. 557, 594–95 (2009) (Scalia, J., concurring).

[81] *Id.*

[82] See Appendix B, *infra.*

And instead of leaving this matter to the courts and the uncertain course of future litigation, Congress should act to preclude or at least limit the disparate-impact approach.

Appendix A: Civil Rights Clarification Act of 2015

To amend the Equal Pay Act of 1963, the Civil Rights Act of 1964, the Equal Credit Opportunity Act, the Age Discrimination in Employment Act, the Fair Housing Act, Title IX of the Education Amendments of 1972, the Equal Educational Opportunities Act of 1974, the Age Discrimination Act of 1975, the Immigration and Reform Control Act of 1986, and other Acts of Congress to clarify that certain provisions of such measures prohibit only disparate treatment, not conduct that has a disparate impact on covered persons without disparate treatment, and to clarify that rules and regulations issued under those provisions must not proscribe conduct that has a disparate impact on covered persons but does not constitute disparate treatment.

SECTION 1. SHORT TITLE.

This Act may be cited as the "Civil Rights Clarification Act of 2015."

SECTION 2. AMENDMENT TO EQUAL PAY ACT OF 1963.

PROHIBITION OF SEX DISCRIMINATION.—Section 3 of such Act (29 U.S.C. § 206(d)) is amended by adding at the end the following new subsection:

"(5) This subsection proscribes conduct that constitutes disparate treatment on the basis of sex and not conduct that has a disparate impact on the basis of sex without disparate treatment. No regulation shall be issued to effectuate the provisions of this subsection that proscribes conduct that has a disparate impact on the basis of sex but does not constitute disparate treatment on the basis of sex."

SECTION 3. AMENDMENT OF CIVIL RIGHTS ACT OF 1964.

(a) PLACES OF PUBLIC ACCOMMODATION.—(1) Section 201 of such Act (42 U.S.C. § 2000a) is amended by adding at the end the following new subsection:

"(f) Disparate treatment

"This section proscribes conduct that constitutes disparate treatment on the ground of race, color, religion, or national origin and not conduct that has a disparate impact on the ground of race, color, religion, or national origin without disparate treatment. No regulation shall be issued to effectuate the provisions of this section that proscribes conduct that has a disparate impact on the ground of race, color, religion, or national origin but does not constitute disparate treatment on the ground of race, color, religion, or national origin."

(2) Section 202 of such Act (42 U.S.C. § 2000a-1) is amended by adding at the end "This section proscribes conduct that constitutes disparate treatment on the ground of race, color, religion, or national origin and not conduct that has a disparate impact on the ground of race, color, religion, or national origin without disparate treatment. No regulation shall be issued to effectuate the provisions of this section that proscribes conduct that has a disparate impact on the ground of race, color, religion, or national origin but does not constitute disparate treatment on the ground of race, color, religion, or national origin."

(b) FEDERALLY ASSISTED PROGRAMS.—(1) Section 601 of such Act (42 U.S.C. § 2000d) is amended by adding at the end "This section proscribes conduct that constitutes disparate treatment on the ground of race, color, or national origin and not conduct that has a disparate impact on the ground of race, color, or national origin without disparate treatment."

(2) Section 602 of such Act (42 U.S.C. § 2000d-1) is amended by adding at the end "No such rule, regulation, or order shall be issued to effectuate the provisions of section 601 of this title (42 U.S.C. § 2000d) that proscribes conduct that has a disparate impact on the ground of race, color, or national origin but does not constitute disparate treatment on the ground of race, color, or national origin."

SECTION 4. AMENDMENT TO AGE DISCRIMINATION IN EMPLOYMENT ACT.

PROHIBITION OF AGE DISCRIMINATION.—(a) Section 4 of such Act (29 U.S.C § 623) is amended by adding at the end of the following new subsection:

"(n) Disparate treatment

"This section proscribes conduct that constitutes disparate treatment on the basis of age and not conduct that has a disparate impact on the basis of age without disparate treatment."

(b) Section 9 of such Act (29 U.S.C. § 628) is amended by adding at the end "No such rule or regulation shall be issued to carry out this chapter that proscribes conduct that has a disparate impact on the basis of age but does not constitute disparate treatment on the basis of age."

SECTION 5. AMENDMENT TO EQUAL CREDIT OPPORTUNITY ACT.

CREDIT TRANSACTIONS.—(a) Section 701 of such Act (15 U.S.C. § 1691) is amended by adding at the end the following new subsection:

"(f) This section proscribes conduct that constitutes disparate treatment on the basis of race, color, religion, national origin, sex or marital status, or age (provided the applicant has the capacity to contract) and not conduct that has a disparate impact on the basis of race, color, religion, national origin, sex or marital status, or age without disparate treatment."

(b) Section 703(a) of such Act (15 U.S.C. § 1691b(a)) is amended by adding at the end the following new subsection:

"(6) No regulation prescribed to carry out the purposes of this subchapter shall proscribe conduct that has a disparate impact on the basis of race, color, religion, national origin, sex or marital status, or age (provided the applicant has the capacity to contract) but does not constitute disparate treatment on the basis of race, color, religion, national origin, sex or marital status, or age (provided the applicant has the capacity to contract)."

SECTION 6. AMENDMENT TO FAIR HOUSING ACT.

FAIR HOUSING.—(a) Section 804 of such Act (42 U.S.C. § 3604) is amended by adding at the end the following new subsection:

"(g) This section proscribes conduct that constitutes disparate treatment on the basis of race, color, religion, sex, familial status, or national origin and not conduct that has a disparate impact on the basis of race, color, religion, sex, familial status, or national origin without disparate treatment."

(b) Section 805 of such Act (42 U.S.C. § 3605) is amended by adding at the end the following new subsection:

"(d) This section proscribes conduct that constitutes disparate treatment on the basis of race, color, religion, sex, familial status, or national origin and not conduct that has a disparate impact on the basis of race, color, religion, sex, handicap, familial status, or national origin without disparate treatment."

(c) Section 806 of such Act (42 U.S.C. § 3606) is amended by adding at the end "This section proscribes conduct that constitutes disparate treatment on the basis of race, color, religion, sex, handicap, familial status, or national origin and not conduct that has a disparate impact on the basis of race, color, religion, sex, handicap, familial status, or national origin without disparate treatment."

(d) Section 815 of such Act (42 U.S.C. § 3614a) is amended by adding at the end "No such rule made to carry out this subchapter shall proscribe conduct that has a disparate impact on the basis of race, color, religion, sex, handicap, familial status, or national origin but does not constitute disparate treatment on the basis of race, color, religion, sex, handicap, familial status, or national origin."

SECTION 7. AMENDMENT TO TITLE IX OF EDUCATION AMENDMENTS OF 1972.

PROHIBITION OF SEX DISCRIMINATION.—(a) Section 901 of such Title (20 U.S.C. § 1681) is amended by adding at the end the following new subsection:

"(d) This section proscribes conduct that constitutes disparate treatment on the basis of sex and not conduct that has a disparate impact on the basis of sex without disparate treatment."

(b) Section 902 of such Title (20 U.S.C. § 1682) is amended by adding at the end "No rule, regulation, or order of general applicability shall be issued to effectuate the provisions of section 901 of this title (20 U.S.C. § 1681) that proscribes conduct that has a disparate impact on the basis of sex but does not constitute disparate treatment on the basis of sex."

SECTION 8. AMENDMENT TO EQUAL EDUCATION OPPORTUNITIES ACT OF 1974.

PROHIBITION OF DENIEL OF EQUAL EDUCATIONAL OPPORTUNITY.—Section 204 of such Act (20 U.S.C. § 1703) is amended by adding at the end "This section proscribes conduct that constitutes disparate treatment on the basis of race, color, sex, or national origin but does not constitute disparate impact on the basis of race, color, sex, or national origin without disparate treatment. No regulation shall be issued to effectuate the provisions of this section that proscribes conduct that has a disparate impact on the basis of race, color, sex, or national origin but does not constitute disparate treatment on the basis of race, color, sex, or national origin."

SECTION 9. AMENDMENT TO AGE DISCRIMINATION ACT OF 1975.

PROHIBITION OF DISCRIMINATION BASED IN AGE.—(a) Section 303 of such Act (942 U.S.C. § 6102) is amended by adding at the end "This section proscribes conduct that constitutes disparate treatment on the basis of age and not conduct that has a disparate impact on the basis of age without disparate treatment."

(b) Section 304(a)(1) of such Act (42 U.S.C. § 6103(a)(1)) is amended by adding at the end "No general regulation shall be published to carry out the provisions of section 303 of this title (42 U.S.C. § 6102) that proscribes conduct that has a disparate impact on the basis of age but does not constitute disparate treatment on the basis of age."

SECTION 10. AMENDMENT TO IMMIGRATION AND REFORM CONTROL ACT OF 1986.

PROHIBITION OF DISCRIMINATION BASED ON NATIONAL ORIGIN OR CITIZENSHIP STATUS.—(a) Section 102(a) of such Act (8 U.S.C. § 1324b(a)) is amended by adding at the end the following new subsection:

"(7) Disparate treatment

"Paragraph (1) proscribes conduct that constitutes disparate treatment on the basis of national origin or citizenship status and not conduct that has a disparate impact on the basis of national origin or citizenship status without disparate treatment. No regulation shall be issued to effectuate the provisions of this section that proscribes conduct that has disparate impact on the basis of national origin or citizenship status but does not constitute disparate treatment on the basis of national origin or citizenship status."

SECTION 11. APPLICABILITY TO OTHER ANTI-DISCRIMINA-TION LAWS.

For any and all Acts of Congress that are not expressly amended by this Act, which contain provisions that prohibit discrimination by proscribing conduct that constitutes disparate treatment but do not explicitly state that they proscribe conduct that has a disparate impact on covered persons without disparate treatment, those provisions shall not be construed to proscribe conduct that has a disparate impact on covered persons but does not constitute disparate treatment, and no regulation shall be issued to effectuate those provisions that proscribes conduct that has a disparate impact on covered persons but does not constitute disparate treatment.

Appendix B: Good Faith Civil Rights Act of 2015

To amend the Civil Rights Act of 1964, as amended, and the Voting Rights Act of 1965, as amended, to allow nondiscriminatory intent as an affirmative defense in claims brought under those statutes that do not allege disparate treatment.

SECTION 1. SHORT TITLE.

This Act may be cited as the "Good Faith Civil Rights Act of 2015."

SECTION 2. AMENDMENT TO THE CIVIL RIGHTS ACT OF 1964, as amended.

In any action brought under 42 U.S.C. §§ 2000e-2(k), no respondent shall be found liable if it can demonstrate that the challenged practice was neither adopted with the intent of discriminating on the basis of race, color, religion, sex, or national origin nor applied unequally on the basis of race, color, religion, sex, or national origin.

SECTION 3. AMENDMENTS TO THE VOTING RIGHTS ACT OF 1965, as amended.

(a) For any allegation or part thereof under 42 U.S.C. § 1973 that does not assert discriminatory intent, no defendant shall be held liable if it can demonstrate that the challenged voting qualification or prerequisite to voting or standard, practice, or procedure was neither adopted with the intent of discriminating on the basis of race, color, or membership in a language minority group nor applied unequally on the basis of race, color, or membership in a language minority group.

(b) In any matter or part thereof before the Attorney General or the United States District Court for the District of Columbia under 42 U.S.C. § 1973c in which discriminatory intent is not at issue, the State or subdivision shall not be prevented from enacting or administering any voting qualification or prerequisite to voting, or standard, practice, or procedure with respect to voting, if it can demonstrate that in making a change, it lacks an intent to discriminate on the basis of race, color, or membership in a language minority group.

Freedom of Competition and the Rhetoric of Federalism: *North Carolina Board of Dental Examiners v. FTC*

*by Timothy Sandefur**

The novice might imagine that the antitrust laws that forbid "every" restraint of trade[1] would bar the government from prohibiting competition for the benefit of established businesses. After all, legal barriers to trade are the most obvious tool for those seeking to establish a cartel. Without such barriers, a cartel is inherently unstable because whenever it tries to raise prices above market levels, it will face either the threat of new firms entering the trade and offering products or services at lower prices, or the threat that members of the cartel will defect and do the same. Legal barriers to entry can therefore shore up the structural weaknesses that doom cartels in a free market. Empowered to punish defectors and block new entrants, the cartel need not satisfy consumers to survive and may raise prices and relax efforts at innovation. Legal barriers to entry such as licensing laws raise the cost of living and deprive entrepreneurs of economic opportunity and their constitutionally protected right to pursue the lawful vocation of their choice.[2]

*Principal Attorney and Director of the Program for Judicial Awareness, Pacific Legal Foundation, and adjunct scholar, Cato Institute. The author drafted and filed the amicus brief of the Pacific Legal Foundation and the Cato Institute in Support of the Respondents in *North Carolina Board of Dental Examiners v. FTC*, 135 S. Ct. 1101 (2015). Thanks to Jonathan Wood and Wencong Fa for helpful comments.

[1] Sherman Antitrust Act, 15 U.S.C. § 1.

[2] Though much neglected in the literature, this right was recognized as far back as seventeenth century common law. See generally Timothy Sandefur, The Right to Earn a Living: Economic Freedom and the Law 17–25 (2010).

But the reality is that today's antitrust laws do not bar government from creating cartels.[3] On the contrary, thanks to the doctrine of *Parker* antitrust immunity, the one entity that can most effectively engage in anti-competitive conduct—the government—may do so with impunity, and states may effectively nullify federal antitrust laws on behalf of private monopolists. *Parker* immunity has led to the bizarre result that private parties who collude among themselves are liable to prosecution and punishment, even though market forces typically render such efforts futile—whereas if their efforts are backed by state regulatory agencies, they are immune from prosecution and yet are much more likely to inflict the harms that the antitrust laws are supposed to prevent.

This is the dilemma at the heart of *North Carolina Board of Dental Examiners v. Federal Trade Commission*.[4] In this case, the FTC sued a state board charged with regulating the dental profession after the board used licensing laws to bar non-dentists from offering teeth-whitening services, not to protect the general public, but to prevent competition against licensed dental practitioners. To what degree will federal laws against monopolist activities apply to state regulators who wield the state's power to block competition to benefit industry members?

I. The *Parker* Immunity Doctrine

A. Origins of Parker Immunity

The shield allowing states—and private parties deputized by states—to indulge in anti-competitive activities that federal law otherwise punishes as a crime is called the *Parker* immunity doctrine, named for the 1943 case of *Parker v. Brown*.[5] That case involved the California Agricultural Prorate Act, one of the many Depression-era

---

[3] Courts are divided as to whether the Constitution does so. The Fifth, Sixth, and Ninth Circuits have held that states may not use licensing laws simply to protect established firms against competition. See St. Joseph Abbey v. Castille, 712 F.3d 215, 222-23 (5th Cir.), cert. denied, 134 S. Ct. 423 (2013); Craigmiles v. Giles, 312 F.3d 220, 224 (6th Cir. 2002); Merrifield v. Lockyer, 547 F.3d 978, 991 n. 15 (9th Cir. 2008). The Tenth Circuit has held that they may. Powers v. Harris, 379 F.3d 1208, 1221 (10th Cir. 2004).

[4] 135 S. Ct. 1101 (2015).

[5] 317 U.S. 341 (1943).

laws that restricted competition in the agriculture industry to keep food prices up.

The act allowed raisin producers to establish "prorate marketing plans" which—subject to alteration by a government commission and approval by a certain number of raisin producers—would govern raisin production in California's central valley, where perhaps half of all raisins are produced. The 1940 plan required producers to divide their crop into categories, handing over a large portion to the commission to sell "in such manner as to obtain stability in the market."[6] Producers were free to sell 30 percent of their standard-grade raisins but were forced to pay the commission a fee for each ton sold. (Basically the same regulatory apparatus remains in place today, and the Supreme Court addressed some of its constitutional implications this term.[7])

This was the very model of a modern major cartel, and raisin packer Porter Brown sued to challenge its legality.[8] Although the Court acknowledged that the Sherman Antitrust Act prohibits "*every* contract . . . in restraint of trade," and that the raisin program would likely have been illegal if it had been "organized and made effective solely by virtue of a contract, combination or conspiracy of private persons," it nevertheless found that the Sherman Act could not apply because the program "derived its authority and its efficacy from the legislative command of the state."[9] The justices saw no reason to believe that the act was intended to apply to state governments, and to "nullify a state's control over its own officers and agents" would unduly interfere with the federalist system.[10] Thus neither the state,

---

[6] *Id.* at 348.

[7] See Michael W. McConnell, The Raisin Case, 2014–2015 Cato Sup. Ct. Rev. 313 (2015); Horne v. Dep't of Agric. 135 S. Ct. 2419 (2015). The Court addressed a procedural aspect of this case in Horne v. Dep't of Agric., 133 S. Ct. 2053 (2013). During the oral argument, Justice Elena Kagan called the California raisin marketing statute "the world's most outdated law" and Justice Antonin Scalia agreed, calling it "a crazy statute." Transcript of Oral Arg. at 40, 49, Horne v. Dep't of Agric., 133 S.Ct. 2053 (No. 12-123).

[8] Brown also argued that it violated the Commerce Clause and was preempted by the Federal Agricultural Marketing Agreement Act. Parker, 317 U.S. at 348-49. Brown did not initially make a Sherman Act claim; that question was raised by the Supreme Court on its own motion. See Cantor v. Detroit Edison Co., 428 U.S. 579, 585-89 (1976).

[9] Parker, 317 U.S. at 350 (quoting Sherman Act, 15 U.S.C. § 1) (emphasis added).

[10] *Id.* at 351.

nor private parties acting under state law, could be prosecuted for antitrust violations.

This conclusion is not as obvious as it may seem. The theory behind the antitrust laws is that restraints on free competition harm consumers by raising prices and harm businesses by limiting the opportunity to engage in a trade. But such restraints can be accomplished either by private collusion or by the government, which legislates against low prices, or restricts entry into a trade, or otherwise bars competition. There is no difference in the consequences between these two—except that private collusion is less likely to succeed than government-created schemes, given the incentives that free competition gives for defection or new entry. This factor suggests that antitrust prosecutors should, if anything, monitor the behavior of government more skeptically than they do private entities.

In fact, one of the first Supreme Court decisions applying the Sherman Act, *United States v. Trans-Missouri Freight Association*,[11] seemed to say just that. There, the Court rejected the argument that railroads were exempt from the Sherman Act because, being subject to heavy government regulation and vested with special government privileges, such as the use of eminent domain, they were not the sort of private entities at which the act was aimed. The railroads had even submitted their price schedules to the Interstate Commerce Commission for approval. How, then, could their price-setting be an illegal restraint of trade?

Yet the Court refused to exempt them from the Sherman Act's reach because the act's plain language applies to *all* restraints of trade, and the Court refused to infer an exemption where none was expressed in the statute. The Court acknowledged that railroads are "of a public nature"[12] and are not ordinary private businesses, but it found that this was actually reason for *more* stringent enforcement of the antitrust laws. Purely private contracts "must be unreasonable in their nature to be held void," but "different considerations" would probably apply "in the case of public corporations." In the latter case, *any* restriction on competition "must . . . be prejudicial to the

---

[11] 166 U.S. 290 (1897).

[12] *Id*. at 321–22.

public interests."[13] At the very least, the harm to be anticipated from anti-competitive acts "is substantially of the same nature"[14] whether done by public or private entities, and "the evil to be remedied is similar."[15] There was thus no basis for exempting the anti-competitive conduct of public entities from the antitrust laws.

Forty-six years later, the *Parker* Court reasoned differently. It found that the Sherman Act's silence regarding government-sponsored cartels—which to the *Trans-Missouri* Court was proof that no exception was available—was sufficient reason to infer an exemption for government-sponsored cartels. *Parker* made no reference to the theory of antitrust laws or to the fact that consumers suffer the same, or worse, harm when public entities block competition. Instead, it focused on the preservation of state autonomy. "In a dual system of government in which, under the Constitution, the states are sovereign, save only as Congress may constitutionally subtract from their authority," the Court wrote, "an unexpressed purpose to nullify a state's control over its officers and agents is not lightly to be attributed to Congress."[16]

This formulation begged the question. The Sherman Act purports to be an exercise of Congress's authority to regulate interstate commerce, which of its own force preempts state laws to the contrary, and therefore it cannot be said to unduly interfere with the "dual system of government."[17] And the act forbids "every" restraint of trade without exceptions. Interpreting that expansive term to bar restraints imposed under color of state law would not be "lightly" attributing anything to Congress but simply giving the statute its literal meaning. At best, *Parker*'s invocation of the clear statement rule is unavailing, since courts also should not "lightly" infer exemptions in a statute phrased so broadly.[18]

---

[13] *Id*. at 334. See further Alan J. Meese, Liberty and Antitrust in the Formative Era, 79 B.U. L. Rev. 1, 45–47 (1999).

[14] Trans-Missouri Freight, 166 U.S. at 322.

[15] *Id*. at 324–25.

[16] Parker, 317 U.S. at 351.

[17] See Ronald E. Kennedy, Of Lawyers, Lightbulbs, and Raisins: An Analysis of the State Action Doctrine under the Antitrust Laws, 74 Nw. U. L. Rev. 31, 72 (1979) ("State sovereignty is not injured when the federal government validly acts in the sphere to which it is delimited.").

[18] The Court has frequently said that antitrust immunity should not be lightly inferred. FTC v. Ticor Title Ins. Co., 504 U.S. 621, 636 (1992); Nat'l Gerimedical Hosp. &

Finally, the *Parker* Court's examination of history left out important details. The anti-monopoly tradition that gave rise to the Sherman Act was—beginning with the 17th-century Whig campaign against legal monopolies and culminating in the 1623 Statute of Monopolies—focused largely on the evils of government-imposed restraints on trade.[19] There is no basis in the text or history of the Sherman Act to presume that its authors meant to categorically immunize state-imposed cartels.[20]

B. Federalism and Rent-Seeking

Parker's motivating concern was state autonomy, but it serves that interest clumsily, creating a unique form of "reverse preemption," which allows states to block the operation of federal statutes, in apparent conflict with the Supremacy Clause.[21] In no other circumstance may a state shield citizens from the operation of federal law in quite that way. *Parker* immunity thus justifies one critic's claim that "the ideology of federalism has displaced a national model of competition for one favoring state-based resolutions."[22] Yet "federalism" is an imprecise word here, because genuine federalism balances state autonomy and federal oversight for the purpose of protecting individual freedom.[23] The *Parker* Court was not motivated by this

---

Gerontology Ctr. v. Blue Cross of Kansas City, 452 U.S. 378, 388–89 (1981); Cantor, 428 U.S. at 596–98; United States v. Nat'l Ass'n of Sec. Dealers, Inc., 422 U.S. 694, 719 (1975); United States v. Philadelphia Nat'l Bank, 374 U.S. 321, 348 (1963). See also Northrop Corp. v. McDonnell Douglas Corp., 705 F.2d 1030, 1056 (9th Cir. 1983).

[19] See generally Steven G. Calabresi & Larissa C. Leibowitz, Monopolies and the Constitution: A History of Crony Capitalism, 36 Harv. J.L. & Pub. Pol'y 983 (2013); William Letwin, Law and Economic Policy in America: The Evolution of the Sherman Antitrust Act 18–52 (1965).

[20] See, e.g., Paul E. Slater, Antitrust And Government Action: A Formula for Narrowing *Parker v. Brown*, 69 Nw. U. L. Rev. 71, 83 (1974) ("In truth, a full reading of the legislative history of the Sherman Act is not likely to help answer the *Parker* question one way or the other . . . . [I]f the legislative history reveals anything, it is that the purpose of the act is to strike down arrangements which have anti-competitive effects . . . . regardless of whether the state is a participant.").

[21] Einer Richard Elhauge, The Scope of Antitrust Process, 104 Harv. L. Rev. 667, 669–70 (1991).

[22] E. Thomas Sullivan, Antitrust Regulation of Land Use: Federalism's Triumph Over Competition, the Last Fifty Years, 3 Wash. U. J.L. & Pol'y 473, 511 (2000).

[23] See The Federalist No. 51 (James Madison) at 351 (Jacob Cooke ed. 1961) ("In the compound republic of America, the power surrendered by the people, is divided

carefully balanced conception of federalism, but by a cruder desire to protect state power, even though the antitrust laws manifest no such concern.

Not only is *Parker's* conception of federalism incorrect, but the decision has had unfortunate consequences for the marketplace thanks to regulatory capture—the tendency of regulatory bodies to be dominated by the private entities they purport to regulate. As public choice scholars have emphasized, private parties who stand to gain or lose from the actions of regulatory agencies will devote time and effort to persuading those agencies to act in ways that will benefit them.[24] Thus businesses will frequently lobby regulators to adopt licensing rules or other barriers to entry so that they can haul up the ladder behind them—pretending public benefit, intending private, as Sir Edward Coke put it.[25] Such regulations cast a cloak of officialdom over policies that protect the private actors from competition with only a flimsy connection to the public welfare.

Parker itself is a prime example. The California raisin law prohibited competition in agriculture for the express purpose of raising food prices, not just in California, but nationwide—at a time of national economic depression, no less. To declare it immune from the antitrust laws is, as Richard Epstein has observed, "quite perverse from every angle."[26] Or consider *Southern Motor Carriers Rate Conference, Inc. v. United States*, in which a group of private shipping companies adopted a price-fixing schedule that was approved by the regulatory agencies of several states.[27] Such price-fixing would certainly have violated the antitrust laws if done privately, but the Court gave it a pass because it had received the blessing of state governments. *Parker* immunity thus rewards and encourages what the Founders called the "mischiefs of faction."[28] By putting the power to

---

between two distinct governments . . . . Hence, a double security arises to the rights of the people. The different governments will controul each other; at the same time that each will be controuled by itself."); *Id.* No. 45, at 309 ("as far as the sovereignty of the States cannot be reconciled to the happiness of the people, the voice of every good citizen must be, let the former be sacrificed to the latter.").

[24] See generally James Buchanan & Gordon Tullock, The Calculus of Consent (1962).

[25] Ronald Coase, The Firm, the Market, and the Law 196 (1990).

[26] Richard A. Epstein, How Progressives Rewrote the Constitution 84 (2006).

[27] 471 U.S. 48 (1985).

[28] The Federalist No. 10 (Madison), *supra* note 23, at 61.

nullify the antitrust laws into the hands of the same bureaucracies that establish all the other rules for an industry—the bureaucracies existing firms are already most likely to lobby and influence—the *Parker* doctrine ensures that the industry groups that gain sway over regulators and acquire the power to impose restraints on their competitors also become exempt from the anti-monopoly laws. The game of regulatory capture is therefore "winner-takes-all."

These concerns are particularly acute in the realm of occupational licensing. Although licensing laws are supposed to prevent dishonest or unqualified practitioners from entering a trade and endangering consumers, such laws have been exploited for centuries by established firms seeking to block new competition.[29] Business owners therefore often invest time and effort to obtain this power. Consider the efforts of the American Society of Interior Designers, a trade organization that has lobbied state legislatures to adopt stringent licensing requirements for the practice of interior design.[30] If there is any such thing as a harmless business, it is interior decorating. Yet the ASID has sought, successfully in some cases, to persuade states to allow only college graduates with special certification to practice that trade. Worse, state officials often delegate their licensing and regulatory powers to long-established businesses, often by deputizing them as regulators, thus ignoring the obvious conflict of interest inherent in empowering established firms to bar their own competition. This should warrant more antitrust scrutiny, not less. As Professors Aaron Edlin and Rebecca Haw observe, "[t]hat the consortium of competitors is called a state board and given power by the state to regulate its profession does not make it more trustworthy. The grant simply makes the board more powerful and therefore more dangerous."[31]

C. Other Anomalous Immunities

In the years since *Parker*, immunity doctrines have carved antitrust law into two spheres, where what's law for thee is not law for me. In

---

[29] See Sandefur, Right to Earn a Living, *supra* note 2, at 145-63.

[30] See generally Dick M. Carpenter, II, Designing Cartels: How Industry Insiders Cut Out Competition (Institute for Justice 2007), available at http://www.ij.org/images/pdf_folder/economic_liberty/Interior-Design-Study.pdf.

[31] Aaron Edlin & Rebecca Haw, Cartels by Another Name: Should Licensed Occupations Face Antitrust Scrutiny?, 162 U. Pa. L. Rev. 1093, 1143 (2014).

City of Lafayette v. Louisiana Power & Light,[32] the Court held that city governments were subject to the antitrust laws. The source of *Parker* immunity, the Court explained, was a concern with *state* autonomy, which was not present in cases involving cities.[33] Nor would the Court adopt a naïve presumption that city governments represent the public interest. Municipalities were just as prone to pursuing "their own parochial interests" as were private parties.[34] A blanket exemption for all government entities would create "a serious chink in the armor of antitrust protection . . . at odds with the comprehensive national policy" of antitrust.[35] Chief Justice Warren Burger emphasized this point in a concurring opinion: if the antitrust laws were "'meant to deal comprehensively and effectively with the evils resulting from contracts, combinations and conspiracies in restraint of trade,'" it would be "wholly arbitrary" to treat government-imposed restraints of trade as categorically "beyond the purview of federal law."[36] But when *Louisiana Power & Light* inspired successful lawsuits challenging cities' anti-competitive conduct, Congress rushed to pass the Local Government Antitrust Immunity Act.[37]

More problematic is the question of immunity in cases in which government acts as a "market participant." *Parker* focused on immunizing the government when it acted as a sovereign implementing official policies, not when it simply operated a business. But subsequent rulings have expanded immunity even into cases where the government is just another business owner. Thus in *Sea-Land Services v. Alaska Railroad*, the D.C. Circuit held that a government-run railroad was immune simply because it was government-run, without considering the conduct at issue or the fact that the government was acting solely as a market participant.[38] More recently, in *U.S. Postal Service v. Flamingo Industries*, the Court held that the Postal Service was immune from suit even for matters *not* involving its mail delivery operations, because, notwithstanding the Postal Reorganization

32 435 U.S. 389 (1978).

33 *Id.* at 412.

34 *Id.* at 408.

35 *Id.*

36 *Id.* at 419 (Burger, C.J., concurring) (quoting Atlantic Cleaner & Dyers, Inc. v. United States, 286 U.S. 427, 435 (1932)).

37 15 U.S.C. §§ 34–36.

38 659 F.2d 243 (D.C. Cir. 1981).

Act, it "remains part of the Government."[39] Chief Justice Burger's warning that focusing on the character of the defendant instead of the nature of its conduct proved prescient: antitrust immunity now revolves almost entirely around the formalistic question of whether courts regard the defendant as a government entity or a private one, instead of the substantive questions of consumer welfare that courts have said is the focus of antitrust law.

Not only are private entities shielded from antitrust scrutiny when they receive state approval, they are also exempt when they endeavor to persuade the government to grant them such monopoly status. Under the *Noerr-Pennington* doctrine,[40] the First Amendment trumps the antitrust laws in cases where private entities lobby the government to block competition against them. *Noerr-Pennington*'s concern for the security of First Amendment rights is understandable, but speech as part of a conspiracy to violate the law has never been protected in any other context. As one critic notes, "when a group of competitors or a single firm influence governmental process for the purpose of restraining trade or monopolizing the market, the statutory objectives of the Sherman Act are placed in serious jeopardy . . . . [Failure to] regulate this form of predatory 'petitioning of government' . . . threatens federal competition policy . . . by allowing competitors to use governmental process as a 'loophole.'"[41]

These anomalies reinforce the overall theme: antitrust immunity doctrines have created a body of law under which government—which enjoys exclusive power to illegalize competition—is not only exempt from laws that purport to forbid *every* restriction on free competition, but it can even grant waivers to private parties who engage in the most obvious example of monopolistic conduct: using coercion to block their competitors. Meanwhile, private parties who conspire between themselves to set prices or to bar new firms from entering their industry face massive damages and even criminal

[39] U.S. Postal Serv. v. Flamingo Indus., 540 U.S. 736, 746 (2004) (citing 39 U.S.C. § 401). This act dissolved the U.S. Post Office and replaced it with the Postal Service as "an independent establishment of the executive branch of the Government."

[40] Named for two cases, E. R. R. Presidents Conference v. Noerr Motor Freight, Inc., 365 U.S. 127 (1961), and United Mine Workers of Am. v. Pennington, 381 U.S. 657 (1965).

[41] Gary Minda, Interest Groups, Political Freedom, and Antitrust: A Modern Reassessment of the *Noerr-Pennington* Doctrine, 41 Hastings L.J. 905, 908–09 (1990).

liability, even though their cartelizing efforts are inherently unlikely to succeed because they lack power to fine or jail potential competitors. What's national economic policy for the goose is a series of judicially created immunities for the gander.

II. The Limits of *Parker* Immunity

The *Parker* Court seemed to detect these problems when it declared that a state "does not give immunity to those who violate the Sherman Act by authorizing them to violate it, or by declaring that their action is lawful."[42] Later decisions have insisted that *Parker* immunity must not be expanded to allow organized business to thwart the "national policy in favor of competition . . . by casting . . . a gauzy cloak of state involvement over what is essentially a private [anti-competitive] arrangement."[43] Yet the Court has not explained the precise limits on the power states enjoy to give away "get out of antitrust free" cards.

Instead, the Court has fashioned two standards which a state must satisfy before *Parker* immunity may apply: first, the anti-competitive policy must be "clearly articulated" by the state, and, second, the parties engaging in the anti-competitive conduct must be "actively supervised" by state officials. These requirements have often proven to be little more than formalities.

The "clear articulation" rule began as a stringent requirement that the anti-competitive conduct at issue be actually compelled by state law before immunity would be granted. Thus in *Goldfarb v. Virginia State Bar*, the Court denied immunity to state bar officials who established a price-fixing scheme for lawyers.[44] The first question to ask when deciding whether immunity applied, said the Court, "is whether the activity is required by the State acting as sovereign."[45] But Virginia statutes were silent on the matter, so that "it cannot fairly be said that the State . . . required the anti-competitive activities."[46] Although this silence might be interpreted as allowing the bar to

[42] Parker, 317 U.S. at 351.

[43] California Retail Liquor Dealers Ass'n v. Midcal Aluminum, Inc., 445 U.S. 97, 106 (1980).

[44] 421 U.S. 773 (1975).

[45] *Id*. at 790.

[46] *Id*.

decide whether or not to set prices for lawyers, the Court found that it was "not enough" that the anti-competitive conduct was merely "'prompted' by state action; rather, anti-competitive activities must be compelled by direction of the State acting as a sovereign" for immunity to apply.[47] Two years later, in *Cantor v. Detroit Edison Co.*, the Court was again tight-fisted, refusing to grant a blanket exemption for all private conduct required by state law, and noting that "state authorization, approval, encouragement, or participation in restrictive private conduct confers no antitrust immunity."[48] Even where the state participates in the anti-competitive conduct of private parties, those parties can still be liable if they exercise "sufficient freedom of choice" that they "should be held responsible for the consequences."[49] And the next year, in *Bates v. State Bar of Arizona*, it granted immunity to the state bar because it "act[ed] as the agent of," and "its role [was] completely defined by," the state government—unlike in previous cases, where the anti-competitive conduct had been engaged in "with only the acquiescence of the state."[50]

But later cases have watered down the "clear articulation" requirement. In *Southern Motor Carriers*, the Court declared that anti-competitive conduct need not be actually *compelled* by state law to qualify for immunity; it was enough that state law simply allowed bureaucrats to decide whether or not to impose an anti-competitive policy. That case involved "collective rate-making"—in other words, price-fixing—by groups of shipping companies in several states. The shippers submitted their rate agreements for review and approval by government regulators in their states, but these agreements were only allowed, not required, by state law. Still, the Supreme Court held that immunity applied, saying that "a state policy that expressly *permits*, but does not compel, anti-competitive conduct" is enough to invoke *Parker* immunity.[51] Thus states may empower private parties to engage in price-fixing and other illegal activities with impunity, so long as the state "intends to adopt a *permissive policy*" allowing

---

[47] *Id.* at 791.

[48] Cantor, 428 U.S. at 592–93.

[49] *Id.* at 593.

[50] 433 U.S. 350, 361–62 (1977).

[51] 471 U.S. at 61 (emphasis original).

such conduct.[52] Since then, write Edlin and Haw, "the Court has made clear that virtually any colorable claim to state authority can be all the articulation necessary."[53]

The second requirement for *Parker* immunity, "active supervision," has also been diluted. This requirement is meant to provide "realistic assurance that a private party's anti-competitive conduct promotes state policy, rather than merely the party's individual interests."[54] Yet the Supreme Court does not demand this showing from a category of entities that it considers sufficiently accountable to the public. In *Town of Hallie v. City of Eau Claire*, decided the same day as *Southern Motor Carriers*, the Court suggested that lower courts could give *Parker* immunity to city governments and state agencies without first ensuring that they were actively supervised by state officials, because such entities could be presumed to act in the public interest.[55]

Since then, courts have granted immunity to state regulatory agencies on the theory that they automatically operate in the public interest—disregarding the risk that businesses will gain sway over the regulatory agency and use its powers to prevent free competition. In *Earles v. State Board of Certified Public Accountants of Louisiana*, the Fifth Circuit held that the active supervision requirement did not apply to a group of CPAs deputized by the state to regulate the practice of accountants.[56] "Despite the fact that the Board is composed entirely of CPAs who compete in the profession they regulate," the court was satisfied that "the public nature of the Board's actions means that there is little danger of a cozy arrangement to restrict competition."[57] And in *Hass v. Oregon State Bar*, the Ninth Circuit held that state agencies are exempt from the antitrust laws because their acts are sufficiently public as to assuage any concern that they are exploiting public power for private benefit.[58]

These decisions have largely transformed the limits on *Parker* immunity into empty gestures. The "clear articulation" requirement

---

[52] *Id.* at 62 (emphasis added).

[53] Edlin & Haw, *supra* note 31, at 1120.

[54] Patrick v. Burget, 486 U.S. 94, 101 (1988).

[55] 471 U.S. 34, 45 (1985).

[56] 139 F.3d 1033 (5th Cir. 1998).

[57] *Id.* at 1041.

[58] 883 F.2d 1453, 1460 (9th Cir. 1989).

can be met by a flimsy "permissive policy," and the "active super-vision" requirement was rendered inapplicable to state entities by the presumption that they act in the public interest. This did indeed allow private trade organizations to cast a "gauzy cloak of state in-volvement" over their efforts to bar free competition.[59]

III. The North Carolina Dental Board Case

A. Proceedings in the FTC and the Fourth Circuit

The North Carolina Board of Dental Examiners is a group of prac-ticing dental professionals deputized by the state to regulate the practice of dentistry. Crucially, they are elected to their positions by other practicing dentists, not by the general public or by government officials.[60] About a decade ago, the board began receiving complaints from dentists about the growing practice of "teeth-whitening," a cosmetic procedure in which a plastic strip treated with peroxide is placed on the teeth for a few minutes in order to make them brighter.

This practice is safe and can even be done at home with a kit avail-able over the counter at the grocery store. There is no evidence that it is dangerous; even the Food and Drug Administration refused to regulate teeth-whitening as a risk to consumer health.[61] Many peo-ple choose to have it done while visiting a nail salon or shopping at the mall. But licensed dentists have labored to exclude anyone but themselves from offering this service, and it is now against the law in at least 14 states to apply a whitening strip to someone else's teeth without having a dental or dental hygienist license. Such a license cannot be obtained without meeting expensive and time-consuming education and testing requirements.[62]

---

[59] Midcal Aluminum, 445 U.S. at 106.

[60] In the Matter of the N.C. Bd. of Dental Examiners, 152 F.T.C. 640, 2011 WL 11798463 at *3 (Dec. 2, 2011).

[61] See Letter from Janet Woodcock to Charles Norman, et al., Apr. 22, 2014 (FDA Docket No. FDA-2009-P-0566), available at http://www.regulations.gov/contentStre amer?objectId=09000064816c224b&disposition=attachment&contentType=pdf.

[62] See Angela C. Erickson, White Out: How Dental Industry Insiders Thwart Com-petition from Teeth-Whitening Entrepreneurs (Institute for Justice 2013), available at http://www.ij.org/white-out.

Responding to complaints by licensed dental workers—not consumers[63]—the board issued 47 cease-and-desist orders to small business owners who offered "teeth-whitening" in stores and malls throughout North Carolina, and urged the state's Board of Cosmetic Art Examiners to bar cosmetologists from offering teeth-whitening services.[64] The Dental Board contended that teeth-whitening qualified as the practice of dentistry and therefore required a license.

When the FTC learned of the board's efforts to block competition for teeth-whitening, it initiated an unlawful competition proceeding, alleging that the board was exploiting its licensing powers to restrict competition. The board responded by asserting immunity under *Parker*. The FTC rejected the immunity argument, and the U.S. Court of Appeals for the Fourth Circuit agreed. *Parker* immunity, the judges held, was unavailable because the board was not adequately supervised by accountable state officers.

The board contended that the active supervision requirement should not apply, because, being a state agency, courts should presume that its acts were in the public interest. The court of appeals rejected this argument. Such a presumption could apply only to entities that answer to voters or to government officials, but the board was accountable only to licensed dentists with a strong private interest in protecting their collective turf.[65] The active supervision requirement therefore did apply, and the board could not pass that test. It sent its cease and desist orders without oversight from any state agency, and although the board was required to file regular public reports of its operations, this was merely "generic oversight" which could not qualify as active state supervision.[66]

Having dispensed with the board's assertion of *Parker* immunity, the court went on to affirm the FTC's finding that the board had violated the antitrust laws. Judge Barbara Milano Keenan wrote a concurring opinion to emphasize the narrowness of the holding: were

[63] In the Matter of the N.C. Bd. of Dental Examiners, 152 F.T.C. 640 (2011), 2011 WL 11798463 at *4. The FTC found evidence of only four instances of possible harm to consumers. The Dental Board failed to investigate two of them. The other two appeared to have resulted from unrelated conditions. In the Matter of the N.C. Bd. of Dental Examiners, 2011 WL 11798463, at *28.

[64] N.C. Bd. of Dental Examiners v. F.T.C., 717 F.3d 359, 365 (4th Cir. 2013).

[65] *Id*. at 369.

[66] *Id*. at 370.

the board appointed by elected officials, she wrote, it would have a stronger argument for immunity. But "the fact that the Board is comprised of private dentists elected by other private dentists, along with North Carolina's lack of active supervision of the Board's activities, leaves us with little confidence that the state itself, rather than a private consortium of dentists, chose to regulate dental health in this manner at the expense of robust competition."[67]

B. The Supreme Court's Holding

The Supreme Court granted certiorari to address just the *Parker* immunity question, and in a 6–3 decision written by Justice Anthony Kennedy, it ruled that *Parker* immunity did not apply, because the state agency was not sufficiently supervised by elected officials. Private parties "cannot be allowed to regulate their own markets free from antitrust accountability."[68] Thus, when considering whether to grant or withhold immunity, a court's primary concern is "political accountability for anti-competitive conduct" that the entity "permit[s] and control[s]."[69]

The Court therefore refused to give the board the blanket exemption that municipalities enjoy. The latter are "electorally accountable" and pursue a broader range of goals than private market actors do, which diminishes the likelihood that they will use regulatory power for private enrichment.[70] Because the private market participants serving on the Dental Board—elected by other private market participants—operated free of these checks and balances, they would have to satisfy the "active supervision" test to qualify for *Parker* immunity.

Justice Kennedy rejected the board's argument that it should be automatically deemed exempt because the state had designated it as the official regulator. Immunity must turn "not on the formal designation" or on legal "nomenclature," but "on the risk that active market participants will pursue private interests in restraining trade."[71] Given "the risks licensing boards dominated by market participants may pose to the free market," it was important to ensure that such

---

[67] *Id.* at 377 (Kennan, J., concurring).

[68] N.C. Bd. of Dental Exam'rs, 135 S. Ct. at 1111.

[69] *Id.*

[70] *Id.* at 1112.

[71] *Id.* at 1114.

boards are accountable to the public, by being answerable either to voters or elected officials on one hand, or to antitrust laws on the other.[72] The active supervision requirement is not a matter of the regulators' good or bad faith, but of the "structural risk" that they will "confus[e]" their private interest with the public good[73]—a particularly realistic concern in a profession like medicine, where regulators can find the two hard to separate.[74]

The Court emphasized that this focus on structural incentives was required by the fact that, once immunized from antitrust law, even a regulator's bad-faith decisions are shielded from antitrust scrutiny. In *Columbia v. Omni Outdoor Advertising*, the Court granted exemption to a municipality even though it had conspired with a private corporation to engage in anti-competitive conduct that benefited the corporation.[75] The justices ruled that there was "no such conspiracy exception" that might deprive officials of immunity. *Parker* immunity is justified by "our national commitment to federalism" and judicial deference, and a bad-faith exception to the immunity doctrine would "shift . . . judgment from elected officials to judges and juries."[76] The only recourse for citizens harmed by officials who abuse their antitrust immunity is to vote the offenders out of office. This, Kennedy wrote in *Dental Examiners*, makes it "all the more necessary to ensure the conditions for granting immunity are met in the first place."[77]

The Dental Board made no effort to argue that it could satisfy the "active supervision" requirement, and the Court spent little time on that question. State law did not expressly define teeth-whitening as the practice of dentistry, and it was therefore unclear whether the board had acted within its ambit when it issued the cease-and-desist

[72] *Id*. at 1116.

[73] *Id*. at 1114.

[74] For example, the American Medical Association was successfully sued for antitrust violations for taking steps to discourage patients from visiting chiropractors, even though those efforts were scientifically well grounded and arguably required by the doctors' Hippocratic Oaths. See Wilk v. Am. Med. Ass'n, 671 F. Supp. 1465 (N.D. Ill. 1987), aff'd, 895 F.2d 352 (7th Cir. 1990).

[75] 499 U.S. 365 (1991).

[76] *Id*. at 374–77.

[77] N.C. Bd. of Dental Exam'rs, 135 S. Ct. at 1113.

orders.[78] The Court provided few details as to how a state might satisfy the active supervision requirement for antitrust immunity in the future—since whether the supervision is adequate "will depend on all the circumstances of a case."[79] But at a minimum, an accountable state actor must review the anti-competitive act to ensure that it complies with state policy, and "the state supervisor may not itself be an active market participant."[80]

C. The Dissent: State Autonomy Trumps

Justices Samuel Alito, Antonin Scalia, and Clarence Thomas dissented. They objected to withholding antitrust immunity simply because the Dental Board was "not structured in a way that merits a good-government seal of approval."[81] In their view, the danger that regulatory entities may "be captured by private interests"[82] was beside the point: antitrust laws simply do not apply to state agencies, and since the Dental Board is a state agency, "that is the end of the matter."[83]

According to the dissenters, *Parker* immunity was fashioned in response to the expansion of federal Commerce Clause authority during the New Deal. In 1890, when the Sherman Act was passed, federal power over interstate commerce was understood as limited in such a way that none of the act's supporters would have imagined that the act might someday be used to interfere with a state's regulatory conduct, regardless of whether such conduct was anti-competitive or not. But by the time *Parker* was decided, the Court had broadened the Commerce Clause so much that state and federal regulatory powers were brought into conflict. The *Parker* Court could only resolve that conflict by devising an immunity doctrine that would shield state regulation from federal oversight. *Parker*, the dissenters acknowledged, "was not based on either the language of the Sherman Act or anything in the legislative history," but on the assumptions of the act's authors about the limits on federal power, which, in light of the

[78] *Id.* at 1116.
[79] *Id.* at 1117.
[80] *Id.*
[81] *Id.* (Alito, J., dissenting).
[82] *Id.* at 1112.
[83] *Id.* at 1118.

New Deal's erosion of those limits, required the creation of an immunity doctrine to give states discretion to regulate without federal oversight, the way they had been allowed to do in 1890.[84]

As for *Parker*'s acknowledgement that immunity would not apply on the state's mere say-so, the dissenters viewed that as referring only to cases in which the state tried to authorize *private* entities to engage in illegal conduct, which was not occurring here. The Dental Board is not a private trade association but "a full-fledged state agency"[85] to which the state gave "the power to regulate."[86] This was just like the raisin cartel at issue in *Parker* itself—and the city's behavior in *Omni Outdoor*—in both of which the anti-competitive conduct was declared immune because the entity involved was a government entity.[87] In the dissent's view, these cases demonstrated that *Parker* immunity does not hinge on the acts of the regulator, whether anti-competitive or even corrupt, but solely on considerations of state autonomy.[88] That autonomy would be compromised by aggressively applying antitrust laws against regulatory boards. The risk of liability could undermine the states' ability to employ the expertise of chosen professionals to help "regulat[e] a technical profession in which lay people have little expertise."[89]

Finally, the dissenters observed, it makes little sense to stop the inquiry at whether the regulatory agency is staffed by practitioners in the regulated trade. If one took the majority's approach of focusing on the national policy against anti-competitive conduct instead of state independence, then there was no reason not to make the inquiry broader and determine "whether this regulatory body has been captured by the entities that it is supposed to regulate," regardless of who serves on the board.[90] The reason the majority did not go so far, wrote Justice Alito, was because it is "no simple task" to determine "when regulatory capture has occurred." But this is just why courts should be "reliev[ed] . . . from the obligation to make

---

[84] *Id.* at 1119.
[85] *Id.* at 1122.
[86] *Id.* at 1120.
[87] *Id.* at 1122.
[88] *Id.*
[89] *Id.*
[90] *Id.* at 1123.

such determinations at all,"[91] and should simply immunize all state entities, regardless of their behavior.

D. Summary

It is no surprise that the dissent was signed by the Court's most steadfast proponents of state autonomy and judicial deference. Justices Alito, Scalia, and Thomas are hardly ignorant of the danger that regulatory entities may abuse their powers to benefit the politically influential, but, in their view, that is simply not a matter for the courts—and efforts by judges to combat such abuses are only judicial meddling. Courts ought therefore to leave it to the political process to police the conduct of regulatory bodies.

This argument is unpersuasive. Given that *Parker* immunity, like so much else in antitrust law, is a wholly judge-made doctrine to begin with, it seems a little late to sound the alarm about judicial "activism" or interference with state authority. In fact, although the dissent phrases its concerns as somehow more fundamental or objective than the majority's considerations of regulatory policy, the dissent is no less rooted in policy considerations. The dissenters argue that "[t]he Sherman Act . . . is not an anticorruption or good-government statute,"[92] but by that logic, state entities should be accorded *no immunity at all*, since the antitrust laws are also not state-autonomy statutes. On the contrary, the Court has often said that the primary concerns of the antitrust laws are "the protection of competition,"[93] the promotion of "fundamental national values of free enterprise and economic competition,"[94] and the preservation of a "national policy in favor of competition."[95] These laws make no reference to state immunity.[96] As the dissent admits, the immunity doctrine itself is based solely on the Court's vision of what makes for "good government"—namely, the "dual system" which gives states a degree of independence never mentioned in the words of the antitrust statutes. State autonomy in antitrust is therefore just a

---

[91] *Id.*

[92] *Id.* at 1122.

[93] Brown Shoe Co. v. United States, 370 U.S. 294, 320 (1962).

[94] FTC v. Phoebe Putney Health Sys., Inc., 133 S. Ct. 1003, 1010 (2013).

[95] Midcal Aluminum, 445 U.S. at 106.

[96] N.C. Bd. of Dental Exam'rs, 135 S. Ct. at 1114.

policy consideration like any other. As with Eleventh Amendment immunity, the dissent's arguments for judicial deference in antitrust have taken on an "activist" life of their own, which throws the statutory text overboard in the service of policy considerations about the proper federal-state balance.

Because *Parker* immunity is a creation of judicial grace, it is up to the courts to decide the conditions on which they will grant that immunity. Good economics teaches us to regard state immunity with suspicion, as it is likely to encourage factionalism and rent-seeking. Good federalism teaches that state autonomy should be sacrificed when necessary to protect individual rights. Thus both wise policy and fidelity to the text of the statutes counsels for narrowing, not expanding, state antitrust immunity.

IV. A Path for the Future

A. The Constitutional Dimension

Although the Court was right to deny blanket immunity to the agency, the decision appears to have little applicability beyond the facts of this case. The structure of the North Carolina Board of Dental Examiners was unusual in that members were chosen not by elected officials or the general public, but by other practicing members of the profession, thus blurring what the Court might otherwise consider a clear line between a public entity and a private trade association.

Justice Kennedy's closing statement—that courts must assess "all the circumstances of a case"[97] when deciding questions of antitrust immunity—makes it hard to predict how future courts will use the decision. Yet it seems that states should find it easy to structure agencies in ways that will satisfy the courts that regulators are being adequately supervised. Moreover, of the two factors that determine whether *Parker* immunity applies, it is the other one—the "clear articulation" requirement—that is more troubling. Under the current rule of *Southern Motor Carriers*, states can satisfy this requirement with a vague "permissive policy," which undermines democratic accountability much more than the "active supervision" requirement does. But the Court did not address this issue. Thus the *Dental Examiners* case seems unlikely to cause much change. It is at

[97] *Id*. at 1117.

least gratifying to see the FTC taking steps to protect entrepreneurs against some of the worst abuses.

A better solution would be to narrow the antitrust immunities drastically, not only through a rigid "active supervision" requirement and a reinvigorated "clear articulation" rule, but also by adopting a third restriction on *Parker* immunity, rooted in a concern that went largely unaddressed in the North Carolina litigation: the constitutional right to earn a living without unreasonable government interference.

The Constitution guarantees to every person the right to pursue the vocation of his or her choice.[98] This right was well recognized by common law courts as far back as the 17th century, when English courts and Parliament took steps to block the government from creating monopolies that denied people the right to take up trades or enter into professions.[99] Although much neglected today,[100] this right is nevertheless firmly rooted in the nation's history and tradition, and courts have held, even recently, that the government may not arbitrarily deprive people of the right to earn a living—a right Justice William Douglas called "the most precious liberty that man possesses."[101]

This right is very often the victim of licensing regimes that exclude entrepreneurs from the marketplace for the benefit of existing industries. Some licensing requirements impose unnecessary and burdensome education or training requirements on people wishing

---

[98] See, e.g., Greene v. McElroy, 360 U.S. 474, 492 (1959).

[99] See, e.g., The Case of Monopolies, 11 Co. Rep. 84b, 77 Eng. Rep. 1260 (Q.B. 1603); City of London's Case, 8 Co. Rep. 121b, 77 Eng. Rep. 658 (K.B. 1610); Dr. Bonham's Case, 8 Co. Rep. 107a, 77 Eng. Rep. 638 (C.P. 1610). See also Bernard Siegan, Economic Liberties and the Constitution 36 (1980).

[100] To cite just one example, Justice Scalia has asserted that "the 'liberties' protected by Substantive Due Process do not include economic liberties." Stop the Beach Renourishment, Inc. v. Florida Dep't of Envtl. Prot., 560 U.S. 702, 721 (2010). This is simply not true. No court has ever categorically excluded economic liberty from the protections of the Due Process Clause. While economic liberty today receives low-yield "rational basis" review, that review is still *some* degree of protection, and in practice courts have protected that right under the Due Process Clause even in recent years. See, e.g., Merrifield, 547 F.3d at 991; Bruner v. Zawacki, 997 F. Supp. 2d 691 (E.D. Ky. 2014).

[101] Barsky v. Bd. of Regents of Univ., 347 U.S. 442, 472 (1954) (Douglas, J., dissenting).

to practice a business.[102] Others impose no requirements relating to skill or honesty, but simply bar people from entering trades if the government believes no more competition is "necessary."[103] Such exploitation of government's regulatory power is a danger not only to wise policy-making and to consumer welfare, but also to constitutionally protected economic liberty.

B. A New Way

This constitutional dimension suggests that antitrust immunity should be only rarely accorded to private entities that are deputized by the government to enforce rules restricting entry into trades. Future decisions should impose a three-part test to determine whether to immunize private entities who wield state power to block competition.

First, the "active supervision" requirement should be consistently applied in the manner promised in *North Carolina Board of Dental Examiners*. The Court's refusal to waive this consideration simply because the board wears a state badge is gratifying, but it is only a first step, and, as the dissent notes, important questions remain unanswered. The Court says that "active supervision" requires state officials to "'have and exercise power to review particular anti-competitive acts of private parties and disapprove those that fail to accord with state policy,'"[104] and that "the 'mere potential for state supervision is not an adequate substitute for a decision by the State.'"[105] It also says that the state agent doing the supervising "may not itself be an active market participant."[106] But beyond that, adequacy "will

---

[102] See, e.g., Craigmiles, 312 F.3d at 222 (law required two years of training as an undertaker before selling coffins); Cornwell v. Hamilton, 80 F. Supp. 2d 1101 (S.D. Cal. 1999) (law required 1,600 hours of training in unrelated subjects to obtain a license to braid hair).

[103] See Timothy Sandefur, A Public Convenience and Necessity and Other Conspiracies Against Trade: A Case Study from the Missouri Moving Industry, 24 Geo. Mason U. Civ. Rts. L.J. 159 (2014); Timothy Sandefur, State "Competitor's Veto" Laws and the Right to Earn a Living: Some Paths to Federal Reform, 38 Harv. J. L. & Pub. Pol'y 1009 (2015).

[104] N. C. Bd. of Dental Exam'rs, 135 S. Ct. at 1112 (quoting Patrick, 486 U.S. at 101)

[105] *Id.* at 1116 (quoting Ticor, 504 U.S. at 638).

[106] *Id.* at 1117.

depend on all the circumstances of a case."[107] This leaves unanswered such questions as whether a regulator qualifies as an "active market participant" if he simply takes a year off to work for the regulatory board, or if he limits his practice in part, but continues to operate on the side.[108] If a dentist serving on the board chooses not to offer teeth-whitening services, but otherwise maintains his practice, is he an "active market participant" vis-à-vis the teeth-whitening trade? Such issues can only be resolved by further litigation, but the courts should err on the side of protecting competition, not state autonomy.

Second, the "clear articulation" requirement should be reinvigorated, to require something more than mere "permissive policy." *Southern Motor Carriers* should be overruled, and the stricter requirement of *Goldfarb* reinstated. As Michael E. DeBow notes, *Southern Motor Carriers* "evidenced a complete lack of interest in the public choice explanation" for how regulatory agencies can fall into the hands of politically powerful businesses at the expense of entrepreneurs and consumers.[109] That case premised its enfeeblement of the "clear articulation" requirement on the idea that limiting immunity to situations in which state laws actually *compel* the anti-competitive conduct would "reduce[] the range of regulatory alternatives available to the State."[110] But many federal laws reduce the states' range of regulatory alternatives, and if "[t]he antitrust laws reflect a basic national policy favoring free markets over regulated markets,"[111] then any state law contradicting that policy must yield.[112] In fact, the Supreme Court has declared that by applying a consistent presumption against immunity from the antitrust laws and "adhering in most cases to fundamental and accepted assumptions about the benefits of competition," the courts actually "increase the States' regulatory flexibility."[113]

The lax *Southern Motor Carriers* rule reduces accountability by encouraging states to delegate authority to less-accountable

---

[107] *Id.*

[108] *Id.* at 1123 (Alito, J., dissenting).

[109] Michael E. DeBow, Understanding (and Misunderstanding) Public Choice: A Response to Farber and Frickey, 66 Tex. L. Rev. 993, 1012 n. 4 (1988).

[110] Southern Motor Carriers, 471 U.S. at 61.

[111] Omni Outdoor, 499 U.S. at 388.

[112] Sola Elec. Co. v. Jefferson Elec. Co., 317 U.S. 173, 176 (1942).

[113] Ticor, 504 U.S. at 636.

enforcement arms, and to couch their economic policies in vague terms that give regulators the broadest possible power and elected officials the greatest degree of plausible deniability. This encourages regulatory capture. Also, a statute that simply lets regulators decide whether to block competition does not give clear instructions to the private parties who wield dangerous power to impose anti-competitive rules contrary to federal antitrust policy. A non-specific "permissive policy" lets them limit free competition without concern for whether they are targeting precisely the aspect of competition that elected officials meant to curtail.[114] Private entities can then exercise "unguided discretion" to choose how much to displace competition—making it "illusory to view the state legislature as the 'politically accountable' source of a state policy that in fact has been adopted by the agency itself."[115]

The *Southern Motor Carriers* Court tried to answer this concern by requiring "evidence [that] *conclusively shows* that a State intends to adopt a permissive policy,"[116] but this does little since vague "permissive policies" are not made less vague by the fact that the law "conclusively shows" that the state has adopted a vague policy! An instruction like "engage in whatever anti-competitive conduct you choose" would *conclusively* delegate broad power, but it would not define the contours of that power. Thus the "permissive policy" rule encourages judges to "use [their] imagination liberally in determining whether particular anti-competitive conduct was a foreseeable or logical result of the regulatory delegation" and to grant immunity when they conclude in the affirmative.[117] Yet this conflicts with the Court's often-asserted reluctance to infer state-action immunity

---

[114] See John F. Hart, "Sovereign" State Policy and State Action Antitrust Immunity, 56 Fordham L. Rev. 535, 571 (1988) ("The displacement-of-competition standard, in supporting immunity for a substantial class of restraints instituted by state agencies or local government that cannot plausibly be said to implement state policy, defeats the Court's objective of confining immunity to those restraints that implement state policy.").

[115] C. Douglas Floyd, Plain Ambiguities in the Clear Articulation Requirement for State Action Antitrust Immunity: The Case of State Agencies, 41 B.C. L. Rev. 1059, 1106 (2000).

[116] Southern Motor Carriers, 471 U.S. at 62 (emphasis added).

[117] Thomas M. Jorde, Antitrust and the New State Action Doctrine: A Return to Deferential Economic Federalism, 75 Cal. L. Rev. 227, 244 (1987).

lightly.[118] To the extent that *Southern Motor Carriers* was motivated by valid federalism concerns, those considerations are sufficiently addressed by a rule that allows immunity to private parties only when their anti-competitive conduct is explicitly compelled by state law. This would respect state autonomy while more effectively ensuring the transparency and accountability that the Court emphasizes in *North Carolina Board of Dental Examiners.*

But these two procedural restrictions on *Parker* immunity would remain inadequate even if they were ratcheted up to a workable degree. Any state-imposed limit on competition should also satisfy some substantive judicial scrutiny as well. That substantive test should accord states sufficient discretion to regulate trades in ways that will protect the public interest in health, safety, and honesty, while preventing states from adopting laws that simply let private parties block legitimate competition.

Several antitrust scholars have called for such a substantive requirement. Edlin and Haw, for example, have proposed that the Court apply a Rule of Reason in such cases.[119] Ronald E. Kennedy suggested that courts require a showing, similar to that used in dormant Commerce Clause cases, that the state's interests significantly outweigh federal interests.[120] Other writers suggested that the Court require some evidence of market failure which the restraint would redress,[121] and the FTC's own State Action Report has suggested a multi-tiered approach under which the "clear articulation" and "active supervision" requirements would be more stringently imposed in proportion to "the seriousness of the alleged anti-competitive conduct."[122] I suggest that a "substantial advancement" test—requiring that any restriction on competition must substantially advance a significant government interest—would ensure a more workable tradeoff between regulation and the right to economic liberty.

---

[118] See, e.g., Ticor, 504 U.S. at 636; Phoebe Putney, 133 S. Ct. at 1010.

[119] *Supra* note 31, at 40.

[120] *Supra* note 17, at 46–47, 72–73.

[121] John Shepard Wiley Jr., A Capture Theory of Antitrust Federalism, 99 Harv. L. Rev. 713, 756 (1986); Peter Hettich, Mere Refinement of the State Action Doctrine Will Not Work, 5 DePaul Bus. & Com. L.J. 105, 147-50 (2006) (proposing a "reasonableness" inquiry).

[122] John T. Delacourt & Todd J. Zywicki, The FTC and State Action: Evolving Views on the Proper Role of Government, 72 Antitrust L.J. 1075, 1089 (2005).

This proposal is bolstered, ironically, by a point made by the dissenters. In arguing that *Parker* immunity must be understood in its historical context, they observe that in 1890, when the Sherman Act was passed, "the regulation of the practice of medicine and dentistry was regarded as falling squarely within the States' sovereign police power," and the act's authors would have thought it unnecessary to carve out explicit protections for state regulatory authority.[123] Only in the New Deal era, when changes in Commerce Clause doctrine magnified federal power, was it necessary to read into the act an immunity doctrine that would shield state powers that the act's authors could not have meant to hinder. But that argument cuts both ways. The Sherman Act was also passed at a time when constitutional protections against abusive licensing requirements were more vigilantly enforced than they are now. Indeed, the dissent cited the case of *Dent v. West Virginia*[124] to support its assertion that states in the 1890s faced little hindrance when regulating professions. But that case actually stands for the opposite proposition. It was the first Supreme Court decision on the constitutionality of occupational licensing under the Fourteenth Amendment; it set forth a substantive limit on licensing laws under the Due Process Clause, holding that if a state imposed a requirement that was not "appropriate to the calling or profession, [or] attainable by reasonable study or application," such a law would unconstitutionally "deprive [a person] of his right to pursue a lawful vocation."[125] Written at the dawn of the so-called *Lochner* era,[126] *Dent* asserted federal protections for economic liberty.[127] The authors of

[123] N.C. Bd. of Dental Examiners, 135 S. Ct. at 1119 (Alito, J., dissenting).

[124] 129 U.S. 114 (1889).

[125] *Id.* at 122.

[126] This term, as David E. Bernstein reminds us, is slippery. See David E. Bernstein, *Lochner* Era Revisionism, Revised: *Lochner* and the Origins of Fundamental Rights Constitutionalism, 92 Geo. L.J. 1, 10-11 (2003) ("in practice there was not one *Lochner* era, but three."). Bernstein dates it from Allgeyer v. Louisiana, 165 U.S. 578 (1897), but the principle of freedom of contract and the right to pursue the occupation of one's choice predates that by centuries. See Sandefur, Right to Earn a Living, *supra* note 2, at 17-24. What appears in retrospect to be a "*Lochner* era" is actually an artifact of the advent of the Fourteenth Amendment, which for the first time made state restrictions on economic liberty a matter for federal court review.

[127] *Dent* was written by Justice Stephen J. Field, one of the godfathers of laissez-faire constitutionalism. See generally John C. Eastman & Timothy Sandefur, Stephen Field: Frontier Justice or Justice on the Natural Rights Frontier?, Nexus: J. Opinion 121 (2001).

the Sherman Act could no more have anticipated today's excessively deferential "rational basis" test than they could have anticipated the changes in Commerce Clause doctrine.[128] If historical context justified the *Parker* Court's choice to read state-action immunity into antitrust law, then it also would justify courts today in reading into the same body of law protections against state restrictions on economic liberty that the Sherman Act's authors would likewise have taken for granted. At the very least, it warrants a sliding scale whereby state antitrust immunity expands only if constitutional protections for economic liberty grow with it. Unless the dissenters are willing to accept the latter, they should not argue for the former.

If state immunity from the antitrust laws is granted "out of respect for . . . the State, not out of respect for the economics of price restraint,"[129] then the flexibility accorded to states under the antitrust laws should mirror the flexibility accorded to states when they deviate from other federal legal or constitutional baselines. The Court should apply a rule that presumes in favor of antitrust liability, unless limiting competition is necessary to accomplish an important end. Such an intermediate form of means–ends scrutiny would require a state to articulate an important goal to be accomplished by restricting competition, and should require that the exemption serve that end in reality.[130]

Anything more lenient, such as rational basis deference, is unwarranted, because such deference should apply only when the political

---

A resolute critic of licensing laws and other monopolistic restrictions, Field wrote Cummings v. Missouri, 71 U.S. (4 Wall) 277 (1866), dissented in the Slaughter-House Cases, 83 U.S. (16 Wall.) 36 (1873), and wrote other important decisions pioneering federal protections against state laws that restricted economic liberty under the guise of the police power. He also joined Justice Brewer's dissent in Budd v. People, 143 U.S. 517, 550-51 (1892), which explained that "[t]here are two kinds of monopoly—one of law, the other of fact. The one exists when exclusive privileges are granted. Such a monopoly, the law which creates alone can break, and, being the creation of law, justifies legislative control. A monopoly of fact any one can break, and there is no necessity for legislative interference."

[128] See Sandefur, Right to Earn a Living, *supra* note 2, at 123–40.

[129] Ticor, 504 U.S. at 633.

[130] Cf. Lingle v. Chevron U.S.A. Inc., 544 U.S. 528, 542 (2005) ("substantial advancement" test "asks, in essence, whether a regulation of private property is effective in achieving some legitimate public purpose."); Craig v. Boren, 429 U.S. 190, 197–98 (1976) (substantial advancement test not satisfied by "administrative ease and convenience" or other weak justifications).

process is thought sufficient safeguard for the individual rights at stake. But the political process is not enough to prevent private parties vested with state authority from engaging in anti-competitive and self-interested behavior.[131] The general public is typically unaware of anti-competitive conduct, and although the public genuinely suffers from it, the rewards for those who benefit from it are great enough to ensure that they can prevent any serious reform efforts by injured consumers and taxpayers.

This substantial advancement proposal finds an analogy in cases involving the Federal Arbitration Act. That law—which, like the antitrust laws, was passed under Congress's power to regulate commerce—holds that an arbitration agreement is valid as a matter of federal law and must be enforced, except when the agreement is invalid for reasons of state law.[132] Some states—notably, California— have tried to exploit this exception to invalidate arbitration agreements, in spite of federal policy, and have adopted various strategies to do so.[133] The Supreme Court has frequently been forced to reverse the state courts' efforts to devise common law rules that contradict the federal law.[134] It has not allowed states to escape the Arbitration Act's requirements merely because they "articulate" an anti-arbitration policy or "supervise" state officials who contradict it. Instead, it has used a substantive test: arbitration agreements may be held invalid as a matter of state law only where that state law "arose to govern issues concerning the validity, revocability, and enforceability of contracts generally."[135] This rule blocks state courts from inventing special rules so as to "effect what . . . . the state legislature cannot," namely, a violation of the federal law that requires enforcement of such contracts.[136] A similar rule should apply to *Parker* immunity: while states may, for certain limited reasons, act in ways that would otherwise violate federal law, courts should apply a substantive test

---

[131] Hettich, *supra* note 122, at 143.

[132] Perry v. Thomas, 482 U.S. 483, 492 n. 9 (1987).

[133] See generally Stephen A. Broome, An Unconscionable Application of the Unconscionability Doctrine: How the California Courts Are Circumventing the Federal Arbitration Act, 3 Hastings Bus. L.J. 39 (2006).

[134] See, e.g., AT&T Mobility LLC v. Concepcion, 131 S.Ct. 1740 (2011); Preston v. Ferrer, 552 U.S. 346 (2008).

[135] Perry, 482 U.S. at 492 n.9.

[136] *Id.*

to determine when such acts are valid, so as to ensure that states do not use procedural devices to evade the federal antitrust law.[137] And that test should be grounded on protecting the right of entrepreneurs to earn a living free of unjust government-created monopolies.

V. Conclusion: Antitrust, the Government, and Economic Liberty

There is much about antitrust law that is deplorable. Its vagueness and malleability threaten the stability we expect of law; the fact that it penalizes non-coercive, often socially beneficial conduct renders it morally objectionable; and many of its economic assumptions are so flimsy that it is incoherent as social policy.[138] But whatever its flaws, antitrust doctrine is only worsened by state-action immunities that allow the worst offenders against economic freedom and competition to escape unscathed. As Dominick Armentano concludes, "antitrust has always been irrelevant to the actual monopoly problem in America"[139]—that real problem being the use of government power to prohibit free competition. The fact that the ancestor of today's antitrust law was a body of legal doctrine devoted to freeing individuals from oppressive licensing restrictions and government-sanctioned cartels makes today's backwardness all the more distressing.

---

[137] The state's choice to deputize private market participants, of course, should not bar application of a substantive legal test rooted in constitutional safeguards. Where a private actor serves as an instrument of the state, it may be required to comply with such standards. See, e.g., Evans v. Newton, 382 U.S. 296, 299 (1966). For example, private parties acting as instruments of the government must obtain a warrant when conducting a search, Skinner v. Ry. Labor Executives' Ass'n, 489 U.S. 602, 614 (1989), and a government-created private corporation must comply with the First Amendment in its dealings with citizens, Lebron v. Nat'l R.R. Passenger Corp., 513 U.S. 374, 399 (1995).

[138] Reforms in the vein of the Chicago School, whose motto was that antitrust law should protect competition and not competitors, have remedied some of the worst instances. For example, rules against "predatory pricing," which once punished businesses that simply lowered their prices, are now sharply limited thanks to decisions such as Brooke Grp. Ltd. v. Brown & Williamson Tobacco Corp., 509 U.S. 209 (1993). But while such reforms have taken place at the federal level, many states continue to impose reactionary antitrust laws. For example, the California Court of Appeal has rejected the *Brooke Group* rule, and held that the state's Cartwright Act is intended to "protect[]...smaller, independent retailers" against competition. Bay Guardian Co. v. New Times Media LLC, 187 Cal. App. 4th 438, 457 (Cal. Ct. App. 2010). Thus businesses can be sued in California simply for cutting prices.

[139] Dominick T. Armentano, Antitrust and Monopoly: Anatomy of a Policy Failure 273 (2d ed. 1990).

Although superficially plausible, the rhetoric of state autonomy that underlies the *Parker* immunity doctrine and the dissent here is simply not compatible with the text of the antitrust laws, the national policy they embody, the historical context typically used to justify that doctrine, or the realities of politics and economics. On the contrary, a rational antitrust policy would not only apply to government agencies, but would target them first and foremost. *North Carolina Board of Dental Examiners* holds out some hope on this front: entrepreneurs wrongly deprived of their constitutional right to economic liberty may find it a useful weapon of self-defense, and the most egregious violations of the right to economic liberty may indeed be subject to some limits. But if antitrust law is to serve what the Court calls "'the fundamental national values of free enterprise and economic competition,'"[140] then the immunity doctrines the Court has invented must be much more sharply limited.

---

[140] N.C. Bd. of Dental Exam'rs, 135 S. Ct. at 1110 (quoting Ticor, 504 U.S. at 636).

Hook, Line & Sinker: Supreme Court Holds (Barely!) that Sarbanes-Oxley's Anti-Shredding Statute Doesn't Apply to Fish

John G. Malcolm*

"What do the former employees of Enron and I have in common? According to the Department of Justice, we're both guilty of the same crime. They spent their nights purging documents in order to hide massive financial fraud. I was accused of disposing of several purportedly undersized red grouper into the Florida surf from which I caught them."[1] This is how John Yates describes the ordeal that culminated in the Supreme Court's closely divided opinion in *Yates v. United States*, in which a bare majority held that an anti-shredding provision in the Sarbanes-Oxley Act did not extend to the act of tossing undersized red grouper back into the sea.[2]

A Fine Kettle of Fish

John Yates's plight began on August 23, 2007, when the *Miss Katie*, a commercial fishing vessel, was boarded off the coast of Cortez, Florida, in the Gulf of Mexico by John Jones, a field officer with the Florida Fish and Wildlife Conservation Commission. Jones had also been deputized as a federal agent by the National Marine Fisheries Service, empowering him to enforce federal fisheries laws. Yates had been hired to serve as captain of the three-member crew, and the *Miss Katie* was six days into its voyage to catch red grouper.

---

* Director, Edwin Meese III Center for Legal and Judicial Studies, and the Ed Gilbertson and Sherry Lindberg Gilbertson Senior Legal Fellow, Heritage Foundation.

[1] John Yates, A Fish Story: I Got Busted for Catching a Few Undersized Grouper. You Won't Believe What Happened Next, Politico Magazine, Apr. 24, 2014, available at http://www.politico.com/magazine/story/2014/04/a-fish-story-106010.html.

[2] 135 S. Ct. 1074 (2015).

At that time, federal law required that harvested red grouper be at least 20 inches long. Upon boarding the vessel, the officer spotted three red grouper that appeared to be undersized. He proceeded to spend the next several hours inspecting the more-than 3,000 fish in the ship's hold, ultimately determining that 72 grouper measured between 18-3/4 and 19-3/4 inches.

Harvesting undersized grouper is not a crime. It is, however, a civil violation under the Magnuson-Stevens Act, punishable by a fine of up to $500 and possible suspension of one's fishing license.[3] Before departing, Officer Jones issued Yates a citation, placed the undersized fish in wooden crates (but did not seal them with evidence tape), and instructed Yates to leave them there until the ship returned to the dock.

Two days after the *Miss Katie* returned, Officer Jones re-measured the fish and determined that although 69 (not 72) of the fish still measured less than 20 inches, the majority of those fish were much closer to 20 inches than the fish he had inspected at sea. Fishy behavior was clearly afoot—Jones suspected that these were not the same fish. Federal agents then spoke to Thomas Lemmons, one of the other crew members, who eventually admitted that Yates had directed him to remove the undersized fish from the unsealed crate, throw them overboard, and replace them with other fish from the catch, which he did.

Nearly three years later, in May 2010, John Yates was charged in a three-count felony indictment. Specifically, he was charged with violating 18 U.S.C. § 2232(a) (which carries a potential five-year sentence) for throwing the undersized fish overboard in order to prevent the government from taking possession of them; 18 U.S.C. § 1001(a)(2) (which carries a potential five-year sentence) for falsely stating to federal agents that the fish that were measured on the dock were the same fish Officer Jones had measured at sea; and, 18 U.S.C. § 1519 (better known as Sarbanes-Oxley's anti-shredding provision, which carries a potential 20-year sentence) for destroying, concealing, and covering up the undersized fish with the intent to impede, obstruct, and influence the investigation and proper administration of the catching of red grouper under the legal minimum size limit. Somewhat ironically, the regulation governing

[3] 16 U.S.C. §§ 1857–1858.

size limits for grouper has been amended, reducing the permissible length from 20 to 18 inches—so had the inspection taken place today, all of the fish aboard the *Miss Katie* would have been in the clear.

The jury acquitted Yates on the Section 1001 false statement count but convicted him on the remaining two counts, specifically, Section 1519 and Section 2232(a).

Section 1519 of Title 18 provides:

> Whoever knowingly alters, destroys, mutilates, conceals, covers up, falsifies, or makes a false entry in any record, document, or tangible object with the intent to impede, obstruct, or influence the investigation or proper administration of any matter within the jurisdiction of any department or agency of the United States or any case filed under title 11, or in relation to or contemplation of any such matter or case, shall be fined under this title, imprisoned not more than 20 years, or both.

And Section 2232(a) of Title 18 provides:

> Destruction or Removal of Property to Prevent Seizure. Whoever, before, during, or after any search for or seizure of property by any person authorized to make such search or seizure, knowingly destroys, damages, wastes, disposes of, transfers, or otherwise takes any action, or knowingly attempts to destroy, damage, waste, dispose of, transfer, or otherwise take any action, for the purpose of preventing or impairing the Government's lawful authority to take such property into its custody or control or to continue holding such property under its lawful custody and control, shall be fined under this title or imprisoned not more than 5 years, or both.

Although the Sentencing Guidelines range was 21 to 27 months' imprisonment, the judge sentenced Yates to 30 days' imprisonment, followed by three years' supervised release. Yates's conviction was affirmed on appeal, and he subsequently sought a writ of certiorari, which the Supreme Court granted, challenging his conviction under Section 1519, but not the other count of conviction under Section 2232(a).

Why did the Court agree to review the case? After all, it was highly unlikely that anyone else would be prosecuted for violating

Section 1519 under a similar fact pattern in the future. Moreover, Yates was convicted on another felony charge, which he was not challenging, and received a sentence well below the applicable guideline range—much less the 20-year statutory maximum in Section 1519 and even the five-year statutory maximum in Section 2232(a). As the King of Siam said in Rodgers and Hammerstein's *The King and I*, "Is a puzzlement."[4]

Trawling for Evidence

Section 1519 is part of the Sarbanes-Oxley Act of 2002, which was enacted in the aftermath of the Enron Corporation fiasco. According to its reported earnings, Enron was, before its collapse, the seventh largest corporation in America. It was, however, a mirage.

On October 23, 2001, shortly after Enron announced that it was writing down over $1 billion in losses due to bad investments, David Duncan, the Arthur Andersen partner in charge of the Enron account, ordered his staff, in anticipation of a formal investigation and under the guise of complying with the company's existing document retention policy, to destroy literally tons of documents pertaining to Enron. For the next two-and-a-half weeks, Andersen employees at home and abroad worked around the clock doing precisely that. The purge, however, was not limited to documents, but extended to computer hard drives and an email system that contained copious records related to Enron. It was not until Duncan received a subpoena from the Securities and Exchange Commission on November 8 that the infamous Enron shredding party stopped.[5]

Within one month, Enron declared bankruptcy, and while certain insiders prospered to the tune of millions of dollars, the scandal left over 20,000 employees unemployed with worthless retirement accounts. Enron defrauded investors and pension funds out of billions of dollars, causing investors to question the financial reporting of other public companies. Congress responded with the Sarbanes-Oxley Act,

[4] Rodgers & Hammerstein, A Puzzlement, on "The King and I" (Decca 1951).

[5] See generally Arthur Andersen LLP v. United States, 544 U.S. 696, 699–702 (2005); S. Rep. No. 107-146, at 2–5 (2002) (Comm. Rep.); Michael Brick, Andersen Fires Lead Enron Auditor, N.Y. Times, Jan. 15, 2002, available at http://www.nytimes.com/2002/01/15/business/15CND-ENRON.html; Richard A. Oppel, Jr. & Kurt Eichenwald, Arthur Andersen Fires an Executive for Enron Orders, N.Y. Times, Jan. 16, 2002, available at http://www.nytimes.com/2002/01/16/business/16ENRO.html.

whose goal, as set forth in its preamble, was "[t]o protect investors by improving the accuracy and reliability of corporate disclosures made pursuant to the securities laws,"[6] and which was designed to ensure that, in the words of President George W. Bush at the bill signing ceremony, "No boardroom in America is above or beyond the law."[7]

Section 1519 of Sarbanes-Oxley was designed "to clarify and close loopholes in the existing criminal laws relating to the destruction or fabrication of evidence and the preservation of financial and audit records."[8] These loopholes posed a problem for prosecutors in the ultimately ill-fated criminal case against Arthur Andersen. One of the problems that this section sought to address was the fact that federal obstruction of justice statutes in effect at that time did not cover the destruction, alteration, or fabrication of documents *prior to* the formal initiation of a federal investigation. Another problem this law was designed to address was that the existing witness tampering statute, 18 U.S.C. § 1512, made it a crime to "persuade[] another person" to destroy evidence but not to destroy evidence oneself, which forced prosecutors in the Arthur Andersen case "to proceed under the legal fiction that the defendants are being prosecuted for telling other people to shred documents, not simply for destroying evidence themselves."[9]

While it's clear that Section 1519 criminalized the destruction or alteration of corporate records with the intent to frustrate an actual or contemplated federal investigation, the precise scope of its parameters remained unclear. Could it extend to John Yates? The government sure thought so.

The Government's Fishing Expedition

The government contended that Section 1519, located in Chapter 73 of Title 18 which covers "Obstruction of Justice,"[10] was always envisioned to be a broad and general evidence-destruction provision,

---

[6] Sarbanes-Oxley Act of 2002, Pub. L. No. 107–204, 116 Stat. 745 (2002).

[7] Elisabeth Bumiller, Corporate Conduct: The President; Bush Signs Bill Aimed at Fraud in Corporations, N.Y. Times, July 31, 2002, available at http://www.nytimes.com/2002/07/31/business/corporate-conduct-the-president-bush-signs-bill-aimed-at-fraud-in-corporations.html.

[8] 148 Cong. Rec. 104, S7418–21 (daily ed. July 26, 2002) (statement of Sen. Patrick Leahy).

[9] S. Rep. No. 107–146, at 7 (2002) (Comm. Rep.).

[10] 18 U.S.C. § 1501 et seq.

something long sought by legal reformers. Further, Section 1519 was meant to be paired with Section 1512(c), the witness-tampering statute, which, among other things, makes it a crime to make unavailable any "record, document, or other object" in an official proceeding, whether pending or not, or to corruptly persuade, intimidate, force, mislead, or otherwise induce someone else to "alter, destroy, mutilate, or conceal an object with the intent to impair the object's integrity or availability for use" in such a proceeding. It was undisputed that Section 1512(c), which uses similar language to Section 1519, applies to all types of physical items, not just business records.

The government argued that Section 1519's use of the phrase "any . . . tangible object" unambiguously covers the destruction of any and all types of physical evidence—including undersized grouper—so long as it's done with the requisite obstructive intent and pertains to an investigation or administration of "any matter within the jurisdiction of any department or agency of the United States." The government further noted that it had "used these provisions to prosecute the destruction of a wide array of physical evidence—including human bodies, bloodstains, guns, drugs, cash, and automobiles—in order to cover up offenses ranging from terrorism and the unreasonable use of lethal police force to violations of environmental and workplace-safety laws."[11] The government also argued that it would make little sense for Congress to pass a statute that prohibited a murderer from destroying a threatening letter to his victim—in other words, a document—"but not the murder weapon, his victim's body, or the getaway car."[12]

The government maintained that Yates's arguments based on canons of statutory construction and the rule of lenity, discussed below, were unavailing because of the plain meaning of the language used in Section 1519. While canons of construction and the rule of lenity are appropriate to resolve any ambiguity or uncertainty in the meaning of a statute, neither existed here. It was the government's position that

> The objective of both Chapter 73 and Section 1519 is to protect the integrity of government operations, promote

[11] Brief for Respondent at 5–6, n.1, Yates v. United States, 135 S. Ct. 1074 (2015) (No. 13-7451) (listing cases).

[12] *Id.* at 47.

fairness to all parties in official proceedings, and ensure that government determinations of factual matters are accurate and true. Those goals are threatened by the destruction of *any* relevant evidence, regardless of its particular form.[13]

Slipping Through the Net

Yates contended, on the other hand, that the meaning of the phrase "tangible object" is "chameleon-like," adapting "to whatever context it is used in."[14] To illustrate his point that "tangible object" can mean different things in different contexts, Yates noted in his brief that, "if a person says, 'General Motors sells tangible objects,' one would naturally understand the person to be referring to automobiles, automobile parts, and the like. But if a person says, 'Apple sells tangible objects,' one would not think of automobiles; rather, one would ordinarily understand the person to be referring to MacBooks, iMacs, iPhones, iPads, and other similar electronic 'i' products."[15]

To ascertain the true meaning of "tangible object" as used in Section 1519, Yates and many of the amici curiae supporting him urged the Court to apply two well-known canons of statutory construction, both of which are designed to narrow the potential universe of meanings that could attach to a statutory term in order to avoid giving unintended breadth to those terms: *noscitur a sociis* and *ejusdem generis*. The former instructs that "words grouped in a list should be given related meaning,"[16] while the latter advises that where general or vague words follow specific words in a statute, the "general words are construed to embrace only objects similar in nature to those objects enumerated by the preceding specific words."[17]

McBoyle v. United States[18] is illustrative of this approach. McBoyle transported from Illinois to Oklahoma an airplane that he knew had

[13] *Id.* at 18 (emphasis in original).

[14] Brief for Petitioner at 12, Yates v. United States, 135 S. Ct. 1074 (2015) (No. 13-7451).

[15] *Id.* at 13–14.

[16] Dole v. United Steelworkers of America, 494 U.S. 26, 36 (1990) (quoting Mass. v. Morash, 490 U.S. 107, 114 (1989)). See also Third Nat'l Bank in Nashville v. Impac Ltd., 432 U.S. 312, 322 (1977); United States v. Williams, 553 U.S. 285, 294 (2008).

[17] Washington State Dep't of Social & Health Servs. v. Guardianship Estate of Keffeler, 537 U.S. 371, 384 (2003) (quoting Circuit City Stores, Inc. v. Adams, 532 U.S. 105, 114–15 (2001)).

[18] 283 U.S. 25 (1931).

been stolen. He was subsequently convicted of violating the National Motor Vehicle Theft Act and sentenced to three years' imprisonment and ordered to pay a $2,000 fine. On appeal, McBoyle argued that the act, which made it a crime to transport a "motor vehicle" in interstate commerce that the defendant knows to have been stolen, did not encompass the interstate transportation of a stolen aircraft. The act defined "motor vehicle" as including "an automobile, automobile truck, automobile wagon, motor cycle, or any other self-propelled vehicle not designed for running on rails," and there is no question that an airplane is clearly a "self-propelled vehicle not designed for running on rails." Nonetheless, Justice Oliver Wendell Holmes, writing for a unanimous Court, held that an aircraft was not a vehicle for purposes of the act. Although acknowledging that, "etymologically it is possible to use the word to signify a conveyance working on land, water or air," the Court cautioned:

> Although it is not likely that a criminal will carefully consider the text of the law before he murders or steals, it is reasonable that a fair warning should be given to the world, in language that the common world will understand, of what the law intends to do if a certain line is passed. To make the warning fair, so far as possible, the line should be clear. When a rule of conduct is laid down in words that evoke in the common mind only the picture of vehicles moving on land, the statute should not be extended to aircraft simply because it may seem to us that a similar policy applies, or upon the speculation that, if the legislature had thought of it, very likely broader words would have been used.[19]

In that case, the Court concluded, "[i]t is impossible to read words that so carefully enumerate the different forms of motor vehicles and have no reference of any kind to aircraft, as including airplanes under a term that usage more and more precisely confines to a different class."[20] Similarly, the Court in *Begay v. United States*[21] rejected the government's argument that drunk driving was a "violent felony" for purposes of the catch-all provision of the Armed Career Criminal Act, because unlike the other crimes listed in the act, drunk driving

[19] *Id.* at 26–27.
[20] *Id.* at 27.
[21] 553 U.S. 137 (2008).

"is a crime of negligence or recklessness, rather than violence or aggression."[22] The presence of the other crimes "indicates that the statute covers only *similar* crimes, rather than *every* crime that 'presents a serious potential risk of physical injury to another.'"[23]

Perhaps most significantly, in *Bond v. United States*[24]—a strange case decided the previous term—the Court stated, "We are reluctant to ignore the ordinary meaning of 'chemical weapon' when doing so would transform a statute passed to implement the international Convention on Chemical Weapons into one that also makes it a federal offense to poison goldfish."[25] *Bond* involved the federal prosecution of Carol Anne Bond for her clumsy attempts to harm her former best friend after discovering that she was having an affair with Bond's husband and was pregnant with his child, by spreading common chemicals which left a distinctive color on the woman's car door, mailbox, and front doorknob, resulting in a minor chemical burn on the woman's thumb. Rather than leaving this garden-variety crime to local authorities, federal authorities charged Bond with violating the Chemical Weapons Implementation Act of 1998 (CWIA), a statute designed to implement the United States' treaty obligations under the 1993 Chemical Weapons Convention, thought to be reserved for actions such as the 1995 Sarin gas attack on the Tokyo subway system by members of the doomsday cult Aum Shinrikyo. In an opinion by Chief Justice John Roberts, the Court gave a narrowing construction to the CWIA and held that it did not extend to such criminal activity, stating "[t]he global need to prevent chemical warfare does not require the Federal Government to reach into the kitchen cupboard, or to treat a local assault with a chemical

[22] *Id.* at 146 (quoting United States v. Begay, 470 F.3d 964, 980 (10th Cir. 2006) (McConnell, J., dissenting)).

[23] *Id.* at 142. See also, Gustafson v. Alloyd Co., 513 U.S. 561, 575–76 (1995) ("[T]he term 'written communication' must be read in context to refer to writings that . . . are similar to the terms 'notice, circular, [and] advertisement,'" which appeared in the same list; holding that the word 'communication' applied only to "communications held out to the public at large," which would exclude person-to-person communications even though a dictionary definition might include such communications.); Robinson v. Shell Oil Co., 519 U.S. 337, 343–44 (1997) (explaining that the word "employees" took on different meanings within different sections of the Civil Rights Act of 1964).

[24] 134 S. Ct. 2077 (2014).

[25] *Id.* at 2091.

irritant as the deployment of a chemical weapon."[26] Indeed, as I will discuss below, I suspect that the specter of the *Bond* case was evident throughout the *Yates* case and played an important role in Yates's narrow victory.

In this case, Yates argued, the meaning of the phrase "tangible object" in Section 1519 must be ascertained by reading it within the context of the statutory scheme, its placement within the statute as a whole, and the verbs and surrounding objects that precede it. When taken altogether, and applying the standard canons of statutory construction, Yates claimed that the only sensible reading of "tangible object" within the meaning of this statute must be to refer to a thing that is used to preserve information, such as a computer, server, or other storage device.

Here, Yates asserted, the Sarbanes-Oxley Act was passed in response to the concerted effort by Enron and Arthur Andersen to destroy records, documents, and other things used to store them—such as computer hard drives, DVDs, flash drives, and email systems—in anticipation of a federal investigation. The anti-shredding provision, entitled "Destruction, alteration, or falsification of *records* in Federal investigations and bankruptcy," was placed in Title VIII of the act, more specifically within Section 802, which was itself entitled "Criminal Penalties for Altering *Documents*."[27] Moreover, the phrase "tangible object" in Section 1519 was immediately preceded by the nouns "record" and "document," which share a common meaning in everyday usage of being things that contain and preserve information—an attribute not shared by fish. The phrase is also preceded by the verbs "alters, destroys, mutilates, conceals, covers up, falsifies, or makes a false entry in." While it might be the case that some of these verbs could apply to an undersized red grouper, one could certainly never make a false entry in one.

Although conceding that Section 1519 falls within the chapter entitled "Obstruction of Justice," Yates pointed out that the provisions immediately preceding that section address acts of obstruction in specific contexts, including federal audits, examinations of

[26] Bond, 134 S. Ct. at 20–21.

[27] Pub. L. 107-2014, Title VIII, § 802, 116 Stat. 745 (emphasis added). See R.R. Trainmen v. Balt & O. R. Co., 331 U.S. 519, 528 (1947) (While not dispositive, titles are useful aids that provide "a short-hand reference to the general subject matter involved.").

financial institutions, bankruptcy investigations, and healthcare-related offenses, and that the section immediately following it was aimed at the destruction of corporate audit records, requiring that such records be retained for five years. In short, these provisions fit neatly within the category of requiring that corporate records be preserved for use as evidence in various contexts to discover and punish fraudulent conduct.

Further, while Section 1519 utilizes similar language to the witness-tampering statute, Section 1512(c), it is not identical. While Section 1512(c) established a broad prohibition on the destruction or alteration of any kind of object, including fish, it applies to a more narrow circumstance—evidence being used in an "official proceeding"—which would be more likely to put someone on notice of their obligation to preserve such evidence. Indeed, if the government's argument was correct, Section 1512(c) would likely be rendered superfluous, since a prohibition on destroying (either by oneself or inducing someone else to do so) any conceivable physical object if done to obstruct, impede, or influence an investigation—including a contemplated investigation—or the administration of any matter within the jurisdiction of any department or agency of the United States, would surely encompass any attempt to destroy a physical object to prevent its availability for use in an "official proceeding." Indeed, if the phrase "tangible object" in Section 1519 was meant to encompass every conceivable physical object, then the words "record" and "document" would also be superfluous.[28]

Finally, if any doubt remained as to the meaning of "tangible object" in the anti-shredding provision, Yates argued that doubt should be resolved in his favor under the well-established—but rarely applied—rule of lenity.[29] The rule of lenity functions as both a tie-breaker and a rule of constitutional avoidance, underscoring

[28] Kungys v. United States, 485 U.S. 759, 778 (1988) ("[N]o provision [of a statute or document] should be construed to be entirely redundant.").

[29] See, e.g., McNally v. United States, 483 U.S. 350, 359–60 (1987) (observing that the rule of lenity requires that "when there are two rational readings of a criminal statute, one harsher than the other, we are to choose the harsher only when Congress has spoken in clear and definite language"); Skilling v. United States, 561 U.S. 358, 404, 410 (2010) (holding that the honest-services statute "presents no vagueness problem" when narrowly construed to apply only to "fraudulent schemes to deprive another of honest services through bribes or kickbacks supplied by a third party"; any "ambiguity concerning the ambit of criminal statutes should be resolved in favor of lenity").

the value of providing fair warning to people about what conduct is and is not illegal to ensure that they are not subject to undue punishment for violating vague prohibitions. As the Supreme Court has said on many occasions, because "[n]o one may be required at peril of life, liberty or property to speculate as to the meaning of penal statutes,"[30] criminal statutes must provide "fair warning . . . in language that the common world will understand, of what the law intends to do if a certain line is passed. To make the warning fair, so far as possible the line should be clear."[31]

The Scales of Justice

The potential for abuse by the government and potential reach of Section 1519 appeared to weigh heavily on the justices' minds in this case. It did not escape the justices' attention that Yates had been charged with two obstruction of justice charges, one of which carried a potential 5-year penalty (Section 2232(a)), the other of which carried a potential 20-year penalty (Section 1519). In enacting Section 1519, was it really Congress's intent to pass a new law that criminalized essentially the same conduct as an existing law, and was it really Congress's intent to *quadruple* the potential penalty for obstruction of justice?[32] Could Congress really have meant to punish somebody who violated a fishing regulation, a civil infraction that did not even rise to the level of a misdemeanor, with a potential twenty-year prison sentence? If so, this would give the

---

[30] Lanzetta v. New Jersey, 306 U.S. 451, 453 (1939).

[31] McBoyle, 283 U.S. at 27. See also, United States v. Harriss, 347 U.S. 612, 617 (1954) ("The constitutional requirement of definiteness is violated by a criminal statute that fails to give a person of ordinary intelligence fair notice that his contemplated conduct is forbidden by the statute."); United States v. Lanier, 520 U.S. 259, 265 (1967); Kolender v. Lawson, 461 U.S. 352, 357 (1983) ("[A] penal statute [must] define the criminal offense with sufficient definiteness that ordinary people can understand what conduct is prohibited and in a manner that does not encourage arbitrary and discriminatory enforcement.").

[32] It is worth noting that, in addition to Section 2232(a), the vast majority of other federal obstruction of justice statutes also carry a potential five-year penalty. See, e.g., 18 U.S.C. § 245(b) (2006) (obstruction of civil rights); 18 U.S.C. § 505 (2006) (court forgeries); 18 U.S.C. § 1505 (2006) (obstruction before departments, agencies, and committees, unless terrorism is involved, in which case the penalty rises to eight years); 18 U.S.C. § 1510 (2006) (obstruction of criminal investigations).

government a tremendous amount of discretion in terms of the charges it could file and considerable leverage over defendants in plea negotiations. What defendant facing a potential twenty-year sentence wouldn't be tempted to charge bargain or plea bargain even if he truly believed he was innocent? And if the government could wield such a heavy hammer in this case—one involving throwing some undersized grouper back into the sea—who else might be at risk of facing the same charge for similarly benign conduct?

During oral argument, the justices peppered the government's attorney, Assistant Solicitor General Roman Martinez,[33] with questions about the potential scope of the statute. For instance, Justice Samuel Alito asked whether someone could be prosecuted under Section 1519 and subjected to a potential 20-year sentence if he caught an undersized fish on federal land and threw it back in the lake when he saw an inspector approaching.[34] Indeed he could, replied Martinez.[35]

---

[33] Whose writing has appeared in these pages. See Gregory G. Garre and Roman Martinez, Looking Ahead: October Term 2011, 2010–2011 Cato Sup. Ct. Rev. 357 (2011).

[34] Transcript of Oral Argument at 50–51, Yates v. United States, 135 S. Ct. 1074 (2015) (No. 13-7451). Several amici who filed briefs in support of Yates raised similar hypotheticals urging the Court to read Section 1519 narrowly to avoid such absurd results. See, e.g., Brief for Cato Institute as Amici Curiae Supporting Petitioner, Yates v. United States, 135 S. Ct. 1074 (2015) (No. 13-7451) at 4 (suggesting that "a smoker stealing the last few puffs of his cigarette as he enters the lobby of a government building could be criminally charged for dousing that cigarette in his coffee cup as he approaches the metal detectors manned by a federal officer"); Brief of Cause of Action, et al. as Amicus Curiae Supporting Petitioner, Yates v. United States, 135 S. Ct. 1074 (2015) (No. 13-7451) at 10 (suggesting that "a person who destroys a misappropriated image of 'Smokey Bear,' conceals evidence of a surfboard being used on a beach designated for swimming, throws away a bag of chips from a workplace restroom prior to an OSHA inspection, fails to declare an item on a customs form at the airport, gets rid of a bat used in a teenager's game of 'mailbox baseball,' or discards an empty container of medicine purchased from a foreign pharmacy" could be prosecuted under Section 1519) (citations omitted); See Clinton v. City of New York, 524 U.S. 417, 429 (1998) (When one possible interpretation of a statute "would produce an absurd and unjust result which Congress could not have intended," a court should adopt an alternative reading.); Haggar Co. v. Helvering, 308 U.S. 389, 394 (1940) ("A literal reading of [statutes] which would lead to absurd results is to be avoided when they can be given a reasonable application consistent with their words and with the legislative purpose.").

[35] Transcript, *supra* note 34, at 51.

Justice Antonin Scalia seemed incredulous that a federal prosecutor bothered to pursue this case, at one point asking, "Is this the same guy that ... brought the prosecution in *Bond* last term? ... What kind of a mad prosecutor would try to send this guy up for 20 years or risk sending him up for 20 years?"[36] The justices did not seem mollified when Martinez stated that the government had not sought a 20-year sentence in this case, especially after informing them that his "understanding of the U.S. Attorney's Manual is that the general guidance that's given is that the prosecutor should charge—once the decision is made to bring a criminal prosecution, the prosecution should charge the . . . offense that's the most severe under the law. That's not a hard and fast rule, but that's kind of the default principle."[37] This prompted Justice Scalia to exclaim, "Well, if that's going to be the Justice Department's position, then we're going to have to be much more careful about how extensive statutes are. I mean, if you're saying we're always going to prosecute the most severe, I'm going to be very careful about how severe I make statutes . . . or how much coverage I give to severe statutes."[38]

Perhaps the most significant statement during the oral argument, in terms of affecting the final outcome, came from Chief Justice John Roberts who, after Martinez explained that "we do not prosecute every fish disposal case," stated:

> But the point is that you could, and the point is that once you can, every time you get somebody who is throwing fish overboard, you can go to him and say: Look, if we prosecute you you're facing 20 years, so why don't you plead to one year, or something like that. It's an extraordinary leverage that the broadest interpretation of this statute would give Federal prosecutors.[39]

---

[36] *Id.* at 27–28.

[37] *Id.* at 28–29. Indeed, Chapter 27 of Title 9 of the U.S. Attorneys' Manual provides: "Except as provided in USAM 9–27.330 (pre-charge plea agreements), once the decision to prosecute has been made, the attorney for the government should charge, or should recommend that the grand jury charge, the most serious offense that is consistent with the nature of the defendant's conduct, and that is likely to result in a sustainable conviction."

[38] Transcript, *supra* note 35, at 29.

[39] *Id.* at 31.

In fairness, the U.S. Attorneys' Manual explicitly states that, "[c]harges should not be filed simply to exert leverage to induce a plea."[40] I suspect, however, that many if not all of the justices were quite reasonably concerned that the temptation to overcharge in order to induce a guilty plea out of someone who engaged in trivial, albeit criminal, behavior might be too great for some federal prosecutors to resist.

The One That Got Away

The Court issued its decision in *Yates* on February 25, 2015, and John Yates prevailed—but barely.

Writing for the plurality, Justice Ruth Bader Ginsburg, joined by the chief justice and Justices Stephen Breyer and Sonia Sotomayor, noted that the government's reading of Section 1519 "covers the waterfront, including fish from the sea"[41] but that such an interpretation "would cut §1519 loose from its financial fraud mooring."[42] The plurality concluded that the phrase "tangible object" in Section 1519 "is better read to cover only objects one can use to record or preserve information, not all objects in the physical world."[43]

Justice Ginsburg conceded, of course, that fish would qualify under the ordinary dictionary meaning of "tangible object," but that "[i]n law as in life, however, the same words, placed in different contexts, sometimes mean different things,"[44] and that while "dictionary definitions of the words 'tangible' and 'object' bear consideration, they are not dispositive of the meaning of 'tangible object' in §1519."[45]

Justice Ginsburg then proceeded to note that the heading for Section 1519 ("Destruction, alteration, or falsification of records in

[40] U.S.A.M. 9–27.300. See also U.S.A.M. 9–27.320 ("Proper charge selection also requires consideration of the end result of successful prosecution—the imposition of an appropriate sentence under all the circumstances of the case. In order to achieve this result, it ordinarily should not be necessary to charge a person with every offense for which he/she, may technically be liable (indeed, charging every such offense may in some cases be perceived as an unfair attempt to induce a guilty plea).").

[41] Yates v. United States, 135 S. Ct. 1074, 1081 (2015).

[42] *Id.* at 1079.

[43] *Id.* at 1081.

[44] *Id.* at 1082.

[45] *Id.*

Federal investigations and bankruptcy") "conveys no suggestion that the section prohibits spoliation of any and all physical evidence, however remote from records," nor did the title of the section in Sarbanes-Oxley in which the section was placed ("Destruction of corporate audit records").[46] She stated that "[w]hile these headings are not commanding, they supply cues that Congress did not intend 'tangible object' in §1519 to sweep within its reach physical objects of every kind, including things no one would describe as records, documents, or devices closely associated with them."[47]

The plurality saw additional clues of congressional intent in the fact that Section 1519 was placed at the end of Chapter 73 of Title 18 among several sections prohibiting obstructive acts in specific contexts, rather than among the sections of that Chapter that more broadly address obstructive acts as they relate to official proceedings and criminal trials.[48] The plurality was also persuaded by the fact that, as noted above, if the government's interpretation of Section 1519 is correct, Section 1512(c)(1), which was passed at roughly the same time, would be rendered superfluous,[49] as would Section 2232(a), which imposed a maximum penalty of only five years.[50] The plurality also employed the *noscitur a sociis* and *ejusdem generis* canons of construction and determined that Yates's interpretation of the statute was more reasonable than the government's,[51] especially given that "Yates would have had scant reason to anticipate a felony prosecution, and certainly not one instituted at a time when even the smallest fish he caught came within the legal limit."[52]

---

[46] *Id.* at 1077.

[47] *Id.* at 1083.

[48] *Id.* at 1083–84.

[49] *Id.* at 1085.

[50] *Id.* at 1085 n.6.

[51] *Id.* at 1085–88.

[52] *Id.* at 1087 (citing *Bond* as another example in which the Court rejected a "boundless reading" of a statutory term because of the "deeply serious" consequences that such a reading would entail). The government urged the Court to consider that the phrase "record, document or tangible object" in Section 1519 had its origins in a 1962 Model Penal Code provision that would have imposed liability on anyone who "alters, destroys, mutilates, conceals, or removes a record, document or thing"; however, the plurality noted that the MPC provision described a misdemeanor, not a 20-year felony, and that the MPC provision and federal proposals based on it contained certain built-in limits that are lacking in Section 1519, *id.* at 1092–93 (Kagan, J., dissenting).

And finally, the plurality stated that "if our recourse to traditional statutory tools of statutory construction leaves us any doubt about the meaning of 'tangible object,' as that term is used in §1519, we would invoke the rule that ambiguity concerning the ambit of criminal statutes should be resolved in favor of lenity."[53] The plurality believed "[t]hat interpretive principle is relevant here, where the Government urges a reading of §1519 that exposes individuals to 20-year prison sentences for tampering with *any* physical object that might have evidentiary value in *any* federal investigation into *any* offense, no matter whether the investigation is *pending or merely contemplated*, or whether the offense subject to investigation is *criminal or civil*."[54] A frightening prospect, to be sure.

Justice Alito wrote a short separate opinion concurring in the judgment, thereby providing the decisive fifth vote for Yates. Believing that the "case can and should be resolved on narrow grounds," Justice Alito concluded that "though the question is close, traditional tools of statutory construction confirm that John Yates has the better of the argument."[55] He continued: "Three features of 18 U.S.C. § 1519 stand out to me: the statute's list of nouns, its list of verbs, and its titles. Although perhaps none of these features by itself would tip the case in favor of Yates, the three combined do so."[56]

In a powerful, sometimes biting dissent, replete with entertaining cultural references—what other Supreme Court opinion makes reference to Dr. Seuss[57] and, for those old enough to remember, Mad Libs[58]—Justice Elena Kagan, joined by Justices Antonin Scalia, Clarence Thomas, and Anthony Kennedy, did not buy what the plurality was selling. While the plurality interpreted "tangible object" to cover "only objects one can use to record or preserve information,"

---

[53] *Id.* at 1088 (citation omitted).

[54] *Id.* (emphasis added).

[55] Yates, 135 S. Ct. at 1089 (Alito, J., concurring in judgment).

[56] *Id.*

[57] See *id.* at 1091 (Kagan, J., dissenting) ("A fish is, of course, a discrete thing that possesses physical form. See generally, Dr. Seuss, One Fish Two Fish Red Fish Blue Fish (1960).").

[58] See *id.* at 1099 ("But §1519's meaning should not hinge on the odd game of Mad Libs the concurrence proposes. No one reading §1519 needs to fill in a blank after the words 'records' and 'documents.' That is because Congress, quite helpfully, already did so—adding the term 'tangible object.'").

and Justice Alito interpreted it to cover "something similar to re-cords or documents," the dissenters believed that "conventional tools of statutory construction all lead to a more conventional result: A 'tangible object' is an object that's tangible,"[59] which would cover undersized red grouper. The dissenters expressed the view that the plurality employed the canons of construction to create ambiguity rather than resolve it and that "the canons have no such transforma-tive effect on the workaday language Congress chose."[60]

Justice Kagan stated that the dissenters' "interpretation accords with endless uses of the term in statute and rule books as construed by courts" and cited several federal statutes, state statutes, and federal cases to support the point.[61] And while agreeing "with the plurality (really, who does not?) that context matters in interpreting statutes" and that sometimes "the dictionary definition of a disputed term cannot control," Justice Kagan contended that "this is not such an occasion, for here the text and its context point the same way."[62] The dissenters stressed how the words surrounding "tangible ob-ject" in Section 1519 "reinforce the breadth of the term at issue,"[63] and noted the similarity of this grouping of words to those in other evidence-tampering laws that had been broadly interpreted.[64] And, perhaps in a deferential nod to Justice Scalia, who has a longstand-ing and noted distaste for relying on legislative history in interpret-ing statutes,[65] Justice Kagan added, that "legislative history, for those who care about it, puts an extra icing on a cake already frosted."[66]

Justice Kagan stated that while "the plurality searches far and wide for anything—anything—to support its interpretation" of

[59] Id. at 1091.

[60] Id. at 1097.

[61] Id. at 1091.

[62] Id. at 1092.

[63] Id.

[64] Id. at 1092–93.

[65] See, e.g., Graham County Soil and Water Conservation Dist. v. U.S. ex rel. Wilson, 559 U.S. 280, 302 (2010) (Scalia, J., concurring) ("Anyway, it is utterly impossible to discern what the Members of Congress intended except to the extent that intent is manifested in the *only* remnant of 'history' that bears the unanimous endorsement of the majority in each House: the text of the enrolled bill that became law"); Zedner v. United States, 547 U.S. 489, 511 (2006) (Scalia, J., concurring) ("[T]he use of legislative history is illegitimate and ill advised in the interpretation of any statute.").

[66] Yates, 135 S. Ct. at 1093 (Kagan, J., dissenting).

the statute, "its fishing expedition comes up empty."[67] In her view, the plurality's opinion is doomed from the outset, finding that its reliance on the title of Section 1519 is "already a sign something is amiss,"[68] since she is aware of no other case in which the Court has begun its interpretation or relied on a title "to override the law's clear terms,"[69] and that the plurality's attempt to "divine meaning" from the section's position within Chapter 73 is a "move . . . yet odder than the last."[70] And where the plurality saw surplusage, the dissenters did not, noting that "[o]verlap—even significant overlap—abounds in the criminal law,"[71] and that, regardless, while there is significant overlap between Section 1519 and Section 1512(c)(1), "each applies to conduct the other does not."[72]

Justice Kagan also criticized the plurality for giving a narrower interpretation of the phrase "object" in Section 1519 than in Section 1512(c)(1) and in other statutes that deal with obstruction of justice because those other statutes describe less serious offenses carrying a less severe penalty. She believed this should make no difference whatsoever. According to Justice Kagan, "[h]ow and why that distinction affects application of the *noscitur a sociis* and *ejusdem generis* canons is left obscure: Count it as one more of the plurality's never-before-propounded, not-readily-explained interpretive theories," and that "[t]he canons, in the plurality's interpretive world, apparently switch on and off whenever convenient."[73]

In discussing the subject and purpose of Section 1519, Justice Kagan stated:

> The plurality characterizes records and documents as things that preserve information—and so they are. But just as much, they are things that provide information, and thus potentially serve as evidence relevant to matters under review. And in a statute pertaining to obstruction of federal investigations, that evidentiary function comes to the fore. The destruction

[67] *Id.* at 1094.
[68] *Id.*
[69] *Id.*
[70] *Id.* at 1094–95.
[71] *Id.* at 1095.
[72] *Id.*
[73] *Id.* at 1098.

of records and documents prevents law enforcement agents from gathering facts relevant to official inquiries. And so too does the destruction of tangible objects—of whatever kind. Whether the item is a fisherman's ledger or an undersized fish, throwing it overboard has the identical effect on the administration of justice.[74]

The dissenters made short shrift of the plurality's invocation of the rule of lenity, finding it inapplicable since a statute's breadth is not "equivalent to ambiguity," and that Section 1519 is "very broad . . . [and] also very clear."[75] They made even shorter shrift of Justice Alito's concurring opinion, which they described as a "shorter, vaguer version of the plurality's."[76] Citing Justice Alito's reliance on "Latin canons plus §1519's verbs plus §1519's title to 'tip the case' for Yates," Justice Kagan wryly opined that "the sum total of three mistaken arguments is . . . three mistaken arguments. They do not get better in the combining."[77]

Bigger Fish to Fry?

So why did five justices vote to overturn Yates's conviction? Justice Kagan and the other dissenters believe they have the answer: the "real issue" that motivated the other justices was "overcriminalization and excessive punishment in the U.S. Code"[78] (and, she could have added, by extension, the Code of Federal Regulations).[79] And, while

---

[74] *Id.* at 1097–98.

[75] *Id.* at 1098.

[76] *Id.* at 1099.

[77] *Id.* at 1100.

[78] *Id.*

[79] For examples of some of the rich literature by academicians and legal commentators on overcriminalization, see, e.g., Douglas Husak, Overcriminalization: The Limits of the Criminal Law (2007); Andrew Ashworth, Conceptions of Overcriminalization, 5 Ohio St. J. of Crim. L. 407 (2008); Sara Sun Beale, The Many Faces of Overcriminalization: From Morals and Mattress Tags to Overfederalization, 54 Am. U. L. Rev. 747 (2005); Darryl K. Brown, Can Criminal Law Be Controlled?,108 Mich. L. Rev. 971 (2010); Stuart P. Green, Why It's a Crime to Tear the Tag Off a Mattress: Overcriminalization and the Moral Content of Regulatory Offenses, 46 Emory L.J. 1533 (1997); Sanford H. Kadish, The Crisis of Overcriminalization, 374 Annals Am. Acad. Pol. & Soc. Sci. 157 (1967); Sanford H. Kadish, Some Observations on the Use of Criminal Sanctions to Enforce Economic Regulations, 30 U. Chi. L. Rev. 423 (1963); Erik Luna, Overextending the Criminal Law, in Go Directly to Jail: The Criminalization

Justice Kagan would have affirmed Yates's conviction and thinks that "the plurality somewhat—though only somewhat—exaggerates the matter,"[80] she wholeheartedly agreed that Section 1519 "is a bad law—too broad and undifferentiated, with too-high maximum penalties, which gives prosecutors too much leverage and sentencers too much discretion," and, in fact, would "go further" in that she believes that "§1519 is unfortunately not an outlier, but an emblem of a deeper pathology in the federal criminal code."[81]

Mind you, I think that the plurality and concurrence have the better arguments. After all, as the Court has said before, the government should not be able to convict somebody of violating a criminal law that cannot be understood by a person of ordinary intelligence.[82] What non-judge or non-lawyer—and probably many judges and lawyers—of average intelligence would have suspected beforehand that Section 1519 would apply to throwing fish overboard? As Justice Alito noted in his concurring opinion, in applying the standard interpretive canons to the nouns in that section, "the term 'tangible object' should refer to something similar to records or documents. A fish does not spring to mind—nor does an antelope, a colonial farmhouse, a hydrofoil, or an oil derrick. All are 'objects' that are 'tangible.' But who wouldn't raise an eyebrow if a neighbor, when

---

of Almost Everything (Gene Healy ed., 2004); Ellen S. Podgor, Overcriminalization: The Politics of Crime, 54 Am. U. L. Rev. 541 (2005); Paul H. Robinson & Michael T. Cahill, The Accelerating Degradation of American Criminal Codes, 56 Hastings L.J. 633 (2005); Stephen F. Smith, Overcoming Overcriminalization, 102 J. of Crim. L. & Criminology 537 (2012); Stephen F. Smith, A Judicial Cure for the Disease of Overcriminalization, Heritage Foundation Legal Memorandum No. 135 (Aug. 21, 2014); William J. Stuntz, The Pathological Politics of Criminal Law, 100 Mich. L. Rev. 505 (2001); Paul J. Larkin, Jr., Public Choice Theory and Overcriminalization, 36 Harv. J.L. & Pub. Pol'y 715, 726 (2013); Edwin Meese III & Paul J. Larkin Jr., Reconsidering the Mistake of Law Defense, 102 J. Crim. L. & Criminology 725 (2012); Michael B. Mukasey & Paul J. Larkin, Jr., The Perils of Overcriminalization, Heritage Foundation Legal Memorandum No. 146 (Feb. 12, 2015); Paul J. Larkin, Jr., A Mistake of Law Defense as a Remedy for Overcriminalization, 26 A.B.A. J. Crim. Just. 10 (Spring 2013); John Malcolm, Criminal Law and the Administrative State: The Problem with Criminal Regulations, Heritage Foundation Legal Memorandum No. 130 (Aug. 6, 2014).

[80] Yates, 135 S. Ct. at 1100 (Kagan, J., dissenting).

[81] *Id.* at 1101.

[82] See, e.g., United States v. Harriss, 347 U.S. 612, 617 (1954) (government cannot enforce a criminal law that cannot be understood by a person of "ordinary intelligence"); Connally v. Gen. Constr. Co., 269 U.S. 385, 391 (1926) (discussing persons of "common intelligence").

asked to identify something similar to a 'record' or 'document,' said 'crocodile'?"[83] And while Justice Alito conceded that many of the verbs in that section "could apply to nouns as far-flung as salamanders, satellites, or sand dunes, the last phrase in the list—'makes a false entry in'—makes no sense outside of filekeeping. How does one make a false entry in a fish?" Like Justice Alito, I believe that the government's "argument, though colorable, [is] too implausible to accept."[84] Nonetheless, I suspect that Justice Kagan may be on to something, which may also explain why the Court took the case in the first place.

As 18 prominent criminal law professors noted in an amicus brief filed in the case:

> The modern federal criminal code is vast and unwieldy: some 4,500 laws criminalize conduct ranging from stockpiling biological weapons to falsely representing oneself as a 4-H Club representative. Moreover, a host of these laws are redundant. Indeed, some federal crimes—notably fraud and false statements—are independently prohibited by over two hundred different statutes. Combined with over 300,000 federal criminal regulations, the canon benefits only the Government, which has a near-endless menu of charging options in a typical prosecution. [¶] Redundancy, however, is but one troubling consequence of the ever-growing criminal code.[85]

Other problems include the complexity of and ambiguity in many of today's criminal laws. The professors continued: "As James Madison wrote in Federalist No. 62, '[i]t will be of little avail to the people . . . if the laws be so voluminous that they cannot be read, or so incoherent that they cannot be understood[.]' Yet these words provide an apt description of today's U.S. criminal code."[86]

---

[83] Yates, 135 S. Ct. at 1089 (Alito, J., concurring).

[84] Id. at 1090. Nor am I persuaded by the dissent's rejoinder that if Justice Alito wished to ask his "neighbor a question, I'd recommend a more pertinent one: Do you think a fish (or, if the concurrence prefers, a crocodile) is a 'tangible object'? As to that query, 'who wouldn't raise an eyebrow' if the neighbor said 'no'?" Id. at 1099 (Kagan, J., dissenting).

[85] Brief of Eighteen Criminal Law Professors as Amici Curiae Supporting Petitioner, Yates v. United States, 135 S. Ct. 1074 (2015) (No. 13-7451) at 6 (citations omitted).

[86] Id. at 9.

Like *Bond* from the previous term, the overarching theme in *Yates* may well have been a concern with overcriminalization, overly aggressive prosecutions based on questionable interpretations that have the effect of expanding the scope of federal criminal statutes, and a concern about the government having too much leverage to induce guilty pleas from people who might otherwise have eminently defensible cases. When that happens, a majority of the Supreme Court appears willing to rein in the government. After all, while it should not be unduly onerous for the federal government to prosecute those who engage in what is arguably criminal conduct, it shouldn't be like shooting fish in a barrel either.

The Right "to Be Secure": *Los Angeles v. Patel*

Luke M. Milligan*

I. Introduction

The U.S. Supreme Court addressed the Fourth Amendment rights of hotel and motel operators in *Los Angeles v. Patel*.[1] The Court held that an ordinance requiring operators to make guest registries available to police on demand was facially unconstitutional because it denied them the opportunity for precompliance review.

The decision can be studied on several levels. On a doctrinal level, *Patel* makes notable alterations to the law of search and seizure: first by loosening the restrictions on Fourth Amendment facial challenges; and second, by tightening the administrative exception to the warrant requirement.

Yet the real significance of *Patel* lies in its reasoning. When studied on this level, *Patel* leaves the reader both frustrated and intrigued. It frustrates because it purports to rest on little more than precedent. It omits discussion of Fourth Amendment text and values, and makes only vague, passing references to the practical consequences at stake. With that said, *Patel's* reliance on case law also intrigues, prompting one to reflect on the influences it left unarticulated.[2]

I argue in this short article that the *Patel* majority was quietly influenced by the "to be secure" text of the Fourth Amendment. At the time of the founding, the right "to be secure" guaranteed not simply a right to be "spared" unreasonable searches and seizures, but also a right to be left "tranquil" or "confident" against such

* Professor of law, University of Louisville School of Law. The author would like to thank Dave Johnson for research assistance.

1 Los Angeles v. Patel, 135 S. Ct. 2443 (2015).

2 Jerome Frank, Are Judges Human?, 80 U. Pa. L. Rev. 17, 37, (1931) ("Identity of the language of artificial, rule-worded, published opinions does not mean identity of the undisclosed 'real' reasons for decisions.").

government actions.[3] The influence of the "to be secure" text on *Patel* can be gleaned, I think, from the majority's emphasis on the "relative power" of hotel operators during police encounters, respondents' counsel Tom Goldstein's focus on "tranquility" at oral argument, and the Electronic Frontier Foundation's lengthy discussion as amicus on the original meaning of "to be secure." The upshot is that the original meaning of the Fourth Amendment appears to have played a silent but important role in *Patel*.

II. Facts and Procedural History

The *Patel* litigation involved a Fourth Amendment challenge to Los Angeles Municipal Code § 41.49. Section 41.49 required hotels, motels, and other places of overnight accommodation (hereinafter hotels) to record and keep specific information about their guests for a 90-day period.[4] Subsection (3)(a) of the ordinance authorized police to inspect such records without consent or a warrant: guest records "shall be made available to any officer of the Los Angeles Police Department for inspection . . . at a time and in a manner that minimizes any interference with the operation of the business."[5] The failure of a hotel operator to comply with § 41.49 was a criminal misdemeanor.[6]

The city enacted § 41.49 to "discourag[e] the use of hotel and motel rooms for illegal activities, particularly prostitution and narcotics offenses."[7] It described as "particularly problematic" the "parking-meter motels" where "[g]uests pay small hourly rates, in cash, to conduct their illicit business, and slink in and out anonymously and

---

[3] See discussion *infra* Part IV.D.

[4] § 41.49(2)(a) (2015) (providing that registries include basic information about guests, including: name; address; make, model, and license plate number of the guest's vehicle; date and time of the guest's arrival and scheduled departure; room number; rate charged; and method of payment for the room).

[5] § 41.49(3)(a). The ordinance is not uncommon. The city's brief makes references to 100 similar laws in cities and counties across the country. Petitioner's Brief at 36-37 n.3, Los Angeles v. Patel, 135 S. Ct. 2443 (2015) (No.13-1175).

[6] § 41.49(3)(a). A hotel operator's failure to make guest records available for police inspection was punishable by up to six months in jail and a $1,000 fine. § 11.00(m) (general provision applicable to entire LAMC).

[7] L.A., Cal., Ordinance No. 177966 (Oct. 6, 2006), available at http://clkrep.lacity.org/onlinedocs/2006/06-0125_ord_177966.pdf.

undetected."[8] But the city also made clear (in a nod to Elliot Spitzer) that illegality thrives in "establishments as reputable as the Mayflower Hotel."[9] In order to stamp out such crime, officers depend on the element of surprise. Criminal activity in hotels cannot be sufficiently deterred, the city argued, without warrantless, on-demand inspections of guest registries: "Prostitutes, johns, dealers, and other criminals who know that the police can scan a hotel's register at any time think twice about conducting their illicit activities in the hotel."[10]

In 2003, a group of hotel operators and a lodging association sued the City of Los Angeles, challenging the constitutionality of § 41.49(3)(a).[11] The parties "agree[d] that the sole issue in the . . . action [would be] a facial constitutional challenge" to § 41.49(3)(a) under the Fourth Amendment.[12] The parties further stipulated that hotel operators had been subjected to warrantless, nonconsensual inspections under the ordinance.[13] Following a bench trial, the district court entered judgment in favor of the city, holding that the hotel operators lacked a reasonable expectation of privacy in the guest registries subject to inspection.[14] On appeal, a Ninth Circuit panel affirmed on separate grounds, holding that the facial challenge failed because the operators "cannot 'establish that no set of circumstances exist under

[8] Petitioner's Brief, *supra* note 5, at 2. Justice Scalia articulated the harms in dissent. Patel, 135 S. Ct. at 2457 (Scalia, J., dissenting) ("Offering privacy and anonymity on the cheap, they have been employed as prisons for migrants smuggled across the border and held for ransom, and rendezvous sites where child sex workers meet their clients on threats of violence from their procurers." (citations omitted)).

[9] Petitioner's Brief, *supra* note 5, at 2; see also Dana Millbank, At the Mayflower, Client 9's Sinking Ship, Wash. Post, Mar. 11, 2008, available at http://www.washingtonpost.com/wp-dyn/content/article/2008/03/10/AR2008031002724.html.

[10] Petitioner's Brief, *supra* note 5, at 2. The city asserts this deterrence has a long tradition. "The City of Los Angeles passed a version of the ordinance more than 100 years ago—long before the emergence of parking-meter motels and, indeed, before common folk had motor vehicles. Throughout, the ordinance has required hotels to make the registers available for police inspection." *Id.*

[11] The plaintiffs sought both declaratory and injunctive relief.

[12] Patel, 135 S. Ct. at 2448.

[13] *Id.* This stipulation satisfied the standing requirements of Article III. See Clapper v. Amnesty Int'l, 133 S. Ct. 1138 (2013) (stating that Article III standing requires an injury that is actual or "certainly impending").

[14] Petitioner's Brief, *supra* note 5, at 9, see also Katz v. United States, 389 U.S. 347 (1967).

which the Act would be valid.'"[15] On rehearing en banc,[16] a majority reversed, holding that a police officer's nonconsensual inspection of hotel records under § 41.49(3)(a) constitutes a Fourth Amendment "search" because "[t]he business records covered by § 41.49 are the hotel's private property" and the hotel operator "has the right to exclude others from prying into the[ir] contents."[17] The majority further held that § 41.49(3)(a) searches are "unreasonable" as they do not afford operators "an opportunity to 'obtain judicial review of the reasonableness of the demand prior to suffering penalties for refusing to comply.'"[18] The Supreme Court granted certiorari to consider whether hotel operators may bring a Fourth Amendment facial challenge to § 41.49(3)(a), and, if so, whether the warrantless inspections authorized by § 41.49(3)(a) violate the Fourth Amendment.

III. The *Patel* Opinions

The hotel operators won on both issues. Seven justices agreed that the operators could proceed with a facial challenge to § 41.49(3)(a), and five justices held that § 41.49(3)(a) violated the Fourth Amendment.[19] The majority opinion was authored by Justice Sonia Sotomayor, and joined by Justices Anthony Kennedy, Ruth Bader Ginsburg, Stephen Breyer, and Elena Kagan. Dissenting opinions were authored by Justices Antonin Scalia (joined by Chief Justice John Roberts and Justice Clarence Thomas) and Samuel Alito (joined by Justice Thomas).

---

[15] 686 F.3d 1085, 1086 (2012) (quoting United States v. Salerno, 481 U.S. 739, 745 (1987)). The Ninth Circuit panel held that they "cannot meet the standard for a successful facial challenge." *Id.* Like the district court, the panel found it unnecessary to decide whether the ordinance could also be justified as a "warrantless administrative search under *Burger*." Petitioner's Brief, *supra* note 5, at 10.

[16] Los Angeles v. Patel, 738 F.3d 1058, 1065 (9th Cir. 2013).

[17] *Id.* at 1061.

[18] *Id.* at 1063–65 (quoting See v. City of Seattle, 387 U.S. 541, 545 (1967)). The Ninth Circuit dismissed the claim that hotels were subject to the more lax standard for "closely regulated businesses" in a footnote, stating only that "no serious argument can be made that the hotel industry has been subjected to the kind of pervasive regulation that would qualify it for treatment under the *Burger* line of cases." *Id.* at 1064 n.2.

[19] Justices Thomas and Alito dissented on both issues, while Chief Justice Roberts and Justice Scalia dissented on only the merits issue. Los Angeles v. Patel, 135 S. Ct. at 2457 (Scalia, J., dissenting) ("I assume that respondents may bring a facial challenge to the City's ordinance under the Fourth Amendment.").

A. *Fourth Amendment Facial Challenge Permissible*

The first holding of *Patel* is that the hotel operators can proceed with a facial challenge to § 41.49(3)(a). To support its holding, the majority placed dictum from *Sibron v. New York* in context, and casted the "no set of circumstances" test from *United States v. Salerno* in broad terms.

1. Giving Context to *Sibron*

The *Patel* majority observed that while facial challenges may be the "the most difficult . . . to mount successfully," the Court has "never held that these claims cannot be brought under any otherwise enforceable provision of the Constitution." [20] It went on to explain that because there is nothing unique about the Fourth Amendment in this regard, facial challenges relating to unreasonable searches and seizures are not "categorically barred or especially disfavored."[21]

The city had argued to the contrary, claiming that Fourth Amendment facial challenges were foreclosed by the Court's 1968 decision in *Sibron v. New York*.[22] In *Sibron*, the Court wrote that "[t]he constitutional validity of a warrantless search is pre-eminently the sort of question which can only be decided in the concrete factual context of the individual case."[23] Writing 47 years later for the majority in *Patel*, Justice Sotomayor explained that *Sibron*'s dictum "must be understood in the broader context of that case."[24] She pointed to the fact that the *Sibron* opinion emphasizes that the challenged New York law was relatively ambiguous ("'susceptible of a wide variety of interpretations'") and new ("'passed too recently for the State's highest court to have ruled upon many of the questions involving potential

---

[20] Patel, 135 S. Ct. at 2449 (citing Sorrell v. IMS Health Inc., 131 S. Ct. 2653 (2011) (First Amendment); District of Columbia v. Heller, 554 U.S. 570 (2008) (Second Amendment); Chicago v. Morales, 527 U.S. 41 (1999) (Due Process Clause of the Fourteenth Amendment); Kraft Gen. Foods, Inc. v. Iowa Dep't. of Revenue & Finance, 505 U.S. 71 (1992) (Foreign Commerce Clause).

[21] Patel, 135 S. Ct. at 2449 ("A facial challenge is an attack on a statute itself as opposed to a particular application.").

[22] 392 U.S. 40 (1968).

[23] *Id*. at 59.

[24] Patel, 135 S. Ct. at 2449.

intersections with federal constitutional guarantees.'").[25] The *Patel* majority instructed that when *Sibron* is read in this broader context, it

> stands for the simple proposition that claims for facial relief under the Fourth Amendment are unlikely to succeed when there is substantial ambiguity as to what conduct a statute authorizes: Where a statute consists of "extraordinary elastic categories," it may be "impossible to tell" whether and to what extent it deviates from the requirements of the Fourth Amendment.[26]

To bolster its interpretation, the majority cited several post-*Sibron* instances in which the Court had invalidated statutes on Fourth Amendment grounds.[27]

2. Narrowing "Work Done" Pursuant to *Salerno*

The city contended in the alternative that if the operators' facial challenge is not generally barred by *Sibron*, it is nonetheless precluded by the "no set of circumstances" test from *United States v. Salerno*.[28] *Salerno* is commonly read to bar facial challenges unless a plaintiff can "'establish that no set of circumstances exists under which the [statute] would be valid.'"[29] The city argued that the hotel operators' facial challenge is improper because, even if the operators won on the merits of their claim, § 41.49(3)(a) would still be valid in various alternative circumstances. The city pointed to situations where the police respond to an exigency, where the subject of the search consents to inspection, and where police act pursuant to a warrant.

---

[25] *Id.* at 2450 (quoting Sibron, 392 U.S. at 60 n.20).

[26] *Id.* (quoting Sibron, 392 U.S. at 59, 61 n.20).

[27] *Id.* (citing Ferguson v. Charleston, 532 U.S. 67, 86 (2001); Chandler v. Miller, 520 U.S. 305, 308–09 (1997); Vernonia Schl. Dist. 47 v. Acton, 515 U.S. 646, 648 (1995); Skinner v. Railway Labor Executives' Assn., 489 U.S. 602, 633 n.10 (1989); Payton v. New York, 445 U.S. 573, 574, 576 (1980); Torres v. Puerto Rico, 442 U.S. 465, 466, 471 (1979)).

[28] 481 U.S. 739, 745 (1987).

[29] Patel, 135 S. Ct. at 2450 (quoting Salerno, 481 U.S. at 745). *Patel* explains that "[u]nder the most exacting standard the Court has prescribed for facial challenges, a plaintiff must establish that a 'law is unconstitutional in all of its applications.'" *Id.* (quoting Wash. St. Grange v. Wash. St. Republican Party, 552 U.S. 442, 449 (2008)).

The *Patel* majority rejected the city's argument for two reasons. The first focused on its flawed "logic."[30] The city's line of reasoning would allow the state to block any Fourth Amendment facial challenge by simply pointing out that the search or seizure authorized by the challenged statute could be alternatively based on consent, exigent circumstances, or a warrant.[31] "For this reason alone," wrote Sotomayor, "the City's argument must fail."[32]

The "illogic" of the city's argument aside, the majority pressed a second criticism. While *Salerno* asks whether the "work done" by the challenged statute is valid under "no set of circumstances," it is important that courts applying *Salerno* not overstate the amount of "work done."[33] The majority cited *Planned Parenthood of Southeastern Pa. v. Casey*, which instructs that "[t]he proper focus of the constitutional inquiry is the group for whom the law is a restriction, not the group for whom the law is irrelevant."[34] As applied to the Fourth Amendment, the majority explained that:

> [I]f exigency or a warrant justified an officer's search, the subject of the search must permit it to proceed irrespective of whether it is authorized by statute. Statutes authorizing warrantless searches also *do no work* where the subject of a search has consented. Accordingly, the constitutional "applications" that petitioner claims prevent facial relief here are irrelevant to our analysis because they do not involve actual applications of the statute.[35]

Because statutes authorizing warrantless searches "do no work" in situations where the search is based on consent, exigent circumstances, or a warrant, the *Patel* majority concluded that they are not to be counted as alternative "sets of circumstances" under the *Salerno* test. As a result, the majority held that the hotel operators

---

[30] *Id.*, at 2451.

[31] *Id.* (stating that the city's argument "would preclude facial relief in every Fourth Amendment challenge to a statute authorizing warrantless searches").

[32] *Id.*

[33] *Id.* ("When assessing whether a statute meets this standard, the Court has considered only applications of the state in which it actually authorizes or prohibits conduct.").

[34] 505 U.S. 833, 894 (1992).

[35] Patel, 135 S. Ct. at 2451 (emphasis added).

met the "no set of circumstances" test from *Salerno* and were able to proceed with their facial challenge to § 41.49(3)(a).

3. Concurring Views on Fourth Amendment Facial Challenges

Dissenting on the merits, Justice Scalia nonetheless assumed that the hotel operators "may bring a facial challenge to the City's ordinance under the Fourth Amendment."[36] His opinion provides "a few thoughts" on how courts have imprecisely discussed "facial invalidations."

> [T]he facial invalidation of a statute is a logical consequence of the Court's opinion, not the immediate effect of its judgment. Although we have at times described our holdings as invalidating a law, it is always the application of a law, rather than the law itself, that is before us.

> The upshot is that the effect of a given case is a function not of the plaintiff's characterization of his challenge, but the narrowness or breadth of the ground that the Court relies upon in disposing of it. . . . I see no reason why a plaintiff's self-description of his challenge as facial would provide an independent reason to reject it unless we were to delegate to litigants our duty to say what the law is.[37]

Scalia's point is that "facial invalidation" occurs only when a court's reasoning is sufficiently broad such that that none of the "work done" by the statute can, as a practical matter, withstand constitutional scrutiny in future litigation.[38] His understanding that

---

[36] *Id.* at 2457 (Scalia, J., dissenting). Justice Scalia's opinion is styled as a dissent because he sides against the hotel operators on the question of whether the ordinance violated their Fourth Amendment rights.

[37] *Id.* at 2457–58.

[38] The more abstract the Court's ruling, the more likely no set of circumstances exists under which the law would be valid and, in turn, the more likely the authorizing statute is, as a practical matter, "facially" invalid. See, e.g., Citizens United v. FEC, 558 U.S. 310, 331 (2010) (explaining that the distinction between facial and as-applied challenges hinges on "the breadth of the remedy employed by the Court, not what must be pleaded in a complaint"); Richard Fallon, Jr., As-Applied and Facial Challenges and Third-Party Standing, 113 Harv. L. Rev. 1321, 1324 (arguing that facial challenges are not "a distinct category of constitutional litigation" but are instead "best conceptualized as incidents or outgrowths of as-applied litigation").

"facial invalidation" is a mere "practical effect of judicial reasoning" challenges the wisdom of treating *Salerno*'s "no set of circumstances" test as an independent ground for dismissal.[39] Put simply, it should make no difference to courts whether a plaintiff styles his complaint "as-applied" or "facial."[40]

4. Dissenting Views on Fourth Amendment Facial Challenges

Justices Alito and Thomas dissented from the Court's holding on facial challenges. Justice Alito wrote that "the Fourth Amendment's application to warrantless searches and seizures is inherently inconsistent with facial challenges."[41] As support, he cited to *Sibron's* dictum that "the constitutional validity of a warrantless search is pre-eminently the sort of question which can only be decided in the concrete factual context of the individual case."[42]

Assuming such facial challenges "ever make sense conceptually," the dissenters went on to criticize the *Patel* majority for misapplying the "no set of circumstances" test from *Salerno*.[43] In response to the majority's claim that the challenged ordinance "does no work" when inspections are based on exigent circumstances or a warrant, Alito wrote that the Los Angeles ordinance created a unique legal sanction for hotel operators who failed to comply with an officer's demand for an inspection.[44] Because this sanction extended to refusals to comply with exigency- or warrant-based inspections, the dissent claims the majority was wrong to conclude that § 41.49(3)(a) "does no work" during such inspections.[45] Alito concluded that *Salerno* prohibits the respondents' facial challenge because even if they prevailed on their

---

[39] Cf. Chem. Waste Mgmt., Inc. v. EPA, 56 F.3d 1434, 1437 (D.C. Cir. 1995) (applying *Salerno* and concluding that "we ... are unable to reach the merits because petitioners have not made a proper facial challenge. . . . [I]f petitioners are to succeed, they must bring a constitutional challenge as applied specifically to them.").

[40] See Alex Kreit, Making Sense of Facial and As-Applied Challenges, 18 Wm. & Mary Bill Rts. J. 657, 659–61 (2010) (discussing the contending views on facial challenges).

[41] Patel, 135 S. Ct. at 2466 (Alito, J., dissenting).

[42] *Id.* (citing Sibron v. New York, 392 U.S. at 59, 62).

[43] *Id.*

[44] *Id.* at 2464–65.

[45] *Id.*

Fourth Amendment claim, some of the "working" parts of § 41.49(3)
(a) would remain valid.[46]

B. Section 41.49(3)(a) Violates the Fourth Amendment

The second holding of *Patel* is that § 41.49(3)(a) violates the Fourth
Amendment. By a 5–4 vote the Court held that the warrantless
inspections authorized by § 41.49 are "unreasonable" because (1)
the ordinance does not provide an opportunity for precompliance
review; and (2) hotels do not fall within the exception for "closely
regulated businesses."

1. Precompliance Review Necessary for Administrative Searches

The Fourth Amendment provides, in relevant part, that "[t]he
right of the people to be secure in their persons, houses, papers, and
effects, against unreasonable searches and seizures, shall not be violated, and no Warrants shall issue, but upon probable cause."[47] The
Fourth Amendment warrant requirement is subject, however, "to a
few specifically established and well-delineated exceptions."[48] Warrantless search regimes may be "reasonable," for instance, where
"'special needs . . . make the warrant and probable-cause requirement impracticable,'" and where the "'primary purpose'" of the
searches is "'[d]istinguishable from the general interest in crime
control.'"[49] As applied to the case at hand, the *Patel* majority wrote:

> [W]e assume that the searches authorized by § 41.49 serve a
> "special need" other than conducting criminal investigations.
> They ensure compliance with the record-keeping requirement,
> which in turn deters criminals from operating on the hotels'

---

[46] *Id.* at 2466 ("Under threat of legal sanction, this law orders hotel operators to
do things they do not want to do."). The majority responded to Justice Alito's point
in summary fashion: "An otherwise facially unconstitutional statute cannot be saved
from invalidation based solely on the existence of a penalty provision that applies
when searches are not actually authorized by the statute." Los Angeles v. Patel, 135 S.
Ct. at 2451 n.1.

[47] U.S. Const. amend. IV.

[48] Arizona v. Gant, 556 U.S. 332, 338 (2009).

[49] Los Angeles v. Patel, 135 S. Ct. at 2452 (quoting Griffin v. Wisconsin, 483 U.S. 868,
873 (1987); Indianapolis v. Edmond, 531 U.S. 32, 44 (2000)).

premises. The Court has referred to this kind of search as an "administrative search."[50]

After classifying § 41.49 inspections as administrative searches, the majority explained that the subjects of administrative searches "must be afforded an opportunity to obtain precompliance review before a neutral decisionmaker."[51] "Precompliance review" is essential, wrote the majority, because it "alters the dynamic" between police and hotel operators.[52] More specifically, it reduces the "intolerable risk" that searches "will exceed statutory limits, or be used as a pretext to harass hotel operators and their guests."[53] The majority explained that the opportunity for precompliance review imposes only *de minimis* burdens on law enforcement. First, actual judicial review is only required in those cases when the subject of a search objects.[54] Second, in the event that an "officer reasonably suspects that a hotel operator may tamper with the registry while the [precompliance review] is pending, he or she can guard the registry until the required hearing can occur."[55]

The *Patel* majority concluded that § 41.49(3)(a) failed to provide hotel operators with an opportunity for precompliance review. Justice Sotomayor explained that "[w]hile the Court has never attempted to prescribe the exact form an opportunity for precompliance review must take, the City does not even attempt to argue that § 41.49 affords hotel operators any opportunity whatsoever."[56] For example, under the ordinance "[a] hotel owner who refuses to give an officer access to his or her registry can be arrested on the spot."[57] This is the case even "if a hotel has been searched 10 times a day, every day,

---

[50] *Id.* at 2452 (quoting Camara v. Mun. Ct. of City & County of San Francisco, 387 U.S. 523, 534 (1967)).

[51] *Id.* (citing See v. Seattle, 387 U.S. 541, 545). Precompliance review for administrative searches differs from a traditional warrant. It does not, for example, require a judicial finding of probable cause. See *id.*

[52] *Id.* at 2454.

[53] *Id.* at 2452–53.

[54] *Id.* at 2453.

[55] *Id.*

[56] *Id.* at 2452.

[57] *Id.*

for three months, without any violation being found."[58] The operator of a hotel faced with such harassment could "only refuse to comply with an officer's demand to turn over the registry at his or her own peril."[59]

2. Hotels Not "Closely Regulated Businesses"

The city argued that it need not provide hotel operators with opportunities for precompliance review because hotels are "closely regulated businesses." In rejecting the argument, Justice Sotomayor wrote that the Supreme Court has only applied the "closely regulated business" exception to four industries: liquor sales, mining, firearms dealing, and automobile junkyards.[60] Unlike these industries, wrote Sotomayor, "nothing inherent in the operation of hotels poses a clear and significant risk to the public welfare."[61] Moreover, the sum of regulations imposed on the hotel industry (e.g., requiring a license, collection of taxes, posting of rates, certain sanitary requirements) does not "establish a comprehensive scheme of regulation that distinguishes hotels from numerous other businesses."[62] As a result, classifying the hotel industry as pervasively regulated "would permit what has always been a narrow exception to swallow the rule."[63]

The *Patel* majority went on to explain that even if hotels fell within the "closely regulated business" exception, § 41.49(3)(a) would still violate the Fourth Amendment. To ensure nonarbitrary enforcement,

[58] *Id.* 2453.

[59] *Id.*

[60] *Id.* at 2454–55 (citing Colonnade Catering Corp. v. United States, 397 U.S. 72 (1970); United States v. Biswell, 406 U.S. 311, 311-12 (1972); Donovan v. Dewey, 452 U.S. 594 (1981); New York v. Burger, 482 U.S. 691 (1987)).

[61] *Id.* (citing Burger, 482 U.S. at 709 ("Automobile junkyards and vehicle dismantlers provide the major market for stolen vehicles and vehicle parts."); Dewey, 452 U.S. at 602 (explaining that the mining industry is "among the most hazardous in the country.")); see also Brief for the Cato Institute as Amicus Curiae in Support of Respondents at 15, Los Angeles v. Patel, 135 S. Ct. 2443 (2015) (No.13-1175) ("Provision of lodging does not have the predisposing relationship to crime that pursuits such as auto dismantling have, so hotels are inapt candidates for 'administrative search.'").

[62] *Id.* at 2455.

[63] *Id.* Moreover, while history is relevant when determining whether an industry is closely regulated, the historical record is not clear in this case.

statutes authorizing warrantless searches of "closely regulated businesses" have long had to satisfy three criteria:

> (1) [T]here must be a "substantial government interest that informs the regulatory scheme pursuant to which the inspection is made"; (2) "the warrantless inspections must be 'necessary' to further [the] regulatory scheme"; and (3) "the statute's inspection program, in terms of the certainty and regularity of its application, [must] provid[e] a constitutionally adequate substitute for a warrant."[64]

The majority concluded that § 41.49(3)(a) failed both the second and third criteria.[65] In relation to the second prong, the city argued that "surprise" inspections pursuant to § 41.49(3)(a) are necessary to deter hotel operators from falsifying guest records. The *Patel* majority disagreed, observing that its holding would not prevent surprise inspections in those situations where the police secured an *ex parte* warrant or identified an exigent circumstance.[66] The majority further explained that officers can make surprise demands without a warrant or an exigency and, should hotel operators request judicial review, the officers can "guard the registry pending a hearing."[67] As to the third prong, the *Patel* majority observed that while the Court had upheld statutes calling for searches "at least four times a year" and on a "regular basis," § 41.49(3)(a) imposed "no comparable standard."[68]

3. Dissenting Views on Constitutionality of § 41.49(3)(a)

Four justices dissented on the merits. They concluded that § 41.49(3)(a) complied with the Fourth Amendment because it met the three criteria for warrantless searches of "closely regulated businesses." Justice Scalia's dissent first attacks the majority's characterization of

---

[64] *Id.* at 2456 (quoting Burger, 482 U.S. at 702–703).

[65] *Id.* The majority did, however, assume the city had a substantial interest in ensuring that hotels keep complete registries. *Id.*

[66] *Id.*

[67] *Id.*

[68] *Id.* Justice Sotomayor explained that the holding does not call into question those parts of § 41.49 requiring hotel operators to keep records. Nor does it prevent police from obtaining access to such records with a warrant, consent, or based on exigent circumstances. *Id.* at 2452.

the "closely regulated business" exception. The exception, he wrote, is based not on the "dangerousness" of the targeted industry, but rather on the "expectations of privacy" of its operators and owners.

> The reason closely regulated industries may be searched without a warrant has nothing to do with the risk of harm they pose; rather, it has to do with the expectations of those who enter such a line of work.[69]

To assess expectations of privacy in this context, Scalia pointed to three factors: the length of the regulatory tradition, the comprehensiveness of regulation, and the imposition of similar regulations by other jurisdictions.[70] Each factor, wrote Scalia, leans toward classifying hotels as "closely regulated." At the time of the founding, warrantless searches "of inns and similar places of public accommodation were commonplace."[71] Moreover, hotels are currently subjected to a vast number of regulations, including requirements to maintain a license, collect taxes, conspicuously post their rates, and meet certain sanitary standards.[72] Lastly, he explained that there are "more than 100 similar register-inspection laws in cities and counties across the country."[73]

The fact that the Court had previously classified only four industries as "closely regulated" mattered little to the dissenters. Scalia explained that the number four says "more about how this Court exercises its discretionary review than it does about the number of industries that qualify as closely regulated."[74] He explained that lower courts which lack discretion to select their cases have extended the "closely regulated business" exception to countless industries (including pharmacies, massage parlors, commercial fishing operations, day-care facilities, nursing homes, jewelers, barbershops, and rabbit dealers).[75]

---

[69] *Id.*, at 2461 (Scalia, J., dissenting).

[70] *Id.* at 2459–60.

[71] *Id.* at 2459 (citing William Cuddihy, Fourth Amendment: Origins and Original Meaning 602–1791, 743 (2009) ("[T]he state code of 1788 still allowed tithingmen to search public houses of entertainment on every Sabbath without any sort of warrant.")).

[72] *Id.*

[73] *Id.* at 2460.

[74] *Id.* at 2461.

[75] *Id.*

After concluding that hotels are "closely regulated," Justice Scalia went on to explain that § 41.49(3)(a) meets the three criteria for warrantless searches of such businesses.[76] First, the city's interest in deterring criminal activity in hotels is "substantial."[77] Second, the warrantless inspections authorized by § 41.49(3)(a) are "necessary" to advance this interest.[78] On this point the dissenters disagreed with the majority's claim that the element of surprise could be preserved without the ordinance. Scalia explained that hotel searches based on exigent circumstances are rare,[79] reliance on *ex parte* warrants is cost-prohibitive,[80] and inviting police to "guard the registry pending a hearing" is "equal parts 1984 and Alice in Wonderland."[81] By this he meant that "[i]t protects motels from government inspection of their registers by authorizing government agents to seize the registers . . . or to upset guests by a prolonged police presence at the motel."[82] The third criterion for warrantless searches of a "closely regulated business" is also met, wrote Scalia, because § 41.49 served as an adequate substitute for a warrant. The ordinance limited warrantless police searches to "pages of a guest register in a public part of a motel," which "circumscribe[d] police discretion in much more exacting terms than the laws we have approved in our earlier cases."[83]

IV. Observations on *Patel*

The *Patel* decision can be assessed on a couple of levels. This section provides a brief survey of *Patel's* doctrinal implications before turning to a more detailed discussion of the majority's reasoning.

[76] See *supra* text accompanying note 68 (stating three guidelines from *Burger* to determine if an industry is "closely regulated).

[77] Patel, 135 S. Ct. at 2461 (Scalia, J., dissenting).

[78] *Id.* at 2464 ("The Court concludes that such minor intrusions, permissible when the police are trying to tamp down the market in stolen auto parts, are 'unreasonable' when police are instead attempting to stamp out the market in child sex slaves.").

[79] *Id.* at 2461 ("[T]he whole reason criminals use motel rooms in the first place is that they offer privacy and secrecy, so that police will never come to discover these exigencies.").

[80] *Id.* 2462.

[81] *Id.*

[82] *Id.*

[83] *Id.* at 2463 (citing Colonnade Catering Corp. v. United States, 397 U.S. 72, 73 n.2 (1970); New York v. Burger, 482 U.S. 691, 694 n.1 (1987); Donovan v. Dewey, 452 U.S. 594, 596 (1981); United States v. Biswell, 406 U.S. 311, 312 n.1 (1972)).

A. Patel's Doctrinal Implications

The *Patel* decision makes several alterations to Fourth Amendment doctrine. First, it loosens the restrictions on Fourth Amendment facial challenges by giving context to *Sibron* and by strictly assessing the "work done" by an authorizing statute in the "no set of circumstances" test from *Salerno*. The practical effect of this doctrinal shift is unclear in light of the Court's 2013 decision in *Clapper v. Amnesty International*.[84] *Clapper* reaffirms that Fourth Amendment litigants lack Article III standing unless they can show they were subjected to an illegal search or seizure that has occurred or is "certainly impending."[85] To meet this standard, Fourth Amendment litigants (including those seeking to make a facial challenge) must allege government action beyond the mere enactment of an authorizing statute. They must allege particularized executive action which will, as a general matter, approximate the facts sufficient to support a conventional as-applied Fourth Amendment challenge. Given the choice between an as-applied and a facial challenge, most plaintiffs and judges will tend to emphasize the former. By framing a challenge as-applied, a plaintiff can avoid scrutiny under *Salerno* yet still invite a judicial holding broad enough to practically invalidate the related statute. Judges in turn tend to prefer as-applied challenges because they can be resolved on narrower constitutional grounds. Since plaintiffs and judges tend to emphasize as-applied challenges, and because any plaintiff able to meet the standing requirements of Article III will almost certainly have the option of an as-applied challenge, it's unlikely that *Patel* will lead to a significant increase in the number of statutes invalidated on Fourth Amendment grounds.

The second doctrinal implication of *Patel* is that it strengthens the protections afforded to businesses under the administrative search doctrine. It does so by reaffirming the importance of precompliance review and by limiting the "closely regulated business" exception to "inherently dangerous" industries. This aspect of *Patel* constitutes a small win for the hundreds of thousands of individuals working in pharmacies, massage studios, day care facilities, nursing homes, jewelry stores, and barbershops. Assuming these businesses are not found "inherently dangerous" in subsequent litigation, statutes

---

[84] 133 S. Ct. 1138 (2013).
[85] *Id.* at 1150.

authorizing regulatory searches of such workplaces will now have to provide their operators with opportunities for precompliance review.

B. Patel *and* Stare Decisis

The holdings of *Patel* purport to rest on little more than case law. In loosening the restrictions on Fourth Amendment facial challenges, the majority opinion offers up a detailed discussion of *Sibron*'s contested dictum, a string citation to facial challenges previously permitted by the Court, and a survey of prior cases applying *Salerno*'s "no set of circumstances" test.[86] *Patel* provides no discussion of how facial challenges (either generally or in the context of the Fourth Amendment) were viewed by the Framers. Nor does it include any pragmatic discussion of how its holding will impact courts and litigants going forward.

The majority's holding on the merits appears similarly reliant on case law. To establish the constitutional value of precompliance review, *Patel* cites precedent and makes a passing reference to the importance of "alter[ing] the dynamic" between police and hotel operators.[87] Moreover, its conclusion that only "inherently dangerous" businesses fall within the "closely regulated business" exception is not attributed to Fourth Amendment text, history, or values, but simply to the fact that the four industries previously classified by the Court as "closely regulated" were each "inherently dangerous."

The majority's disregard for Fourth Amendment text and history was not lost on Justice Scalia:

> The Court reaches its wrongheaded conclusion not simply by misapplying our precedent, but by mistaking our precedent for the Fourth Amendment itself. Rather than bother with the text of that Amendment, the Court relies exclusively on our administrative-search cases. But the Constitution predates 1967, and it remains the supreme law of the land today.[88]

---

[86] Patel, 135 S. Ct. at 2450–51.

[87] *Id.* at 2454. The majority spends several paragraphs, however, explaining the *de minimis* burdens imposed on law enforcement by its precompliance requirement. *Id.* at 2453–54.

[88] *Id.* at 2464 (Scalia, J., dissenting) (citations omitted).

Patel's heavy reliance on case law stands in marked contrast to the Court's recent Fourth Amendment opinions in *Riley v. California* and *United States v. Jones.*[89] In limiting searches of cell phones following an arrest, eight justices in *Riley* affirmed the importance of original constitutional meaning to Fourth Amendment decisionmaking. *Riley* teaches that in the absence of "more precise guidance" from the text,[90] courts should look to Founding-era values:

> The fact that technology now allows an individual to carry such information in his hand does not make the information any less worthy of the protection for which the Founders fought. Our answer to the question of what police must do before searching a cell phone seized incident to an arrest is accordingly simple—get a warrant.[91]

Two years earlier, a majority of the Court relied on Founding-era trespass law to assess the constitutionality of attaching GPS tracking devices to vehicles. Holding that the practice violates the Fourth Amendment, *Jones* explains that "[w]e have no doubt that such a physical intrusion would have been considered a 'search' within the meaning of the Fourth Amendment when it was adopted."[92]

C. Patel's Unstated Influence

Although *Patel* omits reference to constitutional text and history, there is likely more to the majority opinion than meets the eye. I believe that an unstated influence on *Patel* can be gleaned from the majority's reference to "alter[ing] the dynamic" between hotel operators and police. In discussing the value of precompliance review, the majority wrote that

> the availability of precompliance review *alters the dynamic* between the officer and the hotel to be searched, and reduces the risk that officers will use administrative searches as a pretext to harass business owners.[93]

---

[89] Riley, 134 S. Ct. 2473 (2014); Jones, 132 S. Ct. 945 (2012).

[90] Riley, 134 S. Ct. at 2484.

[91] *Id.* at 2495.

[92] Jones, 132 S. Ct. at 949 (citing Entick v. Carrington, 95 Eng. Rep. 807 (C. P. 1765)).

[93] Patel, 135 S. Ct. at 2454; *id.* at 2452 ("Absent an opportunity for precompliance review, the ordinance creates an intolerable risk that searches authorized by it will ex-

Here *Patel* suggests that the opportunity for precompliance review is constitutionally significant not simply because it results in fewer unreasonable searches. Rather, it is constitutionally significant because it "alters the dynamic" between the individual and the state. In other words, precompliance review matters because it strengthens the relative power of hotel owners during police encounters.

Patel's emphasis on "relative power" hints at its unarticulated premise: that the Fourth Amendment guarantees not simply a right to be *spared* unreasonable searches and seizures, but moreover a right to be *confident* against such government illegalities. In other words, the government does not fully comply with the Fourth Amendment by simply not undertaking intrusive searches or seizures (and providing remedies when it does). It must do more. It must not behave in a way that makes the people anxious or fearful about being subjected to such searches or seizures.

Of course the government can ease such anxieties through a remedial scheme (such as the exclusionary rule). But remedial schemes provide only limited degrees of confidence. For instance, the likelihood (even the high likelihood) of a remedy may bring small comfort to a hotel operator worried about private information being revealed during an unreasonable inspection. Sensing a need to bolster the confidence of hotel operators, the *Patel* majority "alters the dynamic" of police encounters, thereby granting operators the power to obtain judicial review before any regulatory inspection takes place.

The claim that Fourth Amendment "confidence" influenced the *Patel* majority finds additional support in the *Patel* briefs and oral arguments. At three points during oral argument, Tom Goldstein (representing the respondents) referenced a Fourth Amendment guarantee of "tranquility." Goldstein argued:

> [W]e make pre-enforcement judicial review [] available, and the reason is the Fourth Amendment protects our sense of *tranquility*. The hotel owners, individuals in other contexts,

---

ceed statutory limits, or be used as a pretext to harass hotel operators and their guests. Even if a hotel has been searched 10 times a day, every day, for three months, without any violation being found, the operator can only refuse to comply with an officer's demand to turn over the registry at his or her own peril."); see also Patel v. City of Los Angeles, 738 F.3d 1058, 1064 (9th Cir. 2013) (en banc) ("Hotel operators are thus subject to the 'unbridled' discretion of officers in the field, who are free to choose whom to inspect, when to inspect, and the frequency with which these inspections occur.").

businesses in other contexts, need to know that beat officers aren't going to, at their whim, conduct these searches.[94]

. . .

But the prospect that there can be an objection and that you can go to a judge is what protects the sense of *tranquility* of the business owner.[95]

. . .

That's—in fact, the principal thing that this Court's precedents have pointed to—and just look at what's missing in this—in this ordinance. Every time the other side will say to you, look, we identified specifically the records. But the question isn't what the records are, it's the loss of the sense of *tranquility* provided by the Fourth Amendment, that we don't know how frequently and for what harassing purpose and how—and for what reasons at all that a police officer is just going to come in over and over again.[96]

Goldstein's repeated references to Fourth Amendment "tranquility" eventually drew questions from Chief Justice Roberts:

C.J. Roberts: Have we used that phrase before?

Mr. Goldstein: Which one, Your Honor?

C.J. Roberts: *Tranquility.*

Mr. Goldstein: I don't think that word is –

C.J. Roberts: We talk about privacy and all that, but I'm not sure that the Fourth Amendment should be expanded to protect the sense of *tranquility.*

Mr. Goldstein: I'm trying to—

J. Scalia: I have a problem imagining *tranquil* hotel owners. It's not what I associate with owning a hotel.

Mr. Goldstein: It is the sense of certainty that the Fourth Amendment provides that you do know is that there are going to be limits on when the

---

[94] Transcript of Oral Argument at 30, Los Angeles v. Patel, 135 S. Ct. at 2443 (2015) (No.13-1175) (emphasis added).

[95] *Id.* at 33–34 (emphasis added).

[96] *Id.* at 48–49 (emphasis added).

police come in and say, show us your papers. Okay? And that's what we're talking about.[97]

A further variation of the "confidence" argument was developed by the Electronic Frontier Foundation (hereinafter EFF) as amicus in *Patel*. The EFF brief argued that the Fourth Amendment is a "shield" which offers "preventative" assurance to individuals.

> The Constitution's framers originally intended the Fourth Amendment to serve as a shield against freestanding authority to conduct general searches. Facial challenges, which can ensure that a statute is struck before the government relies on it to effect an unconstitutional search, support this intent; they ensure the Fourth Amendment does not merely remedy constitutional violations but also prevents them in the first place.
>
> . . .
>
> The Fourth Amendment, like the Establishment Clause, operates as a shield against certain government conduct— *i.e.*, unconstitutional searches.
>
> . . .
>
> The very text and history of the Amendment thus calls for a protective buffer against unreasonable governmental intrusion to ensure that constitutional violations are prevented—not merely dealt with after the fact.[98]

Unlike Goldstein's oral argument, the EFF brief explicitly rooted its claim in the text of the Fourth Amendment.

> Indeed, the Fourth Amendment is not merely a "right" against unreasonable searches, it is also a "right . . . *to be secure*" against unreasonable searches. *See* U.S. Const., amend. IV (emphasis added). The inclusion of this phrase— "to be secure"—demonstrates the Founders' intent for the Amendment to prevent, not merely redress, violations.[99]

Although Fourth Amendment "confidence" was not explicitly referenced in the *Patel* decision, its influence can be inferred from the majority's emphasis on "alter[ing] the dynamic," Tom Goldstein's

---

[97] *Id.* at 49 (emphases added).

[98] Brief of Electronic Frontier Foundation as Amicus Curiae in Support of Respondents and Affirmance at 30–31, Los Angeles v. Patel, 135 S. Ct. at 2443 (2015) (No.13-1175).

[99] *Id.* at 30–31.

arguments about "tranquility," and the EFF's claim that the Fourth Amendment is a "preventative shield."

D. Textual Foundation for "Confidence"

The EFF brief in *Patel* locates Fourth Amendment "confidence" in the textual right "to be secure."[100] The Fourth Amendment provides, in pertinent part, for "the right of the people *to be secure* in their persons, houses, papers, and effects, against unreasonable searches and seizures."[101] Unfortunately, the courts have never explicitly discussed the meaning of "to be secure," and commentators (absent a few exceptions) have shown little interest in the original meaning of these words.[102]

Turning to the dictionaries, "secure" is defined as "free from fear or anxiety" and, alternatively, "sure, not doubting."[103] These meanings closely approximate that of "confidence" ("the mental attitude of trusting in or relying on a person or thing").[104] The interchangeability of "secure" and "confidence" is further demonstrated by influential pre-ratification discourse regarding searches and seizures. In the wake of James Otis's landmark condemnation of the writs of assistance in *Paxton's Case*,[105] it was written anonymously (most likely by Otis):[106]

---

[100] *Id.* at 30–31.

[101] U.S. Const. amend. IV (emphasis added).

[102] See Lawrence Rosenthal, Seven Theses in Grudging Defense of the Exclusionary Rule, 10 Ohio St. J. Crim. L. 523, 536 (2013) ("The term 'secure' is often ignored in discussions of the Fourth Amendment."). But see Thomas Clancy, The Fourth Amendment as a Collective Right, 43 Texas Tech L. Rev. 255, 262 n.57 (2010) (describing the right to be secure as "the right to exclude"); Luke M. Milligan, The Forgotten Right to Be Secure, 65 Hastings L.J. 713, 735–37 (2014) (defining the right "to be secure" as one to be "protected" or "free from fear").

[103] Oxford English Dictionary (2nd ed. 1989), vol. XIV at 851 (defining "secure" as: "free from . . . danger, safe"; "protected from or not exposed to danger"; or being "free from fear or anxiety"); Johnson's Dictionary (W. Strahaned. 1755), at 1777 (defining "secure" as "free from danger, that is safe"; "to protect"; "to insure"; "free from fear"; or "sure, not doubting").

[104] Oxford English Dictionary, *supra* note 103, vol. III at 705.

[105] See generally Boyd v. United States, 116 U.S. 616, 625 (1886) ("'Then and there,' said John Adams, 'then and there was the first scene of the first act of opposition to the arbitrary claims of Great Britain. Then and there the child Independence was born.'").

[106] See Thomas Y. Davies, Recovering the Original Fourth Amendment, 98 Mich. L. Rev. 547, 562 n.20 (2000) (claiming that the article was "probably authored by James Otis").

[E]very hous[e]holder in this province, will necessarily become less *secure* than he was before this writ had any existence among us; for by it, a custom house officer or any other person has a power given him, with the assistance of a peace officer, to enter forcibly into a dwelling house, and rifle any part of it where he shall please to suspect uncustomed goods are lodg[e]d!—Will any man put so great a value on his freehold, after such a power commences as he did before? . . . . Will any one then under such circumstances, ever again boast of [B]ritish honor or [B]ritish privilege?[107]

The author's choice of the terms "less secure" and "every house-holder" is instructive. When he wrote that "every householder . . . will necessarily become less secure," he did not mean that every householder will necessarily be subjected to more actual searches than before the writ was issued. By "less secure" the author likely meant that every householder will necessarily be less confident in relation to such searches. The "confidence" reading of "secure" in this instance is further supported by the author's statement that the cost of being "less secure" is incurred at the moment the "writ had any existence among us." If the author had intended "less secure" to mean "subjected to more actual searches," he would have assigned the *execution* of the writ—not the moment of its mere existence—as the moment when costs were incurred. As a final point, the author makes clear that it is the writ's "power" (rather than its execution) that devalues "freeholds" and silences "boasts of British honor."[108]

The structure of the Fourth Amendment lends further support to the "confidence" interpretation of "to be secure." The amendment is naturally read in two parts: the Reasonableness Clause and the Warrant Clause. The first salient element of the Reasonableness Clause is that it guards the "right of *the people* to be secure."[109] The

---

[107] Josiah Quincy, Jr., Reports of Cases Argued and Adjudged in the Superior Court of the Province of Massachusetts Bay Between 1761 and 1772 (Boston: Little, Brown, & Co. 1865) p. 489 (quoting Boston Gazette, Jan. 4, 1762) (emphasis omitted).

[108] Along these lines, Otis argued that the writs were "most destructive of English liberty" not because of the frequency of their use but rather because they could be used at the whim of government officials: the "liberty of every man [is placed] in the hands of every petty officer." Charles Francis Adams, ed., The Works of John Adams (1850) vol.2 at 523–25.

[109] U.S. Const. amend. IV (emphasis added). Courts and most commentators today treat the Fourth Amendment as safeguarding an individual right. See Dist. of Colum-

term "the people" proves awkward for those who read the Fourth Amendment as a guarantor of the mere right to be "spared" unreasonable searches. For example, one might question when exactly "the people" are no longer "spared" unreasonable searches and seizures. If the government's very first illegal search or seizure is a violation of the collective right to be spared, then the amendment strains common sense: one search or seizure does not cause the people *as a whole* to be searched or seized. But on the other hand, if a critical mass of the population must be illegally searched or seized to trigger a violation, then the amendment serves no practical purpose, for it would not be offended under any plausible scenario.[110] Interpretive frustrations like these are avoided, however, when one reads "secure" as "confident." It is not hard to conceive of a government leaving the people "unconfident" against unreasonable searches and seizures.

The second part of the Fourth Amendment—the Warrant Clause—similarly supports the "confidence" interpretation. The text and drafting history of the amendment indicate that the Framers understood the *issuance* of a general warrant to constitute a violation of the "right to be secure."[111] Yet the mere issuance of a general warrant does not in all cases result in an actual unreasonable search or seizure.[112] Because the issuance of a general warrant necessarily offends the right to be secure, and because such warrants do not always lead to unreasonable searches or seizures, reason demands that the right "to be secure" meant something more than the mere right to be "spared" an unreasonable search or seizure. It is far more

---

bia v. Heller, 554 U.S. 570, 579 (2008) (stating that the Fourth Amendment "unambiguously refer[s] to individual rights, not 'collective' rights, or rights that may be exercised only through participation in some corporate body."); Donald L. Doernberg, "The Right of the People": Reconciling Collective and Individual Interests Under the Fourth Amendment, 58 N.Y.U. L. Rev. 259, 270 (1983) ("These cases clearly contemplate that the rights secured by the [F]ourth [A]mendment are individual rather than a 'right of the people' collectively held."); Anthony G. Amsterdam, Perspectives on the Fourth Amendment, 58 Minn. L. Rev. 349, 367 (1974) ("Plainly, the Supreme Court is operating on the atomistic view.").

[110] Due to constraints on government resources, it is difficult to imagine the situation in which a substantial percentage of the population would be subjected to actual unreasonable searches and seizures.

[111] U.S. Const. amend. IV (stating that "no Warrants shall *issue*, but upon probable cause.") (emphasis added).

[112] The general warrant could, of course, issue but not be executed.

logical to interpret "secure" to mean something akin to "confident." The simple issuance of a general warrant, after all, can make persons less confident against unreasonable searches and seizures.

Interpreting "secure" to mean merely "spared" presents one final structural issue: it suggests the "to be secure" text is a grammatical excess. Had the Framers sought to safeguard a right to be "spared," they could have omitted the "to be secure" language and drafted the amendment to provide for a "right against unreasonable searches and seizures." But if "secure" meant "confidence," then the inclusion of the "to be secure" text would have been essential to give the amendment its intended meaning. Customary rules of interpretation therefore lend further support to the claim that "secure" meant "confident."[113]

The "confidence" interpretation is further substantiated by a study of Founding-era discourse about the harms caused by the *potentiality* of unreasonable searches and seizures. Pre-ratification arguments regarding "potentiality" centered on "risks of exposure," and in turn, criticized the "power," "existence," or "issuance" (rather than "execution") of general warrants. For example, in 1582 an anonymous Catholic documented the anxiety that comes with arbitrary searches: "[F]ellow believers could not enjoy so much as an hour's assurance against sudden, forcible invasion, even in their own dwellings."[114] William Cuddihy has observed that after the 1640s, general warrants attracted criticism because "they furnished an infinite *power* of surveillance" that "*exposed* every Englishman's dwelling to perpetual, capricious intrusion."[115] Examples are many. In 1688, Parliament criticized a tax on stone fireplaces as "a badge of slavery upon the whole people" for it "*expos[ed]* every man's house" to search.[116] In the 1763 decision *Huckle v. Money*, Judge Pratt wrote that a government with the power of general warrants is a government "under which no Englishman would wish to live an hour."[117] The "Inhabitants of Boston" published a report criticizing general

---

[113] See Marbury v. Madison, 5 U.S. (1 Cranch) 137, 174 (1803) ("It cannot be presumed that any clause in the constitution is intended to be without effect.").

[114] Cuddihy, *supra* note 71, at 7.

[115] *Id.* at 122 (emphases added).

[116] *Id.* (emphasis added).

[117] *Id.* at 445; see also Huckle v. Money, 95 Eng. Rep. 768 (C.P. 1763).

warrants in part because "our Houses, even our Bed-Chambers, are *exposed* to be ransacked."[118] James Otis claimed that the writs placed the "liberty of *every* man in the hands of every petty officer."[119] And John Wilkes asserted "the security" of his own house "for the sake of *every* one of my English fellow subjects."[120] Because neither Wilkes nor Otis believed that *every* individual would be subjected to more searches pursuant to general warrants, it seems reasonable to infer that they were warning of the harms that would be incurred by the mere potential for unreasonable searches and seizures.

Of course appeals to the harms of potentiality are not always genuine. Sometimes they are simply a rhetorical means to draw attention to the harms caused by actualities.[121] But Founding-era references to the harms incurred by the risks of unreasonable searches and seizures appear to be genuine, particularly when read in the light of the era's more generalized discourse on searches and seizures. The following paragraphs introduce two relevant strains of pre-ratification discourse: the castle metaphor and allied rights of free expression.

Discourse on general warrants during the Founding era relied on a preferred metaphor: the inhabitant of his home is the king of his castle.[122] "The house of every one is his castle," wrote Chief Justice Coke in the landmark *Semayne's Case*.[123]

> [T]he house of every one is to him as his . . . castle and fortress, as well for his defence against injury and violence, as for his repose; and although the life of man is a thing precious and favoured in law . . . if thieves come to a man's . . . house to rob him, or murder, and the owner or his servants kill any of the thieves in defence of himself and his house, it is not a felony, and he shall lose nothing . . . every one may assemble his friends and neighbours . . . to defend his house against violence.[124]

---

118 Cuddihy, *supra* note 71, at 445 (emphasis added). The "Inhabitants of Boston" was a committee appointed in 1772 to "state the Rights of the Colonists." *Id.* It counted James Otis as a member. *Id.*

119 2 The Works of John Adams, *supra* note 108, at 524–25 (emphasis added).

120 Peter D.G. Thomas, John Wilkes: A Friend to Liberty 32 (1996) (emphasis added).

121 This rhetorical device is used regularly to get an audience "to relate."

122 See generally Thomas K. Clancy, The Framers' Intent: John Adams, His Era, and the Fourth Amendment, 86 Ind. L.J. 979, 1021–25 (2011).

123 Semayne's Case, 77 Eng. Rep. 194, 194 (K.B. 1604); 5 Coke's Rep. 91 a.

124 *Id.* at 195.

Moreover, the castle metaphor anchored William Pitt's famous address to Parliament:

> The poorest man may in his cottage bid defiance to all the forces of the crown. It may be frail—its roof may shake—the wind may blow through it—the storm may enter—the rain may enter—but the King of England cannot enter!—all his force dares not cross the threshold of the ruined tenement![125]

In the colonies, James Otis used the castle metaphor in his 1761 criticism of the writs of assistance: "A man's house is his castle; and while he is quiet, he is as well guarded as a prince in his castle."[126]

The prevalence of the castle metaphor in pre-ratification discourse provides us with insight into the meaning of "to be secure." For some Fourth Amendment scholars, the comparison between the home and the castle is evidence that the Fourth Amendment prohibited only actual intrusions.[127] Yet pre-ratification allusions to "castles" almost certainly evoked an image grander than a dwelling that happened to be spared an actual intrusion. Rather, a "castle" was understood as a place where inhabitants enjoyed a substantial degree of confidence against unreasonable searches and seizures. "Castle" is defined as a building "fortified for defense against an enemy."[128] John Adams realized the centrality of "confidence" to the castle metaphor. He wrote that the home provides "as compleat a security, safety and Peace and Tranquility as if it was surrounded with Walls of Brass, with Ramparts and Palisadoes and defended with a Garrison and Artillery."[129] In this context it seems worth noting that the castle's archetypical inhabitant (the king) enjoyed unique protections from *potential* harms under the common law.[130]

---

[125] Henry Peter Brougham, Historical Sketches of Statesmen Who Flourished in the Time of George III, Vol. 1 41–42 (1839).

[126] Clancy, Collective Right, *supra* note 102, at 258 (quoting 2 The Works of John Adams *supra* note 108, 142–44).

[127] See Thomas K. Clancy, What Does the Fourth Amendment Protect: Property, Privacy, or Security?, 33 Wake Forest L. Rev. 307, 353–54 (1998).

[128] Oxford English Dictionary, *supra* note 103, vol. II at 956.

[129] L. Kinvin Wroth & Hiller B. Zobel, eds., Legal Papers of John Adams, vol. 1 137 (1965).

[130] For a discussion of the protections of the king and the emergence of attempt law, see generally Jerome Hall, Criminal Attempt—A Study of Foundations of Criminal Liability, 49 Yale L.J. 789 (1940). Since the 14th century, "compassing" the death of the

Sensitivity to the harms caused by the mere potential for unreasonable searches and seizures is also reflected in pre-ratification discourse on the relationship between general warrants and the exercise of speech and religious rights. Going back to at least the 16th century, general warrants had been used in England to suppress religious and political dissent.[131] The papers of Sir Edward Coke, for example, were seized during his 1621 imprisonment.[132] *Entick v. Carrington* involved a warrant ordering the king's messengers "to make strict and diligent search for . . . the author, or one concerned in the writing of several weekly very seditious papers."[133] James Otis explicitly referenced searches relating to "breach of Sabbath-day acts."[134] The historical connection between general warrants and freedom of expression has not been lost on the Supreme Court. In *Marcus v. Search Warrant*, the Court observed that "[t]he Bill of Rights was fashioned against the background of knowledge that unrestricted power of search and seizure could also be an instrument for stifling liberty of expression."[135] More recently, in *United States v. Jones*, Justice Sotomayor explained that "[a]wareness that the Government may be watching chills associational and expressive freedoms."[136]

King constituted treason even without an overt act. *Id.* at 795 (stating that treason required "[f]ailure to reveal knowledge about a plot against the king") (citing 21 Richard 2 (1397)).

[131] Cuddihy, *supra* note 71, at 8.

[132] *Id.* at 140–42.

[133] See Entick v. Carrington, 95 Eng. Rep. 807, 807 (K.B. 1765); see also Wilkes v. Wood, 19 Howell St. Trials 1153 (K.B. 1763).

[134] 2 The Works of John Adams, *supra* note 108, at 524–25.

[135] 367 U.S. 717, 729 (1961).

[136] 132 S. Ct. at 956 (Sotomayor, J., concurring) (quoting United States v. Cuevas-Perez, 640 F.3d 272, 285 (7th Cir. 2011) (Flaum, J., concurring)); see also Camara v. Mun. Court, 387 U.S. 523, 531 (1967) (stating that "*possibility* of criminal entry under the guise of official sanction is a serious threat to personal and family security" (emphasis added)); Frank v. Maryland, 359 U.S. 360, 376 (1959) (Douglas, J., dissenting) ("The commands of our First Amendment (as well as the prohibitions of the Fourth and the Fifth) reflect the teachings of *Entick v. Carrington*. These three amendments are indeed closely related, safeguarding not only privacy and protection against self-incrimination but 'conscience and human dignity and freedom of expression as well.'" (citation omitted*)*); Brinegar v. United States 338 U.S. 160, 180–81 (1949) (Jackson, J., dissenting) ("Among deprivations of rights, none is so effective in cowing a population, crushing the spirit of the individual and putting terror in every heart. . . . And one need only briefly to have dwelt and worked among a people possessed of many admirable qualities but deprived of these rights to know that the human personality deteriorates and

An individual's decision to speak or worship often turns, as a practical matter, on a rough assessment of its expected costs and benefits. And one of the risks of engaging in expressive behavior is unwelcomed exposure through government searches or seizures. Here is the critical point: it is the *potential* for an unreasonable search or seizure—not simply its actuality—that affects an individual's decision to exercise his speech or religious rights. This suggests that Founding-era warnings about the harms of potentiality were more than just a rhetorical means to draw attention to the harms resulting from actual unreasonable searches and seizures. Rather, the warnings reflected genuine concerns about the harms caused by the *mere risk* of unreasonable searches and seizures. These concerns for the harms of potentiality ultimately manifested themselves in the text of the Fourth Amendment, which protects not simply the right to be spared unreasonable searches and seizures, but also the right "to be secure" against such government illegalities.

V. Conclusion

The *Patel* decision affects Fourth Amendment doctrine in two notable ways. It loosens the restrictions on Fourth Amendment facial challenges and narrows the administrative search exception to the warrant requirement. Yet the real significance of *Patel* lies in its reasoning. This brief article argues that the *Patel* majority was influenced by the "to be secure" text of the Fourth Amendment. This influence can be gleaned from the majority's emphasis on the "relative power" of hotel operators during police encounters, Tom Goldstein's focus on "tranquility" at oral argument, and the EFF's lengthy discussion as amicus on the original meaning of "to be secure." The upshot is that the original meaning of the Fourth Amendment appears to have played a silent but important role in *Patel*.[137]

---

dignity and self-reliance disappear where homes, persons and possessions are *subject at any hour* to unheralded search and seizure by the police." (emphasis added)).

[137] Assuming this textual influence, the majority's failure to formally discuss the "to be secure" text comes as no surprise. The Supreme Court, after all, has never interpreted the "to be secure" text, and to break such ground in *Patel* would have seemed both onerous and needless to the justices in the majority.

Michigan v. EPA: A Mandate for Agencies to Consider Costs

Andrew M. Grossman*

[M]y way is[] to divide half a sheet of paper by a line into two columns; writing over the one *pro*, and over the other *con*; then, during three or four days consideration, I put down under the different heads short hints of the different motives that at different times occur to me, *for* or *against* the measure. When I have thus got them all together in one view, I endeavor to estimate their respective weights. . . . [A]nd thus proceeding I find at length where the *balance* lies . . . . And though the weight of reasons cannot be taken with the precision of algebraic quantities; yet, when each is thus considered separately and comparatively, and the whole lies before me, I think I can judge better, and am less liable to make a rash step; and in fact I have found great advantage from this kind of equation, in what may be called *moral* or *prudential* algebra.

—Benjamin Franklin[1]

The economic efficiency of subjecting fossil fuel–fired power plants to the Clean Air Act's most prescriptive and onerous regulatory program was probably about the last thing on then-EPA Administrator Carol Browner's mind when she signed the notice to trigger that regulation on December 14, 2000. Two days earlier, the Supreme Court had announced its decision in *Bush v. Gore*, clearing the path for George W. Bush to assume the presidency a little more than a month thereafter. More important for Browner and her colleagues was the defeat of Al Gore, whom many had expected to build on the Clinton Administration's environmental record by

* The author practices appellate litigation in the Washington, D.C., office of Baker & Hostetler LLP, is an adjunct scholar of the Cato Institute, and served as counsel for the Cato Institute as amicus curiae in *Michigan v. EPA*.

[1] Memoirs of the Life and Writings of Benjamin Franklin 12 (William Temple Franklin ed. 1818) (quoting letter from Benjamin Franklin to Joseph Priestly (Sept. 19, 1772)).

requiring even greater reductions in emissions of air pollution by American industry. The centerpiece of the first-term Gore agenda would have been imposing "maximum achievable control technology" (MACT) requirements on power plants under Section 112 of the Clean Air Act. But now there would be no Gore agenda. So Administrator Browner signed the cursory seven-page notice finding that Section 112 regulation was "appropriate and necessary"—irrespective of cost—thereby triggering regulation, with the expectation that even a Bush Administration EPA would have little choice but to issue implementing standards and little ability to blunt Section 112's stringency.

That action was fateful, but not only in the way that those cheering Browner's finding anticipated. Yes, the finding did ultimately lead to MACT standards for power plants known as the Mercury and Air Toxics Standards Rule (MATS Rule)—after a dozen years of false starts and litigation and the election of another Democratic president, Barack Obama. But the Clinton EPA's haste in 2000 boxed in its Obama Administration successors, who sought to backstop the finding against legal challenges even while being constrained to do no more than "affirm" its reasoning, lest they cast doubt on its sufficiency. And that, in turn, led to the Supreme Court's decision in *Michigan v. EPA* holding that the EPA acted "unreasonably when it deemed cost irrelevant to the decision to regulate power plants."[2] Whatever its ultimate impact on the EPA's Section 112 regulation, the Court's decision marks a modest turning point in the law governing the activities of the regulatory state.

Michigan establishes as a baseline principle of administrative law that agencies must give some consideration to costs when regulating under statutes that do not preclude them from doing so. This marks a turnabout from earlier decisions, which were wary of cost-benefit analysis, and even from more recent ones, which focused on agency discretion.

After *Michigan*, all agencies will have to pay some attention to the costs of their actions. On the whole, this will be no great change for executive agencies, which are already subject to executive orders mandating cost-benefit analysis and consideration of alternative approaches. But it could be a sea change for independent regulatory

---

[2] 135 S. Ct. 2699, 2712 (2015).

agencies—including the financial regulators—which have long resisted the application of cost-benefit principles to rulemaking. In addition, *Michigan* provides an opportunity to obtain judicial review of how agencies regard costs.

But greater judicial scrutiny of the substance of agencies' consideration of costs is in itself unlikely to prove much of a check on agency discretion and, more broadly, on the regulatory state. *Michigan* requires only that agencies take some consideration of cost—one that is reasonable in the circumstances—not necessarily that they attempt to monetize costs or measure them against monetized benefits in an attempt to maximize social welfare. In some instances, simply eyeballing the anticipated results of an action may be enough; in others, more formal analysis may be necessary. Agencies are likely to receive substantial deference on what places they choose on that continuum. But even were courts inclined to require more formal, quantitative analyses, it still would not make much of a difference due to increasing sophistication among the "protection-oriented" (i.e., pro-regulatory) community in using cost-benefit analysis to justify a more aggressive regulatory agenda and to block deregulatory measures. And where there are disputes over costs and benefits, the courts are more likely than anything to defer to agency determinations, citing the agencies' relative expertise and policymaking discretion.

That said, *Michigan* may have a real impact in leading courts to focus on the proper scope of agencies' consideration of costs and benefits. While both the majority justices and dissenters agree on the presumption that agencies must consider cost, the difference in their positions is whether cost consideration must be tied to the particular authorities and objectives that Congress legislated, with the majority requiring such a nexus. This and other features of the majority opinion suggest a wariness of agencies' use of co-benefits—that is, ancillary benefits unrelated to statutory objectives—to justify regulatory actions. That would be a major blow to the EPA, which has relied on contestable projections of co-benefits attributable to reductions in particulate-matter emissions to justify many of its recent air rules—including the MATS Rule and its greenhouse-gas regulations.

I. Agencies' Consideration of Costs: From Negative Presumption to Discretion to Obligation

Prior to *Michigan*, the Supreme Court's decisions dealing with agencies' consideration of costs were limited to passing on the requirements of particular statutory schemes—whether they required, forbade, or allowed costs to be taken into account. Such statutory questions are typically subject to review under the two-step framework associated with *Chevron v. Natural Resources Defense Council, Inc.* Under *Chevron*, a court first applies the traditional tools of statutory interpretation to determine whether Congress has spoken directly to the question.[3] If the statute is silent or ambiguous with respect to the question, then in step two a court defers to the agency's interpretation of the statute so long as it is reasonable.[4]

Michigan addresses a more fundamental question than the meaning of a single statute. It considers whether an agency's failure to take account of costs in exercising statutory authority that is silent on the issue is irrational and therefore violates *Chevron's* second step and the Administrative Procedure Act's (APA) bar on "arbitrary and capricious" agency action.[5] The Supreme Court set forth the applicable test in *Motor Vehicle Manufacturers Association v. State Farm*: "Normally, an agency rule would be arbitrary and capricious if the agency has relied on factors which Congress has not intended it to consider, *entirely failed to consider an important aspect of the problem*, offered an explanation for its decision that runs counter to the evidence before the agency, or is so implausible that it could not be ascribed to a difference in view or the product of agency expertise."[6]

Because it proceeds in this manner, *Michigan* breaks new ground, establishing that consideration of costs is a central aspect of reasoned

---

[3] 467 U.S. 837, 842–43 (1984).

[4] *Id*. See also City of Arlington v. FCC, 133 S. Ct. 1863, 1868 (2013).

[5] 5 U.S.C. § 706(2)(A). The Clean Air Act contains an analogous review provision. See, 42 U.S.C. § 7607(d)(9); W. States Petroleum Ass'n v. EPA, 87 F.3d 280, 283 (9th Cir. 1996) ("We review final administrative actions of the EPA pursuant to the Clean Air Act under the same standard as set forth in the Administrative Procedure Act."). On the relationship between *Chevron's* second step and arbitrary-and-capricious review, see United States v. Mead Corp., 533 U.S. 218, 227 (2001) ("any ensuing regulation is binding in the courts unless . . . arbitrary or capricious in substance.").

[6] 463 U.S. 29, 43 (1983) (emphasis added).

decisionmaking and therefore required under any statutory scheme but for those that preclude it.

A. Presumptions Every Which Way

Although the Court had never had the occasion to directly rule on the necessity of cost-benefit analysis in statutes that do not explicitly require or prohibit the practice, its decisions were not completely silent on the point, either. *Michigan's* predecessors generally called on the Court to address the permissibility of consideration of costs in specific statutory contexts. The case that set the mold was *American Textile Manufacturers Institute, Inc. v. Donovan*, a challenge to an agency's refusal to balance costs and benefits in setting a standard limiting exposure to cotton dust, a cause of "brown lung" disease, under the Occupational Safety and Health Act.[7] The act required the agency to "'set the standard which most adequately assures, *to the extent feasible*, on the basis of the best available evidence, that no employee will suffer material impairment of health or functional capacity.'"[8] The agency interpreted that language "to require adoption of the most stringent standard to protect against material health impairment, bounded only by technological and economic feasibility" and, on that basis, rejected a more lenient standard proposed by the textile industry that took account of compliance costs.[9] Although the Court upheld that interpretation based principally on the statutory text—the "plain meaning" of "feasible," it said, was "capable of being done"—it also observed that "Congress uses specific language when intending that an agency engage in cost-benefit analysis" and drew a negative implication from the absence of such language in the act.[10] In this respect, *American Textile Manufacturers Institute* at least suggests a presumption against consideration of costs in the absence of such language.[11]

---

[7] 452 U.S. 490 (1981).

[8] *Id.* at 508 (emphasis in original) (quoting 29 U.S.C. § 655(b)(5)).

[9] 452 U.S. at 503–04.

[10] *Id.* at 508–11.

[11] See also Union Elec. Co. v. EPA, 427 U.S. 246, 257 n.5 (1976) ("Where Congress intended the [EPA] Administrator to be concerned about economic and technological infeasibility, it expressly so provided.").

The Court's 2001 decision in *Whitman v. American Trucking Associations* applied the same logic to National Ambient Air Quality Standards under the Clean Air Act.[12] The act requires the EPA to set standards for ambient concentrations of certain pollutants at levels "requisite to protect the public health" with "an adequate margin of safety."[13] That language, the Court concluded, made it "fairly clear" that the act "does not permit the EPA to consider costs in setting the standards."[14] But what about the point that "the economic cost of implementing a very stringent standard might produce health losses sufficient to offset the health gains achieved in cleaning the air—for example, by closing down whole industries and thereby impoverishing the workers and consumers dependent upon those industries"?[15] A clever argument, but one the Court rejected based on the same negative implication as in *American Textile Manufacturers Institute*: given that "authorization to consider costs . . . has elsewhere, and so often, been expressly granted," the Court refused to find such authority "implicit in ambiguous sections of the [act]."[16] Thus, only "a textual commitment of authority to the EPA to consider costs" would suffice.[17]

At this point, following *American Trucking*, it may have seemed that the case law had all but established a default presumption against consideration of costs. But *Entergy Corp. v. Riverkeeper, Inc.*, in 2009, dispelled that notion.[18] At issue was the EPA's use of cost-benefit analysis to set standards for "impingement" (that is, squashing) and "entrainment" (capture) of aquatic organisms by power-plant cooling-water intake structures under a statute requiring that such structures "'reflect the best technology available for minimizing adverse environmental impact.'"[19] The Court rejected the view of the U.S. Court of Appeals for the Second Circuit—stated in an opinion by then-Judge Sonia Sotomayor—that this language precluded consideration of

---

[12] 531 U.S. 457.

[13] 42 U.S.C. § 7409(b)(1).

[14] 531 U.S. at 465.

[15] *Id.* at 466.

[16] *Id.* at 467.

[17] *Id.* at 468.

[18] 556 U.S. 208.

[19] *Id.* at 213 (quoting 33 U.S.C. § 1326(b)).

costs. Instead, deferring to the EPA's interpretation, it reasoned that "'best technology' may . . . describe the technology that *most efficiently* produces some good" and that "minimize" need not refer to the "greatest possible reduction."[20] Seemingly reversing the presumption against consideration of costs cited in previous decisions, the Court explained that, when Congress has "wished to mandate the greatest feasible reduction," irrespective of cost, it has employed absolute language, like "elimination" or "no discharge."[21] An agency "retains some discretion" to consider costs, it concluded, when Congress "does not unambiguously preclude cost-benefit analysis."[22]

The Court reaffirmed that holding, and then some, in *EPA v. EME Homer City Generation, L.P.*, a challenge to the EPA's Cross-State Air Pollution Rule.[23] The rule implemented the Clean Air Act's "Good Neighbor Provision," which requires states to prohibit in-state sources "'from emitting any air pollutant in amounts which will . . . contribute significantly to nonattainment in . . . any other State with respect to'" ambient air quality standards.[24] To reduce compliance costs, the EPA required states to eliminate emissions that (1) contribute more than a *de minimis* amount to nonattainment in a downwind state and (2) could be eliminated most cost-effectively.[25] This latter means that, rather than address emissions from states in proportion to their contribution to downwind nonattainment, the rule instead required reductions by the least-cost avoider. According to the majority, this cost-centric approach was a reasonable interpretation of the word "amounts," given that multiple upwind states may contribute to nonattainment in a downwind state, that there must be some means of apportioning the offending emissions among the upwind states, and that the statute is silent on how exactly to do that.[26] Using costs, the majority concluded, "makes good sense" because it "is an efficient and equitable solution to the allocation problem the Good

[20] *Id.* at 218–19.

[21] *Id.* at 219 (citing statutory language).

[22] *Id.* at 219–20.

[23] 134 S. Ct. 1584 (2014).

[24] *Id.* at 1593 (alterations in original) (quoting 42 U.S.C. § 7410(a)(2)(D)(i)).

[25] *Id.* at 1597.

[26] *Id.* at 1603–04.

Neighbor Provision requires the Agency to address."[27] Writing in dissent, Justice Antonin Scalia (also the author of *American Trucking* and *Entergy*) argued, with some persuasive force, that the only relevant factor under the statutory text was the "amounts" of air pollution that "contribute" to downwind states' nonattainment.[28] And, he added, there was no distinguishing *American Trucking*, and so its presumption against costs consideration in the absence of authorizing language ought therefore to control.[29]

But as this discussion suggests, that negative presumption was never definitive, bolstering conclusions principally supported by traditional statutory interpretation. And whatever force the presumption may have had—*American Textile Manufacturers Institute* and *American Trucking* have certainly been read to support a principle broader than statute-by-statute analysis—has surely waned, as cases like *Entergy* and *EME Homer* appear to adopt a presumption in favor of agency discretion to consider costs. At the least, "it is difficult not to get the impression that the Court has become more receptive to the use of [cost-benefit analysis] in the thirteen years since *American Trucking* was decided."[30]

B. Michigan *Identifies Consideration of Costs as Fundamental to Reasoned Decisionmaking*

Michigan continues that trend, moving well beyond mere deference to an agency's choices. At issue is the application of the Clean Air Act's hazardous air pollutants program, contained in Section 112 of the act, to power plants. The Section 112 program targets stationary-source emissions of a number of listed hazardous air pollutants.[31] The program's focus is on categories of sources (for example, petroleum refineries and industrial process cooling towers) that emit those pollutants. The EPA is required to "list" all categories of sources that emit hazardous air pollutants and then issue

---

[27] *Id.* at 1607.

[28] *Id.* at 1611 (Scalia, J., dissenting).

[29] *Id.* at 1616 (Scalia, J., dissenting).

[30] Caroline Cecot & W. Kip Viscusi, Judicial Review of Agency Benefit-Cost Analysis, 22 Geo. Mason L. Rev. 575, 586–87 (2015).

[31] 42 U.S.C. § 7412.

emissions standards for each listed category.[32] Unlike other pollution-control programs, Section 112 provides little discretion in setting minimum standards for "major sources"—those emitting or with the potential to emit more than 10 tons of a single pollutant or more than 25 tons of a combination of pollutants per year.[33] In general, under the "maximum achievable control technology" standard, major sources are subject to a "floor" based on "the average emission limitation achieved by the best-performing 12 percent of the existing sources."[34] The EPA then may in some circumstances go "beyond the floor"—that is, make them even more stringent—based on cost considerations and other factors.[35] But the general idea of Section 112 and MACT is that every major source—no matter its age or unique characteristics—is required to minimize emissions of hazardous air pollutants to the same extent as the very best-performing sources in the same category.[36]

When Congress created the current Section 112 program in the 1990 Clean Air Act Amendments, it required the EPA to identify, list, and regulate nearly all categories of sources emitting hazardous air pollutants but made an exception for fossil fuel–fired power plants. Recognizing that other provisions of the amendments would directly lead to significant reductions in power plants' emissions of hazardous air pollutants through market-based measures and could therefore render Section 112 regulation unnecessary, it directed the EPA to study the plants' emissions and review "alternative control strategies."[37] It then directed the EPA to regulate power plants under Section 112 only if it "finds such regulation is *appropriate and necessary* after considering the results of the study."[38]

That was the regulatory finding that EPA Administrator Browner signed in the final days of the Clinton Administration. While the

---

[32] *Id.* § 7412(c)(1)–(2).

[33] *Id.* § 7412(a)(1).

[34] *Id.* § 7412(d)(3)(A).

[35] Michigan, 135 S. Ct. at 2705.

[36] See generally Nat'l Lime Ass'n v. EPA, 233 F.3d 625, 633–34 (D.C. Cir. 2000); S. Rep. No. 101-228, at 131–33 (1989), reprinted in 1990 U.S.C.C.A.N. 3385, 3516–18.

[37] 42 U.S.C. § 7412(n)(1)(A). See also 136 Cong. Rec. 3493 (Mar. 6, 1990) (statement of Sen. Symms); 136 Cong. Rec. H12911, 12934 (daily ed. Oct. 26, 1990) (statement of Rep. Oxley).

[38] 42 U.S.C. § 7412(n)(1)(A) (emphasis added).

notice encompasses seven pages, the core of the finding amounts to just a few sentences:

> It is *appropriate* to regulate HAP [hazardous air pollutant] emissions from coal- and oil-fired electric utility steam generating units under section 112 of the CAA because, as documented in the utility RTC [report to Congress] and stated above, electric utility steam generating units are the largest domestic source of mercury emissions, and mercury in the environment presents significant hazards to public health and the environment. . . . Further, it is *appropriate* to regulate HAP emissions from such units because EPA has identified a number of control options which EPA anticipates will effectively reduce HAP emissions from such units. It is *necessary* to regulate HAP emissions from coal- and oil-fired electric utility steam generating units under section 112 of the CAA because the implementation of other requirements under the CAA will not adequately address the serious public health and environmental hazards arising from such emissions identified in the utility RTC and confirmed by [another] study, and which section 112 is intended to address.[39]

Although the notice contains no explanation of the agency's interpretation of the statutory "appropriate and necessary" trigger, its view can be inferred from the finding itself. Regulation is *appropriate,* in the agency's view, if power plants emit a listed hazardous air pollutant that poses risks to public health or the environment and if controls are available to reduce those emissions. Regulation is *necessary* if other Clean Air Act programs do not eliminate those risks. The costs of regulation—in this instance, the application of the Clean Air Act's most stringent program to the nation's largest category of industrial sources—are not part of the equation.

And there things stood—for purposes of this article[40]—until the Obama Administration, which picked up where the Clinton EPA left off. Pursuant to a consent decree, the EPA proposed MACT standards for power plants in May 2011 and published a final rule in Feb-

---

[39] 65 Fed. Reg. 79,825, 79,830 (Dec. 20, 2000) (emphases added).

[40] For an account of what did happen in the interim, see 76 Fed. Reg. 24,976, 24,984–86 (May 3, 2011) (discussing the Bush Administration's revocation of the 2000 finding and promulgation of standards under Clean Air Act Section 111 and the D.C. Circuit's invalidation of those actions in New Jersey v. EPA, 517 F.3d 574 (2008)).

ruary 2012.[41] Attempting to backfill the deficiencies of the 2000 finding, the final rule's preamble features a dense 54-page discussion of the basis for regulation, ultimately "affirm[ing]" that application of Section 112 to power plants remained "appropriate and necessary."[42] Although greatly expanded, the 2012 analysis relies on the same interpretation of the statutory trigger as the 2000 finding—most likely out of concern that it would be required to defend its action solely by reference to the 2000 finding and therefore did not wish to undercut that finding in advance of litigation.[43]

The agency did, however, respond to comments that it was required to consider costs in assessing the "appropriate[ness]" of regulation. According to the EPA, it was reasonable to make the decision listing power plants without consideration of the costs of regulation because it is forbidden from considering costs when making listing decisions under Section 112 for other source categories.[44] It also claimed discretion to adopt an interpretation of "appropriate" turning only on the ability of Section 112 regulation to address power plants' emissions of hazardous air pollutants. "Cost," it concluded, "does not *have to be read* into the definition of 'appropriate.'"[45] In this, the agency appeared to argue that it had discretion to consider costs but was not obligated to do so. And so it decided not to, on the view that Section 112 was geared to reducing hazards to human health and the environment.[46]

Although the EPA did not take into account costs when determining whether to regulate, it did produce a "Regulatory Impact Analysis" tabulating the expected costs and benefits of the standards. The regulation would force power plants to bear costs of $9.6 *billion* per year[47]—making the rule one of the most expensive in the history of

---

[41] *Id.* For an account of the events leading up to entry of the consent decree, see Andrew M. Grossman, Regulation Through Sham Litigation: The Sue and Settle Phenomenon 5–7 (2014), available at http://www.heritage.org/research/reports/2014/02/regulation-through-sham-litigation-the-sue-and-settle-phenomenon.

[42] 77 Fed. Reg. 9,304, 9,310–64 (Feb. 16, 2012).

[43] See *id.* at 9,311.

[44] *Id.* at 9,327.

[45] *Id.* (emphasis added).

[46] See *id.*

[47] *Id.* at 9,305–06.

the federal government.[48] It projected monetized direct benefits—that is, benefits flowing directly from reduced emissions of hazardous air pollutants, particularly mercury, that could be quantified—of $4–6 *million* per year, chiefly from "avoided IQ loss" resulting from reduced mercury exposure.[49] It also projected ancillary benefits attributable to reductions in emissions of particulate matter (and to a much lesser extent, carbon dioxide) amounting to $37–90 billion per year, while acknowledging that these particulate matter "co-benefits" are subject to "uncertainty" based on limitations in its research linking particulate-matter levels with health outcomes.[50]

The rule was challenged on numerous grounds but ultimately upheld by the D.C. Circuit, over the dissent of Judge Kavanaugh, who argued that it was "entirely unreasonable for EPA to exclude consideration of costs in determining whether it is 'appropriate' to regulate electric utilities under the MACT program."[51] In Judge Kavanaugh's view, the result was the same "whether one calls it an impermissible interpretation of the term 'appropriate' at *Chevron* step one, or an unreasonable interpretation or application of the term 'appropriate' at *Chevron* step two, or an unreasonable exercise of agency discretion under *State Farm*."[52] The Supreme Court granted three petitions raising that point and directed the parties to address a single question that it had formulated: "Whether the Environmental Protection Agency unreasonably refused to consider cost in determining whether it is appropriate to regulate hazardous air pollutants emitted by electric utilities."[53] Notably, the question did not distinguish between the EPA's statutory authority—analogous to the issues

---

[48] White Stallion Energy Ctr., LLC v. EPA, 748 F.3d 1222, 1263 (D.C. Cir. 2014), (Kavanaugh, J., concurring in part and dissenting in part) (citing James E. McCarthy, Congressional Research Service, R42144, EPA's Utility MACT: Will the Lights Go Out? 1 (2012)).

[49] See 77 Fed. Reg. at 9,306, Table 2, 9,427–28. For a description of the EPA's convoluted approach to estimating and monetizing these benefits, see Brief for the Cato Institute as Amicus Curiae, Michigan v. EPA, 135 S. Ct. 2699 (2015) (No. 14-46) [hereinafter "Cato Michigan Brief"].

[50] 77 Fed. Reg. at 9,306 & Table 2.

[51] White Stallion, 748 F.3d at 1261 (Kavanaugh, J., concurring in part and dissenting in part).

[52] *Id.*

[53] 135 S. Ct. 702 (2014).

addressed in the Court's prior cases on consideration of costs—and the reasonableness of its exercise of discretion.

The Court's opinion in *Michigan*, authored by Justice Scalia, takes the latter issue as its starting point, forcefully declaring, "'Not only must an agency's decreed result be within the scope of its lawful authority'"—that is, within its statutory authority—"'but the process by which it reaches that result must be logical and rational.'"[54] And that process, it continues, must rest "'on a consideration of the relevant factors'"—a direct quotation from *State Farm's* explication of the arbitrary and capricious standard.[55]

The opinion reasons that there is a presumption that agencies will consider the costs of their actions. "Agencies," it says, "have long treated cost as a centrally relevant factor when deciding whether to regulate. Consideration of cost reflects the understanding that reasonable regulation ordinarily requires paying attention to the advantages *and* the disadvantages of agency decisions."[56] And it is not "even rational, never mind 'appropriate,' to impose billions of dollars in economic costs in return for a few dollars in health or environmental benefits."[57] Accordingly, to overcome the presumption that costs will be taken into account, the EPA's burden was to identify "an invitation to ignore cost."[58]

The "appropriate and necessary" language, the Court concluded, is not anything of the sort. While recognizing that the word "appropriate" is "capacious[]," which would ordinarily provide an agency a wide scope of interpretative discretion, the majority explains that a reasonable statutory interpretation may not, like any agency action, "'entirely fai[l] to consider an important aspect of the problem'"— which "naturally" includes costs.[59] After all, "[n]o regulation is 'appropriate' if it does significantly more harm than good."[60] For example, an agency could not reasonably deem something like emissions

---

[54] 135 S. Ct. at 2706 (quoting Allentown Mack Sales & Serv., Inc. v. NLRB, 522 U.S. 359, 374 (1998)).

[55] *Id.* (quoting State Farm, 463 U.S. at 43).

[56] *Id.* at 2707.

[57] *Id.*

[58] *Id.* at 2708.

[59] *Id.* at 2707 (quoting State Farm, 463 U.S. at 43) (alteration in original).

[60] *Id.*

limitations "appropriate" if "the technologies needed to eliminate these emissions do even more damage to human health."[61]

Moreover, the Court buried whatever vestige of the presumption against consideration of costs might have survived *Entergy* and *EME Homer*. The opinion rejects as "unreasonable" the government's argument that, "by expressly making cost relevant to other decisions, the Act implicitly makes cost irrelevant to the appropriateness of regulating power plants."[62] And it commensurately narrows the holding of *American Trucking*, stating that it stands for nothing more than "the modest principle that where the Clean Air Act expressly directs EPA to regulate on the basis of a factor that on its face does not include cost, the Act normally should not be read as implicitly allowing the Agency to consider cost anyway."[63] That principle, of course, "has no application here."[64]

For two reasons, *Michigan* should be taken as establishing a baseline principle of administrative law that agencies generally must consider costs to avoid having their actions condemned as unreasonable or arbitrary and capricious. First is the deliberate sequence of the Court's reasoning, which begins with that principle and then places the burden on the EPA to identify some statutory basis to disregard costs. In that respect, *Michigan* is very different from its predecessors, which began and ended with statutory analysis and never addressed agencies' general obligation of reasoned decisionmaking within the bounds of those statutes. Second, even if *Michigan* could be viewed as a statutory case, its *Chevron* step-two reasonableness analysis parallels arbitrary-and-capricious review, drawing the kernel of its reasoning from *State Farm* and denying that the decision to ignore costs, absent some statutory bar to consideration of costs, is "rational."[65] This is in accord with recent decisions recognizing that *Chevron's* second step requires a court to "ask whether an agency

---

[61] *Id.*

[62] *Id.* at 2709.

[63] *Id.*

[64] *Id.*

[65] See *id.* at 2707.

interpretation is 'arbitrary or capricious in substance.'"[66] Viewed either way, the result is the same.

Justice Elena Kagan's dissent—which will be discussed further below—confirms as much. She "agree[s] with the majority—let there be no doubt about this—that the EPA's power plant regulation would be unreasonable if '[t]he Agency gave cost no thought *at all.*'"[67] She continues:

> Cost is almost always a relevant—and usually, a highly important—factor in regulation. Unless Congress provides otherwise, an agency acts unreasonably in establishing "a standard-setting process that ignore[s] economic considerations." *Industrial Union Dept., AFL–CIO v. American Petroleum Institute*, 448 U.S. 607, 670 (1980) (Powell, J., concurring in part and concurring in judgment). At a minimum, that is because such a process would "threaten[] to impose massive costs far in excess of any benefit." *Entergy Corp. v. Riverkeeper, Inc.*, 556 U.S. 208, 234 (2009) (Breyer, J., concurring in part and dissenting in part). And accounting for costs is particularly important "in an age of limited resources available to deal with grave environmental problems, where too much wasteful expenditure devoted to one problem may well mean considerably fewer resources available to deal effectively with other (perhaps more serious) problems." *Id.*, at 233. . . . [A]bsent contrary indication from Congress[,] an agency must take costs into account in some manner before imposing significant regulatory burdens.[68]

Notably, Justice Kagan's point of disagreement with the majority is the EPA's obligation to consider costs when making its "appropriate and necessary" determination, rather than later in the standard-setting process. Accordingly, in the view of Justice Kagan (joined by Justices Ruth Bader Ginsberg, Stephen Breyer, and Sotomayor), the agency's obligation does not arise from the statutory language at issue—which she does not read to address consideration of costs—but from background principles of administrative law. Between the majority and the dissenters, the Court is unanimous on this point,

---

[66] See, e.g., Judulang v. Holder, 132 S. Ct. 476, 483 n.7 (2011) (quoting Mayo Found. for Med. Educ. & Research v. United States, 131 S. Ct. 704, 711 (2011)).

[67] 135 S. Ct. at 2714 (Kagan, J., dissenting) (quoting majority opinion).

[68] *Id.* at 2716–17 (Kagan, J., dissenting).

even if they may disagree as to how this obligation applies in particular cases.

In just 14 years, the Court went from requiring "a textual commitment of authority" for agencies to consider costs to requiring a statutory "invitation to ignore cost" for agencies to disregard them. In fairness, the whiplash is not quite so great—*American Trucking*, if not necessarily *American Textile Manufacturers Institute*, would almost certainly be decided the same today—particularly in light of increased use of and comfort with cost-benefit analysis in the administrative state.

II. Where *Michigan* Matters

Michigan reflects the ascendancy of cost-benefit analysis in administrative practice, and for that reason, it is not exactly a watershed opinion. On the margins, however, it will have practical effects, in terms of both agencies' consideration of costs and judicial review of agency action.

In order to understand the impact of *Michigan* on agency practice, one must first recognize the near-pervasive use of cost-benefit analysis in administrative proceedings. As the epigram commencing this article suggests, systematically weighing the expected benefits of some proposed course of action against its costs is nothing new and just common sense. Little surprise, then, that its use in government has grown in tandem with the rise and regularization of the administrative state. As best anyone can tell, the first formal use of cost-benefit analysis by a federal agency involves the Army Corps of Engineers, which employed the technique as far back as 1902 to identify the most promising and urgent flood-control projects.[69] (Or, for the more cynical, the Corps' actual aim may have been to facilitate logrolling among members of Congress hoping to see projects constructed in their states and districts.[70]) In any case, Congress in 1936 enacted a statutory requirement that the Corps undertake only those projects whose "benefits. . . . are in excess of the estimated costs."[71]

[69] John C. Coates IV, Cost-Benefit Analysis of Financial Regulation: Case Studies and Implications, 124 Yale L.J. 882, 899–901 (2015) (discussing Theodore M. Porter, Trust in Numbers: The Pursuit of Objectivity in Science and Public Life 148–90 (1995)).

[70] *Id.* at 899–900.

[71] 33 U.S.C. § 701a.

While various other statutes require consideration of costs, current use of cost-benefit analysis by agencies can be traced to President Reagan's Executive Order 12,291 in 1981, which required agencies not to act "unless the potential benefits to society for the regulation outweigh the potential costs to society," to select regulatory objectives so as "to maximize the net benefits to society," and, when choosing among alternative approaches to achieve an objective, to select "the alternative involving the least net cost to society."[72] To carry out these requirements, agencies were directed to perform a "regulatory impact analysis" for all major rules, defined as those with an annual effect on the economy of $100 million or more.[73] "The executive order also increased agency accountability to the White House by formalizing a system of review of agency action headed by the Office of Information and Regulatory Affairs ('OIRA') within [the Office of Management and Budget] that continues in substantial part to the present."[74]

The general approach of Executive Order 12,291 was affirmed by President Clinton in Executive Order 12,866 and has been retained through subsequent administrations.[75] Thus, each year executive agencies conduct cost-benefit analyses for most major rules (also referred to as "significant regulatory actions"), and those analyses are in turn reviewed by OIRA, which can recommend that the agency perform additional analysis, change the details of its rule, or scrap its approach altogether. And these agencies are expected in all instances—whether or not a major rule is involved—to assess costs as possible, consider alternatives, and act "in the most cost-effective manner to achieve the regulatory objective."[76] (That said, consideration of costs is not carried out in all instances, as the EPA's decision

[72] Exec. Order No. 12,291, § 2, 46 Fed. Reg. 13,193 (Feb. 17, 1981). President Reagan's initiative, in turn, built on less prescriptive initiatives by Presidents Nixon, Ford, and Carter. For example, an executive order by President Carter required agencies to prepare regulatory impact analyses and consider alternative approaches. Exec. Order No. 12,044, 43 Fed. Reg. 12,661 (Mar. 23, 1978).

[73] Exec. Order No. 12,291, §§ 1(b), 3(a).

[74] Cecot & Viscusi, *supra* note 30, at 581.

[75] See Exec. Order No. 12,866, 58 Fed. Reg. 51,735 (Sept. 30, 1993) (superseding, but in substance only amending, Executive Order 12,291); Exec. Order No. 13,258, 67 Fed. Reg. 9,385 (Feb. 26, 2002) (amending Executive Order 12,866); Exec. Order No. 13,563, 76 Fed. Reg. 3,821 (Jan. 18, 2011) (supplementing Executive Order 12,866).

[76] Exec. Order No. 12,866 § 1(b)(5).

to ignore costs when deciding to regulate power plants under Section 112 demonstrates.) Congress has supplemented the presidential regulatory review process with statutes requiring cost-benefit analysis—although not necessarily consideration of costs in formulating policy—in such statutes as the Unfunded Mandates Reform Act (requiring "a qualitative and quantitative assessment of the anticipated costs and benefits" of rules that impose substantial unfunded mandates on state, local, and tribal governments),[77] the Paperwork Reduction Act,[78] and the Regulatory Flexibility Act (requiring agencies to assess costs of proposed rules on small entities).[79]

Almost none of this, however, applies to independent regulatory agencies,[80] which since 2011 have been merely "encouraged to give consideration" to the principles of Executive Order 12,866 and its successors.[81] They are in some instances required to perform cost-benefit analyses—although not in all instances to actually consider costs—under the Paperwork Reduction Act and Regulatory Flexibility Act. In other instances, independent agencies' authorizing statutes require that they take costs into account in certain respects. For example, the Securities and Exchange Commission is required to consider whether its regulatory actions under the Investment Company Act "will promote efficiency, competition, and capital formation"[82]—a mandate that the courts have construed as requiring consideration of costs.[83] But again, the scope of this requirement is limited, to rules promulgated under particular statutory authority.

Accordingly, *Michigan's* most visible impact may be to more effectively "encourage"—under the real threat of invalidation of regulatory actions—independent regulatory agencies to consider costs

---

[77] 2 U.S.C. § 1532(a)(2).

[78] 44 U.S.C. §§ 3501 et seq.

[79] 5 U.S.C. §§ 601 et seq.

[80] See 44 U.S.C. § 3502(5).

[81] Memorandum from Cass R. Sunstein, Administrator of OIRA, "Executive Order 13563, 'Improving Regulation and Regulatory Review,'" Feb. 2, 2011, available at http://www.whitehouse.gov/sites/default/files/omb/memoranda/2011/m11-10.pdf. See also Exec. Order No. 13,579, 76 Fed. Reg. 41,587 (July 1, 2011) (encouraging independent regulatory agencies to follow the principles of Exec. Order No. 13,563 without actually requiring them to do anything).

[82] 15 U.S.C. § 80a-2(c).

[83] See Chamber of Commerce v. SEC, 412 F.3d 133, 144 (D.C. Cir. 2005).

when issuing regulations. This is no small thing. Nearly all of the major financial regulators are independent regulatory agencies, as are the Federal Communications Commission, the Federal Energy Regulatory Commission, and the National Labor Relations Board.[84] And these agencies' consideration of costs to date has been, at best, inconsistent. For example, from October 2012 through September 2013, the independent regulatory agencies issued 18 major rules.[85] According to the Office of Management and Budget (OMB), 13 of those "provided *some* information on the benefits and costs of the regulation."[86] Only two provided analyses that monetized portions of the costs; none included monetized estimates of benefits.[87] This is roughly consistent with the independent regulatory agencies' performance over the past decade.[88] As OMB concluded, "[t]he absence of such information is a continued obstacle to transparency, and it might also have adverse effects on public policy."[89]

To be sure, *Michigan* does not necessarily require an agency to conduct exhaustive, quantitative cost-benefit analyses—a point considered further below—but it should at least prompt agencies to identify costs in all circumstances and to monetize them when necessary to support reasoned judgment. It could even push hitherto reluctant agencies to finally give in to conducting rigorous cost-benefit accounting.

Michigan will also affect judicial review. Agency compliance with Executive Order 12,866 and its brethren is not subject to judicial review.[90] Limited judicial review is available under the Regulatory Flexibility Act[91]—the typical result in a successful challenge is for the agency to redo its analysis without altering its substantive

---

[84] 44 U.S.C. § 3502(5).

[85] Office of Management and Budget, 2014 Report to Congress on the Benefits and Costs of Federal Regulations and Unfunded Mandates on State, Local, and Tribal Entities 34, June 2015, available at https://www.whitehouse.gov/sites/default/files/omb/inforeg/2014_cb/2014-cost-benefit-report.pdf.

[86] *Id.* (emphasis added).

[87] *Id.*

[88] See *id.* at 106–07.

[89] *Id.* at 34.

[90] Helicopter Ass'n Int'l, Inc. v. FAA, 722 F.3d 430, 439 (D.C. Cir. 2013).

[91] 5 U.S.C. § 611(a)(4).

regulation[92]—and under the Unfunded Mandates Reform Act, which allows suits only to compel the agency to produce analyses, not to challenge their substance or conclusions.[93]

By contrast, agency regulatory actions are generally subject to potential vacatur under the APA's judicial review provisions and analogous statutory provisions.[94] And as *Michigan* teaches, proper consideration of costs is a component of "logical and rational" agency decisionmaking.[95] An agency's refusal to consider costs therefore renders its action arbitrary and capricious because it has "'entirely fail[ed] to consider an important aspect of the problem.'"[96] Accordingly, *Michigan* opens the door to judicial review of agencies' use of costs in regulating, even outside of areas where consideration of costs is specifically required by statute.

In sum, *Michigan* should prod agencies to take account of costs in more instances and should provide at least the potential for relief through litigation for affected parties when they do not.

III. Cost Consideration as a Check on the Regulatory State?

Even so, those hoping that *Michigan*—and greater use of cost-benefit analysis generally—will provide a potent check on regulatory agencies are likely to be disappointed. In the main, *Michigan's* impact is likely to be marginal. Indeed, recent experience suggests that it could even be used to justify greater regulation or to block deregulatory measures.

To begin with, *Michigan* does not say what exactly, short of not entirely ignoring costs, an agency is required to do. The majority opinion denies that, in making what it assumed would necessarily be a "preliminary estimate" of the costs and benefits of Section 112 regulation for power plants, the EPA was required "to conduct a formal cost-benefit analysis in which each advantage and disadvantage is assigned a monetary value."[97] Instead, in the first instance, "[i]t

[92] See, e.g., U.S. Telecom Ass'n v. FCC, 400 F.3d 29, 42–43 (D.C. Cir. 2005).

[93] 2 U.S.C. § 1571(a)(2)(A).

[94] See 5 U.S.C. §§ 702, 706. See also 42 U.S.C. § 7607(b)(1), (d)(9) (analogous provisions applicable to certain actions under the Clean Air Act).

[95] 135 S. Ct. at 2706.

[96] *Id.* at 2707 (quoting State Farm, 463 U.S. at 43).

[97] *Id.* at 2711.

will be up to the Agency to decide (as always, within the limits of reasonable interpretation) how to account for cost."[98]

One may expect that, as with other applications of arbitrary-and-capricious review, courts will be particularly deferential to agency views regarding the assessment and consideration of costs. An agency's approach need only be "rational" to survive, and "a court is not to substitute its judgment for that of the agency."[99] Judicial deference is typically even greater regarding technical matters and matters within an agency's area of expertise.[100] And, "[i]n practice, a [cost-benefit analysis] is the kind of analysis that often requires an agency to make many predictions based on available scientific and technical evidence—such as, for example, predictions about the emission-reduction benefits associated with a particular air-pollution-control technology or predictions about the cost of implementing a particular workplace-safety regulation."[101] In the main, courts are unlikely to reverse such decisions due to flaws in consideration of costs "simply because there are uncertainties, analytic imperfections, or even mistakes" in an agency's analysis, but "only when there is such an absence of overall rational support as to warrant the description 'arbitrary or capricious.'"[102]

The result is that agencies will continue to have substantial flexibility in terms of how they consider costs and their ultimate conclusions. As a practical matter, the term "cost-benefit analysis" "can refer to a wide and divergent array of procedures and practices. At one end of the spectrum is the 'prudential algebra' Ben Franklin described. . . . At the other end of the spectrum is a highly technical and theorized branch of welfare economics that attempts to quantify and monetize all social costs and benefits for a whole range of alternatives using formal techniques—including discounting future costs and benefits to present net value—and then attempts to pinpoint the course of action for which marginal benefits are just equal

---

[98] *Id.*

[99] State Farm, 463 U.S. at 42–43.

[100] See, e.g., Troy Corp. v. Browner, 120 F.3d 277, 283 (D.C. Cir. 1997) (agency determinations are due "considerable deference, especially where the agency's decision rests on an evaluation of complex scientific data within the agency's technical expertise.").

[101] Cecot & Viscusi, *supra* note 30, at 590.

[102] Ctr. for Auto Safety v. Peck, 751 F.2d 1336, 1370 (D.C. Cir. 1985).

to marginal costs."[103] *Michigan,* and *Entergy* before it, suggest that what agencies are required to do lies somewhere in between these two extremes, quantifying costs when possible while also making qualitative judgments—for example, determining that particular items are *de minimis* and need not be considered or, Ben Franklin-style, analyzing based on magnitudes of expected cost and benefit items.[104] In short, there's no reason to believe that many rules will be vacated due to courts' disagreement with the rigor or substance of agency cost-benefit analyses.

And that may be for the best. As Michael Livermore and Richard Revesz have observed, the Obama Administration in particular "has shown that cost-benefit analysis can be used to support a regulatory agenda that substantially increases environmental and public-health protections."[105] They describe how "protection-oriented groups" have become increasingly sophisticated in their use of the tools of cost-benefit analysis to promote regulation and beat back deregulatory initiatives.[106] As much as free-market advocates have come to view consideration of cost as a defense against excessive regulation, their opponents on the other side of the issue increasingly view cost-benefit analysis as a powerful weapon in their own arsenal.[107] To the extent that there is some force to both sides' arguments in this debate, judicial review that defers substantially to agencies' view of things just is not going to make much difference on the whole.

In sum, no one should expect that courts will use *Michigan* to carefully scrutinize the particulars of agency cost accounting and thereby rein in regulatory overreach. But it will matter at the margins,

[103] Amy Sinden, Formality and Informality in Cost-Benefit Analysis, 2015 Utah L. Rev. 93, 99 (footnote omitted).

[104] Michigan, 135 S. Ct. at 2711; Entergy, 556 U.S. at 225–26 (authorizing "some form of cost-benefit analysis").

[105] Michael Livermore & Richard Revesz, Retaking Rationality Two Years Later, 48 Hous. L. Rev. 1, 28 (2011).

[106] *Id.* at 29–33. See also Coates, *supra* note 69, at 916 ("[Cost-benefit analysis] law can slow or stop *de*regulation as easily as it can slow or stop new regulation, particularly if consumer or investor advocates develop and fund their own [cost-benefit analysis] litigation agendas.") (emphasis in original).

[107] But see Bruce Kraus & Connor Raso, Rational Boundaries for SEC Cost-Benefit Analysis, 30 Yale J. on Reg. 289, 291 (2013) (describing OIRA oversight and increased use of cost-benefit analysis as "a Trojan horse for more *Business Roundtable*-style anti-regulatory litigation").

spreading cost consideration to areas where it has been absent until now—presumably because regulatory activities in those areas could not be easily justified in cost-benefit terms—and encouraging agencies to act rationally in using costs as an input to formulating rules. So confined, *Michigan* may have a modest anti-regulatory effect, as agencies that would prefer to ignore excessive costs are forced to account for them.

IV. Judicial Review of Scope, Not Substance, as a Constraint on Agency Decisionmaking

While courts may be reluctant to police the *substance* of agency cost-benefit analyses—due to lack of expertise and the norm of deference—they are on firmer ground in reviewing the *scope* of cost and benefit considerations. Put in APA terms, courts are perfectly competent and well-placed to review whether an agency "relied on factors which Congress has not intended it to consider" or "failed to consider an important aspect of the problem."[108] *Michigan* provides additional support for this approach, recognizing that costs and benefits are just additional factors that Congress intended would be considered in agency reasoning, absent statutory indication to the contrary. In that respect, *Michigan* may be an effective constraint on agency discretion, one that is more amenable to judicial implementation than second-guessing the details of cost-benefit analyses.

This aspect of the decision is reflected in the duel of metaphors between the majority and the dissent. To the majority, consideration of cost is not to be undertaken in gross, but with respect to the specific determinations and actions to which it is relevant. That's why the majority rejects the EPA's argument that "it need not consider cost when first deciding *whether* to regulate power plants because it can consider cost later when deciding *how much* to regulate them."[109] This logic is like someone deciding "to buy a Ferrari without thinking about cost, because he plans to think about cost later when deciding whether to upgrade the sound system."[110]

In the dissenting justices' view, the majority's metaphor "run[s] off the road" because the "EPA knows from past experience and

---

[108] State Farm, 463 U.S. at 43.

[109] 135 S. Ct. at 2709 (emphasis in original).

[110] *Id.*

expertise alike that it will have the opportunity to purchase that good in a cost-effective way."[111] The dissent proposes its own analogy, "to a car owner who decides without first checking prices that it is 'appropriate and necessary' to replace her worn-out brake-pads, aware from prior experience that she has ample time to comparison-shop and bring that purchase within her budget."[112]

But the dissent's analogy falls short in two illuminating respects. For one, what if, upon checking prices, the car owner learns that there are none within her budget? In that instance, she can change course and buy a bus pass. An agency, however, lacks such an easy option, having already exercised its discretion in a way with legal effect—more so than an idle or tentative decision by an individual consumer. Second, it is completely artificial to separate a decision to act from consideration of the costs and benefits of that act. When the dissent's car owner "decides" to replace her brake pads, she assumes that she will be able to afford new ones. And when she learns that brake pads have become excessively expensive, she can factor that into her thinking and then *change her decision*—in other words, she is still engaged in the decisionmaking process. There is, as the majority recognizes, a close nexus between an action and consideration of the factors relevant to undertaking that action. This is just common sense: one properly considers the pluses and minuses of taking a particular action before doing so. Unless, that is, one has already prejudged the matter without reasonable consideration of the circumstances, which may itself be arbitrary and capricious.[113]

Under the majority's approach, then, a court must scrutinize the scope of an agency's analysis of costs and benefits, ensuring that all aspects of an action are supported by adequate analysis and that the agency's analysis is appropriately aligned with the statutory authority at issue. This is essentially the approach taken by the D.C. Circuit in a series of cases vacating rules by the Securities and Exchange Commission due to shortcomings in that agency's evaluation and consideration of costs with respect to the statutory objectives of promoting

---

[111] *Id.* at 2725 (Kagan, J., dissenting).

[112] *Id.*

[113] See, e.g., Consumers Union of U.S., Inc. v. Consumer Prod. Safety Comm'n, 491 F.2d 810, 812 (2d Cir. 1974).

"efficiency, competition, and capital formation."[114] The first, *Chamber of Commerce v. SEC,* involved a rule requiring mutual funds to have boards with at least 75 percent independent directors and to have an independent chairman.[115] The court identified three flaws in the agency's reasoning: (1) it made no attempt to estimate the costs associated with electing independent directors; (2) it made no attempt to estimate the costs to funds of the possibility that independent chairman would hire additional staff; and (3) it failed to consider, as an alternative to the independent-chairman condition, a less burdensome disclosure requirement. While "uncertainty may limit what the Commission can do" the court explained, "it does not excuse the Commission from its statutory obligation to do what it can to apprise itself . . . of the economic consequences"—which the court defined by reference to statutory objectives—"of a proposed regulation before it decides whether to adopt the measure."[116] Likewise, *American Equity Investment Life Insurance Co. v. SEC* vacated a rule subjecting certain annuity contracts to federal regulation due to the Commission's failure to evaluate the rule's potential economic effects consistent with the same statutory objectives.[117] And *Business Roundtable v. SEC* vacated a "proxy access" rule requiring public companies to provide shareholders with information about and the ability to vote for shareholder-nominated board candidates.[118] The agency, the court found, "inconsistently and opportunistically framed the costs and benefits of the rule; failed adequately to quantify the certain costs or to explain why those costs could not be quantified; neglected to support its predictive judgments; contradicted itself; and failed to respond to substantial problems raised by commenters."[119] Again, the court measured the agency's shortcomings by reference to the statutory objectives.[120]

What these cases have in common (with the possible exception of portions of *Business Roundtable* that more carefully scrutinize the SEC's accounting), and what they share with *Michigan,* is that they methodically

---

[114] 15 U.S.C. § 80a-2(c).

[115] 412 F.3d 133, 135 (D.C. Cir. 2005).

[116] *Id.* at 144.

[117] 613 F.3d 166, 176–79 (D.C. Cir. 2009).

[118] 647 F.3d 1144 (D.C. Cir. 2011).

[119] *Id.* at 1148–49.

[120] See, e.g., *id.* at 1148, 1155.

check that the agency did its homework, ensuring that all relevant costs and benefits have been considered with respect to each aspect of agency action, without second-guessing the agency's determinations and weighing of the evidence.[121] In this way, the D.C. Circuit has navigated an administrable middle course between abdication of any reviewing role and substitution of the court's views for the agency's own.

This approach is likely to have currency in litigation over the use of ancillary benefits, or "co-benefits," in cost-benefit analysis, including with respect to the EPA's Section 112 regulations on remand. In recent years, the EPA has relied extensively on particulate-matter co-benefits to justify regulations targeting power plants and other industrial sources, particularly under statutory authority other than that concerned with particulate-matter emissions.[122] For example, although the EPA projects that its MATS Rule will have little in the way of benefits from reducing power plants' emissions of hazardous air pollutants (the ostensible target of Section 112), the agency projects benefits of $36 to $89 billion per year from reductions in particulate-matter emissions due to plant shutdowns and the controls that must be installed to address emissions of hazardous air pollutants.[123] This is consistent with the EPA's approach in other recent air rulemakings.[124] For example, in its proposed carbon-dioxide regulations for

[121] See, e.g., Chamber of Commerce, 412 F.3d at 144 (tying cost issues to impacts on statutory factors of "efficiency and competition"); Business Roundtable, 647 F.3d at 1148 (same). For another good example of judicial review in this vein, see Corrosion Proof Fittings v. EPA, 947 F.2d 1201, 1215–17 (5th Cir. 1991) (same approach, under different statutory regime).

[122] In general, consideration of co-benefits is consistent with OMB guidance, although the guidance warns against "double-counting of benefits," as the EPA has been accused of doing with respect to projected particulate-matter reductions. See Office of Management and Budget, Circular A–4, at 26–27 (2003). Particulate matter is subject to an EPA-set National Ambient Air Quality Standard that is, in turn, enforced through several of the Clean Air Act's cooperative federalism programs. See generally 42 U.S.C. §§ 7408–7410, 7470–7479, 7501 et seq.

[123] 77 Fed. Reg. at 9,306, Table 2.

[124] See, e.g., 75 Fed. Reg. 35,520, 35,588/3 (June 22, 2010) (claiming $2.2 million in direct benefits from revised sulfur-dioxide standard and $15 billion to $37 billion in co-benefits due to reductions in particulate matter); 75 Fed. Reg. 9,648, 9,669/3 (Mar. 3, 2010) (promulgating Section 112 standards for stationary compression ignition engines used in power plants and other facilities and projecting monetized benefits only for particulate-matter co-reductions); RIA, Existing Stationary Spark Engine Hazardous Air Pollutant Rule at 1-3, Table 1-1 (Jan. 2013) (projecting monetized benefits only for incidental co-reductions of particulate matter and its precursors); RIA, Industrial,

existing power plants under Clean Air Act Section 111(d) (which the agency calls the "Clean Power Plan"), the EPA projects annual net monetized benefits from the proposed rule of between $46 billion and $84 billion.[125] Projected reductions in emissions of particulate matter and its precursors account for almost all of that amount.[126]

The *Michigan* dissenters accept the EPA's lopsided co-benefits estimate uncritically, citing it as reason enough to justify the EPA's decision to regulate.[127] Their credulity is easy to understand: courts aren't really in the business of second-guessing agency scientific determinations. Then again, a more inquisitive jurist might wonder why, if particulate-matter emissions are responsible for as much premature mortality and morbidity as the EPA claims, the agency doesn't crack down on them more through the Clean Air Act programs that actually target particulate matter but that do not allow the EPA to directly target particular disfavored source categories.[128] Such a judge would discover that the EPA's benefit estimates are based on aggressive extrapolation from limited epidemiological studies; are subject to significant uncertainty, such that zero benefits cannot be ruled out; lead to seemingly absurd results, such as the conclusion that up to a quarter of deaths are related to particulate-matter concentrations; and are primarily the result of reductions below the level that the EPA recently identified as "requisite to protect human health."[129]

Commercial, and Institutional Boilers and Process Heaters Hazardous Air Pollutant Rule, at 1-4 to 1-5, Tables 1-1 & 1-2, 7-21, Tables 7-2 & 7-3 (Feb. 2011) (same); RIA, Final Ozone NAAQS at 34, Figs. S2.5 & S2.6 (July 2011) (showing particulate-matter monetized benefits greatly outweighing ozone benefits); RIA, New Source Performance Standards and Existing Source Emission Guidelines for Sewage Sludge Incineration Units at 1-3, Table 1-1, 5-10, Table 5-3 (Sept. 2010) (projecting particulate-matter-related benefits of $110 to $270 million, out of total monetized benefits of $130–320 million).

[125] 79 Fed. Reg. 34,830, 34,840–41, Table 2 (June 18, 2014).

[126] *Id.* at 34,937–39, Tables 14–16.

[127] See 135 S. Ct. at 2725–26 (Kagan, J., dissenting).

[128] Compare 42 U.S.C. § 7410 (authorizing states to develop implementation plans to achieve ambient air quality standards for "criteria" pollutants, including particulate matter), with *id.* § 7412 (authorizing the EPA to directly regulate emissions of hazardous air pollutants from listed source categories). See also Cato Michigan Brief, *supra* note 49, at 30–33.

[129] See Sean Mulholland & James Broughel, Comment on Control of Air Pollution from Motor Vehicles, Mercatus Center, June 28, 2013, available at http://mercatus. org/sites/default/files/Mulholland_EPA_PIC_062813.pdf (surveying literature).

But a judge need not be especially skeptical to wonder whether it is proper for the EPA to use a program aimed at emissions of certain hazardous air pollutants to achieve a completely different purpose. *Michigan* suggests that it is not: an agency directed to determine whether "[Section 112] regulation is appropriate and necessary" must take that problem as Congress has framed it and may not "rel[y] on factors which Congress has not intended it to consider."[130] Under *Michigan's* logic, that includes projected benefits relating to things other than the statutory objective of reducing emissions of hazardous air pollutants. Such considerations are untethered from the EPA's Section 112 authority and from the provision's objective of addressing emissions of hazardous air pollutants.

Without definitively resolving this question, the *Michigan* majority flags it as one of concern and hints at its answer. The opinion pointedly observes that, per the EPA's projections, "[t]he costs to power plants [of regulation] were thus between 1,600 and 2,400 times as great as the quantifiable benefits from reduced emissions of hazardous air pollutants."[131] When describing the EPA's attribution of billions in benefits to the rule, it notes that these are due almost entirely to reductions in emissions of "substances that are not covered by the hazardous-air-pollutants program."[132] The majority declines to "uphold the EPA's action because the accompanying regulatory impact analysis shows that, once the rule's ancillary benefits are considered, benefits plainly outweigh costs" on the ground that the agency did not follow that reasoning, while criticizing the dissent for looking to co-benefits at all.[133] And then, of course, there is the majority's reasoning regarding the relationship between statutory authority and consideration of cost.

Moreover, consideration of co-benefits chafes against broader principles of administrative law, as well as the constitutional separation of powers. At base, arbitrary-and-capricious review constrains agency discretion to the parameters set by Congress, prophylactically ensuring that agencies are carrying out the law rather than

---

[130] State Farm, 463 U.S. at 43. Cf. Mass. v. EPA, 549 U.S. 497, 533 (2007) ("But once EPA has responded to a petition for rulemaking, its reasons for action or inaction must conform to the authorizing statute."); see also Am. Trucking, 531 U.S. at 466–67.

[131] 135 S. Ct. at 2706.

[132] *Id.*

[133] *Id.* at 2711.

creating it.[134] One need not be a separation-of-powers formalist to recognize the problem inherent in, say, the EPA administrator setting a particularly stringent emissions standard with the expectation that it will force the development of technology that may prove beneficial to his first love, space exploration. Even if that expectation is rational—that is, the technology likely will be developed and will be an enormous boon to spaceflight and to the nation as a whole—the consideration of that benefit when setting emissions standards is not rational, for the simple reason that space exploration is not an objective of any provision of the Clean Air Act.[135] With respect to the authority conferred by Congress to issue emissions standards, its advancement is an irrelevant consideration. Deeming that advancement a "benefit" doesn't change the result.[136]

Yet that is the approach that the EPA appears poised to adopt in reaffirming the MATS Rule on remand.[137] And it is the approach that the agency is being encouraged to take in future rules targeting greenhouse-gas emissions—to use co-benefit projections as "an overarching justification for setting more stringent GHG reduction targets and timelines."[138] But if the lower courts are faithful to *Michigan's* logic, that approach will be soundly rejected.

[134] At the outer limits, failure to constrain agencies in this fashion—particularly with respect to the use of co-benefits—may raise nondelegation issues. See C. Boyden Gray, The Nondelegation Canon's Neglected History and Underestimated Legacy, 22 Geo. Mason L. Rev. 619, 643 (2015).

[135] Cf. Mass. v. EPA, 549 U.S. at 533 ("Under the clear terms of the Clean Air Act, EPA can avoid taking further action only if it determines that greenhouse gases do not contribute to climate change or if it provides some reasonable explanation as to why it cannot or will not exercise its discretion to determine whether they do. To the extent that this constrains agency discretion to pursue other priorities of the Administrator or the President, this is the congressional design.") (citation omitted).

[136] Cf. Bluestone Energy Design, Inc. v. FERC, 74 F.3d 1288, 1294–95 (D.C. Cir. 1996) (holding that agency acted impermissibly when it considered "staff time and resources"—a cost factor—in making its determination).

[137] David Doniger, Steady as She Goes: Lessons for the Clean Power Plan from the Supreme Court's Mercury and Healthcare Decisions, Huffington Post (July 6, 2015), http://www.huffingtonpost.com/david-doniger/steady-as-she-goes-lesson_b_7737828.html (citing co-benefit projections as evidence that "the MATS rule can be easily fixed" on remand); Dan Farber, Interpreting *Michigan v. EPA*, LegalPlanet.org (June 29, 2015), available at http://legal-planet.org/2015/06/29/interpreting-michigan-v-epa (similar).

[138] Alice Kaswan, Climate Change, the Clean Air Act, and Industrial Pollution, 30 UCLA J. Envtl. L. & Pol'y 51, 74 (2012).

V. Conclusion

The majority opinion in *Michigan* does not stand alone, but is one of a number of recent opinions concerned with the enormous power and policymaking discretion wielded by the administrative state. Despite its modesty, it may have—in the near term, at least—the greatest impact of them all. *King v. Burwell*, for example, places limits on judicial deference to agencies' statutory interpretations,[139] but it is much too soon to tell how broadly applicable its reasoning may be or whether its approach was entirely opportunistic. Likewise, *Horne v. Department of Agriculture*[140] and *Yates v. United States*[141] both pushed back against dramatic government overreaching, albeit with reasoning that may be "a ticket good for one day only."[142] And across six separate opinions this past term—including one in *Michigan*—Justice Clarence Thomas laid out an originalist approach to the issues of administrative law, calling into question agency rulemaking, judicial deference to agencies, and certain agency adjudications.[143] If these seeds of doubt ever do bear fruit, it will not be for years or decades. And momentum continues to build for denying deference to agencies' interpretations of their own regulations, but with a majority decision supporting that result still elusive.[144]

But *Michigan* addresses more mundane matters and for that reason may have real impact. Every day, federal agencies take actions

---

[139] 135 S. Ct. 2480, 2488–89 (2015) (denying *Chevron* deference in "extraordinary case[]" of "deep economic and political significance" where agency lacks relevant expertise) (quotations omitted). That said, *King* may prove relevant to the lawfulness of the EPA's "Clean Power Plan" greenhouse gas regulations. See, e.g., Jeremy Jacobs, Lawyers Mine Health Care Ruling for Clean Power Plan Clues, Greenwire (June 25, 2015), available at http://www.eenews.net/greenwire/stories/1060020908/climate_digest.

[140] 135 S. Ct. 2419 (2015).

[141] 135 S. Ct. 1074 (2015).

[142] Richard M. Re, On 'A Ticket Good for One Day Only,' 16 Green Bag 2d 155 (2013), available at http://www.greenbag.org/v16n2/v16n2_articles_re.pdf.

[143] See Brian Lipshutz, Justice Thomas and the Originalist Turn in Administrative Law, Yale L.J. Forum, July 18, 2015, available at http://www.yalelawjournal.org/pdf/LipshutzForumEssayForWebsitePDF_zxeyeenu.pdf.

[144] See, e.g., Perez v. Mortg. Bankers Ass'n, 135 S. Ct. 1199, 1210–11 (2015) (Alito, J., concurring in part and concurring in judgment) (questioning validity of this form of deference); *id.* at 1211–12 (Scalia, J., concurring in judgment) (same); *id.* at 1213 (Thomas, J., concurring in judgment) (same).

where costs should be a relevant consideration. After *Michigan*, agencies no longer have discretion to disregard the costs of their actions, or to proceed with actions whose costs are disproportionate to their benefits, in most instances. If one subscribes to the view that agencies, in some proportion of proceedings, disregard or downplay cost considerations so as to pursue preferred policies that may not pass cost-benefit muster, then this new attention to the costs of regulatory actions should promote cost-effectiveness and efficiency, at least at the margins. Given the enormous scope of federal agency activity, even a marginal improvement in overall efficiency can translate into substantial economy-wide benefits.

And that's just the small stuff. *Michigan* stands as an impediment to several of the Obama EPA's major actions under the Clean Air Act due to their reliance on co-benefits to justify otherwise excessive costs. While the majority opinion does not definitively resolve the permissibility of considering co-benefits in agency decisionmaking, its logic clearly constrains agencies to focus on the factors and objectives identified by Congress. Of all the Court's recent decisions attempting to cabin agency discretion, *Michigan* is the most modest and yet may also be the most consequential.

The Raisin Case

*Michael W. McConnell**

Any law teacher will say that simple and obvious cases often are the most illuminating because they bring fundamental issues to the fore. *Horne v. Department of Agriculture,* known as *The Raisin Case,* is an example.[1] Each year, an obscure federal government entity, the Raisin Administrative Committee (RAC), requires that all raisin growers withhold a certain percentage of their crop (often quite large) from the market, for the stated purpose of "stabilizing"—propping up—raisin prices, and to deliver those excess raisins to the RAC, for no payment. The RAC disposes of these "reserve raisins" at its discretion. It gives away some of them to school lunch programs and the like. Most it sells to large packers, using the proceeds for export subsidies and administrative expenses. If any money is left over, it is remitted to the raisin growers on a proportionate basis. In the relevant years for this case, 2002–2003 and 2003–2004, the government seized 47 percent and 30 percent of the crop, respectively, and remitted a tiny sum in one year and nothing in the other. The question in the case was whether this was a "taking" of private property without just compensation, in violation of the Fifth Amendment. In an opinion by Chief Justice John Roberts, by a vote of 8–1, the Court held that the raisin program constitutes a taking. (The Court split 5–3 on the question of remedy.)

This seems like an easy question. The government took raisins, sold them, spent most of the proceeds, and remitted far less than market value (in one year, zero). How could this not be a taking? Yet

* Richard & Frances Mallery Professor of Law and Director of the Constitutional Law Center, Stanford Law School, and Senior Fellow, Hoover Institution. Professor McConnell was counsel for Marvin and Laura Horne in the subject case. The author thanks Brian Leighton, Stephen Schwartz, and Max Raskin for both their invaluable assistance in the case and also their comments on an earlier draft, and Trevor Ezell for research assistance.

[1] 135 S. Ct. 2419 (2015).

the case took three published opinions in the U.S. Court of Appeals for the Ninth Circuit, which decided against the property claim each time (on different theories) and two trips to the U.S. Supreme Court. It even earned a mock investigative report on Comedy Central.[2]

In the course of concluding that the raisin program constitutes an uncompensated taking, the Supreme Court confronted four issues of some complexity. To be sure, the Court did not bring full clarity to any of these questions, but it took a step in that direction, making the jurisprudence of the Takings Clause somewhat less convoluted—and certainly more hospitable to property rights claims.

I. When Has There Been a Taking?

Takings Clause jurisprudence is plagued with misleading terminology. The two large categories are called "per se" takings and "regulatory" takings. This starts off on the wrong track, because those two terms are not parallel: "per se" tells us nothing about the nature of the government's action, but only about the legal consequence; "regulatory" tells us the nature of the government's action, but nothing about the legal consequence. Try to draw a Venn diagram. And why depart from the clear English of the Fifth Amendment itself? The clause is about the obligation of the government to pay just compensation when it "takes" (not "regulates") property for the purpose of public "use." Much of the confusion in Takings Clause jurisprudence could be avoided if we just paid more attention to its words.[3]

According to current doctrine, per se takings occur when the government seizes an ownership interest in what was previously private property or when it effects a permanent or recurring physical invasion of the property. (I will discuss a third version of "per se" takings in a moment.) A better term for this would be an actual "taking." When there is a taking, the government must pay the value of the property taken. It does not matter what the government's reasons are for the taking or how much property is left to the owner afterward; the government must pay for what it takes. This requirement of just compensation is based on the proposition that, as a matter

---

[2] The Daily Show with Jon Stewart: Raisin Growers Lawsuit (Comedy Central television broadcast Aug. 13, 2013), available at http://thedailyshow.cc.com/videos/pm-rodj/raisin-growers-lawsuit.

[3] See Jed Rubenfeld, Usings, 102 Yale L.J. 1077 (1993).

of justice, taxpayers as a whole rather than the particular property owner should bear the cost of achieving the governmental purpose. But there is also an economic logic: if the government has to pay the value of the property taken, it is unlikely to take it unless the public use is more valuable than the market value.

So-called "regulatory takings" are not takings in any traditional sense of the term. They are use restrictions that reduce the value of the property without transferring that value to the government. Regulatory takings are subject to a vague and forgiving balancing test—the *Penn Central* test[4]—that almost never results in compensation being due. In truth, this branch of Takings Clause jurisprudence is nothing but economic substantive due process in different garb. Its primary function in real-world litigation is to allow courts that do not wish to recognize actual takings to pretend that they are still affording property *some* Fifth Amendment protection, even if that protection is essentially illusory. For example, in *The Raisin Case* the Ninth Circuit could say that personal property is still protected by the Fifth Amendment, just not on a per se basis. That sounds less unreasonable than saying personal property is outside the Takings Clause altogether, but it does the owner of personal property confiscated by the government little practical good.

The Supreme Court has carved out one subset of use restrictions and treated them as per se takings: those that eliminate substantially all the value of the property. This is the *Lucas* doctrine.[5] *The Raisin Case* had nothing to do with the *Lucas* doctrine, but both the Ninth Circuit and the dissenting justice thought it did, so I will return to it below as it becomes relevant. The *Lucas* doctrine is peculiar because it kicks in only when substantially all the value of the property is destroyed, which leads to unanswerable questions about how to define "all" of the property. Does the government have to pay if it destroys all the value of a separable part of the property? What is the numerator and what is the denominator? When real takings are involved, this question does not arise, because the government simply pays for what it takes, whether that is the entire property, a particular piece of it, or a particular use of it.

---

[4] Penn. Cent. Transp. Co. v. New York City, 438 U.S. 104 (1978).

[5] Lucas v. S.C. Coastal Council, 505 U.S. 1003 (1992).

The term "regulatory taking" is misleading because it suggests a dichotomy between takings effectuated by means of regulation versus takings effectuated in other ways, such as through eminent domain. The raisin program is plainly "regulatory" in the sense that it is imposed via regulations promulgated by the Department of Agriculture. This inspired the government at one stage in the litigation to assert that it never took "title" to the reserve raisins, but merely regulated the terms of their sale (by taking control of the reserve raisins and selling or giving them away). But it does not matter what species of power the government claims to be exercising; what matters is whether the government has taken ownership and control. The majority opinion used the terms "direct appropriations," "government acquisitions of property," and "physical taking," to distinguish real takings from use restrictions.[6] This helpfully reorients Takings Clause terminology from the technical but meaningless terms "per se" and "regulatory" toward the realistic difference between government seizure of ownership and control versus use restrictions.

Justice Sonia Sotomayor's dissent underscores the importance of distinguishing clearly between takings and use restrictions. She maintained that the raisin program is not a per se taking because it "does not deprive the Hornes of all of their property rights. . . . Simply put, the retention of even one property right that is not destroyed is sufficient to defeat a claim of a *per se* taking."[7] Under the raisin program, she explained, growers "retain at least one meaningful property interest in the reserve raisins: the right to receive some money for their disposition."[8] This is incorrect factually, but it is more importantly wrong as a matter of Takings Clause doctrine.

It is incorrect factually because the raisin grower does not retain any property interest in the property taken, namely their own raisins. Those raisins now belong to the government. The grower instead is given a different form of property: a contingent interest in the proceeds of the raisin reserve as a whole, if any money is left. As the U.S. Court of Appeals for the Federal Circuit explained in another case, "once the raisins were transferred to the RAC, [the producer] no longer had a property interest in the raisins themselves,

---

[6] Horne, 135 S. Ct. at 2427–28.

[7] *Id.* at 2437 (Sotomayor, J., dissenting).

[8] *Id.* at 2438–39.

but only in its share of the reserve pool proceeds as defined by the regulations."[9] Even under the dissent's legal theory, therefore, there was a taking, because the growers retain no property interest in the raisins that were taken. The growers' collective interest in the reserve pool proceeds is relevant to whether there has been compensation for the raisins, but does not affect whether there was a taking.

More importantly, as the majority observed,[10] Justice Sotomayor's claim that there cannot be a per se taking if the property owner retains "even one property right" confuses the two categories of taking. Under the *Lucas* doctrine a use restriction is treated as a per se taking if and only if it destroys substantially all the economic value of the property. But this principle is wholly inapposite to actual takings. When the government actually takes possession and control of property, it must pay for what it takes—and it does not matter how much property the owner has left. If the government takes one acre from my 100-acre plot to build a post office, it must pay for that acre, even though I retain the other 99. If the government asserts an easement across my land, it must pay for the easement, even though I retain every other property interest in the land.[11] This is clear even from the precedent on which the dissent primarily relies: *Loretto v. Teleprompter Manhattan CATV Corp.*[12] In that case, the Court held that requiring the owner of an apartment dwelling to permit installation of a cable TV box on the exterior of the structure was a per se taking because it was a permanent physical intrusion. Obviously, installation of a cable TV box did not deprive the apartment owner of "all" of its property rights in the apartment. But because it was a physical invasion, it counted as an actual taking. (The just compensation due, however, was negligible; the property owner was awarded one dollar.)

---

[9] Lion Raisins, Inc. v. United States, 416 F.3d 1356, 1369 n.9 (Fed. Cir. 2005). Justice Sotomayor also erred in thinking that the amount of the remittance depends on "market forces for which the Government cannot be blamed." 135 S. Ct. at 2439 (Sotomayor, J., dissenting). In fact, the amount of the remittance depends largely on how much of the revenues from sale of the reserve raisins is spent on export subsidies and other activities of the Raisin Committee.

[10] Horne, 135 S. Ct. at 2429.

[11] See Dolan v. City of Tigard, 512 U.S. 374 (1994); Nollan v. Cal. Coastal Comm'n, 483 U.S. 825 (1987); Kaiser Aetna v. United States, 444 U.S. 164 (1979).

[12] 458 U.S. 419 (1982), cited in Horne, 135 S. Ct at 2437–40, 2441 n.3, 2442 (Sotomayor, J., dissenting).

The total-loss rule has long been recognized as a conceptual disaster area, incapable of objective and consistent administration.[13] It should be abandoned where it now holds sway—as an upper bound on permissible uncompensated use restrictions—not extended to the core and settled territory of actual takings. If Justice Sotomayor's approach were adopted, it would be a relatively simple matter for governments to avoid their just-compensation obligation by allowing the property owner to retain some slight "property interest" even as it takes the rest. The cavalry could commandeer your horses, so long as it allows you to retain the contingent right to get them back at the end of the war (assuming they are alive). It is a blessing that no other justice joined the dissent.

One quibble with the majority opinion is that it did not supply a bit more theory about why this key distinction between actual takings and use restrictions makes sense. Why do the full protections of the Fifth Amendment apply when the government takes possession and control of property, though property owners must suffer use restrictions of comparable economic impact, with only the lame protections of "regulatory takings" jurisprudence (that is, substantive due process)? It makes little sense to attach dramatically different constitutional consequences to government actions that have similar purposes and effects.

This is not merely an abstract question. The stated purpose of the raisin program is to stabilize and increase prices of raisins by prohibiting growers from selling their entire crop. In theory, the size of the raisin reserve is set each year in accordance with expected crop size and market conditions, to maximize the total income of the raisin industry. In other words, it is a cartel. Note, however, that the Raisin Administrative Committee could accomplish its cartel objective without taking possession and control of the reserve raisins. Many agricultural programs operate that way, restricting acreage or crop yield or sales, or the timing or nature of sales, without actually appropriating any of the crop. The raisin program is unusual because, in addition to the sales cap, the government demands physical transfer of the excess raisins, which it then sells or gives away. It is only the latter aspect of the program—the expropriation—that the

---

[13] For a summary of the literature, as well as a cogent statement of the problem, see Jed Rubenfeld, Usings, 102 Yale L.J. 1077, 1081–97, 1106–10 (1993).

Hornes challenged. They conceded that, if the Department of Agriculture merely told them not to sell the reserve portion of their raisin crop, rendering it worthless, that would be nothing but a regulatory taking—a claim they did not consider worth bringing.

The majority noted that "[t]he Government thinks it 'strange' and the dissent 'baffling' that the Hornes object to the reserve requirement, when they nonetheless concede that 'the government may prohibit the sale of raisins without effecting a per se taking.'"[14] But the majority supplied only half an answer. The Court explained, correctly, that this "distinction flows naturally from the settled difference in our takings jurisprudence between appropriation and regulation."[15] True: when the government *takes* property it has a categorical obligation to pay, but when it imposes *use restrictions*—even very costly ones—it does not. But why would a sensible constitution draw this line, if it is true, as the majority says, that "[a] physical taking of raisins and a regulatory limit on production may have the same economic impact on a grower"?[16] The majority provides no real answer to its question, noting only that the Constitution "is concerned with means as well as ends."[17]

There is an answer. It lies, I think, not with any difference in economic impact on the grower, but with the political and economic incentives of the government. The government has little incentive to impose use restrictions whose costs exceed the regulatory benefits (assuming there is no animus against the property owner). That is certainly no guarantee of wise or efficient regulation, but, overall, one would expect the benefits to exceed the costs, at least roughly. When the government takes the property, however, it now has a thing of value that it can use for its own purposes, or to please constituents and supporters. In the absence of a just compensation requirement, one would expect the government to take from disfavored Class A and give to favored Class B, even if the losses to A exceed the benefits to B.

The raisin program is Exhibit A of this phenomenon. It is highly unlikely, for reasons we will discuss below, that the raisin volume

14 Horne, 135 S. Ct. at 2428.

15 *Id.*

16 *Id.*

17 *Id.*

controls would be imposed in the absence of the expropriation of the excess raisins. Farmers have already expended labor and capital in producing the raisins, and any requirement that they refrain from selling a portion of the crop would constitute a pure loss. It would make sense to impose a percentage cap on sales only if the price of the remaining raisins increased by prodigious amounts. Indeed, in a year like 2002–2003, when the raisin reserve was 47 percent of the crop, the price of the remaining raisins would have to increase by nearly 90 percent to make the pure volume control profitable.

But in fact the Raisin Administrative Committee takes possession of the excess raisins; they are not a pure loss. The RAC sells them or gives then away at its own discretion. In 2002–2003 it sold the vast majority of the reserve raisins, receiving $118,280,587 in revenues, of which it devoted $53,360,854 to export subsidies. In 2003–2004 the RAC sold its reserve raisins for $111,242,849, spending $99,807,957 on export subsidies.[18] It is obvious that the big winners from the raisin program are the few large firms that engage in the export trade. It will come as no surprise to readers of this journal that a program of economic regulation supposedly enacted in the interest of small raisin farmers in fact works to the benefit of the largest players in the industry.

My conceptual point is that there is a large practical difference between value-destroying use restrictions and takings. When the government actually takes possession of private property, it can exploit the value of that property for what the Fifth Amendment calls "public use" and what, in practice, means politically advantageous uses. There will often be a political constituency for those uses (here, large exporters), even if the costs exceed the benefits. The majority opinion notes that the economic impact on the Hornes of pure volume controls would be the same as the economic impact of the taking. But large special interests do not specially benefit from pure volume controls, making abuse less likely. The constitutional line between takings and use restrictions reflects the reality that government is more likely to invade property rights if it thereby gains control over valuable resources that can be redistributed to its friends.

---

[18] Supplemental Appendix to the Petition for Writ of Certiorari at 2a, Horne v. Dep't of Agric., 135 S. Ct. 2419 (2015) (No. 14-275) (annual report of the Raisin Admin. Comm.), available at http://object.cato.org/sites/cato.org/files/ articles/raisin-administrative-committee-statement.pdf.

The distinction also rests on a moral difference—often deconstructed and disliked by economists—between harm and benefit. The effect of the distinction is to allow government to prevent property owners from harming others, but not to allow government to require property owners to benefit others. This is not the occasion to delve into the philosophical depths of this important question. Suffice it to say that much of our law, of ordinary moral intuitions about justice, and of constitutional structure, depends on it. I may not drown a stranger in a pond, but I do not have to fish him out if I was not responsible for his being there. The Takings Clause seems to follow the same intuition.

The majority quite properly did not extend its reasoning to Takings Clause problems beyond *The Raisin Case* itself, but its emphatic insistence on the line between "appropriations" and "use restrictions" hints at a fundamental reformulation of the jurisprudence of "regulatory takings." That jurisprudence is utterly vacuous and has been so from its inception. The first regulatory takings case, *Pennsylvania Coal Co. v. Mahon*, unhelpfully stated that a use restriction becomes a Taking when it "goes too far."[19] More recently, the Court's balancing test for regulatory takings, the *Penn Central* test, provides no meaningful criteria whatsoever. But if the majority is correct in *Horne*, there is a path out of the morass. A regulation in the form of a use restriction should be deemed a taking if the government thereby exploits (or in Fifth Amendment language "uses") the resource for its own affirmative purposes, but not if it simply prevents its use by the owner. Thus, a regulation effectively shutting down a coal-fired plant is not a "taking," but a regulation requiring the owner of an historic building to maintain its historic character for the pleasure and edification of society might be. If the government orders raisin growers to destroy part of their crop, this is not a taking; but if the government orders raisin growers to transfer part of their crop to the government, for sale or other disposition, it is.[20] Professor Rubenfeld enunciates the "test" this way: "If the state's interest in taking or regulating something would be equally well served by destroying the thing altogether (putting aside any independent considerations

[19] 260 U.S. 393, 415 (1923).

[20] This suggestion closely resembles the position advocated by Professor Rubenfeld. See *supra* note 3. Readers curious about how to apply this line of reasoning should consult his article.

that might make such destruction undesirable to the state for other reasons), no use-value of the thing is being exploited."[21]

Interestingly, the line between physical and regulatory takings is assailed from both "sides" of the issue. Some, like Justice Sotomayor, wish to relegate all or almost all takings—even actual appropriations, like the one here—to the tender mercies of *Penn Central* balancing. Others, like Professor Richard Epstein, who calls the difference between physical and regulatory takings "an indefensible intellectual distinction," wish to extend the rigorous protections of just compensation to the wide expanses of improvident regulation.[22] I would speculate that Justice Sotomayor is more prescient on this matter than Professor Epstein: that erasure of the distinction would be more likely to water down existing protections for property than to expand judicial review of the substance of economic regulation. But the common ground between Sotomayor and Epstein highlights that the Takings Clause, as interpreted by the majority, occupies a middle ground that protects private property from confiscation but does not augur a return to the substantive-due-process solicitude for economic liberty of the *Lochner* sort.[23]

II. Protections for Personal Property

The Raisin Case is most likely to be remembered—and cited—for the proposition that the Takings Clause protects personal property (such as raisins) no less than it protects real property (land). Surprisingly, the Court had never squarely addressed that question before, perhaps because no one ever doubted that the Takings Clause applies fully to personal property. The Court has applied the Clause (in its "per se" form) in the past to such personal property as patents, steamboats, machinery, and money,[24] but it did so casually, without explanation, until *Horne*. In *Horne*, the Ninth Circuit panel held that

[21] Rubenfeld, *supra* note 3, at 1116.

[22] Richard Epstein, Raisin' A Raw Deal, Defining Ideas, Hoover Institution (July 6, 2015), http://www.hoover.org/research/raisin-raw-deal.

[23] Lochner v. New York, 198 U.S. 45 (1905). I appreciate that many readers of this journal may not find that an ominous possibility, but if we are to build consensus for stronger protections for property rights, our coalition must be broader than *Lochner* advocates.

[24] See Webb's Fabulous Pharmacies, Inc. v. Beckwith, 449 U.S. 155 (1980) (money); United States v. General Motors Corp., 323 U.S. 373 (1945) (machinery); United States

"per se" takings rules (which I prefer to call actual takings) do not apply to personal property. (To its credit, the government did not suggest this line of argument to the court of appeals and disdained to defend it before the Supreme Court.) That surprising holding attracted much of the attention the case received from the bar, and may have been the reason the Court granted the petition for certiorari.

That the Takings Clause applies fully to personal property may be the takeaway holding of *The Raisin Case*, but it raises little in the way of intellectual interest. Of course the Takings Clause applies fully to personal property. Nothing in the text, history, or logic of the clause suggests otherwise. As the majority wrote: "The Government has a categorical duty to pay just compensation when it takes your car, just as when it takes your home."[25] There was no dissent on this point.

Indeed, as the majority observed, protection of personal property—and especially of farmers' crops—has been a central concern of takings jurisprudence since the Magna Carta. One provision of that fountainhead of Anglo-American constitutionalism provided that "[n]o constable or other of Our bailiffs shall take corn or other chattels of any man without immediate payment, unless the seller voluntarily consents to postponement of payment."[26] In the colonial era, Section 8 of the Massachusetts Body of Liberties (1641) protected personal property alone from uncompensated takings. As an historical matter, uncompensated takings of personal property such as horses, vehicles, food, blankets, and supplies by the army likely were the animating events that led to the Takings Clause. Henry St. George Tucker, author of the first treatise on the United States Constitution, observed that the Takings Clause was "probably" enacted in response to "the arbitrary and oppressive mode of obtaining supplies for the army, and other public uses, by impressment, as was too frequently practiced during the revolutionary war, without any compensation whatever."[27] As early as 1778, John Jay, later the first

---

v. Russell, 80 U.S. 623 (1871) (steamboats); United States v. Palmer, 128 U.S. 262 (1888) (patents)

[25] Horne, 135 S. Ct. at 2426.

[26] Magna Carta, § 28 (1215), reprinted in A.E. Dick Howard, Magna Carta: Text and Commentary 43 (1964).

[27] 1 St. George Tucker, Blackstone's Commentaries: With Notes of Reference, to the Constitution and Laws, of the Federal Government of the United States; and of the Commonwealth of Virginia 305–06 (1803).

chief justice of the United States, wrote an essay decrying the practice by military quartermasters in New York of impressing "horses, teems [sic], and carriages" without the protections of the law.[28] Many questions surrounding the law of private property are controversial, but it is hard to see under what point of view it could be permissible for the government to take your chattels without payment but not your land.

The sole support for the Ninth Circuit's holding was language in *Lucas* that suggested—without holding, for the case did not actually involve the issue—that personal property might not be included in the special rule that use restrictions that render property economically worthless are treated as per se takings.[29] Once again, the analytical confusion wrought by *Lucas* takes its toll. *Lucas* is not a case about an actual taking. It is a case about a use restriction that effectively destroyed all of the land's economic value. The intuition behind *Lucas* is that a regulation that destroys all economic value of land must necessarily "go too far." That intuition is less likely to hold water in the case of personal property; many regulations render specific forms of personal property valueless. But as the majority recognized, none of this has any bearing when the government actually takes possession. When the government takes personal property and uses it (or sells the property and uses the proceeds), it must pay.

III. "Voluntary" Transactions and Unconstitutional Conditions

The most sweeping of the government's arguments in support of the raisin program was that raisin growers "voluntarily" choose to participate in the program in exchange for the "benefit" of selling their remaining raisins in interstate commerce. If they do not like the reserve requirement, said the government, they can plant different crops or use their grapes to make wine instead of raisins. The majority responded acerbically: "'Let them sell wine' is probably not much more comforting to the raisin growers than similar retorts have been to others throughout history."[30]

---

[28] John Jay, A Freeholder, A Hint to the Legislature of the State of New York (1778), reprinted in 5 The Founders' Constitution 312–13 (Philip B. Kurland & Ralph Lerner, eds., 1987).

[29] Horne v. Dep't of Agric., 750 F.3d 1128, 1139–40 (9th Cir. 2014) (citing Lucas, 505 U.S. at 1027-28).

[30] Horne, 135 S. Ct. at 2430.

It is sometimes true that a person can be required to waive exercise of a constitutional right in exchange for a government benefit. But if being allowed to engage in business is a "benefit," not much would remain of constitutional rights. During the middle decades of the last century, the Court—led by its liberals, and especially Justice William Brennan—developed a line of analysis called "unconstitutional conditions" doctrine to define and limit the scope of the government's power to condition benefits on the waiver of constitutional rights.[31] The doctrine is not always clear and it is not always applied consistently.[32] A simple summary is that the government may not require a person to waive a constitutional right in exchange for a generally available public benefit unless that waiver is closely related ("germane") to the reason the benefit is being granted.

The Court has gradually, sometimes haltingly, extended these principles to virtually all constitutional rights. One of the first was freedom of speech. Justice Brennan expressed the logic of the doctrine in *Speiser v. Randall*, a case involving the grant of certain tax benefits to veterans only to those willing to take a loyalty oath:

> To deny an exemption to claimants who engage in certain forms of speech is in effect to penalize them for such speech. Its deterrent effect is the same as if the State were to fine them for this speech. The appellees are plainly mistaken in their argument that, because a tax exemption is a "privilege" or "bounty," its denial may not infringe speech.[33]

The doctrine was extended to the Takings Clause (though without mentioning its name) in *Loretto v. Teleprompter Manhattan CATV Corp.*[34] The government had argued that it could require property owners to permit installation of cable TV boxes without compensation for the intrusion, as a condition of permission to rent the

---

[31] See Richard A. Epstein, The Supreme Court 1987 Term: Foreword: Unconstitutional Conditions, State Power, and the Limits of Consent, 102 Harv. L. Rev. 4 (1988); Seth F. Kreimer, Allocational Sanctions: The Problem of Negative Rights in a Positive State, 132 U. Pa. L. Rev. 1293 (1984); Kathleen M. Sullivan, Unconstitutional Conditions, 102 Harv. L. Rev. 1413 (1989).

[32] See, e.g., Christian Legal Soc'y v. Martinez, 561 U.S. 661 (2010) (allowing state university to require waiver of freedom of association as a condition to being allowed to use an otherwise open speech forum).

[33] 357 U.S. 513, 518 (1958).

[34] 458 U.S. 419 (1982).

apartments. Justice Thurgood Marshall's opinion for the Court rejected this argument, explaining:

> It is true that the landlord could avoid the requirements of § 828 by ceasing to rent the building to tenants. But a landlord's ability to rent his property may not be conditioned on his forfeiting the right to compensation for a physical occupation. Teleprompter's broad "use-dependency" argument proves too much. For example, it would allow the government to require a landlord to devote a substantial portion of his building to vending and washing machines, with all profits to be retained by the owners of these services and with no compensation for the deprivation of space. It would even allow the government to requisition a certain number of apartments as permanent government offices. The right of a property owner to exclude a stranger's physical occupation of his land cannot be so easily manipulated.[35]

The argument applies equally to the raisin program. The right of raisin growers to sell their product cannot be conditioned on forcing them to give a portion of their crop to the government.

Unfortunately, there is a precedent that at least seems to go the other way: *Ruckleshaus v. Monsanto Corp.*[36] That case involved an Environmental Protection Agency requirement that certain pesticide manufacturers disclose health and safety information, including trade secrets, which then were made public. It is possible that this requirement could have been upheld on other grounds, but the Court did so on the ground that Monsanto had waived its property right in exchange for a "valuable Government benefit"—namely, the permission to sell the pesticides.[37] More broadly, the Court wrote that the disclosure requirement was the price the company had to pay for "'the advantage of living and doing business in a civilized community.'"[38] The Court made no mention of the unconstitutional conditions doctrine, no mention of *Loretto*, no attempt to distinguish contrary cases, and no attempt to identify limits to this argument.

---

[35] *Id.* at 439 n.17.

[36] 467 U.S. 986 (1984).

[37] *Id.* at 1007.

[38] *Id.* (quoting Andrus v. Allard, 444 U.S. 51, 67 (1979)).

It would probably be preferable if the Court in *Horne* had simply stated that *Monsanto* was wrongly decided, or at least wrongly reasoned. But that is not the way constitutional law usually works. Faced with an erroneous precedent, the Court more commonly distinguishes it, sometimes on spurious grounds, effectively limiting the precedent to its facts. To some extent, the Court had already done that to *Monsanto*. In *Nollan v. California Coastal Commission*,[39] an important and careful application of unconstitutional conditions doctrine to the Takings Clause, the Court had held that "the right to build on one's own property . . . cannot remotely be described as a 'government benefit,'" and so does not allow the government to demand property as part of the bargain.[40] This is an important point: it is not a "benefit" for the government simply to refrain from forbidding a person to do something he would otherwise be free to do. Raisin farmers have the right to sell raisins, and the government is doing them no favors when it gets out of the way.

Not content with *Nollan*'s limitation of the reach of the decision, Chief Justice Roberts went on to distinguish *Monsanto* on the ground that selling pesticides is dangerous to public health, while "[r]aisins . . . are a healthy snack."[41] Justice Sotomayor's dissent may be right that this ground of distinction does not "hold up"—that "nothing in *Monsanto* . . . turned on the dangerousness of the commodity at issue."[42] But that is a product of the alarmingly sweeping language of the *Monsanto* opinion. In fact, the regulatory action in *Monsanto* might have been justifiable under the doctrine, frequently applied in land use permitting, that property owners can sometimes be required to disgorge property when this serves to mitigate the damage their actions would otherwise inflict on the public. They might, for example, have to pay for improvements to

---

[39] 483 U.S. 825 (1987).

[40] *Id.* at 833 n.2.

[41] Horne, 135 S. Ct. at 2431.

[42] *Id.* at 2441 n.2 (Sotomayor, J., dissenting). Justice Sotomayor was on far weaker ground in relying on *Andrus v. Allard*, 444 U.S. 51 (1979), which upheld a bar on the sale of eagle feathers, rendering them economically (but not culturally or religiously) valueless. *Andrus* was a mere use restriction; the government neither took possession of the feathers nor appropriated any aspect of their value. In *Monsanto*, the government and the public made use of the company's trade secrets.

sewers or roads, or dedicate open space to the public, if a development would strain existing infrastructure.[43]

It has been suggested that this principle covers the raisin program, on the theory that the sale of raisins somehow "harms" other members of the raisin industry by depressing prices. I personally believe this strains the idea of "harm" beyond its breaking point. But even if it is a "harm", the argument might justify capping the number of raisins a grower may sell, but it provides no justification for the further requirement that the growers transfer those raisins, without compensation, to the government. Those transfers do nothing to benefit growers, apart from any remittances they might generate.

IV. The Question of Offsetting Benefits

Justice Stephen Breyer, joined by Justices Ruth Bader Ginsburg and Elena Kagan, dissented in part, on the theory that a remand is necessary to determine whether the benefit to the Hornes of higher raisin prices caused by the reserve requirement might constitute just compensation. The majority rejected this suggestion, largely on the ground that the government "has already calculated the amount of just compensation in this case, when it fined the Hornes the fair market value of the raisins: $483,843.53. The Government cannot now disavow that valuation . . . ."[44] The proper remedy, the majority held, is to reverse the decision upholding the fine. That seems to be an adequate response, but Justice Breyer's partial dissent invites further reflection, both about the nature of Takings remedies and about the economics of the raisin program.

There is a more fundamental reason why the proper remedy in *The Raisin Case* was simply to reverse the fine: there was no taking, not yet, and therefore no legal basis for doing the just compensation calculations that the partial dissent contemplated. The *Horne* litigation was neither an eminent domain proceeding nor an inverse condemnation proceeding; rather, it was an injunctive action to prevent an unconstitutional taking before it occurred. The raisin program is unconstitutional not (as the partial dissent would have it) because

---

[43] See Koontz v. St. Johns River Water Mgmt. Dist., 133 S. Ct. 2586 (2013), and Dolan v. City of Tigard, 512 U.S. 374 (1994), for explanations of these cases and their constitutional limits.

[44] Horne, 135 S. Ct. at 2433 (citation omitted).

compensation was inadequate, but because the statutory scheme did not contemplate compensation in the first place. The Agricultural Marketing Agreement Act, the exclusive legal avenue by which the Hornes could challenge the order to turn over their raisins, refers to the district court as exercising "jurisdiction in equity"—and an equity court does not have authority to calculate or award damages.[45]

As Professor Thomas Merrill explains in his recent article, *Anticipatory Remedies for Takings*, there is nothing wrong in principle with injunctive or declaratory actions to prevent takings where the legislature has made no provision for compensation.[46] Indeed, although the Court has not noted the fact or explained what it is doing, there have been numerous cases in recent years enjoining takings where there was no legal provision for just compensation.[47] *The Raisin Case* was such a case. It may help to resurrect the original understanding of remedies under the Fifth Amendment, which prevailed until the early 20th century. When the government proposes to effectuate a taking and the legislature has provided for compensation, the remedy is for the property owner to sue for compensation; but if the government proposes to effectuate a taking and the legislature has not provided for compensation; (implicitly or explicitly—a question of statutory interpretation), the proper remedy is to sue for an injunction or declaration that the uncompensated taking is unconstitutional.[48]

The economic reasoning of the partial dissent also warrants comment. It rests on the speculation that the raisin reserve must necessarily have benefitted raisin growers like the Hornes (albeit at the expense of consumers). Why else would the program exist?

There are both empirical and theoretical reasons to doubt that the raisin reserve program actually raises the price of raisins over the long run. The only serious academic study of the consequences of the program—a study cited by the government in its brief—concluded

---

[45] 7 U.S.C. § 608c(15)(B) (2015).

[46] Thomas M. Merrill, Anticipatory Remedies for Takings, 128 Harv. L. Rev. 1630 (2015).

[47] See Joshua D. Hawley, The Beginning of the End? *Horne v. Department of Agriculture* and the Future of *Williamson County*, 2012–2013 Cato Sup. Ct. Rev. 245, 256 n.58 (2013) (collecting cases).

[48] See Robert Brauneis, The First Constitutional Tort: The Remedial Revolution in Nineteenth-Century State Just Compensation Law, 52 Vand. L. Rev. 57 (1999).

that "grower net return . . . averaged zero under the volume control program, suggesting that profits were not above normal" relative to an unregulated market, though prices were less variable.[49] Even the Department of Agriculture's estimates of the effects of the reserve turn out to predict that growers are made worse off. Take the 2003–2004 crop year as an example. That year, the field price for raisins was $810 per ton.[50] The department's econometric model estimated that the price would have been $63 per ton less without the reserve, or $747 per ton.[51] Using that figure, a producer of 1,000 tons of raisins could have sold them in an unregulated market for $747,000, from which should be deducted the state mandatory advertising fee of almost $5 per ton. Under the marketing order, however, the producer could sell only 70% of his crop, yielding $567,000. He received nothing for his reserve raisins that year, meaning he was worse off by $175,000. This is according to the government's own numbers.

What is the explanation? Why wouldn't a cartel dominated by the industry benefit the industry? There are at least three reasons why the raisin reserve program was not well designed to increase the incomes of raisin farmers. First, if the volume controls actually have the effect of maintaining above-market prices, hence supracompetitive profits to growers, this would simply attract more producers into the industry, dissipating any benefits over the long run. Even in the shorter run, volume controls calculated as a percentage of crops already grown—in contrast to volume controls based on reducing acreage or production levels—have the perverse effect of stimulating production while discouraging marketing. If you grow more raisins, you may sell proportionately more raisins. Second, it is likely that the Raisin Administrative Committee's own sales and give-aways have a depressive effect on prices. Third, given that raisins grown abroad may be imported into the United States without being subject to the volume controls, it is likely that volume controls hurt American farmers while driving up world prices, to the benefit of foreign growers. In a world market, it is not possible to enrich

---

[49] Ben C. French & Carole Frank Nuckton, An Empirical Analysis of Economic Performance Under the Marketing Order for Raisins, 73 Am. J. Agric. Econ. 581, 592 (1991).

[50] Petition for Writ of Certiorari at 41a, Horne, 135 S. Ct. 2419 (No. 14-275).

[51] Brief for the Respondent at 10, Horne, 135 S. Ct. 2419 (No. 14-275).

American growers by restricting their sales, when Turkish and other competitors can pick up the slack.

Again, one may wonder why the Raisin Administrative Committee, which is elected by members of the industry (then formally appointed by the secretary of agriculture) would continue a program that likely hurts its constituents. The most likely answer is that *exporters* benefit from the export subsidies that are financed by sale of the reserve raisins. The raisin industry is highly concentrated, with one large cooperative commanding a plurality of the seats on the RAC. Since that cooperative is the largest exporter, it seems probable that this is the explanation for the political support for the raisin reserve. Interestingly, though, for the last five years the RAC has set the reserve at zero, and the cooperative has petitioned to cancel it altogether.[52] Apparently, even with the export subsidies, the raisin program has come to be a loser for even the large players who previously were its supporters.

No one would expect Supreme Court justices to research the empirical evidence or to engage in economic analysis of the program, but it is somewhat disappointing that Breyer's partial dissent, written by the justice most versed in economic regulation and its perversities, showed so little skepticism about the government lawyers' claim that the raisin reserve program, on balance, benefitted growers like the Hornes. Very likely, it did not.

V. Conclusion

The Raisin Case made little new law. It affirmed that the Takings Clause protects personal as well as real property, but this had not genuinely been in doubt. It reaffirmed application of the unconstitutional conditions doctrine to takings, which is important—but not a change. And it gave new emphasis to the crisp distinction between actual governmental appropriations of property and mere use restrictions. All too many takings cases in the past avoided clear lines and pushed in the direction of vague and muddy standards, which work to the advantage of government. If the Court applies the logic of this distinction rigorously to other issues arising under the

---

[52] Sun-Maid Sends Initiative to Eliminate the Raisin Reserve, Am. Vineyard, Jan. 2015, at 19.

Takings Clause, it could clear up much of the confusion that plagues this area of the law.

The decision, however, has a significance that is more than the sum of its individual holdings. The great obstacle to enforcement of the Takings Clause has been the willingness—nay, in some cases, the seeming eagerness—of courts to blur lines, magnify technicalities, and construct procedural and doctrinal roadblocks to recovery. The lower court decisions in this case illustrate the point: the panel published an initial decision based on the idea that the taking was a voluntary transaction; on petition for rehearing *en banc* the panel substituted a decision that the issue was not ripe and there was no jurisdiction; and then on remand it discovered two new reasons why this straightforward example of a classic taking of property could be relegated to what it called the "doctrinal thicket of the Supreme Court's regulatory takings jurisprudence."[53] A decade ago, the case would have died on the vine. That the Supreme Court twice granted petitions to review, once on jurisdiction and once on the merits, and concluded there had been a taking in a short, clear, commonsensical, and almost unanimous opinion, suggests that the tide has turned. Twenty years ago, Chief Justice William Rehnquist observed that there was "no reason why the Takings Clause of the Fifth Amendment, as much a part of the Bill of Rights as the First Amendment or Fourth Amendment, should be relegated to the status of a poor relation."[54] *The Raisin Case* suggests that Rehnquist's admonition is bearing fruit.

---

[53] Horne, 750 F.3d at 1138.
[54] Dolan, 512 U.S. at 392.

Perez v. Mortgage Bankers: Heralding the Demise of Auer Deference?

*Adam J. White**

Judging solely from the justices' votes, *Perez v. Mortgage Bankers Association* was one of the simplest cases before the Supreme Court this year: the justices unanimously reversed the U.S. Court of Appeals for the D.C. Circuit in a brisk 14-page slip opinion.

Indeed, if one does not look beyond the Court's characterization of the case, then the question presented was so simple that to ask it is to answer it: The Administrative Procedure Act's Section 553(b)(A) expressly exempts "interpretative rules" from the requirements of notice and comment. The Labor Department issued an interpretative rule. Can the D.C. Circuit require the department to undertake notice and comment proceedings for the rule? *Of course not.*[1]

But, in fact, the case was not so simple. Indeed, *Mortgage Bankers* raises some of the thorniest issues in modern administrative law: the gap between nominal form and actual substance; the theoretical divide between lawmaking and legal "interpretation"; and, most important, the courts' role in ensuring that unelected agency officials remain accountable to the political branches, the courts, and ultimately the people—through *ex ante* notice-and-comment procedures, *ex post* judicial review, or perhaps even both. These considerations surrounded the *Mortgage Bankers* case, spurring specific discussion from several justices in 30 pages of concurrences, and thus spotlighting the issues to be litigated in future cases.

The place of administrative agencies in our constitutional system has been contentious for nearly a century. The Constitution instructs, in seemingly simple terms, that "[a]ll legislative Powers

---

* Counsel at Boyden Gray & Associates; adjunct fellow with the Manhattan Institute.

[1] See generally Perez v. Mortgage Bankers Ass'n, 135 S. Ct. 1199, 1206–07 (2015) (citing Vermont Yankee Nuclear Power Corp. v. Natural Res. Def. Council, 435 U.S. 519, 524 (1978)).

herein granted shall be vested in a Congress,"[2] that "[t]he executive Power shall be vested in a President,"[3] and that "[t]he judicial Power of the United States . . . shall be vested in one supreme Court, and in such inferior Courts as the Congress may from time to time ordain and establish."[4] To many, these structural provisions imply that administrative agencies must be part of the executive branch and thus should be subject to plenary presidential control.[5] But the Supreme Court famously disagreed with that reading of the Constitution, in the New Deal era.[6] And that disagreement persists today.[7]

Moreover, agencies wield immense powers delegated to them by Congress. The Supreme Court has held that such delegations violate the Constitution only in the most extreme cases—namely, when Congress's grant of power to the agency is so open-ended as to contain no "intelligible principle" guiding and limiting the agency's discretion.[8] In practice, the Supreme Court has only twice held that statutes violated that requirement, and both of those cases were decided in a single year, eight decades ago.[9]

Thus, regulators unaccountable to the people effectively "make" most of the federal law, either through their regulations or through

---

[2] U.S. Const. art. I, § 1.

[3] U.S. Const. art. II, § 1, cl. 1.

[4] U.S. Const. art. III, § 1.

[5] See, e.g., Stephen G. Calabresi & Christopher S. Yoo, The Unitary Executive 3 (2008).

[6] See, e.g., Humphrey's Ex'r v. United States, 295 U.S. 602 (1935) (allowing Congress to make a commission "independent" of the president).

[7] See, e.g., Free Enter. Fund v. PCAOB, 130 S. Ct. 3138, 3146–47 (2008) (reiterating that the president's power to remove agency officials "is not without limit," and that therefore "Congress can, under certain circumstances, create independent agencies run by principal officers appointed by the President, whom the President may not remove at will but only for good cause.").

[8] Whitman v. Am. Trucking Ass'ns, 531 U.S. 457, 474 (2001).

[9] A.L.A. Schechter Poultry Corp. v. United States, 295 U.S. 495, 550 (1935); Pan. Ref. Co. v. Ryan, 293 U.S. 388, 433 (1935). The Supreme Court's reluctance to hold statutes unconstitutional under the nondelegation doctrine spurred Cass Sunstein to quip in 2000 that the doctrine "has had one good year, and 211 bad ones (and counting)." Cass R. Sunstein, Nondelegation Canons, 67 U. Chi. L. Rev. 315, 322 (2000). But see generally C. Boyden Gray, The Nondelegation Canon's Neglected History and Underestimated Legacy, 22 Geo. Mason L. Rev. 619 (2015) (explaining how the nondelegation doctrine has been used much more often as a canon of construction, narrowing statutes' scopes in order to avoid constitutional problems).

their adjudications. This state of affairs draws vigorous criticism from a band of administrative law scholars,[10] other legal scholars and political scientists,[11] and even the occasional Supreme Court justice.[12]

The Administrative Procedure Act (APA) was enacted by Congress in 1946 to impose at least some structure on the workings of the administrative state, in the interests of both democratic accountability and legal legitimacy.[13] Its provisions included the requirement that agencies subject rulemakings (with some exceptions) to *ex ante* public scrutiny through the notice-and-comment process,[14] and the codification of an *ex post* judicial review process in which courts would "decide all relevant questions of law, interpret constitutional and statutory provisions, and determine the meaning or applicability of the terms of an agency action," and set aside rulemakings that fail to satisfy the APA's standards of review.[15]

As noted earlier, the APA does not require *all* rulemakings to undergo the notice-and-comment process. Rather, the APA exempts a number of rulemakings from that requirement, including "interpretative rules."[16] (The APA does not specifically assign a label to the sorts of rules that *are* subject to notice and comment, but they

[10] See generally, e.g., Gary Lawson, The Rise and Rise of the Administrative State, 107 Harv. L. Rev. 1231 (1994) ("The post-New Deal administrative state is unconstitutional, and its validation by the legal system amounts to nothing less than a bloodless constitutional revolution.").

[11] See, e.g., Philip Hamburger, Is Administrative Law Unlawful? 7 (2014) ("Administrative law constrains outside the paths of regular law and adjudication, and in securing legal deference, it also rises above the law and the courts."); Charles Murray, By The People 71–75 (2015) ("To call the regulatory state an extralegal state within the state is not hyperbole but a reasonable description of the facts on the ground.").

[12] Morrison v. Olson, 487 U.S. 654, 726 (Scalia, J., dissenting) (writing that "one must grieve for the Constitution" in light of the Court's broad endorsement of Congress's power to restrict the president from removing officers at will).

[13] Its sponsor, Senator Pat McCarran, called the APA "a comprehensive charter of private liberty and a solemn undertaking of official fairness.... It upholds the law and yet lightens the burden of those on whom the law may impinge. It enunciates and emphasizes the tripartite form of our democracy and brings into relief the ever essential declaration that this is a government of law rather than of men." Administrative Procedure Act: Legislative History, S. Doc. No. 79-248, 2d Sess., p. III (1946) (Foreword).

[14] 5 U.S.C. § 553(b).

[15] *Id.* § 706.

[16] *Id.* § 553(b)(A).

have come to be known colloquially as "legislative" or "substantive" rules.[17])

Perhaps the interpretative-rule exception seemed narrow in 1946. But 70 years later, as agencies wield exponentially greater power and become much savvier in avoiding procedural requirements,[18] such exceptions loom much larger.

For years, the D.C. Circuit attempted to prevent that exception from swallowing the rule, beginning with *Paralyzed Veterans of America v. D.C. Arena L.P.*[19] Ultimately that line of D.C. Circuit cases gave rise to—and then was nullified by—*Mortgage Bankers.*

But discussion surrounding *Mortgage Bankers* ultimately came to focus less on notice-and-comment requirements *per se* than on the broader debate over modern doctrines of judicial "deference" to agency interpretations, as evidenced by the amicus briefs filed in the case and, ultimately, by several justices' concurring opinions. For that reason, *Mortgage Bankers* may be remembered less for the Court's specific holding on notice-and-comment procedures than for several justices' concurring opinions considering—or even demanding—the abolition of a major doctrine of judicial deference.

From "Considerable Smog" to *Paralyzed Veterans*

What is the difference between an "interpretative" and a "legislative" (or "substantive") rule? At a certain level of abstraction the difference is simple, as explained by the courts. An "interpretative rule" is a rule that interprets either a statute or a legislative rule,[20] but which does not itself have "the force of law" and therefore does not itself have any "binding" effect on the public.[21] A legislative

---

[17] See, e.g., Thomas W. Merrill & Kathryn T. Watts, Agency Rules with the Force of Law: The Original Convention, 116 Harv. L. Rev. 467, 477 (2002) ("Such rules are typically referred to as either 'legislative rules' or 'substantive rules' for short").

[18] See, e.g., Michael S. Greve & Ashley C. Parrish, Administrative Law Without Congress, 22 Geo. Mason L. Rev. 501, 504 (2015) (criticizing "procedural shell games and manipulation" and "broad regulatory waivers without or in excess of a statutory warrant").

[19] 117 F.3d 579 (D.C. Cir. 1997).

[20] See, e.g., Am. Hosp. Ass'n v. Bowen, 834 F.2d 1037, 1045 (D.C. Cir. 1987) ("interpretive rules are statements as to what an administrative officer thinks the statute or regulation means").

[21] *Id.* at 1046. An agency's power to issue legislative rules is defined by Congress: "an agency has the power to issue binding legislative rules only if and to the extent

rule might itself contain an interpretation, but if it has independent binding effect on the public, then it is a legislative rule rather than a merely interpretative rule.

At least that's the basic theory. In practice, distinguishing "legislative" rules from merely "interpretative" rules (or, as they tend to be called today, "interpretive" rules) is often no easy task. Or, as the *en banc* D.C. Circuit observed three decades ago, "the distinction between legislative and nonlegislative rules" is "enshrouded in considerable smog."[22] The APA's vague distinction between legislative and interpretative rules has given rise to "decades of less than successful judicial efforts to distinguish between legislative rules and interpretative rules."[23]

In the 1990s, two different panels of the D.C. Circuit attempted to lay down relatively specific standards for distinguishing between legislative and interpretative rules. In the first, *American Mining Congress v. MSHA* (D.C. Cir. 1993), the panel identified four factors, any one of which would render a rule legislative rather than interpretative: (1) if the underlying statute would not itself give the agency "an adequate legislative basis" for an "enforcement action or other agency action to confer benefits or ensure the performance of duties"; (2) if the agency has published the rule in the Code of Federal Regulations; (3) if the agency explicitly invokes its legislative authority when promulgating the rule; or (4) if the rule effectively amends a prior legislative rule.[24]

Just three years after announcing the *American Mining Congress* factors, however, a different D.C. Circuit panel (albeit with one of the three *AMC* judges) announced another framework to distinguish *truly* interpretative rules from rules that are nominally "interpretative" but that effectively "amend" previous legislative rules and therefore require notice and comment (under 5 U.S.C. § 551(5)).[25]

Congress has authorized it to do so"; interpretative rules, by contrast, "have no power to bind members of the public, but only the potential power to persuade a court[.]" Richard J. Pierce, Jr., 1 Administrative Law Treatise 422 (5th ed. 2010).

[22] General Motors Corp. v. Ruckelshaus, 742 F.2d 1561, 1565 (D.C. Cir. 1984).

[23] Richard J. Pierce, Jr., 1 Administrative Law Treatise 448 (5th ed. 2010).

[24] American Mining Congress v. MSHA, 995 F.2d 1106, 1112 (D.C. Cir. 1993).

[25] See 5 U.S.C. § 551(5) (defining "rule making" as any "agency process for formulating, *amending*, or repealing a rule" (emphasis added)).

Specifically, in *Paralyzed Veterans of America v. D.C. Arena*, the D.C. Circuit announced that when the agency has previously provided an "authoritative" interpretation of its own prior legislative rule, then the agency's subsequent re-interpretation is itself a "legislative" rule, because the new interpretation effectively "amends" the underlying legislative rule—that is, it effectively amends the underlying legislative rule as understood through the prior interpretation.[26] Thus, the court held, because a rulemaking that "amends" a prior rule is itself a "rulemaking,"[27] notice and comment would be required for a new interpretation that effectively amends the rule.[28] In such a case, the court held, the APA's exemption for merely "interpretative" rules would not apply.[29]

Paralyzed Veterans arose from a dispute over Washington's MCI Center, in which wheelchair-bound sports fans argued that the arena's seating arrangement would make it difficult for them to watch the action, in violation of the Americans with Disabilities Act. The Justice Department (DOJ) had adopted a legislative rule, pursuant to the ADA, requiring sports arenas to provide disabled spectators "a choice of admission prices and lines of sight comparable to those for members of the general public."[30]

DOJ issued that legislative rule in 1991, and then it proceeded to further interpret its standards in a series of "Technical Assistance Manuals." For years, DOJ's interpretation of its legislative rule on "comparable lines of sight" did not go so far as to require (as advocates urged) that the arena ensure that wheelchair seats provide lines of sight over standing spectators. But in 1994, DOJ abruptly issued a rule announcing that it would henceforth interpret the "comparable lines of sight" standard as requiring unobstructed wheelchair seat sightlines over standing spectators.[31]

The arena argued that DOJ's 1994 interpretation was a significant enough change that it should be deemed a legislative rule requiring notice and comment. The D.C. Circuit disagreed, finding that DOJ

[26] 117 F.3d 579 (D.C. Cir. 1997).
[27] 5 U.S.C. § 551(5).
[28] 117 F.3d at 586.
[29] *Id.*
[30] *Id.* at 581.
[31] *Id.* at 581–82.

had not changed an interpretation, since its earlier manuals' silence on sightlines over standing spectators never explicitly, authoritatively adopted a position that such sightlines are not required. But in dicta, the Court pondered the question of whether an interpretative about-face could actually rise to such a degree as to necessitate notice-and-comment processes.

"Under the APA," the court explained, "agencies are obliged to engage in notice and comment before formulating regulations, which applies as well to '*repeals*' or '*amendments*.'"[32] And on this point, the court eschewed formalism for an explicitly functionalist approach: "To allow an agency to make a fundamental change in its interpretation of a substantive regulation obviously would undermine those APA requirements."[33]

The Court did not pause in *Paralyzed Veterans* to spell out in precise terms the logic underlying its view of that "obvious" conclusion. But another panel of the D.C. Circuit spelled it out, two years later, in *Alaska Professional Hunters Association v. FAA*. There, the court focused on the FAA's departure from what had been the agency's "authoritative departmental interpretation" of regulations governing Alaskan pilots. Invoking the dictum of *Paralyzed Veterans*, the court held that "[w]hen an agency has given its regulation a definitive interpretation, and later significantly revises that interpretation, the agency has in effect amended its rule, something that it may not accomplish without notice and comment."[34]

The *Paralyzed Veterans* doctrine was not the product of any particular ideological or methodological agenda. Despite Cass Sunstein's and Adrian Vermeule's recent characterization of *Paralyzed Veterans* as an example of "libertarian administrative law" run amok on the D.C. Circuit,[35] the six judges who decided *Paralyzed Veterans* and *Alaska Hunters*—Edwards, Henderson, Randolph, Sentelle, Silberman, and Tatel—were appointed by Republican and Democratic presidents alike, reflecting the full spectrum of judicial methodol-

---

[32] 117 F.3d at 586 (emphasis in original).

[33] *Id.*

[34] 177 F.3d 1030, 1034 (D.C. Cir. 1999) ("Alaska Hunters"). Note that the court spoke in terms of a prior "definitive" interpretation, a term it offered as a synonym for "authoritative" interpretation. *Id.*

[35] Cass R. Sunstein & Adrian Vermeule, Libertarian Administrative Law, 82 U. Chi. L. Rev. 393, 428–31 (2015).

ogies. Yet the six judges embraced the *Paralyzed Veterans* standard unanimously.

While those judges may not have realized it, their instincts echoed the analysis of leading administrative scholars of the APA's founding era who sometimes endorsed the practical point at the heart of the D.C. Circuit's approach in *Paralyzed Veterans*—summarily rejected by the Supreme Court in *Mortgage Bankers*—that sometimes an interpretative rule, with the passage of time, "becomes seasoned . . . something upon which people justifiably rely," which ought to limit the agency's discretion in so easily changing that interpretation years later.[36] Or, as Kenneth Culp Davis later wrote, an "interpretative rule may or may not have the force of law, depending on such factors as . . . *whether the rule is one of long standing.*"[37]

Nevertheless, legal scholars were virtually unanimous in their *denunciation* of the D.C. Circuit's approach. Cataloging the array of senior administrative law scholars who had inveighed against the case, Professor Richard Murphy in 2006 noted pithily (and accurately) that "[a]cademic commentary" on the *Paralyzed Veterans* doctrine "has been scathing." (And then he damned the doctrine with the faintest possible praise: "Student commentary has been mixed."[38]) Similarly, in his *Administrative Law Treatise*, Professor Richard Pierce urged the Supreme Court to terminate the doctrine because it "is inconsistent with the APA, unsupported by precedents, inconsistent with scores of precedents, and it has terrible effects"—namely, "it discourages agencies from issuing interpretative rules and encourages them instead to rely entirely on ad hoc adjudication to adopt interpretations of ambiguous language in statutes and legislative rules."[39]

---

[36] Erwin N. Griswold, A Summary of the Regulations Problem, 54 Harv. L. Rev. 398, 413–16 (1941).

[37] Kenneth Culp Davis, 1 Administrative Law Treatise § 5.03 (1st ed. 1958) (emphasis added). The Cato Institute's brief in *Mortgage Bankers* elaborated on this historical point.

[38] Richard W. Murphy, Hunters for Administrative Common Law, 58 Admin. L. Rev. 917, 918 (2006).

[39] Richard J. Pierce, Jr., 1 Administrative Law Treatise 456 (5th ed. 2010). Agencies enjoy broad discretion to choose either rulemakings or adjudications as the form by which they announce policies or interpretations. SEC v. Chenery Corp., 332 U.S. 194, 202–03 (1947); see generally M. Elizabeth Magill, Agency Choice in Policymaking Form, 71 U. Chi. L. Rev. 1383 (2004).

The scholars' criticism was rooted in *Vermont Yankee*, the Supreme Court's seminal 1978 decision prohibiting federal courts from burdening agencies with procedural requirements above and beyond the minimal requirements of the Administrative Procedure Act. "Absent constitutional constraints or extremely compelling circumstances," then-Justice William Rehnquist wrote for the unanimous Court, "the administrative agencies should be free to fashion their own rules of procedure and to pursue methods of inquiry capable of permitting them to discharge their multitudinous duties."[40] For the same reason, Pierce and his colleagues argue, *Vermont Yankee* forbids the D.C. Circuit's *Paralyzed Veterans* approach, because the court cannot require agencies to use notice-and-comment procedures for interpretative rules when neither the APA nor any "agency rule, statute, or provision of the Constitution . . . even arguably requires an agency to engage in notice-and-comment procedure when it issues an interpretative rule."[41] So long as the APA specifically exempts interpretative rules from notice-and-comment rulemaking and no other law requires it, Pierce and others urged, the D.C. Circuit cannot impose such procedural requirements on an agency's interpretative rules—which, again, are expressly exempt from notice and comment.[42]

The sheer volume of scholarly criticism of *Paralyzed Veterans* dwarfed that case's actual impact in the courts. One other circuit adopted the D.C. Circuit's rule, while several others rejected it. Indeed, in the 15 years after *Paralyzed Veterans* was decided in 1997, the D.C. Circuit itself invoked the doctrine only *three* times to vacate agency actions. First, as mentioned above, there was the court's unanimous decision in *Alaska Hunters*, holding that the FAA's rule was invalid because it did not undergo notice and comment.[43]

Second, in 2005 the court applied the doctrine (once again unanimously and bipartisanly) to vacate an EPA rule interpreting a legislative rule regarding standards for monitoring emissions from stationary sources. Specifically, the court held that the agency's interpretation reversed the agency's prior, "definitive" interpretation

---

[40] Vermont Yankee Nuclear Power Corp. v. NRDC, 435 U.S. 519, 543 (1978).

[41] Richard J. Pierce, Jr., 1 Administrative Law Treatise 458 (5th ed. 2010).

[42] 5 U.S.C. § 553(b)(A).

[43] Alaska Hunters, 177 F.3d at 1034, 1036.

of the legislative rule, and therefore the new interpretation required notice and comment under *Paralyzed Veterans*.[44]

And third, in 2013, the D.C. Circuit employed it to strike down the Labor Department's revised interpretation of rules governing working conditions for loan offices—and that was the case that finally brought the matter before the Supreme Court: *Mortgage Bankers*.

Perez v. Mortgage Bankers Association

In 2010, pursuant to the Fair Labor Standards Act of 1938 (FLSA), the deputy administrator of the Labor Department's Wage and Hour Division announced that mortgage loan officers are entitled to overtime wages because they do not fall within the category of "administrative" employees exempt from overtime benefits. She announced this in an informal "Administrator's Interpretation" issuance, rather than going through full notice-and-comment proceedings.[45] That was problematic because her interpretation of the FLSA explicitly reversed the agency's 2006 opinion letter—which, the government conceded on appeal, had been a "definitive" interpretation of the FLSA.[46]

The Mortgage Bankers Association, a trade association representing real estate finance companies, promptly sued the Labor Department, arguing that the agency had violated *Paralyzed Veterans* by significantly changing a prior definitive interpretation without notice and comment.

Before the D.C. Circuit, the issue was not whether to keep the *Paralyzed Veterans* doctrine but merely how to apply it. As noted above, the court required agencies to undertake notice-and-comment rulemaking before making a "significant change" to a prior "definitive" or "authoritative" interpretation. But the intervening years produced dicta implying that the Court had added a third criterion to *Paralyzed Veterans*: namely, that parties challenging the reversal also demonstrate sufficient "reliance" on the previous interpretation.[47]

---

[44] Envtl. Integrity Project v. EPA, 425 F.3d 992, 997–98 (D.C. Cir. 2005).

[45] Mortgage Bankers Ass'n v. Harris, 720 F.3d 966, 968 (D.C. Cir. 2013).

[46] *Id.*

[47] See, e.g., Alaska Hunters, 177 F.3d at 1035 (discussing guide pilots' and lodge operators' reliance on the prior interpretative rule).

Presented with that narrow issue, the D.C. Circuit disposed of the case swiftly. In a short opinion, it held that "reliance" was not a stand-alone criterion in the *Paralyzed Veterans* framework—instead, regulated parties' reliance on an agency's interpretation is but one indicator that the interpretation was "definitive." Definitiveness could be proven even without reliance, the D.C. Circuit unanimously held, and the court remanded the case to the district court to re-apply *Paralyzed Veterans'* two-step framework.[48]

But the case would not return to the district court. Instead, the government seized upon the case as an opportunity to finally achieve what Professor Pierce and his colleagues long had sought: a Supreme Court reversal of *Paralyzed Veterans*.

Petitioning for certiorari, the Obama administration attacked *Paralyzed Veterans* head-on, asking the Court to decide "[w]hether a federal agency must engage in notice-and-comment rulemaking before it can significantly alter an interpretive rule that articulates an interpretation of an agency regulation."[49] Embracing the categorical distinction between interpretation and legislation, the administration's merits brief argued that when an agency alters a rule it "no more 'amends' a legislative regulation than a judicial interpretation 'amends' the source of law it interprets."[50] And the agency's interpretation, unlike the underlying legislative rule, "do[es] not have the force and effect of law."[51]

In this case, the government urged, the deputy administrator's action was an interpretative rule, not a legislative one. But the government did not argue this point so much as assert it, telling the Court that "[t]here is no dispute between the parties that the 2010 [interpretation] is an interpretative rule." And given that premise, the government urged, the case before the Court was an easy one. The APA "categorically exempts" interpretative rules from the APA's notice-and-comment requirements, and under *Vermont Yankee* that is the end of the matter because courts may not "require more than

48 Mortgage Bankers Ass'n, 720 F.3d at 971–72.

49 Gov't Petition for Writ of Certiorari at I, Perez v. Mortgage Bankers Ass'n, 135 S. Ct. 1199 (2015) (No. 13-1041).

50 Gov't Opening Br. at 12, Perez v. Mortgage Bankers Ass'n, 135 S. Ct. 1199 (2015) (Nos. 13-1041, 13-1052).

51 *Id.* at 11.

the APA's 'minimum' procedural requirements for rulemaking in 5 U.S.C. 553."[52]

Perhaps recognizing that some of the justices might pause before categorically exempting a class of rules from notice and comment, the government argued that Congress included that exemption in the APA for one "plain" reason: administrative efficiency and convenience. "Congress presumably determined that it would be an unwarranted encroachment," the government argued in its opening brief, "to force agency decisionmakers to dedicate limited agency time and resources to undertake notice-and-comment rulemaking simply to inform the public about the agency's own views on the meaning of relevant statutory and regulatory provisions."[53] To that end, the government quoted portions of the APA's legislative history in which members of Congress argued that an agency "should be as free as it can be" to issue interpretative rules, "for the simple reason that those types of regulations are the kind that agencies should be encouraged to make" in order to apprise the public of the agency's current interpretations of the law.[54]

The government's characterization of the APA's purpose contrasted sharply with the characterization offered by the Mortgage Bankers Association in their merits brief defending *Paralyzed Veterans*. The "overriding goal" of the APA was not administrative efficiency but "procedural fairness in agency dealings." And the *Paralyzed Veterans* doctrine "plays a critical role in enforcing the APA's mandate of procedural fairness by restraining agencies from abruptly changing positions without at least providing notice and an opportunity to comment on the contemplated agency action."[55]

Moreover, *Paralyzed Veterans* vindicates not just the spirit of the APA, the Mortgage Bankers continued, but also the letter, because when an agency significantly revises its definitive interpretation of a regulation "it has effectively amended the regulation itself—and the APA requires notice and comment before an agency can do that."[56]

[52] *Id.* at 6, 27.

[53] *Id.* at 21.

[54] *Id.* at 22 (quoting Administrative Procedure: Hearings on the Subject of Federal Administrative Procedure Before the House Judiciary Comm., 79th Cong., 1st Sess. 30 (1945)).

[55] Br. for Respondent at 16–17, Perez, 135 S. Ct. 1199 (2015) (Nos. 13-1041, 13-1052).

[56] *Id.* at 20–21.

Fully embracing a realist's view of legal interpretation, the Mortgage Bankers argued that, "once clarified by a definitive interpretation," the "regulation is no longer ambiguous—and the definitive interpretation becomes part of the regulation itself."[57]

But the brief that attracted the most attention was not one filed by the government, the private petitioners, the Mortgage Bankers Association, or the various amici supporting the association. Rather, it was the short brief filed by Richard Pierce and 71 other administrative law scholars in support of the government's petition. The brief reiterated quite bluntly the criticism that scholars had aimed at *Paralyzed Veterans* from the very beginning: that the D.C. Circuit's doctrine added new procedural requirements above and beyond those required by the APA, in violation of *Vermont Yankee*. But perhaps the brief's most significant impact was not its characterization of the law so much as its characterization of the legal academy:

> *All* scholars and most courts have reacted critically to the *Paralyzed Veterans* doctrine. . . . We are not aware of a single scholar who agrees with the doctrine. Indeed, when counsel for amici circulated a draft of this brief, *not a single scholar declined to join it on the ground that the position of the D.C. Circuit was correct.*[58]

In the end, the scholars' virtual unanimity foreshadowed an even more important unanimity—that of the justices themselves, all nine of whom voted in *Perez v. Mortgage Bankers* to reverse the D.C. Circuit and end the *Paralyzed Veterans* doctrine. In the opinion for the Court (although not for Justices Antonin Scalia and Clarence Thomas, who concurred only in the judgment and wrote separately), Justice Sonia Sotomayor cut swiftly through the issues. The deputy administrator's action was without question an interpretative rule—even the Mortgage Bankers Association conceded this claim, the Court asserted. And the APA explicitly exempts *all* interpretative rules from the notice-and-comment requirement, the Court explained; true, the APA's definition of "rule making" includes those that "repeal" or "amend" an existing rule, but that does not detract from the fact

---

[57] *Id.* at 20–21.

[58] Br. of Administrative Law Scholars as Amici Curiae in Support of the Petitions at 9, Perez, 135 S. Ct. 1199 (2015) (Nos. 13-1041, 13-1052) (emphasis added).

that the APA "exempts interpretive rules"—*all* interpretive rules—"from the notice-and-comment requirements that apply to legislative rules."[59]

And that, the Court held, is the end of the matter. An agency is not required to use notice-and-comment proceedings to promulgate its initial interpretation, and it faces no additional procedural requirements to revise its interpretation. The D.C. Circuit's attempt to impose a new "judge-made procedural right" violates *Vermont Yankee*: imposing requirements above and beyond the APA's procedures "may be wise policy," or "it may not," but "[r]egardless, imposing such an obligation is the responsibility of Congress or the administrative agencies, not the courts."[60] Simply put, the Court found the question presented supremely easy to answer.

Perhaps too easy. For it must be noted that the Court's brisk analysis rested on a factual premise that was not quite as obvious as the Court insisted—namely, whether the deputy administrator's action was, in fact, an "interpretative rule." The Court assumed that the Mortgage Bankers Association had conceded that the action was an interpretative rule. "From the beginning," the Court insisted, "the parties litigated this suit on the understanding that the Administrator's Interpretation was—as its name suggests—an interpretative rule."[61]

But a review of the Mortgage Bankers Association's briefs suggests the very opposite. In its merits brief, it stressed that, "[c]ontrary to the government's contentions . . . the Association did not 'acknowledge'" in the lower courts that the agency's action "was an interpretative rule."[62] To be sure, the association "did acknowledge that it was an *'interpretation'*," but that did not itself make the rule an *interpretative rule*.[63]

Indeed, the Court's very characterization of *Paralyzed Veterans* reflected the same questionable assumption: the Court suggested that "if [the Mortgage Bankers Association] did not think the Administrator's Interpretation was an interpretative rule, then its decision to

---

[59] *Id.* at 1206.

[60] *Id.* at 1207.

[61] *Id.* at 1210.

[62] Br. for Respondent, *supra* note 55, at 46 n.8.

[63] *Id.* (emphasis added).

invoke the *Paralyzed Veterans* doctrine in attacking the rule is passing strange."[64] "After all," the Court concluded, "*Paralyzed Veterans* applied only to interpretative rules."[65] But that is not obviously true either: the D.C. Circuit explained in *Alaska Hunters* that an agency's significant change to a definitive interpretation requires notice and comment because the agency "has in effect amended its rule"—suggesting that the D.C. Circuit viewed such re-interpretations as *legislative* rules.[66] Indeed, even Richard Pierce, the doctrine's staunchest critic, had written in his treatise that *Paralyzed Veterans* was a test that the D.C. Circuit "use[s] to *distinguish between legislative rules and interpretative rules.*"[67]

But in the end, these criticisms of the Court's decision are of limited significance. The justices plainly saw *Paralyzed Veterans* as a doctrine that adds procedural requirements to interpretative rules, something that lower courts simply cannot do under *Vermont Yankee* and the APA. The Court saw it as a simple case, and made it so.

Were *Mortgage Bankers* simply a case about the APA's notice-and-comment requirements, it would have attracted little attention beyond insular administrative-law circles. Given the nearly two decades of overwhelming scholarly criticism of the *Paralyzed Veterans* doctrine there seemed little reason to doubt that the Supreme Court would reverse the D.C. Circuit. And given that the D.C. Circuit virtually never applied *Paralyzed Veterans* anyway, the issue's practical impact seemed minuscule. As the Mortgage Bankers Association suggested in its brief opposing certiorari, the notice-and-comment issue before the Court "arises infrequently and has limited practical importance."[68]

But *Mortgage Bankers* took on much greater practical importance due to a broader and more fundamental administrative law debate that came to surround and, ultimately, permeate the case—namely, the debate over modern judicial deference to agencies' interpretations of their own regulations.

[64] Mortgage Bankers, 135 S. Ct. at 1210.

[65] *Id.*

[66] Alaska Hunters, 177 F.3d at 1034.

[67] Richard J. Pierce, Jr., 1 Administrative Law Treatise 454 (5th ed. 2010) (emphasis added).

[68] Br. in Opp'n to Cert. at 19, Mortgage Bankers, 135 S. Ct. 1199 (2015) (Nos. 13-1041, 13-1052).

Deference's Discontents

Throughout *Mortgage Bankers*—indeed, throughout nearly two decades of debate over *Paralyzed Veterans* and interpretative rules—it was said repeatedly that interpretative rules do not bind the public but merely advise the public. Whether that was true as a matter of theoretical legal formalities, it seems much less obvious as a matter of practical reality. Courts not only give utmost deference to an agency's interpretation of its own regulations such that agencies interpretative rules will very rarely be struck down, but in the *Mortgage Bankers* litigation the same administration that told the Supreme Court that its interpretation was not "binding" had told the lower courts that the interpretation was *"controlling"* with respect to the courts.[69] Such *Auer* deference (or, as it is sometimes called, *"Seminole Rock* deference"[70]) is an increasingly controversial doctrine that ultimately came to be deeply intertwined with the legal arguments before the Court in *Mortgage Bankers*.

For all the deference that courts give agencies' interpretations of Congress's statutes, they give ever more deference to agencies' interpretations of the agencies' own regulations. As the Court explained in *Auer v. Robbins* (1997), an agency's interpretation of its own regulation is "controlling" unless "plainly erroneous or inconsistent with the regulation."[71]

Unlike its explanations of *Chevron* deference, the Court has been less comprehensive in attempting to justify *Auer* deference. But the primary justification is one of agency expertise. "Because applying an agency's regulation to complex or changing circumstances calls upon the agency's unique expertise and policymaking prerogatives," the Court has explained, "we presume that the power authoritatively to interpret its own regulations is a component of the agency's delegated lawmaking powers."[72] Elsewhere, the Court had justified *Auer* deference in terms of the agency's political accountability, or

---

[69] Defs.' Reply to Pls.' Opp. to Defs.' Cross Motion to Dismiss or, in the Alternative, for Summary Judgment at 9, Mortgage Bankers Ass'n v. Solis, (No. 11-73, Doc. 20) (D.D.C. May 17, 2011) (emphasis added).

[70] Bowles v. Seminole Rock & Sand Co., 325 U.S. 410 (1945).

[71] 519 U.S. 452, 461 (1997).

[72] Martin v. Occupational Safety and Health Review Comm'n, 499 U.S. 144, 151 (1991).

the agency's superior historical familiarity with the particular regulation at issue.[73]

Whatever its underlying justification, the existence of *Auer* deference forecloses the vast majority of challenges to agency regulatory interpretations. According to the 2008 study of Supreme Court litigation by Professors William Eskridge and Lauren Baer, the government wins more than 90 percent of cases that enjoy *Auer* deference.[74] (The government likely has even greater success in the lower courts, where the cases tend to be more technically esoteric, and less controversial, than those attracting Supreme Court attention.)

For a long time, *Auer* or *Seminole Rock* deference was relatively uncontroversial. Indeed, in *Auer*, Justice Scalia wrote for a unanimous Court, giving overwhelming deference to an interpretation the agency had offered, not in a rulemaking but in an amicus brief in that very case.

But the justices' complacent embrace of *Auer* deference changed abruptly in 2011 when Scalia published a startling concurrence in *Talk America v. Michigan Bell Telephone Co.* He shared the Court's ultimate conclusion in that case that the FCC's interpretation of a regulation was the best interpretation, but he took care to stress that he would have reached that conclusion even *without* the application of *Auer* deference. And then he expressed his first public doubts on the doctrine that he had for so long embraced:

> [W]hile I have in the past uncritically accepted that rule, I have become increasingly doubtful of its validity. On the surface, it seems to be a natural corollary—indeed, an a fortiori application—of the rule that we will defer to an agency's interpretation of the statute it is charged with implementing. . . . But it is not.[75]

---

[73] See, e.g., Matthew C. Stephenson & Miri Pogoriler, Seminole Rock's Domain, 79 Geo. Wash. L. Rev. 1449, 1461 (2011); John F. Manning, Constitutional Structure and Judicial Deference to Agency Interpretations of Agency Rules, 96 Colum. L. Rev. 612, 627–31 (1996).

[74] William N. Eskridge, Jr. & Lauren E. Baer, The Continuum of Deference: Supreme Court Treatment of Agency Statutory Interpretations from *Chevron* to *Hamdan*, 96 Geo. L.J. 1083, 1104 (2008).

[75] Talk America, Inc. v. Mich. Bell Tel. Co., 131 S. Ct. 2254, 2266 (Scalia, J., concurring).

The difference, Scalia continued, lay in structural considerations. On questions of *statutory* interpretation, the agency is interpreting a law written by another branch of government; thus the lawmaker is distinct from the law-interpreter. But on questions of *regulatory* interpretation, the agency is interpreting a law written by the agency itself, thus making the agency both the lawmaker and the law-interpreter.

This "seems contrary to fundamental principles of separation of powers to permit the person who promulgates a law to interpret it as well," Scalia stressed.[76] Such an arrangement runs afoul of Montesquieu's famous warning that when "the legislative and executive powers are united in the same person, or in the same body of magistrates, there can be no liberty."[77] But it also creates perverse incentives for the agency:

> [D]eferring to an agency's interpretation of its own rule encourages the agency to enact vague rules which give it the power, in future adjudications, to do what it pleases. This frustrates the notice and predictability purposes of rulemaking, and promotes arbitrary government.[78]

Scalia did not hesitate to credit a law review article authored by his former clerk, Professor John Manning, for these insights.[79] A year later, a majority of justices—specifically, the more conservative wing of the Court—acknowledged Scalia's and Manning's concerns in dicta, in *Christopher v. SmithKline Beecham Corp.*, but did not need to reach the issue.[80]

But in 2013, Scalia moved from mere concerns to outright condemnations. In *Decker v. Northwest Environmental Defense Center* he dissented from the Court's deference to an EPA regulatory interpretation:

> For decades, and for no good reason, we have been giving agencies the authority to say what their rules mean, under

[76] *Id.*

[77] XI Montesquieu, Spirit of the Laws 151–52 (O. Piest ed., T. Nugent Transl. 1949).

[78] Talk America, 131 S. Ct. at 2266.

[79] Constitutional Structure and Judicial Deference to Agency Interpretations of Agency Rules, 96 Colum. L. Rev. 612 (1996).

[80] 132 S. Ct. 2156, 2168 (2012).

the harmless-sounding banner of 'defer[ring] to an agency's interpretation of its own regulations.' . . . [But] however great may be the efficiency gains derived from *Auer* deference, beneficial effect cannot justify a rule that not only has no principled basis but contravenes one of the great rules of separation of powers: He who writes a law must not adjudge its violation. [81]

Scalia's remarkable about-face on *Auer* deference coincided with a rising tide of criticism of judicial deference more broadly. Recent years have witnessed significant and widespread reconsideration of judicial deference among conservative and libertarian legal scholars[82]—even when much of that deference originated in, or was reinforced by, Reagan-era judges and scholars critical of the then-liberal courts' efforts to stymie President Reagan's deregulatory agenda.[83]

To be clear, *Mortgage Bankers* was not a case that turned on *Auer* deference. The question before the Court was not the substance of the Labor Department's new interpretation but the procedure by which the Labor Department arrived at that interpretation. Nevertheless, the gathering storm surrounding *Auer* deference quickly came to overshadow the narrow procedural issue decided by the Court, because advocates—and, ultimately, several justices—recognized that the question of *ex ante* procedure was tied closely to *ex post* deference. If *Auer* deference is problematic in and of itself, it is all the more problematic when agencies receive *Auer* deference for interpretations that were not subjected to notice and comment in the first place, such as in interpretative rules. As Scalia had highlighted in his scathing *Decker* dissent:

> *Auer* deference encourages agencies to be "vague in framing regulations, with the plan of issuing 'interpretations' to create the intended new law without observance of notice

---

[81] 133 S. Ct. 1326, 1339, 1342 (2013) (Scalia, J., concurring in part and dissenting in part) (citing Talk America, 131 S. Ct. at 2265 (Scalia, J., concurring)).

[82] See, e.g., Philip Hamburger, Is Administrative Law Unlawful? 316 (2014) (arguing that judicial deference to an agency's statutory interpretation "is an abandonment of judicial office").

[83] See, e.g., Adam J. White, The Regulatory Court, Weekly Standard, Aug. 26, 2013, at 20–25 (describing the history of the D.C. Circuit and the development of deference doctrines).

and comment procedures." . . . [It is] a dangerous permission slip for the arrogation of power.[84]

After several amicus briefs supporting the Mortgage Bankers Association highlighted the connection between the Labor Department's avoidance of notice-and-comment proceedings and its claimed *Auer* deference for the resulting interpretation, justices pressed the issue at oral argument.[85] "I understand [that the *Auer* issue is] not before the Court," Scalia told the deputy solicitor general, "but my perception of what is before the Court would be altered if I didn't think that courts had to give deference to these flip-flops."[86]

Similarly, Justice Samuel Alito questioned the Labor Department's argument that its new interpretation did not "bind" anyone (and thus was merely "interpretative"), given the amount of deference that the agency's interpretation would receive. "In this case," Alito asked, "didn't the government say explicitly that its interpretation would be entitled to controlling deference?" And "if it has controlling deference, does it have the force of law?" When the deputy solicitor general replied that despite *Auer* deference the courts would still ultimately be the ones responsible for reviewing the interpretation, Alito suggested that his formalistic description of the Court's role paled in comparison to the "practical" reality.[87]

Other justices were noticeably less eager to bring the *Auer* issue into the heart of the case. "We needn't go into those matters in this case," Justice Stephen Breyer offered, "and I surely hope we don't."[88]

Ultimately, the *Auer* issue did not affect any of the justices' votes—all nine sided with the Labor Department and against the *Paralyzed Veterans* doctrine—but several of them wrote separately to further stress their concerns about *Auer* deference. Scalia reiterated and expanded the themes he previously raised in *Talk America* and *Decker* and rejected the formalistic distinction drawn by the administration

---

[84] 133 S. Ct. at 1341.

[85] The Cato Institute's brief was among the amicus briefs that highlighted the problem of courts giving *Auer* deference to agency rules that have not undergone notice and comment.

[86] Transcript of Oral Argument at 10–11, Perez v. Mortgage Bankers Ass'n, 135 S. Ct. 1199 (2015) (Nos. 13-1041, 13-1052).

[87] *Id.* at 11–12.

[88] *Id.* at 21.

(and by Sotomayor's opinion for the majority)—namely, that an interpretative rule enjoys *Auer*'s "controlling" deference yet does not "bind" the public because ultimately the Court, not the agency, has the final say. "After all," Scalia wrote,

> if an interpretive rule gets deference, the people are bound to obey it on pain of sanction, no less surely than they are bound to obey substantive rules . . . Interpretive rules that command deference *do* have the force of law. The Court's reasons for resisting this obvious point would not withstand a gentle breeze.[89]

Justice Thomas, too, concurred in the judgment and wrote at length to criticize *Auer* deference. "This line of precedents undermines our obligation to provide a judicial check on the other branches, and it subjects regulated parties to precisely the abuses that the Framers sought to prevent."[90]

Justice Alito did not go quite so far. He wrote separately to acknowledge the "substantial reasons" offered by Scalia and Thomas to end *Auer* deference: he "await[s] a case in which the validity of [the doctrine] may be explored through full briefing and argument"— an openness that he had signaled in his opinion for the Court in *SmithKline*, which had acknowledged Scalia's initial *Talk America* concerns.[91] Indeed, Chief Justice Roberts and Justice Anthony Kennedy had joined that majority in *SmithKline*, indicating that there are at least five judges strongly entertaining the notion of ending *Auer* deference, including the firmly committed Justices Scalia and Thomas.[92]

"Pay Me Now, or Pay Me Later"

Thus, the *Mortgage Bankers* litigation cast in stark relief the increasingly tenuous status of *Auer* deference in modern administrative law; and with a spotlight shining on that issue, litigants will no doubt be encouraged to tee up a case that ultimately presents *Auer* deference squarely before the Court.

---

[89] Mortgage Bankers, 135 S. Ct. at 1212 (Scalia, J., concurring in the judgment).

[90] *Id.* at 1213 (Thomas, J., concurring in the judgment).

[91] *Id.* at 1210–11 (Alito, J., concurring in part and concurring in the judgment).

[92] See Christopher v. SmithKline Beecham Corp., 132 S. Ct. 2156 (2012).

But *Mortgage Bankers* also highlighted something else: the government's utterly one-sided characterization of the Administrative Procedure Act's purpose and history. Throughout the litigation the government asserted that the Congress that enacted the APA had exempted interpretative rules from notice-and-comment requirements for one and only one reason: administrative convenience.

The government's opening brief offers a particularly stark example of this narrative:

> The reason for exempting interpretive rules from notice-and-comment rulemaking is plain. . . . Congress presumably determined that it would be an unwarranted encroachment to force agency decisionmakers to dedicate limited agency time and resources to undertake notice-and-comment rulemaking simply to inform the public about the agency's own views on the meaning of relevant statutory and regulatory provisions.[93]

But that rationale and the selective legislative history that the government quoted to support that narrative tell only half the story—if that. For while bureaucratic efficiency was indeed *one* of Congress's reasons for categorically exempting interpretative rules from the burdens of notice and comment, Congress's *other* reason, which the government neglected to mention, was no less important.[94]

Specifically, the APA's framers chose to exempt interpretative rules from the APA's notice-and-comment requirements because they fully expected the courts to conduct robust, "plenary" judicial review of those interpretative rules. Judicial review of interpretative rules would provide *ex post* protection for the public that would offset the absence of *ex ante* procedural protection. Legislative rules, by contrast, were not expected to face such intense judicial review, and therefore the *ex ante* protection of notice-and-comment rulemaking was necessary.[95]

[93] Gov't Opening Br., *supra* note 50, at 20–21.

[94] See, e.g., Administrative Procedure Act: Legislative History, S. Doc. No. 79-248, 2d Sess., p. 18 (1946) (Staff of S. Comm. on the Judiciary, 79th Cong. (Comm. Print 1945)).

[95] See, e.g., *id.* The fact that the APA's framers expected legislative rules to enjoy significant judicial deference might lend credence to the theory that *Chevron* deference for statutory interpretations is more consistent with the APA than *Auer* deference. Cf. United States v. Mead, 533 U.S. 218, 242–43 (2001) (Scalia, J., dissenting) ("There is some question whether *Chevron* was faithful to the text of the [APA], which it did not even bother to cite. But it was in accord with the origins of federal-court judicial

The APA's sponsor, Senator Pat McCarran, put this point well, stressing both the presence of plenary judicial review *and* the value of administrative efficiency in justifying the exemption.

> The pending bill exempts from its procedural requirements all interpretative . . . rules, because under present law interpretative rules, being merely adaptations of interpretations of statutes, are subject to a more ample degree of judicial review, and because the problem with respect to the other exempted types of rules is to facilitate their issuance rather than to supply procedures.[96]

Similarly, Attorney General Robert H. Jackson's influential 1941 committee report on administrative law made this point, explaining that agencies' interpretations "are ordinarily of an advisory character," and that they "are not binding upon those affected for, if there is disagreement with the agency's view, the question may be presented for a determination by a court," where the judges may "be influenced though not *concluded* by the administrative opinion."[97] (As with its descriptions of legislative history, in *Mortgage Bankers* the government's description of the attorney general's committee report neglected to mention his focus on rigorous judicial review.)

The scholars of that era expressly recognized the dangers of depriving the public of both the *ex ante* protections of public participation and the *ex post* protections of judicial review. Writing in 1938, Professor Ralph Fuchs (who would later serve as a member of the attorney general's aforementioned committee) explained that if a regulation "is subject to challenge in all of its aspects after its promulgation, the need of advance formalities is reduced or eliminated." But when "a regulation presents affected parties with . . . only limited opportunity or none at all to challenge its correctness [after it is

---

review. . . . Statutory ambiguities, in other words, were left to reasonable resolution by the Executive."), cited in Mortgage Bankers, 135 S. Ct. at 1212 (Scalia, J., concurring) ("the rule of *Chevron*, if it did not comport with the APA, at least was in conformity with the long history of judicial review of executive action").

[96] Administrative Procedure Act: Legislative History, S. Doc. No. 79-248, 2d Sess., p. 313 (1946).

[97] Report of the Attorney General's Committee on Administrative Procedure in Government Agencies 27 (1941).

promulgated], the need is evident for an antecedent opportunity to influence its content or be heard in regard to it."[98]

Indeed, Kenneth Culp Davis, one of the era's leading administrative law scholars, recognized precisely the danger that *Auer's* forerunner, *Seminole Rock*, threatened to the public if courts were to extend their deference to interpretative rules. "It would be *absurd* to hold that the courts must subordinate their judgment as to the meaning of a statute or regulation to the mere unsupported opinion of associate counsel in an administrative department," he observed in a footnote to his seminal text, *Administrative Law* (1951).[99]

Today, scholars refer to these considerations as the "pay me now or pay me later" principle.[100] (Or, as President Franklin Roosevelt's influential "Brownlow Committee" put it a bit more colorfully in 1937, rulemaking procedures are "prenatal safeguards," while judicial review is the "postnatal" safeguard.)[101] When the APA was enacted, lawmakers and scholars widely recognized that administrative law must hold agencies fully accountable either at the beginning of the rulemaking process or at its end. If *Mortgage Bankers* is indicative, judges seem to be recognizing it again.

But this return to the APA's legislative history is instructive for another crucial reason. In recent years, Congress has repeatedly considered legislation to reform administrative law: by supplementing the APA with additional procedures (as in the Regulatory Accountability Act), by making Congress more directly responsible for agencies' rulemakings (as in the REINS Act), or by other measures. Some of these measures have even been passed by the House of Representatives, although none has yet become law.[102] Such proposals to reform the APA tend to be met by a specific criticism: namely, they

[98] Ralph F. Fuchs, Procedure in Administrative Rule-Making, Faculty Publications, Paper 1595, 271–72 (1938).

[99] Kenneth Culp Davis, Administrative Law 202 n.72 (1951).

[100] See, e.g., Matthew C. Stephenson & Miri Pogoriler, Seminole Rock's Domain, 79 Geo. Wash. L. Rev. 1449, 1464 (2011).

[101] The President's Committee on Administrative Management, Report of the Committee: With Studies of Administrative Management in the Federal Government 337 (1937).

[102] E.g., Regulatory Accountability Act of 2015, H.R. 185, 114th Cong. (2015) (passing the House but under review by the Senate); Regulations from the Executive in Need of Scrutiny Act of 2015, H.R. 427, 114th Cong. (2015) (passing the House but under review by the Senate).

impose too much burden on regulators and will incentivize regulators to devise ways to evade those new requirements by eschewing rulemaking for other regulatory avenues.[103]

Our debate over these proposals should be informed by the approach that Congresses, scholars, and other experts of the mid-20th century took in framing the original APA. First, they recognized that it was appropriate to place at least some burdens on regulators through administrative law. For as important as regulatory efficiency might be, the APA's framers also recognized that it was but one value at stake in administration; affording the public an opportunity to participate and to challenge the agency, either *ex ante* or *ex post*, was no less important.

Thus, when faced with the criticism that added procedures might prove unduly burdensome or even counterproductive, we should take such considerations seriously—but we should also keep in mind that such considerations are not dispositive. Indeed, the addition of such burdens is not inherently bad. For, as Professor Manning put it in his influential article, "even if [the] rejection" of *Auer* or *Seminole Rock* deference "marginally increased agency reluctance to rely on rulemaking . . . that result would be attributable to the fact that agencies would finally be internalizing the cost of adopting unobvious or vague regulations."[104]

And the APA's history should remind us that its framers were not simply theorists. They were practical lawmakers. In crafting the APA they studied the actual workings of the administrative state as it then existed, and they crafted rules responsive to those practical realities, not to abstract theories.[105]

---

[103] See, e.g., Letter from Law Professors to Rep. Lamar Smith and Rep. John Conyers, Jr. (Oct. 24, 2011) ("We seriously doubt that agencies would be able to respond to delegations of rulemaking authority or to congressional mandates to issue rules if this bill were to be enacted. Instead it would likely lead to rulemaking avoidance by agencies—increasing use of underground rules, case-by-case adjudication, or even prosecutorial actions, to achieve policies without having to surmount the additional hurdles presented by the new Section 553. Executive officials would find it practically impossible to use rulemaking either to create new regulations or to undo old regulations.").

[104] John F. Manning, Constitutional Structure and Judicial Deference to Agency Interpretations of Agency Rules, 96 Colum. L. Rev. 612, 694 (1996).

[105] The Cato Institute's brief in *Mortgage Bankers* discussed the history of the APA—both the APA's legislative history and the scholarly and political debates that preceded and followed its enactment—in detail.

We should expect no less practical an approach in our time. To the extent that administrative agencies and processes have evolved to a point where particular provisions of administrative law no longer serve their original purpose, or to a point where administrators see the APA less as a substantive check on their discretion than as a collection of mere formalities, then those parts of the administrative law should be reformed in the same spirit that animated the framers of the original Administrative Procedure Act.

To that end, Congress must take seriously the extent to which the APA fails to impose meaningful constraints upon agency discretion—the extent to which agencies can effectively bind the public with rules not subjected to notice-and-comment rulemaking, and the extent to which such rules receive deference from the courts. As matters currently stand, the APA increasingly fails to deliver on either of its original promises: to make agencies more accountable to the people, and to ensure that agencies' actions are subjected to meaningful judicial review.

The Regulatory Accountability Act, which at this writing has already passed the House by a significant majority and now awaits action in the Senate, would amend the APA to prohibit courts from deferring to interpretative rules that were not subjected to notice and comment.[106]

But it should not require congressional action to solve a problem of the Court's own making. The Court should abolish *Auer* deference and subject agency interpretations to more significant judicial review—at the very least, it should withhold *Auer* deference from an agency interpretation that had not been subject to the *ex ante* protections of notice and comment.

---

[106] H.R. 185, 114th Cong. § 7 (amending 5 U.S.C. § 706); 161 Cong. Rec. H271–72 (Jan. 13, 2015) (passing H.R. 185 in Roll Call No. 28, by a vote of 250–175).

The Shadow Debate over Private Nondelegation in *DOT v. Association of American Railroads*

*Alexander "Sasha" Volokh**

I. Introduction

The nondelegation doctrine has an uneasy place in constitutional law. On the one hand, it's a structural, separation-of-powers doctrine, founded on the Vesting Clause of Article I, Section 1 of the Constitution—and thus presumptively important. (Indeed, I spend about a week every year teaching it in my administrative-law course.) The Vesting Clause—"All legislative powers herein granted shall be vested in a Congress of the United States . . . ."—has been interpreted as barring any delegation of legislative power.[1] Since our modern administrative state relies on agencies wielding massive rulemaking power, clearly compliance with the nondelegation doctrine—making sure that delegations of power aren't forbidden delegations of *legislative* power—is crucial for preventing the unconstitutionality of the whole edifice.[2]

On the other hand, this interpretation of the Vesting Clause seems hardly obvious:[3] Why should a power *vested* in Congress be nontransferable? Surely we can transfer our vested property rights or

---

*Associate Professor, Emory Law School, avolokh@emory.edu. I am grateful to Ryan Pulley for his able research assistance.

[1] See, e.g., Whitman v. Am. Trucking Ass'ns, 531 U.S. 457, 472 (2001) (Am. Trucking II) (citing Loving v. United States, 517 U.S. 748, 771 (1996)).

[2] See Gary Lawson, The Rise and Rise of the Administrative State, 107 Harv. L. Rev. 1231, 1237–41 (1994).

[3] See Am. Trucking II, 531 U.S. at 487–90 (Stevens, J., concurring in part and concurring in the judgment).

vested stock options.[4] And indeed, some commentators deny that any nondelegation principle exists at all.[5]

Back to the first hand, though, the basic principle is surely sound. Imagine Congress passes a law saying, "President Obama, you get to make all laws (within Congress's power, of course) through the end of the current Congress. We'll just go home now." Is that constitutional? Anyone who says "no" believes that there's some sort of nondelegation doctrine, whatever its precise doctrinal basis; the only question is how strict the doctrine should be.

The other hand responds that, though the Supreme Court agrees with the soundness of the doctrine in principle and has long accepted the nondelegation reading of the Vesting Clause,[6] it's hard to find it in action, at least until this year. The nondelegation doctrine has been used only twice to strike down an act of Congress, both times in 1935.[7] The current doctrine—do the terms of the congressional delegation state an "intelligible principle" sufficient to guide the delegate's discretion?[8]—has been capacious enough to uphold virtually every statute, including one directing agencies to act in the "public interest"[9] or set prices that are "fair and equitable."[10]

Cass Sunstein argues that the doctrine has gone underground and now functions more as a canon of interpretation;[11] this may be true, but even in this new role, it's not always easy to find. This shadow

---

[4] See, e.g., In re Silicon Graphics Inc. Sec. Litig., 183 F.3d 970, 986 (9th Cir. 1999); Joseph William Singer, Property Law: Rules, Policies, and Practices 590 (2d ed. 1997) (quoting the traditional Rule Against Perpetuities: "No interest is good unless it must vest, if at all, no later than 21 years after the death of some life in being at the creation of the interest.").

[5] See Eric A. Posner & Adrian Vermeule, Interring the Nondelegation Doctrine, 69 U. Chi. L. Rev. 1721 (2002).

[6] See, e.g., Wayman v. Southard, 23 U.S. (10 Wheat.) 1 (1825).

[7] See A.L.A. Schechter Poultry Co. v. United States, 295 U.S. 495 (1935); Panama Ref. Co. v. Ryan, 293 U.S. 388 (1935); Cass R. Sunstein, Nondelegation Canons, 67 U. Chi. L. Rev. 315, 315–16, 322 (2000) ("[T]he conventional doctrine has had one good year, and 211 bad ones (and counting).").

[8] J.W. Hampton, Jr., & Co. v. United States, 276 U.S. 394, 409 (1928).

[9] See NBC v. United States, 319 U.S. 190, 225–26 (1943); N.Y. Cent. Sec. Corp. v. United States, 287 U.S. 12, 24–25 (1932).

[10] See Yakus v. United States, 321 U.S. 414, 420, 423–26 (1944).

[11] See Sunstein, *supra* note 7, at 315.

doctrine shows up explicitly in a couple of cases.[12] Otherwise, detecting its traces—possibly in places like the *Chenery I*[13] doctrine of administrative law,[14] or in the modern-day resistance to the expansive *Chevron* doctrine[15]—has been the subtle job of legal academics.

Our two hands also duel on the policy question of whether the nondelegation doctrine is a good idea: to David Schoenbrod's critique that extensive delegation to agencies reduces political accountability (of members of Congress) and leads to worse policy,[16] there is Jerry Mashaw's defense (also found in cases like *Chevron*[17]) that agencies *should* make more political decisions since they're both more politically accountable (through the president) and more expert than Congress.[18]

For nondelegation doctrine buffs, then, this term has had good news and bad news. The good news is that there has finally been a

[12] See Indus. Union Dep't, AFL-CIO v. Am. Petrol. Inst., 448 U.S. 607, 646 (1980) (plurality opinion); Nat'l Cable Television Ass'n, Inc. v. United States, 415 U.S. 336, 341–42 (1974); cf. Arizona v. California, 373 U.S. 546, 626–27 (1963) (Harlan, J., dissenting in part) (using constitutional doubts raised by a broad delegation to "buttress the conviction, already firmly grounded in [a statute] and its history," that an agency lacked certain power under the statute).

[13] SEC v. Chenery Corp., 318 U.S. 80 (1943); see also Kevin M. Stack, The Constitutional Foundations of *Chenery*, 116 Yale L.J. 952, 981–1004 (2007).

[14] Nondelegation concerns also show up in general concerns about limiting agency discretion and requiring reasoned decisionmaking. See, e.g., FCC v. Fox Television Stations, Inc., 556 U.S. 502, 536–37 (2009) (Kennedy, J., concurring in part and concurring in the judgment).

[15] See Michigan v. EPA, 135 S. Ct. 2699, 2712–14 (2015) (Thomas, J., concurring); City of Arlington v. FCC, 133 S. Ct. 1863, 1877–86 (2013) (Roberts, C.J., dissenting); United States v. Mead Corp., 533 U.S. 218 (2001); see also 1 Laurence H. Tribe, American Constitutional Law § 5-19, at 997 n.71 ("[R]econciling *Chevron* deference with the nondelegation doctrine would appear to require a particularly heroic degree of self-deception."); *id.* at 999 n.74 ("[W]hen courts treat agencies operating under *Chevron* delegations as free to pick any meaning they wish within a congressionally specified range (and then to change their minds as the political situation changes), those courts are effectively (even if inadvertently) conceding that what Congress delegates under *Chevron* is, contra nondelegation theory and the separation of powers, nothing less than the power to legislate.").

[16] See David Schoenbrod, Power Without Responsibility: How Congress Abuses the People Through Delegation (1993).

[17] Chevron U.S.A., Inc. v. Nat. Res. Def. Council, Inc., 467 U.S. 837, 865–66 (1984).

[18] See Jerry L. Mashaw, Prodelegation: Why Administrators Should Make Political Decisions, 1 J.L. Econ. & Org. 81 (1985).

major new nondelegation case—for the first time since *Whitman v. American Trucking Ass'ns* in 2001.[19] The case is *DOT v. Ass'n of American Railroads*,[20] which centered on regulatory power delegated to the National Passenger Railroad Corp., colloquially called Amtrak.

The case had the added attraction that it presented the interesting question of whether congressional delegations to private parties were evaluated using the same "intelligible principle" rule that applies to public agencies. (The opinion below, written by D.C. Circuit Judge Janice Rogers Brown, had struck down the statute delegating power to Amtrak on the ground that private delegations by Congress were per se unconstitutional.)[21] And it ended up producing an interesting separation-of-powers opinion by Justice Samuel Alito[22] and an interesting originalist opinion by Justice Clarence Thomas.[23]

The bad news for nondelegation buffs is that—in a display of the minimalism famously championed by Chief Justice John "Philip Glass" Roberts[24]—the Supreme Court ignored all the interesting arguments (including the ones in my own amicus brief[25]) by deciding the case on the narrowest possible, most Amtrak-specific theory. The Court held that Amtrak is in fact public, and not private, for purposes of the nondelegation doctrine, without explaining whether this matters. As a result, the troublesome question of whether there exists a special private nondelegation doctrine remains troublesome. Having held that Amtrak is public, the Court resolved no other question, but sent the case back to the D.C. Circuit for further litigation. We'll have to wait a bit longer to see how the case comes out, but the Supreme Court might no longer be involved, and the resolution may end up having nothing to do with the nondelegation doctrine.

[19] 531 U.S. 457.

[20] 135 S. Ct. 1225 (2015) (AAR II).

[21] Ass'n of Am. R.Rs. v. DOT, 721 F.3d 666 (D.C. Cir. 2013) (AAR I), vacated and remanded by AAR II, 135 S. Ct. 1225.

[22] AAR II, 135 S. Ct. at 1234–40 (Alito, J., concurring).

[23] *Id.* at 1240–54 (Thomas, J., concurring in the judgment).

[24] See Chief Justice Says His Goal Is More Consensus on Court, N.Y. Times (May 22, 2006), http://www.nytimes.com/2006/05/22/washington/22justice.html ("'If it is not necessary to decide more to a case, then in my view it is necessary not to decide more to a case,' Chief Justice Roberts said.").

[25] See Br. of Prof. Alexander Volokh as Amicus Curiae in Support of Pet'rs, AAR II, 135 S. Ct. 1225 (No. 13-1080).

II. The Regulatory Scheme

Congress created Amtrak via a 1970 federal statute, the Rail Passenger Service Act, to act as a for-profit passenger railroad corporation; its purpose was to revive the national passenger railroad system.[26] Railroads that offered passenger service had been incurring heavy losses, and many of them had petitioned the Interstate Commerce Commission for permission to withdraw from that market. Now they could arrange for Amtrak to take over their passenger service responsibilities in exchange for agreeing to a number of other conditions—one of which was granting Amtrak preferential access to their tracks and other facilities. By statute, except in emergency conditions, an Amtrak passenger car has precedence over another railroad's freight car when they both need the same facilities. Most railroads were more than happy to agree to these conditions, which were formalized in various bilateral operating agreements.[27]

Many years later, in 2008, Congress passed the Passenger Rail Investment and Improvement Act, requiring the development or improvement of "metrics and minimum standards for measuring the performance and service quality of intercity passenger train operations."[28] These performance and service quality measures should include "cost recovery, on-time performance and minutes of delay, ridership, on-board services, stations, facilities, equipment, and other services."[29]

These metrics aren't just of academic interest: they're a way of enforcing Amtrak's statutory precedence over other railroads. If an intercity passenger train fails to meet these metrics and standards for two consecutive quarters, or if a complaint is filed, the statute authorizes the Surface Transportation Board (STB) to investigate who's at fault. If the STB determines that the failure to meet the standards is "attributable to a rail carrier's failure to provide preference to Amtrak over freight transportation as required," the STB may assess

[26] See 49 U.S.C. § 24301 (2012).

[27] See AAR I, 721 F.3d at 668; Alexander Volokh, A New Private Delegation Doctrine?, Reason Found., (Aug. 1, 2013), http://reason.org/news/show/private-delegation-doctrine-amtrak.

[28] AAR I, 721 F.3d at 669 (quoting Passenger Rail Investment and Improvement Act of 2008 [hereinafter PRIIA], Pub. L. No. 110-432, § 207(a) (codified at 49 U.S.C. § 24101 (2012))).

[29] *Id.*

damages.[30] Moreover, the standards have an immediate regulatory effect: Amtrak and the railroads must incorporate them into their operating agreements "[t]o the extent practicable."[31]

Amtrak has a special role in developing these standards. Both Amtrak and the Federal Railroad Administration, an agency within the Department of Transportation, must agree on any metrics or standards before they can be implemented; in the event of a disagreement, the statute allows Amtrak and the FRA to petition the STB "to appoint an arbitrator to assist [them] in resolving their disputes through binding arbitration."[32]

The FRA and Amtrak eventually developed the required metrics. These included

> "effective speed" (the ratio of route's distance to the average time required to travel it), "endpoint on-time performance" (the portion of a route's trains that arrive on schedule), and "all-stations on-time performance" (the degree to which trains arrive on time at each station along the route).[33]

But wait a minute: Wasn't Amtrak created as a for-profit corporation? Believing that this was fishy, and that the statute giving Amtrak this (joint) rulemaking power was unconstitutional, the Association of American Railroads (AAR) sued to invalidate these metrics. Two of the principal arguments were that the statute (1) violates the nondelegation doctrine and separation-of-powers principles by giving Amtrak, a private entity, regulatory power over its own industry, and (2) violates the Due Process Clause by letting Amtrak self-interestedly regulate its own competitors.

III. A New-Fangled Doctrine

The AAR lost at the district court, but convinced the D.C. Circuit, which ruled in favor of the AAR based on the nondelegation doctrine. This required the court to sign on to two nonobvious conclusions: first, that Amtrak is private; and second, that Congress "cannot

---

[30] *Id.*

[31] *Id.* (quoting 49 U.S.C. § 24101 (2012)).

[32] *Id.*

[33] *Id.* at 669–70.

delegate regulatory authority to a private entity," even with an intelligible principle.[34]

A. Is Amtrak Private?

As an initial matter, any argument that Amtrak should be considered private for constitutional purposes runs into a problem: the Supreme Court's 1995 decision in *Lebron v. National Railroad Passenger Corp.*[35] In that case, Michael Lebron wanted to display a political ad, commenting on the Coors family's support of the Nicaraguan contras, in Amtrak's Penn Station. Amtrak—which, together with the billboard owner, had joint power to approve the content of ads—vetoed the ad. Lebron sued Amtrak for violating (among other things) his First Amendment rights. This claim would have been a nonstarter unless Amtrak was a "state actor,"[36] which indeed is what the Supreme Court held.

Amtrak was created by federal statute to serve federal goals.[37] The whole board of directors is politically appointed in one way or another. At the time of the case, the president appointed six directors out of nine (some with Senate confirmation and some without, with the secretary of transportation serving ex officio). Two more directors were selected by the holders of Amtrak's preferred stock—but since all that stock was held by the federal government, those directors were in fact selected by the secretary of transportation. A ninth director, the president, was selected by the other eight. Amtrak was required to submit reports to the president and Congress, one of which was made part of the Department of Transportation's annual report to Congress.

Amtrak, the Supreme Court noted, is part of a long tradition of "corporations created and participated in by the United States for the achievement of government objectives," from the banks of the United States to the Tennessee Valley Authority and the Federal Deposit Insurance Corp.[38]

[34] *Id.* at 670.

[35] 513 U.S. 374 (1995).

[36] See, e.g., Rendell-Baker v. Kohn, 457 U.S. 830 (1982); The Civil Rights Cases, 109 U.S. 3 (1883).

[37] Lebron, 513 U.S. at 383–84.

[38] *Id.*

In light of all of this, the statutory labeling of Amtrak as "not an agency or establishment of the United States government"[39] doesn't govern how it should in fact be treated for constitutional purposes:

> It surely cannot be that government, state or federal, is able to evade the most solemn obligations imposed in the Constitution by simply resorting to the corporate form. On that thesis, *Plessy v. Ferguson* can be resurrected by the simple device of having the State of Louisiana operate segregated trains through a state-owned Amtrak.[40]

Thus, the Court concluded, "where, as here, the Government creates a corporation by special law, for the furtherance of governmental objectives, and retains for itself permanent authority to appoint a majority of the directors of that corporation, the corporation is part of the Government for purposes of the First Amendment."[41] Because the state action doctrine is transsubstantive,[42] a holding of state action as to the First Amendment also applies as to the Due Process Clause,[43] the Equal Protection Clause,[44] and other rights provisions.

How, then, could the D.C. Circuit panel in this case get around *Lebron* and hold that Amtrak was private? It did so by holding that, while Amtrak might be a state actor for purposes of constitutional *rights* provisions, it might still be private for purposes of the nondelegation doctrine.[45] The most important part of Judge Brown's analysis was functional: the purposes of the public-private distinction in the nondelegation doctrine are to ensure democratic accountability and disinterested decisionmaking.[46] But the labeling of Amtrak as "not an agency or establishment of the United States government" distances Amtrak's decisions from democratic accountability, and

---

[39] *Id.* at 391.

[40] *Id.* at 397 (citation omitted).

[41] *Id.* at 400.

[42] See Mark D. Rosen, Was *Shelley v. Kraemer* Incorrectly Decided? Some New Answers, 95 Calif. L. Rev. 451, 475 (2007).

[43] See, e.g., Am. Mfrs. Mut. Ins. Co. v. Sullivan, 526 U.S. 40 (1999).

[44] See, e.g., Moose Lodge No. 107 v. Irvis, 407 U.S. 163 (1972).

[45] AAR I, 721 F.3d at 677.

[46] *Id.* at 675.

the statutory command to operate as a for-profit corporation actively discourages disinterested decisionmaking.[47]

Where the *Lebron* Court worried that the government could insulate itself from constitutional rights provisions by using the corporate form, the D.C. Circuit worried that considering such corporations state actors for *all* purposes would likewise allow the government to insulate itself from structural provisions like the nondelegation doctrine.[48]

B. The Rule Against Private Delegation?

But do we care? All this discussion assumes that whether Amtrak is public or private makes a difference to the nondelegation analysis. According to the D.C. Circuit, being private makes all the difference. "We open our discussion with a principle upon which both sides agree: Federal lawmakers cannot delegate regulatory authority to a private entity."[49] While a public agency can receive delegated power as long as an intelligible principle exists, even an intelligible principle can't save a statute that places regulatory authority in the hands of private parties. And, said the D.C. Circuit, the Supreme Court has never approved a private delegation of this extent.[50]

Consider, for instance, *Currin v. Wallace*.[51] The Tobacco Inspection Act of 1935 allowed the secretary of agriculture to designate a tobacco market; in a designated market, no tobacco could be sold until it had been inspected and certified according to certain standards.[52] But the secretary wasn't allowed to designate a market unless two-thirds of the growers approved the designation in a referendum.[53] The statute thus delegated to private parties—the regulated community—an "on-off switch," the power to decide whether regulations would go into effect. The Supreme Court upheld this delegation.

The Supreme Court also upheld the statutory scheme in *Sunshine Anthracite Coal Co. v. Adkins*, where Congress allowed a commission

[47] *Id.* at 675–76.
[48] *Id.* at 675.
[49] *Id.* at 670.
[50] *Id.* at 671.
[51] 306 U.S. 1 (1939).
[52] *Id.* at 6.
[53] *Id.*

of private coal industry members to propose regulations.[54] There was nothing unconstitutional about this delegation, since the private parties were doing nothing more than proposing regulations; the decision to "approve[], disapprove[], or modify[]" them was left solely to the government agency.[55]

But, said the D.C. Circuit, the statute here went far beyond both of those statutes. Amtrak's authority was more than merely advisory and went further than merely vetoing a regulation written by another; in fact, Amtrak enjoyed regulatory authority equal to the FRA's.[56] The government argued that the metrics and standards merely triggered future STB investigation—so the relevant regulatory activity, and a check on Amtrak's power, would be the future STB investigation.[57] But the D.C. Circuit responded that the metrics and standards are the enforcement mechanism for the obligation to provide preference to Amtrak trains; moreover, the statute immediately imposes the regulatory requirement that the metrics and standards be incorporated in Amtrak's operating agreements with other carriers.[58]

The D.C. Circuit held that the delegation here was more similar to the kind that was invalidated in *Carter v. Carter Coal Co.*[59] That case concerned the Bituminous Coal Conservation Act of 1935, which allowed the producers of two-thirds of the coal in any "coal district" to set wages and hours for all coal producers in the district, after negotiation with unions representing a majority of mine workers in the district. The Supreme Court invalidated this delegation of coercive power to private actors, calling it "legislative delegation in its most obnoxious form."[60] And the delegation to Amtrak, wrote the D.C. Circuit, "is as close to the blatantly unconstitutional scheme in *Carter Coal* as we have seen."[61]

---

[54] 310 U.S. 381, 387–88 (1940).

[55] *Id.* at 388, 397.

[56] AAR I, 721 F.3d at 671.

[57] *Id.* at 672.

[58] *Id.*

[59] 298 U.S. 238 (1936).

[60] *Id.* at 311.

[61] AAR I, 721 F.3d at 673.

C. Nondelegation vs. Due Process

Perhaps, as the court said, both sides did agree that the nondelegation doctrine prohibits Congress from "delegat[ing] regulatory authority to a private entity," and that the source of this prohibition was *Carter Coal*.[62] But then both sides, and the court, were wrong. *Carter Coal*, properly read, is a case about the Due Process Clause. There is therefore no Supreme Court case that strikes down a delegation to private parties based on the nondelegation doctrine: *Currin v. Wallace* should be taken to stand for the proposition that private delegations are not per se illegal.

I would go even further. In *Currin*, the Court upheld the delegation by stating that it was comparable to the delegation *to the president* that was upheld in *J.W. Hampton, Jr. & Co. v. United States*.[63] Thus, *Currin* stands for a stronger proposition: that private delegations should be judged by the same nondelegation doctrine that applies to public officials. I've argued elsewhere that *Currin* was wrongly decided on its own terms, since the "on-off" power delegated to the industry participants was so unconstrained as to lack an intelligible principle.[64] But whether or not *Currin* properly applies the nondelegation doctrine, it's still good law on the more general question of whether the doctrine should apply identically in public and private cases.

And that general proposition has the added advantage of being correct: The nondelegation doctrine is about whether Congress has given up so much authority as to have abdicated its legislative power. It's about whether too much power has been given up, not about who receives that power.[65]

---

[62] The government accepted the characterization that *Carter Coal* prevents Congress from making an "absolute delegation of regulatory authority to private parties," Br. for the Appellees, AAR I, 721 F.3d 666, at 28, but argued that *Carter Coal* was distinguishable because of the government's "structural control" over Amtrak, *id.* at 29–31, the involvement of the FRA and the other railroads in the development of the standards, *id.* at 31, and the requirement that STB itself find a violation of the "separate and longstanding statutory preference requirement" before any fines can be assessed. *Id.* So the D.C. Circuit seems to be correct in characterizing the government's position: a private delegation (unlike a public delegation) violates the nondelegation doctrine if not accompanied by sufficient safeguards.

[63] 276 U.S. 394 (1928).

[64] Alexander Volokh, The New Private-Regulation Skepticism: Due Process, Non-Delegation, and Antitrust Challenges, 37 Harv. J.L. & Pub. Pol'y 931, 960–61 (2014).

[65] *Id.* at 957 n.134.

1. How to Interpret *Carter Coal*

My thesis on *Currin v. Wallace* and the (nonexistence of the) private nondelegation doctrine depends on undermining the association of *Carter Coal* with the nondelegation doctrine. So it's important to read *Carter Coal* carefully. Here's the text from the portion of *Carter Coal* that supposedly invokes that doctrine:

> The power conferred upon the majority is, in effect, the power to regulate the affairs of an unwilling minority. This is legislative delegation in its most obnoxious form; for it is not even delegation to an official or an official body, presumptively disinterested, but to private persons whose interests may be and often are adverse to the interests of others in the same business. . . . The difference between producing coal and regulating its production is, of course, fundamental. The former is a private activity; the latter is necessarily a governmental function, since, in the very nature of things, one person may not be entrusted with the power to regulate the business of another, and especially of a competitor. And a statute which attempts to confer such power undertakes an intolerable and unconstitutional interference with personal liberty and private property. The delegation is so clearly arbitrary, and so clearly a denial of rights safeguarded by the due process clause of the Fifth Amendment, that it is unnecessary to do more than refer to decisions of this court which foreclose the question.[66]

Two things about this block quotation could be taken to suggest that the Court might be referring to the nondelegation doctrine: the Court says "delegation" three times, and it cites the nondelegation case *Schechter Poultry*.

But the citation to *Schechter Poultry* isn't highly probative, since *Schechter Poultry* wasn't actually decided on the basis of delegation to private parties. The statutory scheme in *Schechter Poultry* involved industry codes of "fair competition"—comprehensive regulations of entire industries—which members of that industry could propose and the president could then adopt. The Supreme Court was, in the first place, highly dubious that Congress could delegate such

---

[66] Carter Coal, 298 U.S. at 311 (citing A.L.A. Schechter Poultry Corp. v. United States, 295 U.S. 495 (1935); Eubank v. City of Richmond, 226 U.S. 137 (1912); Washington ex rel. Seattle Title Trust Co. v. Roberge, 278 U.S. 116 (1928)).

comprehensive regulatory power over industries to the industries themselves:

> [W]ould it be seriously contended that Congress could delegate its legislative authority to trade or industrial associations or groups so as to empower them to enact the laws they deem to be wise and beneficent for the rehabilitation and expansion of their trade or industries? Could trade or industrial associations or groups be constituted legislative bodies for that purpose because such associations or groups are familiar with the problems of their enterprises? And could an effort of that sort be made valid by such a preface of generalities as to permissible aims as we find in [the preamble to the statute]? The answer is obvious. Such a delegation of legislative power is unknown to our law, and is utterly inconsistent with the constitutional prerogatives and duties of Congress.[67]

But this is dictum. The Court went on to strike down the statute because *the president* had insufficient guidance on whether or not to approve the industry-proposed codes. And this isn't a blanket disapproval of all private delegation—just of extremely broad private delegation. Phrased that way, I agree: of course Congress couldn't delegate such an unconstrained power to private industry, because it couldn't delegate such an unconstrained power to *anyone*, not even the president.

In any event, this dictum just says the delegation would be unconstitutional, without being totally clear on why: Is it unconstitutional because it violates the nondelegation doctrine, or because it violates some other constitutional doctrine? (Admittedly, the block quotation, with its talk of "trade or industrial associations or groups be[ing] constituted legislative bodies" and "the constitutional prerogatives and duties of Congress," does suggest a separation-of-powers, i.e. nondelegation, rationale, but it doesn't come out and say it.)

This last point is important: saying the word "delegation" doesn't mean one is talking about the nondelegation doctrine. For example, a delegation of governmental power to religious groups can violate the Establishment Clause.[68] An excessively vague delegation of power to

---

[67] Schechter Poultry, 295 U.S. at 537.

[68] See Bd. of Educ. of Kiryas Joel Vill. Sch. Dist. v. Grumet, 512 U.S. 687 (1994); Larkin v. Grendel's Den, Inc., 459 U.S. 116 (1982).

courts and juries to determine what acts are criminal violates the Fifth and Sixth Amendments.[69] A delegation of "private attorney general" power to a *qui tam* plaintiff might violate the Appointments Clause.[70] And a delegation of regulatory power to self-interested private parties could also violate the Due Process Clause.[71]

Thus—now leaving *Schechter Poultry* and going back to *Carter Coal*—when the *Carter Coal* Court talks about "legislative delegation in its most obnoxious form," it's much more plausible that this refers to the Due Process Clause. First, note that *Eubank* and *Roberge* are cited right after *Schechter Poultry*. While *Schechter Poultry* may be a problematic citation, *Eubank* and *Roberge* are precisely on point, since they're exactly about the unconstitutionality of delegations of regulatory authority to self-interested private parties—under the Due Process Clause alone, since these cases involved state governments. (Not that there's any specific due process doctrine against regulation by private parties: the same line of cases also bars regulation by *public* actors whose compensation gives them incentives not to act disinterestedly.[72] But obviously non-disinterestedness can be easier to show when the regulators have a clear profit motive, which in turn is easier to find in the case of private actors.)

Carter Coal also explicitly mentions the "denial of rights safeguarded by the due process clause of the Fifth Amendment." And it notes that the statutory scheme works "an intolerable and unconstitutional interference with personal liberty and private property"—reciting the terms "liberty" and "property," which are predicates for the Due Process Clause to apply.[73]

Perhaps this is why the Supreme Court has characterized *Carter Coal* as a due process case, and not a nondelegation case, on the few occasions the question has come up over the last 30 years.[74]

[69] United States v. L. Cohen Grocery Co., 255 U.S. 81, 92 (1921).

[70] See Vt. Agency of Nat. Res. v. United States ex rel. Stevens, 529 U.S. 765, 778 n.8 (2000) (noting this argument but not deciding it).

[71] See Roberge, 278 U.S. 116; Eubank, 226 U.S. 137.

[72] See, e.g., Aetna Life Ins. v. Lavoie, 475 U.S. 813 (1986); Ward v. Vill. of Monroeville, 409 U.S. 57 (1972); Tumey v. Ohio, 273 U.S. 510 (1927).

[73] See Bd. of Regents of State Colls. v. Roth, 408 U.S. 564, 572 (1972).

[74] See Am. Trucking II, 531 U.S. at 474 (noting that *Schechter Poultry* and *Panama Refining* were the only two cases where a statute was struck down on nondelegation grounds, completely excluding *Carter Coal*); Mistretta v. United States, 488 U.S. 361

Nor, as the panel suggested, is the D.C. Circuit's own precedent to the contrary.[75] In *National Ass'n of Regulatory Utility Commissioners v. FCC (NARUC)*, the D.C. Circuit had indeed spoken critically of private delegations, but it was dictum (no such delegation was found in that case), and it cited *Carter Coal* without discussing whether the case was based on nondelegation or due process.[76]

Moreover—in a footnote (still dictum) specifically focused on the nondelegation doctrine—the *NARUC* court stated that the harm of delegations is "doubled in degree in the context of a transfer of authority from Congress to an agency and then from an agency to private individuals."[77] O.K., but is that because the delegation is private, or because there are two levels of delegation (as opposed to only one level of delegation in Amtrak's case)?

The *NARUC* court also stated that "[t]he vitality of challenges to" transfers of authority from Congress to an agency "is suspect," but from an agency to private individuals, "unquestionable." But again, Amtrak's case isn't about agency-to-private delegations but rather about Congress-to-private delegations. And saying that the vitality of a certain type of legal challenge is unquestionable isn't the same as saying that this kind of challenge always wins. Nor does it make clear why the vitality is unquestionable: is it because the legal test is different, or because delegations to private parties are more likely to lack the requisite intelligible principle?

In short, this supposed D.C. Circuit precedent doesn't carry much weight. Anything it says on the matter is (1) dictum, (2) ambiguous as to whether the nondelegation doctrine or due process is involved, (3) ambiguous as to whether there's any per se rule, or (4) focused on agency-to-private delegations, not Congress-to-private delegations.

(1989) (also excluding *Carter Coal* from the list of nondelegation cases); see also INS v. Chadha, 462 U.S. 919 (1983) (White, J., dissenting) (similarly excluding *Carter Coal* from the discussion of nondelegation cases). Even then-appellate judge Antonin Scalia noted (albeit as one-third of a *per curiam* opinion) that *Carter Coal* spoke of the nondelegation doctrine but rested its holding primarily upon denial of substantive due process. Synar v. United States, 626 F. Supp. 1374, 1383 n.8 (D.D.C. 1986) (three-judge panel) *(per curiam)*, aff'd sub nom. Bowsher v. Synar, 478 U.S. 714 (1986).

[75] AAR I, 721 F.3d at 671 n.3.

[76] 737 F.2d 1095, 1143 (D.C. Cir. 1984).

[77] *Id.* at 1143 n.41.

2. What Difference Does It Make?

In a footnote, the D.C. Circuit acknowledged the argument that *Carter Coal* should be interpreted as a due process case instead of a nondelegation case, but decided that this didn't make much difference. The difference, the panel wrote, was only of "scholarly interest" and "neither court nor scholar has suggested a change in the label would effect a change in the inquiry."[78] Oh, but (speaking as a scholar) it does.

First, would the doctrine of this case apply to federal delegations only, or also to state delegations? The nondelegation doctrine derives from the Vesting Clause of Article I and therefore applies only to delegations by Congress. The Due Process Clause applies to both the federal government and state governments through the Fifth and Fourteenth Amendments.[79] Sure, this wouldn't make a difference in this case, but getting the theory correct is important because the greatest value of cases is as precedent.

It doesn't help to treat private delegation as a hybrid nondelegation and due process problem, as some courts and commentators have done.[80] The Due Process Clause has one line of doctrine, and the nondelegation doctrine has another.[81] If we're talking about a federal delegation, how do these two lines of doctrine mix? And if we're talking about a state delegation, how does such a due-process-only analysis proceed differently from a federal case where both doctrines apply?

Second, are damages available? In federal delegation cases, plaintiffs prefer to win on due process grounds rather than nondelegation grounds, because due process cases can be litigated under *Bivens v.*

---

[78] AAR I, 721 F.3d at 671 n.3.

[79] U.S. Const. amend. V; U.S. Const. amend. XIV, § 1; see Note, The Vagaries of Vagueness: Rethinking the CFAA as a Problem of Private Nondelegation, 127 Harv. L. Rev. 751, 764 (2013); David N. Wecht, Note, Breaking the Code of Difference: Judicial Review of Private Persons, 96 Yale L.J. 815, 825 n.57 (1987).

[80] See, e.g., McGautha v. California, 402 U.S. 183, 272 n.21 (1971) (Brennan, J., dissenting); A. Michael Froomkin, Wrong Turn in Cyberspace: Using ICANN to Route Around the APA and the Constitution, 50 Duke L.J. 17, 151, 153 (2000); Paul R. Verkuil, Public Law Limitations on Privatization of Government Functions, 84 N.C. L. Rev. 397, 422 (2006).

[81] The due process line of cases involves *Mathews v. Eldridge*, 424 U.S. 319 (1976), *Roth*, and *Roberge*. The nondelegation line of cases includes *Schechter Poultry* and *J.W. Hampton*.

Six Unknown Named Agents of the Federal Bureau of Narcotics, which allows for damages against federal actors responsible for the due process violation.[82] *Bivens* hasn't been extended to cases under the nondelegation doctrine and is unlikely to be.[83]

Third, how do we determine who's a state actor? If the case involves due process, we rely on *Lebron* and find that Amtrak is a state actor. If the case involves the nondelegation doctrine, we rely on the D.C. Circuit's new, ad hoc theory related to the underlying goals of the nondelegation doctrine. (Well, not anymore, since, as we'll see, that part of the holding was reversed by the Supreme Court.) Perhaps we shouldn't have a multiplicity of state-action doctrines for different constitutional contexts, or perhaps the different contexts make different tests appropriate. What's clear, though, is that nondelegation and due process are not at all interchangeable in this respect.

Finally, and most important, the Due Process Clause just makes more sense here, because of the internal logic of the doctrines themselves. The nondelegation doctrine—true to its roots in the Vesting Clause—ensures that legislative authority stays with Congress.[84] Due process, though, is about fairness.

What's the difference between nondelegation and fairness? Consider *Whitman v. American Trucking Assn's*, which involved a nondelegation challenge to the Clean Air Act.[85] Before *American Trucking* reached the Supreme Court, the D.C. Circuit held that the Clean Air Act lacked an intelligible principle for Congress to properly delegate regulatory authority to the EPA.[86] But, said the D.C. Circuit, all would be fine if the EPA adopted a limiting construction of the overly broad delegation[87]—a theory advanced by administrative law scholar Kenneth Culp Davis, who wrote that such limiting constructions would

---

[82] 403 U.S. 388 (1971) (recognizing the availability of damages for federal officials' violation of the Fourth Amendment); see also Davis v. Passman, 442 U.S. 228 (1979) (extending *Bivens* to the Due Process Clause).

[83] See Alexander Volokh, The Modest Effect of *Minneci v. Pollard* on Inmate Litigants, 46 Akron L. Rev. 287 (2013).

[84] See text accompanying note 65, *supra*.

[85] 531 U.S. 457.

[86] *Id*. at 463 (citing Am. Trucking Ass'ns, Inc. v. EPA, 175 F.3d 1027, 1034 (D.C. Cir. 1999) (Am. Trucking I), rev'd, Am. Trucking II, 531 U.S. 457).

[87] *Id*. (citing Am. Trucking I, 175 F.3d at 1038).

adequately serve the nondelegation doctrine's concern with limiting "arbitrariness" and "uncontrolled discretionary power."[88]

The Supreme Court rejected all of that. First, it held that the delegation wasn't too broad. Second, it held that even if the delegation were too broad, it would make no sense to say that the EPA could cure that deficiency by adopting a limiting construction: the EPA's voluntarily limiting its own authority would itself be an exercise of the forbidden legislative power.[89] But note that, while an appropriate limiting construction couldn't cure a nondelegation problem, it would provide notice and could even provide other elements of due process if these were lacking in the statute. Thus, *American Trucking* shows that a nondelegation doctrine violation need not violate due process as well.

Similarly, a violation of due process need not violate the nondelegation doctrine. Congress could pass a statute allowing officials to withdraw certain beneficiaries' welfare payments without any process; such a statute would presumably violate due process,[90] but it would be perfectly consistent with the nondelegation doctrine if the officials' discretion were sufficiently circumscribed.

The two theories are related in various ways—for instance, the presence of procedures can satisfy due process and can also help to alleviate nondelegation concerns[91]—but they don't necessarily go together. So, despite the D.C. Circuit's footnote suggesting otherwise, keeping the two doctrines separate is important for both academic and very practical reasons.

In sum, here the D.C. Circuit got the doctrine wrong: delegation to a private, self-interested party is a due process problem, not a nondelegation problem. That said, the panel's bottom line was sound. I think there is enough of an intelligible principle—the command

---

[88] Kenneth Culp Davis, A New Approach to Delegation, 36 U. Chi. L. Rev. 713, 713 (1969). The D.C. Circuit had already used this approach in *Amalgamated Meat Cutters & Butcher Workmen AFL-CIO v. Connally*, 337 F. Supp. 737, 758–59 (D.D.C. 1971) (three-judge panel).

[89] Am. Trucking II, 531 U.S. at 472–73.

[90] See Goldberg v. Kelly, 397 U.S. 254 (1970).

[91] See, e.g., Fahey v. Mallonee, 332 U.S. 245, 253 (1947); Yakus, 321 U.S. at 426; Schechter Poultry, 295 U.S. at 539–40.

that Amtrak be run as a profit-making enterprise.[92] But the same principle that saves the delegation under the nondelegation doctrine should be enough to doom it under the Due Process Clause. As a (quasi-?) for-profit enterprise, Amtrak has a fiduciary duty to undermine other railroads by any legal means if this would maximize its own profits. Amtrak could exercise its ability to create metrics and standards, as well as its veto power, self-interestedly. This conflict of interest violates due process.

IV. A Narrow Overruling

The Supreme Court overruled the D.C. Circuit but didn't disapprove of the private nondelegation doctrine. Rather, it sidestepped the issue entirely, merely holding that Amtrak is a governmental actor for purposes of the nondelegation doctrine. This limited holding makes it unimportant (for this case) whether a special private doctrine even exists. (Of course, if there's no special private doctrine, it doesn't matter whether Amtrak is public. So the Supreme Court's opinion might be completely irrelevant.)

The Supreme Court's opinion is awfully reminiscent of *Lebron*—which is indeed cited repeatedly as an opinion that "provides necessary instruction."[93] As in *Lebron*, the labeling of Amtrak as not-an-agency and the requirement that it operate as a profit-making entity aren't dispositive of the constitutional question.[94] As in *Lebron*, it's relevant that the government holds the majority of Amtrak's stock and that virtually all the board members are government officials. The statute has changed a bit since *Lebron*; now, eight of nine board members are government officials, including the secretary of transportation and seven others who are appointed by the president and confirmed by the Senate. Their salaries are limited by Congress and, according to the attorney general, they're removable by the president without cause.[95]

The government has a lot of supervisory authority over Amtrak: Amtrak has to submit certain annual reports to Congress and the

---

[92] See 49 U.S.C. § 24301(a) (2012) ("Amtrak . . . shall be operated and managed as a for-profit corporation.").

[93] AAR II, 135 S. Ct. at 1233.

[94] *Id.* at 1231.

[95] *Id.* (citing 49 U.S.C. §§ 24302(a)(1), 24303(b) (2012); 27 Op. Atty. Gen. 163 (2003)).

president, receives large subsidies, is subject to the Freedom of Information Act, and must maintain an inspector general similar to other governmental agencies.[96] Congress frequently conducts oversight hearings to determine Amtrak's budget, routes, and prices.[97] And while it's required to maximize profits, it also has to pursue various other statutory goals, including "provid[ing] efficient and effective intercity passenger rail mobility," "provid[ing] reduced fares to the disabled and elderly," and "ensur[ing] mobility in times of national disaster."[98]

As a result, "[g]iven the combination of these unique features and its significant ties to the Government, Amtrak is not an autonomous private enterprise."[99] (Unique indeed: this laundry list of factors is awfully Amtrak-specific, and—even if public or private status is relevant for the nondelegation doctrine—may not be very helpful next time a similar case comes up involving a different organization.) "[T]he practical reality of federal control and supervision" suffice to make *Lebron*'s holding (in a rights context) applicable in this separation-of-powers context too; after all, "[t]he structural principles secured by the separation of powers protect the individual as well."[100]

Having decided this, the Court remanded to the D.C. Circuit for further litigation.[101] There remain several constitutional issues in the case: whether the Amtrak board's selection of its president, who isn't appointed by the president or confirmed by the Senate, violates the Appointments Clause; whether the arbitrator provision, which allows Amtrak or the FRA to appoint a (possibly private) binding arbitrator if neither party can agree on metrics and standards, violates the nondelegation doctrine or the Appointments Clause; and (the real *Carter Coal* issue) whether Congress violated the Due Process Clause by granting Amtrak regulatory authority over the industry.

---

[96] *Id.* at 1232 (citing 49 U.S.C. § 24315 (2012)).

[97] *Id.*

[98] *Id.* (quoting 49 U.S.C. §§ 24101, 24307 (2012)).

[99] *Id.*

[100] *Id.* at 1233 (quoting Bond v. United States, 131 S. Ct. 2355, 2365 (2011)).

[101] *Id.* at 1234.

V. The More Interesting Concurrences

The concurrences are more interesting than the majority opinion—not surprisingly, since just about anything is more interesting than the majority opinion. Justice Alito wrote a strong concurrence opining on the remaining separation of powers issues (and, unfortunately, endorsing the private nondelegation theory). Justice Thomas used the opportunity to present his complete originalist theory of the nondelegation doctrine (which is likewise somewhat confused on private nondelegation).

A. Justice Alito's Structural Concurrence

Justice Alito, stressing that "[l]iberty requires accountability,"[102] addressed a number of structural issues that might arise on remand. (Justice Alito apparently likes to address issues that he feels might become significant in the case down the road but that aren't addressed in the narrower majority opinion.[103])

First, Amtrak board members don't swear an oath or (apparently) receive a commission from the president, both of which are required of officers of the United States.[104] These requirements are important if Amtrak board members are "officers," an issue that Justice Alito returns to shortly.

Second, the statute is indisputably regulatory—and yet, this regulatory power can be wielded, in case of disagreement between Amtrak and the FRA, by an arbitrator. But the statute "says nothing . . . about who the arbitrator should be."[105] Clearly, the arbitration provision can be challenged here even though no arbitration has occurred—what actually happens occurs in the shadow of what could happen. And the arbitration provision, Justice Alito writes, is unconstitutional:[106] First, if the arbitrator is private, he's unconstitutional because of the private delegation doctrine. The government suggested that the arbitrator should be interpreted to be public, for

---

[102] *Id.* at 1234 (Alito, J., concurring).

[103] See, e.g., EEOC v. Abercrombie & Fitch Stores, Inc., 135 S. Ct. 2028, 2035 (2015) (Alito, J., concurring in the judgment); T-Mobile S., LLC v. City of Roswell, 135 S. Ct. 808, 819 (2015); Volkman v. United States, 135 S. Ct. 13 (2014).

[104] AAR II, 135 S. Ct. at 1234 (Alito, J., concurring).

[105] *Id.* at 1236.

[106] *Id.* at 1237–39.

exactly these constitutional avoidance reasons—though the plain meaning of "arbitrator" usually refers to a private arbitrator. But second, it doesn't matter because, even if he's public, he's unconstitutional. As someone who wields significant federal authority without a superior, he's a principal officer, and because he's not nominated by the president with Senate confirmation, his appointment violates the Appointments Clause. Justice Alito thus endorses the D.C. Circuit's private nondelegation analysis.

Finally, the appointment of Amtrak's president raises structural issues. He's just appointed by the other eight board members (who themselves are presidential appointees). Since he has no superior and can cast the deciding vote, he also seems to be a principal officer, and therefore also requires presidential nomination and Senate confirmation. But even if he's an inferior officer, his appointment may likewise be unconstitutional because the rest of the Amtrak board, which appoints him, might not be properly considered a "Head" of a "Department" within the meaning of the Appointments Clause.[107]

Justice Alito's arguments are bound to shape the parties' arguments on remand—at least the separation-of-powers arguments, since Justice Alito didn't address any due process arguments.

B. Justice Thomas's Originalist Concurrence

1. The Promised Theory of Nondelegation

On February 27, 2001, the Supreme Court issued *Whitman v. American Trucking Ass'ns*, easily upholding the Clean Air Act's delegation to the EPA of the authority to set National Ambient Air Quality Standards.[108] Everyone accepted the "intelligible principle" doctrine as a way of distinguishing between valid and invalid delegations[109]—except for Justice Thomas, who wrote:

---

[107] AAR II, 135 S. Ct. at 1239–40 (citing Free Enter. Fund v. Pub. Co. Accounting Oversight Bd., 561 U.S. 477, 511 (2010)).

[108] 531 U.S. 457.

[109] The *American Trucking* majority, in line with prevailing doctrine, would use the principle to distinguish between delegations of *legislative* power and delegations of authority that fall short of being legislative delegations. Am. Trucking II, 531 U.S. at 472–73. Justice Stevens's concurrence would use the principle to distinguish between valid and invalid delegations of legislative power. *Id.* at 489–90 (Stevens, J., concurring in part and concurring in the judgment).

The parties to these cases who briefed the constitutional issue wrangled over constitutional doctrine with barely a nod to the text of the Constitution. Although this Court since 1928 has treated the "intelligible principle" requirement as the only constitutional limit on congressional grants of power to administrative agencies, the Constitution does not speak of "intelligible principles." Rather, it speaks in much simpler terms: "*All* legislative Powers herein granted shall be vested in a Congress." I am not convinced that the intelligible principle doctrine serves to prevent all cessions of legislative power. I believe that there are cases in which the principle is intelligible and yet the significance of the delegated decision is simply too great for the decision to be called anything other than "legislative."

As it is, none of the parties to these cases has examined the text of the Constitution or asked us to reconsider our precedents on cessions of legislative power. On a future day, however, I would be willing to address the question whether our delegation jurisprudence has strayed too far from our Founders' understanding of separation of powers.[110]

March 9, 2015, was that future day. Justice Thomas has now given us his complete originalist theory of delegation.[111]

First, Justice Thomas engages in an extended historical overview—notably focusing on the controversial use of the proclamation power by Henry VIII and James I, which deeply influenced the Framers—to establish that only the legislative branch can "make 'law' in the Blackstonian sense of generally applicable rules of private conduct."[112]

---

[110] *Id.* at 487 (Thomas, J., concurring) (citations omitted).

[111] Justice Thomas's concurrence in the judgment here goes together with his concurrence in the judgment in *Perez v. Mortgage Bankers Ass'n*, 135 S. Ct. 1199, 1213 (2015), handed down the same day, as well as his concurrence in *Michigan v. EPA*. In *Perez*, Justice Thomas discusses administrative deference under *Auer v. Robbins*, 519 U.S. 452 (1997), and *Bowles v. Seminole Rock & Sand Co.*, 325 U.S. 410 (1945); and in *Michigan v. EPA*, he discusses administrative deference under *Chevron*. See Michigan v. EPA, 135 S. Ct. at 2712–14 (Thomas, J., concurring) (questioning *Chevron* deference on nondelegation grounds but merely calling it "potentially unconstitutional" and granting that "[p]erhaps there is some unique historical justification for deferring to federal agencies" (citing Mead, 533 U.S. at 243 (Scalia, J., dissenting))). Deference to agencies has always been rooted in concepts of implicit delegation—*Chevron* deference explicitly so. See Chevron, 467 U.S. at 843–44.

[112] AAR II, 135 S. Ct. at 1242–45 (Thomas, J., concurring in the judgment).

Next, he goes through the history of American delegation cases, showing that early delegations to the executive branch were generally in the form of conditional legislation, by which a fully formed congressional regime sprang in or out of being when the president or another executive official found a particular fact.[113] (One early example is Congress's enactment of an embargo, conditional on the president's determination as to whether or not France was violating the neutral commerce of the United States.)[114] To be sure, some of this fact-finding involved implicit policy determinations, and to that extent was problematic (except if the determinations involved core executive areas like foreign affairs).[115] But even when such delegations came before the Court at the turn of the 20th century, the Court upheld them, not because it endorsed the view that the president could make generally applicable rules of private conduct, but because it (perhaps wrongly) denied that any such implicit policymaking was going on.[116]

Only in the 20th century did courts truly start endorsing delegates' power to make binding rules of conduct. These cases purported to rely on Chief Justice Marshall's early opinion in *Wayman v. Southard*,[117] but that case—which upheld congressional delegation to the judiciary of power to make procedural rules—was about rules for governmental bodies to enforce their own judgments, not about rules of private conduct.[118] And today, "the Court has abandoned all pretense of enforcing a qualitative distinction between legislative and executive power," so that the executive branch is now allowed to "craft significant rules of private conduct" and even "decide which policy goals it wants to pursue."[119]

In Justice Thomas's view, "[w]e should return to the original meaning of the Constitution: The Government may create generally

---

[113] *Id.* at 1247.

[114] Cargo of Brig Aurora v. United States, 11 U.S. (7 Cranch) 382 (1813).

[115] AAR II, 135 S. Ct. at 1247–48.

[116] *Id.* at 1248–49 (citing J.W. Hampton, 276 U.S. at 410–11; Field v. Clark, 143 U.S. 649, 692–93 (1892)).

[117] 23 U.S. (10 Wheat.) 1.

[118] AAR II, 135 S. Ct. at 1249–50 (Thomas, J., concurring in the judgment).

[119] *Id.* at 1250–51.

applicable rules of private conduct only through the proper exercise of legislative power."[120]

Moving on to the current case, Justice Thomas endorses the D.C. Circuit's view that, if Amtrak were private, a delegation to it would be unconstitutional based on *Carter Coal*.[121] But because here he agrees with the majority that Amtrak is governmental, the above theory applies. Amtrak's joint development of metrics and standards "alter[s] the railroads' common-carrier obligations," so Amtrak is making binding rules of private conduct, which is a legislative function. Therefore, the delegation to Amtrak is invalid.[122] *Currin v. Wallace*, the case discussed above involving industry veto of agency regulations,[123] and its companion case, *United States v. Rock-Royal Cooperative, Inc.*,[124] "have been discredited and lack any force as precedents," since they conflict with the more recent decision in *INS v. Chadha*[125] that a one-house legislative veto is an exercise of legislative power. (Under Justice Thomas's theory, *Currin* is of course incorrect, as is most of the rest of nondelegation case law. But here, Justice Thomas is making a narrower point about the consistency of *Currin* with *Chadha*, and this point is certainly incorrect: Of course, the decision to deport Chadha was a legislative act, but only because it was performed by the House of Representatives. Everyone agrees that it would have been unambiguously an executive, not a legislative, act if the executive branch had made the same decision. So *Chadha* has no bearing on whether the industry members' veto in *Currin* is an exercise of legislative power.)

Of course, the D.C. Circuit is required to apply current doctrine on remand, so the delegation to Amtrak is likely to survive under the "intelligible principle" doctrine. Thus, the next step is to "determine whether Amtrak is constitutionally eligible to exercise executive power"—which involves applying constitutional doctrines related

[120] *Id.* at 1252.

[121] *Id.*

[122] *Id.* at 1253.

[123] See text accompanying notes 51–53, 63–65, *supra*.

[124] 307 U.S. 533 (1939).

[125] 462 U.S. 919.

to appointment and removal.[126] On this point, Justice Thomas refers back to Justice Alito's concurrence.

2. Evaluating Justice Thomas's Theory

Does Justice Thomas's theory have originalist support? Eric Posner and Adrian Vermeule have argued for a drastically different nondelegation doctrine—they call their view the "naïve"[127] view—that would merely prevent legislators from delegating their formal "authority to vote on federal statutes or to exercise other de jure powers of federal legislators."[128] A Congress that allows an agency to make rules isn't *delegating* its legislative power; it's *exercising* its legislative power. And an agency that uses this power to make rules isn't exercising *legislative* power; it's doing what Congress told it to do, that is, executing the federal statute, that is, exercising *executive* power.[129]

The originalist argument against this naïve view is that the term "legislative power" was understood—for instance, by Locke, Montesquieu, and Blackstone—as meaning "the power to make laws/rules for the governance of society," not "the power to vote on legislation."[130] Thus, when Congress passes such a statute, it's *both exercising and delegating* legislative power, and when an agency uses the delegated power, it's exercising *both legislative and executive* power.[131]

But why should the Vesting Clause prevent transfers of legislative power, rather than just announcing where the legislative power lies initially?[132] Justice Thomas doesn't address this question—he simply assumes that the three Vesting Clauses announce where particular powers should lie forever—but Gary Lawson, one of the leading

---

[126] AAR II, 135 S. Ct. at 1254 (Thomas, J., concurring in the judgment).

[127] Posner & Vermeule, *supra* note 5, at 1725–26.

[128] *Id.* at 1723.

[129] *Id.* at 1725–26.

[130] Larry Alexander & Saikrishna Prakash, Reports of the Nondelegation Doctrine's Death Are Greatly Exaggerated, 70 U. Chi. L. Rev. 1297, 1310 (2003); see also AAR II, 135 S. Ct. at 1244 (Thomas, J., concurring in the judgment) (quoting William Blackstone, 1 Commentaries 44).

[131] Alexander & Prakash, *supra* note 130, at 1319.

[132] See text accompanying notes 3–4, *supra*.

academic defenders of the nondelegation doctrine from an originalist perspective, does.[133]

Lawson poses the following hypothetical: Suppose Congress passes a Goodness and Niceness Act, where section 1 outlaws any transaction in interstate or foreign commerce not promoting goodness and niceness, and section 2 gives the president the power to define the content of the statute by promulgating regulations.[134] Section 1 is justified by the Commerce Clause, but section 2 has no support in any congressional power. Section 2 doesn't itself regulate commerce; nor is it justified under the Necessary and Proper Clause unless the delegation is both "necessary" and "proper." Many delegations will prove to be not "necessary"[135]—though for this to have bite, one will have to reconsider the modern scope of necessity, possibly going all the way back to *McCulloch v. Maryland*.[136] And most delegations will prove to be "improper," where the standard of propriety includes background constitutional principles of limited government (as illustrated by the precise list of congressional functions in Article I) and divided government (in light of the division of functions between Congress and the president).[137]

Lawson thus places the nondelegation doctrine not in the Article I Vesting Clause but rather in the Necessary and Proper Clause as informed by background principles derived from the overall structure of the document; but his analysis supports the basic structure of the doctrine, even if not its precise doctrinal location.[138]

But if a nondelegation doctrine, limiting anyone but Congress's ability to make binding rules of private conduct, can be traced back

---

[133] See Gary Lawson, Delegation and Original Meaning, 88 Va. L. Rev. 327 (2002); Gary Lawson, Discretion as Delegation: The "Proper" Understanding of the Nondelegation Doctrine, 73 Geo. Wash. L. Rev. 235 (2005); see also Michael B. Rappaport, The Selective Nondelegation Doctrine and the Line Item Veto: A New Approach to the Nondelegation Doctrine and Its Implications for *Clinton v. City of New York*, 76 Tul. L. Rev. 265 (2001).

[134] Lawson, Discretion as Delegation, *supra* note 133, at 238.

[135] *Id.* at 242–48.

[136] 17 U.S. (4 Wheat.) 316 (1819); Lawson, Discretion as Delegation, *supra* note 133, at 248 & n.78 (questioning whether *McCulloch* itself is really as broad as later generations have made it out to be).

[137] Lawson, Discretion as Delegation, *supra* note 133, at 255–67.

[138] *Id.* at 243–44.

to original meaning, does that mean that the limitation is as extreme as Justice Thomas makes it out to be?

Justice Thomas would allow delegations of power to determine the organization of governmental functions, like the grant to the judiciary to determine its rules of procedure upheld in *Wayman v. Southard*.[139] He would apparently also allow delegations, even of the power to make binding rules of private conduct, where the power granted by Congress relates closely enough to core executive functions—as, perhaps, in *United States v. Curtiss-Wright Export Corp.*,[140] where the president was given the power to ban arms sales in connection with the Chaco War between Bolivia and Paraguay if he found that it "may contribute to the reestablishment of peace between" the warring countries.[141]

Justice Thomas would allow delegations of a fact-finding power, like whether France had ceased to violate the neutral commerce of the United States.[142] But even in this category, he holds out the possibility that "fact-finding power" cases like *Field v. Clark* or *J.W. Hampton* were incorrectly decided because they wrongly held that the president was given no discretion.[143]

And in fact, the president certainly held substantial discretionary power in those cases. Modern scholars would be inclined to—correctly—detect discretion and implicit policymaking in most (or all?) fact-finding. Review of formal agency findings of fact under the Administrative Procedure Act,[144] which (roughly speaking) upholds such findings if they could have been made by any reasonable fact finder,[145] has taught us as much, since it recognizes that a broad range of fact-finding can be nonarbitrary. So even most fact-finding delegation should be considered suspect under Justice Thomas's theory. (Conversely, if we try to get around this by just exempting any fact-finding from the nondelegation doctrine—which Justice

---

[139] 23 U.S. (10 Wheat.) 1.

[140] 299 U.S. 304 (1936).

[141] *Id.* at 330–31; see also Rappaport, *supra* note 133, at 353–54.

[142] See text accompanying note 114 *supra*.

[143] AAR II, 135 S. Ct. at 1249 (Thomas, J., concurring in the judgment).

[144] See 5 U.S.C. § 706(2)(A), (E) (2012) (laying out the standard of review for formal agency findings).

[145] See, e.g., Universal Camera Corp. v. NLRB, 340 U.S. 474, 477 (1951); Gary Lawson, Federal Administrative Law 473–75 (6th ed. 2013).

Thomas wouldn't do—one can probably recreate a lot of the status quo in more complicated form: Congress will just reenact a lot of statutes in the form of complex conditional legislation.)

It's not just most or all of the administrative state that becomes suspect: What about the executive branch's authority to prosecute someone who violates a statute? Presumably they're just executing the statute, and the prosecutor's authority is to find the fact that a suspect may have violated the various elements of the statute. But this is precisely the sort of discretion-laden fact-finding power that is suspect. The inconsistency of Justice Thomas's theory with basic functions that would have been accepted at the Founding suggests that his theory is too strict.

But this doesn't mean that a slightly less strict theory isn't viable. In Gary Lawson's view, the nondelegation doctrine "permits Congress to grant discretion with respect to matters ancillary to a statutory scheme but forbids grants of discretion on fundamental matters."[146] This sort of ancillary-fundamental distinction is admittedly hard to apply, but it would accommodate reasonable structural concerns about delegation while at the same time giving Congress realistic flexibility and not requiring it to legislate impossibly precisely.

3. Unpacking the Theory of Private Delegation

Justice Thomas grounds the per se rule against private delegations not just in *Carter Coal*, but in more fundamental considerations of constitutional structure. It's worth unpacking his structural argument, which turns out to be (only) partially right and broader than just the nondelegation doctrine. He writes:

> Although no provision of the Constitution expressly forbids the exercise of governmental power by a private entity, our so-called "private nondelegation doctrine" flows logically from the three Vesting Clauses. Because a private entity is neither Congress, nor the President or one of his agents, nor the Supreme Court or an inferior court established by Congress, the Vesting Clauses would categorically preclude it from exercising the legislative, executive, or judicial powers of the Federal Government. In short, the "private nondelegation doctrine" is merely one application of the provisions of the

[146] Lawson, Discretion as Delegation, *supra* note 133, at 266.

Constitution that forbid Congress to allocate power to an ineligible entity, whether governmental or private.

For this reason, a conclusion that Amtrak is private—that is, not part of the Government at all—would necessarily mean that it cannot exercise these three categories of governmental power.[147]

It's not clear that Justice Thomas's view that Congress may allocate no power outside of the three branches is correct. For instance, federal law incorporates state law quite a lot, from state definitions of spouses and children (for purposes of income taxes or Social Security) to state tort law (for purposes of tort suits against the federal government). By changing their family law or tort law, states can alter one's tax liability and eligibility for federal benefits or expand the scope of the federal government's waiver of its sovereign immunity. Congress has indisputably allocated power to non-federal entities, but it seems inconceivable that dynamically incorporating state law for these sorts of purposes is unconstitutional.

But—ignoring that problem for now—consider the difference between conventional nondelegation doctrine and Justice Thomas's view.

Conventional doctrine agrees that legislative power can never be delegated (though it disagrees with Justice Thomas on what makes a delegation legislative), but the conventional doctrine is based on Article I's Vesting Clause alone—on the principle that Congress can't give up its legislative power.

Here, Justice Thomas is briefly setting forth a complete view of governmental power: each of the three branches is limited to exercising its own distinctive type of power, and no entity outside those branches may exercise any governmental power. A mere Article I-based view would be insufficient to establish that there's a separate doctrine for private delegates. If no one but Congress may establish binding rules of private conduct, what difference should it make whether the maker of such rules is Barack Obama or Bill Gates? Either way, it's a forbidden exercise of legislative power; there's nothing distinctive about the private party.

---

[147] AAR II, 135 S. Ct. at 1252–53 (Thomas, J., concurring in the judgment).

What's doing the work in ruling out private parties is not Article I, but rather Article II (or, in private adjudicator cases, Article III).[148] Private parties can't exercise any delegated power—even if it's nonlegislative, like the power to find facts or make internal governmental rules—because they're not "the President or one of his agents"; that is, they're not part of the executive branch.

In that sense, this discussion resembles Justice Alito's discussion. Recall that Justice Alito (wrongly, in my view) endorsed the private nondelegation doctrine as to the private arbitrator—but then argued that a public arbitrator was likewise invalid because he would exercise significant governmental power without oversight and was thus a principal officer of the United States who must be presidentially appointed with Senate confirmation.[149] It's not an Article I–based theory of how much power Congress can delegate, but an Article II–based theory of who can exercise the delegated power.

But Justice Alito gets the better of this resemblance. Justice Alito was clear: if you're within the executive branch and you exercise significant federal governmental authority, you're an officer, and therefore you need to be properly appointed. Justice Thomas even says so later:

> [T]he Court of Appeals must then determine whether Amtrak is constitutionally eligible to exercise executive power. . . .
>
> As noted, Article II of the Constitution vests the executive power in a "President of the United States of America." Amtrak, of course, is not the President of the United States, but this fact does not immediately disqualify it from the exercise of executive power. Congress may authorize subordinates of the President to exercise such power, so long as they remain subject to Presidential control.
>
> The critical question, then, is whether Amtrak is adequately subject to Presidential control. Our precedents treat appointment and removal powers as the primary devices of executive control, and that should be the starting point of the Court of Appeals' analysis. As Justice Alito's concurrence demonstrates, however, there are other constitutional requirements that the Court of Appeals should also scrutinize

---

[148] Cf. Thomas v. Union Carbide Agric. Prods. Co., 473 U.S. 568 (1985) (involving whether a private arbitrator was granted the Article III judicial power).

[149] See text accompanying note 106, *supra.*

> in deciding whether Amtrak is constitutionally eligible to
> exercise the power [the statute] confers on it.[150]

But note the possible contrast with what he had written in the previous block quotation: "Because a private entity is . . . [not] the President or one of his agents . . . , the [Article II] Vesting Clause[] would categorically preclude it from exercising the . . . executive . . . power[] of the Federal Government. . . . For this reason, a conclusion that Amtrak is private—that is, not part of the Government at all—would necessarily mean that it cannot exercise . . . governmental power."[151]

As a matter of first principles, can a private party *never* be part of the executive branch? Can it *never* be an "agent" or "subordinate" of the president? What if a private party goes through the proper appointment process?[152] Would it be categorically impossible for an entity to be appointed, and does it matter whether it's a Senate confirmation appointment or a vested appointment? Does this have something to do with whether it's possible for an entity to take an oath? (If an entity can't take an oath, what if all the employees of the entity took the oath for as long as the entity exercises the power?)

These are interesting questions[153]—I'm inclined to think that there's nothing wrong in principle with anyone, public or private, being part of the executive branch as long as they're properly appointed—but Justice Thomas doesn't address them, so we end up

---

[150] AAR II, 135 S. Ct. at 1254 (Thomas, J., concurring in the judgment) (citations omitted).

[151] *Id.* at 1252–53. See also text accompanying note 148, *supra.*

[152] Under current doctrine, one isn't an "officer of the United States" subject to the Appointments Clause unless one has a position of "continuing and permanent" employment within the federal government. See United States v. Hartwell, 73 U.S. (6 Wall.) 385, 393 (1868); United States v. Germaine, 99 U.S. 508, 512 (1879); Auffmordt v. Hedden, 137 U.S. 310, 327 (1890). But here we are talking about first principles.

[153] The status of military contracting, prison privatization, and *qui tam* suits is unclear under some super-strong separation-of-powers views. For discussions of possible Appointments Clause issues surrounding privatization, see, e.g., Paul R. Verkuil, Outsourcing Sovereignty: Why Privatization of Government Functions Threatens Democracy and What We Can Do About It 106–13 (2007); Evan Caminker, The Constitutionality of *Qui Tam* Actions, 99 Yale L.J. 341, 374–80 (1989); Neil Kinkopf, Of Devolution, Privatization, and Globalization: Separation of Powers Limits on Congressional Authority to Assign Federal Power to Non-Federal Actors, 50 Rutgers L. Rev. 331 (1998); Jon D. Michaels, Beyond Accountability: The Constitutional, Democratic, and Strategic Problems with Privatizing War, 82 Wash. U. L.Q. 1001, 1070–73 (2004).

with two theories in tension: (1) private parties can never exercise governmental power because they're not part of the government, and (2) a subordinate of the president can exercise executive power if (among other things) he's properly appointed.

The tension could be easily resolved by *defining* "private" as "not properly appointed"; that works when talking about individuals (if you're properly appointed, you're an officer, otherwise you're just a private person), but this isn't how we typically use the word "private" when talking about entities. A profit-making entity whose shares are traded on the stock market and that isn't a "state actor" for constitutional purposes definitely falls within the generally accepted meaning of "private," so it would be strange to have a per se rule against private delegations that *allows* delegations to such an entity if that entity is properly appointed. Certainly defining "private" as "not properly appointed" is not identical to the majority's (and the *Lebron* Court's) list of public-vs.-private factors; one would want to use a word different than "private" to refer to this concept.

Likewise, the tension could be easily resolved by asserting that such a profit-making entity could never be properly appointed under the Appointments Clause, but it's not clear to me that this is correct, and Justice Thomas doesn't engage that question. Indeed, it would seem hard to take this position without begging the question of what it *means* to be private—an issue I've discussed at length elsewhere.[154]

The proper answer to Justice Thomas's endorsement of a per se rule against private delegations is thus: (1) as discussed earlier, *Carter Coal* doesn't establish such a rule, (2) the private prohibition doesn't follow from Justice Thomas's rule against congressional delegation of the power to make binding rules of private conduct, (3) Justice Thomas's view that Congress may not allocate power outside of the three branches is probably incorrect, and (4) any prohibition against private exercise of executive power flows not from a theory of congressional delegation but from a theory of how the executive branch must be constituted—a theory that need not categorically exclude private actors.

---

[154] See Alexander Volokh, Privatization and the Elusive Employee-Contractor Distinction, 46 U.C. Davis L. Rev. 133 (2012).

VI. Conclusion

In the end, *DOT v. Ass'n of American Railroads* is unlikely to have much direct effect. Its decision is the narrowest, most fact-based, most Amtrak-specific decision one could imagine. Its significance lies in what one can divine of the Court's thinking by reading between the lines.

As to Justices Alito and Thomas, not much divining is necessary, since they were considerate enough to tell us their thinking. Unlike Justices Alito and Thomas, the majority neither endorsed nor rejected the D.C. Circuit's *Carter Coal*–based private nondelegation theory. But some language from Chief Justice Roberts's dissent in *Wellness International Network, Ltd. v. Sharif,* a separation-of-powers opinion issued two months later, might give us a clue as to the thinking of some of the other justices. This part of his opinion was joined only by Justice Scalia:

> It is a fundamental principle that no branch of government can delegate its constitutional functions to an actor who lacks authority to exercise those functions. *See Whitman v. American Trucking Ass'ns; Carter v. Carter Coal Co.* Such delegations threaten liberty and thwart accountability by empowering entities that lack the structural protections the Framers carefully devised. *See DOT v. Ass'n of American Railroads* (Alito, J., concurring); *id.* (Thomas, J., concurring in the judgment); *Mistretta v. United States* (Scalia, J., dissenting).[155]

So perhaps there is at least a substantial minority that accepts the D.C. Circuit's theory. The reference to Justice Scalia's dissent in *Mistretta*[156] suggests even another possible (though related) theory: that "a certain degree of discretion, and thus of lawmaking, *inheres* in most executive or judicial action," and that lawmaking is thus "ancillary to" the executive and judicial branch's exercise of their powers.[157] Delegation should thus, in Justice Scalia's view, be considered per se invalid when the recipient of the delegation has no proper executive or judicial powers—as the Sentencing Commission in *Mistretta*. Here, it would be Amtrak, though perhaps one might say that

---

[155] Wellness Int'l Network, Ltd. v. Sharif, 135 S. Ct. 1932, 1957–58 (2015) (Roberts, C.J., dissenting) (citations altered or omitted).

[156] 488 U.S. at 417–22 (Scalia, J., dissenting).

[157] *Id.* at 417.

Amtrak is exercising the executive function of helping to enforce the statutory requirement that private trains yield to Amtrak trains. Whether that executive power is properly exercised now becomes a question for other constitutional provisions like the Appointments Clause—which could make this theory, in the end, much like Justice Alito's.

Even as to the Amtrak case, the resolution is quite limited: the Court has reversed the D.C. Circuit's finding as to Amtrak's public-private nature, while keeping its private nondelegation theory alive for possible use in re-invalidating the scheme based on the arbitrator provision. As Justice Alito points out, the scheme may yet be invalidated on a host of separation-of-powers grounds. And there remains my own favorite, the due process theory: the fundamental unfairness of putting the regulation of an industry in the hands of an entity that has a profit-making interest in the outcome of the regulation.

Looking Ahead: October Term 2015

John P. Elwood and Conor P. McEvily*

If the Supreme Court watchers you know have been looking exhausted recently, there's a reason for that: It's only 2015, and we're already on about our *third* "Term of the Century."[1] The recently completed term has a better claim to that title than most. It not only had more than its share of blockbuster cases that would make any term memorable—same-sex marriage;[2] Obamacare II, Electric Boogaloo;[3]

---

* John P. Elwood is a partner in the D.C. office of Vinson & Elkins LLP, specializing in Supreme Court and appellate litigation. He has argued nine cases before the Supreme Court and previously served both as an assistant to the solicitor general and as senior deputy assistant attorney general in the Office of Legal Counsel. Conor P. McEvily is an appellate associate in the Houston office of Vinson & Elkins. The authors are regular contributors to the semi-humorous and largely factual *Relist Watch* on SCOTUSblog. The authors wish to thank their colleague Lyle Denniston for his invaluable insights about the cases still in the cert. pipeline. See pp. 423–28, *infra*.

[1] The nominees (from the past decade) are: (1) October Term 2011, see, e.g., Adam Liptak, A Significant Term, With Bigger Cases Ahead, N.Y. Times (June 28, 2011) ("'Next term [October Term 2011] is going to be the term of the century,' said Thomas C. Goldstein, a leading Supreme Court advocate and the publisher of Scotusblog."), available at http://goo.gl/tbEjMJ; Bill Mears, Justice Ginsburg Suggests 'Sharp Disagreement' over Hot-Button Cases, CNN (June 16, 2012) (Justice Ginsburg, speaking shortly before Obamacare individual mandate was upheld as a tax, stated that "The term has been more than usually taxing, some have called it the term of the century."), http://goo.gl/y2Avqr; (2) October Term 2012, cf. Kannon K. Shanmugam & James M. McDonald, Looking Ahead: October Term 2012, 2011–2012 Cato Sup. Ct. Rev. 393, 393 (2012) (noting that "many pundits predicted that the 2011 Supreme Court term would be the term of the century" but "the 2012 term looks like it could be even more significant than 2011"; "in October Term 2012, the Court will be jumping from the frying pan into the fire"); and (3) October Term 2014, see Adam Liptak, Supreme Court's Robust New Session Could Define Legacy of Chief Justice, N.Y. Times (Oct. 4, 2014) ("'I'm more excited about the next 12 months at the Supreme Court than about any Supreme Court term in its modern history,' said Thomas C. Goldstein."; "'This term [October Term 2014] could become the "déjà vu all over again" term of the century,' said Pratik A. Shah, a Supreme Court specialist."), available at http://goo.gl/ICKWcX.

[2] Obergefell v. Hodges, 135 S. Ct. 2584 (2015).

[3] King v. Burwell, 135 S. Ct. 2480 (2015).

the constitutionality of independent redistricting;[4] disparate impact under the Federal Housing Act;[5] specialty license plates as government speech;[6] the constitutionality of lethal injection;[7] a campaign-finance law the Roberts Court actually likes;[8] and the first decision ever to "accept[] a President's direct defiance of an Act of Congress in the field of foreign affairs."[9] October Term (OT2014) also marked the best term for liberals since the Warren Court.[10] As a result, the Supreme Court's approval ratings among Republicans hit record lows usually seen only for ISIS, or even teachers' unions, while with Democrats, the Court polled nearly as well as subsidized housing for transgendered baby seals.[11] Some on the left looked past the unusually high percentage of 5–4 decisions this term (26 percent versus just 14 percent for OT2013[12]), and made appreciative comments about how John Roberts really was calling balls and strikes after all.[13]

The coming term has a lot to live up to, and so far, relatively few cases to do it with: just 35 granted as of this writing, versus 39 as OT2014 began and 47 at this point the term before that. But the new term already has more than its share of high-profile cases, and those granted already have observers speculating that it may reverse the leftward drift of the Roberts Court. In the memorable-if-nerdy phrase of one academic commentator, if last term was *Return of the*

---

[4] Ariz. State Legislature v. Ariz. Indep. Redistricting Comm'n, 135 S. Ct. 2652 (2015).

[5] Texas Dep't. of Housing & Cmty. Affairs v. Inclusive Communities Project, Inc., 135 S. Ct. 2507 (2015).

[6] Walker v. Texas Div., Sons of Confederate Veterans, Inc., 135 S. Ct. 2239 (2015).

[7] Glossip v. Gross, 135 S. Ct. 2726 (2015).

[8] Williams-Yulee v. Florida Bar, 135 S. Ct. 1656 (2015).

[9] Zivotofsky v. Kerry, 135 S. Ct. 2076, 2113 (2015) (Roberts, C.J., dissenting).

[10] Alicia Parlapiano, Adam Liptak, & Jeremy Bowers, The Roberts Court's Surprising Move Leftward, N.Y. Times (June 29, 2015), available at http://goo.gl/hLPxqU; see also Adam Liptak, Right Divided, a Disciplined Left Steered the Supreme Court, N.Y. Times (June 30, 2015), available at http://goo.gl/H4lxN8.

[11] Pew Research Center, Negative Views of Supreme Court at Record High, Driven by Republican Dissatisfaction (July 29, 2015), http://goo.gl/TRqDN9.

[12] See Stat Pack, October Term 2014, SCOTUSblog (July 30, 2015), http://goo.gl/gBdExP.

[13] Jeffrey Rosen, John Roberts, the Umpire in Chief, N.Y. Times (June 27, 2015), available at http://goo.gl/jxX9Qg.

Jedi, next term may be *The Empire Strikes Back.*[14] The implications are obvious—and grave. First: October Term 2015 is a term of sequels. Second: If present trends continue, it is only a matter of time before an activist and antidemocratic judiciary inflicts a jurisprudential Jar Jar Binks on the nation.

So what—besides the prospect of a bumbling Gungan buzzkill with an inexplicable Jamaican accent—is causing all the fuss? In the next few pages we aim to tell you a bit about the Court's "coming attractions."

I. First Amendment

Readers familiar with past Terms of the Century may recall OT2011's *Knox v. Service Employees International Union, Local 1000.*[15] That case concerned a fairly narrow question of how to implement *Abood v. Detroit Board of Education,* which held that public-sector unions can bill nonmembers for expenses related to collective bargaining to keep nonmembers from free-riding on the union's efforts on behalf of workers, but unions may not require nonmembers to fund political or ideological efforts.[16] *Knox* involved a public-sector union that imposed a temporary dues increase to fund the union's political operations for an upcoming special election. In an opinion by Justice Samuel Alito, joined by the Court's four other conservatives, the Court held that where a union imposes a special assessment or dues increase levied to meet expenses that were not disclosed when its regular assessment was set, it has to provide a new notice and may not exact additional funds from nonmembers without their affirmative consent. But that was not the half of it. As one pair of halfwits put it:

> Even more significantly, the opinion went on to express skepticism of using compelled assessments even to *finance collective bargaining.* The majority said that compulsory fees for collective bargaining "constitute a form of compelled speech and association that imposes a 'significant impingement on First Amendment rights,'" and the Court's past "tolera[nce]"

[14] Kimberly Robinson, Twitter (July 13, 2015), https://goo.gl/itBnzD (quoting Dean Erwin Chemerinsky of the University of California Irvine School of Law). Yes, we realize that reverses the order of the films, but details should never stand in the way of a good metaphor.

[15] 132 S. Ct. 2277 (2012).

[16] 431 U.S. 209 (1977).

of the practice was an "anomaly." The majority all but invited requests to revisit that line of cases, which could set the stage for a *Citizens United*-style reconsideration in the area of union dues.[17]

Two terms later, the Court in *Harris v. Quinn* (in another opinion authored by Justice Alito) refused to extend *Abood* to personal rehabilitation assistants, and in the process threw enough cold water on *Abood* to fill Lake Erie.[18]

Then, in the waning days of OT2014, the Court granted review in a case, *Friedrichs v. California Teachers Association*, which involves a challenge to California's "agency shop" law. That law requires public-school teachers either to be union members (and thus pay dues) or contribute an equivalent fee to the teachers' union. *Friedrichs* presents the question whether *Abood* should be overruled and public-sector "agency shop" arrangements invalidated under the First Amendment, and whether it violates the First Amendment to require public employees each year to affirmatively *object* to funding the union's political speech rather than requiring employees' affirmative *consent* before such funds can be collected. For the real nerderati, *Friedrichs* also sets something of a record for pre-grant pleadings, with *nine* amicus briefs, *three* briefs in opposition, and *two* reply briefs.

Because a majority of the Court has twice previously expressed skepticism of the continuing validity of *Abood*, the Court seems poised to overrule the case. This Court has a very broad view of free speech, and this is a subject about which the remaining swing justice doesn't, well, swing much. Because the case was decided on motions for judgment on the pleadings, respondents argue the record is inadequate and that arguments against opt-out are premised on facts and issues not presented on this record. It remains to be seen whether those arguments gain traction. If the Court invalidates *Abood*, it could have enormous implications for "[p]ublic sector

---

[17] John Elwood & Eric White, What Were They Thinking: The Supreme Court in Revue, October Term 2011, 15 Green Bag 2d 405, 417 (2012), available at http://goo.gl/fDvxDQ; see also Adam Liptak, With Subtle Signals, Supreme Court Justices Request the Cases They Want to Hear, N.Y. Times (July 6, 2015), available at http://goo.gl/jRiyKm.

[18] 134 S. Ct. 2618 (2014).

unions, which represent one of the last bastions of strong unionism in the U.S."[19] Because nonmembers would no longer have to contribute to the union, and the practical difference between (required) union dues and (opt-in) nonmember fees would be so great, it could prompt "thousands of members" to leave unions, and cost unions "millions of dollars" in dues and fees,[20] causing public-sector unions to "potentially wither into insignificance."[21] The case thus has the potential to be a watershed in labor law.

Check for union seals printed on the covers of amicus briefs. It's likely to be a record number for the 21st century.

II. Equal Protection

There is so much going on in OT2015 that the Equal Protection Clause comes *second*.

Readers familiar with past Terms of the Century may recall OT2012's *Fisher v. University of Texas at Austin*. The case involves equal protection claims raised by Abigal Fisher, a white (now former) student from Sugar Land, Texas, who argues that in 2008, she was denied admission to the University of Texas at Austin ("UT") because of her race.

After the U.S. Court of Appeals for the Fifth Circuit invalidated an earlier UT affirmative-action policy in 1996,[22] the Texas legislature enacted the "Top 10% Law," which required the university to admit any Texas student who graduated in the top 10 percent of his or her high school class. The Top 10% Law still accounts for the vast majority of undergraduate admissions each year (around 80 percent), but after the Supreme Court in *Grutter v. Bollinger* upheld the University of Michigan Law School's use of race as a "plus" factor in admission decisions,[23] UT modified its admissions plan to reintroduce race as a consideration for admitting the portion of the class not filled based

---

[19] Moshe Z. Marvit, The Supreme Court Case That Could Decimate American Public Sector Unionism, In These Times (Feb. 3, 2015), available at http://goo.gl/xSTRvp.

[20] *Id.*

[21] Laura Moser, Why an Upcoming Supreme Court Case Has Teachers' Unions Feeling Very, Very Nervous, Slate (July 8, 2015), http://goo.gl/hRDmkn.

[22] Hopwood v. Texas, 78 F.3d 932 (5th Cir. 1996).

[23] 539 U.S. 306 (2003).

on class rank. This was the basic admissions scheme in place at the time UT denied Fisher's application, and it remains in place today.

During the case's *first* trip through the court system, a Fifth Circuit panel (with Judge Emilio Garza writing separately to note his doubts about the correctness of *Grutter*) upheld UT's admissions system. With Justice Elena Kagan recused (because, as solicitor general, she had approved the Justice Department's decision to support UT as amicus in the lower courts), the Supreme Court granted review. Some 257 days after argument (making it the longest-pending decision of the term by a 47-day margin[24]), the Court issued a 13-page, 7–1 opinion that essentially restated existing law. The opinion stated that the Fifth Circuit had been too deferential to UT and that strict scrutiny requires a showing that the reviewing court must "be satisfied that no workable race-neutral alternatives would produce the educational benefits of diversity."[25] Because it does not take the better part of a year to prepare such a short, straightforward, and largely unanimous opinion, the clear implication—borne out by interviews with the justices—was that earlier iterations of the opinion had gone further, and had done so by a more closely divided (or splintered) vote.[26]

The case returned to the Fifth Circuit, which, by a divided vote, again upheld UT's admissions policy. The majority stated that while Fisher (who in 2012 graduated from Louisiana State University) likely lacked standing because her test scores were low enough that she would not have been admitted even if her race were a plus factor, it was constrained to resolve the case on the merits because the Supreme Court did not "address the issue of standing, although it was squarely presented to it."[27] The majority called UT's program "nearly indistinguishable from the . . . program [upheld] in *Grutter*," and agreed with UT's conclusion that the Top 10% Plan did not produce "sufficient

[24] Stat Pack, October Term 2012, Time Between Oral Argument and Opinion, SCO-TUSblog (June 27, 2013), http://goo.gl/9QEgJC.

[25] 133 S. Ct. 2411, 2420 (2013).

[26] See Joan Biskupic, Breaking In: The Rise of Sonia Sotomayor and the Politics of Justice 201–210 (2014) ("[C]onversations with a majority of justices" indicated that Justice Sonia Sotomayor initially wrote a dissent comparable to the "attention-getting fiery statements that were the trademark of Justice Scalia," but Sotomayor "dropped her dissenting statement" after Kennedy narrowed his majority opinion to "le[ave] intact the central holding of *Grutter*.").

[27] Fisher v. University of Texas at Austin, 758 F.3d 633, 640 (5th Cir. 2014).

numbers of minorities for critical mass" the university said it needed to obtain the benefits of diversity. In other words, the court held that the university "has demonstrated that race-conscious holistic review is necessary to . . . patch[] the holes that a mechanical admissions program leaves in its ability to achieve the rich diversity that contributes to its academic mission."[28] In dissent, Judge Garza wrote that UT had "failed to define th[e] term ['critical mass'] in any objective manner," so it was "impossible to determine whether the University's use of racial classifications in its admissions process is narrowly tailored."[29]

When Fisher again sought cert., the Court relisted the case a whopping *five times*, suggesting that the justices might be attempting a summary disposition of the case or maybe someone was dissenting from denial of review—or perhaps they simply weren't sure they were ready to revisit such a divisive subject. Finally, the Court granted review with the penultimate group of grants before heading out for the summer recess.

Fisher does not seek to revisit *Grutter,* but argues that the Fifth Circuit again failed to apply traditional strict scrutiny and that the record contains no evidence or analysis of students demonstrating that those admitted under the Top 10% Law lack the "unique talents or higher test scores" required to enrich the diversity of the student body such that consideration of race is necessary. Fisher also argues that UT impermissibly adopted a new rationale to defend its program while on remand and that the university should be held to the original rationale it asserted at the time of its adoption. She argues that UT presented no evidence to substantiate an unmet need for "qualitative" diversity, and that such a rationale could not survive strict scrutiny.

Since the Court has gone to the trouble of granting cert. a second time, it seems unlikely that the decision in *Fisher II* will be the nothingburger that the Court's earlier opinion was. It also seems unlikely that the Court will overrule *Grutter,* which would go beyond what Fisher's lawyers have sought in *this* case—although they are separately challenging *Grutter* in actions against Harvard University and the University of North Carolina at Chapel Hill. Instead, the Court likely will provide further guidance (we almost said "clarification")

[28] *Id.* at 653, 657, 659.
[29] *Id.* at 661–62 (Garza, J., dissenting).

on the application of strict scrutiny in education. Picking up on one of Judge Garza's key complaints in dissent, the Court may provide additional guidance on the meaning of "critical mass"—that is, the point at which a college admissions plan produces enough minority students to achieve the academic goal of diversity. Lastly, it is worth noting that Justice Kennedy dissented in *Grutter*, so any further gloss on that decision that has his endorsement may have the effect of making strict scrutiny more exacting.

III. Election Law

The new term is shaping up to be an especially important one in the field of election law.

A. One-Person, One-Vote

In 1964's landmark decision *Reynolds v. Sims*, the Supreme Court held that states must make election districts "as nearly of equal population as is practicable" to ensure equal voting rights under the Fourteenth Amendment.[30] This "one-person, one-vote" principle prevents states from apportioning voting districts along county (or other geographic) lines, heedless of population. Next term's *Evenwel v. Abbott* will resolve a question that seems long overdue, a half-century later: What's a person?

Sims did not specify what the Court meant by "population"—the total population, the population of registered voters, or something else entirely. Two years later, the Court held in *Burns v. Richardson* that Hawaii could use either *total* population or *voting* population in drawing district lines, writing, "The decision to include or exclude any such group involves choices about the nature of representation with which we have been shown no constitutionally founded reason to interfere."[31] There, the Court upheld a plan that drew district lines based on registered voters, but took pains to state that, "We are not to be understood as deciding that the validity of the registered voters basis as a measure has been established for all time or circumstances, in Hawaii or elsewhere."[32] Since then, some thought "[i]t ha[d] been settled . . . that states have discretion" whether to use total

[30] 377 U.S. 533, 577 (1964).

[31] Burns v. Richardson, 384 U.S. 73, 92 (1966).

[32] *Id.* at 96.

population or registered voters in "put[ting] the one-person, one-vote principal into effect."[33] Federal appeals courts have uniformly held that it is *permissible* to use total population. Judge Alex Kozinksi wrote in a 1990 partial dissent that whether one-person, one-vote entailed "representational equality" (equal total populations) or "electoral equality" (equal voting populations) "deserves a more careful examination."[34] In 2001, Justice Clarence Thomas dissented from the Court's denial of cert. to review the redistricting plan in *Chen v. Houston*, writing that the Court "ha[d] an obligation to explain to States and localities what [population] actually means."[35] Saying he had not prejudged the question of which population governed, Justice Thomas noted that districts in *Chen* having a total population variance of less than 10 percent (which is presumptively constitutional under current doctrine) could have a much higher variance among the citizens-of-voting-age population—there, on the order of 20–30 percent.[36]

Petitioners in *Evenwel* say the variance at issue there is more on the order of 30–55 percent. Sue Evenwel and Edward Pfenninger live in rural Texas. They say that rural Texas state senate districts are heavy with registered voters, while more urban districts have fewer, so rural votes are diluted and urban voters have undue sway. While the challengers do not appear to be saying that legislatures should be forever forbidden from using total population as a districting measure, they argue that Texas's current districting "distributes voters or potential voters in a grossly uneven way," denying them equal protection. The case is very significant, particularly in "border states, like California, Texas, Arizona and Nevada, that have the largest proportions of noncitizens."[37] Election law expert Professor Richard Hasen explains, "Urban areas are much more likely to be filled with people who cannot vote: noncitizens (especially Latinos), released

[33] Tierney Sneed, 5 Points on How 'One Person, One Vote' Is Suddenly in Jeopardy, Talking Points Memo (May 27, 2015), http://goo.gl/b9X6Wb (quoting election-law expert Richard L. Hasen).

[34] Garza v. County of Los Angeles, 918 F.2d 763, 784 (9th Cir. 1990) (Kozinski, J., concurring in part and dissenting in part).

[35] 532 U.S. 1046, 1046 (2001) (Thomas, J., dissenting from denial of cert.).

[36] Id.

[37] Adam Liptak, Supreme Court Agrees to Settle Meaning of 'One Person One Vote,' N.Y. Times (May 26, 2015), available at http://goo.gl/NVHtUk.

felons whose voting rights have not been restored, and children."[38] He forecasts that a ruling for petitioners would favor Republicans. Others argue that just as it "was intolerable for a rural district with 500 voters to have the same representation in a state legislature as an urban district with 5000 voters, it's now constitutionally suspect to have that disparity between a heavily (non-citizen) foreign-born district and one with mostly native-born citizens. In each case, the Supreme Court must intervene to maintain voter equality."[39] Some are skeptical that the Court will hold that basing districts on registered voters will be deemed mandatory: they note many states used total population both at the time of the Founding and at the time the Fourteenth Amendment was ratified, and the census no longer collects citizenship information, which would make it difficult to obtain adequate information for redistricting.[40] The case was brought by the Project on Fair Representation,[41] the group behind both *Fisher v. University of Texas* and *Shelby County v. Holder,* which successfully challenged the constitutionality of the Voting Rights Act provision establishing which areas of the country were subject to preclearance before new voting rules could take effect. [42]

Although *Evenwel* involves the districting for state legislatures, which is governed by the Equal Protection Clause of the Fourteenth Amendment, it seems likely that if the challengers are successful, others will argue it should also be applied to drawing congressional districts (not to be confused with apportioning House seats among the states).

B. Redistricting and Preclearance

Readers familiar with past Terms of the Century may recall OT2014's *Arizona State Legislature v. Arizona Independent Redistricting*

---

[38] Richard L. Hasen, Only Voters Count? Conservatives Ask the Supreme Court to Restrict States' Rights and Overturn Precedent, Slate (May 26, 2015), http://goo.gl/CJODGE.

[39] Ilya Shapiro, Symposium: Taking Voter Equality Seriously, SCOTUSblog (July 29, 2015), http://goo.gl/WrVyBT.

[40] See Richard Pildes, Symposium: Misguided Hysteria over Evenwel v. Abbott, SCOTUSblog (July 30, 2015), http://goo.gl/ZPNSqV.

[41] See Project on Fair Representation, Our Cases, https://goo.gl/YZoGtJ (last visited Aug. 17, 2015).

[42] 133 S. Ct. 2612 (2013).

Commission, in which the Court, by a 5–4 vote, held that Arizona voters' decision to amend their state constitution by referendum to entrust redistricting to an independent districting commission, instead of the legislature itself, was constitutional.[43] Just one day later, the Court noted probable jurisdiction in *Harris v. Arizona Independent Redistricting Commission,* an appeal that alleges that the commission wrongly used race and partisanship in drawing Arizona's state legislative district boundaries in the wake of the 2010 Census.

A group of 11 Republican Arizona voters brought suit, arguing, in relevant part, that the commission's maps, which were used in 2012 state elections, violated the "one person, one vote" requirement by packing Republican voters into districts to enhance minority voter strength in other, relatively underpopulated districts. The challengers emphasized that all but one Republican-leaning district has *more* voters than the ideal district size (thus diluting each voter's power), while all but two Democratic-leaning districts have *fewer* voters than ideal (thus enhancing each voter's power).

A divided three-judge district court rejected the challenge. The courts' two appellate judges (Richard Clifton, a George W. Bush appointee, largely joined by Roslyn O. Silver, a Clinton appointee) held that the redistricting was constitutional, concluding that "the population deviations were primarily a result of good-faith efforts" "to obtain preclearance [of the redistricting scheme] from the Department of Justice" before its plan could be used for the then-upcoming elections, consistent with the requirement of Section 5 of the Voting Rights Act for covered jurisdictions (those with a history of voting discrimination).[44] The majority noted that "[m]ost of the underpopulated districts have significant minority populations," and to obtain preclearance, "the Commission had to show that any proposed changes" would not violate the Voting Rights Act's "anti-retrogression" principle—that is, they would not "diminish the ability of minority groups to elect the candidates of their choice."[45] The commission believed that the Justice Department was under the impression that under the previous district scheme, there were 10 districts where

---

[43] 135 S. Ct. 2652 (2015).

[44] Harris v. Ariz. Indep. Redistricting Comm'n, 993 F. Supp. 2d 1042, 1046–47 (D. Ariz. 2014).

[45] *Id.* at 1047.

minorities were able to elect the candidate of their choice, and so to obtain preclearance, it would be advisable to create a 10th such district in their plan.[46] To do so, the commission increased overpopulation in two districts. To further increase the chances of preclearance, the commission then underpopulated some districts and overpopulated others to make an *11th* district closer to a minority ability-to-elect district. While the majority concluded that "[p]artisanship may have played some role" in district lines (mainly, the majority concluded, because one Democratic commissioner sought to make one district more politically competitive), "the primary motivation was [a] legitimate" desire to obtain preclearance so the district lines could be used in upcoming elections.[47] The majority acknowledged that the Supreme Court's 2013 decision in *Shelby County v. Holder* had invalidated the coverage formulas governing Section 5 preclearance, so Arizona voting plans were no longer subject to preclearance, but concluded that obtaining preclearance was still a legitimate objective at the time the maps were drawn.

Judge Silver concurred in part, dissented in part, and concurred in the judgment, to emphasize that the challengers had failed to prove partisanship motivated changes, and also noted that after the redistricting, Republicans were overrepresented in the legislature in proportion to party registration.

The Court's decision to grant review has to have been driven in substantial part by the powerful opinion of District Judge Neil V. Wake (a George W. Bush appointee) concurring in part, dissenting in part, and dissenting from the judgment. He emphasized that "[o]f 30 legislative districts, the 18 with population deviation greater than ±2% from ideal population correlate perfectly with Democratic Party advantage," and that "the statistics of their plan are conclusive."[48] He argued that seeking Voting Rights Act preclearance "is insufficient as a matter of law" to justify population deviations in districting, saying that "[p]ending civil cases must be decided in accordance with current law," under which Arizona is no longer subject

---

[46] *Id.* at 1056–57.

[47] *Id.* at 1060–61.

[48] *Id.* at 1092 (Wake, J., concurring in part, dissenting in part, and dissenting from the judgment).

to Section 5 preclearance.[49] In a passage that seems likely to resonate with the four justices who subscribed to Chief Justice Roberts' statement that "[t]he way to stop discrimination on the basis of race is to stop discriminating on the basis of race,"[50] Judge Wake argued that it was categorically illegitimate to deviate from population equality in an effort to obtain preclearance, saying, "there is no basis in statutory text, administrative interpretation, or precedent . . . to systematically dilute people's equal voting rights for any reason, least of all as a protection of equal voting rights."[51] He accused the commission of "coin-clipping the currency of our democracy—everyone's equal vote—and giving all the shavings to one party, for no valid reason."[52]

The Court has agreed to review (1) whether the constitution permits intentionally overpopulating legislative districts to gain partisan advantage and (2) whether the desire to obtain preclearance justifies deviating from the one-person, one-vote principle. Two days after noting probable jurisdiction in the case, the Court amended its order to state that it would not review the third question the challengers had presented, which asked whether it was constitutional to overpopulate Republican districts to create districts in which Hispanics would have greater electoral influence. While both (1) and (2) may be the subject of questioning at argument, it seems likely that if the case goes against Arizona, the opinion will center on preclearance. Seeking partisan advantage is a much more complex question—with, one imagines, a fairly substantial historical pedigree. Meanwhile, preclearance is already wounded after *Shelby County*.

IV. Federal Jurisdiction

The law of Article III standing is like *Star Trek*: Those who care about it care *a lot*—and everyone else thinks those people are dorks.

---

[49] *Id.* at 1100.

[50] Parents Involved in Cmty. Schools v. Seattle Schl. Dist. No. 1, 127 S. Ct. 2738, 2768 (2006) (plurality opinion).

[51] Harris, 993 F. Supp. 2d at 1102 (Wake, J., concurring in part, dissenting in part, and dissenting from the judgment).

[52] *Id.* at 1092.

A. Injury

Like *Star Trek*, *Spokeo, Inc. v. Robins*, is one installment in a series. *Spokeo* is "The Wrath of Khan"[53] to *First American Financial Corp v. Edwards's*[54] "The Motion Picture."[55] Readers familiar with past Terms of the Century may recall that OT2011's *First American* presented the question whether a technical violation of a federal statute satisfies the injury-in-fact requirement for Article III standing—or, to put it differently, whether Congress can by legislation confer Article III standing upon a plaintiff who suffers no concrete harm by authorizing a private right of action based on a bare violation of a federal statute. *First American* asked whether Congress could create a cause of action under the Real Estate Settlement Procedures Act of 1974 ("RESPA," which gave us the HUD-1 Form every homeowner pretends to read at closing) for buyers of real-estate settlement services for statutory violations that do not affect the price, quality, or other characteristics of the transaction. *First American* was argued in November 2011 and the majority opinion was apparently assigned to Justice Thomas (the only justice with no majority opinion from that sitting); but on the last day of the term (213 days later—the term's longest-pending case by an 18-day margin[56]), the Court dismissed the case as improvidently granted in a one-sentence order.

Four terms later, the Court apparently has recovered from whatever unpleasantness transpired and is ready to face the issue once again. *Spokeo* involves whether a bare violation of the Fair Credit Reporting Act is enough to establish Article III standing. Respondent Thomas Robins instituted a putative class action against Spokeo, operator of a "people search engine" that aggregates publicly available information, saying that Spokeo search results associated with his name falsely indicated that he has more education and professional experience than he actually has, that he is married, and that he is wealthier than he is. Robins claims that this misinformation—which in the pre-digital age was the *sole purpose* of class reunions—harmed his employment prospects and caused him anxiety and stress.

[53] See Stak Trek II: The Wrath of Khan (1982); see also *id.* ("Khaaaaan!!").

[54] No. 10-708, October Term 2011.

[55] Star Trek: The Motion Picture (1979).

[56] Stat Pack, October Term 2011, Days Between Oral Argument and Opinion, SCOTUSblog (June 30, 2013), http://goo.gl/1voOIK.

Spokeo countered that he had not suffered any actual concrete harm, just speculative anxiety and concern about what might happen. The district court dismissed his claims on the grounds that he had not alleged any actual or imminent harm, but the U.S. Court of Appeals for the Ninth Circuit reversed. After Spokeo petitioned for certiorari, the Court sought the views of the solicitor general, who recommended that the Court deny cert. In part of what at least *feels* like a trend, the Court departed from its usual practice of following the SG's denial recommendation and granted review.[57]

The issue may sound like the classic dispute about whether Kirk or Picard is better. But the case has tremendous practical importance—as demonstrated by the remarkable 10 amicus briefs supporting Spokeo filed at the cert stage, and 17 at the merits stage—because it is poised to determine the extent to which Congress can give people who have not suffered a traditional "injury" a right to sue. Just don't try explaining to a layperson why the case is important; it's like bragging that you speak Klingon.

B. Mootness

Campbell-Ewald Company v. Gomez involves a lingering question of the federal courts' jurisdiction: whether a defendant's offer to settle a lawsuit for everything the named plaintiff is seeking renders a case moot. If there is only one party suing to advance a claim, some federal courts have ruled that if there is an offer to give the plaintiff everything he or she is seeking, that ends the case, whether the party accepts the offer or not—the theory is that the plaintiff has won and has no cognizable legal interest in pursuing the case, even if she won't take "yes" for an answer. Cutting the other way (in federal court at least) is Federal Rule of Civil Procedure 68, which provides that "[a]n unaccepted [settlement] offer is considered withdrawn." And some courts have held that when the lawsuit is brought on behalf of a putative class as well as the named plaintiff, the case remains live despite the settlement offer because the absent class plaintiffs have live

---

[57] David C. Thompson & Melanie F. Wachtell, An Empirical Analysis of Supreme Court Certiorari Petition Procedures: The Call for Response and the Call for the Views of the Solicitor General, 16 Geo. Mason L. Rev. 237, 276 (2009) (noting Court historically denied cert. in 75 percent of cases in which the solicitor general recommended denial during 1998–2000 and 83 percent during 2001–2004).

concerns.[58] The question is of obvious interest both to corporations (which have a strong interest in having suits dismissed, especially class actions) and the people who sue them (who have a strong interest in maximizing recovery and, not incidentally, their fees).

Enter Campbell-Ewald Company, an advertising agency that conducts recruiting campaigns for the U.S. Navy. The agency developed a recruiting text message and sent it to 150,000 cell phones, and surpassed all expectations by yielding five recruits, seven online stalkers, 15 marriage proposals, and 149,973 lawsuits. Respondent Jose Gomez received the Navy's call to service and was so moved that he immediately enlisted . . . the assistance of counsel to commence a class-action lawsuit under the Telephone Consumer Protection Act. Campbell-Ewald offered Gomez $1503 per text message he received and stipulated to an injunction prohibiting it from sending more such messages—more than matching the statutory $500 per violation (with trebling) and injunctive relief Gomez could obtain if he prevailed in the litigation. Nevertheless, this was an offer Gomez could (and did) refuse. The district court held that the offer had not mooted Gomez's claims, but granted Campbell-Ewald summary judgment, concluding that because it was acting as a Navy contractor, it was entitled to derivative sovereign immunity. On appeal, the Ninth Circuit agreed that the claim was not moot, but reversed the sovereign immunity ruling, holding that derivative sovereign immunity applied only in the context of property damage resulting from public works projects.

Campbell-Ewald asks (1) whether a case becomes moot when the plaintiff receives an offer of complete relief on his claim; (2) whether a case becomes moot when the plaintiff has asserted a class claim but receives an offer of complete relief before any class is certified; and (3) whether the doctrine of sovereign immunity recognized for government contractors in *Yearsley v. W.A. Ross Construction Co.*[59] is restricted to claims arising out of property damage caused by public works projects. If the first two questions sound familiar, it's either an obscure neurological condition affecting the brain's FedJur cortex, or you're a reader familiar with past Terms of the Century

---

[58] See, e.g., Stein v. Buccaneers Ltd. P'ship, 772 F.3d 698, 704–09 (11th Cir. 2014); Lucero v. Bureau of Collection Recovery, Inc., 639 F.3d 1239, 1247–50 (10th Cir. 2011).

[59] 309 U.S. 18 (1940).

who recalls OT2012's *Genesis Healthcare Corp. v. Symczyk*.[60] *Genesis* sought to resolve those questions, but the Court could not reach the question because Symczyk (coincidentally, Polish for "my type-writer's jammed!") had conceded before the court of appeals that an unaccepted-but-fully-satisfactory Rule 68 offer renders a claim moot.[61] *Genesis* went off on a 5–4 vote split along ideological lines, with Justice Kagan writing a clever if vituperative dissent that force-fully argued that an unaccepted settlement offer can never moot a case (and inviting the reader to "relegate the majority's decision to the furthest reaches of your mind"[62]). The Court's four liberals have solidly staked out their position; the question remains whether this famously disciplined group[63] can peel off the one conservative vote it will take to make a majority.

V. Class Actions

Although the Court has in recent terms taken an active interest in delineating limits to class actions under Federal Rule of Civil Proce-dure 23, the area remains "a messy corner of the law,"[64] where "the Supreme Court and the lower courts appear out of step."[65] In *Tyson Foods, Inc. v. Bouaphakeo*, the Court aims to clear up two recurring issues: (1) whether damages for class members can be determined using statistical sampling techniques, and (2) whether a class may be certified that contains members who were not injured.

Plaintiffs are current and former employees at Tyson's Storm Lake, Iowa, pork-processing plant, who work in occupations whose names are not likely to make you crave a ham sandwich: "Slaughter" and "Fabrication." (Fabrication?) Such employees must wear (or wield) various professional accouterments—hard hats, hair nets, smocks, mesh sleeves, knives, scabbards, and, ominously, "belly guards,"

---

[60] 133 S. Ct. 1523 (2013).

[61] *Id.*

[62] *Id.* at 1533 (Kagan, J., dissenting).

[63] Adam Liptak, Right Divided, a Disciplined Left Steered the Supreme Court, N.Y. Times (June 30, 2015), available at http://goo.gl/IdseLi.

[64] Editorial, Class Action Spring Cleaning, Wall. St. J. (June 12, 2015), available at http://goo.gl/WqbhyY.

[65] Tim Bishop, Archis A. Parasharami, & Chad Clamage, Supreme Court to Revisit Class-Certification Standards in Tyson Foods, Inc. v. Bouaphakeo, Class Defense Blog (June 8, 2015), https://goo.gl/NPAVK6.

raising the fundamental question whether the guard protects the belly in question or those within its gravitational field. Tyson paid its employees for a fixed amount of extra time each day (around four to eight minutes) to compensate workers for "donning" and "doffing" their occupational garb. In 2007, plaintiffs filed a class action claiming that Tyson failed to adequately compensate them for overtime work spent donning and doffing, in violation of both the Fair Labor Standards Act ("FLSA") and a related Iowa statute. Plaintiffs successfully moved for class certification under Federal Rule 23(b)(3) (and for a collective action under the FLSA). After the Court issued its landmark decision in *Wal-Mart Stores, Inc. v. Dukes*, which reemphasized that class actions could be certified only when "questions of law or fact common to the class" "predominate over any questions affecting only individual members"[66] (and disapproving of "trial by formula," determining liability for a "sample set" of class members and then "appl[ying it] to the entire remaining class"[67]), the plaintiffs successfully opposed decertification.

Invoking *Wal-Mart*, Tyson took aim at two experts used to prove and measure plaintiffs' alleged damages: the first measured how much time a sample of employees took for donning/doffing-related activities, and used those figures to arrive at averages for both Fabrication and Slaughter employees (18 and 21 minutes, respectively); the second, assuming that all class members spent this average amount of time donning/doffing their equipment (the 18 and 21 minutes), used a computer program to determine how much overtime compensation would be due to an employee if he or she was credited for the average donning/doffing time each workday. Tyson protested that this was precisely the type of "trial by formula" that *Wal-Mart* prohibited and vitiated Tyson's right to demonstrate that *individual* members were not entitled to overtime pay. Subsequent trial testimony showed that (1) Tyson employees wore different equipment, depending on their job; (2) Tyson employees donned and doffed this equipment in different order, and in different places; and (3) over 200 employees appeared to suffer no injury at all because even adding up the average donning/doffing time did not result in these employees working uncompensated "overtime" (that is, over 40 hours in a

66 Fed. R. Civ. P. 23(a), (b)(3).
67 131 S. Ct. 2541, 2561 (2011).

single week). Nevertheless, the trial court denied Tyson's motions for decertification and entered a nearly $6 million judgment for the plaintiffs.

The U.S. Court of Appeals for the Eighth Circuit affirmed, over the dissent of Judge C. Arlen Beam. Though the appellate court acknowledged that plaintiffs "rel[ied] on inference from average donning [and] doffing" times, it reasoned that, because Tyson had a "specific company policy" that applied to all class members, and the class members worked at the same plant, "this inference was allowable under [the Supreme Court's decision in] *Anderson v. Mt. Clemens Pottery Co.*"[68] The court likewise rejected Tyson's argument that decertification was necessary because evidence showed that some class members suffered no harm.

Before the Supreme Court, Tyson points to "undisputed evidence" showing substantial variance in the time employees spent in donning/doffing-related activities, and contends that plaintiffs cannot "prove" liability and damages using statistical evidence that presumes that all class members are identical to the average observed in a sample. Regarding the question of uninjured plaintiffs, Tyson draws on the holding of *Lujan v. Defenders of Wildlife*[69] to argue that Rule 23 must be interpreted consistently with the basic Article III requirement that plaintiffs who invoke federal courts' jurisdiction must establish that they have standing to sue under the "case or controversy" requirement. Rule 23, Tyson says, is a limited procedural device for aggregating liability and damages claims; it should not be used to expand federal court jurisdiction and compensate individuals who have suffered no injury, lack Article III standing, and are entitled to no damages.

The case is still being briefed, but plaintiffs' best argument so far may be the Court's nearly 70-year-old *Mt. Clemens* FLSA decision that the Eighth Circuit invoked to uphold class certification. There, the Court held that where an employer has failed to keep records of time worked, "an employee has carried out his burden [in seeking overtime] if he proves that he has in fact performed work for which he was improperly compensated and if he produces sufficient

---

[68] Bouaphakeo v. Tyson Foods, Inc., 765 F.3d 791, 797 (8th Cir. 2014) (citing 328 U.S. 680 (1946)).

[69] 504 U.S. 555 (1992).

evidence to show the amount and extent of that work *as a matter of just and reasonable inference.*"[70] Plaintiffs contend that *Mt. Clemens* used the "just and reasonable inference" principle to allow 300 employees in a FLSA collective action to make out a claim based on the representative testimony of eight employees whose estimates of uncompensated time spent walking to work stations ranged from 30 seconds to 8 minutes, and where walking distances varied from 130 feet to 890 feet. A similar result should follow here because Tyson failed to keep the requisite records. For its part, Tyson italicizes a different portion of this *Mt. Clemens* quote to suggest individualized proof is required: "*he* . . . performed work for which *he* was improperly compensated."[71]

This is a question that arises constantly. *Tyson* was just one of at least three cases raising similar issues about resort to statistics and allegedly unharmed class members vying for a spot on OT2015's docket; that means that even if *this* case is resolved based on the peculiarities of FLSA collective actions, there are other cases behind it in line to serve as vehicles to address any distinct Rule 23 question.[72] All eyes will be on the justices during argument—and not just to watch them try to pronounce the lead plaintiff's name (which, if you're buying vowels, is a much more expensive proposition than "Symczyk"). But on that score, it can't hold a candle to the league-leader from a prior Term of the Century, OT2011's epic *Match-E-Be-Nash-She-Wish Band of Pottawatomi Indians v. Patchak*, which the chief justice may have rehearsed more than the oath of office.[73]

---

[70] Anderson v. Mt. Clemens Pottery Co., 328 U.S. 680, 687 (1946).

[71] Cert. Pet. at 19, Tyson Foods, Inc. v. Bouaphakeo (No. 14-1146).

[72] Among the other cases were: Wal-Mart Stores v. Braun, involving a $187 million judgment entered on behalf of a certified class of 187,000 Wal-Mart employees who claimed that they had not been paid for rest breaks and off-the-clock work; Dow Chemical v. Industrial Polymers, arising from a $1.1 billion judgment in an antitrust class action alleging coordinated price announcements; and Allstate Insurance Co. v. Jimenez, also involving unpaid overtime. See John Elwood, Relist Watch, SCOTUSblog (May 29, 2015), http://goo.gl/9wI0t4. With the exception of Allstate (in which the Court denied cert. in June), the other cases appear to remain on hold until a decision is rendered in Tyson.

[73] Barack Obama Oath of Office, YouTube, Jan. 20, 2009, https://goo.gl/iq3CUg.

VI. Criminal Law

A. *Right to Counsel*

Our next case involves a subject close to every attorney's heart: making sure the lawyer gets paid. The Court touched on this issue in OT2013's *Kaley v. United States*, but the seminal cases were decided 25 years ago on the same day: *United States v. Monsanto* and *Caplin & Drysdale, Chartered v. United States*.

All three cases involved 21 U.S.C. § 853, a federal forfeiture statute authorizing a court to freeze a convicted or indicted defendant's assets under certain circumstances. In *Caplin & Drysdale*, the Court rejected arguments that, under the Sixth Amendment or the Fifth Amendment's Due Process Clause, money a *convicted* defendant has agreed to pay his attorney *from tainted assets* is exempt from forfeiture: "A defendant has no [constitutional] right to spend another person's money for services rendered by an attorney, even if those funds are the only way that that defendant will be able to retain the attorney of his choice."[74] *Monsanto*, in turn, held that, *even before* trial, when the presumption of innocence still applies, the government may constitutionally use Section 853 to freeze assets of an indicted defendant "based on a finding of probable cause to believe that the property will ultimately be proved forfeitable."[75] As a practical matter, that determination requires a two-part inquiry: first, whether there is probable cause to think a defendant has committed an offense permitting forfeiture; and second, whether there is probable cause that the property has the requisite criminal connection. "[I]f the Government may, post-trial, forbid the use of forfeited assets to pay an attorney, then surely no constitutional violation occurs when, after probable cause is adequately established, the Government obtains an order, barring a defendant from frustrating that end by dissipating his assets prior to trial."[76]

Neither *Monsanto* nor *Caplin & Drysdale* considered whether the Due Process Clause requires a hearing to establish probable cause—though, in the wake of those decisions, most courts did. (Section 853 itself is silent on the matter.) Lower courts split on whether, at

[74] 491 U.S. 617, 626 (1989).
[75] 491 U.S. 600, 615 (1989).
[76] *Id.* at 616.

such a hearing, criminal defendants are constitutionally entitled to contest the first prong of the *Monsanto* inquiry—a grand jury's prior determination of probable cause to believe the defendant committed the crimes charged. In *Kaley*, the Court held by a 6–3 vote that indicted defendants "cannot challenge the grand jury's conclusion that probable cause supports the charges against them."[77] Justice Kagan's majority decision drew a dissent from Chief Justice Roberts, who (joined by Justices Stephen Breyer and Sonia Sotomayor) faulted the majority for failing to explain "why the District Court may reconsider the grand jury's probable cause finding as to traceability [of the asset to a crime] . . . but may not do so as to the underlying charged offense."[78] The chief justice argued that the "Court's opinion pays insufficient respect to the importance of an independent bar as a check on prosecutorial abuse and governing."[79]

Fast forward to OT2015. The same attorney who argued *Kaley* is back with *Luis v. United States*, this time to determine whether it matters that the assets to be used for paying the lawyer are "untainted"—that is, not connected to the commission of a crime.[80] The case implicates a different (if similar) statute. Like Section 853, 18 U.S.C. § 1345 authorizes the government to initiate a civil action in order to "preserve the defendant's assets until a judgment requiring restitution or forfeiture can be obtained."[81] But unlike Section 853, Section 1345 authorizes the court to enter an order restraining "property, obtained as a result of a banking law violation . . . or property

[77] 134 S. Ct. 1090, 1105.

[78] *Id.* at 1108 (Roberts, C.J., dissenting).

[79] *Id.* at 1107, 1114 (quoting United States v. Gonzales-Lopez, 548 U.S. 140, 147–48 (2006)).

[80] Fear not: He has other clients who are permitted to pay him. The same attorney has succeeded (so far at least) in preventing the public release of photos of Justin Bieber "reliebing" himself by the roadside after his DUI arrest. Although, however much an attorney is paid for such a representation, it remains in some deeper sense work done *pro bono publico*. See David Ovalle, Justin Bieber's Privates Will Remain Private for Now as Miami-Dade Judge Weighs Public Urination Footage, Miami Herald (Feb. 19, 2014), available at http://goo.gl/JrUano (noting that "footage" of incident will remain sealed while the judge reviews the videos in chambers; in unrelated news, judicial internship applications from Miami middle school students have soared); see also https://goo.gl/6KffC8 (videotape of hearing).

[81] United States v. DBB, Inc., 180 F.3d 1277, 1284 (11th Cir. 1999).

which is traceable to such violation ... *or property of equivalent value.*"[82] The *Luis* trial court held that the "equivalent value" language meant "that when some of the assets that were obtained as a result of fraud cannot be located, a person's substitute, *untainted* assets may be restrained instead."[83] The U.S. Court of Appeals for the Eleventh Circuit affirmed, in tension with a Fourth Circuit holding that under Section 853, a defendant "still possesses a qualified Sixth Amendment right to use wholly legitimate funds to hire the attorney of his choice."[84]

In support of her argument that the Fifth and Sixth Amendments prohibit pretrial restraint of a criminal defendant's untainted assets needed to retain counsel of choice, the petitioner notes that, in all of the Court's cases addressing the constitutionality of restraining and forfeiting funds earmarked for attorneys' fees, those assets have been tainted; and indeed, *Kaley* emphasized that fact.[85] Cases involving untainted assets thus do not implicate the oft-repeated maxim that a defendant "'has no Sixth Amendment right to spend another person's money' for legal fees."[86] Luis concedes that, under the "relation-back" doctrine, the government has a vested interest in property tainted by virtue of being traceable to, or instrumentalities of, a crime. But no aspect of the Court's prior holdings, Luis contends, suggests that pretrial restraint of *untainted* assets would meet a similar fate. Luis's petition is seasoned with appeals to both English common law and the Framers' intent—catnip for the originalists, part-time originalists, and even "faint hearted" originalists on the Court.[87] Frequently referenced in the argument is the hypothetical bank robber who uses his ill-gotten proceeds to cover legal costs,

[82] 18 U.S.C. § 1345(a)(2)(B)(i) (emphasis added).

[83] United States v. Luis, 966 F. Supp. 2d 1321, 1325 (S.D. Fla. June 21, 2013) (emphasis added).

[84] United States v. Farmer, 274 F.3d 800, 804 (4th Cir. 2001).

[85] See Kaley, 134 S. Ct. at 1097 ("[N]o one contests that the assets in question derive from, or were used in committing, the offenses.").

[86] *Id.* at 1029 (quoting Caplin & Drysdale, 491 U.S. at 626).

[87] Antonin Scalia, Originalism: The Lesser Evil, 57 U. Cin. L. Rev. 849, 862 (1989) ("It is, I think, the fact that most originalists are faint-hearted."). But see Jenifer Senior, In Conversation: Antonin Scalia, New York Magazine (Oct. 6, 2013), available at http://nymag.com/news/features/antonin-scalia-2013-10/# (Senior: "You've described yourself as a fainthearted originalist. But really, how fainthearted?" Scalia: "I described myself as that a long time ago. I repudiate that.").

who made his first appearance in *Caplin & Drysdale*, and was later revived by Justice Kagan in her majority opinion in *Kaley*. Something tells me we haven't heard the last of this guy.

If the government is able to restrain untainted assets needed to pay counsel, it could have a far more sweeping effect on defendants than *Monsanto* and *Caplin & Drysdale*, because it could deprive them of all assets to retain a lawyer.

B. Capital Punishment

Cases involving the death penalty will be especially closely watched in October Term 2015, in the wake of last term's contentious lethal-injection case *Glossip v. Gross*, which saw two more members of the Court express the view that the death penalty is likely categorically unconstitutional.[88] But the new term finds the Court continuing to "tinker with the machinery of death."[89]

In OT2001's *Ring v. Arizona*,[90] the Court held that the Sixth Amendment jury trial guarantee, as construed by *Apprendi v. New Jersey*,[91] requires jurors and not judges to find aggravating circumstances that justify imposing the death penalty. Ever since, Florida's capital sentencing scheme has seemed, like Florida itself,[92] precariously positioned. Nevertheless, the scheme has fended off

---

[88] See Glossip v. Gross, 135 S. Ct. 2726, 2756 (2015) (Breyer, J., dissenting) ("[T]he death penalty, in and of itself, now likely constitutes a legally prohibited 'cruel and unusual punishment[].'"); accord Baze v. Rees, 553 U.S. 35, 86 (2008) (Stevens, J., concurring in the judgment) ("[T]he imposition of the death penalty represents the pointless and needless extinction of life . . . . A penalty with such negligible returns to the state [is] patently excessive and cruel and unusual punishment violative of the Eighth Amendment." (internal quotations omitted)); Callins v. Collins, 510 U.S. 1141, 1145–46 (1994) (Blackmun, J., dissenting) ("[T]he inevitability of factual, legal, and moral error gives us a system that we know must wrongly kill some defendants, a system that fails to deliver the fair, consistent, and reliable sentences of death required by the Constitution.").

[89] Callins, 510 U.S. at 1145 (Blackmun, J., dissenting).

[90] 536 U.S. 584 (2002).

[91] 530 U.S. 466 (2000).

[92] See Michael Kuhne, Will This Season Bring an End to Florida's Decade-Long Hurricane Drought?, AccuWeather.com (June 3, 2015), http://www.accuweather.com/en/weather-news/florida-decade-hurricane-drought-atlantic-2015/47137699 (noting that Florida "has been hit by seven of the [ten] most costly and damaging hurricanes in U.S. history").

13 years of Sixth Amendment attacks post-*Ring*.[93] That streak may be coming to an end.

The Court granted cert. in *Ring* to "allay uncertainty in the lower courts caused by the manifest tension between *Walton* [*v. Arizona*] and the reasoning of *Apprendi*."[94] In *Walton*, rendered in 1990, the Court held that it was permissible under the Sixth Amendment to allow a trial judge, sitting alone, to determine the presence or absence of aggravating factors supporting imposition of the death penalty.[95] *Walton* drew support from *Hildwin v. Florida*, which had, by summary affirmance, upheld that state's sentencing scheme, under which the jury enters an advisory sentence the judge is free to override, "without a specific finding by the jury that sufficient aggravating circumstances exist to qualify the defendant for capital punishment."[96] But a decade after *Walton*, the Court declared in *Apprendi* that the Sixth Amendment does not allow a defendant to be "expose[d] to ... a penalty exceeding the maximum he would receive if punished according to the facts reflected in the jury verdict alone."[97] While *Apprendi* papered over the tension with *Walton*, two terms later, the Court explicitly held in *Ring* that "the Sixth Amendment's jury trial guarantee ... requires that the aggravating factor determination be entrusted to the jury," and "overrule[d] *Walton* to the extent that it allows a sentencing judge, sitting without a jury, to find an aggravating circumstance necessary for imposition of the death penalty."[98]

That brings us to next term's *Hurst v. Florida*, which asks "[w]hether Florida's death sentencing scheme violates the Sixth Amendment or the Eighth Amendment in light of ... *Ring*."[99] Hurst, who was convicted of murdering a co-worker at Popeye's Fried Chicken, notes that in addition to providing the jury only an advisory role in sentencing, Florida law requires only a majority vote

---

[93] See, e.g., Peterson v. State, 94 So. 3d 514, 538 (Fla. 2012) ("We have consistently rejected claims that Florida's death penalty statute is unconstitutional" under *Ring*.).

[94] Ring, 536 U.S. at 596.

[95] 497 U.S. 639, 649 (1990).

[96] 490 U.S. 638, 640–41 (1989) (per curiam).

[97] 530 U.S. 466, 483 (2000).

[98] 536 U.S. 584, 597, 609 (2002).

[99] Hurst v. Florida, 147 So.3d 435 (Fla. 2014), cert. granted, 135 S. Ct. 1531 (U.S. March 9, 2015) (No. 14-7505).

is necessary for a jury's recommendation of death—and even then, the jurors need not agree on *which* aggravators are present, nor do they make express findings on aggravating circumstances. The trial judge typically conducts a separate hearing in which he may consider evidence, arguments, and aggravators that were not presented to the jury. If a court imposes the death sentence, it renders its findings in writing; and these findings, rather than the jury's verdict, furnish the basis of the Florida Supreme Court's review.[100] Hurst argues that by assigning the fact-finding responsibilities to a court, rather than to a jury, Florida's capital-sentencing scheme contravenes *Ring*. Hurst also claims the Eighth Amendment requires the death penalty to be imposed by a jury, which embodies "the community's moral sensibility." Finally, Hurst claims that even if Florida's scheme does satisfy *Ring*, his death sentence violates the Sixth and Eighth Amendments for other reasons, including: the misleading minimization of the jury's sense of responsibility for determining the appropriateness of death; Florida's simple majority vote on the death penalty offends the Constitution; and the aggregate effects of the scheme's subversion of the jury's deliberative function. There are very few cases in which judicial fact-finding related to sentencing has survived *Apprendi* challenges. Florida has its work cut out for it.

C. Hobbs Act

The Hobbs Act, the Court observed a few years ago in *Sekhar v. United States*, punishes "one of the oldest crimes in our legal tradition": extortion.[101] Under the act, extortion is defined to include "the obtaining of property from another, with his consent, . . . under the color of official right."[102] At issue in *Ocasio v. United States* is whether a conspiracy to commit extortion requires that the co-conspirators agree to obtain property from someone *outside* the conspiracy.

Ocasio arises from misconduct by members of the Baltimore Police Department—albeit a fairly mild form of misconduct by BPD

---

[100] Grossman v. State, 525 So.2d 833, 839 (Fla. 1988).

[101] Sekhar v. United States, 133 S. Ct. 2720, 2724 (2013).

[102] 18 U.S.C. § 1951(b)(2).

standards, if news accounts are to be believed.[103] After an extensive FBI investigation, 17 Baltimore police officers were arrested and indicted for participating in a kickback scheme with brothers Hernan Alexis Moreno Mejia ("Moreno") and Edwin Javier Mejia ("Mejia"), the owners of the Majestic Auto Repair Shop 'n' Graft Emporium.[104] Over the course of several years, the brothers paid BPD cops, as the first responders to car accidents, to refer accident victims to Majestic for repairs. Though Moreno, Mejia, and most of the officers pleaded guilty to the crimes, Ocasio and another officer contested the charges. By a superseding indictment, the two were charged with three counts of substantive extortion under the Hobbs Act and one count of conspiracy to commit extortion. The conspiracy charge forms the basis of Ocasio's petition.

Under the indictment, Ocasio allegedly conspired "with Moreno and Mejia to obstruct, delay, and affect commerce and the movement of any article and commodity in commerce by extortion, that is, to unlawfully obtain under color of official right, money and other property from Moreno, Mejia, and [the Majestic Auto Repair Shop], with their consent . . . in violation of [the Hobbs Act]."[105] "In other words," Ocasio says, the indictment "accused the defendant[] of conspiring *with* [*his*] *bribers* to obtain property *from the bribers themselves*"[106]—an offense he argues the Hobbs Act does not recognize. Relying on *United States v. Brock,* an opinion by Sixth Circuit Judge Jeffrey Sutton (whose opinion in *United States v. Jeffries* was influential in another statutory construction case in the most recent Term of the Century, *Elonis v. United States*[107]), Ocasio argued that, to conspire to obtain property "from another" under the act, conspirators must have agreed to obtain property from someone *outside the*

---

[103] See Conor Friedersdorf, The Brutality of Police Culture in Baltimore, The Atlantic (April 22, 2015), available at http://goo.gl/OSGJmb; Meredith Cohn, Two More Men Allege 'Rough Rides' in Baltimore Police Van, Baltimore Sun (May 1, 2015), available at http://goo.gl/WvxR2O. See generally The Wire, "Port in a Storm," Season 2, Episode 12 (originally aired August 24, 2003) (Major Valchek: "F**k you. This is the Baltimore Police Department, not the Roland Park Ladies Tea.").

[104] Name partially made up. See Majestic Auto Repair Shop, Baltimore Sun, http://goo.gl/wnY16v.

[105] Cert. Pet. at 5, Ocasio v. United States, (No. 14-361) (quoting indictment).

[106] *Id.*

[107] Elonis v. United States, 135 S. Ct. 2001, 2008, 2011 (2015) (citing United States v. Jeffries, 692 F.3d 473, 483–84 (6th Cir. 2012) (Sutton, J., concurring *dubitante*)).

conspiracy, not from a person participating *in* the conspiracy. But the trial court concluded that the argument was foreclosed by Fourth Circuit law. Because of the inclusion of the conspiracy charge, Ocasio says that the trial judge admitted "a great deal of evidence (offered to prove the conspiracy) that otherwise would not have been admitted."[108] After his co-defendant pleaded guilty on the last day of trial, Ocasio was found guilty on all counts and sentenced to serve 18 months in prison.

The U.S. Court of Appeals for the Fourth Circuit affirmed. While appearing to acknowledge (like the Sixth Circuit) that the Hobbs Act clause requiring conspirators to obtain "property from another" and do so "with his consent" does not "appl[y] naturally to the conspirators' own property or to their own consent,"[109] the panel nevertheless held that the "from another" provision simply "refers to a person or entity other than the public official."[110] Which is to say, the requirement "provides only that a public official cannot extort himself."[111] Thus, nothing in the Hobbs Act forecloses the possibility that the "another" can also be a coconspirator of the public official.

Before the Court, Ocasio contends, not without force, that the text of the Hobbs Act requires that a conspiracy involve an agreement to obtain *someone else's* property. "If two people agree that one will pay the other a bribe," Ocasio argues, "no speaker of English would say they have agreed to 'obtain property from another, with his consent.'"[112] There is the further question (noted by Judge Sutton) of "How do (or why would) people conspire to obtain their own consent?"[113] The Fourth Circuit's reading would transform every bribe into a criminal conspiracy, effectively transforming the Hobbs Act into an anti-bribery statute. In response, the government observes that the Hobbs Act "does not state that the defendant must agree to obtain property from someone outside of the conspiracy,"

---

[108] Cert. Pet. at 6, *supra* note 105.

[109] United States v. Ocasio, 750 F.3d 399, 410 (4th Cir. 2014) (quoting United States v. Brock, 501 F.3d 762, 768 (6th Cir. 2007)).

[110] 750 F.3d at 411.

[111] *Id.*

[112] Pet. Br. at 23, Ocasio v. United States, No 14-361 (U.S. June 1, 2015).

[113] *Id.* at 24 (quoting Brock, 501 F.3d at 767).

"[n]or do its terms imply such a limitation."[114] "Whoever" refers to the defendant official; and property from "another" refers to property not belonging to that official. Ocasio's reading, the government argues, would produce anomalous results. "Petitioner does not contest in this Court that he committed substantive Hobbs Act violations by accepting payments from Moreno. But if a bribe-payer such as Moreno can be 'another' under [§] 1951(b)(2) for purposes of a substantive Hobbs Act violation, it is difficult to see how that same person can lose his status as 'another' solely by virtue of a conspiracy charge."[115] Assisted by an amicus brief filed by numerous prominent former U.S. Attorneys, Ocasio seeks to harness the sentiment that the case reflects prosecutorial overreaching, à la OT2014's pun-fest *Yates v. United States*[116] (*wearily*: yes, the fish case). Oral argument will help reveal which OT2014 criminal case *Ocasio* most closely resembles: *Henderson v. United States* (a "controlled implosion" of the government's position[117]), *Yates* (a disturbing prosecution, but legally a close question), or *Whitfield v. United States* (a prosecution that seemed outrageous at the time of the grant, but turned out quite reasonable once the Court took a careful look).[118]

VII. Cases in the Pipeline

In case the last 28 pages of rampant speculation about the cases the Court will be hearing next term is not enough for you, we thought we'd end this essay by engaging in some truly wild guesses about cases that the Court hasn't even decided to review yet.

A. Environmental Law

Kent Recycling Services, LLC v. U.S. Army Corps of Engineers, 14-493. Mention your rehearing petition around the Supreme Court *cognoscenti*, and you will get a look like you just said you've received an email from a deposed prince promising to pay you handsomely to

---

[114] Govt. Brief in Opposition at 7, Ocasio v. United States, No. 14-361 (U.S. Dec. 29, 2014).

[115] *Id.* at 8.

[116] 135 S. Ct. 1074, 1100–01 (Kagan, J., dissenting).

[117] See Richard M. Re, Argument Analysis: A Controlled Implosion, SCOTUSblog (Feb. 25, 2015), http://goo.gl/Q7zCnU.

[118] 135 S. Ct. 785 (2015).

move his assets through your bank account. That is because both situations have approximately the same odds of a happy ending.[119] They *never* work—except when they do. The Court grants rehearing once in a blue moon, just to ensure people keep legal printers fully employed preparing rehearing petitions in hopeless cases.[120] The most recent example of the Court granting cert. on rehearing is *Boumediene v. Bush*, 553 U.S. 723 (2008).

So back to *Kent Recycling*. The petition principally presented the question whether a "jurisdictional determination" by the Army Corps of Engineers that a property contains "waters of the United States" subjecting it to costly regulation under the Clean Water Act ("CWA") is final agency action subject to immediate review under the Administrative Procedure Act, even if the agency has not ordered the property owner to do (or refrain from doing) something to comply with the CWA. Readers familiar with past Terms of the Century may recall Justice Alito's concurrence in OT2011's *Sackett v. EPA*, suggesting that a jurisdictional determination alone might be reviewable.[121] Soon after the Court denied Kent Recycling's petition as splitless in March 2015, the Eighth Circuit held that a jurisdictional determination itself *is* reviewable, and Kent Recycling filed a petition for rehearing. The Court took the unusual step of ordering the government to file a response. The government acknowledged the circuit split but told the Court to deny cert. because it was filing a rehearing petition to give the Eighth Circuit the opportunity to bring its law into line. But in July, the Eighth Circuit denied rehearing, cementing the split. As this goes to press, the rehearing petition remains pending. The Court's conservatives like EPA's regula-

---

[119] That is true even when the rehearing petition is meritorious. Just take our word for it that the Court should have at least granted the petition, vacated the judgment below, and remanded ("GVR'd") in light of the rehearing petition in British American Tobacco (Investments) Ltd. v. United States, after Morrison v. National Australia Bank, 561 U.S. 247 (2010). Both involved the correct test for the extraterritorial application of U.S. law. It didn't work out. See British American Tobacco (Investments) Ltd. v. United States, 131 S. Ct. 57 (2010). The Court is generally a bit more indulgent in granting rehearing to GVR. See, e.g., Liberty University v. Geithner, 133 S. Ct. 679 (2012); Melson v. Allen, 561 U.S. 1001 (2010). Hat tip to Sean Marotta and Bryan Gividen. See https://goo.gl/SCaZWi.

[120] It's possible that that may not be their actual motivation.

[121] 132 S. Ct. 1367, 1375 (Alito, J., concurring) ("property owners like petitioners will have the right to challenge the EPA's jurisdictional determination under the [APA]").

tion of "waters of the United States" (redefined in a recent rule[122]) about as much as they like the Armed Career Criminal Act's residual clause.[123]

B. Abortion

Recent years have seen a variety of new restrictions placed on the provision of abortion, including requirements that providers comply with certain health and safety regulations or have admitting privileges at local hospitals, requirements that the mother be shown an ultrasound, and measures prohibiting abortion outright past a certain number of weeks of gestation.

Currier v. Jackson Women's Health Organization seeks review of the Fifth Circuit's decision to invalidate a Mississippi law requiring abortion clinics (er, *clinic*—there is only one statewide) to comply with health and safety regulations applicable to other outpatient facilities and have admitting privileges. The Fifth Circuit held—over the dissent of, you guessed it, Judge Garza—that it was an undue restriction on the constitutionally recognized right to an abortion to "effectively clos[e] the one abortion clinic in the state."[124] The Court has already relisted *Currier* six times, making clear that the justices were giving the case close consideration. A second panel of the Fifth Circuit *upheld* a Texas measure that required those who perform abortions to have admitting privileges at local hospitals and have facilities equal to those available at a surgical center.[125] Near the end of the term, the Court, by a 5–4 vote, stayed the Fifth Circuit's judgment in that case and thus temporarily blocked Texas from enforcing its abortion law,[126] reflecting that a majority concluded that there is "a reasonable probability that th[e] Court will grant certiorari, [and] a fair prospect

---

[122] Environmental Protection Agency, Clean Water Rule: Definition of 'Waters of the United States, 80 Fed. Reg. 37054 (2015), available at http://goo.gl/ULCQR6.

[123] See Johnson v. United States, No. 13-7120 (U.S. June 26, 2015) (finally putting the clause out of its constitutional misery after several fruitless attempts to give lower courts guidance regarding its meaning).

[124] Jackson Women's Health Org. v. Currier, 760 F.3d 448, 458 (5th Cir. 2014).

[125] Whole Woman's Health v. Cole, 790 F.3d 563, as modified by 790 F.3d 598 (5th Cir. 2015). The Court did, however, enjoin its application to one isolated facility along the Mexican border.

[126] Whole Woman's Health v. Cole, 135 S. Ct. 2923 (2015).

that the Court will then reverse the decision below."[127] Separately, the Eighth Circuit, in the course of invalidating North Dakota's law prohibiting abortion after a fetus has a detectable heartbeat, urged the Supreme Court that "good reasons exist for the Court to reevaluate its jurisprudence" because the Court's "viability standard . . . gives too little consideration to the substantial state interest in potential life."[128] It seems inevitable that the Court will have at least *one* high-profile abortion case on its docket next term.

C. Fourth Amendment

It's great how your cellphone can give turn-by-turn directions from your precise location. It's less great when prosecutors use the same "cell site location information" ("CSLI") to tie you to a string of armed robberies that results in a 162-*year* prison sentence. That is the situation that Quartavious Davis finds himself in, and he is not alone: CSLI has become an everyday tool in criminal prosecutions.

The Fifth Circuit has held that no warrant is required before the government obtains CSLI records, reasoning that because cellphone users permit service providers to access that information, people lack an expectation of privacy in it.[129] This is known as the "third party doctrine," best associated with *Smith v. Maryland*.[130] The Third Circuit, by contrast, has concluded that "[a] cell phone customer has not 'voluntarily' shared his location information with a cellular provider in any meaningful way," and suggested that a warrant might be required where disclosure of information "would implicate the Fourth Amendment, as it could if it would disclose location information about the interior of a home."[131]

When Davis appealed his conviction, a panel of the Eleventh Circuit, in an opinion written by visiting D.C. Circuit Judge David Sentelle, held that a warrant was required. But on rehearing *en banc*, the

[127] Maryland v. King, 133 S. Ct. 1, 2 (2012) (Roberts, C.J., in Chambers) (internal quotation marks omitted).

[128] MKB Mgmt. Corp. v. Stenehjem, No. 14-2128, 2015 WL 4460405, at *4 (8th Cir. July 22, 2015).

[129] In re Application of the U.S. for Historical Cell Site Data, 724 F.3d 600 (5th Cir. 2013).

[130] 442 U.S. 735 (1979).

[131] In re Application of U.S. for an Order Directing a Provider of Elec. Commc'n Serv. to Disclose Records to Gov't, 620 F.3d 304, 317–18 (3d Cir. 2010).

full court joined the Fifth Circuit in applying the third-party doctrine.[132] While Davis's petition for certiorari was pending (indeed, between the due date for this article and the date it was actually delivered), a divided panel of the Fourth Circuit in *United States v. Graham* explicitly disagreed with the Fifth and Eleventh Circuits and held that users have an expectation of privacy because "a cell phone user does not 'convey' CSLI to her service provider at all—voluntarily other otherwise—and therefore does not assume any risk of disclosure to law enforcement."[133] The Fourth Circuit *also* adopted the so-called "mosaic" theory associated with the D.C. Circuit opinion in *United States v. Maynard* (and some of the concurring opinions when the case later reached the Supreme Court as *United States v. Jones*) that long-term monitoring infringes privacy interests because of its ability to reveal "an intimate picture" of a person's life.[134]

There is now a clear split. But both *Davis* and *Graham* seem like longshots—regardless of whether the government seeks rehearing in *Graham*. In both cases, the courts held that the CSLI evidence was admissible under the good-faith exception to the exclusionary rule, and in both cases *that* issue appears to implicate no circuit split and is not obviously certworthy.[135] Thus, it seems unlikely that the Court would grant review since a ruling in Davis's or Graham's favor would not affect the outcome. It seems inevitable, however, that the Court *will* pass on the question whether (and under what circumstances) individuals have an expectation of privacy in CSLI. Such cases arise quite frequently, so there is a real prospect that the Court will have the opportunity to address this issue in OT2015. The Court seems increasingly interested in privacy and electronic surveillance, as exemplified by recent decisions in OT2013's *Riley v. California* (requiring a warrant for a cellphone search)[136] and OT2011's *United States v. Jones* (requiring a warrant for GPS monitoring).[137] And since Justice

---

[132] United States v. Davis, 785 F.3d 498 (11th Cir. 2015) (en banc).

[133] United States v. Graham, No. 12-4659, slip op. at 43 (4th Cir. Aug. 5, 2015), available at http://goo.gl/ydxlYn.

[134] United States v. Maynard, 615 F.3d 544, 561-64 (D.C. Cir. 2010), aff'd sub nom. United States v. Jones, 132 S. Ct. 945 (2012).

[135] Cert. Pet. at 36–39, Davis v. United States, (No. 15-146); Graham, *supra* note 133, slip op. at 60–65.

[136] 134 S. Ct. 2473 (2014).

[137] 132 S. Ct. 945 (2012).

Sotomayor's *Jones* concurrence questioned whether the third-party doctrine remain appropriate in the digital age,[138] and *"Riley* can be viewed as a signal ... that old Fourth Amendment precedents may be narrowed in light of new digital technologies,"[139] there is every reason to believe that a major reconsideration may be in the offing.

*   *   *

That is just the beginning. The Court will be granting cases to be argued during OT2015 for several more months, which may result in many more grants to talk about on Twitter with your law-nerd friends, perhaps involving the required mental state (and benefit a participant must receive) to be convicted of insider trading,[140] the standard for obtaining a religious accommodation under the Affordable Care Act's contraceptive mandate,[141] the lawfulness of Texas's voter-ID law,[142] the use of military commissions,[143] and the National Security Agency's collection of telephone metadata.[144] And perhaps, if we are really lucky, we'll get a truly hot-button issue that is sure to galvanize public attention and inspire protests from both Left and Right: whether ERISA permits a court to retroactively reassign retirement benefits after the plan participant's death.[145]

OT2015 might fairly be called a "term of sequels," as numerous questions three previous Terms of the Century failed to resolve will be returning. With several other important issues, the coming term is shaping up to be interesting indeed. While we would hesitate to

---

[138] Jones, 132 S. Ct. at 957; see also Elwood & White, 15 Green Bag 2d at 410 (noting that Sotomayor's opinion "may loom large in future Fourth Amendment cases.").

[139] Richard M. Re, Narrowing the Third-Party Doctrine from Below, PrawfsBlawg (Aug. 6, 2015 8:11AM), http://goo.gl/itz3XO.

[140] United States v. Newman, 773 F.3d 438 (2d Cir. 2014), cert. pet. filed, No. 15-137 (July 30, 2015).

[141] Little Sisters of the Poor Home for the Aged v. Burwell, No. 13-1540, 2015 WL 423206 (10th Cir. July 14, 2015), cert. pet. filed, No. 15-105 (July 23, 2015).

[142] Veasey v. Abbott, No. 14-41127 (5th Cir. Aug. 5, 2015), available at http://goo.gl/iINmkf.

[143] Al Bahlul v. United States, No. 11-1324, 2105 WL 3687457 (D.C. Cir. June 12, 2015).

[144] American Civil Liberties Union v. Clapper, 785 F.3d 787 (2d Cir. 2015).

[145] Cowser-Griffin v. Griffin, 753 S.E.2d 574 (Va. 2015), cert. pet. filed, No. 14-1531 (June 26, 2015). One of the authors is sorta counsel for petitioner in that case.

say that this is another candidate to be the Term of the Century, we can all agree that OT2015 is a strong contender to be the outstanding term of the third fifth of the 20-teens.

Contributors

Jonathan H. Adler is the inaugural Johan Verheij Memorial Professor of Law and director of the Center for Business Law & Regulation at the Case Western Reserve University School of Law, where he teaches courses in environmental, administrative, and constitutional law. Adler is the author or editor of five books and over a dozen book chapters, and several dozen academic articles. His writing has appeared in publications ranging from the *Supreme Court Economic Review* and *Harvard Journal of Law & Public Policy* to the *Wall Street Journal* and *USA Today*, and his scholarship has been cited in the U.S. Supreme Court. A 2007 study identified Adler as the most cited legal academic in environmental law under age 40 and three years earlier he received the Paul M. Bator Award, given annually by the Federalist Society to an academic under 40 for excellence in teaching, scholarship, and commitment to students. Adler is a senior fellow at the Property & Environment Research Center in Bozeman, Montana, and serves on the editorial board of the *Cato Supreme Court Review*, the board of directors of the Foundation for Research on Economics and the Environment, and the Environmental Law Institute's *Environmental Law Reporter* and ELI Press Advisory Board. Before joining the faculty at Case Western, Adler clerked for Judge David B. Sentelle on the U.S. Court of Appeals for the D.C. Circuit. From 1991 to 2000, Adler worked at the Competitive Enterprise Institute, where he directed CEI's environmental studies program. He holds a B.A. magna cum laude from Yale University and a J.D. summa cum laude from the George Mason University School of Law.

James F. Blumstein is a University Professor of Constitutional Law and Health Law & Policy at Vanderbilt Law School, a professor of management at the Owen Graduate School of Management, and director of Vanderbilt's Health Policy Center. He ranks among the nation's most prominent scholars of health law, law and medicine, and voting rights. As the director of Vanderbilt's Health Policy Center,

Blumstein has served as the principal investigator on numerous grants concerning managed care, hospital management, and medical malpractice. His peers recognized his leadership in health law and policy by electing Blumstein to the National Academy of Sciences' Institute of Medicine, and he was awarded the Earl Sutherland Prize, which is Vanderbilt's preeminent university-wide recognition for lifetime scholarly contributions. In 2007, he received the prestigious McDonald-Merrill-Ketcham Memorial Award for Excellence in Law and Medicine from the University of Indiana and delivered the award lecture on hospital-physician joint-venture relationships. Blumstein has been the Olin Visiting Professor at the University of Pennsylvania Law School, an Adjunct Professor at Dartmouth Medical School, and a Visiting Professor at Duke Law School and at Duke's Institute of Policy Sciences and Public Affairs. He has served as former Tennessee Governor Phil Bredesen's counsel on TennCare reform and has participated actively in a number of Supreme Court cases, arguing three. A dedicated teacher, Blumstein has received the law school's student-sponsored Hartman Teaching Award. He joined Vanderbilt's law faculty in 1970.

Michael F. Cannon is the Cato Institute's director of health policy studies. Cannon has been described as "an influential health-care wonk" (*Washington Post*), "ObamaCare's single most relentless antagonist" (*The New Republic*), "the man who could bring down ObamaCare" (Vox.com), and "ObamaCare's fiercest critic" (*The Week*). He has appeared on all major TV and cable networks. His articles have been featured in the *Wall Street Journal*, the *New York Times*, SCOTUSBlog, *Forum for Health Economics & Policy*, the *Harvard Health Policy Review*, *Health Matrix: Journal of Law-Medicine*, the *Journal of Health Politics, Policy, and Law*, and the *Yale Journal of Health Policy, Law, and Ethics*. Cannon is the co-editor of *Replacing Obamacare* and co-author of *Healthy Competition*. Previously, he served as a domestic policy analyst for the U.S. Senate Republican Policy Committee, where he advised the Senate leadership on health, education, labor, welfare, and the Second Amendment. He holds a B.A. in American government from the University of Virginia, and an M.A. in economics and a J.M. in law and economics from George Mason University.

Roger Clegg is president and general counsel of the Center for Equal Opportunity, where he writes, speaks, and conducts research on legal issues raised by the civil rights laws. The Center for Equal Opportunity is a conservative research and educational organization based in Falls Church, Virginia, that specializes in civil rights, immigration and assimilation, and bilingual education issues. Clegg also is a contributing editor at *National Review Online*, and writes frequently for other popular periodicals and law journals. From 1982 to 1993, Clegg held a number of positions at the U.S. Department of Justice, including Assistant to the Solicitor General, where he argued three cases before the United States Supreme Court, and the number-two official in the Civil Rights Division and in the Environment Division. From 1993 to 1997, Clegg was vice president and general counsel of the National Legal Center for the Public Interest, where he wrote and edited a variety of publications on legal issues of interest to business. He is a graduate of Rice University and Yale Law School.

John P. Elwood is an appellate partner in the Washington office of Vinson & Elkins LLP and adviser to the University of Virginia School of Law's Supreme Court Litigation Clinic. Elwood has argued nine cases in the U.S. Supreme Court and has appeared before most of the federal courts of appeals. He is a regular contributor to the Supreme Court legal blog SCOTUSblog. Before joining V&E, Elwood served for seven years as the senior deputy in the Justice Department's Office of Legal Counsel and as an assistant to the solicitor general. He received both the Attorney General's Award for Exceptional Service and the Attorney General's Award for Distinguished Service—the Justice Department's two top awards for lawyers. Elwood is a former law clerk to Supreme Court Associate Justice Anthony M. Kennedy and the late Judge J. Daniel Mahoney of the U.S. Court of Appeals for the Second Circuit. He is a graduate of Yale Law School and Princeton University.

William N. Eskridge Jr. is the John A. Garver Professor of Jurisprudence at Yale Law School. His primary legal academic interest has been statutory interpretation. Together with Professor Philip Frickey, he developed an innovative casebook on legislation. In 1990-95, Professor Eskridge represented a gay couple suing for recognition of their same-sex marriage. Since then, he has published a field-establishing casebook, three monographs, and dozens of law review articles articulating a legal and political framework for proper state treatment of sexual and gender minorities. The historical materials in the book on "Gaylaw" formed the basis for an amicus brief he drafted for the Cato Institute and for much of the Court's (and the dissenting opinion's) analysis in *Lawrence v. Texas* (2003), which invalidated consensual sodomy laws. His most recent books are *Dishonorable Passions: Sodomy Laws in America*, 1861-2003 (Viking 2008), and *A Republic of Statutes: Our New American Constitution* (Yale 2010) (with John Ferejohn). Professor Eskridge received his B.A., summa cum laude, from Davidson College, his masters in History from Harvard, and his J.D. from Yale.

Andrew M. Grossman is an associate at the Washington office of Baker & Hostetler LLP and adjunct scholar at the Cato Institute. He has represented states in challenges to the constitutionality of federal statutes and the legality of federal environmental regulations, and is also active in commercial litigation. He is experienced in Supreme Court practice, authoring or contributing to many certiorari-stage filings, merits briefs, and amicus briefs, and frequently "mooting" the nation's top Supreme Court litigators and state solicitors general before their oral arguments. Before joining BakerHostetler, Grossman was a senior legal analyst for the Center for Legal and Judicial Studies at the Heritage Foundation, where his research focused on law and finance, bankruptcy, national security law, and the constitutional separation of powers. Grossman has testified before Congress on a variety of issues and is a frequent commentator on radio and television. His legal commentary has also appeared in dozens of magazines and newspapers, including the *Wall Street Journal*, *USA Today*, *Washington Post*, and many others. Grossman has written and published research on criminal law and "overcriminalization," constitutional law, civil liberties and privacy, domestic intelligence operations, the legal aspects of economic regulation and civil justice reform. He served as a judicial clerk to Chief Judge Edith H. Jones of the U.S. Court of Appeals for the Fifth Circuit. In 2007, the Burton Foundation and the Library of Congress presented Grossman with the Burton Award for Legal Achievement, citing his research on federal evidentiary law and Internet communications technologies.

John G. Malcolm oversees the Heritage Foundation's work to increase understanding of the Constitution and the rule of law as director of the think tank's Edwin Meese III Center for Legal and Judicial Studies. Malcolm, who also is Heritage's Ed Gilbertson and Sherry Lindberg Gilbertson Senior Legal Fellow, brings to the challenge a wealth of legal expertise and experience in both the public and private sectors. Before being named director of the Meese Center in July 2013, Malcolm spearheaded the center's rule of law programs. His research and writing focuses on criminal law, immigration, national security, religious liberty, and intellectual property. In addition to his duties at Heritage, Malcolm is chairman of the criminal law practice group of the Federalist Society. He serves on the board of directors of Boys Town Washington, D.C., which provides homes and services to troubled children and families, and Enough Is Enough, which strives to protect children from online predators and other dangers. Before joining Heritage, Malcolm was general counsel at the U.S. Commission on International Religious Freedom, as well as a distinguished practitioner in residence at Pepperdine Law School. From 2004 to 2009, Malcolm was executive vice president and director of worldwide anti-piracy operations for the Motion Picture Association of America. He served as a deputy assistant attorney general in the Department of Justice's Criminal Division from 2001 to 2004, where he oversaw sections on computer crime and intellectual property, domestic security, child exploitation and obscenity, and special investigations. Before that, he was a partner in the Atlanta law firm of Malcolm & Schroeder, LLP. From 1990 to 1997, Malcolm was an assistant U.S. attorney in Atlanta, assigned to the fraud and public corruption section, and also an associate independent counsel, investigating fraud and abuse in the Department of Housing and Urban Development. He was honored with the Director's Award for Superior Performance for his work in the successful prosecution of Walter Leroy Moody Jr., who assassinated an 11th Circuit judge and the head of the Savannah chapter of the NAACP. Malcolm began his law career as a law clerk to a federal district court judge and a federal appellate court judge as well as an associate at the Atlanta-based law firm of Sutherland, Asbill & Brennan. Malcolm is a graduate of Harvard Law School and holds a bachelor's degree in economics from Columbia College.

Michael W. McConnell is the Richard and Frances Mallery Professor of Law at Stanford Law School and a leading authority on freedom of speech and religion, the relation of individual rights to government structure, originalism, and various other aspects of constitutional history and constitutional law. He is author of numerous articles and co-author of two casebooks: *The Constitution of the United States* (Foundation Press) and *Religion and the Constitution* (Aspen). In addition to teaching, he is the director of the Stanford Constitutional Law Center, which was founded in 2006 to explore and improve public understanding of the most pressing constitutional issues. McConnell brings wide practical experience to bear on his teaching and scholarship. Before joining Stanford in 2009, he served as a federal judge on the U.S. Court of Appeals for the Tenth Circuit and was frequently mentioned as a possible nominee to the Supreme Court. He is the only full-time professor of law in the nation who has previously served as a federal appellate judge. He also has been involved in extensive appellate litigation, including arguing 15 cases in the U.S. Supreme Court, including one during October Term 2009. Before his appointment to the bench, McConnell was Presidential Professor of Law at the S.J. Quinney College of Law at the University of Utah, and before that the William B. Graham Professor of Law at the University of Chicago Law School. He has taught five times as a visiting professor at Harvard Law School. McConnell served as law clerk to then-Chief Judge J. Skelly Wright of the U.S. Court of Appeals for the D.C. Circuit, and to Supreme Court Justice William J. Brennan Jr. McConnell was an assistant general counsel at the Office of Management and Budget and an assistant to the solicitor general in the Department of Justice under President Ronald Reagan. He is also a senior fellow at the Hoover Institution.

Conor P. McEvily is an associate in the Houston office of Vinson & Elkins LLP, where his principal area of practice is appellate litigation. He received his B.A. from the University of Notre Dame, and his J.D. from Georgetown University Law Center, where he was the senior administrative editor and a senior board member of the Georgetown Law Journal.

Luke M. Milligan is a professor of law at the University of Louisville's Brandeis School of Law, with an expertise in privacy and criminal procedure. Milligan got his start at Williams & Connolly LLP in Washington, where he defended business executives charged with fraud and related corporate crimes. Since entering academia, he has represented individuals at the trial level in criminal matters ranging from identity theft to terroristic threatening to murder. Milligan is a former law clerk to Judge Edith Brown Clement of the U.S. Court of Appeals for the Fifth Circuit and Judge Martin L.C. Feldman of the U.S. District Court for the Eastern District of Louisiana. He has taught criminal law, criminal procedure, and jurisprudence, winning the alumni award for teaching excellence in 2013. Milligan's writings focus on criminal procedure, with recent projects calling for a strong libertarian reading of the Fourth Amendment's "to be secure" text. His articles have appeared in the *Boston University Law Review*, *Emory Law Journal*, *Georgia Law Review*, *Hastings Law Journal*, and *Washington and Lee Law Review*, among other journals. Milligan has held visiting teaching positions at Emory Law School, University of Turku (Finland), University of KwaZulu-Natal (South Africa), and University of Mainz (Germany).

Walter Olson is a senior fellow at the Cato Institute's Center for Constitutional Studies. Prior to joining Cato, Olson was a senior fellow at the Manhattan Institute, and has been a columnist for Great Britain's *Times Online*, as well as *Reason*. His writing appears regularly in such publications as the *Wall Street Journal*, *New York Times*, and *New York Post*. He has appeared numerous times before Congress and advised many public officials. The *Washington Post* has dubbed him the "intellectual guru of tort reform." His approximately 400 broadcast appearances include all the major networks, CNN, Fox News, PBS, NPR, and "Oprah." Olson's most recent book, *Schools for Misrule: Legal Academia and an Overlawyered America* (Encounter Books), appeared in 2011 and was described by Publisher's Weekly as "cutting-edge commentary," "astute," "witty" and "hard-hitting." His previous book on mass litigation, *The Rule of Lawyers*, was hailed in leading publications including *Forbes*, *The American Lawyer*, and *Barron's*. *The Excuse Factory*, his 1997 book on lawsuits in the workplace, was met with accolades in the *London Times* and the *ABA. Journal*. Olson's widely discussed first book, *The Litigation Explosion*, was cited by Justice Sandra Day O'Connor in a major Supreme Court case. He founded and continues to run Overlawyered.com, widely cited as the oldest blog on law as well as one of the most popular.

Roger Pilon is Cato's vice president for legal affairs, the founding director of Cato's Center for Constitutional Studies, and the founding publisher of the *Cato Supreme Court* Review. He holds Cato's B. Kenneth Simon Chair in Constitutional Studies and is an adjunct professor of government at Georgetown University through The Fund for American Studies. Prior to joining Cato, Pilon held five senior posts in the Reagan administration, at OPM, State, and Justice, and was a National Fellow at Stanford's Hoover Institution. In 1989 the Bicentennial Commission presented him with its Benjamin Franklin Award for excellence in writing on the U.S. Constitution. In 2001 Columbia University's School of General Studies awarded him its Alumni Medal of Distinction. Pilon lectures and debates at universities and law schools across the country and testifies often before Congress. His writing has appeared in the *Wall Street Journal*, *Washington Post*, *New York Times*, *L.A. Times*, *National Law Journal*, *Harvard Journal of Law & Public Policy*, *Stanford Law & Policy Review*, and elsewhere. He has appeared on ABC's *Nightline*, CBS's *60 Minutes II*, Fox News Channel, NPR, CNN, MSNBC, CNBC, and other media. Pilon holds a B.A. from Columbia University, an M.A. and a Ph.D. from the University of Chicago, and a J.D. from the George Washington University School of Law.

Timothy Sandefur is a principal attorney at the Pacific Legal Foundation, where he directs the Economic Liberty Project, devoted to protecting the constitutional right to earn a living. He has won important victories for economic freedom in California, Kentucky, Missouri, Oregon, and elsewhere. He is an adjunct scholar with the Cato Institute and has authored three books—*Cornerstone of Liberty: Property Rights in 21st Century America* (the second edition of which, coauthored with his wife Christina Sandefur, will be published in 2016), *The Right to Earn A Living* (2010), and *The Conscience of The Constitution* (2014)—as well as some 50 scholarly articles on subjects ranging from economic liberty to eminent domain, copyright, slavery and the Civil War, and legal issues in Shakespeare and ancient Greek drama. His articles have appeared in *National Review*, the *Claremont Review of Books*, *Regulation*, the *San Francisco Chronicle*, and elsewhere, and he is a frequent guest on radio and television programs, including John Stossel, Kennedy, and The Armstrong & Getty Show. He is a graduate of Hillsdale College and Chapman University School of Law.

Ilya Shapiro is a senior fellow in constitutional studies at the Cato Institute and editor-in-chief of the *Cato Supreme Court Review*. Before joining Cato, he was a special assistant/adviser to the Multi-National Force in Iraq on rule-of-law issues and practiced international, political, commercial, and antitrust litigation at Patton Boggs and Cleary Gottlieb. Shapiro is the co-author of *Religious Liberties for Corporations? Hobby Lobby, the Affordable Care Act, and the Constitution* (2014). He has contributed to a variety of academic, popular, and professional publications, including the *Wall Street Journal, Harvard Journal of Law & Public Policy, L.A. Times, USA Today, National Law Journal, Weekly Standard, New York Times Online*, and *National Review Online*. He also regularly provides commentary for various media outlets, including CNN, Fox News, ABC, CBS, NBC, Univision and Telemundo, *The Colbert Report*, and NPR. Shapiro has testified before Congress and state legislatures and, as coordinator of Cato's amicus brief program, has filed more than 100 "friend of the court" briefs in the Supreme Court. He lectures regularly on behalf of the Federalist Society, is a member of the Legal Studies Institute's board of visitors at The Fund for American Studies, was an inaugural Washington Fellow at the National Review Institute, and has been an adjunct professor at the George Washington University Law School. Before entering private practice, Shapiro clerked for Judge E. Grady Jolly of the U.S. Court of Appeals for the Fifth Circuit, while living in Mississippi and traveling around the Deep South. He holds an A.B. from Princeton, an M.Sc. from the London School of Economics, and a J.D. from the University of Chicago Law School (where he became a Tony Patiño Fellow). Shapiro is a member of the bars of New York, D.C., and the U.S. Supreme Court.

Diane S. Sykes is a judge on the U.S. Court of Appeals for the Seventh Circuit, having been nominated by President George W. Bush and confirmed by the Senate in 2004. Prior to her appointment to the federal bench, Judge Sykes served as a justice on the Wisconsin Supreme Court. Governor Tommy G. Thompson appointed her in September 1999 to fill a mid-term vacancy and she was elected to a full ten-year term in April 2000. From 1992–1999, Judge Sykes served on the state trial bench in Milwaukee County (elected in 1992 and re-elected in 1998). From 1985–1992, Judge Sykes practiced law with the Milwaukee firm of Whyte & Hirschboeck, S.C., and from 1984–1985, was a law clerk to Judge Terence T. Evans, then on the federal district court for the Eastern District of Wisconsin. Born and raised in the Milwaukee area, Judge Sykes earned a bachelor's degree in journalism from Northwestern University in 1980 and a law degree from Marquette University Law School in 1984. Between college and law school, Judge Sykes worked as a reporter for the *Milwaukee Journal*.

Alexander "Sasha" Volokh is an associate professor of law at Emory University. He earned his B.S. from UCLA and his J.D. and Ph.D. in economics from Harvard University. He clerked for Judge Alex Kozinski of the U.S. Court of Appeals for the Ninth Circuit and for Supreme Court Justices Sandra Day O'Connor and Samuel Alito. Before coming to Emory, he was a visiting associate professor at Georgetown University Law Center and a visiting assistant professor at University of Houston Law Center. His interests include law and economics, administrative law and the regulatory process, antitrust, privatization, corrections, and legal history.

Adam J. White is counsel at Boyden Gray & Associates and an adjunct fellow with the Manhattan Institute. He works, writes, and speaks often on constitutional and regulatory issues. His writing appears in publications such as the *Wall Street Journal, Weekly Standard, Commentary*, and SCOTUSblog; he is a contributing editor with *City Journal, National Affairs*, and *The New Atlantis*; and he has published scholarly articles in the *Harvard Journal of Law & Public Policy* and the *Albany Law Review*. He also serves as a council member leading the ABA's section of administrative law and regulatory practice, where he also co-chairs the section's judicial review committee and co-directs its Supreme Court series. He studied at Harvard Law School and the University of Iowa, and clerked for Judge David Sentelle of the U.S. Court of Appeals for the D.C. Circuit.

Cato Institute

Founded in 1977, the Cato Institute is a public policy research foundation dedicated to broadening the parameters of policy debate to allow consideration of more options that are consistent with the principles of limited government, individual liberty, and peace. To that end, the Institute strives to achieve greater involvement of the intelligent, concerned lay public in questions of policy and the proper role of government.

The Institute is named for Cato's Letters, libertarian pamphlets that were widely read in the American Colonies in the early 18th century and played a major role in laying the philosophical foundation for the American Revolution.

Despite the achievement of the nation's Founders, today virtually no aspect of life is free from government encroachment. A pervasive intolerance for individual rights is shown by government's arbitrary intrusions into private economic transactions and its disregard for civil liberties. And while freedom around the globe has notably increased in the past several decades, many countries have moved in the opposite direction, and most governments still do not respect or safeguard the wide range of civil and economic liberties.

To address those issues, the Cato Institute undertakes an extensive publications program on the complete spectrum of policy issues. Books, monographs, and shorter studies are commissioned to examine the federal budget, Social Security, regulation, military spending, international trade, and myriad other issues. Major policy conferences are held throughout the year, from which papers are published thrice yearly in the Cato Journal. The Institute also publishes the quarterly magazine Regulation.

In order to maintain its independence, the Cato Institute accepts no government funding. Contributions are received from foundations, corporations, and individuals, and other revenue is generated from the sale of publications. The Institute is a nonprofit, tax-exempt, educational foundation under Section 501(c)3 of the Internal Revenue Code.

CATO INSTITUTE
1000 Massachusetts Ave., N.W.
Washington, D.C. 20001
www.cato.org